ESSENTIALS OF MARKETING

E S S E N T I A L S   O F

MARKETING

E. Jerome McCarthy
Michigan State University

Stanley J. Shapiro
Simon Fraser University

- FIRST CANADIAN EDITION
- 1983
- RICHARD D. IRWIN, INC.
- Homewood, Illinois 60430

ISBN 0-256-02941-5

Library of Congress Catalog Card No. 82–83441

Printed in the United States of America

2 3 4 5 6 7 8 9 0 K 0 9 8 7 6 5

PREFACE

Essentials of Marketing is a shortened version of the Third Canadian Edition of *Basic Marketing*—a book that has been widely used in the first marketing course. In cutting the material down to its *Essentials,* considerable time and effort was devoted to defining terms carefully and to finding words and phraseology that would speed understanding. Similarly, figures, pictures, and illustrations were selected to help today's increasingly visual student better "see" the material. Although approximately three fifths the length of *Basic Marketing,* this *Essentials* text covers in less detail much of the same material. The few topics that have been entirely omitted, such as control in marketing and response functions, are ones many instructors prefer to discuss in a second-level marketing management course.

Essentials of Marketing retains *Basic Marketing*'s strategy planning emphasis—seeing marketing through the marketing manager's eyes. It begins with four chapters on the nature of marketing and its environment. Then five chapters are concerned with finding opportunities and selecting target markets. Included here are chapters on marketing opportunity analysis, marketing research, customer behavior, segmenting markets, and forecasting sales.

The bulk of the book is concerned with developing a marketing mix out of McCarthy's now famous four Ps—Product, Place (that is, channels and institutions), Promotion, and Price. Chapter 20 applies the ideas in the text to international marketing. The final chapter considers many criticisms of marketing, evaluates the effectiveness of both micro- and macro-marketing, and discusses whether any changes are needed.

Since *Essentials* is a shorter book, it does not have quite as much Canadian content as the new Canadian edition of *Basic Marketing.* Nevertheless, this volume contains the most relevant and recent statistical material on the economic and demographic dimensions of the Canadian market. Unlike its American counterpart, *Essentials of Marketing,* First Canadian Edition, has an entire chapter devoted to population, income levels, and spending patterns. Similarly, Canadian marketing law is covered in far more detail than McCarthy devotes to U.S. legislation. Of course, any Canadianization should be more Canadian than the original, usually American, source document. This follows from the relative abundance of other outlets for U.S. material as compared to the all-but-complete absence of Canadian journals and advanced Canadian marketing texts.

Apparently, a sizable market segment prefers a somewhat shorter introductory text. Since we are committed to taking our marching orders from the market, a Canadian edition of *Essentials of Marketing* has been designed to meet that customer need. We expect this volume to be exceedingly well received by both students and colleagues. However, we may be somewhat biased and unduly optimistic. The market must decide and we now eagerly await that judgment.

The authors also await comments, suggestions, and corrections on any subject. Canadian issues might best be discussed with me as I am solely responsible for the Canadian content of the text.

Stanley J. Shapiro

ACKNOWLEDGEMENTS

No textbook emerges, fully grown and fully dressed, from the forehead of its author. Inevitably, many different people contribute in a variety of ways to the completion of each project. This has certainly been the case as I prepared in tandem the Third Canadian Edition of McCarthy's *Basic Marketing* and the First Canadian Edition of his *Essentials of Marketing*. Now that both manuscripts have been completed, the time has come for me to express my thanks to all those who gave so graciously of their assistance. I wish, first of all, to recognize Mr. D. Buskas of Selkirk College, Mr. M. Chandross of George Brown College, Mr. T. F. Funk of the University of Guelph, Mr. K. Jensen of Ryerson Polytechnical Institute, Mr. W. G. Lyon of Fanshawe College, Mr. R. Marcus, a long-time friend associated with both Dawson College and McGill University, Dr. H. Matsusako of the University of Calgary, and Mr. J. I. Rubinstein of Vanier College for responding in some detail to a letter asking for user views on how a new revision might be strengthened. This same letter eventually generated a meeting at which Mr. G. Abbott, Mr. P. Cherry, Mr. G. Jacob, and Ms. C. Nelson, all of the British Columbia Institute of Technology, made a number of helpful suggestions.

All of these written and oral comments received very serious consideration. Many of them have been incorporated into the text or otherwise adopted. When the suggested changes were not made, this was usually due to the fact that such modifications would have involved my going beyond the assigned mandate to "Canadianize" McCarthy.

Change, of course, should only be made for the better. Ten outside contributors prepared original cases for the Second Canadian Edition of *Basic Marketing*. These cases have stood the test of time so well that they now appear, with some minor modifications, not only in the new edition of *Basic Marketing* but also in the first Canadianization of the *Essentials* text. The honor roll of repeat case contributors includes: D. Aronchick, Ryerson Polytechnical Institute; G. Byers, Humber College; J. Graham, University of Calgary; W. Kalaher, Humber College; J. Liefeld, University of Guelph; H. Overgaard, Wilfrid Laurier University; P. Rosson, Dalhousie University; R. Rotenberg, Brock University; R. Tamilia, University of Quebec, at Montreal; and R. Wyckham, Simon Fraser University. In addition, I am beholden to Professor W. Balderson of the University of Lethbridge for an additional Canadian case that has not been previously published.

Once again, Professor Tamilia has earned an additional vote of thanks for his helpful review of the revised section on the French Canadian market. I also greatly appreciated his perceptive comments on many other aspects of the Canadian marketing scene. Indeed, I eagerly await his publication of the ideas he expressed to me privately so that others might benefit from them as well.

Other academic colleagues providing helpful comments or useful references included Professors J. Forbes and R. Kelley of the University of British Columbia, V. H. Kirpalani of Concordia University, and two new colleagues, Drs. L. Meredith and R. Schwindt of Simon Fraser University. The following members of the business community and the public sector also provided references or helpful background material: Mr. F. Leonard of the Purchasing Commission of the Province of British Columbia, Ms. C. Farquahar of the Conference Board in Canada, Mr. A. Hazen of Salesforce Development Ltd., and Mr. R. Oliver of the Advertising Standards Council.

Carl Lawrence of Queens University, a friend and colleague for some 25 years, is the "outside" academic to whom I am clearly most in debt. Fortunately for me, Carl "went West" to spend a sabbatical year at Simon Fraser. Since he shared an office with me, he was soon caught up in efforts to revise *Basic Marketing*. He was the one to whom I turned when undecided as to whether material should be added, dropped, rephrased, or repositioned. In addition, Carl both researched and wrote the sections in both books dealing with the demographic and economic dimensions of the Canadian consumer market. He also prepared all of the Canadian material on wholesaling and retailing. Professor Lawrence's accumulated expertise in the analysis of statistical data is clearly reflected in his contributions. Carl, in turn, was greatly assisted by Ms. Karen Calderbank of the Statistics Canada Advisory Services in Vancouver, our primary source for the most recent and relevant data.

The various forms of assistance provided by new associates at Simon Fraser University must also be acknowledged. Both Bob Brown, Dean of Arts and the administrator to whom Business was reporting when I arrived at Simon Fraser, and Cal Hoyt, the first Dean of our new Faculty of Business Administration, provided much needed support. The necessary typing services were cheerfully and efficiently provided by Jean Last, Felicity Warburton, Bernice Ferrier, and Jenny Tjosvold. As Appendix B indicates, Mary Roberts of the SFU Library System did a truly brilliant job of updating previously published material on Canadian sources of marketing information. Though my demands may have put Simon Fraser to the test, I am happy to report that SFU passed with flying colors.

Finally, Shaheen. I have once again been blessed with a research associate who proved to be especially skilled at putting it all together and making it happen. I could not have prepared the two volumes without Ms. Shaheen Lalji's assistance; sometimes I think I would not even have tried. Canadianization of a textbook is, in many respects, an exercise in infinite detail. A thousand different things must be done, almost simultaneously and all with great care. Imagination and intelligence, patience and persistence, knowledge and know-how—these are the skills required and these are the skills Ms. Lalji possesses in abundance. She also seems to sense just when a trade-off must be made between additional research and the necessity to meet deadlines. Assisted when necessary by the also very able Mr. Karim Lalji, Shaheen did indeed make it all happen. More than anyone else, she is responsible for there being both a Third Canadian Edition of *Basic Marketing* and a new Canadianization of the *Essentials* text.

S. J. S.

CONTENTS

xi

ESSENTIALS OF MARKETING

When you finish this chapter, you should:

1. *Know what marketing is—and why you should learn about it.*

2. *Know why and how macro-marketing systems develop.*

3. *Know why marketing specialists—including middlemen and facilitators—develop.*

4. *Know the marketing functions—and who performs them.*

5. *Recognize the important new terms (shown in red).*

MARKETING'S ROLE IN SOCIETY

1

Marketing affects almost every aspect of your daily life.

You are probably reading this book because you have to. It's required reading in a course you have to take. Therefore, we want to tell you why you should study this book.

MARKETING—WHAT'S IT ALL ABOUT?

If you are a typical student taking your first course in marketing, it's a pretty safe bet that you have little, if any, idea of what marketing is all about. Don't worry—you're not alone! Few Canadians really understand what marketing is. In fact, even some business managers would have a hard time giving an exact definition of marketing.

Marketing is more than selling or advertising

If forced to define marketing, most people would probably say that marketing means ''selling'' or ''advertising.'' But this is not true. It is very important for you to see that selling and advertising are only *part* of marketing. Marketing is much more than selling and advertising.

How did all those tennis raquets get here?

Let's think about the marketing of tennis racquets. None of us was born with a tennis racquet in our hand. Nor do we make our own tennis racquets. Instead, they are made by such firms as Wilson, Spalding, Slazenger, Davis, Head, and Bancroft.

Most tennis racquets look pretty much alike. All are intended to do the same thing—hit the ball over the net. Even so, a tennis player can choose among a wide assortment of racquets. There are different weights, handle sizes, materials, and strings. You can spend less than $10 on a prestrung racquet or more than $100 for just a frame! This variety in sizes and materials complicates the production and sale of tennis racquets. The following list gives just some of the many things a firm should do when it decides to manufacture tennis racquets.

1. Estimate how many people will be playing tennis over the next several years—and how many tennis racquets they will buy.
2. Predict exactly when people will want to buy tennis racquets.
3. Determine which handle sizes and weights people will want—and how many of each.
4. Decide what materials to use—as well as where and how to get them.
5. Estimate what price different tennis players will be willing to pay for their racquets.
6. Determine where these tennis players will be—and how to get the firm's racquets to them.
7. Decide which methods of promotion should be used to tell potential customers about the firm's tennis racquets.
8. Estimate how many other firms will be manufacturing tennis racquets—and how many racquets they will produce, what kind, at what prices, and so on.

The above activities are *not* part of **manufacturing**—actually producing goods and services. Rather, they are part of a larger process—called marketing—which can provide needed direction for manufacturing and

Manufacturers have to decide how big their markets are and what is wanted before they can even start production.

help to make sure that the right products find their way to interested consumers. You can see that this includes far more than selling or advertising. As you move through the book, you will learn much more about these activities. For now, however, it is important to see that marketing plays a necessary role in providing consumers with goods and services that satisfy their needs.

HOW MARKETING RELATES TO MANUFACTURING

Manufacturing is a very important economic activity. Whether for lack of skill, resources, or just lack of time, most people don't make most of the products they use. Picture yourself, for example, building a 10-speed bicycle, a color television, or a digital watch—starting from scratch! Clearly, the high standard of living that most Canadians enjoy would not be possible without modern manufacturing know-how.

Tennis racquets, like mousetraps, don't sell themselves

Although manufacturing is a necessary economic activity, some people tend to overrate its importance in relation to marketing. Their attitude is reflected in the old saying: "If a man . . . makes a better mousetrap . . . the world will beat a path to his door."

The mousetrap theory probably wasn't true in your grandfather's time—and it certainly is not true today. In modern economies, the grass grows high on the path to the Better Mousetrap Factory—if the new mousetrap is not properly marketed. We have already seen, for example, that there is a lot more to marketing tennis racquets than simply manufacturing them. This is true for most products.

The point is that manufacturing and marketing are both important parts of an economic system aimed at providing consumers with need-satisfying goods and services. Together they provide the four basic economic utilities—form, time, place, and possession utility—which are commonly needed to provide consumer satisfaction. Here, **utility** means the power to satisfy human needs.

Tennis racquets do not automatically provide utility

Form utility is provided when a manufacturer makes something (say a tennis racquet) out of other materials. But contrary to those who believe in the mousetrap theory, just making tennis racquets does not result in consumer satisfaction. Time, place, and possession utility must also be provided.

Time utility means having the product available *when* the customer wants it. And **place utility** means having the product available *where* the customer wants it. For example, how much satisfaction would a tennis player in British Columbia get from a tennis racquet in a manufacturer's warehouse in Winnipeg? That tennis racquet wouldn't win many games unless it was available *when* (time utility) and *where* (place utility) the tennis player wanted it. And to have the legal right to use the tennis racquet, the tennis player would have to pay for it before enjoying possession

This player needs a new racquet immediately (time utility) at the court (place utility) or the game has to stop.

utility. **Possession utility** means completing a transaction and gaining possession so that one has the right to use the product.

Stated simply, the job of manufacturing is to create form utility, while marketing's job is to provide time, place, and possession utility. And marketing information may help decide what products to produce. So it can also be argued that marketing helps create form utility.

You can see that successful manufacturing depends on successful marketing. How marketing creates time, place, and possession utility will be explored later in this chapter. First, we want to tell you why you should study marketing—and then we must define marketing.

MARKETING AND YOU

Why you should study marketing

One reason for studying marketing is that—as a consumer—you pay for marketing activities. It's estimated that marketing costs about 50 percent of each consumer's dollar.[1]

Marketing organizes producers to satisfy consumers' needs.

Another important reason for learning about marketing is that marketing affects almost every part of your daily life. The products you buy. The stores where you shop. All that advertising you are exposed to. They are all a part of marketing. Even your job résumé is part of a marketing campaign to sell yourself to some employers.

Another reason for studying marketing is that there are many exciting and rewarding career opportunities in marketing. Marketing is often the road to the top. Throughout this book you will find information about opportunities in various areas of marketing.

Those of you who are looking for nonmarketing positions in business will have to work with marketing people. Knowing something about marketing will help you understand them better. It will also help you do your own job better. Remember, a company that cannot successfully sell its products won't need accountants, computer programmers, financial managers, personnel managers, production managers, and so on. It's often said, "Nothing happens unless the cash register rings."

Even if you are not planning a business career, marketing ideas and methods will be very useful for you. Nonprofit organizations are beginning to realize this. The same approaches used to sell soap can also be used to "sell" ideas, politicians, mass transportation, health care services, energy conservation, and museums.

A final and even more basic reason for studying marketing is that marketing plays a big part in economic growth and development. Marketing stimulates research and change—resulting in new products. If these products attract customers, this can lead to fuller employment, higher incomes, and a higher standard of living. An effective marketing system is important, therefore, to the future of our nation—and all nations.

HOW SHOULD WE DEFINE MARKETING?

As noted earlier, most people would probably define marketing as selling or advertising. On the other hand, one famous marketing expert called marketing: "The creation and delivery of a standard of living."[2]

Micro- or macro-marketing?

There is a big difference between these two definitions. The first definition focuses on the activities of an individual firm. The second focuses on the economic welfare of the entire society.

Which view is correct? Is marketing a set of activities performed by individual organizations, or is it a social process?

To answer this question, let's go back to our tennis racquet example. We saw that a manufacturer of tennis racquets would have to perform several customer-related activities besides simply producing racquets. The same would be true for an art museum or a welfare agency. This supports the idea of marketing as a set of activities performed by individual organizations.

On the other hand, people cannot live on tennis racquets and art museums alone! In an advanced economy like ours, it takes thousands of goods and services to satisfy the many needs of society. A large supermarket may handle as many as 10,000 items. A typical K mart stocks 15,000 different items. A society needs some sort of marketing system to organize all the producers needed to satisfy the needs of all its citizens. So it would appear that marketing is an important social process.

The answer to our question then is that marketing is *both* a set of activities performed by organizations *and* a social process. Therefore, we will present two definitions of marketing—one for micro-marketing and another for macro-marketing. The first looks at customers and organizations. The second one takes a broad view of our whole production-distribution system.

MICRO-MARKETING DEFINED

Micro-marketing is the performance of activities which seek to accomplish an organization's objectives by anticipating customer or client needs and directing a flow of need-satisfying goods and services from producer to customer or client.

Let's look at this definition.

Applies to profit and nonprofit organizations

To begin with, this definition applies to both profit and nonprofit organizations. Their customers or clients may be individual consumers, business firms, nonprofit organizations, government agencies, or even foreign nations. While most customers and clients will probably have to pay for the goods and services they receive, others may receive them free of charge or at a reduced cost—through private or government subsidies.

It is more than selling and advertising

Is micro-marketing only personal selling and advertising? Unfortunately, many executives think this is true. They feel that the job of marketing is to "get rid of" the product that has been produced and priced by the production, accounting, and finance executives.

This narrow view of marketing should be rejected. As noted management consultant Peter Drucker has stated:

> There will always, one can assume, be need for some selling. But the aim of marketing is to make selling superfluous. The aim of marketing is to know and understand the customer so well that the product or service sells itself.
>
> Ideally, marketing should result in a customer who is *ready* to buy. All that should be needed then is to make the product or service available.[3]

Thus, when we define micro-marketing as those activities which anticipate customer or client needs and direct a flow of need-satisfying goods and services, we mean just that.

Begins with customer needs

Marketing should begin with potential customer needs—not with the production process. Marketing should try to anticipate needs. And then, marketing rather than production should determine what products are to be made—including decisions about product development, product design,

Marketers should know their markets so well that their products sell themselves.

and packaging; what prices or fees are to be charged; credit and collection policies; transporting and storing policies; when and how the products are to be advertised and sold; and after-sale warranty, service, and perhaps even disposal policies.

Provides a sense of direction

This does *not* mean that marketing should take over production, accounting, and financial activities. Rather, it means that marketing—by interpreting consumers' needs—should provide direction for these activities and helps to coordinate them. After all, the purpose of a business or nonprofit organization is to satisfy customer or client needs. It is *not* to supply goods or services which are *convenient* to produce and which *might* sell or be accepted free.

THE FOCUS OF THIS TEXT—BUSINESS-ORIENTED MICRO-MARKETING

Assuming that you are preparing for a business career, the main focus of this text will be on micro-marketing. We will see marketing through the eyes of the marketing manager. Much of this material will also be useful for those who plan to work for nonprofit organizations.

It is very important, however, that marketing managers never forget that their organizations are just small parts of a larger macro-marketing system. Therefore, for the rest of this chapter we will look at the macro—the big picture—view of marketing. Let's begin by defining macro-marketing and then reviewing some basic concepts.

MACRO-MARKETING DEFINED

Macro-marketing is a social process which directs an economy's flow of goods and services from producers to consumers in a way which effectively matches supply and demand and accomplishes the objectives of society.

Like micro-marketing, macro-marketing is concerned with the flow of need-satisfying goods and services from producer to consumer. When we talk about macro-marketing, however, the emphasis is not on the activities of *individual* organizations. Rather, the emphasis is on how the *whole system* works.

EVERY SOCIETY NEEDS AN ECONOMIC SYSTEM

All societies must provide for the needs of their members. Therefore, every society needs some sort of **economic system**—the way an economy is organized (with or without the use of money) to use *scarce* productive resources (which could have alternative uses) to produce goods and services and distribute them for consumption—now and in the future—among various people and groups in the society.[4]

How an economic system operates depends upon a society's objectives and its political system. But, all economic systems must decide *what and how much* is to be produced *by whom and when* and distributed *to whom*. How these decisions are made may vary from nation to nation—but the macro-level objectives are basically the same: to create goods and services and make them available when and where they are needed to maintain or improve each nation's output.

HOW ECONOMIC DECISIONS ARE MADE

There are two basic kinds of economic systems: planned systems and market-directed systems. Actually, no economy is *entirely* planned or market-directed. Most developing or advanced economies are a mixture of the two kinds.

The assortment of goods and services may be limited in a planned economy.

*Government planners
may make the decisions*

A **planned economic system** is one in which government planners decide what and how much is to be produced and distributed by whom, when, and to whom. Producers generally have very little choice about product design. Their main job is to meet their assigned production quotas. Prices are set by government planners and tend to be very rigid—not changing according to supply and demand. Consumers usually have some freedom of choice. It is impossible to control every single detail! But the assortment of goods and services may be quite limited. Activities such as market research, branding, and advertising may receive little emphasis—and sometimes are not done at all.[5]

Government planning may work fairly well as long as the economy is simple—and the variety of goods and services is small. It may even be necessary under certain conditions—during wartime, for example. However, as economies become more complex, government planning becomes more difficult. It may even break down. Planners may face too many complex decisions. And consumers may lose patience if the planners don't meet their needs.

*A market-directed
economy runs itself*

A **market-directed economic system** is one in which the individual decisions of the many producers and consumers make the macro-level decisions for the whole economy.

A pure market-directed economy is free from the government controls that go with government planning. Consumers make a society's production decisions when they make their choices in the marketplace. They decide what is to be produced and by whom—through their dollar "votes." The prices in the marketplace serve roughly as a measure of the social importance of goods and services. If consumers are willing to pay the market prices, then apparently they feel they are getting at least their money's worth.

Whenever a new consumer need arises, an opportunity is created for some profit-minded business. All consumer needs which can be served profitably will encourage producers to meet those needs. Ideally, control of the economy is completely democratic. Power is spread throughout the economy.

Greatest freedom of choice

Consumers in a market-directed economy enjoy maximum freedom of choice. They are not forced to buy any goods or services except those that must be provided for the good of society—things like national defense, schools, police and fire protection, mass transportation, and public health services. These are provided by the community—and citizens are taxed to pay for them.

In a market-directed economy, people have free choice in finding work that is satisfying to them. Producers are free to produce whatever they wish, providing that they stay within the rules of the game established by government *and* that they receive enough dollar votes from consumers.

If they do their job well, they will earn a profit and stay in business. But profit, survival, and growth are not guaranteed.

The Canadian economy is largely—but not completely—market-directed. For example, in addition to setting and enforcing the rules of the game, the federal government controls interest rates and the supply of money, sets import and export restrictions, regulates radio and TV broadcasting, alternately restricts and stimulates agricultural production, sometimes controls prices and wages, and so on. Some of these activities may be necessary to reach short-run goals. But some may get in the way of accomplishing long-run goals. For example, increasing government interference could affect the survival of our market-directed system—and the economic and political freedom that goes with it.[6]

ALL ECONOMIES NEED MACRO-MARKETING SYSTEMS

In general, no economic system—whether planned or market directed—can achieve its objectives without an effective macro-marketing system. To explain why this is true, we will look at marketing in primitive economies. Then we will see how macro-marketing tends to become more and more complex in advanced economic systems.

Marketing involves exchange

In a pure subsistence economy, each family unit produces all the goods that it consumes. There is no need to exchange goods and services. Each producer-consumer unit is totally self-sufficient. Marketing would not take place— because marketing does not occur unless there are two or more parties who want to exchange something for something else.

Almost all economies have gone beyond the pure subsistence stage. There is a need to exchange things.

The term "marketing" comes from the word "market" A **market** is a group of sellers and buyers bargaining the terms of exchange for goods and services. This can be done face-to-face at some physical location (e.g., a farmers' market). Or it can be done indirectly through a complex network of middlemen who link buyers and sellers who are far apart.

In primitive economies, markets tend to be located in central places. **Central markets** are convenient places where buyers and sellers can meet face-to-face to exchange goods and services. We can understand macro-marketing better by seeing how and why central markets develop.

Central markets help exchange

Imagine a small village of five families. Each has some special skill for producing some need-satisfying product. After meeting basic needs, each family might decide to specialize. It is easier for one family to make two pots and another to make two baskets than it is for each one to make one pot and one basket. Specialization makes labor more efficient and more productive. It can increase the total amount of form utility created.

If these five families specialize in one product each, they will have to trade with each other. As Figure 1–1 shows, it would take the 5 families 10 separate trips and exchanges to obtain some of each of the products.

**Figure 1–1: Ten exchanges
required when a central
market is not used**[7]

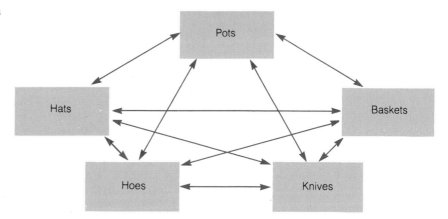

If the families live near each other, the exchange process would be relatively simple. But if they are far apart, traveling back and forth will take time. Who would do the traveling and when?

Faced with this problem, the families can agree to come to a central market and trade on a certain day. Then, each family would need to make only one trip to the market to trade with all the others. This will reduce the total number of trips to five. This would make exchange easier, leave more time for production and consumption, and provide for social gatherings. In total, much more time, place, possession, and even form utility would be enjoyed by each of the five families.

*Money system speeds
trading*

While a central meeting place would simplify exchange, the individual bartering transactions would still take much time. Bartering requires another person who wants what you have and vice versa. Each trader must find others who have products of about equal value. After trading with one group, a family might find itself with some extra hats, knives, and pots. Then it would have to find others willing to trade for these products.

A money system would change all of this. A seller would just have to find a buyer who can either use or sell his product and agree on a price. Then he would be free to spend his money to buy whatever he wants.

*Middlemen help
exchange even more*

The development of a central market and a money system would simplify the exchange process among the five families in our imaginary village. But a total of 10 separate transactions would still be required—once the families arrived at the central market. Thus, it would still take a lot of time and effort to carry out exchange among the five families.

This clumsy exchange process could be made much simpler by the appearance of a **middleman**—someone who specializes in trade rather than production. He would be willing to buy each family's output—and then sell each family whatever goods it needs. This middleman would charge for his service, of course. But this charge might be more than offset by savings in time and effort.

Figure 1-2: Only five
exchanges are required
when a middleman in a
central market is used[8]

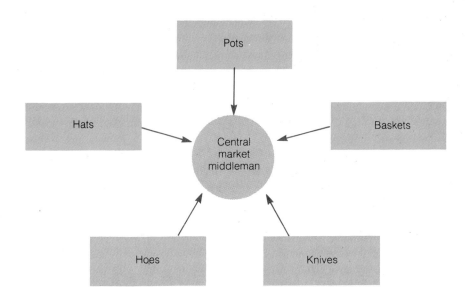

In our simple example, using the services of a middleman at a central market would reduce the number of transactions for all families from 10 to 5. See Figure 1-2. Each family would have more time for production, consumption, and visits to other families. Also, each family could specialize in production—creating greater form utility. Meanwhile, by specializing in trade, the middleman could provide additional time, place, and possession utility. In total, all the villagers might enjoy greater economic utility and greater satisfaction by using a middleman in the central market.

You can see that the reduction in transactions that results from using a middleman in a central market becomes more important as the number of families increases. For example, if the population of our imaginary village were to increase from 5 to 10 families, 45 transactions would be required without a middleman. Using a middleman would reduce the necessary number of transactions to 10—that is, 1 for each family.

Today, such middlemen—offering permanent trading facilities—are known as wholesalers and retailers. The advantages of working with middlemen increase as the number of producers and customers, their distance apart, and the number and variety of competing products increase. That is why there are so many wholesalers and retailers in modern economies.

THE ROLE OF MARKETING IN ECONOMIC DEVELOPMENT

Modern economies have advanced well beyond the five-family village—but the same ideas still apply. The basic purpose of markets and middlemen is to make exchange easier and allow greater time for production, consumption, and other activities—including leisure.

Effective marketing is necessary for economic development

Although it is tempting to decide that more effective macro-marketing systems are the *result* of greater economic development, just the opposite is true. An effective macro-marketing system is *necessary* for economic development. In fact, management expert Peter Drucker has suggested that marketing may even be the key to growth in less-developed nations.[9]

Breaking the vicious circle of poverty

Without an effective macro-marketing system, the less-developed nations may not be able to escape the "vicious circle of poverty."[10] They can't leave their subsistence way of life to produce for the market, because there are no buyers for any goods they might produce. And there are no buyers because everyone else is producing for his own needs. Breaking this vicious circle of poverty may require a major change in the micro- and macro-marketing systems that are typical in less-developed nations.

CAN MASS PRODUCTION SATISFY A SOCIETY'S CONSUMPTION NEEDS?

The growth of cities brings together large numbers of people. They must depend on others to produce most of the goods and services they need to satisfy their basic needs. Also, many consumers have higher incomes. They can afford to satisfy higher-level needs as well. A modern economic system has a big job satisfying all these needs.

Economies of scale mean lower costs

Fortunately, advanced economies can take advantage of mass production with its **economies of scale**—which means that as a company produces larger numbers of a particular product, the cost for each of these products goes down. For example, a one-of-a-kind, custom-built car would cost *much* more than a mass-produced standard model.

It may be hard for marketing to have an effect in underdeveloped countries if everyone's at the subsistence level.

Modern manufacturing skills can help produce great quantities of goods and services to satisfy large numbers of consumers. But mass production alone can't solve the problem of satisfying a society's needs. Effective marketing is needed also.

Effective marketing is needed to link producers and consumers

Effective marketing means delivering the goods and services that consumers need and want. And it means getting the goods to them at the right time, in the right place, and at a price they're willing to pay. This is no easy job, especially if you think about the big variety of goods a highly developed economy can produce—and the many kinds of goods and services consumers want.

Effective marketing in an advanced economy is more difficult because producers are separated from consumers in several ways—as Figure 1–3 shows.[11] It is also complicated by "discrepancies of quantity" and "discrepancies of assortment" between producer and consumers. This means that individual producers specialize in producing and selling large amounts of a narrow assortment of goods and services, but each consumer wants only small quantities of a wide variety of goods and services.

Universal marketing functions must be performed

The purpose of a macro-marketing system is to overcome these separations and discrepancies. The "universal functions of marketing" do this.

Figure 1–3: **Marketing facilitates production and consumption**[12]

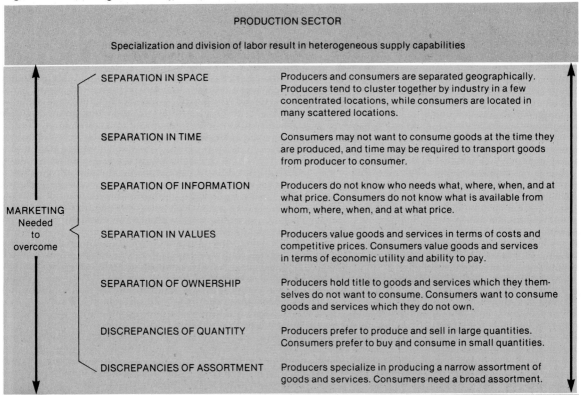

The **universal functions of marketing** are: buying, selling, transporting, storing, standardization and grading, financing, risk-taking, and market information. These marketing functions are *universal* in the sense that they must be performed in *all* macro-marketing systems. *How* these functions are performed and by *whom* may differ among nations and economic systems, but they are needed in any macro-marketing system. Let's take a closer look at them now.

The **buying function** means looking for and evaluating goods and services. The **selling function** involves promoting the product. It would include the use of personal selling, advertising, and other mass selling methods. This is the best known, and some people feel the only, function of marketing.

Transporting function means the movement of goods from one place to another. The **storing function** involves holding goods.

Standardization and grading involve sorting products according to size and quality. This simplifies buying and selling by reducing the need for inspection and sampling. **Financing** provides the necessary cash and credit to manufacture, transport, store, promote, sell, and buy products. **Risk taking** involves bearing the uncertainties that are a part of the marketing process. A firm can never be sure that customers will want to buy its products. And the products could also become damaged, stolen, or outdated. The **market information function** involves the collection, analysis, and distribution of information needed to plan, carry out, and control marketing activities.

WHO PERFORMS MARKETING FUNCTIONS?

Producers, consumers, and marketing specialists

From a macro-level viewpoint, these functions are all part of the marketing process—and must be done by someone. None of them can be skipped or eliminated. In a planned economy, some of the functions might be performed by government agencies. Others might be left to individual producers and consumers. In a market-directed economy, these marketing functions are performed by producers, consumers, and various marketing specialists. See Figure 1–4.

Earlier in this chapter, we saw that adding a middleman to a simple five-family village of producers and consumers made exchange easier—and increased the total amount of economic utility. This effect is even greater in a large, complicated economy. This helps explain why most of the products sold in Canada are distributed through wholesalers and retailers—instead of directly from producers to consumers.

You saw how producers and consumers benefited when a marketing specialist (middleman) helped in buying and selling. Producers and consumers also benefit when marketing specialists perform the other marketing functions. So we find marketing functions being performed by a variety of other specialists. These include advertising agencies, marketing research firms, independent product-testing laboratories, public warehouses,

Figure 1–4: **Model of Canadian macro-marketing system**[13]

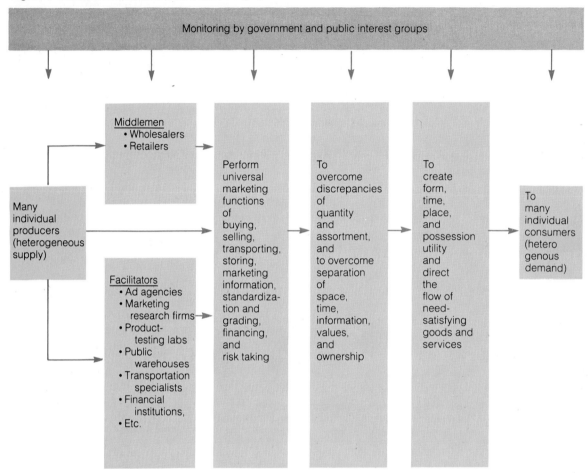

transportation firms, and banks. Through specialization and economies of scale, specialists are often able to perform the marketing functions at a lower cost than producers or consumers could. This allows producers and consumers to spend more time on production and consumption.

Functions can be shifted and shared

From a macro viewpoint, all of the marketing functions must be performed by someone. But from a micro viewpoint not every firm must perform all of the functions. Some marketing specialists perform all the functions. Others specialize in only one or two. For example, marketing research firms specialize only in the market information function.

Sometimes several specialists are used between producer and consumer. Then some of the marketing functions may be performed several times. But the key point to remember is this: *Responsibility for performing the marketing functions can be shifted and shared in a variety of ways, but no function can be completely eliminated!*

HOW WELL DOES OUR MACRO-MARKETING SYSTEM WORK?

It connects remote producers and consumers

A macro-marketing system does more than just deliver goods to consumers—it allows mass production with its "economies of scale." Also, with mass communication and transportation, our system allows the products of our farms to be shipped where they are needed. Wheat from the Prairies is sold even in the Maritimes, and toys are manufactured throughout the year for sale in December.

It encourages growth and new ideas

In addition to making mass production possible, our market-directed macro-marketing system encourages new ideas. Competition for the consumers' dollars forces firms to think of new and better ways of satisfying consumer needs.

It has its critics

In trying to explain marketing's role in society, we have emphasized the good points of our macro-marketing system. In general, we feel this approach is right—because our macro-marketing system has provided us with one of the highest standards of living in the world. We have to admit, however, that marketing—as we know it in Canada—has many critics. Marketing activity is especially open to criticism because it is the part of business most visible to the public. There is nothing like a pocketbook issue for getting consumers excited!

Typical complaints about marketing include:

Advertising is annoying, dishonest, and wasteful.

Product quality is terrible—they just don't build things like they used to!

Marketing makes people too materialistic—it motivates them toward the "almighty dollar" instead of social needs.

Easy consumer credit makes people buy things they don't need and can't really afford.

Too many unnecessary products are offered.

Packaging and labeling are often confusing and deceptive.

Middlemen add to the cost of distribution and raise prices without providing anything in return.

Marketers are destroying our environment.

Advertising is corrupting the minds of children—and putting too much sex and violence on TV.

Greedy business people create monopolies which limit output and raise prices.

Distribution costs are too high.

Retailers are cheating the public.

There are too many unsafe products on the market.

Marketing serves the rich and exploits the poor.

Consumers' complaints should be taken seriously.

Such complaints cannot and should not be taken lightly. They show that many Canadians aren't happy with some parts of our marketing system. The strong public support that consumer advocates like Ralph Nader and Phil Edmonston have received shows that not all consumers feel they are being treated like kings and queens. If business people ignore these complaints, there could be strong pressure for the government to reshape our macro-marketing system. Already, some of our nation's leaders are calling for national economic planning—instead of depending on a market-directed system.[14]

CONCLUSION

In this chapter we have defined two levels of marketing: micro-marketing and macro-marketing. A close review of the complaints against marketing suggests that there are basically two levels of criticism also. Some are concerned with marketing's overall role in society (macro-marketing). Others are concerned with the activities of individual organizations (micro-marketing).

The chapter has gone into macro-marketing in some detail because organizations are just small parts of a bigger macro-marketing system. We saw how economic decisions are made—in both planned and market-directed economies. We talked about the nature of markets and how and why central markets develop. Finally, the role of marketing in economic development and in

mass production was considered. The importance of the universal marketing functions was emphasized.

Although the major emphasis in this chapter was on macro-marketing, the emphasis of this book is on micro-marketing. We believe that most criticisms of marketing are the result of ineffective decision making at the micro level. Therefore, the best way to answer some of this criticism is to educate future business people—like you—to be more efficient and socially responsible decision makers. This will help improve the performance of individual organizations. Eventually, it should also make our macro-marketing system work better.

The effect of micro-level decisions on society

will be discussed throughout the text. Then, in Chapter 21—after you have begun to understand how and why producers and consumers think and behave the way they do—we will return to macro-marketing. We will try to evaluate how well both macro-marketing and micro-marketing perform in our market-directed economic system.

QUESTIONS FOR DISCUSSION

1. It is fairly easy to see why people do not beat a path to the mousetrap manufacturer's door, but would they be similarly indifferent if some food processor developed a revolutionary new food product which would provide all necessary nutrients in small pills for about $100 per year per person?

2. Distinguish between macro- and micro-marketing. Then explain how they are interrelated, if they are.

3. Distinguish between how economic decisions are made in a centrally planned economy and in a market-directed economy.

4. Explain *(a)* how a central market facilitates exchange and *(b)* how the addition of a middleman facilitates exchange even more.

5. Identify a "central market" in your own city and explain how it facilitates exchange.

6. Discuss the nature of marketing in a socialist economy. Would the functions that must be provided and the development of wholesaling and retailing systems be any different?

7. Describe a recent purchase you have made and indicate why that particular product was available at a store and, in particular, at that store.

8. Explain, in your own words, why the emphasis in this text is on micro-marketing.

9. Why is satisfying consumers apparently considered of equal importance with satisfying an organization's objectives in the text's definition of micro-marketing?

10. On the streets of cities in many developing countries, one sees old women and small boys selling cigarettes one at a time. The price per cigarette is higher than if the customer purchased a package or carton, as is typical in Canada. Some Canadians are appalled at the unhygienic aspects of this method of distribution. Some are also appalled at the "inefficiency" of this method of distribution. Is this an inefficient method of distribution? Are consumers getting "ripped off"? If so, by whom? Who is benefiting?

SUGGESTED CASES

2. Tom's Cleaning Company
28. Cando, Ltd.

When you finish this chapter, you should:

1. *Know what the marketing concept is—and how it should affect a firm's strategy planning.*

2. *Understand what a marketing manager does.*

3. *Know what marketing strategy planning is—and why it will be the focus of this book.*

4. *Be familiar with the four Ps in a marketing mix.*

5. *Know the difference between a strategy, a strategic plan, and a marketing program.*

6. *Recognize the important new terms (shown in red).*

MARKETING'S ROLE IN THE FIRM

2

"A master plan to hit the target" is not a James Bond story line—but the goal of a good marketing manager.

Marketing and marketing management are important in our society—and in business firms. As you saw in Chapter 1, marketing is concerned with anticipating needs and directing the flow of goods and services from producers to consumers. This is done to satisfy the needs of consumers—and accomplish both the economy's (the macro view) and the firm's (the micro view) objectives.

To get a better understanding of both macro- and micro-marketing, we are going to emphasize micro-marketing. That is, we are going to look at things from the point of view of the marketing manager—the one who makes a company's important marketing decisions.

MARKETING'S ROLE HAS CHANGED A LOT OVER THE YEARS

In a modern economy, marketing management is very important. But this hasn't always been true. It is only recently that more and more producers, wholesalers, and retailers have begun to see the importance of marketing planning. These companies used to think mainly about making a product. Now they focus on customers—and try to aim the company's total effort toward satisfying them.

From the production era to the marketing era

The story of this change was told very well by R. J. Keith—a top manager of Pillsbury, Inc.—a manufacturer of flour, cake mixes, and animal feeds.[1]

From the production to the sales era

The marketing concept was a long time coming to Pillsbury. The company was formed in 1869—and continued until about 1930 in what Keith called the production era. The **production era** is a time when a company focuses on production—perhaps because few products are available in the market. Beginning in 1930, the company went into the sales era. The **sales era** is a time when a company emphasizes selling—because competition is increasing. Pillsbury increased selling effort as it became aware that it was very important to attract both its middlemen and the middlemen's customers.

To the marketing department era

The sales era continued until about 1950. By then, Pillsbury had developed many new products. Sales were growing rapidly. Someone was needed to tie together the efforts of production, research, purchasing, and sales. As Pillsbury faced up to this job, the sales era was replaced by the marketing department era. The **marketing department era** is a time when all marketing activities are brought under the control of one department—to improve short-run policy planning—to try to tie together the firm's activities. Finding people trained in short-run marketing policy making was difficult. For three or four years the company worked at learning how to turn ideas into products—and products into profits.

To the marketing company era

In a relatively few years, Pillsbury had developed a staff with a marketing management view. Then, in 1958, the company went all the way—into the marketing company era. The **marketing company era** is a time when—in addition to short-run marketing planning—the whole company effort is guided by the *marketing concept*. Now, Pillsbury's marketing specialists look and plan 3 to 10 years ahead.

What does the marketing concept mean in business?

The **marketing concept** means that a firm aims all its efforts on satisfying its customers—at a profit. This is really a new idea in business. It replaces the production-oriented way of thinking. **Production orientation** means making products which are easy to produce—and *then* trying to sell them. **Marketing orientation** means trying to carry out the marketing concept.

The marketing concept calls for changing the firm's ways of doing things. Instead of trying to get customers to buy what the firm has produced, a marketing-oriented firm would try to produce what customers want.

Those who believe in the marketing concept feel that customers' needs

marketing Concept is to try and produce what the customer wants!!!

A firm with a "marketing company" thrust tries to plan for its market's long term needs.

should be the firm's main focus. They feel that the firm's resources should be organized to satisfy those needs.

Three basic ideas are included in the definition of the marketing concept:

1. A customer orientation.
2. A total company effort.
3. Profit—not just sales—as an objective of the firm.

Carrying out the marketing concept, therefore, might require three related changes:

1. A change in management attitudes.
2. A change in the firm's organization structure.
3. A change in its management methods and procedures.

Changes in all three areas would probably be needed if the firm really wanted to adopt the marketing concept.

The typical production orientation is a roadblock

Give the customers what they need—this may seem so obvious and logical that it may be hard for you to understand why the marketing concept is such a new idea. However, people haven't always done the logical and obvious. In a typical company, production managers thought mainly about getting out the product. Accountants were interested only in balancing the books. Financial people looked after the company's cash position. And sales people were mainly concerned with getting orders. Each person saw the rest of the business working around him. No one was concerned with whether the whole system made sense. As long as the company made a profit, each department went merrily on—doing its own thing. Unfortunately, this is still true in most companies today.

"Production orientation" refers to the typical lack of a central focus in a business firm. To be fair to the production people, however, it also is seen in sales-oriented sales representatives, advertising-oriented agency people, finance-oriented finance people, and so on. We will use "production orientation" to cover all such narrow thinking.

It should be a "sharing" situation

Ideally, all managers should work together—because the output from one department may be the input to another. But managers in production-oriented firms tend to build "fences" around their own departments—as seen in Figure 2–1(A). Each department runs its own affairs for its own benefit. There may be committees to try to get them to work together. But usually each department head comes to such meetings with the idea of protecting his department's interests.

It's easy to slip into a production orientation

It is very easy to slip into a production-oriented way of thinking. Production managers, for example, might prefer to have long production runs of easy-to-produce, standardized products. And retailers might prefer only daytime weekday hours—avoiding nights, Saturdays, and Sundays, when many customers would prefer to shop. Differences in outlook between production-oriented and marketing-oriented managers are shown in Figure 2–2.

Work together . . . do a better job

In a firm that has accepted the marketing concept, however, the fences come down. There are still departments, of course, because there are efficiencies in specialization. But the total system's effort is guided by what customers want—instead of what each department would like to do.

In such a firm, it is more realistic to view the business as a box with both an internal and an external section. See Figure 2–1(B). Here, there are some internal departments concerned mainly with affairs inside the firm—production, accounting, and research and development (R&D). And there are external departments concerned with outside matters—sales, advertising, and sales promotion. Finally, there are departments that must be concerned with both the internal and the external sections—warehous-

Figure 2–1

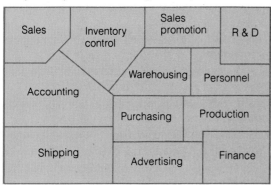

A. A business as a box
    (most departments have high fences)

B. Total system view of a
    business (implementing marketing concept;
    still have departments but all guided by
    what customers want)

Figure 2–2: Some differences in outlook between adopters of the marketing concept and the typical production-oriented managers[2]

Marketing orientation	Attitudes and procedures	Production orientation
Customer needs determine company plans	← Attitudes toward customers →	They should be glad we exist, trying to cut costs and bring out better products
Company makes what it can sell	← Product offering →	Company sells what it can make
To determine customer needs and how well company is satisfying them	← Role of marketing research →	To determine customer reaction, if used at all
Focus on locating new opportunities	← Interest in innovation →	Focus is on technology and cost cutting
A critical objective	← Importance of profit →	A residual, what's left after all costs are covered
Seen as a customer service	← Role of customer credit →	Seen as a necessary evil
Designed for customer convenience and as a selling tool	← Role of packaging →	Seen merely as protection for the product
Set with customer requirements and costs in mind	← Inventory levels →	Set with production requirements in mind
Seen as a customer service	← Transportation arrangements →	Seen as an extension of production and storage activities, with emphasis on cost minimization
Need-satisfying benefits of products and services	← Focus of advertising →	Product features and quality, maybe how products are made
Help the customer to buy if the product fits his needs, while coordinating with rest of firm— including production, inventory control, advertising, etc.	← Role of sales force →	Sell the customer, don't worry about coordination with other promotion efforts or rest of firm

ing, shipping, purchasing, finance, and personnel. The efforts of *all* of these departments are aimed at satisfying some market needs—at a profit.

Marketing concept forces changes
The marketing concept is really very powerful—if taken seriously. It forces the company (1) to think through what it is doing, and why, and then (2) to develop a plan for accomplishing its objectives. Where the marketing concept has been wholeheartedly accepted and carried out, it has led to major changes in the way the firm operates—and often to higher profits.

ORGANIZING TO IMPLEMENT THE MARKETING CONCEPT

Pointing the company toward its goal
The first and most important step in applying the marketing concept is a serious commitment to a customer orientation. Without acceptance of this idea—at least by top management—any change in the organization structure won't really matter.

Some organization helps　　　After top management has accepted the marketing concept, some formal reorganization is usually desirable. The product planning function is often under the production or R&D (research and development) department. Pricing is under the finance or accounting department. And sales and advertising are often separate departments.

　　　All these activities involve the customer, so they should be under the direction of the marketing manager. The marketing manager should report directly to top management—along with the heads of production, R&D, finance, and accounting. The arrangement of a particular marketing department depends on the strategies of that company—and the personalities involved. Organization charts in one company before and after adoption of the marketing concept are shown in Figure 2–3.[3]

Who should organize and run the total system?　　　Top management is responsible for developing and running a *total system* designed to meet the needs of target customers. Ideally, the whole company becomes customer-oriented—all departments pull together to

Figure 2–3: **A company's organization chart before and after acceptance of the marketing concept**

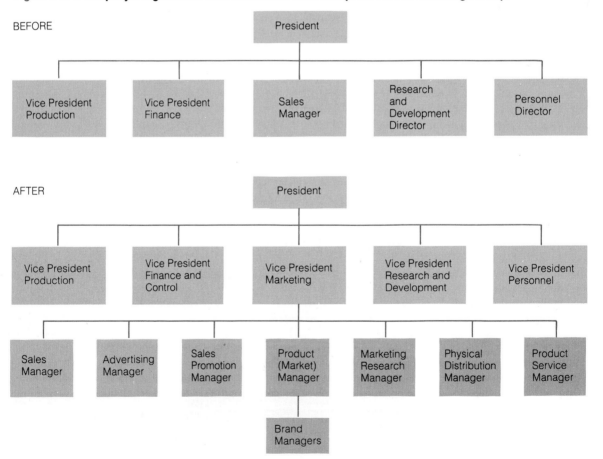

reach its objectives. We will still have departments—because there are advantages in job specialization. But instead of battles between various departments, a marketing-oriented system would do some marketing research, perhaps run some market tests, and figure potential costs and *company* (not departmental) profits for possible strategies. Then it would decide what is best for the *firm*—not just what is best for any one department.

In such a system, the marketing manager helps develop this "total system" attitude within the firm. He must work regularly with customers—and is in an ideal position to tie things together.

Who is suited to lead a marketing-oriented company?

Many marketing managers probably will come out of sales management—because they are more likely to be familiar with target customers. But this isn't always true. The marketing manager and a marketing-oriented president could come from any specialty. In one cosmetic company—as might be expected in this type of business—the advertising and sales promotion manager gradually assumed major planning and coordinating responsibilities. In another firm, however—which produced highly technical custom-built products—the production manager was the leader in applying the marketing concept.

The most important point is that the prospective marketing manager and top manager accept the marketing concept.

ADOPTION OF THE MARKETING CONCEPT HAS NOT BEEN EASY OR UNIVERSAL

The marketing concept seems so logical that you would think that it would have been quickly accepted by most firms. In fact, it was not. Further, there are still many firms which are production-oriented. In fact, the majority

Many managers are naturally product oriented and must make a conscious effort to apply the marketing concept.

*Marketers of services—
including professionals—
are being forced into a
marketing orientation by
competition.*

are either production-oriented—or regularly slip back that way—and must consciously bring the customers' interests to bear in their planning.

The marketing concept was first accepted by consumer goods companies—such as General Electric and Procter & Gamble.[4] Competition was intense in some of their markets—and trying to satisfy customers' needs more fully was a way to win in this competition.

Slow acceptance in many markets

Producers of industrial commodities—steel, coal, paper, glass, chemicals—have accepted the marketing concept more slowly—if at all. Similarly, many retailers have been slow to accept the marketing concept—in part because they are so close to the final consumer that they feel that they really know their customers.

In the last 10 years or so, service industries—including banks, airlines, lawyers, physicians, accountants, and insurance companies—have begun to consider the marketing concept. Acceptance varies widely in these industries. The government has even promoted more emphasis on marketing—by encouraging advertising and price competition among lawyers, accountants, and other professional groups. This has led many in these professions to pay more attention to their customers' needs. And some have been forced into it by aggressive competitors who are advertising and using price to attract new customers—which is contrary to long-accepted professional practice.

THE MARKETING CONCEPT IS USEFUL FOR NONPROFIT ORGANIZATIONS, TOO

Most of this book will focus on how to apply the marketing concept in a business firm. But the same general principles can be applied directly to nonprofit organizations. The Red Cross, art museums, and government agencies are all trying to satisfy some consumer groups. The objectives are different—but the marketing concept works here, too![5]

THE MANAGEMENT JOB IN MARKETING

Hitting the target customers

The marketing manager wants to satisfy the needs of a particular group of customers—the target—with a particular good or service. Out of all the products offered to customers, the marketing manager wants to be sure that *his* product will succeed. How can he do this?

First, the marketing manager is a manager. So let's see first what a manager does.

The marketing management job is continuous

The **marketing manager's job** consists of three basic tasks: planning, implementing, and control. See Figure 2–4. The planning job consists of two parts: (1) finding attractive opportunities and (2) developing marketing strategies. The marketing manager can't be satisfied with only planning present strategies. In a competitive marketplace, he is always looking for new opportunities—and making plans for new strategies. Developing marketing strategies is the main focus of this book. Without a well-defined strategy, there are no guidelines for implementing or control.

Planning strategies to guide the whole company is called **strategic planning**—the managerial process of developing and maintaining a match between the resources of an organization and its market opportunities. This is even bigger than developing marketing strategies—because it includes planning for production, research and development, and other functional areas in more detail than is necessary when planning marketing strategies.

We will not get into such detail in this text—but it is important to see that the marketing department's plan is not the whole company plan. On the other hand, it is clear that a good company plan should be market-oriented—and the marketing department's strategies can set the tone and direction for the whole company. In other words, if the marketing department applies the marketing concept, this could lead the whole company to do so.

Only after the basic marketing strategy is developed can managers begin to carry out (implement) that strategy (personnel selection, salary

Figure 2–4: **The marketing management process**

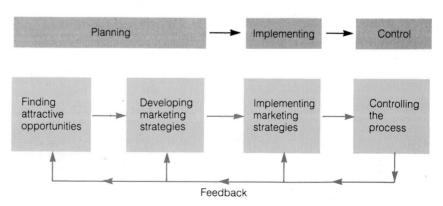

A manager needs good strategic plans to run a company smoothly and profitably.

administration, retailer selection, and so on). Making the plan work may, in fact, take a greater part of the manager's time.

We will discuss control, too, since it provides feedback that may lead to changing marketing strategies. The tools most frequently used by the marketing manager are data processing, marketing research, and accounting.

All marketing jobs require planning

At first, it might seem that planning should concern only the top management of large companies. This isn't true. Even the smallest farmer, retailer, or wholesaler must plan a strategy.

WHAT IS MARKETING STRATEGY PLANNING?

Marketing planning means finding attractive opportunities—and developing profitable marketing strategies. But what is a "marketing strategy?" We have used these words rather casually so far. Now let's see what they really mean.

What is a marketing strategy?

A **marketing strategy** is a target market and a related marketing mix. It is a "big picture" of what a firm will do in some market. Two interrelated parts are needed:

1. A **target market**—a fairly homogeneous (similar) group of customers to whom a company wishes to appeal.
2. A **marketing mix**—the controllable variables which the company puts together to satisfy this target group.

The importance of target customers in this process can be seen in Figure 2–5, where the customer—the "C" in the center of the diagram—

Figure 2–5: A marketing strategy

The marketing mix

C

is surrounded by the controllable variables which we call the "marketing mix." A typical marketing mix would include some product, offered at a price, with some promotion to tell potential customers about the availability of the product.

Coca-Cola's strategy for Coke is to aim at young people around the world with a refreshing drink which Coca-Cola packages or dispenses in various ways—in as many retail outlets as it can reach. While its pricing is more or less competitive, the company supports the whole effort with much promotion—including advertising, personal selling, and sales promotion.

Strategy planning takes place within a framework

A marketing manager's planning does not take place in a vacuum. Instead, the manager works within a framework with many uncontrollable variables. He has to consider these variables even though he can't control them. Figure 2–6 illustrates this framework. It shows that the typical market-

Figure 2–6: Marketing manager's framework

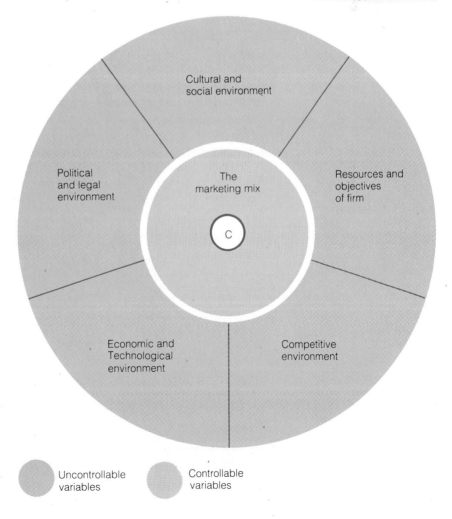

Cultural and social environment

Political and legal environment

Resources and objectives of firm

The marketing mix

C

Economic and Technological environment

Competitive environment

Uncontrollable variables

Controllable variables

ing manager has to be concerned about the cultural and social environment, the political and legal environment, the economic and technological environment, the competitive environment, and the resources and objectives of the firm. We will talk about these uncontrollable variables in more detail in Chapters 3 and 4.

SELECTING A MARKET-ORIENTED STRATEGY IS TARGET MARKETING

Target marketing is not mass marketing

It is important to see that a marketing strategy focuses on some target customers. We will call this market-oriented approach "target marketing"—to distinguish it from "mass marketing." **Target marketing** focuses on some specific target customers. **Mass Marketing**—the typical production-oriented approach—focuses on "everyone." Production-oriented managers just assume that everyone is the same—and will want whatever their firms offer. They don't try to find out what *some* customers might want. Instead, everyone is considered a potential customer. See Figure 2–7.

"Mass marketers" may do target marketing

Commonly used terms can be confusing here. The words "mass marketing" and "mass marketers" do not mean the same thing. Far from it! "Mass *marketing*" means selling to "everyone" as explained above—while "mass *marketers*" like General Electric, Procter & Gamble, and Simpson's Sears are *not* aiming at "everyone." They do aim at clearly defined target markets. The confusion with "mass marketing" occurs because their target markets usually are large—and spread out.

We'll use the words "strategy planning" to mean "marketing strategy planning" and "target marketing." We want to avoid "mass marketing."

Figure 2–7: Production-oriented and marketing-oriented managers have different views of the market

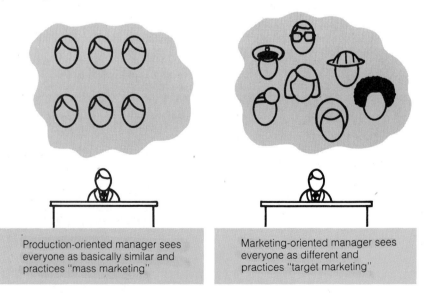

Production-oriented manager sees everyone as basically similar and practices "mass marketing"

Marketing-oriented manager sees everyone as different and practices "target marketing"

DEVELOPING MARKETING MIXES FOR MARKETING STRATEGIES

*There are many
marketing mix variables*

There are many possible ways to satisfy the needs of target customers. A product can have many different features, colors, appearances and goods/services combinations—or it may be only a service. A package can be of various sizes, colors, or materials. Brand names and trademarks can be changed. Various advertising media (newspapers, magazines, radio, television, billboards) may be used. A company's own sales force or other sales specialists can be used. Different prices can be charged—and so on. With so many variables available, the question is: Is there any way of simplifying the selection of marketing mixes? And the answer is *yes*.

*The four "Ps" make up a
marketing mix*

It is useful to reduce the number of variables in the marketing mix to four basic ones:

Product
Place
Promotion
Price

*Figure 2–8: A marketing
strategy—showing the 4 Ps
of a marketing mix*

It helps to think of the four major parts of a marketing mix as the "four Ps." Figure 2–8 emphasizes their relationship—and their focus on the customer—"C."

Customer is not part of the marketing mix

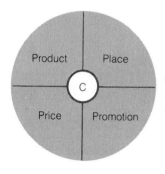

The customer is shown surrounded by the four Ps in Figure 2–8. This has led some students to think that the customer is part of the marketing mix. This is not true. The customer should be the target of all marketing efforts. The customer is placed in the center of the diagram to show this—the C stands for the target market.

Table 2–1 shows some of the variables in the four Ps which will be discussed in later chapters. For now, let's just describe each P briefly.

*Table 2–1: Strategic decision
areas*

Product	Place	Promotion	Price
Features	Channels	Promotion blend	Flexibility
Accessories	Market exposure	Kind of sales people	Level
Installation	Kinds of middlemen	Selection	Introductory pricing
Instructions	Who handles storing	Motivation	Discounts
Service	and transporting	Kind of advertising	Allowances
Warranty	Service levels	Media type	Geographic terms
Product lines		Copy thrust	
Package		Publicity	
Brand name		Sales promotion	

Product—the right one for the target

The Product area is concerned with developing the right "product" for the target market. This product may involve a physical good and/or service. The important thing to remember in the Product area is that your product—good and/or service—should satisfy some customers' needs.

Under Product we will cover problems connected with developing products and product lines. We will also talk about the characteristics of various kinds of products—so that you will be able to make generalizations about product classes. This will help you develop whole marketing mixes more quickly. Although most of this text will be concerned with physical goods and goods/services combinations, the principles also apply to pure services. This is important because the service side of our economy is large and growing.

Place—reaching the target

Place is concerned with getting the right product to the target market. A product isn't much good to a customer if it isn't available when and where it's wanted. In the Place area, we will see where, when, and by whom the goods and services can be offered for sale.

Goods and services move to consumers through channels of distribution. A **channel of distribution** is any series of firms (or individuals) from producer to final user or consumer. A channel can include several kinds of middlemen. Marketing managers work with these channels. So our study of Place is very important to marketing strategy planning.

Sometimes a channel system is quite short. It may run directly from a producer to a final user or consumer. Usually, it is more complex—involving many different kinds of middlemen. And if a marketing manager has several different target markets, several channels of distribution might be needed. See Figure 2–9.

Figure 2–9: Four possible (basic) channels of distribution for consumer goods

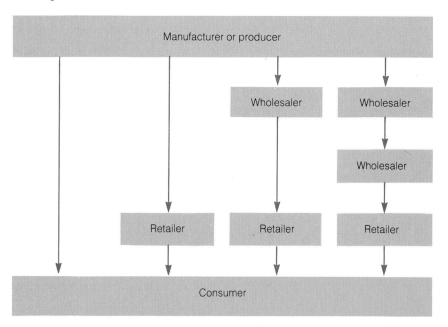

Promotion—telling and selling the customer

The third P, Promotion, is concerned with telling the target market about the "right" product. Promotion includes personal selling, mass selling, and sales promotion. It is the marketing manager's job to blend these methods.

Personal selling involves direct face-to-face relationships between sellers and potential customers. Personal selling lets the salesperson adapt the firm's marketing mix to each potential customer. But this individual attention comes at a price. Personal selling can be very expensive. Often, this personal effort has to be blended with mass selling and sales promotion.

Mass selling is communicating with large numbers of customers at the same time. **Advertising** is any paid form of nonpersonal presentation of ideas, goods, or services by an identified sponsor. It is the main form of mass selling.

Sales promotion refers to those promotion activities which complement personal selling and mass selling. This can involve designing and arranging for the distribution of novelties, point-of-purchase materials, store signs, catalogs, and circulars. Sales promotion people try to help the personal selling and mass selling specialists.

Price—making it right

In addition to developing the right Product, Place, and Promotion, marketing managers must also decide the right Price. In setting a price, they must consider the nature of competition in the target market. They must also try to estimate customer reaction to possible prices. Besides this, they also must know current practices as to markups, discounts, and other terms of sale. Further, they must be aware of legal restrictions on pricing.

If customers won't accept the Price, all of the planning effort will be wasted. So you can see that Price is an important area for the marketing manager.

Relative importance of the four Ps

All four Ps are needed in a marketing mix. In fact, they should all be tied together. But is any one more important than the others? Generally speaking, the answer is *no*. When a marketing mix is being developed, all decisions about the Ps should be made at the same time. That's why the four Ps are arranged around the customer (C) in a circle—to show that they all are equally important.

Strategy guides implementing

Let's sum up our discussion of marketing mix planning this far. We develop a *Product* that we feel will satisfy the target customers. We find a way *(Place)* to reach our target customers. *Promotion* tells the target customers about the availability of the product that has been designed for them. Then, the *Price* is set—after estimating expected customer reaction to the total offering and the costs of getting it to them.

These ideas can be seen more clearly with an example in the home decorating market.

A British paint manufacturer looks at the home decorating market

The experience of a paint manufacturer in England illustrates the strategy planning process—and how strategic decisions help decide how the plan is carried out.

First, this paint manufacturer's marketing manager interviewed many potential customers—and studied their needs for the products he could offer. By combining several kinds of customer needs and some available demographic data, he came up with the view of the market shown in Figure 2–10. In the following description of these markets, note that useful marketing mixes come to mind immediately.

There turned out to be a large market for "general-purpose paint"— about 60 percent of the potential for all kinds of paint products. The manufacturer did not consider this market—because he did not want to compete "head-on" with the many companies already in this market. The other four markets—which were placed in the four corners of a market diagram simply to show that they were different markets—he called Helpless Homemaker, Handy Helper, Crafty Craftsman, and Cost-Conscious Couple.

The Helpless Homemaker—the manufacturer found out—really didn't know much about home painting or specific products. This customer needed a helpful paint retailer who could supply not only paint and other supplies but also much advice. And the retailer who sold the paint would want it to be of fairly good quality—so that the homemaker would be satisfied with the results.

The Handy Helper was a jack-of-all-trades who knew a great deal about paint and painting. He wanted a good-quality product and was satisfied to buy from an old-fashioned hardware store or lumberyard—which usually sells mainly to men. Similarly, the Crafty Craftsman was willing to buy from a retailer who would not attract female customers. In fact, these

Figure 2–10: The home decorating market (paint area) in England

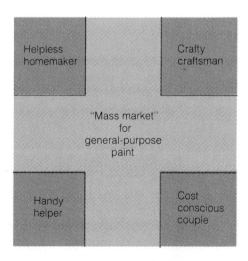

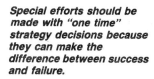

Special efforts should be made with "one time" strategy decisions because they can make the difference between success and failure.

older men didn't want to buy paint at all. They wanted pigments, oils, and other things to mix their own paint.

Finally, the Cost-Conscious Couple was young, had low income, and lived in an apartment. In England, an apartment dweller must paint the apartment during the course of the lease. This is an important factor for at least some tenants as they choose their paint. If you were a young apartment dweller with limited income, what sort of paint would you want? Some couples in England—the manufacturer discovered—did not want very good paint! In fact, something not much better than whitewash would do fine.

The paint manufacturer decided to cater to Cost-Conscious Couples with a marketing mix flowing from the description of that market. That is, knowing what he did about them, he offered a low-quality paint (Product), made it available in lower-income apartment neighborhoods (Place), aimed his price-oriented ads at these areas (Promotion), and, of course, offered an attractive low price (Price). The manufacturer has been extremely successful with this strategy—giving his customers what they really want, even though the product is of low quality.

THE IMPORTANCE OF MARKETING STRATEGY PLANNING

Most of our emphasis in this book will be on the planning phase of the marketing manager's job—for a good reason. The "one time" strategy decisions—the decisions that decide what business the company is in and the general strategy it will follow—may be more important than has been realized. In fact, an extremely good plan might be carried out badly and still be profitable—while a poor but well-executed plan can lose money. The case histories that follow show the importance of planning—and why we are going to emphasize strategy planning throughout this text.

Sears, Roebuck found its own market

Sears, Roebuck has had success since World War II because of a good new strategy. While other large retailers were concentrating downtown, Sears tried a new strategy—developing stores with their own parking in suburban areas where the population was growing fast. Some conventional retailers predicted Sears would fail. But the company knew what it was doing. Sears placed its new units away from competition. It provided ample parking space—and built stores so large and well stocked that customers could do all their shopping under one roof.

Instead of trying to meet competition head-on, Sears developed a strategy for reaching *some* target markets that had not been completely satisfied before. At the same time, people were shifting to the suburbs. Their new strategy was a big success—for many years.

Sears has not been doing as well lately, however, as new kinds of retailers have moved to the outlying areas. These newer competitors included various kinds of specialized discounters—with experienced salespeople. These newcomers, like K mart and Woolco emphasized lower prices—some with service and some self-service—as they moved right near Sears' previously well-chosen locations.

So you can see, that while Sears had a successful strategy for a while, newcomers have come along with different—and perhaps better—strategies which "chip away" at Sears. These competitors are attracting customers who might have been satisfied with Sears' marketing mix—until they were offered different marketing mixes.

Henry Ford's strategy worked—until General Motors caught up

Henry Ford is remembered for developing the mass production techniques that produced a car for the masses. His own view of his approach, however, is that mass production developed *because* of his basic decision to build a car for the masses. In those days, cars were almost custom-built for the wealthy, the sports drivers, and other specialty buyers. Ford decided on a different strategy. He wanted to produce a car that could appeal to the majority of potential buyers.

Certainly, new production ideas were needed to carry out Ford's strategy. But the really important decision was the initial *market-oriented* decision that there was a market for millions of cars in the $500 price range. Much of what followed was just carrying out this decision. Ford's strategy

Henry Ford saw a market and developed the technology to satisfy it.

to offer a low-priced car was an outstanding success—and millions of Model Ts were sold in the 1910s and 1920s. But there was a defect in his strategy. To keep the price down, a very basic car was offered with "any color you want as long as it's black."

In the 1920s, General Motors' management felt that there was room for a new strategy. Their basic decision was to add colors and styling—even if this meant raising prices. They also hit upon the idea of looking at the market as having several segments (based on price and quality)—and then offering a full line of cars with entries at the top of each of these price ranges. They planned to appeal to quality-conscious consumers—always offering good values. The General Motors strategy was not an immediate success. But they stuck with their plan through the 1920s and slowly caught up with Ford. Finally, in May 1927, Ford closed down his assembly line for 18 months and switched his strategy to meet the new competition. He stopped producing the long-successful Model T and introduced the more market-oriented Model A. But General Motors was already well on its way to the commanding market position it now holds.[6]

The watch industry sees new strategies

The conventional watchmakers—both domestic and foreign—had always aimed at customers who thought of watches as high-price, high-quality symbols to mark special events—like graduation, retirement, and so on. These manufacturers produced expensive watches—and stressed their symbolic appeal in advertising. Their promotion was heavily concentrated in the gift-buying seasons of Christmas and graduation time. Jewelry stores were the main retail outlets—charging large markups.

This commonly accepted strategy of the major watch companies ignored those who just wanted to tell the time—and were interested in low-priced watches that kept time reasonably well. So the U.S. Time Company developed a successful strategy around its Timex watches—and became the world's largest watch company.[7]

U.S. Time completely upset the watch industry—both foreign and domestic—by not only offering a good product (with a one-year guarantee) at a lower price, but also by using new, lower-cost channels of distribution. Its watches are widely available in drug stores, discount houses, and nearly any other retail outlet which will carry them.

Now, Timex itself faces competition from the digital watchmakers. Electronics firms have entered the market with an entirely new time-keeping idea. They have also been cutting prices drastically—while following Timex's lead into widespread distribution. Some of the traditional watchmakers are closing their factories. Even Timex is threatened because it is not deeply involved in electronics. Here, technological improvements—combined with modern marketing strategy planning—may completely change this whole industry in only a few years.[8]

Creative strategy planning needed for survival

Such dramatic shifts in strategy may surprise conventional production-oriented managers. But they are becoming much more common—especially in industries where some of the firms have accepted the marketing concept.

What all this means is that a marketing manager—and his firm—may have to pay less attention to finding ways to use a company's present resources—a typical production-oriented approach—and pay more attention to locating new market opportunities. By looking for breakthrough opportunities, a company may find profit possibilities which might otherwise be missed.

Creative strategy planning is becoming even more important because profits no longer can be won just by spending more money on plant and equipment. Moreover, domestic and foreign competition threatens those who can't create more satisfying goods and services. New markets, new customers, and new ways of doing things must be found if companies are to operate profitably in the future—and contribute to our macro-marketing system.

STRATEGIC PLANS AND PROGRAMS MUST BE DEVELOPED—EVENTUALLY

Our focus has been—and will continue to be—on developing marketing strategies. But it is also important to see that, eventually, marketing managers must develop strategic plans—and marketing programs. However, detailed study of these ideas is beyond the scope of this book. We can only discuss them briefly here. See Figure 2–11.

What is a strategic plan?   A strategy is a "big picture" of what a firm will do in some market. A strategic plan goes farther. A **strategic plan** includes a strategy and the time-related details for carrying out the strategy. It should spell out the following in detail: (1) what marketing mix is to be offered to whom (i.e., the target market), and for how long; (2) what company resources (shown as costs) will be required, at what rate (month by month, perhaps); and (3) what results are expected (sales and profits, perhaps month by month). It should also include some control procedures—so that whoever is to carry out the plan will know when things are going wrong. This might be something as simple as comparing actual sales against expected sales—with a "warning flag" to be raised whenever total sales fall below a certain level.

Several plans make a program   Most companies have more than one strategic plan at the same time. Typically, they aim at several target markets—and prepare different marketing mixes for each one. A **marketing program** blends all of a firm's strategic plans into one "big" plan. This program, then, is the responsibility of the whole company.

Figure 2–11: Elements of a firm's marketing program

$$\left.\begin{array}{c}\text{Target market}\\+\\\text{Marketing mix}\end{array}\right\} = \begin{array}{c}\text{Marketing}\\\text{strategy}\end{array} + \begin{array}{c}\text{Time related}\\\text{details and}\\\text{control}\\\text{procedures}\end{array} = \left.\begin{array}{c}\text{Strategic}\\\text{plan}\\+\\\text{Other}\\\text{strategic}\\\text{plans}\end{array}\right\} \begin{array}{c}\text{A firm's}\\\text{marketing}\\\text{program}\end{array}$$

CONCLUSION

Marketing's role within a marketing-oriented firm is to tie the company together. The marketing concept provides direction. It stresses that the firm's efforts should be focused on satisfying some target markets—at a profit. Production-oriented firms tend to forget this. Often, the various departments within such a firm let their natural conflicts of interest lead to building "fences" around their areas. Then, even coordinating committees may not be able to redirect the firm's efforts.

Complete acceptance of the marketing concept would probably lead to new organization arrangements. But the really important matter is acceptance—by top management—of the marketing concept. Without this, new arrangements probably won't make much difference.

The job of marketing management is one of continuous planning, implementing, and control.

The marketing manager must constantly study the environment—seeking attractive opportunities. And new strategies must be planned continually. Potential target markets must be matched with marketing mixes that the firm can offer. Then attractive strategies are chosen for implementation. Controls are needed to be sure that the plans are carried out successfully. If anything goes wrong along the way, this continual feedback should cause the process to be started over again—with the marketing manager planning more attractive marketing strategies.

A marketing mix has four variables—the four Ps: Product, Place, Promotion, and Price. Most of this text is concerned with developing profitable marketing mixes for clearly defined target markets. So, after several chapters on selecting target markets, we will discuss each of the four Ps in greater detail.

QUESTIONS FOR DISCUSSION

1. Define the marketing concept in your own words, and then explain why profit is usually included in this definition.

2. Define the marketing concept in your own words, and then suggest how acceptance of this concept might affect the organization and operation of your college.

3. Distinguish between "production orientation" and "marketing orientation," illustrating with local examples.

4. Explain why a firm should view its internal activities as part of a "total system." Illustrate your answer for (a) a large grocery products manufacturer, (b) a plumbing wholesaler, and (c) a department store chain.

5. Does the acceptance of the marketing concept almost require that a firm view itself as a "total system"?

6. Distinguish clearly between a marketing strategy and a marketing mix. Use an example.

7. Distinguish clearly between mass marketing and target marketing. Use an example.

8. Why is the customer placed in the center of the four Ps in the text diagram of a marketing strategy?

Explain, using a specific example from your own experience.

9. Explain, in your own words, what each of the four Ps involves.

10. Evaluate the text's position that "a marketing strategy guides implementing."

11. Distinguish between a strategy, a strategic plan, and a marketing program—illustrating for a local retailer.

12. Outline a marketing strategy for each of the following new products:

   a. A radically new design for a haircomb.
   b. A new fishing reel.
   c. A new "wonder drug."
   d. A new industrial stapling machine.

13. Provide a specific illustration of why marketing strategy planning is important for all business people, not just for those in the marketing department.

14. Recently the U.S. government accused Sears, Roebuck of dealing unfairly with customers. The government argued that Sears' print and television campaign for Lady Kenmore dishwashers between 1972 and 1975 was misleading because it suggested that the appliances would remove

all food residue without presoaking. Part of the government's evidence came from Sears' owner's manual, which suggests that one scour baked-on foods before putting dishes in the machine. Assuming the government is correct in its argument, how could this situation come about? That is, how is it that a company could say one thing in one place and another in another place?

SUGGESTED CASES

  1. Quenton, Limited
  3. Kemek Manufacturing Company
  29. Rundle Manufacturing Company

ECONOMICS FUNDAMENTALS

APPENDIX A

When you finish this appendix, you should:

1. Understand the "law of diminishing demand."
2. Know what a market is.
3. Understand demand and supply curves—and how they set the size of a market and its price level.
4. Know about elasticity of demand and supply.
5. Recognize the important new terms (shown in red).

A marketing manager should be an expert on markets and the nature of competition in different kinds of markets. The economists "demand and supply" analysis give us useful tools for studying the nature of demand. In particular, you should master the ideas of a demand curve and demand elasticity. A firm's demand curve shows how the target customers see the firm's offering. And the effect of both demand and supply curves helps set the size of the market and the market price. These ideas are discussed more fully in the following sections.

PRODUCTS AND MARKETS AS SEEN BY CUSTOMERS AND POTENTIAL CUSTOMERS

Economists provide useful insights

The way potential customers (not the firm) see a firm's good or service has an important effect on how much they are willing to pay for it, where it should be made available, and how eager they are to obtain it. In other words, it has a very direct effect on marketing strategy planning.

Economists have been concerned with these basic problems for years. Their tools can be quite helpful in showing how customers view products and how markets behave.

45

**Economists see
individual customers
choosing among
alternatives**

Economics is sometimes called the "dismal" science because it shows that customers just can't buy everything they want. Since most customers have a limited income over any period of time, they must balance their needs and the costs of various products.

Economists usually assume that customers have a fairly definite set of preferences. When they are given a set of alternatives, it is assumed that they evaluate these alternatives in terms of whether they will make them feel better (or worse) or in some way improve (or change) their situation.

But what exactly is the nature of the customer's desire for a particular product?

Usually the argument is given in terms of the extra utility (value) the customer can get by buying more of a particular product or how much utility would be lost if he had less of the product. (Students who wish more discussion of this approach should refer to indifference curve analysis in any standard economics text.)

Utility is a theoretical idea. It may be easier to understand if we look at what happens when the price of one of the customer's usual purchases changes.

**The law of diminishing
demand**

Suppose that a consumer were buying potatoes in 10-pound bags at the same time he bought other foods—such as meat and vegetables. If the consumer is mainly interested in buying a certain amount of foodstuffs, and the price of potatoes drops, it seems reasonable to expect that he will switch some of his food money to potatoes—and away from some other foods. But if the price of potatoes goes up, you would expect our consumer to buy fewer potatoes and more of other foods.

The general relation of price and quantity shown by this example is called the **law of diminishing demand**—which says that if the price of a product is raised, a smaller quantity will be demanded—and if the price of a product is lowered, a greater quantity will be demanded.

**A group of customers
makes a market**

A market has a group of consumers who buy in a similar way. If price drops, the total quantity demanded by the group will increase. But if the price rises, the quantity demanded will decrease. "Real world" data supports this reasoning—especially for general product classes or "commodities" like potatoes.

The relationship between price and quantity demanded in the market for potatoes is shown in Table A–1. It is an example of what economists call a "demand schedule." Notice that as the price decreases, the quantity demanded increases. Total dollar sales or total revenue of the potato market is shown in the third column. Notice, however, that as prices go lower, the total *unit* sales increases—but the total revenue (total dollar sales) decreases. It is suggested that you fill in the missing blanks and watch the behavior of total revenue—an important figure for the marketing manager. We will explain what you should have seen—and why—a little later.

**Table A–1: Demand
schedule for potatoes**

Point	(1) Price of potatoes per bag (P)	(2) Quantity demanded (bags per month) (Q)	(3) Total revenue per month (P× Q= TR)
A	$0.80	8,000,000	$6,400,000
B	0.65	9,000,000	
C	0.50	11,000,000	5,500,000
D	0.35	14,000,000	
E	0.20	19,000,000	

*The demand curve—
usually down-sloping*

If your only interest is seeing at which price customers would be willing to pay the greatest total revenue, the demand schedule may be enough. But a demand curve may be more helpful. A **demand curve** is a "picture" of the relationship between price and quantity in a market—assuming that all other things stay the same. It is a graph of the demand schedule. Figure A–1 shows the demand curve for potatoes—really just a plotting of the demand schedule. It shows how many potatoes would be demanded by potential customers at various possible prices. This is known as a "down-sloping demand curve."

Most demand curves are down-sloping. It just shows that if prices were lowered, the quantity that customers will buy would increase.

Note that the demand curve only shows how customers would react to various prices. Usually, in a market, we see only one price at a time—not all of these prices. The curve just shows what quantities will be demanded—depending upon what price is set. You can see that most business people would like to set the price at a point where the resulting income was large.

Before talking about this, however, we should think about the demand schedule and curve for another product—to get a better picture of demand curves.

**Figure A–1: Demand curve
for potatoes (10-pound
bags)**

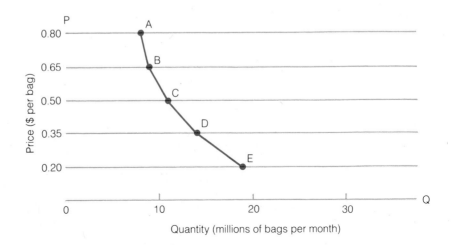

Table A–2: Demand schedule for refrigerators

Point	(1) Price per refrigerator (P)	(2) Quantity de- manded per year (Q)	(3) Total revenue per year (P× Q= TR)
A	$300	20,000	$ 6,000,000
B	250	70,000	17,500,000
C	200	130,000	26,000,000
D	150	210,000	31,500,000
E	100	310,000	31,000,000

A refrigerator demand curve looks different

A different kind of demand curve is the one for refrigerators shown in Table A–2. Column (3) shows the total revenue that would be earned at various possible prices and quantities. Again, as the price of refrigerators goes down, the quantity demanded goes up. But here, unlike the potato example, total revenue increases—at least until the price drops to $150.

Every market has a demand curve—for some time period

These general demand relationships are true for all products. But each product has its own demand curve in each potential market—no matter how small the market. In other words, a particular demand curve has meaning only when tied to a particular market. We can think of demand curves for individuals, regions, and even countries. And the time period covered really should be stated. This is often ignored, however, because monthly or yearly periods are usually implied.

The difference between elastic and inelastic

The demand curve for refrigerators—see Figure A–2—is down-sloping. But note that it is "flatter" than the curve for potatoes. It is quite important that you understand what this flatness means.

We will look at the flatness in terms of total revenue—since this is what interests business managers.*

When you filled in the total revenue column for potatoes, you should have noticed that total revenue would continue to decrease if the price were reduced. This is bad from a manager's point of view, and shows inelastic demand. **Inelastic demand** means that although the quantity demanded would increase if the price were decreased, the quantity de- manded would not "stretch" enough—that is, it is not elastic enough— to increase total revenue.

In contrast, **elastic demand** means that if prices were dropped, the quantity demanded would stretch enough to increase total revenue. The upper part of the refrigerator demand curve is an example of elastic de- mand.

But note that if the refrigerator price were dropped from $150 to $100,

---

* Strictly speaking, two curves should not be compared for flatness if the graph scales are different, but for current purposes we will do so to illustrate the idea of "elasticity of demand." Actually, it would be more correct to compare two curves for one commodity— on the same graph. Then, both the shape of the demand curve and its position on the graph would be important.

Figure A–2: Demand curve for refrigerators

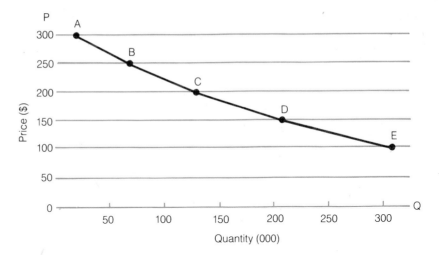

total revenue would *decrease.* We can say, therefore, that between $150 and $100, demand is inelastic—that is, total revenue would decrease if price were lowered to $100.

Thus, elasticity is defined in terms of changes in total revenue. If total revenue would *increase* if price were lowered, then demand is said to be elastic. If total revenue would *decrease* if price were lowered, then demand is said to be inelastic.

Total revenue may decrease or increase if price is raised

A point that is often missed in talking about demand is what happens when prices are raised instead of lowered. With elastic demand, total revenue will decrease if the price is raised. With inelastic demand, total revenue would increase if the price is raised. If total revenue remains the same when prices change, then we have a special case known as "unitary elasticity of demand."

The possibility of raising price and increasing total revenue at the same time should be of special interest to managers. This occurs if the demand curve is inelastic—and is an attractive situation because total costs probably would not increase and might actually go down at smaller quantities!

The ways total revenue changes as prices are raised are shown in Figure A–3. Here, total revenue is shown as a rectangular area formed by a price and its related quantity.

P_1 is the original price here. The total potential revenue with this original price is shown by the area in red. The possible total revenue with the new price, P_2, is shaded in gray. At both prices, there is some overlap. So the important areas are those with lighter shadings. Note that in the left-hand figure—where demand is elastic—the revenue added when price is increased is less than the revenue lost. (Compare only the light-shaded

Figure A–3: Changes in total revenue as prices increase

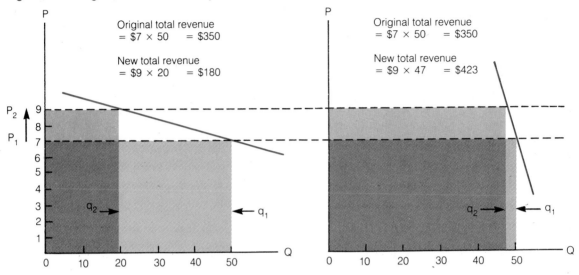

areas.) When demand is inelastic, however, only a small lighter-shaded revenue area is given up for a much larger one when price is raised.

An entire curve is not elastic or inelastic

It is important to see that it is wrong to talk about a whole demand curve as elastic or inelastic. Instead, elasticity for a particular curve refers to the change in total revenue between two points on a curve—and not along the whole curve. The change from elastic to inelastic can be seen in the refrigerator example.

Generally, however, nearby points are either elastic or inelastic. So it is common to refer to a whole curve by the elasticity of the curve in the price range that normally is of interest—the relevant range.

Demand elasticities affected by availability of substitutes and urgency of need

At first, it may be hard to see why one product should have an elastic demand and another an inelastic demand. Many things—such as the availability of substitutes, the importance of the item in the customer's budget, and the urgency of the customer's need and its relation to other needs—affect demand for a particular product. By looking at one of these factors—the availability of substitutes—we should better understand why demand elasticities vary.

Substitutes are goods and/or services that offer a choice to the buyer. The greater the number of good substitutes available, the greater the elasticity of demand will be. The term *good* here refers to the amount of similarity that customers see. If they see the products as extremely different—then a particular need cannot be satisfied by easily exchanging them—and the demand for the most satisfactory product may be quite inelastic.

For example, if the price of hamburger is lowered—and other prices stay the same—the quantity demanded will increase a lot. And so will

Figure A–4: Demand curve for hamburger (a product with many substitutes)

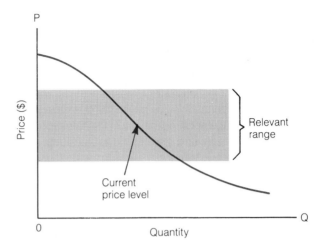

total revenue. The reason is that not only will regular hamburger users buy more hamburger, but those consumers who used to buy hot dogs, steaks, or bacon probably will buy hamburger too. But if the price of hamburger rises, the quantity demanded will decrease—perhaps sharply—depending on how much the price has risen, their individual tastes, and what their guests expect. See Figure A–4.

In contrast to a product which has many "substitutes"—such as hamburger—consider a product with few or no substitutes. Its demand curve will tend to be inelastic. Salt is a good example. Salt is needed to flavor food. Yet no one person or family uses great quantities of salt. And even with price changes within a reasonable range, it is not likely that the quantity of salt wanted will change much. Of course, if the price dropped to an extremely low level, manufacturers might buy more—say for low-cost filler instead of clay or sand. See Figure A–5. Or, if the price rose to a very

Figure A–5: Demand curve for salt (a product with few substitutes)

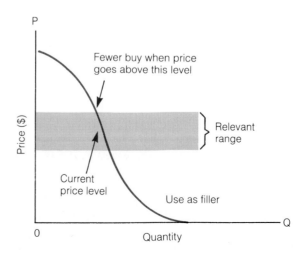

high figure, many people would have to do without. But these extremes are outside of the relevant range.

MARKETS AS SEEN BY SUPPLIERS

Demand curves are introduced here because the elasticity of demand shows how potential customers feel about the product—and especially whether there are substitutes for the product. But to get a better understanding of markets, we must study the supply side of "demand and supply." Customers may want a product, but if suppliers aren't willing to offer it, then there is no market.

Note: economists often use the kind of analysis we are discussing here to explain pricing in the marketplace. We aren't trying to do that. Here we are interested in markets and the relation between customers and potential suppliers. The discussion in this appendix does not explain how individual firms set prices. We'll talk about that in Chapters 18 and 19.

Supply curves reflect supplier thinking

Generally speaking, suppliers' costs affect the quantity of products they are willing to offer during any time period. In other words, their costs affect their supply curves. While a demand curve shows the quantity of goods customers would be willing to buy at various prices, a **supply curve** shows the quantity of goods that would be offered at various possible prices by all suppliers together. With a demand curve, it shows the attitudes and probable behavior of buyers and sellers toward a particular product in a particular market.

Some supply curves are vertical

We usually assume that supply curves slope upward—that is, that suppliers will be willing to offer greater quantities at higher prices. If a product's market price is very high, you can see why producers will want to produce more of the product. They might even put workers on overtime or perhaps hire additional workers to increase the quantity they can offer. To go further, it seems likely that producers of other products will switch their resources—farms, factories, and labor—to the product that is in great demand.

If, however, a very low price is being offered for a particular product, you might expect producers to switch to other products—reducing supply.

A supply schedule (Table A–3) and a supply curve (Figure A–6) for

Table A–3: Supply schedule for potatoes

Point	Possible market price per 10-lb.bag	Number of bags sellers will supply per month at each possible market price
A	$0.80	17,000,000
B	0.65	14,000,000
C	0.50	11,000,000
D	0.35	8,000,000
E	0.20	3,000,000

Note: This supply schedule is for a month to emphasize that farmers might have some control over when they delivered their potatoes. There would be a different schedule for each month.

Figure A–6: Supply curve for potatoes (10-pound bags)

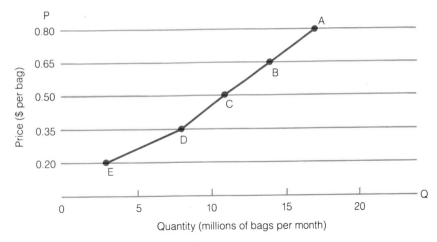

potatoes illustrate these ideas. This supply curve shows how many potatoes would be produced and offered for sale at each possible market price in a given month.

In the very short run—say, over a few hours, a day, or a week—suppliers may not be able to increase the supply at all. So we would see a vertical supply curve. This situation is often important in the market for fresh fruits and vegetables. Fresh strawberries, for example, will spoil and suppliers want to sell them quickly—hopefully, at a higher price—but they want to sell them at any price.

If the product is a service, it may not be easy to expand the supply. And there is no way to "store" it either. Additional barbers or medical doctors are not quickly trained and licensed. And they have only so much time to give each day. When the day is done, the unused "supply" is lost. Further, the hope of much higher prices in the near future will not expand the supply of many services. A good play or an "in" restaurant or nightclub may be limited in the amount of "product" it can offer at a particular time.

Elasticity of supply

The term *elasticity* also is used to describe supply curves. An extremely steep or almost vertical supply curve—often found in the short run—is called **inelastic supply**—the quantity supplied does not stretch much (if at all) if the price is raised. A flatter curve is called **elastic supply**—the quantity supplied does stretch if the price is raised. A slightly up-sloping supply curve is typical of longer-run market situations. Given more time, suppliers have a chance to change their offerings and competitors may enter or leave the market.

DEMAND AND SUPPLY INTERACT TO ESTABLISH THE SIZE OF THE MARKET AND PRICE LEVEL

We have talked about demand and supply forces separately. Now we must bring them together to show their relationship. The intersection of

Figure A–7: **Equilibrium of supply and demand for potatoes**

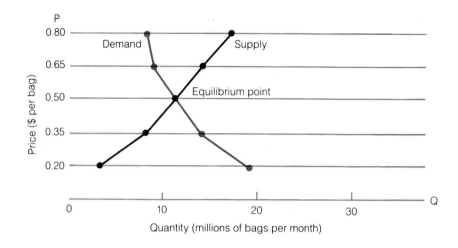

these two forces decides the size of the market and the market price. At this point, the market is said to be in equilibrium (balanced).

The intersection of demand and supply is shown in Figure A–7 for the potato data discussed above. In this potato market, the demand is inelastic—the total revenue of all the potato producers would be greater at higher prices. But the market price is at the **equilibrium point**—where the quantity and the price that sellers are willing to offer are equal to the quantity and price that buyers are willing to accept. The $0.50 equilibrium price for potatoes gives a smaller total revenue to potato producers than would a higher price. This lower equilibrium price comes about because the many producers are willing to supply enough potatoes at the lower price. Demand is not the only fact that decides price level! Cost also must be considered—via the supply curve.

DEMAND AND SUPPLY HELP UNDERSTAND THE NATURE OF COMPETITION

The elasticity of demand and supply curves and their interaction help predict the kind of competition a marketing manager is likely to meet. For example, extremely inelastic demand curves together with the usual up-sloping supply curves mean that the firm will have much choice in its strategy planning. Apparently customers like the product and see few substitutes. They are willing to pay higher prices before cutting back too much on their use of the product.

Clearly, the elasticity of a firm's demand curves is important for strategy planning. But there are other facts which affect the nature of competition. Among these are the number and size of competitors and the uniqueness of each firm's marketing mix. These ideas are discussed more fully in Chapter 3 in the section on "competitive environment." That discussion is based on a real understanding of the contents of this appendix. So now you should be ready to handle that and later material dealing with pricing—especially Chapters 18 and 19.

CONCLUSION

The economist's traditional demand and supply analysis provides useful tools for studying the nature of demand and market situations. It is important that you master the ideas of a demand curve and demand elasticity. The way demand and supply act together helps set the size of a market and its price level. It also helps explain the kind of competition in different market situations. These ideas are discussed in Chapter 3 and then built upon throughout the text. So careful study of this appendix will build a good foundation for later work.

QUESTIONS FOR DISCUSSION

1. Explain in your own words how economists look at markets and arrive at the "law of diminishing demand."

2. Explain what a demand curve is and why it is usually down-sloping.

3. What is the length of life of the typical demand curve? Illustrate your answer.

4. If the general market demand for men's shoes is fairly elastic, how does the demand for men's dress shoes compare with it? How does the demand curve for women's shoes compare with the demand curve for men's shoes?

5. If the demand for fountain pens were inelastic above and below the present price, should the price be raised? Why or why not?

6. If the demand for steak is highly elastic below the present price, should the price be lowered?

7. Discuss what factors lead to inelastic demand and supply curves. Are they likely to be found together in the same situation?

When you finish this chapter, you should:

1. Know the uncontrollable variables the marketing manager must work with.

2. Know how—and how quickly—the cultural and social environment can change.

3. Know why you could go to prison by ignoring the political and legal environment.

4. Know the effect of the different kinds of market situations on strategy planning.

5. Understand how the economic environment can affect strategy planning.

6. Recognize the important new terms (shown in red).

UNCONTROLLABLE ENVIRONMENTS AFFECTING MARKETING MANAGEMENT

3

Marketing managers do not plan strategies in a vacuum. They have to work with several uncontrollable variables when choosing target markets and developing the four Ps.

As we saw in Chapter 2, the uncontrollable variables managers must work with fall into the following categories:

1. Cultural and social environment.
2. Political and legal environment.
3. Economic environment.
4. Competitive environment.
5. Resources and objectives of the firm.

In the long run, marketing managers may affect some or all of these variables. In the short run, however, they must be considered as "givens."

Now we will see how the first four factors add to the complexity and challenge of marketing management. And in Chapter 4, we will see how the resources and objectives of the firm can limit its opportunities—as well as the strategies it eventually chooses.

CULTURAL AND SOCIAL ENVIRONMENT

Cultural similarities and differences

Is there a distinct Canadian culture? Do differences and so-called national characteristics have an effect on the way Canadians live, work, and consume? It is easy to ask such questions but difficult to answer them in a manner helpful to marketers. All that we can do now is provide some awareness of cultural similarities and differences.

The Canadian personality is often presented as somewhat subdued, less assertive, and more tolerant of dissenting viewpoints than its American counterpart. Internationally, Canadians are perceived as reserved, conservative, and a trifle self-conscious. Americans, in contrast, are usually described as gregarious, outspoken, ethnocentric, self-confident, and proud. Other significant English Canadian characteristics are presented in Figure 3–1. Nevertheless, the similarities in values, living patterns, work roles, family relationships, and consumer behavior are much more obvious than the differences between American and English Canadian families.[1]

Canada is indeed a "mosaic"

The Canadian population is not at all homogeneous. The presence of regional differences is one of the very important characteristics of the Canadian market. The United States is often considered as a "melting pot." In Canada it is best to think in terms of a mosaic, where the pieces at times converge and other times remain very far apart. Incomes, consumption patterns, life-styles, dialects, and attitudes vary from province to province. For example, disposable income per household, family size, and number of persons per dwelling in Ontario is substantially higher than in Prince Edward Island. Unemployment is generally higher in the Atlantic Provinces than in the rest of Canada.[3] Life in the Prairie Provinces is usually

Canada is not a homogenous whole—so markets must be analyzed carefully by marketing managers.

Figure 3–1: Summary of significant English Canadian characteristics[2]

A. As a function of being a part of the North American reality:
   Modern orientation.
   Openness to new ideas.
   Egalitarianism.
   A rich developing society with many needs and high materialistic expectations.
   Growing, more diffuse "middle class."
B. In relation to the United States:
   Conservative tendencies.
   Traditional bias.
   Greater confidence in bureaucratic institutions.
   Collectivity orientation—reliance on such institutions as state, big business, and the church versus personal risk taking.
   Less achievement oriented.
   Lower optimism—less willing to take risks.
   Greater acceptance of hierarchical order and stratification.
   Tolerance for diversity—acceptance of cultural mosaic.
   Family stability.

more relaxed than in other regions. It is also in the Prairies that "western hospitality" is expected and is often experienced.

Cultural differences similar to those found between regional areas are also common within large urban areas. Montreal and Toronto, for example, have large Italian, Greek, Jewish, and Chinese communities. That more than 200,000 residents of Toronto report Italian as their mother tongue is an important fact marketers cannot overlook. Food stores, newsstands, travel agencies, credit unions, and restaurants cater specifically to this and other culturally defined markets.

Women are being liberated

The past 10 years has seen a shift in thinking about women's roles in our culture. Women are now free to seek any kind of job they want—and many are doing so. Greater financial freedom is making many women less dependent on marriage as a career. More women are not marrying at all—or are marrying later. They plan to have fewer children, as we saw already. This is having an effect on manufacturers of housing, baby foods, convenience foods, clothing, and cosmetics.

It is clear that this is a big shift in North American thinking and must be considered in strategy planning. It will affect not only what is offered to consumers—but also how and by whom. We will see many more women in manager positions. Others will have important selling and advertising jobs. Ineffective and untrained males are in for some real shocks as more women get business training and go out to compete as equals. They will take jobs that once might have gone to less able males. This is happening already.

Work and growth are important to some

We also have to consider changing attitudes toward life and work. The North American culture encourages the idea that hard work leads to achievement and material rewards. Americans and Canadians are willing

Many North Americans are taking a more leisurely, less goods-oriented view toward their life-styles.

to work. But they also expect rewards and material comforts. This had led us to place great emphasis on growth—and producing and distributing goods and services. Much of our study of Canadian markets will be within this cultural framework.

In some other societies, however, more importance is placed on leisure and enjoyment of life. More holidays are built into the working year. The output of such economies may not be quite as high—but the people don't feel that they are suffering because of this.

Our growing interest in the "quality of life" may reflect a desire for less goods-oriented solutions to our problems. This may lead to reducing our productivity and income. In time, we may learn to live a slower-paced, less goods-oriented life. This obviously will affect marketers.

Changes come slowly

It is important to see, however, that changes in basic values come slowly. An individual firm could not hope to encourage big changes in the short run. Instead, it should identify these attitudes and plan accordingly.

Sometimes, however, strong outside forces—such as energy shortages, riots, or boycotts—may force more rapid changes in the cultural and social environments. And these may affect the political and economic environments.

POLITICAL ENVIRONMENT

The attitudes of people, social critics, and governments are becoming more important to the marketing manager. They all affect the political environment.

Consumerism is here and basic

Consumerism is a social movement seeking to increase the rights and powers of consumers and buyers. Its recent growth is due to a change in thinking that was captured by President Kennedy's "Consumer Bill of Rights." Although the listed rights did not become law, they have affected people's thinking—including government agencies and some courts.

President Kennedy's "Consumer Bill of Rights" includes the following:

The right to safety.
The right to be informed.
The right to choose.
The right to be heard.

Kennedy did not include "the right to a clean and safe environment"—probably because the environment had not yet become a public concern. But most people are concerned with such a right. More government pressure is being applied on everyone—including businesses and government units—to improve our waste handling, and clean our chimneys and motor exhaust systems. This is probably the outstanding recent example of a rapid change in cultural values that was turned into action by the political authorities.

These consumer "rights" are generally not as easy to obtain as the antipollution changes. Instead, individual firms and government agencies must make basic changes in their attitudes about what is "right" and "wrong." This doesn't happen quickly. So there may be an ongoing need for consumerists to help make sure that the little guy is not ignored by business or government. The consumerism movement is not likely to die overnight.

The Canadian consumer scene

Canadian consumerism has become an important environmental factor. This is due in part to the establishment in 1968 of the Federal Department of Consumer and Corporate Affairs. This action gave one department the task of administering a number of already existing consumer protection laws. It also generated a wide variety of new programs designed to further the interests of the Canadian consumer.

That Department, now Consumer and Corporate Affairs Canada, has moved aggressively in the area of consumer protection. Additional laws have been passed and already existing legislation enforced far more vigorously than was true in the past. The department has also placed great emphasis on educating and informing consumers. It has systematically gathered information on consumer complaints as a method of dealing with specific grievances. At the provincial level, consumer protection bureaus and agencies have also been established or greatly strengthened over the past few years. Some of these units are becoming at least as active as their federal counterpart.

The Consumers' Association of Canada (CAC), attempts to safeguard the legitimate interests of all consumers. It is an especially influential group, at both the provincial and federal level. Since most consumers remain unorganized, the CAC has become widely recognized as "the voice of the Canadian consumer." And that organization does not hesitate to raise its collective voice whenever it believes that consumer interests are threatened.

Increased consumer awareness is also created by educational efforts at every level of government as well as by the *Canadian Consumer* and other CAC publications. Specialized groups such as the Automobile Protection Association are also busy educating consumers. A number of consumer self-help and "rip-off protection" books are now widely sold across Canada. Articles on how to purchase intelligently and columns designed to help complaining consumers obtain a fair deal from local merchants are found in many Canadian newspapers. Also, consumer-oriented programs on network television and radio talk shows frequently deal with marketplace problems.

Not meeting consumers' expectation could be drastic

A recent U.S. poll showed the business community to be out of step with the American public on consumerism issues. Generally, the public seems to like what the consumerists are trying to do.[4] Marketers shouldn't forget that the role of businesses is to satisfy consumers. No firm has a God-given right to operate anyway it wants to.

This means that the marketing manager—as well as top management—should pay more attention to consumers' attitudes in marketing planning. Ignoring the consumer movement could be fatal. The rules governing business could change. Specific businesses might be told they could not operate. Or they might face fines that—in an "antibusiness" environment—could be quite large.

Managers should be aware of consumers who want a better environment.

Nationalism can be limiting in international markets

Strong sentiments of **nationalism**—an emphasis on the country's interests before everything else—may also affect the work of some marketing managers. These feelings can reduce sales—or even block marketing activity in some international markets. Oil and copper mining firms have felt such pressures in recent years—for example, in Latin America, Africa, and the Middle East.

To whom the firms could sell—and how much—have been dictated by national interests. The Arab boycott of firms doing business with Israel is probably the outstanding example in recent years. But the ''Buy Canadian'' policy in many government contracts reflects similar attitudes in Canada. And there is some support for protecting Canadian producers from foreign competition—especially of color TVs, footwear, textiles, and cars. Similarly, Philippines business people have tried to drive ''excessively aggressive'' Chinese merchants out of the Philippines. And some African countries have driven out Indian merchants.

Countries may choose to issue guidelines to foreign firms—as Canada did recently to encourage ''good corporate behavior.'' These guidelines sometimes are backed up with new laws—or the threat of laws. Laws were passed in Canada, for example, to restrict the flow of U.S. advertising and culture—via television—into the Canadian market. British Columbia once banned some types of ads in all media—including the U.S. press.[5]

Such guidelines can be extremely important in both domestic and international business—because often businesses must get permission to operate. In some political environments, this is only a routine formality. In others, a lot of red tape is involved—and personal influence and/or ''bribes'' are sometimes necessary.

Within Canada, the Department of Regional Economic Expansion (DREE) created in the late 1960s uses developmental incentives in the form of monetary grants, accelerated depreciation, guarantee of commercial loans and start-up grants, to help encourage the growth of depressed areas. Upon the creation of DREE, all federal programs with the objective of developing specific regions were placed under its control. Provincial and local governments also try to attract and hold businesses, sometimes with tax incentives.[6]

Some business executives have become very successful by studying the political environment and developing strategies which use these political opportunities.

Impact of anticombines legislation

American law has been a far more important factor in the shaping of prevailing business practices than has corresponding Canadian legislation. Why is this so? First of all, Canada traditionally has not been as committed as the United States to protecting either competition or the existence of a large number of competing small firms. Monopoly has not always been automatically condemned by Canadian economists and legislators.

Note also that Combines Act offenses had to be treated as violations of criminal law. The government, to win a case, must prove guilt ''beyond any reasonable doubt.'' Difficulties in establishing this degree of proof has discouraged prosecution. It has also reduced the likelihood that any firm brought to court would be found guilty.

How effective, then, was the Combines Investigation Act as amended through 1960? The legislation has prevented two kinds of marketing activity—price fixing by competitors and misleading price advertising. Even though resale price maintenance was specifically prohibited in 1951, considerable difference of opinion exists as to how often and how effectively manufacturers still controlled retail prices.

Aside from these two or three areas, the Combines Investigation Act had very little effect on either prevailing marketing practices or the structure of the Canadian economy. No firm was ever found guilty of price discrimination. In two key cases brought to court under the merger provisions, the government lost and did not appeal.[7]

Bill C-2 the "new" Competition Act—Stage I

Dissatisfaction with the Combines investigation Act led to the passage by Parliament, in December of 1975, of Bill C-2, the first part of a proposed two-stage major revision of the existing legislation. The minister who introduced this legislation said the following were its most important features.[8]

1. The bill clarifies and strengthens provisions concerning misleading advertising. It adds new protection in the area of warranties and guaranties. It deals with certain undesirable selling practices, such as pyramid selling, referral selling, bait-and-switch selling, selling at a price higher than advertised, the use of promotional contests, and "double-ticketing."
2. The bill covers some trade practices which could be acceptable in some circumstances but not in others. The Restrictive Trade Practices Commission is authorized to review these practices (refusal to deal, consignment selling, exclusive dealing, tied sales, and market restriction) and to issue orders prohibiting or modifying them.
3. The commission also has the power to issue orders forbidding the implementation within Canada of foreign judgments, laws, or directives where it finds them contrary to the Canadian public interest.
4. The bill makes bid-rigging an indictable offense. It also strengthens the existing provisions regarding resale price maintenance.
5. Services are to be covered by the provisions of the Combines Investigation Act. Service activities have become a very important part of the Canadian economy, and there is no logical case for their continued exclusion from our competition legislation.
6. All economic activity in the private sector is covered by federal competition policy. However, activities regulated or authorized by valid federal or provincial legislation will continue to be exempted from the provisions of the Combines Investigation Act.
7. The bill proposes that in order to prove that an agreement prevents or lessens competition "unduly," it is not necessary to establish complete or virtual elimination of competition in the relevant market.

8. The courts, for the first time, are able to issue interim injunctions to prevent the commission or continuation of suspected offenses against the act until the main issue is settled.
9. Also for the first time the bill provides for bringing civil actions by any one adversely affected by violation of the Act to enable such a person to recover his damages and full costs.

Other federal legislation exists

Other laws and regulations are designed primarily to strengthen and maintain two of the previously mentioned consumer rights—to be protected against the marketing of hazardous goods (the right to safety) and to be safeguarded against deceptive promotion (the right to be informed). It is possible here to mention only a few of the many federal laws and regulations designed to protect public well-being.

The Food and Drug Act regulates the sale of foods, drugs, cosmetics, and medical devices. This legislation deals with quality standards, packaging, labeling, and advertising, as well as the manufacturing practices and selling policies of food and drug manufacturers. Certain forms of misrepresentation in food labeling, packaging, selling, and advertising are specifically outlawed by the Food and Drug Act.

The Canadian Radio-Television Commission regulates broadcast advertising. The Standards Branch of Consumer and Corporate Affairs Canada is but one of the many federal agencies establishing product standards and grades. There are also laws concerning the labeling of wool, furs, precious metals, and flammable fabrics. Particularly noteworthy as a form of promotional self-regulation is the voluntary ban on cigarette advertising on Canadian radio and television, which became effective as of January 1, 1972.

Provincial and local regulations

Marketers must also be aware of provincial and local laws which affect the four Ps. There are provincial and city laws regulating minimum prices and the setting of prices (to be discussed in Chapter 19); regulations for starting up a business (licenses, examinations, and even tax payments); and in some communities, regulations prohibiting certain activities, such as door-to-door selling or selling on Sundays or during evenings. The sale and advertising of alcoholic beverages also is provincially controlled.

The provinces have also become far more active in the protection of consumer rights. All of them have passed laws which regulate the granting of credit and otherwise call for "truth in lending." Purchases are often provided with a "cooling-off period" within which they may cancel the contract, return any merchandise actually received and obtain a full refund. The provinces are also more actively exercising their regulatory authority over car dealers, travel agents, and many other types of business that deal with large numbers of consumers spending considerable amounts of money.

Perhaps the most significant development on the provincial scene has been the passage by a number of governments of "trade practices" legislation. The purpose of such legislation is to protect the consumer from unconscionable and deceptive practices. Though the laws passed by the different provinces are not identical, they are all attempts to deal with the same set of problems.

The legislative environment in Quebec

Like every other major governmental jurisdiction in Canada, Quebec has in recent years passed a number of laws designed to protect its consumers. The most recent piece of Quebec legislation, the Consumer Protection Act of 1978, is modeled after, but goes considerably beyond, trade practices legislation previously passed in British Columbia, Ontario, and Alberta. One Unique feature of this Quebec Statute is its virtual elimination of all advertising directed toward children.

There are also laws that reflect a growing concern with assuring the preeminence of the French language in every aspect of Quebec life. A requirement that French be featured either exclusively or as prominently as any other language on the labels of all food products sold in that province was in force long before the Parti Quebecois came to power. Similar legislation governing billboards, direct mail, and point of sale displays was passed in 1974. Bill 101, enacted in August 1977, provides even greater legal support for the primary and sometimes exclusive use of French in all aspects of advertising and promotion.

Although Quebec is too large a part of the total Canadian market to be neglected by most major North American manufacturers, such firms are certain to incur additional costs in complying with language legislation. Smaller Canadian and foreign corporations, on the other hand, may well cease marketing in Quebec. They could decide that the size of this market, as compared with the rest of North America, does not justify modifying the firm's promotional efforts to the extent compliance would require.

Consumerists and the law say "let the seller beware"

The old rule about buyer-seller relations was "let the buyer beware." Now it seems to be shifting to "let the seller beware." The number of consumer protection laws has been increasing. These proconsumer laws and court decisions suggest that there is more interest now in protecting consumers—instead of protecting competition. This may upset production-oriented managers. But they will just have to adapt to the new political and legal environment. Times have changed.

ECONOMIC ENVIRONMENT

The **economic and technological environment** refers to the way firms—and the whole economy—use resources. We will treat the economic and technological environments separately—to emphasize that the technological environment provides a base for the economic environment. Technical skills and equipment affect the way resources of an economy are changed into output. The economic environment, on the other hand, is affected by the way all of the parts of our macro-economic system interact. This, then, affects such things as national income, economic growth, and inflation.

National income changes make a difference

Changes in the overall level of economic activity are obviously of importance. Even the best possible marketing strategy may prove unsuccessful when Canada is in the midst of a depression or suffering from a rapid business decline. As consumers' incomes go down, people have less money to spend and they spend it in different ways. In a mild recession, for example, firms offering luxury goods can be badly hurt while those offering lower-priced goods may continue to prosper. More serious or more prolonged crises, however, can also hurt those who produce or retail lower priced goods.

Resource shortages may limit opportunities

The growing shortage of some natural resources—and in particular energy resources—may cause real upsets. Plastics manufacturers—who use oil-based resources—find their costs rising so high that they are priced out of some markets. Rising gasoline prices are making consumers less interested in the larger, more profitable (to the auto industry) cars. Further, important shifts in auto-buying patterns are affecting the whole economy because the industry is a major buyer of metals, plastics, fabrics, and tires.

Even lower real incomes are possible in the future because of technological factors. Much of our plant and equipment now depends on lots of low-cost energy. Industrial processes that were profitable with low energy prices are now less profitable. So it is possible that the average job in the future will use less machinery and be less productive. This means that Canadian consumers—and industries—will have to adjust their spending patterns.

Inflation can change mixes

Inflation is a major factor in many economies. The marketing manager must understand this when setting prices. When inflation becomes a way of life, people buy and sell accordingly. Some countries have had 25–100 percent inflation per year for years. In contrast, the 8, 10, or even 12 percent levels reached in Canada in recent years were "low." Still, inflation must be considered in strategy planning. It can lead to government policies which will reduce income, employment, *and* consumer spending. The federal government also considered it necessary in 1975 to introduce legislation which controlled wages, prices, profits, and dividends for a three-year period.[9]

You can see that the marketing manager must watch the economic environment carefully. In contrast to the cultural and social environment, economic conditions change all the time. And they move rapidly—up or down—sometimes requiring strategic responses.

TECHNOLOGICAL ENVIRONMENT

The technological base affects opportunities

Underlying any economic environment is the **technological base**—the technical skills and equipment which affect the way the resources of any economy are converted to output. In tradition-bound societies, relatively little technology is used. And the output is small. In modern economies on the other hand, aggressive competitors continually look for better ways of doing things. They copy the best methods quickly.

Technological developments certainly affect marketing. The modern automobile, for example, lets farmers come to town—and city people go wherever they want. This has destroyed the local "monopolies" of some retailers and wholesalers. Modern trucks and airplanes have opened up national and international markets. Electronic developments have made possible mass promotion by radio, TV, and telephone. Soon we may be able to shop in the home with a combination TV-computer system—eliminating the need for some retailers and wholesalers.

As we move through the text, you should see that some of the big advances in business have come from early recognition of new ways to do things. Marketing managers should help their firms see such opportunities by trying to understand the "why" of present methods—and what is keeping their firms from doing things more effectively. Then, as new developments come along, they will be alert to possible uses—and see how opportunities can be turned into profits.

Marketers also can help decide what technical developments would be acceptable to society. With the growing concern about environmental pollution, the quality of life, working conditions, and so on, it is possible that some potentially attractive developments should be rejected because of their long-run effects. Perhaps what might be good for the firm and the economy's *economic* growth might not fit with the cultural and social environment or the political and legal environment. Closeness to the market could give the marketing manager a better feel for what people are thinking—and help the manager help the firm avoid bad mistakes.[10]

THE COMPETITIVE ENVIRONMENT

(Note: The following materials assume some familiarity with economic analysis—and especially the nature of demand curves and demand elasticity. For those wishing a review of these materials, see Appendix A, which follows Chapter 2.)

The **competitive environment** refers to the number and types of competitors the marketing manager must face—and how they might behave. Although these factors can't be controlled by the marketing manager, the manager can choose strategies which will avoid head-on competition.

A marketing manager will have to operate in one of four kinds of market situations. We will talk about three kinds: pure competition, oligopoly, and monopolistic competition. A fourth type—monopoly—is not found very often and is like monopolistic competition anyway.

Figure 3–2: Some important dimensions regarding market competition

Important dimensions \ Types of situations	Pure competition	Oligopoly	Monopolistic competition	Monopoly
Uniqueness of each firm's product	None	None	Some	Unique
Number of competitors	Many	Few	Few to many	None
Size of competitors (compared to size of market)	Small	Large	Large to small	None
Elasticity of demand facing firm	Completely elastic	Kinked demand curve (elastic and inelastic		
Elasticity of industry demand	Either	Inelastic	Either	Either
Control of price by firm	None	Some (with care)	Some	Complete

Understanding these market situations is quite important because the freedom of a marketing manager—especially control over price—is greatly reduced in some situations. The important aspects of these kinds of competition are outlined in Figure 3–2.

When competition is pure

Many competitors offer the same thing

Pure competition is a market situation which develops when a market has:

1. Homogeneous (similar) products.
2. Many buyers and sellers—who have full knowledge of the market.
3. Ease of entry for buyers and sellers, i.e., new firms have little difficulty starting in business—and new customers can easily come into the market.

More or less pure competition is found in many agricultural markets. In the potato industry, for example, there are tens of thousands of producers—and they are in pure competition. Let's look more closely at these small producers.

In pure competition, these many small producers see almost a perfectly flat demand curve facing each one of them. The relation between the industry demand curve and the demand curve facing the individual farmer in pure competition is shown in Figure 3–3. Although the potato industry

Figure 3–3: Interaction of demand and supply in the potato industry and the resulting demand curve facing individual potato producers

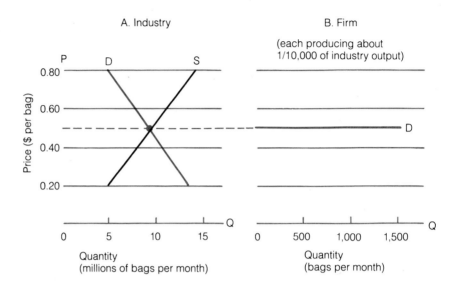

A. Industry

B. Firm

(each producing about 1/10,000 of industry output)

as a whole has a down-sloping demand curve, each individual potato producer has a demand curve that is perfectly flat at the **equilibrium price**—the going market price.

To explain this more clearly, let's look at the demand curve for the individual potato producer. Assume that the equilibrium price for the industry is 50 cents. This means the producer can sell as many potatoes as he chooses at 50 cents. The quantity that all producers choose to sell makes up the supply curve. But acting alone, a small producer can do almost anything he wants to do.

If this individual farmer raises 1/10,000th of the quantity offered in the market, for example, you can see that there will be little effect on the market if he goes out of business—or doubles his production.

The reason an individual's demand curve is flat in this example is that the farmer probably could not sell any potatoes above the market price. And there is no point in selling below 50 cents.

Not many markets are *purely* competitive. But many are close enough to allow us to talk about "almost" pure competition situations—ones in which the marketing manager has to accept the going price.

Squeeze on the orange growers

Florida orange growers, for example, have basically homogeneous products. They have no control over price. When there is a very large supply, prices drop rapidly. When supplies are short, the reverse happens. During one year, the crop was 50 percent larger than the previous crop— and most growers sold their oranges below their costs. Oranges "on the tree" which cost 75 cents a box to grow were selling for 35 cents a box. Supply turned around the next year, however, and oranges were selling for $2.40 to $2.60 a box.[11]

Profit squeeze is on in many markets

Such highly competitive situations are not limited to agriculture. Wherever many competitors sell basically homogeneous products—such as some chemicals, plastic parts, lumber, coal, printing, and laundry services—the demand curve for each producer tends to be flat.

Markets tend to become more competitive. In pure competition, prices and profits may be pushed down until some competitors are forced out of business. Eventually, the price level is only high enough to keep enough firms in the market. That is, none of them makes a profit. Each just covers all its costs.

When competition is oligopolistic

Few competitors offering similar things

Not all markets move toward pure competition. Some become oligopoly situations.

Oligopoly situations are special market situations which develop when a market has:

1. Homogeneous products—such as basic industrial chemicals or gasoline.
2. Relatively few sellers—or a few large firms and many smaller ones who follow the lead of the larger ones.
3. Fairly inelastic industry demand curves.

The demand curve facing each firm is especially interesting in an oligopoly situation. Although the industry demand curve can be inelastic throughout the relevant range, the demand curve facing each competitor looks "kinked." See Figure 3–4. The current market price is at the kink.

There is a "market price" because the competing firms watch each other carefully—and know it is wise to be at the kink. Each marketing manager must expect that raising his own price above the market for such a homogeneous product would cause a big loss of sales. Few, if any, competitors would follow his price increase. So, his demand curve

Figure 3–4: Oligopoly—kinked demand curve—situation

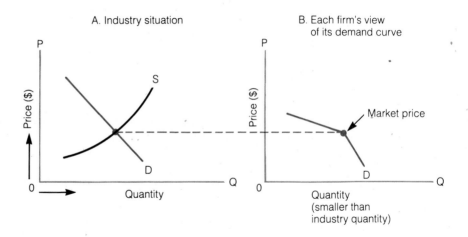

would be relatively flat above the market price. But if he lowers his price, he must expect competitors to follow. Therefore, given inelastic industry demand, his own demand curve would be inelastic at lower prices. Since lowering prices along such a curve would drop total revenue, he probably should not do it. That is, he should leave his price at the kink—the market price.

Actually, however, there are price fluctuations in oligopolistic markets. Sometimes this is caused by firms who don't understand the market situation—and cut their prices to get business. In other cases, big increases in demand or supply change the basic nature of the situation—and lead to price cutting. Sometimes the price cuts are drastic, such as Du Pont's Dacron price cut of 25 percent. This happened when Du Pont decided that industry production capacity already exceeded demand and more was due to start into production.[12]

Price wars are sometimes started

A common example of price fluctuations can be seen in retail gasoline marketing—at a major intersection where there are several obvious competitors. Apparently enough final consumers think of gasoline as homogeneous to create oligopoly conditions. And oligopoly-type price wars are common. These usually start when some gasoline discounter successfully attracts "too much" business—perhaps by cutting his prices one cent a gallon below his usual price. The war proceeds for a time—with everyone losing money—until one of the retailers calls a meeting and suggests that they all "get a little sense." Sometimes these price wars will end immediately after such a meeting—with prices returning to a "reasonable and proper" level.

When competition is monopolistic—A price must be set

You can see why firms would want to avoid pure competition or oligopolistic situations. They would prefer a market in which they have more control.

Monopolistic competition is a market situation which develops when:

1. A market has different (heterogeneous) products—in the eyes of some consumers.
2. Sellers feel they do have some competition in this market.

The word *monopolistic* means that each firm is trying to get control of its own little market. But the word *competition* means that there are still substitutes. The vigorous competition of the purely competitive market is reduced. Each firm has its own down-sloping demand curve. But the shape of the curve depends on the similarity of competitors' products and marketing mixes. Each monopolistic competitor has freedom—but not complete freedom—in its own little "industry."

Judging elasticity will help set the price

Since a firm in monopolistic competition has its own down-sloping demand curve, it must make a price decision as part of its strategy planning.

Here, estimating the elasticity of the firm's own demand curve is helpful. If it is highly inelastic, the firm may decide to raise prices—to increase total revenue. But if demand is highly elastic, this may mean many competitors with acceptable substitutes. Then the price may have to be set near "competition." And the marketing manager probably should try to develop a better marketing mix.

Why some products are offered in pure competition

Why would anyone compete in basically profitless pure competition? One reason is that the firm was already in the industry. Or the firm enters without knowing what is happening—and then must stick it out until it runs out of money. Production-oriented people seem more likely to make such a mistake than market-oriented managers.

Avoiding pure competition seems wise. It certainly fits with our emphasis on target marketing.

CONCLUSION

This chapter was concerned with the forces that are beyond the marketing manager's control yet affect strategy planning. Some uncontrollable variables can change faster than others. But all can change—requiring adjustments in plans. Ideally, possible changes would be considered in the planning.

As we have seen, a marketer must develop mixes appropriate to the customs of the people in his target markets.

The marketing manager must also be aware of legal restrictions—and sensitive to changing political climates. The consumer movement may force many changes.

The economic environment—the chance of recession or inflation—also will affect the choice of strategies. And the marketer must try to anticipate, understand, and deal with such changes as well as changes in the technological base underlying the economic environment.

A manager must also examine the competitive environment. How well established are competitors? What action might they take? What is the nature of competition?

Developing good market-oriented strategies in an uncontrollable environment is not easy. Marketing management, as you can see, is a challenging job.

QUESTIONS AND PROBLEMS

1. For a new design of hair comb, or one of the items mentioned in Question 12 of Chapter 2, discuss the uncontrollable factors that the marketing manager will have to consider.

2. Discuss the relative importance of the uncontrollable variables, given the speed with which these variables move. If some must be neglected because of a shortage of executive time, which would you recommend for neglect?

3. Discuss the probable impact on your hometown of a major technological breakthrough in air transportation which would permit foreign producers to ship into any Canadian market for about the

same transportation cost that domestic producers must incur.

4. If a manufacturer's well-known product is sold at the same price by many retailers in the same community, is this an example of pure competition? When a community has many small grocery stores, are they in pure competition? What characteristics are really needed in order to have a purely competitive market?

5. List three products that are sold in purely competitive markets and three sold in monopolistically competitive markets. Do any of these products have anything in common? Can any generaliza-

tions be made about competitive situations and marketing mix planning?

6. Cite a local example of an oligopoly, explaining why it is an oligopoly.

7. Which way does the Canadian political and legal environment seem to be moving (with respect to business-related affairs)?

8. Why is it necessary to have so many laws regulating business? Why has Parliament not just passed one set of laws to take care of business problems?

9. What and whom is the government attempting to protect in its effort to preserve and regulate competition?

10. For each of the *major* laws discussed in the text, indicate whether in the long run this law will promote or restrict competition. As a consumer, without any financial interest in business, what is your reaction to each of these laws?

11. Are consumer protection laws really new? Discuss the evolution of consumer protection. Is more such legislation likely?

SUGGESTED CASES

1. Quenton Limited
5. Laurentian Steel Company

When you finish this chapter, you should:

1. Understand how to find marketing opportunities.

2. Understand how to define relevant markets, generic markets, and product-markets.

3. Know about the different kinds of marketing opportunities.

4. Understand how to screen and evaluate opportunities.

5. Understand how the resources and objectives of a firm can help in the search for opportunities.

6. Recognize the important new terms (shown in red).

MARKETING OPPORTUNITY ANALYSIS

4

Finding attractive opportunities is part of marketing strategy planning.

In this book we have emphasized marketing strategy planning—an important part of which is finding attractive opportunities. Let's define what we mean by "attractive opportunities"—and then see how the company's objectives and resources can affect the search for these opportunities. Remember, strategic planning tries to match market opportunities to a firm's resources—what it can do—and to its objectives—what it wants to do.

We'll also talk about the kinds of opportunities available—and how to evaluate them. This chapter is important—because attractive opportunities make the rest of marketing strategy planning easier.

WHAT ARE ATTRACTIVE OPPORTUNITIES?

Optimists see opportunities everywhere. Should a marketing manager go after all of the possibilities he finds? Is every one really an attractive marketing opportunity for his firm? The answer, in general, is *no!* Attractive opportunities for a particular firm are those the firm has some chance of doing something about—given its resources and objectives. Usually, attrac-

Figure 4-1: **Finding and evaluating opportunities**

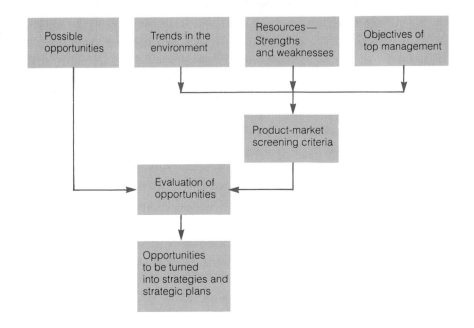

tive opportunities are fairly close to markets the firm already knows. It makes sense to build on a firm's strengths and avoid its weaknesses.

How many opportunities a firm "sees" depends on the thinking of top management—and the objectives of the firm. Some want to be innovators—and eagerly search out new opportunities. Others are willing to be creative imitators of the leaders. And others are willing to be risk-avoiding "me too" marketers.

Figure 4-1 shows the process we will be discussing in this chapter—finding possible opportunities and then screening them to choose the ones which will be turned into strategies and strategic plans. As Figure 4-1 shows, first we will look for possible opportunites—and then evaluate them against screening criteria. These criteria grow out of analysis of the company's resources, the long-run trends facing the company, and the objectives of top management.

Breakthrough opportunities are needed

Throughout this book we will emphasize finding **breakthrough opportunities**—opportunities which help the innovators develop hard-to-copy marketing mixes which will be very profitable for a long time. Really, what we would like to find is attractive enough opportunities so we can win a "competitive advantage" which will give the firm an edge over competitors—and a monopoly in "its own little market"—at least for awhile.

Finding breakthrough opportunities is important—because such opportunities are needed just to survive in our increasingly competitive markets. The "me too" products which production-oriented people like to turn out are not very profitable anymore.[1]

SEARCH FOR OPPORTUNITIES CAN BEGIN WITH DEFINING THE FIRM'S MARKETS

When marketing managers really understand their target markets, they may see breakthrough opportunities—as this Eastman Kodak example shows. Eastman Kodak—well known for cameras and photographic supplies—also produces an industrial good, X-ray film. Until a few years ago, Kodak felt this market wanted faster X-ray pictures at cheaper prices. Their marketing mix was aimed to satisfy those needs. But closer study of this market showed that the real need in hospitals and health-care units was saving the radiologist's time. Time was precious—and just giving the radiologist a faster picture wasn't enough. Something more was needed to help him do the whole job faster. Kodak came to see that its business was not just supplying X-ray pictures, but really helping to improve the health care supplied to patients. As a result, Kodak came up with two new time-savers for the radiologist: a handy cassette film pack—and a special identification camera that records all vital patient data directly on the X-ray at the time the X-ray is made. Before, this tagging had to be done in the darkroom during developing—which took more time and created the risk of error. This was a different marketing mix aimed at satisfying a different need.[2] And it worked very well.

What is a firm's market?

What is a firm's market is an important—but sticky—question. A **market** is a group of potential customers—with similar needs—and sellers offering various products—that is, ways of satisfying those needs.

Companies sometimes avoid the difficulties of defining markets by describing them in terms of the products the firm sells. This production-oriented approach is easy—but it may also make the firm miss opportunities. Producers and retailers of Christmas cards, for example, may define their market very narrowly as the "Christmas-card" market. Or, if they think a little broader, they might call their market the "greeting-card" market—

Really understanding what your market wants and needs can help find opportunities.

including birthday cards, Easter cards, all-occasion cards, and humorous cards. But by taking a more customer-oriented view, the firm might define its market as the "personal-expression" market. And this might lead the firm to offer all kinds of products which could be sent as gifts—to express one person's feelings toward another. The possibilities—besides greeting cards—include jewelry, plaques, candles, puzzles, and so on. Companies like Hallmark have this bigger view—and they have expanded far beyond selling just standard greeting cards for the major greeting-card occasions—birthdays and Christmas.

From generic market to product-markets

It is useful to think of two basic types of market—a generic market and a product-market. A **generic market** is a market in which sellers offer substitute products which are quite different. In contrast, a **product-market** is a market in which sellers offer substitute products which are similar.

A generic market description looks at markets broadly—and from the customers' viewpoint. People seeking status, for example, have several very different ways to satisfy their status needs. A status-seeking consumer might buy an expensive car, take a luxury cruise to Hawaii, or buy designer clothes at an exclusive shop. See Figure 4–2. Any one of these very different products might satisfy the status need. Sellers in this generic status market will have to focus on the *needs* the *customer* wants satisfied—*not* on *how* one seller's product (car or vacation or designer label) is better than that of another producer. By really understanding people's needs and attitudes, it may be possible for producers of "status symbols" to encourage shifts to their particular product.

The fact that quite different products may compete with each other in the same generic market makes it harder to define the market. But if customers see all these products as substitutes—as competitors in the same generic market—then marketers will have to live with this complication.

Suppose, however, that our status-seeking consumer decides to satisfy his status need with a new, expensive car. Then—in this *product*-market—

Figure 4–2: The position of some products in a "status-symbol" market

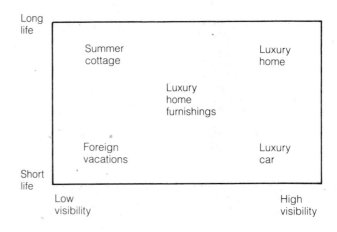

Are these cars in the same generic market or product-market?

Mercedes, Cadillac, or Ferrari may compete with each other for the status-seeker's dollar.

To summarize—in the broad, *generic* market for status—cars, designer clothes, or expensive vacations may all be competing with each other. In a narrower *product*-market concerned with status—consumers compare similar products to satisfy their status needs (e.g., a Ferrari with a Mercedes or a Cadillac).

Most companies quickly narrow their focus to product-markets—because of the firm's past experience, resource commitments, or management preferences. And we will usually be thinking of product-markets when we refer to markets. But this should be done carefully when looking for opportunities—because it is so easy to miss opportunities—as the Christmas-card example showed.

Broaden market definitions for finding opportunities

Broader market definitions—including broader product-market definitions and generic market definitions—are useful for finding opportunities. But deciding what is the relevant market area is a creative process. Too narrow a definition will limit a firm's opportunities—but too broad a definition will make the company's efforts and resources seem worthless.

Our strategic planning process can help define a firm's **relevant market**—the market which is suitable for the firm's purpose. Here, we are trying to match opportunities to the firm's resources and objectives—so the *relevant market for finding opportunities* should be bigger than the firm's present product-market—but not so big that the firm couldn't expand and be an important competitor in this relevant market. A small manufacturer of screwdrivers, for example, shouldn't define its market as broadly as ''the worldwide tool market'' or as narrowly as ''our present screwdriver customers.'' But it might have the production and/or marketing capabilities to consider ''the Canadian hand tool market.'' It might be able to offer hammers, pliers, and wrenches to present customers. Or, this broader market definition might suggest other, smaller markets into which the firm could expand with screwdrivers. These might be other parts of

Identifying the geographic boundaries of a market can suggest new opportunities.

the country—using the same type of channel of distribution—or other kinds of customers—using different kinds of channels.

Naming a market

A product-market description should include some customer-related terms—*not* just product-related terms. Product-related terms are *not*—by themselves—an adequate description of a market. Further, a generic market description would *not* include *any* product-related terms. The emphasis, instead, would be on the needs or benefits sought—for example personal expression, or status, or personal transportation.

It is important to realize that focusing *only* on customer-related terms may lead to dealing with markets which are too broad. So, depending on the company's resources and objectives, it often will have to narrow its relevant market down to one or more product-markets. If an auto manufacturer does not already have a well-known brand which can compete in the status-symbol market—but does have a brand which can compete successfully in the "personal transportation" market—then it might want to define its relevant market so that it only analyzes those market areas where it has some chance of matching opportunities to its own resources.

Identifying geographic boundaries may help

When trying to name present or potential markets, it usually is best to start with the customers' views of the geographic boundary of the market—and then move on to the needs that the company's present offering might satisfy. Just identifying the geographic boundaries of the present market can suggest new opportunities. A supermarket in Vancouver is not catering to all consumers in the Vancouver area—and so there may be opportunities for expansion to unsatisfied customers in that market. In general, it is good practice to identify the geographic boundaries of *all* markets.

Identifying customers' needs can help, too

Potential customers' needs and attitudes toward the products in the general area being considered can help name the relevant product-market or generic market. If the firm were interested in the transportation market, for example, it should think about the basic reasons why people buy transporting "substitutes." In varying degrees, the following products are substitutes—airplanes, pickup trucks, cars, motorcycles, mopeds, bicycles, skateboards, and shoes. And by thinking about why some of these substitutes are better than others, we can convert these product-related solutions to more particular needs or benefits sought. For example, some of these substitutes are better than others with respect to speed, convenience (in all weather), personal versus group transportation, size of load, and cost.

Creative analysis of the needs and attitudes of present and potential target markets—in relation to the benefits being offered by the firm and competitors—will help you see new opportunities. In the next several chapters we will be studying the many possible dimensions of markets—and suggesting ways of segmenting these markets. But, for now, you should see that markets can be defined in various ways—and defining them only in terms of current *products* is *not* the best way of finding new opportunities—and planning marketing strategies. Instead, you should try to define *generic markets* and *product-markets*—with emphasis on the customer-related characteristics, including geographic dimensions—and needs and attitudes.

TYPES OF OPPORTUNITIES TO PURSUE

Most people have unsatisfied needs—and alert marketers can find opportunities all around them. Starting with the firm's present product-markets is useful. This may require marketing research, research and development (R&D), analysis of profitable companies' activities, and analysis of the environmental trends we discussed in the last chapter. It is also possible to go beyond the firm's present activities. It helps to see the kinds of opportunities which may be found. Figure 4–3 shows that there are four possibilities: market penetration, market development, product development, and diversification.

Market penetration

Market penetration: a firm trying to increase sales of its present products in its present markets—probably through a more aggressive marketing mix. The firm might try to increase the customers' rate of use—or attract either the competitors' customers or current nonusers. New promotion appeals might be effective. McDonald's may have Ronald McDonald invite the kids in for a special offer. More stores may be added in present areas—

Figure 4–3: **Four basic types of opportunities**

	Present products	New products
Present markets	Market penetration	Product development
New markets	Market development	Diversification

for greater convenience. Short-term price cuts might be a help. Obviously, effective planning would be improved by a real understanding of why some people are buying now—and what might motivate them to buy more—or motivate others to shift brands or begin or resume buying.

Market development

Market development: a firm trying to increase sales by selling present products in new markets. This might involve, for example, McDonald's adding new stores in new areas—perhaps in downtown locations, in schools or hospital lobbies, or even in foreign countries. Or it might only involve advertising in different media to reach new target customers.

Product development

Product development: a firm offering new or improved products for present markets. Here, the firm should know the market's needs—and might see ways of adding or modifying product features, or creating several quality levels, or adding more types or sizes—to better satisfy the present market. For example, McDonald's now offers breakfast for adults—and cookies for kids.

Diversification

Diversification: a firm moving into totally different lines of business—which might include entirely unfamiliar products, markets, or even levels in the production-marketing system. For example, manufacturers might go into wholesaling or retailing—or buy their suppliers.[3]

Which opportunities come first?

Most firms tend to be production-oriented—and think first of greater market penetration. If they already have as big a share as they can get in their present markets, they may think of market development—finding new markets for their present products—including expanding regionally, nationally, or even internationally.

Marketers who have a good understanding of their present markets may see opportunities in product development—especially because they already have a way of reaching their present customers.

The most challenging opportunities involve diversification. Here, both new products and new markets are included. The further the opportunity is from what the firm is already doing, the more attractive it may look to the optimists—and the harder it will be to evaluate. The firm may have a good understanding of all the problems close to its current operations—that's why it's considering other opportunities! But opportunities which are far from a firm's current operations may involve much higher risks. This is why it is very important to have ways of avoiding wasteful searches for opportunities—as well as for efficiently evaluating those which are finally considered. How this can be done is discussed in the following pages.

COMPANY RESOURCES MAY LIMIT SEARCH FOR OPPORTUNITIES

A smart marketing manager knows that his firm has some resources—perhaps some unique resources—which will help him develop a good strategy. Because of the firm's own history, experience, and personnel, it should have strengths and weaknesses that make it different from other firms. Attractive opportunities should take advantage of these strong points. Resources that should be considered when looking for attractive opportunities are discussed in the following sections.

Financial strength

Some industries (such as steel and public utilities) need large amounts of capital to gain economies of scale. For them, the cost of production per unit goes down as the quantities produced increase. Therefore, smaller producers would be at a great disadvantage if they tried to compete in these lines. On the other hand, large companies often have difficulties when they enter low-investment businesses. For example, a large chemical processor tried to make and sell decorated shower curtains—because it was producing the basic plastic sheets. It lost heavily on the experiment, however. The smaller shower curtain manufacturers and wholesalers were much more flexible—changing their styles and price policies more rapidly. Here, financial strength was an asset in the basic plastic sheet business—but not where style and flexibility in adapting to customer needs was important.

Raw material reserves

Firms that own or have dependable sources of basic raw materials have a head start in businesses that need these resources. But companies—large or small—that don't have this advantage may have difficulty even staying in these businesses. Chemical and paper manufacturers, for example, usually try to control timber supplies. And the metals and oil companies have controlled their own resources. Now that we see a growing shortage of raw materials, it probably would be desirable for a firm to be sure of supplies before building a marketing strategy which depends upon raw materials.

Physical plant

Some kinds of business require large physical plants which must be owned by the firm. If these are well located, this may be an asset. On the other hand, badly located or out-of-date factories—or wholesale or

Some companies that depend on raw materials try to control their own sources of supply.

retail facilities—may be real handicaps. The existing physical plant can affect marketing strategy planning. One of the firm's objectives probably will be to use the existing plant as fully as possible.

Patents

Patents are most important to manufacturers. A patent owner has a 17-year monopoly to develop and use its new product, process, or material as it chooses. If a firm has a patent on a basic process, potential competitors may be forced to use second-rate processes—and they may fail. You can see that if a firm has such a patent, it is a resource. But if its competitors have it, it may be a handicap which cannot be overcome with other parts of a marketing mix.

Brands

If a firm has developed a loyal following of customers who prefer or insist on its good or service, others may have trouble breaking into its market. A strong brand is a valuable asset that a marketing manager can use in developing marketing strategies.

Skill of personnel

Some firms deliberately pay high wages to attract and hold skilled workers—so they can offer high-quality goods or services. A skilled sales force is also an asset. But lack of good sales people may limit strategy planning. Skilled workers may be able to produce a new product, but the sales force may not have the contacts or know-how to sell it. This often happens when a firm moves into new markets.

Management attitudes

The attitudes toward growth are important in strategy planning—especially in developing new products.

The president of a Nova Scotia manufacturing company was excited about the prospects of a new product. But after looking at the attitudes of his company personnel—and especially his management people—he dropped his plans for the product. Why? He found that his employees had no ambition or interest in growth![4]

OBJECTIVES MAY LIMIT THE SEARCH FOR OPPORTUNITIES

A company's objectives should direct the operation of the whole business. If it has already been decided that the firm is to stay small—so the owner has plenty of time for golf—then this objective will obviously limit the firm's opportunities. (Actually, of course, it probably wouldn't even be looking for opportunities!) On the other hand, if a large aggressive firm seeks to maximize profit wherever it can, then the range of opportunities expands quickly.

Objectives should set firm's course

Objectives are important to marketing strategy planning. A business should know where it is going, or it is likely to fall into this trap: "Having lost sight of our objectives, we redoubled our efforts."[5]

In spite of their importance, objectives are seldom stated clearly. They may even be stated *after* the strategies are carried out!

Setting objectives that really guide the present and future development of a company isn't easy. It forces top management to look at the entire business—and relate its present needs and resources to the external environment. Then it can decide what it wants to do in the future.

Three basic objectives provide guidelines

The following three objectives provide a useful starting point for setting objectives for a firm. These three objectives could be stated in many ways. But they should be aimed at together because, in the long run, a failure in even one of the three areas could lead to total failure of the business.

1. Engage in some specific business activity that will be socially and economically useful.
2. Develop an organization to stay in business—and carry out its strategies.
3. Earn enough profit to survive.[6]

Shortsighted top management may straitjacket marketing

Objective setting must be taken seriously—or the objectives may limit marketing strategies—perhaps hurting the whole business.

A few examples will show how the marketing manager might have to choose undesirable strategies.

A quick return on investment is sometimes sought by top management. This might force the marketing manager to choose marketing strategies aimed at quick return in the short run—but kill customer goodwill in the long run.

Some top managements want a large sales volume or a larger market share—just for its own sake. Ampex (an electronics firm) almost went out of business seeking growth for its own sake. And A&P, Ford Motor Company, RCA, and Westinghouse shifted their objectives toward *profitable* sales growth when they realized that sales growth does not necessarily mean profitable growth.[7]

Really understanding a company's objectives will improve its strategy planning.

Figure 4–4: A hierarchy of objectives

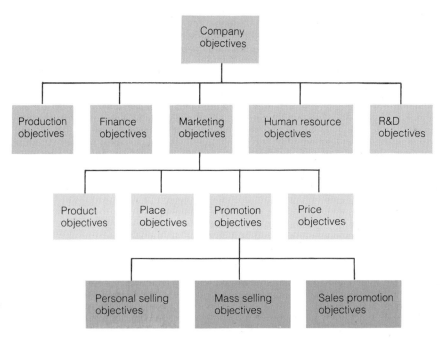

Objectives should guide the whole management process

Ideally, the marketing manager should help set the objectives—and these objectives should guide the search for and evaluation of opportunities—as well as later planning of marketing strategies. As shown in Figure 4–4, there should be a hierarchy of objectives—moving from company objectives, to marketing department objectives. For each marketing strategy, there should also be objectives for each of the four Ps—as well as sub-objectives. For example, in the Promotion area we might need advertising objectives, sales promotion objectives, and personal selling objectives.

HOW TO EVALUATE OPPORTUNITIES

Once some opportunities have been identified, it is necessary to screen and evaluate them. A firm can't possibly pursue all of its opportunities. Instead, it must try to match its opportunities to its resources and objectives. The first step is to quickly screen out the obvious mismatches. Then, it can analyze the remaining ones more carefully. Let's look at some methods for screening and evaluating opportunities.

Developing and applying screening criteria.

We have already evaluated the firm's resources (for strengths and weaknesses), the environmental trends facing the firm, and the objectives of top management. Now these can be combined into a set of product-market screening criteria. These criteria should include both quantitative and qualitative components. The quantitative components outline the objectives of the firm—sales, profit, and return on investment (ROI) targets for each

Figure 4–5: An example of product-market screening criteria for a small retailer ($300,000 annual sales)

1. Quantitative criteria
   a. Increase sales by $100,000 per year for the next five years.
   b. Earn ROI of *at least* 25 percent before taxes on new ventures.
   c. Break even within one year on new ventures.
   d. Opportunity must be large enough to justify interest (to help meet objectives) but small enough so company can handle with the resources available.
   e. Several opportunities should be needed to reach the objectives—to spread the risks.
2. Qualitative criteria
   a. Nature of business preferred.
      1. Goods and services sold to present customers.
      2. "Quality" products which can be sold at "high prices" with full margins.
      3. Competition should be weak and opportunity should be hard to copy for several years.
      4. Should build on our strong sales skills.
      5. There should be strongly felt (even unsatisfied) needs—to reduce promotion costs and permit "high" prices.
   b. Constraints
      1. Nature of businesses to exclude.
         (a) Manufacturing.
         (b) Any requiring large fixed capital investments.
         (c) Any requiring many people who must be "good" all the time and would require supervision (e.g., "quality" restaurant).
      2. Geographic
         (a) United States and Canada only.
      3. General
         (a) Make use of current strengths.
         (b) Attractiveness of market should be reinforced by *more than one* of the following basic trends: technological, demographic, social, economic, political.
         (c) Market should not be bucking *any* of above trends.

strategy.* The qualitative components explain what kind of business the firm wants to be in, what businesses it wants to ignore, what weaknesses it should avoid, and what strengths and trends it should build on.[8] Opportunities that pass the screen should be ones that could be turned into strategies which the firm could carry out with its current resources.

Figure 4–5 illustrates the product-market screening criteria for a small retailer. This whole set would help the firm's managers eliminate unsuitable opportunities—and find attractive ones to turn into strategies and plans.

Whole plans should be evaluated

Forecasts for the possible results of implementing whole strategic *plans* are needed in order to apply the quantitative part of the screening criteria— because it is "implemented plans" which produce sales, profits, and return on investment (ROI). For a rough screening, we only need an estimate of the likely results of implementing alternative opportunities over logical

---

* See Appendix B (following Chapter 18) for definitions of these terms.

planning periods. If a product's life (before withdrawal from the market) is likely to be five years, for example, then a good strategy may not produce profitable results during the first six months to a year. But evaluate the plan over the projected five-year life, and it might look like a winner. When evaluating the potential of alternative opportunities—strategic plans—it is important to evaluate similar things—that is, *whole* strategic plans.

Note that—as shown in Figure 4–6 quite different strategic plans can be evaluated at the same time. In this case, a substantially improved product and product concept (Product A) is being compared with a "me-too" product for the same target market. In the short run, the me-too product would break even sooner and might look like the better choice—if only one's year's results were considered. The new product, on the other hand, will take a good deal of pioneering but—over the five-year life—will be much more profitable.

PLANNING GRIDS HELP EVALUATE DIFFERENT KINDS OF OPPORTUNITIES

When a firm has many possibilities to evaluate, it usually has to compare quite different ones. This can present a real problem—but the problem has been reduced by the development of graphical approaches—such as the nine-box strategic planning grid developed by General Electric.

General Electric looks for green positions

General Electric's strategic planning grid—see Figure 4–7—forces company managers to make three-part judgments (high, medium, and low) about the business strengths and industry attractiveness of all proposed or existing products or businesses.

GE feels that opportunities that fall into the green boxes in the upper left-hand corner of the grid are its growth opportunities—the ones that will lead the company to invest and grow with these businesses. The red boxes in the lower right-hand corner of the grid, on the other hand, suggest a no-growth policy. Existing red businesses might continue to generate earnings—but GE figures they no longer deserve much invest-

Figure 4–6: Expected sales and cost curves of two strategies over five-year planning periods

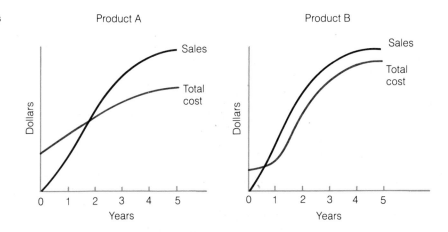

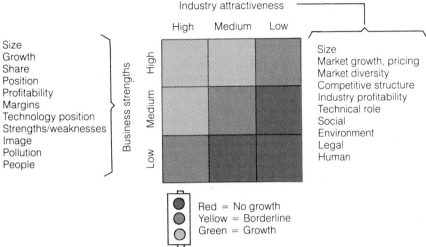

ment. The yellow businesses are the borderline cases—which could go either way. An existing yellow business might be continued and supported—but a proposal for a new yellow business would have a greater chance of being rejected by top management.

GE's "stop-light" evaluation method is a very subjective approach—because GE feels that there are too many possible errors if it tries to use oversimplified criteria—like ROI and market share—for judging "attractiveness" or "strength." Instead, top managers review written summaries of about a dozen factors (see Figure 4–7) which help them make summary judgments. Then they make a collective judgment—based on the importance they attach to each of the factors. GE reports that the approach generally leads to agreement—and a good understanding about why some businesses or new opportunities are supported and others are not. Further, it appears that high-high green businesses are uniformly good on almost any quantitative or qualitative measure used. This interaction among the relevant variables makes it practical to boil them all down into a stop-light framework.[9]

MULTIPRODUCT FIRMS WITH SEVERAL PRODUCTS HAVE A DIFFICULT STRATEGY PLANNING JOB

Firms with many product lines—like General Electric and Procter & Gamble—obviously have a tougher strategic planning job than a firm with only a few products or product lines aimed at the same or similar target markets. They have to develop strategic plans for very different businesses. And the corporate level must try to balance the plans and needed resources for the various businesses in such a way that the whole corporation reaches its objectives—perhaps continued sales and profit growth. This requires analyses of the various alternatives—using approaches similar to the General Electric strategic planning grid—and approving strategic plans which make sense for the *whole* corporation.

Details on how to manage such a complicated firm are beyond our scope. But it is important to know (1) that there are such firms and (2) that the principles we will discuss in this text work—they just have to be extended to develop and control many strategic plans.

CONCLUSION

Innovative strategy planning is needed for survival in our increasingly competitive marketplaces. This requires not only developing marketing strategies but finding attractive opportunities—which was the focus of this chapter.

We discussed ways of finding attractive opportunities—and breakthrough opportunities. And we saw that the firm's own resources and objectives may help limit the search for opportunities.

Eventually, some procedures are needed for screening and evaluating opportunities. We explained an approach for developing screening criteria—from the output of an analysis of the strengths and weaknesses of the company's re-

sources, the environmental trends it faces, and top management's objectives. We also considered some techniques for evaluating opportunities—including the GE strategic planning grid.

Now that we have discussed how to find and evaluate attractive opportunities, we must go on to discuss how we turn these opportunities into profitable marketing strategies. This will require us to get into marketing research (Chapter 5), analyzing customer buying behavior (Chapters 6–8), and segmenting markets (Chapter 9). After these chapters, we will go on to developing marketing mixes and strategies (Chapters 10–20).

QUESTIONS FOR DISCUSSION

1. Distinguish between an attractive opportunity and a breakthrough opportunity.

2. Explain how new opportunities may be seen by defining a firm's markets more precisely. Illustrate for a situation where you feel there is an opportunity—i.e., an unsatisfied market segment—even if it is not very large.

3. Distinguish between a generic market and a product-market. Illustrate your answer.

4. Explain the major differences among the four basic types of opportunities discussed in the text, and cite examples for two of these types of opportunities.

5. Explain why a firm might want to pursue a market penetration opportunity before pursuing one involving product development or diversification.

6. Explain how a firm's resources might limit its

search for opportunities. Cite a specific example for a specific resource.

7. Discuss how a company's financial strength might have a bearing on the kinds of products it might produce. Will it have an impact on the other three Ps as well? If so, how? Use an example in your answer.

8. Explain how a firm's objectives might affect its search for opportunities.

9. Specifically, how would various company objectives affect the development of a marketing mix for a new type of baby shoe? If this company were just being formed by a former shoemaker with limited financial resources, list the objectives he might have and then discuss how they will affect the development of his marketing strategy.

10. Explain the components of product-market

screening criteria—which are used to evaluate opportunities.

11. Explain how you could use the General Electric strategic planning grid to evaluate quite different opportunities. Be sure to distinguish between a "green" and a "red" opportunity.

SUGGESTED CASES

4. Redi, Limited
12. Ski Haus Sports Shop
29. Rundle Manufacturing Company

When you finish this chapter, you should:

1. *Understand a scientific approach to marketing research.*

2. *Know how to go about defining and solving marketing problems.*

3. *Know about getting secondary and primary data.*

4. *Know about marketing information systems.*

5. *Recognize the important new terms (shown in red).*

GATHERING INFORMATION FOR MARKETING PLANNING

5

"Hello. I'm conducting a survey. . . ." Marketing research? Yes, but there's a lot more to the job than that.

Marketing managers need information to plan successful marketing strategies. Ideally, they would like (1) information about potential target markets and how they might react to various marketing mixes, and (2) information about competition and other uncontrollable factors. Marketing research is needed to help the marketing manager gather the information required to make wise decisions. This is not an easy job—because potential customers and competitors are not very predictable. It is a very necessary job though. Without good information, managers can only guess about potential markets. In our fast-changing, competitive economy, this almost guarantees failure.

MARKETING RESEARCHERS HELP SUPPLY MARKETING INFORMATION

Marketing research gathers and analyzes data to help marketing managers make decisions. One of the important jobs of a marketing researcher is to help management get the "facts"—and understand them. Marketing research is much more than a bunch of techniques—or a group of specialists in survey design. Good marketing researchers must keep marketing *and* management in mind—to be sure that their research focuses on real problems.

Managers must know what researchers do

Marketing research details can be handled by staff or outside specialists. But marketing managers must be able to explain the kinds of problems they are facing—and the kinds of information which will help them make decisions. They also must be able to communicate with specialists in *their* language. Marketing managers may only be "consumers" of research, but they have to be able to explain what they want. For this reason, our emphasis won't be on mechanics—but rather on how to plan and evaluate the work of marketing researchers.

OUR STRATEGIC PLANNING FRAMEWORK CAN GUIDE MARKETING RESEARCH

Marketing researchers work on all kinds of problems—from developing wholly new strategies to evaluating current strategies. An important part of their job is providing feedback—which may lead to new plans. Marketing research is a continuing process—involving a wide range of possible jobs.

Finding the right problem level almost solves the problem

The strategic planning framework introduced in Chapter 2 can be especially useful here—helping the researcher to see where the real problem lies. Do we really know enough about target markets? If so, do we know enough to work out all of the four Ps?

The importance of understanding the nature of the problem—and then trying to solve it—can be seen more clearly in the following example of a manufacturer of a new easy-to-use baking mix. Top management had selected apartment dwellers, younger couples, and the too-busy-to-cook crowd as the target market—because it seemed "logical" that the convenience of the new product should appeal to them. A little research on the size of this market indicated that—if these consumers responded as expected—there were enough of them to create a profitable baking mix market. The company decided to aim at this market—and developed a logical marketing mix.

Managers should know what they want and be able to communicate it to researchers.

Why didn't this baking mix sell?

During the first few months, sales results were disappointing. The manufacturer "guessed" that something was wrong with the product—since the promotion seemed to be adequate. At this point, a consumer survey was done—with surprising results. The product was apparently satisfactory, but the target customers just weren't interested in convenience for this kind of product. Instead, the best market turned out to be families who did lots of cooking! They liked the convenience of the mix—especially when they needed a dish in a hurry.

In this case, the original strategy planning was sloppy. The choice of target market was based on guesswork by top management. This led to a poor strategy—and wasted promotion money. Just a little research on consumers—about their needs and attitudes—might have avoided this costly error. Both marketing research and management fumbled the ball—by not studying the target market. Then, when sales results were poor, the company fumbled again by assuming that the product was at fault—instead of checking consumers' real attitudes about the product. Fortunately, research finally uncovered the real problem. Then the overall strategy was changed quickly.

The moral of this story is that our strategic planning framework can be useful for guiding marketing research efforts. Without a logical approach, marketing researchers can waste time working on the wrong problem.

Quick answers are often needed

Marketing research often has to supply information quickly. But researchers still should use the best methods possible. For this reason, we will show that a scientific approach to solving marketing problems makes sense. This scientific approach—combined with our strategic planning framework—can help marketing managers make better decisions—even if they have to be made quickly.

THE SCIENTIFIC METHOD AND MARKETING RESEARCH

Managers want to make the best decisions possible. The scientific method helps them do this. It forces researchers to follow steps that reduce the chances for sloppy work—or guesswork.

The **scientific method** is a research approach which consists of four stages:

1. Observation.
2. Developing hypotheses.
3. Prediction of the future.
4. Testing the hypotheses.

With this method, researchers try to develop **hypotheses**—educated guesses about the relationship between things or what will happen in the future. Then they test each hypothesis. A formal hypothesis statement might be: "There is no significant difference between brands A and B in the minds of consumers."

Managers should study their markets carefully before developing hypotheses.

The scientific approach to pain

To illustrate these stages in a simple nonmarketing case, consider a college student who develops a painful, swollen ankle after a skiing accident. The ankle could be bruised, sprained, or broken. What should he do? If he goes to a doctor, he will probably find the doctor following the scientific method:

1. Observation: Pain seems to increase if foot is twisted, but pain is not unbearable.
2. Developing an hypothesis: Since a sprain would be more painful than this, the ankle is broken.
3. Prediction of the future: Pain and swelling will reduce, but bone may heal improperly if not set.
4. Testing the hypothesis: X-ray the ankle; don't wait to see if hypothesis is correct in this case!

Now let's use the same method to show how a marketing manager might use this method.

The scientific approach to offering shirt wrappers

A manufacturer of men's shirts wanted to develop new opportunities. The approach taken is shown here:

1. Observation: Notice some competitors' sales increasing and many competitors shifting to a new plastic wrapping.
2. Developing hypotheses: Assume *(a)* that plastic wrapping is the main cause of competitors' sales increases and *(b)* that the firm's products are similar.
3. Prediction of the future: Firm's sales ought to increase if it shifts to the new wrapping.
4. Testing hypotheses: Produce some shirts in the new package and test them in the market.

The market test revealed that the prediction was correct—sales did increase. But what if they had not? Here is one important benefit of the scientific method. Through careful control—making certain that the test was correctly designed and run—and evaluation of results, we should be able to see exactly where the hypotheses were wrong.

In this case, either one of the hypotheses could have been wrong. Either increased sales by competitors were not caused by the new wrapping—or this manufacturer's products were not similar.

Assuming that the first hypothesis was wrong, further research might show that competitors' sales increased because their promotion was better. Or, if the second hypothesis was wrong, the firm might find out how the products differed—and change its product.

FOUR-STEP APPROACH TO SOLVING MARKETING PROBLEMS

In marketing research, there is a four-step application of the scientific method: (1) definition of the problem, (2) situation analysis, (3) informal investigation, and (4) formal research project. See Figure 5–1.

Observation—the first stage in the scientific method—is used during the first three marketing research steps. Once the problem is defined, developing hypotheses takes place. Prediction of the future occurs any time before a formal research project is planned. Testing the hypotheses is completed in the formal research project unless—as often happens—informal investigation solves the problem.

You can see that the scientific method is an important part of marketing research. Table 5–1 may help you see the relationships. The exact meaning of these terms is explained in the following pages.

Figure 5–1: Four-step approach to solving marketing problems

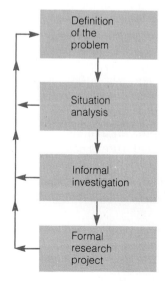

Table 5–1: Relation of scientific method to marketing research

Scientific method stages	Used during the following marketing research steps
Observation	Definition of problem Situation analysis Informal investigation Formal research
Developing hypotheses	Situation analysis Informal investigation Formal research (planning)
Predicting the future . . . . (action implications)	Situation analysis Informal investigation Formal research (planning)
Testing hypotheses	Formal research (unless management is satisfied with an earlier but more intuitive solution)

DEFINITION OF THE PROBLEM—STEP ONE

Defining the problem is the most important—and often the most difficult—job of the marketing researcher. It is slow work. It requires careful observation. Sometimes it takes over half the time spent on a research project. But it is time well spent if the problem is precisely defined. The best research job on the wrong problem is wasted effort. It may even lead to more costly mistakes—the introduction of a poor product or the use of an ineffective advertising approach.

Don't confuse problems with symptoms

Problem definition sounds simple—and that's the danger. It is easy to confuse symptoms with the problem. For example, suppose that a firm's continuing sales analysis shows that the company's sales are decreasing in certain territories—while expenses remain the same—with a resulting decline in profits. Will it help to define the problem by asking: How can we stop the sales decline? Probably not. This would be like asking how to lower a patient's temperature—instead of first trying to find the cause of the fever.

The real problem may be hard to discover. The marketing manager can start with the strategic planning framework—and evaluate what is known about the target market and whether the marketing mix seems to make sense. If there are doubts about one or more of these factors, these problem areas can be explored. But without further evidence, the marketing manager should not assume too quickly that he has defined the real problem. Instead, he should take his list of possible problems and go on to the next step—trying to discover which is the basic cause of the trouble.

SITUATION ANALYSIS—STEP TWO

No talks with outsiders

In a situation analysis, researchers try to size up the situation—but without talking to outsiders. They talk to informed people within the com-

Figure 5–2: **Sources of data**

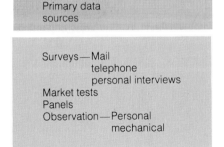

Primary data sources	Secondary data sources
Surveys—Mail telephone personal interviews Market tests Panels Observation—Personal mechanical	Company files Libraries Governments Private research organizations Trade associations University business research bureaus

pany. They study internal company records. They also search libraries for available material.

This research is important—since researchers have to know the environment in which they work. They should study information about their own company and its products. They should know the industry—and the specific markets in which it operates. They must understand their middlemen, the firm's own promotion, and its competitors' activities. Once the researchers have begun to focus on possible problems, they can look for specific kinds of information.

Unless they know what they are looking for, researchers may be confused by all the information available in their own company—or in libraries. Let's take a look at the type of information we're talking about.

Secondary data is available **now**

A situation analysis evaluates **secondary data**—information which is already published or collected. **Primary data** is information which is gathered specifically to solve a current problem. Gathering primary data is discussed later. But it must be emphasized now that too often researchers rush out to gather primary data when there is already plenty of secondary information. And this data may be available immediately—at little or no cost! See Figure 5–2.

One of the first places a researcher should look for secondary data is a good library. Often your local library has the answer you need. Librarians can be a big help. Ask! They're glad to help. They can offer you an excellent list of secondary data from both government and private sources available to the Canadian marketer.

RESEARCH BY SUBSCRIPTION

A number of research firms are in the business of supplying research data that will aid the marketing manager in making a situation analysis. These research firms collect, in a single large study, information on very different product categories. Findings by category are then sold to manufacturers with a particular interest in specific products. Syndicated services can be costly but nowhere near an expensive as if each manufacturer individually tried to collect such data on its own and competing brands.

International Surveys Limited (ISL) makes available information on product movements using data from a consumer panel of more than 3,500 households located throughout the country. These households record in diaries their total purchases from all sources; and they list for each item the day and date of purchase, the type and size of package, and the retail price as well as the source of purchase. This data is used by many large food and drug manufacturers to measure the rate of consumption of their products at the consumer level.

A. C. Nielsen, which audits 750 retail food stores and drugstores also measures movement at the retail level. Nielsen, however, provides additional information about competitors' use of retail displays, two-for-one sales, and other activities. In contrast, ISL furnishes more detailed information on buyer characteristics. For this reason, some large companies subscribe to both services. With such information on hand, they often know more about the customers and sales of smaller competitors than some of these competitors know about themselves.

Syndicated services also provide reliable data on the audience characteristics of both print and broadcast media. Nielsen and the Bureau of Broadcast Measurement (BBM) both provide station-by-station television audience estimates and program ratings. BBM also reports on the size of the Canadian audience, throughout the day, of all its member radio stations.

The Print Measurement Bureau provides equally detailed information to its subscribers on both the readers and the readership of 47 major Canadian magazines. Very specific demographic data is gathered along with information on life-style and exposure to other media. Also of great value to marketing managers is PMB's information bank on actual purchase and usage, by type of customer, of 668 different products or services. Having comparable information available on both purchase and readership greatly facilitates print media planning.[1]

Problem may be solved during the situation analysis

If the problem is clear-cut, it can sometimes be solved at this point—without additional expense. Perhaps someone else already has done a study that answers almost exactly the same question.

The fact that further research may not be necessary is important. Too often researchers rush out a questionnaire to 100 or even several thousand persons or firms. This gives the impression that they are really "doing something." An effective situation analysis, unfortunately, is less impressive. If a supervisor asks the researcher what he is doing, about all he can say is: "I'm sizing up the situation" or "I'm studying the problem."

Actually, the situation analyst is really trying to discover the exact nature of the situation *and* the problem. The person who rushes out all the questionnaires may be doing this too—although he may not even know it.

An effective situation analysis can save research time and money.

The point is that when the results of the questionnaire come in, he may finally see the problem. But he still won't have the answer. He will have to go on to the next step in analysis—just like the more scientific researcher.

INFORMAL INVESTIGATION—STEP THREE

During the informal investigation, the researcher is still trying to define the problem and develop hypotheses. But now the idea is to get outside the company and the library—to talk to informed people. By informed people, we mean intelligent and efficient retailers, wholesalers, and customers. No formal questionnaire is used. The researcher is not yet testing hypotheses—except informally.

When developing machine tools, for example, it would make sense to talk to a few machine operators, plant managers in more efficient factories, design engineers at independent research organizations or universities, and perhaps a few good wholesalers who have close contact with potential customers.

Fast, informative, inexpensive

These talks would be informal—but they should help the researcher zero in on the problem and develop useful hypotheses. By this time, the researcher should have the problem area narrowed down. This is important—asking informed people to discuss general problems would be a waste of time.

An informal investigation takes little time—but can be very informative. Also, it is cheaper than a large-scale survey.

On the basis of the information gathered in a situation analysis and informal investigation, the researcher should now be developing some definite hypotheses. And he may be able to decide on an answer to the problem without further research.

If management has to make a decision quickly—if it can't wait for a formal test—then well-considered hypotheses may lead to a practical solution. In such cases, the extra time and effort spent on more scientific research in the early steps may pay off handsomely.

PLANNING THE FORMAL RESEARCH PROJECT—STEP FOUR

Gathering primary data

If the researcher has failed to solve the problem by this time, the next step is a formal research project—usually to gather primary data. Three basic methods can be used: (1) the observation method, (2) the survey method, or (3) the experimental method.

The **observation method** involves observing potential customers' behavior. This method avoids face-to-face interviews—because asking direct questions may not get very good results. Sometimes, however, asking questions can't be avoided. Then, the **survey method**—which asks potential customers questions—may be helpful. Telephone, mail, or personal interviews can be used for surveys. The **experimental method** uses experiments to test hypotheses. Either the observation method or the survey method or both could be used. But usually control groups are needed.

Managers should share in research design

The actual design of a research project is beyond the scope of this text—but it is very important to the final results. Therefore, marketing managers should be involved in the process. At least, they should be familiar with some of the design details. Then they will be able to evaluate the quality of the research—and be sure that the results will be useful.

Some researchers may imply a great deal about the reliability of their research methods. They may be using samples which are not representative—yet try to pass off the results as reliable. An experienced manager would not be fooled by such sloppy work. He would understand that technical matters such as research design—and the size and representativeness of samples—do affect the quality of the results.

Interviewing informed people can get useful information quickly.

EXECUTION AND INTERPRETATION OF THE RESEARCH PROJECT

We can't discuss here how to conduct and interpret a formal research project. This involves training a field staff—and tabulating, interpreting, and presenting results. It also means following through to make sure results are used effectively. Such matters are explained in most marketing research texts.[2]

Marketing manager and researcher should work together

Marketing research involves some technical details. But it should be obvious that the marketing researcher and the marketing manager should work together—to be sure that they really do solve the problems facing the firm.[3]

When the researcher and the manager have not worked closely together, the interpretation step becomes extremely important. While managers may not be research specialists, they have to be able to evaluate research results. If the research methods and the reliability of the data are not clearly explained, the marketing manager must use even greater judgment in evaluating the data. In fact, if the researcher doesn't explain his methods and suggest specific action, he should not be surprised if the marketing manager ignores the work. This stresses, again, the importance of the two working together to solve problems.

REAL PROBLEM SOLVING MAY REQUIRE ALL FOUR STEPS

Logical flow of steps may help

Marketing research usually must combine several steps to do a good job. This is illustrated by an example of a manufacturer interested in expanding its market for interior decorating products.

The company wanted to increase its sales. But it didn't know how many interior decorators were in the market—or how much money consumers spent on the company's product type (definition of the problem). A review of U.S. Census of Business data indicated that there were approximately 1,300 interior decorators. According to their own sales records (situation analysis), this would not leave much room for expansion of sales volume with their present line. Management considered branching out into other lines (hypothesis that business would improve by producing other products for this or other markets).

Before doing this, the company decided to do additional research in its present market area. They interviewed the company's sales reps—and checked the circulation data of an interior decorators' magazine (more situation analysis). They also made a limited mail survey to check on the size of the market (a formal research project to test the hypothesis that there were more potential customers).

This revealed that there were actually 9,700 interior decorators who spent some $75 million on the company's type of product alone. For some reason (probably their small size) the decorators had not all been included in the published census data. It was clear at this point that the company's biggest and best market was the one which they were already selling.

A thorough situation analysis is vital to solving the real problem.

In this case, no research at all—or a too sketchy situation analysis—would have led to a wrong answer. But further analysis—along with an informal investigation and a limited survey—got results that proved very satisfactory.[4] This type of research is within the reach of even small firms. You should now be able to understand and help in such an effort.

COST AND ORGANIZATION OF MARKETING RESEARCH

Relatively little—perhaps too little—is spent on the typical marketing research department. Often the research department's budget is about 0.2 percent of sales—$100,000 for a company with a $50 million annual sales volume![5] This is in contrast to research and development budgets that frequently run 5 to 10 percent of sales. Unfortunately, this sometimes leads to the development of products with little or no market potential.

Shortcuts cut cost, add risk

Even on small budgets, however, good research work can be done.[6] When a problem is carefully defined, formal research projects may not be necessary. This is especially true for industrial markets—because of the relatively small number of manufacturers. But taking shortcuts increases the risk.

More dependable research can become expensive. A large-scale survey could easily cost from $10,000 to $100,000. And the continuing research available from companies such as A. C. Nielsen can cost a company from $25,000 to $100,000 or more a year.

Who does the work

Most large companies have a separate marketing research department to plan and conduct research projects. Even these departments, however, often use outside specialists—such as interviewing services—to handle specific jobs.

Few companies with sales of less than $2.5 million have separate marketing research departments. They depend on sales personnel—or top executives—for what research they do.[7]

HOW MUCH RESEARCH SHOULD BE DONE?

No firm can afford to do without marketing research

Most companies do some marketing research—whether they know it or not. Most marketing executives would agree with the manager of marketing research for Dow Chemical Co., who states:

> I feel that it is impossible to run a company today without market research, whether it is done by the president, the sales manager, or a separate group set up specifically to perform the function. Few companies are small enough to afford the luxury of having their market research done by the president. No company can afford not to do market research at all.[8]

What is the value of information?

The high cost of good research must be balanced against its probable value to management. You never get all the information you would like to have. Very detailed surveys or experiments may be "too good" or "too expensive" or "too late" if all that is needed is a rough sampling of retailer attitudes about a new pricing plan *by tomorrow*.

Marketing managers must take risks—because of incomplete information. This is part of their job—and always will be. They might like more data. But they must compare the cost of getting it against its likely value. If the risk is not too great, the cost of getting more or better information may be greater than the potential loss from a poor decision. A decision to expand into a new territory with the present marketing mix, for example, might be made with more confidence of success after a $5,000 survey. But simply sending a sales rep into the territory for a few weeks to try to sell the potential customers would cost less than $5,000. And—if successful—the answer is in and so are some sales.

Faced with many risky decisions, the marketing manager should seek help from research only for problems where he feels the risk can be greatly reduced at a reasonable cost.[9]

The cost and time of a research project has to be balanced against the value of the information received and when it's needed.

SOME FIRMS ARE BUILDING COMPUTER-AIDED MARKETING INFORMATION SYSTEMS

In some companies, marketing researchers have high status—and are deeply involved in major marketing decisions. In other companies, they may be just data collectors. They have not managed to sell the idea that good information (not just data) will improve decision making.

Separate department may be needed

Some companies are setting up marketing information systems to improve the quality—and quantity—of information available to their managers. A **marketing information system (MIS)** is an organized way of continually gathering and analyzing data to obtain information to help marketing managers make decisions. Sometimes this means expanding the job of the marketing research department. In other companies, this information function is separated into a new department. Management wants to make sure that it does not get buried in the data-collection activities of the marketing research department.

Figure 5–3: A diagram of a marketing information system showing various inputs to a computer and outputs to managers

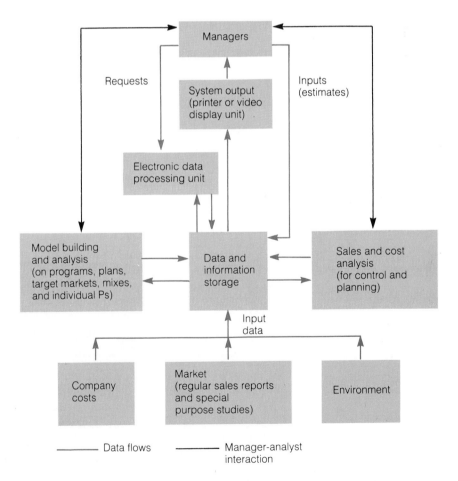

Information may make managers more daring

Once marketing managers see how a working MIS can help their decision making, they are eager for more information. They see that they can improve all of their planning. They can check strategies—comparing results and making necessary changes more quickly. Figure 5–3 shows how the parts in a MIS work together.

Interest in developing information systems is growing—because companies are beginning to see that better information can improve profits. It may also encourage what may seem like "daring" actions. After a series of experiments—and careful data analysis—for example, Anheuser-Busch felt that they better understood how advertising affected their sales. So they cut their advertising budget from $14.8 million down to $10 million a year. While reducing advertising, sales continued to grow and the cost of advertising per barrel dropped in half. Obviously, this had a good effect on profits.[10]

We probably will see more and better marketing information systems as researchers become more experienced—and computer costs continue to go down. The biggest problem may be marketing managers not asking for more useful information—or failing to use it in their decision making. Unfortunately, modern decision-making techniques are not used very much in most companies. There is still lots of room in marketing for able people who can apply research techniques to solve real marketing problems.

CONCLUSION

In this chapter, we saw that marketing research is not a mystery understood only by statisticians. It is a management tool that helps the marketing manager make better decisions based—not on "feel" and guesswork—but on useful information. The marketing researcher should work with the marketing manager—helping him to solve real problems. Without this teamwork, the output of a marketing research department may be useless. And the department may become just a collector of data.

Marketing research should use the scientific method to solve marketing problems. Some organized approach is desirable—because very often a researcher does not have the time or money to complete a full research project. If the early stages of the research effort have been done effectively, he may be able to solve the problem early in the process. A scientific approach to solving marketing problems involves four steps: definition of the problem, situation analysis, an informal investigation, and, if necessary, a formal research project.

The text's strategic planning framework can be a big help in identifying the real problem. By focusing on the real problem, a researcher may be able to move quickly to a useful solution—without the cost and problems of a formal research project. If the manager has more time and money, then he may be able to afford the luxury of a more detailed analysis. Some firms have even developed computer-aided marketing information systems—which help them to learn a great deal about their market areas. This, in turn, helps them to make better decisions.

QUESTIONS FOR DISCUSSION

1. Marketing research entails expense—sometimes much expense. Why does the text recommend the use of marketing research even though a highly experienced marketing executive is available?

2. Explain the steps in the general scientific method and then show how the steps in marketing research are similar.

3. How is the situation analysis any different from the informal investigation? Could both these steps be done at the same time to obtain answers sooner? Is this wise?

4. Explain how you might use each of the research methods (observation, survey, and experiment) to forecast market reaction to a new kind of margarine which is to receive no promotion other than what the retailer will give it. Further, it should be assumed that the new margarine's name will not be associated with other known products. The product will be offered at competitive prices.

5. Distinguish between primary data and secondary data, illustrating your answer.

6. If a firm were interested in determining the distribution of income in the Province of Ontario, how could it proceed? Be specific.

7. If a firm were interested in sand and clay production in Alberta, how could it proceed? Be specific.

8. Go to the library and find (in some government publication) three marketing-oriented "facts" which you did not know existed or were available. Record on one page and show sources.

9. Discuss the concept that some information may be too expensive to obtain in relation to its value. Illustrate.

10. Discuss the concept of a marketing information system and how its output would differ from the output of the typical marketing research department.

11. Discuss what will be needed before marketing information systems become common. Also, discuss the problem facing the marketer in a small firm which is not likely to be able to afford the development of a marketing information system.

SUGGESTED CASES

4. Redi, Ltd.
6. The Capri
7. Sleep-Inn Motel
21. The Niagara Peninsula Rehabilitation Centre
35. Bramalea Realty Ltd.

When you finish this chapter, you should:

1. Know about population and income trends.

2. Understand how population is growing—but at different rates for different age groups.

3. Know about the distribution of income.

4. Know how final consumer spending is related to population, income, family life cycle, and other variables.

5. Know how to estimate likely consumer purchases for broad classes of products.

6. Recognize the important new terms (shown in red).

DEMOGRAPHIC DIMENSIONS
OF THE CANADIAN
CONSUMER MARKET*

6

Markets are people with money to spend to satisfy needs.

The customer is the focal point of all business and marketing activity. Customers in the aggregate make up markets—people with the ability (buying power) and the willingness to spend their money to satisfy their wants. Marketers hope to develop unique marketing strategies by finding unsatisfied customers and offering them more attractive marketing mixes. Finding these attractive opportunities takes really knowing what makes potential customers tick. This means finding those market dimensions that make a difference, in terms of population, income, needs, attitudes, and subsequent buying behavior.

Forget the stereotypes

The marketing manager should not fall into the trap of accepting common stereotypes about the size or potential of various markets. When valid data are available, there is no excuse for decisions based on misconceptions or regional propaganda. Try to see the data in the next few chapters in terms of selecting relevant dimensions and estimating the potential in

---

* The Canadian content of this chapter was researched and written for *Essentials of Marketing,* 1st Canadian Edition, by Professor Carl Lawrence of Queen's University.

different market segments. Also, check your own assumptions against these data. Marketing decisions often must be made in a hurry, under pressure. Then, if you feel you really do know the relevant market dimensions, you may decide to go ahead without even looking at the available data. Now is a good time to get the facts straight.

POPULATION

Present population and its distribution

Table 6–1 shows the population of Canada by province in 1971, 1976, and 1981. The percentage change in each area between 1971 and 1981 is also indicated. The consumer market in 1981 consisted of about 24 million people, with the bulk of them (62 percent) residing in the provinces of Quebec and Ontario. Another 9 percent lived in the Atlantic Provinces, about 8 percent in Manitoba and Saskatchewan, 9 percent in Alberta, and the remaining 12 percent in British Columbia (including the Yukon and the Northwest Territories).

Ontario and Quebec contain slightly more than three fifths of the country's population. They also account for the majority of consumer expenditures and the lion's share of the industrial market. The marketer has an added challenge in that these two provinces have different linguistic and cultural heritages.

Table 6–1: **Population by province—1971, 1976, and 1981**[1]

	1971 Population (000)	1971 Percent of total	1976 Population (000)	1976 Percent of total	1981 Population (000)	1981 Percent of total	Percentage change 1971–1981
Canada	21,568.3	100	22,992.6	100	24,105.2	100	11.8
Atlantic Provinces	2,057.3	9.5	2,181.8	9.5	2,210.0	9.2	7.4
Newfoundland	522.1	2.4	557.7	2.4	562.0	2.3	7.6
Prince Edward Island	111.6	0.5	118.2	0.5	121.3	0.5	8.7
Nova Scotia	789.0	3.7	828.6	3.6	837.8	3.5	6.2
New Brunswick	634.6	2.9	677.3	3.0	688.9	2.9	8.6
Quebec	6,027.8	27.9	6,234.5	27.1	6,377.5	26.5	5.8
Ontario	7,703.1	35.7	8,264.5	35.9	8,551.7	35.5	11.0
Manitoba/Saskatchewan	1,914.5	8.9	1,942.8	8.4	1,974.3	8.2	3.1
Manitoba	988.3	4.6	1,021.5	4.4	1,017.3	4.2	2.9
Saskatchewan	926.2	4.3	921.3	4.0	957.0	4.0	3.3
Alberta	1,627.9	7.5	1,838.0	8.0	2,207.9	9.2	35.6
B.C./Territories	2,237.8	10.4	2,531.0	11.0	2,783.7	11.6	24.4
British Columbia	2,184.6	10.1	2,466.6	10.7	2,716.3	11.3	24.3
Yukon	18.4	0.1	21.8	0.1	22.7	.09	23.4
Northwest Territories	34.8	0.2	42.6	0.2	44.7	.2	28.4

Note: May exceed 100 percent due to rounding. *Population Projections for Canada and Provinces 1976–2001,* Cat. 91–520, February 1979.

Where are the people today and tomorrow?

Glance again at the changes between 1971 and 1981 revealed by Table 6–1. Although all provinces grew over this 10-year period, the greatest percentage growth in population occurred in the western provinces of Alberta and British Columbia. Manitoba, Saskatchewan, and Quebec had the lowest average annual growth rate.

Changes in growth rates that took place within a given period also deserve careful study. For example, Saskatchewan's population grew by some 3.3 percent between 1971 and 1981. However, that province actually experienced a population decline of 1.5 percent during the years 1971–1976. Both Alberta and British Columbia grew by about 13 percent during the 1971–1976 period. However, Alberta grew an amazing 20 percent between 1976 and 1981, while British Columbia growth was at a more modest rate of about 10 percent.

Population will keep growing, but . . .

The Canadian population will continue to grow, at least for the foreseeable future. This leaves us with two big questions: How much? and How fast? Statistics Canada has released an in-depth study of population growth in Canada which tries to answer these questions.[2]

FERTILITY RATE IS DECLINING

Canada's rapid rate of population growth following World War II ended in the late 1950s. The slowdown in the rate of population growth since that time is due mainly to a drop in birthrate, which has declined steadily from a high of 3.95 in 1959 to a low of 1.757 in 1978.

The lower birthrate, in turn, is due to factors which greatly altered the lifestyle of the population. The greater availability of birth control devices made a lower birthrate possible; rising economic expectations made it necessary; and changing social attitudes toward deferring or foregoing child rearing made it acceptable. More women have chosen to remain in the educational system for longer periods of time, and marriages are being delayed. Also the labor force participation rate of women has increased from less than 25 percent in 1956 to nearly 50 percent in the late 1970s. It is not known whether these trends will continue into the future. Some analysts are predicting a mini baby boom, believing that women have merely postponed childbearing.

The decline in the birthrate does not mean that the population of Canada will not grow, nor does a fertility rate at or below the replacement level mean zero population growth. The potential for future population growth is built into the age structure of the current population. The children of the "baby boom" era of 1945–1965 are themselves now reaching the age of fertility. Even if the birthrate were to drop to a level at which each married couple was not replacing itself, Canada's population would still expand because of the absolute increase in the number of women bearing children. Thus Canadian marketers can expect a growing market, at least until the end of the century.

IMMIGRATION CAN ALSO AFFECT GROWTH

Immigration levels fluctuate sharply from year to year depending on economic and political circumstances both within and outside Canada. Net international immigration had a strong influence in Canada's population growth in the early and mid 1950s. However, in recent years that influence has been declining. Net migration contributed about one third to the total population growth during 1971–1976, but only about one sixth during 1976–1979. Statistics Canada is now predicting a net increase from immigration of between 50,000 and 100,000 people each year. Statistics Canada projections also indicate that about 60 percent (as opposed to 62 percent) of these people will live in Quebec and Ontario. However, the relative balance will shift in favor of Ontario (now at 35.5 percent) as Quebec (currently at 26.5 percent) continues to lose population share. The Atlantic Provinces will hold onto their 9–10 percent share of population, but Manitoba and Saskatchewan may not maintain their 8.2 percent. British Columbia and Alberta, in particular, will be the gainers. Together, they will have some 22 percent of the population by the turn of the century. Alberta will likely grow faster than British Columbia so that both will be about the same size by the year 2001.

Obviously, any marketer doing future planning must take such population increases and other related changes into account.

AVERAGE AGE WILL RISE

The average age of the Canadian population is going to rise for many years. The major reason is the post-World War II baby boom. This large group crowded into the schools in the 1950s and 1960s and then into the job market in the 1970s. By the 1980s and 1990s they will be swelling the middle-aged group. And early in the 21st century, they will reach retirement, still a dominant group in the total population. According to one population expert, "It's like a goat passing through a boa constrictor."

Figure 6–1 shows the movement of the bulge through their life cycle, as well as the impact of declining birthrates. The median age will continue to rise as there are fewer young people and more older people. In the 1990s, the median age will be about 35, which is 10 years older than during the 1960s.[3]

The proportion of Canada's population under 15 declined from 32.9 percent in 1966 to 23.5 percent in 1979, an absolute decrease of about 1 million people. The proportion of the population considered to be of working age (15–64) increased from 59.4 percent of the total in 1966 to 67.2 percent in 1979—an absolute increase of more than 4 million people. Immigration has a strong influence on the size and rate of growth of this working age category, especially at its lower end. In 1976, for example, about 47 percent of all immigrants were between 20 and 39 years of age.

Of particular interest are the over-65s, whose percentage of the popula-

Figure 6–1: Canada's moving age bulge[4]

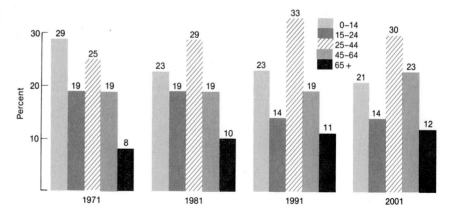

tion has increased from 7.7 in 1966 to 9.3 in 1979. It is now estimated that over-65s will account for 12 percent of the total population by the turn of the century.

Effects on markets will be great

Canada's "youth culture" is giving way to a new kind of society. The population bulge created by the post-World War II baby boom will affect every area of society for the next 50 years. This change in age structure is of great importance to marketers. Accommodating their market offerings of goods and services to this changing demographic profile will cause problems for some firms but offer tremendous opportunities to others. Also, think how such demographic changes affect those in government who must design social and economic programs for aging constituents.

Projected number of families and households

Changes in the size and age structure of the population are important to all marketers. Those involved in the sale and distribution of housing units, consumer durables (televisions, refrigerators, furniture) and other household goods are especially interested in changes associated with the number and composition of households.

During the 15-year period between 1961 and 1976, the number of households increased from 4.6 million to 7.2 million—a gain of about 57 percent. By 1991 it is expected that this number will increase to between 10 and 10.5 million. There could be as many as 11.2 million households by the year 2001. This figure would represent an overall increase of 56 percent between 1976 and the year 2001.[5]

Figure 6–2 shows attention must also be paid to anticipated changes in the structure of households. The husband-wife household will continue to be most common. But note the growth in the number of single-parent families, the increase in the number of households with a female head, and the increasing proportion of households whose members are not related. These shifts reflect some of the population trends noted earlier— the increasing percentage of adults in the population, declining fertility rates, and more elderly persons. In addition, a major contributing factor

Household Types	Percent		
	1961	*1976*	*1991*
1. Husband-wife	79.3%	71.0%	66.0%
Primary family households:			
2. Male head—wife absent	1.4	1.2	1.5
3. Female head—husband absent	4.9	6.0	7.1
Nonfamily households:			
4. Male head	6.3	9.1	11.1
5. Female head	8.1	12.7	14.3

to the growth of single-parent families has been Canada's rising divorce rate—from 55 divorces per 100,000 people in 1968 (the year in which the divorce laws were changed) to 259 divorces per 100,000 people in 1980.[7]

The shift to urban and suburban areas

The shift of population from rural to urban areas is another exceedingly important demographic development. At the time of the first census in 1871, 82 percent of the population lived in rural areas.

The 1976 census figures show an urbanization rate of 76 percent—a figure that is expected to remain unchanged in future years.[8] However, the pace of urbanization is not even across the country. Figure 6–3 shows the uneven distribution of urbanization, with Ontario and Quebec leading the pack.[9]

From city to suburbs to city again

Since World War II, there has been a continual movement to the suburbs. In 1941 only 25 percent of the metropolitan population lived in suburbs. By 1976 72 percent of the urban population were suburbanites. As people moved to the suburbs, retail and service businesses followed.

A movement back to the city is most evident among older and sometimes wealthier families. Their children are usually married or ready to leave home. They feel hemmed in by the rapid expansion of suburbia and especially by the large number of lower-income families moving in. These older families are showing increased interest in condominiums and high-rise apartments close to downtown.

Despite the return of some families to the central cities, the trend to the suburbs seems likely to continue. An expanding population must go somewhere. The suburbs can combine pleasant neighborhoods with easy transportation to higher-paying jobs in the city. The continuing decentralization of industry may also move jobs closer to the suburbs than to downtown. Not only people but industries have been leaving downtown.

Developing a new concept of the urban area

Marketing professionals are more interested in the size of homogeneous marketing areas than in the number of people within political boundaries. To meet this need, Statistics Canada has developed a separate population classification, the **census metropolitan area** (CMA). The CMA is the

Figure 6–3: **Population by province: Urban and rural, 1976**[10]

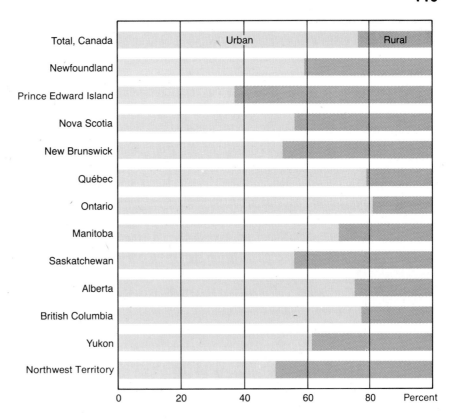

"main labor market area" of a continuous built-up area having 100,000 or more population. It is a zone in which a significant number of people are able to commute on a daily basis to their work places in the main built-up area.[11]

In other words, CMAs represent integrated economic and social units with a large population. They are usually known by the name of their largest city. In 1981 there were 24 CMAs in Canada, with a total population of 13.5 million. This figure amounts to 56 percent of the 1981 Canadian total. Table 6–2 shows the location of Canada's largest urban areas.

These CMA target markets also offer greater sales potential in dollars and cents than population alone would indicate, in part because of generally higher wages in metropolitan areas and the concentration of higher-paying occupations. Densely populated areas offer great opportunities—if the competition is not too strong!

Megalopolis—the continuous city

In 1981 11 of Canada's 24 CMAs fell within Canada's megalopolis. This is a strip of land running approximately 750 miles from Quebec in the east to Windsor in the west, passing through such cities as Trois Rivieres, Montreal, Ottawa, Oshawa, Kitchener, Toronto, Hamilton, London, and St. Catharines. When considered in terms of the country's total land mass, this strip represents less than 2 percent. But it contains 54 percent

Table 6–2: **Population of census metropolitan areas, 1976 and 1981**[12]

	1976 (000)	1981 (000)	Change (percent)
Atlantic Provinces			
Halifax	268.0	274.9	2.6
St. John's, Newfoundland	145.4	153.4	5.5
St. John, New Brunswick	113.0	112.7	− 0.3
Quebec			
Chicontimi	128.6	134.3	4.4
Montreal	2,802.5	2,801.2	− 0.05
Ottawa-Hull	693.3	708.5	2.2
Quebec	542.2	570.1	5.2
Trois-Rivieres	106.0	110.0	4.0
Ontario			
Hamilton	529.4	537.7	1.8
Kitchener	272.2	285.0	4.7
London	270.4	280.5	3.7
Oshawa	135.2	153.4	13.5
St. Catharines	301.9	301.8	− 0.06
Sudbury	157.0	148.9	− 5.2
Thunder Bay	119.8	120.2	0.4
Toronto	2,803.1	2,975.2	6.1
Windsor	247.6	243.3	− 1.7
Manitoba/Saskatchewan			
Regina	151.2	163.0	7.8
Saskatoon	133.8	152.7	14.2
Winnipeg	578.2	580.3	0.4
Alberta			
Calgary	471.4	595.0	26.2
Edmonton	556.3	647.8	16.5
British Columbia			
Vancouver	1,166.3	1,257.1	7.8
Victoria	218.3	231.1	5.9
Total CMAs	12,911.0	13,539.3	4.9
Total Canada	22,992.6	24,105.2	4.8
Percent CMAs	56.2	56.2	

Note: 1976 adjusted to conform to 1981 geography.

of the country's population, 57 percent of disposable income, and 81 percent of manufacturing![13]

Another concentration of population is developing in British Columbia in the vicinity of Vancouver and Victoria. To a lesser degree, population corridors are building up between Calgary and Edmonton, and between Regina and Saskatoon.

The mobile ones are an attractive market

A constantly shifting population is a marketing fact of life. People move, stay awhile, and then move on again. In fact Canada, along with the United States and Australia, has one of the most mobile populations in the world. Residents in these countries move from one place to another an average of 12 times in their lives.[14]

Mobile people make up an important market. Their moves are often caused by promotions and job transfers, and they have money to spend. They must make many market-oriented decisions fairly quickly after their move. New sources of food, clothing, and household goods must be located.

INCOME

So far we have been concerned primarily with demographic characteristics. But unless people have money or are certain of acquiring it, they cannot be regarded as potential customers. The amount of money they can spend will also affect the type of goods they buy. For this reason, marketers must also study income data.

Growth may continue

Income comes from producing and selling goods or services in the marketplace. A widely available measure of the output and the growth of the economy is the **gross national product.** It represents the total market value of goods and services produced in a year.

In 1970 Canada's GNP was $85.7 billion. By 1980 GNP had reached $289.9 billion. Much of that change, however, does not reflect real growth but rather the effects of inflation. In "constant" 1971 dollars, the relevant figures for 1970 were $88.4 billion, and for 1980, $130.2 billion. This is still a very significant increase over the decade of 47.3 percent.

Canadians have for some time been witnessing a continual slowing in their economy's rate of growth. Between 1960 and 1970 the Canadian economy grew in constant 1971 dollars at an average annual rate of 5.2 percent. Between 1970 and 1980 this annual rate of growth declined to 3.9 percent. But the average annual rate of growth can be misleading. Within the decade 1970–1980 there has been a steady decline in this growth rate. For example, the rate was only 2.8 percent for the years 1975–1980, and there was no real growth between 1979 and 1980.

Aggregate GNP figures are more meaningful when converted to family or household income. Although money isn't everything, it does give individuals and families command over goods and services. Both the level of income and its distribution—among individuals and families, between sexes, among occupations, and across different regions of the country—are important to marketers.

Family income continues to rise

The data in Figure 6–4 reveal that in current dollars the average family income in 1971 was $10,368 and grew steadily until it reached $26,610 in 1980. This represents an annual rate of growth of slightly over 11 percent, or 157 percent over the nine-year period. However, note the stark contrast when the same data is presented in real terms (constant 1971 dollars). There was a slow but steady growth in average family income until it reached $12,789 in 1978, but a gradual decline in the last two years. Over the 10-year period, the real income of the average family has increased only at an annual rate of 2.2 percent.

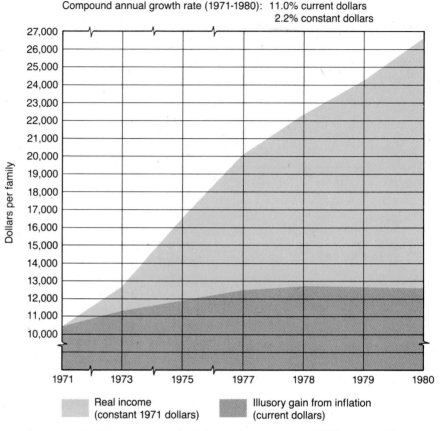

Figure 6–4: **Real family
income growth stops**[15]

Compound annual growth rate (1971-1980): 11.0% current dollars
2.2% constant dollars

Dollars per family

27,000
26,000
25,000
24,000
23,000
22,000
21,000
20,000
19,000
18,000
17,000
16,000
15,000
14,000
13,000
12,000
11,000
10,000

1971   1973   1975   1977   1978   1979   1980

Real income   Illusory gain from inflation
(constant 1971 dollars)   (current dollars)

On a regional basis, average family incomes in 1980 ranged from a low of $21,150 in the Atlantic Provinces to a high of $29,639 in British Columbia. Average family incomes in Ontario, the Prairie Provinces, and Quebec were $28,086, $27,260, and $24,720, respectively.[16] Figure 16–5 presents the relevant data in graphic form.

As would be expected, variations in family incomes follow from differences in family characteristics, such as the age, sex, occupation, and education of the family head. Statistics Canada data reveals that family income rises until the head of the family reaches middle age (45–54), and then family income declines. The average family income in 1979 was $24,245. For families whose head was under 25 years of age, it was $17,686. Families headed by individuals over 70 years of age averaged $14,389. These figures are considerably less than the average incomes of families headed by individuals between 25 and 64. Similarly, the average income of families whose head had a university degree ($35,062) was almost twice that of families whose heads had received eight years of schooling or less ($19,951).[17]

*The income pyramid
capsized*

This general rise in family incomes has produced an upward shift in family and household incomes. Figure 6–6 shows that in 1965 most Cana-

Figure 6–5: **British Columbia leads in average family income**[18]

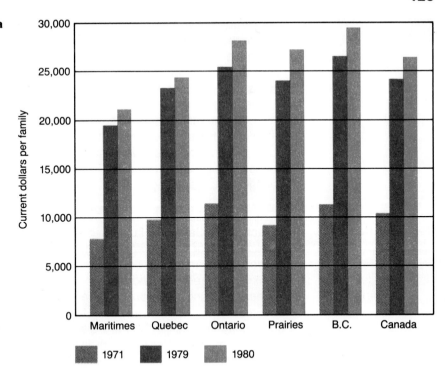

Figure 6–6: **Changing income pyramid**[19]

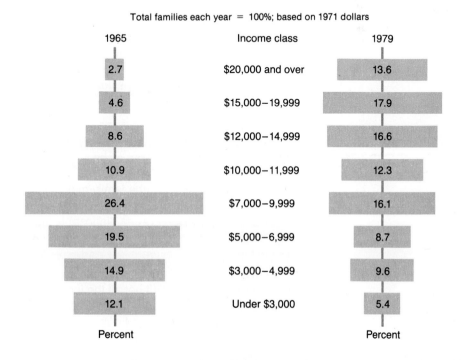

dian families were bunched in the lower income levels. The overall income pattern resembled a pyramid. By 1979 the pyramid was on its way toward becoming an ice cream cone. Since these data are based on constant 1971 dollars, the effects of inflation have already been removed. In other words, real incomes have risen substantially!

This is extremely important to marketers because it means that now more families are important customers. Before this upward shift in real income, markets tended to be characterized by a large number of people at the bottom and a relative handful forming an "elite" market at the top. This is a significant revolution which has broadened markets and drastically changed our marketing system.

How much income is enough?

Not all families received the 1980 average family income of $26,610. In fact many Canadian families must make do on much less. Statistics Canada has for many years used "low income cut-offs" as a measure of well-being and as a basis for welfare and other transfer payments. Families required to spend more than 62 percent of their income on basic necessities, such as food, shelter, and clothing, are said to be in "strained circumstances." The size of the family unit as well as the size of the community in which it lives are also taken into account. (See Figure 6–7.) For example, a family of four living in a rural area had a low income or poverty line cut-off of $9,312 in 1980. For a similar family in a metropolitan area of 500,000, the low income cut-off figure was $12,807.

CONSUMER SPENDING PATTERNS RELATED TO POPULATION AND INCOME

We have been using the term **family income** because consumer budget studies suggest that most consumers spend their incomes as part of a family or household unit. If the wife or children work, they usually pool their incomes with the husband or father when planning family expenditures. Thus most of our discussion will be on how households or families spend their income.

Disposable income is spendable income

It should be remembered, however, that families do not get to spend all of their income. Taxes take a share, and what is left is called **disposable income.** Out of its disposable income—together with gifts, pensions, cash savings, or other assets—the family makes its expenditures. Some families do not spend all their disposable income, saving part of it. Therefore, we should distinguish between disposable income and actual expenditures when trying to estimate potential expenditures.

Discretionary income is elusive

As we have already noted, people's incomes have been growing and may continue to grow. But not all the income is uncommitted. Most households allocate a good portion of their income to "necessities"—food, rent or house payments, car and house furnishings payments, insurance, and so on—which are defined in various ways by different researchers and

Figure 6–7: Incidence of low income by selected family characteristics, 1979[20]

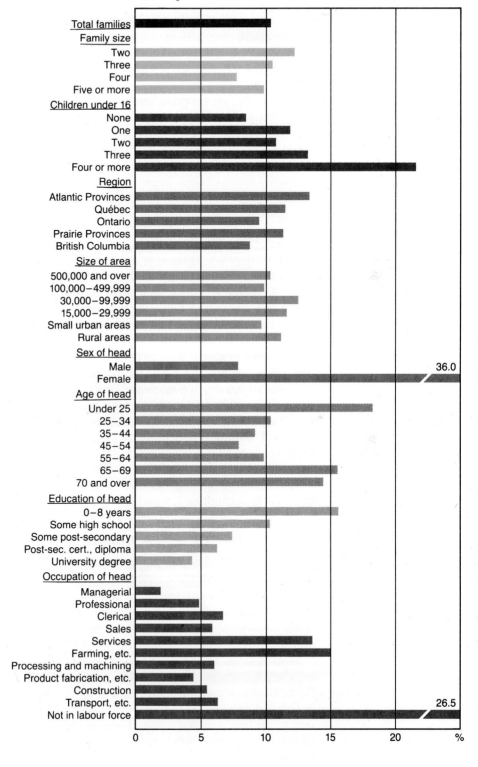

Percentage of families below low income cut-offs

consumers. A family's purchase of "luxuries" comes from what's left, or what is called **discretionary income.**

Discretionary income is a rather elusive concept. The definition of "necessities" varies from family to family and over a period of time. A color television set might be purchased out of discretionary income by a lower-income family, yet be considered a necessity by a higher-income family. But if many people in a lower-income neighborhood start buying color television sets, then they might become a necessity for the others. This would severely reduce the discretionary income available for other purchases.

Estimating how potential customers spend their money

Data such as in Table 6–3 can help a marketing manager understand how potential target customers spend their money. For example, a manager seriously considering consumers in the $16,000–$19,999 income group can analyze how families in this group spend their money, then can consider how they would have to rearrange spending to buy the manager's product. A swimming pool manufacturer could see that such families spend about 4.7 percent of their total expenditures or some $862 on recreation of all kinds. Suppose a particular pool costs $600 a year—including depreciation and maintenance. The average family in this income category would have to make a big change in lifestyle if it bought the pool.

Of course this data will not tell the pool maker whether these potential customers *will* buy the pool. But it does supply useful input to help the manager's planning. If a manager thinks that more information is needed—perhaps about these people's attitudes toward recreation products—then some marketing research may be necessary. For example, a manager may want to make a budget study on consumers who already have swimming pools to see how they adjusted their spending patterns and how they felt before and after the purchase.

Income has a direct effect upon spending patterns. But there are other facts that should not be ignored in any careful analysis of potential markets.

EXPENDITURE PATTERNS VARY WITH OTHER MEASURABLE FACTORS

Income has a direct bearing upon spending patterns, but other factors must be considered in any careful analysis of potential markets. Statistics Canada publications summarize family expenditures from a number of different perspectives, such as family type, family size, family income, home ownership, age of family head, and urban as opposed to rural residence.

When the percentage shares going for various types of expenditure are studied, important regional differences show up. Relative expenditures for clothing are lowest (5 percent) and for recreation highest (6.2 percent) in British Columbia. By contrast, the largest allocation to transportation occurs on Prince Edward Island. As would be expected, there are also differences in how families spend their income depending upon whether they are tenants or homeowners.

Table 6–3: Percentage distributions of family expenditure, by family income, in Canada, 1978—all families and unattached individuals[21]

					Family income					
	All classes	Under $6,000	$6,000–7,999	$8,000–11,999	$12,000–15,999	$16,000–19,999	$20,000–24,999	$25,000–29,999	$30,000–34,999	$35,000 and over
Food	16.8	25.9	25.0	21.2	18.9	17.8	16.7	15.4	14.9	12.9
Shelter	16.1	28.5	23.5	20.5	17.3	17.0	15.9	15.0	13.9	12.6
Rented living quarters	4.4	14.6	10.7	10.0	7.3	4.9	3.8	2.6	2.1	1.3
Owned living quarters	7.5	6.1	5.7	5.4	5.8	8.0	8.3	8.7	8.2	7.5
Other accommodation	.9	.4	.5	.6	.7	.6	.7	.9	.9	1.4
Water, fuel, and electricity	3.3	7.4	6.6	4.6	3.5	3.5	3.1	2.9	2.7	2.4
Household operation	4.1	6.1	5.7	5.2	4.5	4.3	4.0	3.9	3.6	3.4
Household furnishings and equipment	4.6	4.3	4.9	4.4	4.5	4.8	4.5	4.9	4.5	4.2
Furniture	1.5	1.2	1.2	1.3	1.4	1.5	1.5	1.8	1.4	1.4
Household appliances	1.0	1.0	1.2	1.1	1.0	1.1	1.0	.9	.9	.8
Other	2.1	2.2	2.4	2.1	2.1	2.2	2.0	2.2	2.2	2.0
Clothing	6.8	5.8	6.3	6.4	6.5	6.9	6.8	6.9	7.0	7.2
Personal care	1.6	2.1	2.1	1.9	1.8	1.7	1.6	1.6	1.6	1.4
Medical and health care	1.9	2.1	2.3	2.4	2.3	2.1	1.9	1.8	1.8	1.7
Tobacco and alcoholic beverages	3.2	3.6	3.9	4.1	3.9	3.5	3.3	3.0	2.9	2.5
Transportation	12.7	8.3	12.4	13.1	14.3	13.2	13.1	12.9	12.6	11.8
Automobile and truck	11.4	6.5	10.6	11.4	12.9	12.0	11.9	11.7	11.4	10.5
Purchase	5.3	2.6	4.4	4.8	6.2	5.2	5.4	5.5	5.3	5.5
Operation	6.1	3.9	6.1	6.6	6.7	6.7	6.5	6.2	6.0	4.9
Other transportation	1.3	1.8	1.8	1.7	1.4	1.2	1.2	1.2	1.3	1.4
Recreation	5.0	3.7	3.6	4.1	4.6	4.7	5.1	5.4	5.3	5.4
Reading	.6	.8	.7	.7	.6	.6	.5	.5	.5	.5
Education	.6	.7	.5	.5	.4	.4	.6	.6	.6	.9
Miscellaneous expenses	2.4	2.5	2.2	2.5	2.8	2.7	2.4	2.3	2.4	2.2
Total current consumption	76.5	94.3	92.9	86.8	82.4	79.6	76.5	74.2	71.8	66.9
Personal taxes	16.9	1.0	2.6	7.1	11.6	14.3	16.8	18.9	21.2	25.4
Security	4.2	.8	1.2	2.7	3.8	4.0	4.4	4.5	4.6	5.3
Gifts and contributions	2.5	3.9	3.3	3.4	2.2	2.2	2.3	2.3	2.4	2.4
Total expenditure	100.0	100.0	100.0	100.0	100.0	100.0	100.0	100.0	100.0	100.0

Stage of family life cycle affects spending

Two demographic dimensions—age and number of children—affect spending patterns. Put together, these dimensions are concerned with the life cycle of a family. See Figure 6–8 for a summary of life cycle and buying behavior.

Young people and families accept new ideas

Younger people seem to be more open to new products and brands. But they are also careful shoppers. One study of 14–25-year-olds showed that 74 percent of them compared prices—and brands—before buying. The average income of these younger people is lower than that of older groups. But they spend a greater part of their income on "discretionary" items. They do not yet have big expenses for housing, education, and raising a family.[22] Although many are marrying later or deciding not to marry at all, some young people *are* getting married. These younger fami-

Figure 6–8: Stages in the family life cycle[23]

Stage	Characteristics and buying behavior
1. Singles: Unmarried people living away from parents	Feel "affluent" and "free." Buy basic household goods. More interested in recreation, cars, vacations, clothes, cosmetics and personal care items.
2. Divorced or separated	May be financially squeezed to pay for alimony or maintaining two households. Buying may be limited to "necessities"—especially for women who had no job skills.
3. Newly married couples: No children	Both may work and so they feel financially well-off. Buy durables: cars, refrigerators, stoves, basic furniture—and recreation equipment and vacations.
4. Full nest I: Youngest child under six	Feel squeezed financially because they are buying homes and household durables—furniture, washers, dryers, and TV. Also buying child-related products—food, medicines, clothes and toys. Really interested in new products.
5. Full nest II: Youngest child over five	Financially are better off as husband earns more and/or wife goes to work as last child goes to school. More spent on food, clothing, education, and recreation for growing children.
6. Full nest III: Older couples with dependent children	Financially even better off as husband earns more and more wives work. May replace durables and furniture, and buy cars, boats, dental services, and more expensive recreation and travel. May buy bigger houses.
7. Empty nest: Older couples, no children living with them, head still working	Feel financially "well-off." Home ownership at peak and house may be paid for. May make home improvements or move into apartments. And may travel, entertain, go to school, and make gifts and contributions. Not interested in new products.
8. Sole survivor, still working	Income still good. Likely to sell home and continue with previous lifestyle.
9. Senior citizen I: Older married couple, no children living with them, head retired	Big drop in income. May keep home but cut back on most buying as purchases of medical care, drugs, and other health-related items go up.
10. Senior citizen II: Sole survivor, not working	Same as senior citizen I, except likely to sell home, and has special need for attention, affection, and security.

lies (especially those with no children) are still buying durable goods—such as automobiles and furniture. They need less food. It is only as children begin to arrive and grow that the family spending shifts to furniture, clothing, and services—such as education, medical, and personal care. This usually occurs when the household head reaches the 35–44 age bracket.

Teenagers mean shifts in spending

Once the children become teenagers, further shifts in spending occur. Teenagers eat more. Their clothes become more expensive. They develop recreation and education needs that are hard on the family budget. The parents may be forced to change their spending to cover these costs—spending less on durable goods such as appliances, automobiles, furniture, and houses.

Many teenagers do earn much or all of their own spending money, so they are an attractive market. But marketers who have aimed at teenagers are beginning to notice the aging of the population. Motorcycle manufacturers, for example, have already been hurt—as teenagers are their heaviest buyers.[24]

Selling to the "empty nesters"

An important group within the 50–64 age category is sometimes called the "empty nesters." Their children are grown. They are now able to spend their money in other ways. It is the empty nesters who move back into the smaller, more luxurious apartments in the city. They may also be more interested in travel, small sports cars, and other things they couldn't afford before. Much depends on their income, of course. But this is a high-income period for many workers—especially white-collar workers.

Senior citizens are a big new market

Finally, the **senior citizens**—people over 65—should not be neglected. The number of people over 65 is now more than 10 percent of the population and growing.

Although older people generally have reduced incomes, many do have money and very different needs. Some firms are already catering to the senior citizen market. Gerber, for example—faced with a declining baby market—began producing foods for older people.[25] Some firms have gone into special diet supplements and drug products. Others have designed housing developments to appeal to older persons.

Do ethnic groups buy differently?

Language and culture also greatly influence the Canadian marketplace. The majority of Canada's population are of British and French descent, but by the 1970s about one quarter were of some other ethnic origin—

Italian, German, Ukrainian, Dutch, and the like. Increased immigration in recent years from India, East Africa, Asia, and the Caribbean has added further to our ethnic diversity.

More than one quarter (28.7 percent) of Canada's total population comes from a French ethnic background, with its own distinct and separate culture and life-style. More than one quarter (26.1 percent) of the population lists French as the language most often spoken at home. Those marketing nationally must give full weight and attention to this unique feature of the Canadian marketplace. The French Canadian market will be dealt with more fully in Chapter 7.

But Canada is rich, too, in other cultures. The country has often been called a mosaic. In contrast to the United States, where it has been the practice for cultural minorities to assimilate as quickly as possible, the Canadian environment has encouraged cultural diversity. Thus there are still relatively distinct nationality groups (mostly European) that require special consideration.

This wide range of ethnic backgrounds has created a whole host of demands for new products and services. Also, the market for such items as Greek food and bagels is not confined to the original ethnic group. Canadians of all backgrounds are being exposed to a wide range of cultural influences. Their consumption patterns are constantly changing. This factor contributes to the growth of specialized market segments for a wide variety of goods and services. Conversely other markets also expand as ethnic groups become more fully assimilated into the Canadian scene.

According to the 1971 census, the majority of "ethnic Canadians" is found in major metropolitan areas, particularly in Toronto, Hamilton, Winnipeg, and Vancouver. Certain ethnic groups tend to concentrate in specific geographic areas. For example, the Kitchener-Waterloo area in Ontario has a large population of German-Canadians. Winnipeg has many Ukrainian-Canadians and Toronto has attracted large numbers of Italians. Nova Scotia gets its name from the Scottish origin of many early settlers.[26] Figure 6–9 provides more detailed information of the ethnic mix of a number of major cities.

When the wife earns, the family spends

Attention must also be paid to the increasing number of wives working outside the home. In 1965 only 25 percent of all wives worked outside the home. By 1978 wives with full-time employment were to be found in 39 percent of all spending units, and part-time working wives in another 24 percent. These percentages will likely increase in the future for a variety of reasons, including inflation and the pressure to make ends meet.

The family in which the wife is a wage earner is a different family— both economically and psychologically—from one in which the wife is a homemaker fully dependent upon her husband for support. In families in which the wife works, the median family income in 1979 was $23,359, over 27 percent higher than in families with nonworking wives.[27] Families with working wives spend more and their consumption patterns are different. They also make new kinds of demands on the market place. If the

Figure 6–9: Ethnic origin of people in principal cities, 1971 (percent)[28]

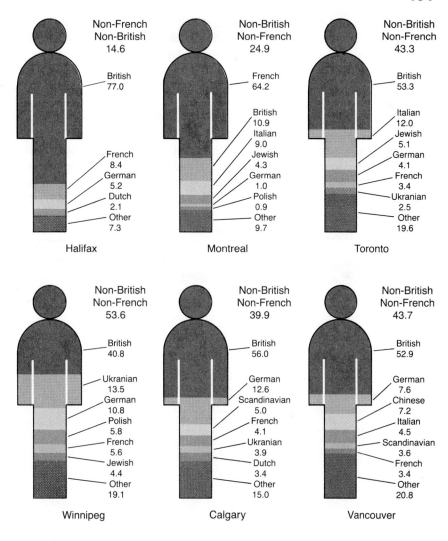

Non-French
Non-British
14.6

British
77.0

French
8.4
German
5.2
Dutch
2.1
Other
7.3

Halifax

Non-British
Non-French
24.9

French
64.2

British
10.9
Italian
9.0
Jewish
4.3
German
1.0
Polish
0.9
Other
9.7

Montreal

Non-British
Non-French
43.3

British
53.3

Italian
12.0
Jewish
5.1
German
4.1
French
3.4
Ukranian
2.5
Other
19.6

Toronto

Non-British
Non-French
53.6

British
40.8

Ukranian
13.5
German
10.8
Polish
5.8
French
5.6
Jewish
4.4
Other
19.1

Winnipeg

Non-British
Non-French
39.9

British
56.0

German
12.6
Scandinavian
5.0
French
4.1
Ukranian
3.9
Dutch
3.4
Other
15.0

Calgary

Non-British
Non-French
43.7

British
52.9

German
7.6
Chinese
7.2
Italian
4.5
Scandinavian
3.6
French
3.4
Other
20.8

Vancouver

trend continues we can expect an increase in the demand for day-care centers and for fast foods. Since less time will be spent on routine household chores, the demand for labor-saving devices should also increase.

Families with working wives spend more on household furnishings and equipment, clothing, transportation and recreation. They spend relatively, but not absolutely, less on food, shelter and medical care. A working wife has a very distinct effect on the spending habits of the family. This fact must be considered when analyzing both current and future markets.

CONCLUSION

In our study of the Canadian consumer, we have moved from the general to the particular. We first studied population data, dispelling various misconceptions about how our 24 million people are spread throughout Canada. In so doing, it became apparent that the potential of a given market cannot be determined by numbers alone. Income, stage in life cycle, geographic location of people, and other factors are important, too.

We also noted the growth of interurbia, such as along the Quebec-Windsor corridor. These urban-suburban systems suggest the shape of future growth in this country. It is also apparent that one of the outstanding characteristics of Canadians is their mobility. For this reason, even relatively new data are not foolproof. The wealth of available data can only aid judgment, not replace it.

Canadian consumers are among the most affluent in the world. And this affluence affects purchasing behavior. Beyond the necessities of life, they are able to buy a wide variety of products. In fact, it could be argued that little they buy is an absolute necessity.

The kinds of data discussed in this chapter can be very useful for estimating the market potential within possible target markets. Unfortunately, they are not very helpful in explaining specific customer behavior—why people buy *specific* products and *specific* brands. And such detailed forecasts are obviously important to marketing managers. Fortunately, improved estimates can come from a fuller understanding of consumer behavior.

In Chapter 7, we discuss the decision-making behavior of individual consumers and household groups.

QUESTIONS AND PROBLEMS

1. Discuss how slower population growth, and especially a decline in the number of babies, will affect the businesses in your local community.

2. Discuss the impact of our "aging culture" on marketing strategy planning.

3. Some demographic characteristics are likely to be more important than others in determining market potential. For each of the following characteristics, identify two products for which this characteristic is *most* important: (a) size of geographic area, (b) population, (c) income, (d) stage of life cycle.

4. If a large, new atomic research installation were being built in a formerly small and sleepy town, how could the local retailers use consumption data in planning for the influx of newcomers, first of construction crews and then of scientists?

5. Name three specific examples (specific products or brands—not just product categories) illustrating how demand will differ by geographic location and market location, that is, with respect to size and location inside or outside a metropolitan market.

6. Explain how the continuing mobility of consumers as well as the development of a "megalopolis" should affect marketing strategy planning in the future. Be sure to consider the impact on the four Ps.

7. Explain how the redistribution of income has affected marketing planning thus far and its likely impact in the future.

8. Explain why the concept of the Census Metropolitan Areas was developed. Would it be the most useful breakdown for retailers?

9. With the growing homogeneity of the consumer market, does this mean there will be fewer opportunities to segment markets? Do you think that all consumers of about equal income will probably spend their incomes similarly and demand similar products?

SUGGESTED CASES

6. The Capri
30. Canadian Foods Ltd.

When you finish this chapter, you should:

1. *Know about the various "black box" models of buyer behavior.*

2. *Understand how the intra- and inter-personal variables affect an individual's buying behavior.*

3. *Have some feel for how all the behavioral variables and incoming stimuli are handled by a consumer.*

4. *Recognize the important new terms (shown in red).*

BEHAVIORAL DIMENSIONS
OF THE CONSUMER MARKET

7

*Which car will the customer buy—the Ford Mustang
or the Audi Fox?*

Data on population, income, and consumer spending patterns is useful for forecasting basic trends and relationships. Unfortunately, however, when many firms sell similar products, such data is of little value in predicting which specific products and brands will be purchased. Yet this is very important to a marketing manager.

To find better answers, we need to understand people better. For this reason, many marketers have turned to the behavioral sciences for help. For the rest of this chapter, we'll be looking at the thinking in psychology, sociology, and the other behavioral sciences.

Buying in a black box

A simple way of summing up the way some behavioral scientists see consumer buying behavior is shown in Figure 7–1. Potential customers are exposed to various stimuli—including the marketing mixes of competitors. Somehow, an individual interprets these stimuli. (This person is usually shown in a mysterious "black box" that we can't see into. See Figure 7–1.) Then, for some reason, the person responds to the stimuli—and may buy a marketer's good or service.

This is the classical model of buying behavior. This **stimulus–response model** says that people respond in some predictable way to a stimulus.

Figure 7–1: Simplified buyer behavior model

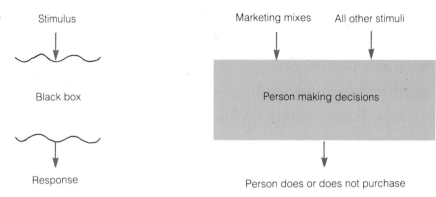

Stimulus

Black box

Response

Marketing mixes   All other stimuli

Person making decisions

Person does or does not purchase

The model does not predict *why* they behave the way they do—only that there is a predictable response to a stimulus. This is the model we were using when discussing spending patterns. There, we hoped to find some relationship between demographic characteristics of customers in the black box, product categories (stimulus), and the customer's buying behavior (response). We did find some relationships. Now we want to go even deeper. This requires a better understanding of how consumer decision making works.

There are many black box theories

Depending on a person's behavioral science training, we find many descriptions of how the black box works. These different theories lead to different forecasts about how consumers will behave.

How the economist views the black box

The economist typically assumes that consumers are **economic men**—people who logically weigh choices in terms of cost and value received—to get the greatest satisfaction from spending their time, energy, and money. Therefore, the economist collects and analyzes demographic data when trying to predict consumer behavior. It was a logical extension of the economic-man theory which led us to look at consumer spending

The economic man theory suggests that people compare among their alternatives to try to get the best value for their money.

Figure 7–2: More complete buyer behavior model

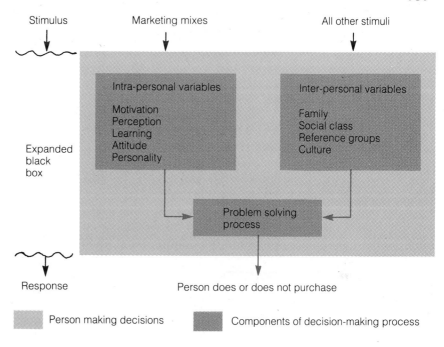

Stimulus Marketing mixes All other stimuli

Expanded black box

Intra-personal variables

Motivation
Perception
Learning
Attitude
Personality

Inter-personal variables

Family
Social class
Reference groups
Culture

Problem solving process

Response Person does or does not purchase

Person making decisions Components of decision-making process

patterns earlier in the chapter. There is value in this approach. Consumers must at least have income to be in the market. But other behavioral scientists suggest that the black box works in a more complicated way than the economic-man model.

How we will view the black box

Consumers have many dimensions. Let's try to combine these dimensions into a better model of how consumers make decisions. Figure 7–2 presents a more detailed view of the black box model. Here, we see both intra-personal and inter-personal variables affecting the person making decisions.

These topics will be discussed in the next few pages. Then, we will look at the consumer's problem-solving process.

INTRA-PERSONAL VARIABLES FOCUS ON THE INDIVIDUAL

Motivation determines what is wanted

Everybody is motivated by needs and wants. **Needs** are the basic forces which motivate an individual to do something. Some needs are concerned with a person's physical body. Other needs are concerned with the individual's view of himself—and his relationship with others. Wants are less basic. **Wants** are "needs" which are learned during an individual's life. For example, everyone has a basic need for food—but some people also have a learned want for a Big Mac.

When a need or want is not satisfied, it leads to a drive. The food need, for instance, leads to a hunger drive. A **drive** is a strong stimulus which causes a tension that the individual tries to reduce by finding ways of satisfying this drive. Drives are, in effect, the reasons behind certain behavior patterns.

Are there hierarchies of needs?

Some psychologists see a hierarchy of needs. Maslow is well known for his five-level hierarchy. But we will discuss a similar four-level hierarchy which is easier to apply. It is supported by more recent research on human motivation.[1] The four levels are illustrated in Figure 7–3. The lowest-level needs are physiological. Then come safety, social, and personal needs. For easy recall, think of the "PSSP needs."

The **physiological needs** are concerned with food, drink, rest, sex, and other biological needs. The **safety needs** are concerned with protection and physical well-being (perhaps involving health, food, drugs, and exercise). The **social needs** are concerned with love, friendship, status, and respect. These are all things that involve a person's interaction with others. The **personal needs,** on the other hand, are concerned with the need of an individual to gain personal satisfaction—unrelated to what others think or do. Examples here include self-respect, accomplishment, fun, freedom, and relaxation.

Motivation theory suggests that humans never reach a state of complete satisfaction. As soon as lower-level needs are reasonably satisfied, those at higher levels become more dominant. It is important to see, however, that a particular physical good or service might satisfy more than one need at the same time. A hamburger in a friendly environment, for example, might satisfy not only the physiological need to satisfy hunger—but also some social need.

Figure 7–3: The PSSP hierarchy of needs

Highest

Personal

Social

Safety

Physiological

Lowest

Economic needs affect how we satisfy basic needs

The four basic needs can help explain *what* we buy. The economic needs help explain *how* we buy—and *why* we want specific product features.

Economic needs are concerned with making the best use of a customer's limited resources—as the customer sees it. Some people look for the best price. Others want the best quality—almost regardless of price. And others settle for the best value. It's helpful to think of eight economic needs:

1. Convenience.
2. Efficiency in operation or use.
3. Dependability in use.
4. Reliability of service.
5. Durability.
6. Improvement of earnings.
7. Improvement of productivity of property.
8. Economy of purchase or use.

With economic needs, measurable factors can be emphasized. These might include specific dollar savings, differences in weight, or length of product life.

Perception determines what is seen and felt

All kinds of stimuli are aimed at consumers. But they may not hear or see anything. This is because we unconsciously apply the following selective processes:

1. **Selective exposure**—our eyes and mind notice only information that interests us.
2. **Selective perception**—we can screen out or modify ideas, messages, and information that conflict with previously learned attitudes and beliefs.
3. **Selective retention**—we remember only what we want to remember.

These selective processes help explain why some people are not at all affected by some advertising—even offensive advertising. They just don't see or remember it.

A person's attitudes affect these selective processes. Further, decisions that the consumer is currently making—and typically concerned about—will affect which attitudes are important. If a consumer is thinking about buying an automobile, for example, then he may become quite interested in available cars, people's attitudes toward them, and car advertising. At the same time, if a house purchase is not being considered at all, housing-related stimuli may be completely screened out.

When planning strategies, it would be useful to know how potential customers perceive their problems, what kind of information they are looking for, and what standards they are using. This would help an advertiser catch the attention of potential buyers as they are receiving the incoming stimuli.

Perception skills are improved by learning. This is why some marketers pay special attention to the learning process.

Learning determines what is remembered

Learning theorists have described a number of steps in the learning process. They define a "drive" as a strong stimulus that motivates an individual. Depending on the **cues**—products, signs, ads, and other stimuli existing in the environment—an individual chooses some specific response. A **response** is an effort to satisfy a drive. The specific response chosen depends on the cues and the person's past experience.

Reinforcement—of the learning process—occurs when a response is followed by satisfaction—that is, reducing the drive tension. Reinforcement strengthens the relationship between the cue and the response. And it may lead to a similar response the next time the drive occurs. Repeated reinforcement leads to the development of a habit—making the decision process routine for the individual. The relationships of the important variables in the learning process are shown in Figure 7–4.

The learning process can be illustrated by a hungry person. The hunger drive could be satisfied in a variety of ways. But if the person happened

Figure 7–4: The learning process

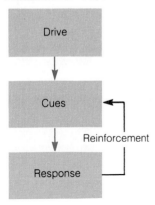

Drive

↓

Cues ←

Reinforcement

↓

Response

to be driving around and saw a McDonald's sign—a cue—he might satisfy the drive by buying a McDonald's hamburger—the response. If the experience is satisfactory, reinforcement would occur. Our friend might be quicker to satisfy this drive in the same way in the future. This emphasizes the importance of developing good products which live up to the promises of the firm's advertising. Note, people could learn to like *or dislike* McDonald's hamburgers. Learning works both ways.

Good experiences can lead to positive attitudes about a firm's product. Bad experiences can lead to negative attitudes—which may be difficult or impossible to change with promotion. In fact, the subject of attitudes is very important to marketers. We'll discuss this more fully in a following section.

Are needs learned?

Trying to separate learned from unlearned needs is not very useful. But brief consideration of the idea is desirable—because some critics feel that marketing "creates" many needs.

It can be argued that people are born with all the basic needs. A small child develops strong desires for "things"—certainly before advertisers have had a chance to influence him.

Even the need for status—which some marketing critics feel is related to the influence of advertising—is found among animals and in human societies where there is no advertising. Studies of birds show that there is a definite pecking order in flocks. In a study of jackdaws, for instance, it was found that the female—upon mating—takes on the status of her mate. Some African villagers raise domesticated cattle and goats purely as signs of wealth and social status. For food, they hunt wild animals.[2]

Wanting a hamburger is learned behavior

Some needs may be culturally (or socially) determined, however. When human babies are born, their needs are simple. But as they grow, they learn complex behavior patterns—to satisfy the drives arising from these needs. As their needs become more sophisticated and specific, the needs can be described as wants. The need for food, for instance, may lead to many specific food wants. The resulting hunger drive may be satisfied only by the specific food desired. The people of Western nations like beef. And their children learn to like it. In India, however, Hindus regard the cow as sacred—and will not eat beef. Hindu children learn to eat and like other foods. Many foods, in other words, can satisfy the hunger drive. But in a particular culture, an individual might want a hamburger. And the hunger drive might not be fully satisfied until he has eaten one.

Attitudes limit what decisions are made

Attitudes are an important topic for marketers—because they affect the selective processes. Attitudes also affect learning—and eventually buying decisions. **Attitudes** are reasonably permanent points of view about an object or class of objects. Attitudes are things people believe strongly

Whether needs are innate or learned, they are still real.

enough to be willing to take some action. Opinions and beliefs are not so action-oriented. It would be possible to have a belief—say that the world was round—without having an attitude about the world.

Attitudes are not the same thing as buying intentions. A person might have a positive attitude toward a Cadillac, for example, without ever intending to buy one. So attitudes must be used with care when trying to predict buying behavior.

Consumers' attitudes—both positive and negative—are learned from experiences with a product, exposure to the attitudes of others, or promotion which affects their own attitudes. If a marketer can learn the attitudes of the firm's potential target markets, he can know whether there are positive attitudes to appeal to. Or maybe he must change existing attitudes. Or perhaps he must create new attitudes. Each of these jobs would require a slightly different approach.

Marketers generally try to understand the attitudes of their potential customers and work with them—perhaps directing positive attitudes toward the firm's own brand. This is much easier and more economical than trying to change attitudes. Changing present attitudes—especially negative ones—is probably the most difficult job that marketers face. If very negative attitudes are held by the target market, it may be more practical to try another strategy.[3]

Personality affects how people see things

Much research has been done on how personality affects people's behavior. The results have been disappointing to marketers. Certainly, personality traits influence how individual people behave. But right now we do not have *general* principles about personality which help us much in strategy planning.

Psychographic and life-style analysis may help

Some marketers are trying to find meaning in sets of consumer-related dimensions. When only personality traits are used, the approach is sometimes called "psychographics." More commonly, however, **psychograph-ics** or **life-style analysis** refers to the analysis of many dimensions—including consumers' demographics, Activities, Interests, and Opinions. The last three sets are referred to as the "AIO variables." Typical life-style dimensions are shown in Table 7–1.

The basic idea behind this kind of analysis is that the more you know about your potential customers, the better you can plan strategies to reach them.

Life-style analysis usually includes many items—perhaps questionnaires as long as 25 pages—because several statements must be answered for each of the AIO variables to get a real understanding of potential custom-ers. For example, if a marketer wanted to learn whether his target market included "sports spectators" he could list statements such as:

"I like to watch or listen to baseball or football games."
"I usually read the sports pages in the daily paper."
"I thoroughly enjoy conversations about sports."
"I would rather go to a sporting event than a dance."[4]

Potential customers would be asked how strongly they agreed with the statements—from "definitely agree" to "definitely disagree." Hundreds of such statements are used. And then a computer tries to find patterns among all of the answers.

Life-style research can provide helpful information about markets. But so far, the results have been special purpose—no general principles have been found. A specific analysis, for example, might isolate clearly defined segments—such as swingers, conservatives, and so on.

The answers to the AIO questions provide the marketer with an in-depth view of how these markets think and buy specific products. Some-times it will show that changing products—or target markets—is needed. White Stag, for example, modified its missy-size sportswear lines when a life-style study showed that what the firm thought was the "missy market" was really five different kinds of women with varied life-styles. This led to new lines for the various sub-markets—and new promotion to consumers and retailers.[6]

Table 7–1: Life-style dimensions[5]

Activities	Interests	Opinions	Demographics
Work	Family	Themselves	Age
Hobbies	Home	Social issues	Education
Social events	Job	Politics	Income
Vacation	Community	Business	Occupation
Entertainment	Recreation	Economics	Family size
Club membership	Fashion	Education	Dwelling
Community	Food	Products	Geography
Shopping	Media	Future	City size
Sports	Achievements	Culture	Stage in life cycle

INTER-PERSONAL VARIABLES AFFECT THE INDIVIDUAL'S BUYING BEHAVIOR

So far we have been discussing findings from psychology. Yet consumer behavior may be determined not only by a person's particular personality and drives, but also by his relations with others.

Social psychologists and sociologists see market behavior as a response to the attitudes and behavior of others. Let's look at their thinking about the interaction of the individual with family, social class, reference groups, and culture.

Family considerations may overwhelm personal ones

Most decisions are made within a framework developed by experience within a family. An individual may go through much thinking about his own preferences for various goods and services. But this analysis may be only one of the influences in the final decision. Social processes—such as power, domination, and affection—may be involved, too. This decision-making behavior is often the result of much social learning.

A boat for father or a TV for mother

The interaction of various social forces can be illustrated by a choice between two products: a television set and a boat with outboard motor.

The husband in a family might be interested in the boat and motor for his camping and fishing trips. Weekend pleasure outings with the family would be secondary. But in his arguments, he can present his preference in the desirable terms of family wants and uses. At the same time, his wife might want a new television set. It would add to the beauty of her home—and also could be used as entertainment for herself, her husband, and the children. She, too, could argue that this purchase is for the family.

The actual outcome in such a situation is unpredictable. It depends on: the strength of the husband's and the wife's preferences; their individual degree of dominance of the family; who contributes the most money to

Families make buying decisions together.

the family's income; the need for affection; and the response of other family members. Yet an individual retail salesclerk in direct contact with the family might sense how the family operates—and be able to adjust the sales presentation to fit.

Who is the real decision maker?

Although one person in the family often makes the purchase, in planning strategy it is important to know who is the real decision maker.

Traditionally, the wife has been considered the family purchasing agent. She had the time to shop—and run the errands. So, most promotion has been aimed at women. But the situation may be changing as more women work—and as night and Sunday shopping become more popular. Men now have more time for—and interest in—shopping.

The nature of the product makes a difference

The husband is usually concerned with buying decisions that involve functional (mechanical or technical) items. Of the two, he tends to be more concerned with matters external to the family. The wife is more likely to make those buying decisions that have expressive values. She is more concerned with internal matters. These distinctions may apply even if the user of a purchased product is the other person. For example, a wife may buy the husband's clothing accessories. The husband might buy household appliances.

The husband and wife may work together where the usual husband-wife roles overlap. Husbands and wives may share in home improvements, for example, because they involve both functional and expressive matters.[7]

Some buy for themselves or others

The question of spending by the family is not limited to wives and husbands. As the life-cycle stages of the family change, children begin to spend more money.

In many cases, the person doing the shopping is just acting as an agent for others. And they may have specified which products should be bought. Small children may want specific brands of cereals. A teenager may want a certain brand of shampoo.

Social class affects buying of specifics

Up to now, we have been concerned with the individual and his relation to his family. Now let's consider how society looks at an individual and the family—in terms of social class. **Social class** is concerned with how an individual fits into the social structure.

In discussing class structure, we will use the traditional technical terms: *upper, middle,* and *lower.* These words seem to suggest "superior" and "inferior." But no value judgment is meant. In fact, it is not possible to say that a particular class is "better" or "happier" than any other. Some people try to enter a different class—because they find that class more attractive. But others are quite comfortable in their own class—and prefer to remain there. A marketer should learn the characteristics and typical buying patterns of each class—not pass judgments.

Characteristics of the U.S. class system

The U.S. class system is an individual and a family system. While a child is a member of a family, his social class will depend on the class of his family. But grown children often "join" a different class than their parents. This happens when they reach higher education levels or take different occupations than their parents.

The U.S. class system is usually measured by occupation, education, and housing arrangements. The *source* of income is related to these variables. *But there is not a direct relation between amount of income and social class.* Some blue-collar workers earn much more than some white-collar workers—but they are usually placed in the "lower" class.

The early work on social class in the United States was done for cities in the 10,000–25,000 population range. Later, the *Chicago Tribune* developed a population breakdown for Chicago—which is probably typical of a big industrial city. Many of the findings are interesting to marketing managers. Let's look at the *Chicago Tribune's* breakdown first—and then consider some of the findings.

1. **Upper Class** (0.9 percent of the total population): This was defined as wealthy old families **(upper-upper class)** and the socially prominent new rich **(lower-upper class).** This group has been the traditional leader in the American community. Most large manufacturers, bankers, and top marketing people belong to it. It represents, however, less than 1 percent of the population. Being so small, the two upper classes are often merged into one.

Less than one percent of Canada is in the upper class.

2. **Upper-Middle Class** (7.2 percent of population): These are the successful business people, professionals and top salespeople. The advertising professional usually is part of this class—reflecting the tastes and codes of the first two groups. Yet, together, groups 1 and 2 still represent only 8.1 percent of the population!

3. **Lower-Middle Class** (28.4 percent of population): These are the white-collar workers—small business people, office workers, teachers, technicians, and most salespeople. The American moral code—and the emphasis on hard work—have come from this class. This has been the most conforming, church-going, morally serious part of society. We speak of America as a middle-class society. But the middle-class value system stops here. *Two-thirds of our society is not middle class.*

4. **Upper-Lower Class** (44.0 percent of population): These are the factory production line workers, the skilled workers, the service workers—the "blue-collar" workers—and the local politicians and union leaders who would lose their power if they moved out of this class.

5. **Lower-Lower Class** (19.5 percent of population): This group includes unskilled laborers—and people in nonrespectable occupations.[8]

Class system in Canada

Canadian sociologists generally agree that Canada has a clearly definable class structure which can be classified according to the above five categories. However, the type of study carried out in the United States has few Canadian counterparts. Instead, Canadian studies of social class have focused more on national or ethnic class profiles, on the factors hindering movement between classes, and on the social background of Canada's economic elite.[9]

What do these classes mean?

The *Chicago Tribune* class studies suggest that an old saying—"A rich man is simply a poor man with more money"—is not true. It appears that a person belonging to the lower class—given the same income as a middle-class person—handles himself and his money very differently. The various classes shop at different stores. They would prefer different treatment from salespeople. They buy different brands of products—even though their prices are about the same—and they have different spending–saving attitudes. Some of these differences are shown in Figure 7–5.

The impact on strategy planning is most interesting. Selection of advertising media should be related to social class, for example. Customers in the lower classes would have little interest in *Fortune, Holiday, Vogue,* or *Ladies' Home Journal.* The middle and upper classes probably would have little desire to read *True Story, Modern Romances,* or *True Confessions.*

Class should also affect product design—and the kinds of goods carried

Figure 7–5: A comparison of attitudes and characteristics of middle and lower social classes[10]

Middle class	Lower class
1. Pointed to the future.	1. Pointed to the present and past.
2. Viewpoint embraces a long expanse of time.	2. Lives and thinks in a short expanse of time.
3. More urban identification.	3. More rural identification.
4. Stresses rationality.	4. Nonrational essentially.
5. Has a well-structured sense of the universe.	5. Vague and unclear structuring.
6. Horizons vastly extended or not limited.	6. Horizons sharply defined and limited.
7. Greater sense of choice making.	7. Limited sense of choice making.
8. Self-confident, willing to take risks.	8. Very much concerned with security and insecurity.
9. Immaterial and abstract in thinking (idea-minded).	9. Concrete and perceptive in thinking (thing-minded).
10. Sees himself tied to national happenings.	10. World revolves around family.

by retailers. The *Chicago Tribune* studies found that lower-class people preferred overstuffed or flashy house furnishings. Those in the middle and upper classes preferred plain, functional styles. Further, those in the lower classes seemed to be confused by variety—and had difficulty making choices. As a result, such buyers looked on furniture salespeople as friends and advisors. The middle-class buyers, on the other hand, were more self-confident. They knew what they wanted. They preferred the salesclerk to be an impersonal guide.

Reference groups are important too

A **reference group** is the people to whom the individual looks when forming attitudes about a particular topic. A person normally has several reference groups—for different topics. Some he meets face-to-face. Others he may just wish to copy. In either case, he may take his values from "them"—and make buying decisions based on what he feels they would accept. *Playboy* magazine editors, for instance—and the "in" people who read it—might be a reference group for *some* readers of *Playboy*.

The importance of reference groups depends on the product—and whether anyone else will be able to "see" which product and which brand is being used. Figure 7–6 suggests the relationships. For example, an individual may smoke cigarettes because his reference group smokes. And the group's preference may even decide the brand he chooses. At the other extreme, most people in our society use laundry soap. But which brand is used is not easily seen. In this case, reference group influence may be small.

Reaching the opinion leaders who are buyers

Opinion leaders are people who influence others. Opinion leaders are not necessarily wealthier or better educated. And opinion leaders on one subject are not necessarily opinion leaders on another subject. Home-

Figure 7–6: **Reference-group influence**[11]

Brand type \ Product class	Weak	Strong
Weak	Canned peaches Laundry soap Refrigerator (brand) Radios	Air conditioners* Instant coffee* TV (black and white)
Strong	Clothing Furniture Magazines Refrigerator (type) Toilet soap	Cars* Cigarettes* Beer (premium versus regular)* Drugs*

* Classification by the extent to which reference groups influence their purchase based on actual experimental evidence. Other products listed are classified speculatively on the basis of generalizations derived from the sum of research in this area and confirmed by the judgment of seminar participants.

makers with large families may be consulted for advice on cooking. Young girls may be leaders in new clothing styles and cosmetics. This may occur within the various social classes—with different opinion leaders in the various classes.[12]

Culture surrounds the whole decision-making process

Culture is the whole set of beliefs, attitudes, and ways of doing things of a similar group of people. We can think of the American culture, the western Canadian culture, the French culture, or the Latin American culture. People in these cultural groupings would be more similar in outlook and behavior than those in other groups. And sometimes it is useful to think of sub-cultures within such groups. For example, within the Canadian culture there are various religious and ethnic sub-cultures.

From a target-marketing point of view, marketers would probably want to aim at people within one culture. So, if a firm developed strategies for two cultures, two different strategies would be needed.[13]

The values, attitudes, and beliefs within a culture change slowly. So once a manager develops a good understanding of the culture for which he is planning, he can focus on the more dynamic variables discussed above.

CONSUMERS USE PROBLEM-SOLVING PROCESSES

Behavioral scientists generally agree that people are problem solvers. How an individual solves a particular problem depends on his own intra-personal and inter-personal variables. However, a common problem-solving process seems to be used by most consumers.

The basic problem-solving process consists of five steps:

1. Becoming aware of—or interested in—the problem.
2. Gathering information about possible solutions.
3. Evaluating alternative solutions—perhaps trying some out.

4. Deciding on the appropriate solution.
5. Evaluating the decision.[14]

A larger version of this basic process is presented in Figure 7–7.

Three levels of problem solving are useful

The basic problem-solving process shows the steps a consumer might go through while trying to find a way to satisfy his needs. But it does not show how long he will take—or how much thought he will give to each step.

It is helpful, therefore, to recognize three levels of problem solving—extensive problem solving, limited problem solving, and routinized re-

Figure 7–7: Consumer's problem-solving process

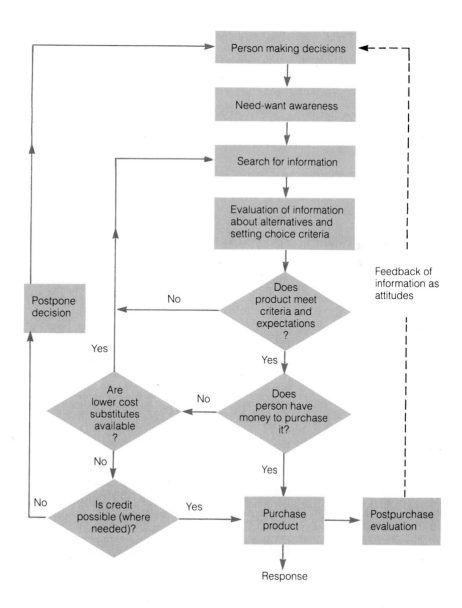

sponse behavior.[15] These problem-solving approaches might be used for any kind of good or service.

Extensive problem solving occurs when a need is completely new to a person—and much effort is taken to understand the need and how to satisfy it. A new college student, for example, may have feelings of loneliness, a need for companionship, a need for achievement, and so on. It may take him some time to figure out how—and what—he wants to do.

Limited problem solving involves *some* effort to understand a person's need and how best to satisfy it. Our college student, for example, might have tried various ways of satisfying his needs and come up with several fairly good choices. So limited problem solving would mean deciding which choice would be best at a particular time.

Routinized response behavior involves mechanically selecting a particular way of satisfying a need whenever it occurs. When our college student feels the need for companionship, for example, it might be quickly solved by meeting with friends in familiar surroundings. A daily trip to the local "hang out" might become the answer to this problem.

New ideas need an adoption process

Really new ideas present a problem solver with a harder job—the adoption process. The **adoption process** means the steps which individuals go through on the way to accepting or rejecting a new idea. See how promotion could affect the adoption process.

The adoption process for individuals moves through some definite stages, as follows:

1. Awareness—The potential customer begins to know about the product—but lacks details. He may not even know how it works—or what it will do.
2. Interest—If he becomes interested, he gathers general information and facts about the product.

Consumers may search for more information after a purchase—to reduce dissonance.

3. Evaluation—He begins to make a mental trial—applying the product to his own situation.

4. Trial—The customer may buy the product so he can actually try it. A product that is either too expensive to try—or can't be found for trial—may have trouble being adopted.

5. Decision—The customer decides on either adoption or rejection. A satisfactory experience may lead to adoption of the product—and regular use. According to learning theory, reinforcement will lead to adoption.

6. Confirmation—The adopter continues to think over his decision—and searches for support for his choice, i.e., further reinforcement.[16]

Dissonance may set in after the decision

After a decision has been made, the buyer may have second thoughts. He may have had to choose from among several attractive choices—weighing the pros and cons—and finally making a decision. Later doubts, however, may lead to **dissonance**—a form of tension growing out of uncertainty about the rightness of a decision. Dissonance may lead a buyer to search for more information—to confirm the wisdom of the decision—and help reduce his tension. You can see how important it is to provide information the consumer might want at this stage. Without this confirmation, the adopter might buy something else next time. Further, he would not give very positive comments to others.[17]

Several processes are related and affect strategy planning

The relation between the problem-solving process, the adoption process, and learning can be seen in Figure 7–8. It is important to see that they can be changed by promotion. Also, note that the problem-solving behavior of potential buyers would affect the design of distribution systems.

Figure 7–8: Relation of problem-solving process, adoption process, and learning (given a problem and drive tensions)

Problem-solving steps	Adoption process steps	Learning steps
1. Becoming aware of or interested in the problem.	Awareness and interest	Drive
2. Gathering information about possible solutions.	Interest and evaluation	Cues
3. Evaluating alternative solutions, perhaps trying some out.	Evaluation, maybe trial	
4. Deciding on the appropriate solution.	Decision	Response
5. Evaluating the decision.	Confirmation	

Reinforcement

If they are not willing to travel far to shop, then more retail facilities may be needed to get their business. Their attitudes may also decide what price is charged. You can see that knowledge of how target customers handle problem solving would make strategy planning easier.

INTEGRATING THE BEHAVIORAL SCIENCE APPROACHES

We have been studying the effect of many variables on a consumer's problem-solving behavior. Now—to tie this all together—we will show the various processes in one diagram. Then, we will suggest how it might help you plan better marketing strategies—and understand new research findings.

Integrated model can aid strategy planning

The integrated buyer behavior model in Figure 7–9 can be useful for predicting the problem-solving behavior the target customers are likely to use in a specific market.

Extensive problem solving may be necessary if there isn't much information at some of the decision-making steps. Then the consumer must get the needed information—and apply it. Routine buying behavior, on the other hand, can result if the consumer is familiar with the incoming stimuli, understands them correctly (at least in his own mind), and has already learned that a particular product will satisfy his needs.

Running through this model could help a marketing manager focus on what he knows—and does not know—about his target customers' buying processes. If he doesn't know how they search for information, for example, he might do some marketing research to be sure he understands how they behave.

If the target customers don't see the product correctly, a promotion effort might try to change the information entering the buyer's "black box." Or if there is confusion about how to use all the information, advertising or personal selling efforts might try to help potential customers choose among the various offerings.

Model can help use new findings

Finally, this model gives marketing managers a way to handle new research findings in a useful way. Instead of just saying, "Well, that's very interesting"—and wondering how it all fits—they can organize their thoughts within the model. This may mean changing their understanding of whichever variables are involved in the research findings.

Intuition and judgment are still needed

The present state of our knowledge of consumer behavior is such that we still must use intuition and judgment to describe the "why" of consumer behavior in specific markets. By applying our model, however, "guesses" should be limited to areas where knowledge is lacking. There is no excuse for "guessing" about the impact of things which have already been well researched.

Some people feel that understanding consumers is just "common sense." Actually they are using some model—perhaps a very simple one.

Figure 7–9: Integrated buyer behavior model

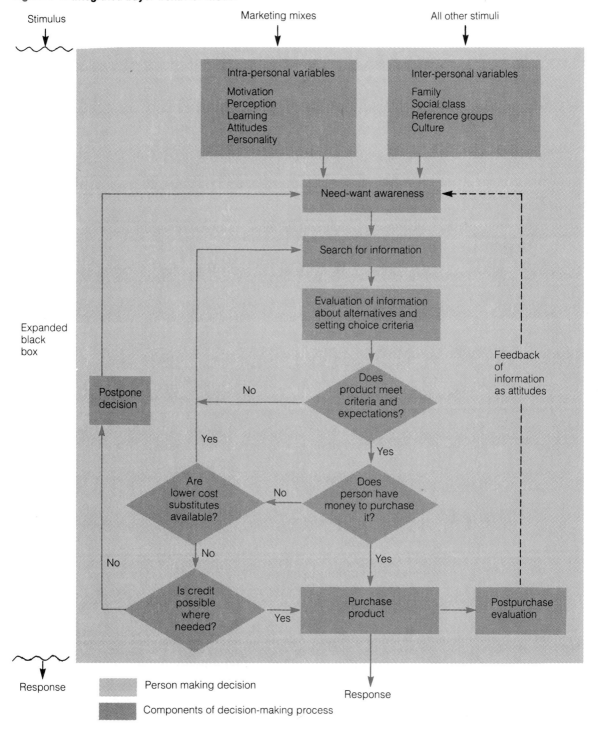

As we have seen, economists tend to use the economic-man model. Some very price-oriented retailers depend on this model. But, consumer behavior is much more complicated. Better strategies can result from making informed judgments about how the intra-personal and inter-personal variables affect the target customers' problem solving in a particular market.

BEHAVIORAL INSIGHTS INTO THE FRENCH CANADIAN MARKET[18]

Will behavioral science help us understand existing differences between French Canadian consumers and their English Canadian counterparts? We shall see that a behavioral approach gives us additional insights not available from economic and demographic data. What is learned however, supplements marketing judgment. It is not a substitute for such judgment.

Size and scope of that market

The following questions must be answered to talk meaningfully about the French Canadian market.

1. *What is a French Canadian consumer?* French Canadians can be defined in many ways. Let's accept the position that a French Canadian consumer is any one whose mother tongue is French or who tends to speak French rather than English at home.[19] However, marketers must realize that a large number of French Canadians are truly bilingual. They watch English language television programs and read English language publications.

2. *Where is the French Canadian market?* Is that market essentially Quebec or should it be defined more broadly? For marketing purposes, Quebec and the French Canadian market are not identical. However, a French Canadian market does not exist in every location where French is the mother tongue of a few consumers. Marketers cannot afford to develop special programs for very small market segments.

One approach defines the French Canadian market to include Quebec, nine adjacent counties in Ontario, and seven counties in the northern part of New Brunswick. The proportion of residents claiming French as their mother tongue in each of these 16 additional counties is at least 25 percent. For the 16 taken together, the mother tongue of 46 percent of the population is French, and 10 percent speak only French.[20]

Of all Canadians reporting French as their mother tongue, 92 percent, or over 5.4 million people, live either in Quebec or in these adjacent counties. The figure includes, of course, immigrants from France, North Africa, Vietnam, Haiti, and other French-speaking nations. A substantial Acadian population in New Brunswick is also unique in some ways. Nevertheless, Acadians are usually considered, for marketing planning purposes, to be part of the larger "French" market.

Differences in consumption?

3. *Are there French-English differences in produce usage?* Yes, and in some cases these differences are very great. One report suggests that, in comparison with their English counterparts, French Canadians buy rela-

tively more packaged soups, instant coffees, olives, wine, cosmetics, ale-type beer, linoleum tile, baby food, Geneva Gin, and soft drinks. They buy relatively less frozen goods, canned fish and meats, chocolate chips, pickles, vinyl tile, tea, and dietetic foods.[21]

A French Canadian sweet tooth may also exist. Quebec leads all other provinces in per capita sales of soft drinks, corn and maple syrup, and molasses, as well as several other sweets and delicacies.[22] Quebecers also prefer dry-mix soups that can be turned into homemade soups. They are not heavy consumers of lemon-flavored products.[23]

The above are but a few of the many differences in product usage and preference that have been reported. However, alert marketers must regularly reexamine the market to find whether such differences or preferences still exist. What the firm should do when differences in consumption are discovered is also not clear. Suppose we find out that lemon-flavored products are now being relatively underconsumed by French Canadians. Does this make Quebec a market that deserves more attention? Perhaps real barriers exist to increasing our sales to French Canadians. In the latter case, marketing could far more profitably be spent elsewhere.

Unique purchasing habits and practices

4. *What is known about the purchasing habits and practices of French Canadians?* French Canadian homemakers seem to like the friendly atmosphere of the boutique and personal contact with store employees. This fact may account for Quebec's omnipresent épicerie (grocery store), charcuterie (butcher shop) and pâtisserie (bakery). It may also help explain, as compared with Ontario, the relatively greater importance in Quebec of small retail outlets.

Household decison making

5. *What about household decision making in the market place?* BCP Publicité, one of Montreal's largest advertising agencies, found the following when it studied middle-aged, middle-class French Canadian couples:

a. Automobiles, insurance, and lodging are viewed primarily as male responsibilities.
b. Food, clothing, and allowances are recognized as female responsibilities.
c. Decisions regarding the education of children are jointly made.
d. Furniture was considered by females as a female responsibility, and men perceived such purchases as a joint decision.
e. Clothing for males was regarded by men as a joint decision, but women claimed it as their area of responsibility.[24]

These findings may have applied to French Canadian consumers in the past. Are they still valid? How have they been affected by the feminist movement and other recent developments? To what extent do such dimensions differentiate French-speaking from English-speaking consumers? Unfortunately, it is impossible to answer these questions.

THE SEARCH FOR THE "REASON WHY"

If French- and English-speaking Canadians differ in product usage, brand preference, and shopping habits, what factors account for such differences? With an answer to that question firms could develop far more effective strategies for these two important segments of the Canadian market. Unfortunately, general agreement is yet to be reached as to the reasons marked variations often exist. What are the different explanations that have been advanced?

Language-related differences in response to advertising do exist. For example, French Canadians are believed to react far more positively when products or services are endorsed by prominent French Canadian athletes or entertainers.[25] French Canadians, a recent study concluded, pay more attention to the source of advertisements (i.e., spokesperson), and English Canadians are more affected by the content of the message.[26] But such differences notwithstanding, language is not generally considered a major cause of existing French-English differences in brand preferences and consumption patterns. We must look beyond language for an explanation.

Is the explanation socioeconomic?

Does the answer lie in the social and economic differences existing between French Canadian consumers and their English-speaking counterparts? It has been argued that a much larger proportion of French Canadian families belong to the lower socioeconomic classes and that they consume accordingly. As evidence of this fact, many parallels between the values of French Canadian women and those of American working-class wives have been cited. The more commonly mentioned marketing differences between French and English Canadian consumers, one observer maintained, are similar to those that American researchers have found between the middle and lower classes.[27]

However, there are those who believe comparable incomes and educations need not necessarily mean similar consumption patterns. They maintain that a different heritage affecting ideas, attitudes, values, and habits could lead to very different French Canadian purchasing patterns.[28] And there is evidence to support this position. Two studies have revealed that consumption patterns differed markedly between Quebec (French language) and Ontario (English language) households of similar size, income level, and educational background.[29]

Does culture make the difference?

That culture, broadly defined, underlies many French-English differences in consumption patterns is also a widely held view. In addition to language, some of the more important French Canadian cultural traits are believed to be:

A more homogeneous society with rigid barriers against assimilating forces.

A philosophical and psychological outlook which tends to be more humanistic, more historically oriented, more emotionally based, and less pragmatic, with lower-achievement motivation.

A relatively stronger sense of religious authority.

A greater role for the family unit and the kinship system.

However, the fundamental upheaval associated with Quebec's Quiet Revolution is recognized as having affected the prevailing philosophical outlook. In particular, it reduced the importance of both church and family.[30]

Unfortunately, a generalized statement that culture and heritage makes the difference does not help in developing more appropriate marketing strategies. We need to know how and why social, psychological, and cultural factors are reflected in the choice of specific brands and products.

And what about social change?

Also deserving attention is the very rapid social and cultural evolution of this market. French Canadian society has transformed itself over the past few years. Today, that society is determined to exercise economic and social authority within the province. There has also been an increasing level of education, a weakening of family ties, and a distinct rejection of religious constraints. Such changes have far-reaching marketing implications. For example, consider how products and markets have been affected by a sharp decline in the Quebec birthrate and a marked increase in the number of working French Canadian women!

What psychographics teaches us

Very little scientifically valid information on French and English Canadian consumers is available. Some published reports were subsequently challenged as being "bad research."[31] Also, many studies of French-English differences in specific product areas are kept confidential by the firms that paid for them. However, some useful information is available from two major investigations.

A life-style study of activities, interests, opinions, and behavior revealed, among other things, that compared with her English counterpart, the French Canadian female is:

1. More oriented toward the home, the family, the children, and the kitchen.
2. More interested in baking and cooking and more negative toward convenience foods.
3. More concerned about personal and home cleanliness and more fashion and personal appearance conscious.
4. More price conscious.
5. Much more concerned about a number of social, political, and consumer issues.
6. More religious, especially in feelings about the life hereafter.
7. More security conscious and less prone to take risks.
8. More positive toward television and less positive toward newspapers.
9. More negative toward bank borrowing and the use of credit cards.
10. Characterized by a set of values described as steady and consistent.[32]

Although the data for this study was collected in 1970, a subsequent life-style investigation some years later produced essentially similar results.

In addition, the French Canadian homemaker, as compared with her English-speaking counterpart, was more liberal and perhaps less prudish in her views, more concerned about education, and less confident about her decision-making abilities. The only significant difference in the two studies concerned the apparent degree of price consciousness. The more recent investigation concluded that French-speaking homemakers were less rather than more price conscious than English-speaking ones.[33]

CONCLUSION

In this chapter, we have analyzed the individual consumer as a problem solver who is influenced by intra- and inter-personal variables. Our "black box" model of buyer behavior helps integrate a large number of variables into one process. A good grasp of this material is needed in marketing strategy planning because an assumption that everyone behaves the way you do—or even like your family or friends do—can lead to expensive marketing errors.

Consumer buying behavior results from the consumer's efforts to satisfy needs and wants. We discussed some reasons consumers buy and saw that consumer behavior can't be explained by only a list of needs.

We also saw that our society is divided into social classes—which does help explain some consumer behavior. The impact of reference groups and opinion leaders were also discussed, and the French Canadian market was investigated in some depth.

A buyer behavior model was presented to help you interpret and integrate the present findings and any new data you might obtain from marketing research. As of now, the behavioral sciences can only offer insights and theories which the marketing manager must blend with intuition and judgment in developing marketing strategies.

Remember that consumers—with all their needs and attitudes—may be elusive but not invisible. We have more data and understanding of consumer behavior than is generally used by business managers. Applying this information may help you find your breakthrough opportunity.

QUESTIONS AND PROBLEMS

1. What is the behavioral science concept which underlies the "black box" model of consumer behavior? Does this concept have operational relevance to marketing managers, i.e., if it is a valid concept, can they make use of it?

2. Explain what is meant by a hierarchy of needs, and provide examples of one or more products which enable *you* to satisfy each of the four levels of need.

3. Cut out two recent advertisements: one full-page color ad from a magazine and one large display from a newspaper. Indicate which needs are being appealed to in each case.

4. Explain how an understanding of consumers' learning processes might affect marketing strategy planning.

5. Explain psychographics and life-style analysis. Explain how it might be useful for planning marketing strategies to reach college students as compared with the "average" consumer.

6. How do society's values have an impact on purchasing behavior? Give two specific examples.

7. How should the social class structure affect the planning of a new restaurant in a large city? How might the four Ps be adjusted?

8. What social class would you associate with each of the following phrases or items?
   a. Sport cars.
   b. *True Story, True Romances,* etc.
   c. *Maclean's.*
   d. *Playboy.*

e. People watching "soap operas."

f. TV bowling shows.

g. Families that serve martinis, especially before dinner.

h. Families who dress formally for dinner regularly.

i. Families which are distrustful of banks (keep money in socks or mattress).

j. Owners of French poodles.

In each case, choose one class, if you can. If you are not able to choose one class, but rather think that several classes are equally likely, then so indicate. In those cases where you believe that all classes would be equally interested or characterized by a particular item, choose all five classes.

9. To illustrate how the reference group concept may apply in practice, explain how you personally are influenced by some reference group for some product. What are the implications of such behavior for marketing managers?

10. What new status symbols are replacing the piano and automobile? Do these products have any characteristics in commmon? If they do, what are some possible status symbols of the future?

11. Illustrate the three levels of problem solving with an example from your own personal experience.

12. On the basis of the data and analysis presented in Chapters 6 and 7, what kind of buying behavior would you expect to find for the following products: *(a)* canned peas, *(b)* toothpaste, *(c)* ball-point pens, *(d)* baseball gloves, *(e)* sport coats, *(f)* dishwashers, *(g)* encyclopedias, *(h)* automobiles, and *(i)* motorboats? Set up a chart for your answer with products along the left-hand margin as the row headings and the following factors as headings for the columns: *(a)* how consumers would shop for these products, *(b)* how far they would go, *(c)* whether they would buy by brand, *(d)* whether they would wish to compare with other products, and *(e)* any other factors they should consider. Insert short answers—words or phrases are satisfactory—in the various grid boxes. Be prepared to discuss how the answers you put in the chart would affect each product's marketing mix.

SUGGESTED CASES

7. Sleep-Inn Motel

9. Annie's Floral

30. Canadian Foods Ltd.

36. Beaver Spirits Ltd.

When you finish this chapter, you should:

1. Know who the organizational customers are.

2. Know about the number and distribution of manufacturers.

3. Understand the problem-solving behavior of manufacturers' purchasing managers.

4. Know the basic methods used in industrial buying.

5. Know how buying by retailers, wholesalers, farmers, and governments is similar to—and different from—industrial buying.

6. Recognize the important new terms (shown in red).

ORGANIZATIONAL CUSTOMERS AND THEIR BUYING BEHAVIOR

8

Organizational customers buy more goods and services than final consumers!

Most purchases are made by "organizational customers." Who are organizational customers anyway? In this chapter, we'll talk about them. Who they are. Where they are. And how they buy.

There are great marketing opportunities in serving organizational customers. A student aiming for a business career has a good chance of working with these customers.

ORGANIZATIONAL CUSTOMERS ARE DIFFERENT

Organizational customers are any buyers between the owners of basic raw materials and final consumers. There are only about ½ million organizational customers in Canada. Compare this with the more than 24 million final consumers. But organizational customers do a wide variety of jobs. Many different market dimensions are needed to describe all these different markets.

The emphasis in this chapter will be on the buying behavior of manufacturers—because we know the most about them. Other organizational customers seem to behave much the same way.

162

Even small differences are important

Understanding how and why organizational customers buy is very important. Competition is often tough in organizational markets. Even small differences may affect the success of a marketing mix.

Sellers usually approach each organizational customer directly—through a sales rep. This makes it possible to adjust the marketing mix for each individual customer. It is even possible that there will be a special marketing mix for each individual customer. This is carrying target marketing to its extreme! But when the customer's sales volume is large, it may be worth it.

Now, let's see how these organizational customers behave.

MANUFACTURERS ARE IMPORTANT CUSTOMERS

There are not many big ones

There are very few manufacturers—compared with final consumers—and most manufacturers are quite small. See Table 8–1. The owners may also be the buyers in these small plants. They are more informal about the buying process than the buyer in the relatively few large plants.

Larger plants, however, employ the majority of workers—and produce a big share of the value added by manufacturing. Plants with 200 or more employees were only 5 percent of the total—yet they employ 51.4 percent of the production employees and produce 60.3 percent of manufacturing shipments. You can see these large plants are an important market.

Customers cluster in geographic areas

Besides concentration by size, industrial markets are concentrated in certain geographic areas. Quebec and Ontario are important industrial markets. So are the big urban areas of the other provinces.

The buyers for some of these large manufacturers are even further concentrated in home offices—often in big cities. One of the large building material manufacturers, for example, does most of its buying for more than 50 plants from its Chicago office. In such a case, a sales rep may be able to sell all over the country without leaving his home city. This makes selling easier for competitors also—and the market may be very competitive.

Iron and steel mills center in Ontario; flour mills are in Saskatchewan; and pulp and allied industries tend to group in Quebec and British Columbia. Other industries have similar concentrations based on the availability of natural or human resources.

Much data is available on industrial markets by SIC codes

In industrial markets, marketing managers can focus their attention on a relatively few clearly defined markets and be near most of the business. Their efforts can be aided by some very detailed information collected by the federal government. The data shows the number of firms, their sales volume, and how many people they employ—broken down by industry, county, and CMA. The data is reported for Standard Industrial Classification code industries (SIC codes). These codes make market analysis easier. Figure 8–1 provides more detailed information on how the SIC code goes from the general to very specific.

Table 8–1: Manufacturing establishments, by number employed, by province, 1979[1]

	Number employed									
	Under 5	5 to 9	10 to 19	20 to 49	50 to 99	100 to 199	200 to 499	500 to 999	1,000 or over	Total
Province:										
Newfoundland	114	44	33	45	32	—41—		—5—		314
Prince Edward Island	56	29	30	—31—		—4—				150
Nova Scotia	262	106	144	130	59	36	27	7	4	775
New Brunswick	194	108	100	97	45	44	29	6	3	626
Quebec	2,717	1,809	1,779	2,026	986	568	362	82	52	10,381
Ontario	3,738	2,319	2,268	2,620	1,356	925	629	170	79	14,104
Manitoba	413	208	225	225	112	101	30	14	—	1,328
Saskatchewan	284	149	117	108	46	24	13	3	—	744
Alberta	738	432	409	400	164	100	48	14	—	2,305
British Columbia	1,468	695	577	510	248	151	124	37	12	3,822
Yukon and Northwest Territories	8	7	9	5	—	—	—	—	—	29
Canada:										
Number of establishments	9,992	5,906	5,691	6,197	3,048	1,994	1,262	338	150	34,578
Percent of establishments	28.90	17.08	16.46	17.92	8.81	5.77	3.65	0.98	0.43	100%
Number of employees	17,042	35,146	66,349	155,989	166,302	220,284	287,353	172,894	239,524	1,360,883
Percent of employees	1.25	2.58	4.88	11.46	12.22	16.19	21.12	12.70	17.60	100%
Percent of manufacturing shipments	.72	1.33	3.04	8.24	10.24	16.10	23.35	14.62	22.36	100%

Figure 8–1: SIC analysis of the corrugated box industry[2]

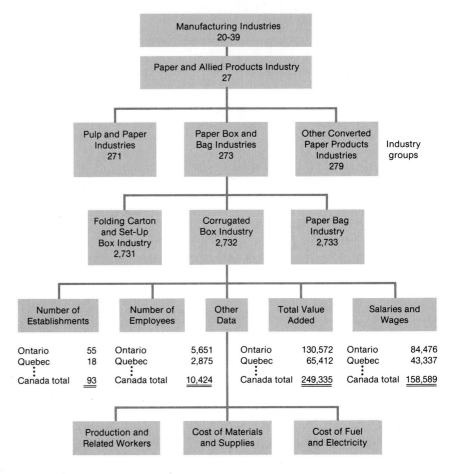

Four-digit detail is not available for all industries in every geographic area. Industries tend to concentrate, and further, the census will not reveal data when only one or two plants are located in an area. But, the point is that a lot of good basic information is available. If companies know their target markets, readily available data organized by SIC codes may be very valuable.

INDUSTRIAL BUYERS ARE PROBLEM SOLVERS

Some people think of industrial buying as entirely different from consumer buying. But there are many similarities. In fact, it appears that the problem-solving framework introduced in Chapter 7 can be applied here.

Three buying processes are useful

In Chapter 7, we discussed three kinds of buying by consumers: extensive, limited, and routine buying. In industrial markets, it is useful to change these ideas a little—and work with three buying processes: a new-task buying process, a modified rebuy process, or a straight rebuy.[3]

New-task buying

New-task buying occurs when a firm has a new need and the buyer wants a lot of information. New-task buying can include setting product specifications and sources of supply.

Modified rebuy buying

A **modified rebuy** is the in-between buying process where some review of the buying situation is done—though not as much as in new-task buying.

Straight rebuy buying

A **straight rebuy** is a routine repurchase which may have been made many times before. Buyers probably would not bother looking for new information—or even new sources of supply. Most of a company's purchases might be this type. But they would take a small amount of a good buyer's time.

The fact that a particular product or service might be bought in any of the three ways is very important. Careful market analysis is needed to learn how the firm's products are bought—and by whom. A new-task buy will take much longer than a straight rebuy—and give much more chance for promotion impact by the seller. This can be seen in Figure 8–2. It shows the time—and the many influences—involved in buying a special drill.

Industrial buyers are becoming specialists

The large size of some manufacturers has led to buying specialists. **Purchasing managers (agents)** are buying specialists for manufacturers. These experts in buying usually must be seen first—before any other employee is contacted. Purchasing managers have a lot of power. In large companies, they may become very specialized—by specific product area. These buyers expect information that will help them buy wisely. They like to know about new products—and possible price changes, strikes, and

Straight rebuys use the same sources routinely, freeing the buyer for more time-consuming purchases.

Figure 8–2: Decision network diagram of the buying situations: Special drill[4]

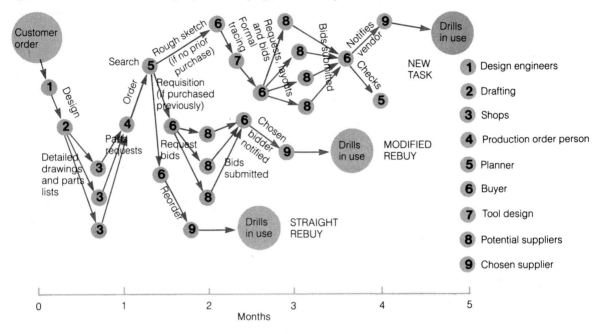

other changes in business conditions. Most industrial buyers are intelligent and well educated. A sales rep should treat them accordingly.

Basic purchasing needs are economic

Industrial buyers are usually less emotional in their buying habits than final consumers. They tend to look for specific product characteristics—including economy, productivity, uniformity, purity, and ability to make the buyer's final product better.

In addition to product characteristics, buyers consider the dependability of the seller and cooperativeness—and the ability to provide speedy maintenance and repair, and fast delivery.

Supply sources must be dependable

The matter of dependability is really important. There is nothing worse for a purchasing manager and a production manager than shutting down a production line because sellers have not delivered their goods. Product quality is important, too. The cost of a small item may have little to do with its importance. If it causes the breakdown of a larger unit, it may cause a large loss—much greater than its own value.

Emotional needs are relevant, too

Industrial purchasing does have an emotional side, however. Buyers are human—and want friendly relationships with suppliers. Some buyers seem eager to copy progressive competitors. Some want to be the first

Multiple buying influence lengthens and complicates the sales job.

to try new products. Such "innovators" might deserve special attention when new products are being introduced.

Buyers also want to protect their own position in the company. "Looking good" is not easy for purchasing managers. They often have to buy a wide variety of products from many sources. They must make decisions involving many factors beyond their control. A new source may deliver low-quality materials, for example, and the buyer may be blamed. Or late delivery may reflect on his ability. Any good, or service, or sales rep, therefore, that helps the buyer look good to higher-ups has a definite appeal. In fact, this might make the difference between a successful and an unsuccessful marketing mix.

A seller's marketing mix should satisfy both the buyer's company needs and the buyer's emotional needs. Therefore, it helps to find some common area where both can be satisfied.

Multiple influence on buying

Most purchases of the typical purchasing manager are straight rebuys which he handles himself. But in some situations—especially in new-task buying—a multiple buying influence may be important. **Multiple buying influence** means the buyer shares the purchasing decision with several managers—perhaps even top management. Each of these buying influences may be interested in different topics.

The sales rep might have to talk to every one of these possible influences—stressing different points. This not only complicates the promotion job—but also lengthens it. Approval of a routine order may take anywhere from a week to several months. On very important purchases—say, the purchase of a new computer system or major equipment—the selling period may stretch out to a year or more.

BASIC METHODS IN INDUSTRIAL BUYING

Should you inspect, sample, describe, or negotiate?

Industrial buyers—really, buyers of all types, including final consumers—can use four basic ways to evaluate and buy products: inspection, sampling, description, and negotiated contracts.

In modern economies, most products are purchased by description or negotiated contracts. In contrast, most buying is done by inspection or sampling in less-developed economies. The reason is doubt about quality—or lack of faith in the seller. Understanding the ''when'' and ''why'' of these buying methods is important in strategy planning.

Inspection looks at everything

Inspection buying means looking at every item. It is used for products that are not standardized—for example, fruits and vegetables, livestock, used buildings, and cars. These products are often sold in open markets—or at auctions. Potential buyers inspect the merchandise—and either bargain over price with the seller or bid against competitors.

Sampling looks at some

Sampling buying means looking at only part of a potential purchase. As products become more standardized—perhaps because of more careful grading and better quality control—buying by sample becomes possible. The general price level may be set by demand and supply factors—but the actual price may be adjusted according to the quality of a specific sample. This kind of buying is used when buying truck or railcar loads of wheat or corn, for example.

Description just describes accurately

Description buying means buying from a written (or verbal) description of the product. The goods are not inspected. This method is used when quality can be controlled and described—as with many branded products. In recent years, more wholesale and retail buyers have come to accept government grading standards for fruits and vegetables. Now, most of these products are packed in the fields and sold without any further inspection or sampling. This, of course, reduces the cost of buying—and is used by buyers whenever possible.

Negotiated contracts explain how to handle relationships

Negotiated contract buying means writing a contract that allows for changing the purchase arrangements.

Sometimes the buyer knows roughly what is needed—but can't describe it exactly. Perhaps the specifications—or total requirements—may change as the job is being done. Or maybe some of the details can't be anticipated. This is found, for example, in research and development work—and in building special-purpose machinery and buildings. In such cases, the general project is described. Then, a basic price may be agreed upon—with allowance for adjustments both upward and downward. The whole contract may even be subject to bargaining as the work proceeds.

Buyers want several supply sources to protect them from shortages due to strikes, fires or natural disasters.

Buyers may favor loyal, helpful suppliers

To be assured of dependable quality, a buyer may develop loyalty to certain suppliers. This is especially important when buying nonstandardized products. When a friendly relationship is developed over the years, the supplier almost becomes a part of the buyer's organization.

Most buyers have a sense of fair play. When a seller suggests a new idea that saves the buyer's company money, the seller is usually rewarded with orders. This encourages future suggestions.

In contrast, buyers who use a bid system exclusively may not be offered much beyond the basic products. They are interested mainly in price. Marketing managers who have developed better goods and services may not seek such business—at least with their better mixes.

But buyers must spread their risk—seeking several sources

Even if a firm has the best marketing mix possible, it probably won't get all the business of its industrial customers. Purchasing managers usually seek several dependable sources of supply. They must protect themselves from unpredictable events—such as strikes or other problems in their suppliers' plants. Still, a good marketing mix is likely to win a larger share of the total business.

Most buyers try to routinize buying procedure

Most firms use a buying procedure that tries to routinize the process. When some department wants to buy something, a **requisition**—a request to buy something—is filled out. After approval by a supervisor, the requisition is forwarded to the buyer—for placement with the "best" seller. Now the buyer is responsible for issuing a purchase order—and getting delivery by the date requested.

Ordering may be routine after requisitioning

Requisitions are converted to purchase orders as quickly as possible. Straight rebuys are usually made the day the requisition is received—by choosing from a list of acceptable suppliers. New-task and modified rebuys take longer. But if time is important, the buyer may place the order by telephone.

It pays to know the buyer

Notice the importance of being one of the regular sources of supply. Buyers do not even call potential suppliers for straight rebuys.

Further, note that if a particular sales rep has won a favorable image, it is likely that he might win a slightly larger share of the orders. Moving from a 20 percent to a 30 percent share may not seem like much from the buyer's point of view. But for the seller it would be a 50 percent increase in sales!

Some buy by computer

Some buyers have been able to turn over a large part of their routine order placing to computers. They develop decision rules that tell the computer how to order—and leave the details of following through to the machine. If economic conditions change, the buyers may modify the instructions to the computer. When nothing unusual happens, however, the computer system can continue to routinely rebuy as needs develop—printing out new purchase orders to the regular suppliers.

Paying taxes affects spending decisions

It is extremely important, then, for a supplier to be in the computer's memory. In such a situation, the critical thing is to be one of the regular suppliers. Obviously, this is a big sale. It requires an attractive marketing mix—perhaps for a whole line of products—not just a lower price for a particular order.

How the cost of a particular purchase affects profits may have a big effect on the buyer. If the cost of a large machine can be charged to the current year's expenses, the company may be more willing to buy it.

There are two general methods of charging costs—as capital and as expense items. The actual rules used have been established by Revenue Canada.

Capital items are depreciated

Capital items are durable goods—such as factories or large machinery—which are charged off over many years, i.e., depreciated. The depreciation period could be 2 to 50 years—depending on the item.

Managers do look at capital investment differently than at expense items. The purchase of capital items is likely to lead to new-task purchasing. The purchase of capital items is a long-term claim against future revenues. Mistakes can affect many years' profits. So, managers avoid quick decisions. Further, there is little agreement on the best approach to capital

The truck itself is a capital item while food and gasoline are expense items.

expenditure decisions.[5] So emotional considerations may become important in strategy planning.

Expense items are expensed

In contrast to capital items, **expense items** are short-lived goods and services which are charged off as they are used—usually in the year of purchase. The potential value is more easily forecast—and can be compared with the cost. Since the company is not spending against its future when it buys these items, it tends to be less concerned about these costs. This is especially true if business is good.

The multiple buying influence is less here. Straight rebuys are more common.

Inventory policy may determine purchases

Industrial firms generally try to maintain an adequate inventory—at least enough to be sure that production lines keep moving. There is nothing worse than to have a production line close down.

Adequate inventory is often stated in number of days' supply—for example, a 60- or 90-day supply. But what a 60- or 90-day supply is, depends upon the demand for the company's products. If the demand rises sharply—say by 10 percent—then total purchases will expand by *more* than 10 percent to maintain regular inventory levels and meet the new needs. On the other hand, if sales drop by 10 percent, actual needs and inventory requirements drop. Buying may even stop while the inventory is being "worked off." During this time, a seller would probably have little success with trying to stimulate sales. The buyer is just "not in the market."

Reciprocity helps sales, but . . .

Reciprocity means trading sales for sales—i.e., "If you buy from me, I'll buy from you." If a company's customers also sell products which the firm buys, then the sales departments of both buyer and seller may try to trade sales for sales. Purchasing managers usually resist reciprocity. But often it is forced upon them by their sales departments.

Reciprocal buying and selling are common in some industries—paints, chemicals, and oil. When both prices and product qualities are competitive, it's hard to ignore the pressures from the sales departments. An outside supplier can only hope to become an alternate source of supply. He has to wait for the "insiders" to let quality slip—or prices rise.

The legality of reciprocal agreements has not been seriously challenged under Canadian law. Any such move in this direction would force those firms that place heavy reliance upon reciprocal dealing to reevaluate their marketing strategies.

RETAILERS AND WHOLESALERS ARE PROBLEM SOLVERS, TOO

They must buy for their customers

Most retail and wholesale buyers see themselves as buyers for their target customers. They believe the old saying: "Goods well bought are half sold." They do *not* see themselves as sales agents for manufacturers. They buy what they think they can sell. They do not try to make value judgments about the desirability of what they are selling. Instead, they focus on the needs and attitudes of their target customers.

They must buy too many items

Most retailers carry a large number of items—drugstores up to 12,000, hardware stores up to 25,000, and grocery stores up to 10,000. They just don't have time to pay close attention to each item. Wholesalers, too, handle so many items that they can't give constant attention to each one of them. A grocery wholesaler may stock up to 20,000 items—and a drug wholesaler up to 125,000 items.

You can see why retailers and wholesalers buy most of their products as straight rebuys. Sellers should recognize the difficulty of the buyer's

Retail buyers consider their target markets when buying—trying to satisfy their needs.

All firms should know how much inventory they're carrying—and how fast it sells.

job. Many of these buyers are annoyed by the number of sales reps who call on them with little to say about only one of the many items they carry. Sales reps should have something useful to say and do when they call. For example, besides just improving relationships, they might take inventory or arrange shelves—while looking for a chance to talk about specific products.

In larger firms, buyers spend more time on individual items. They may even specialize in certain goods. Some large chains even expect buyers to get out of their offices and find additional—and lower-cost—sources of supply.[6]

They watch inventories and computer output

The large number of items stocked by wholesalers and retailers make it necessary to watch inventories carefully. Most modern retailers and wholesalers try to maintain a selling stock and *some* reserve stock. Then they depend on a continual flow through the channel.

Increasingly, even small firms are moving to automatic inventory control methods. Large firms use complicated computer-controlled inventory systems. Large retail discounters have even moved to *unit* control systems—to quickly pinpoint sales of every product on their shelves. As one discounter put it, "We are not satisfied to know what we are selling in a thousand-foot area—we want to know quickly what we are selling on each table.[7]

Buyers who watch their inventory this closely know their needs. They become more demanding about dependable delivery. They also know how goods move—and what promotion help might be needed.

Some are not always "open to buy"

Just as manufacturers sometimes try to reduce their inventory and are "not in the market," retailers and wholesalers may stop buying for similar reasons. No special promotions or price cuts will make them buy.

In retailing, another fact affects buying. A buyer may be controlled by a fairly strict budget. This is a miniature profit and loss statement for each department or merchandise line. In an effort to make a profit, the buyer tries to forecast sales, merchandise costs, and expenses. The figure for "cost of merchandise" is the amount the buyer has to spend over the budget period. If the money has not yet been spent, the buyer is **open to buy**—that is, the buyer has budgeted funds which he can spend in the current time period.

Owners or professional buyers may buy

The buyers in small stores—and for many wholesalers—are the owners or managers. There is a very close relationship between buying and selling. In larger operations, buyers may specialize in certain lines. But they still may supervise the salespeople who sell what they buy. These buyers, therefore, are in close contact with their customers *and* their salespeople. The salespeople are sensitive to the success of the buyer's efforts—especially when they are on commission. A buyer may even buy some items to satisfy the preferences of his salespeople. They should not be ignored in a seller's promotion effort. The multiple buying influence may make the difference.

As sales volumes rise, a buyer may specialize in buying only—and have no responsibility for sales. Sears is an extreme case, to be sure. But it has a buying department of more than 3,000 people—supported by a staff department of over 1,400. These are professional buyers who may know more about prices, quality, and trends in the market than their suppliers. Obviously, these are big potential customers—and should be approached differently than the typical small retailers.[8]

Resident buyers may help a firm's buyers

Resident buyers are independent buying agents who work—in central markets—for several retailers or wholesaler customers in outlying markets. They work in such cities as Montreal, Toronto, and Winnipeg. They buy new styles and fashions—and fill-in items—as their customers run out of stock during the year. Resident buying organizations may buy everything (except furniture, shoes, and food) for their stores. Some resident buyers have hundreds of employees—and buy more than $1 billion worth of goods a year.

Resident buying organizations fill a need for the many small manufacturers who cannot afford large selling organizations. Resident buyers usually are paid an annual fee based on the amount they buy.

Committee buying happens, too

In some large companies, especially in those selling foods and drugs, the major buying decisions may be made by a buying committee. The seller still must contact the buyer. But the buyer does not have final responsibility. The buyer prepares a form summarizing the proposal for a new product. The seller may help complete this form—but he probably won't get to present his story in person to the buying committee.

This rational, almost cold-blooded, approach has become necessary because of the flood of new products. Consider the problem facing grocery chains. In an average week, up to 250 new items are presented to the buying offices of the larger food chains. If all were accepted, 10,000 new items would be added during a single year. This might be more than

A strong marketing mix is essential to compete in committee buying situations.

their present stock! Obviously, buyers must be hard-headed and impersonal. About 90 percent of the new items presented to food stores are rejected.

Clearly, marketing managers must develop good marketing mixes when buying becomes so organized and competitive.

THE FARM MARKET

Farmers are the largest group of intermediate customers. But the number of farms has really dropped in recent years.

Just as in manufacturing, there are still many small units—but the large farms produce most of the output. About half the farmers produce almost 90 percent of the total farm output.

The owners of large farms tend to run their farms as a business. They are impressed by sales presentations stressing savings—and increases in productivity. Further, they are well informed—and open to change. And, they may have the money to act on their decisions.

Many farmers are unwilling to shop around for the lowest price—preferring the convenience of the nearest farm implement or feed dealer. There is some keeping up with the neighbors, too—especially in the purchase of farm machinery. A farmer's home and place of business are the same. A new tractor may offer just as much status as a new car would to an urban resident!

Fitting products to customers' specialization

Another important factor is that farmers are tending to specialize in one or a few products (such as wheat alone, or fruit, or eggs). These farmers are interested in very specific kinds of products.

Marketing mixes may have to be planned for each individual farmer—and in some cases this is happening. Fertilizer producers have moved far beyond selling an all-purpose bag of fertilizer. Now they are able to blend the exact type needed for each farm. Then they load it directly onto fertilizer spreaders. Some producers are working directly with farmers,

Farming is now big business and requires specialized products and sales people.

providing a complete service—including fertilizing, weeding, and debugging—all fitted to each individual farmer's needs.[9]

Agriculture is becoming agribusiness

Of growing importance is the tendency for farmers to go into contract farming. **Contract farming** means the farmer gets supplies and perhaps working capital from local middlemen or manufacturers who agree to buy the farmer's output—sometimes at guaranteed prices. The farmer becomes, in effect, an employee. Such arrangements are found in raising chickens and turkeys—and in growing fresh vegetables for commercial canning. These arrangements give security to the farmer. But they also limit the markets for sellers. It is all part of **agribusiness**—the move toward bigger and more businesslike farms.

Where contract farming is found, marketing managers will have to adjust their marketing mixes. They may have to sell directly to large manufacturers or middlemen who are handling the arrangements—instead of to the farmer.

In summary, the modern farmer is becoming more businesslike. He seems willing to accept help and new ideas—but only when he's sure they will help improve production.

THE GOVERNMENT MARKET

Size and variety

Government is collectively the largest customer in Canada. A substantial proportion of our national income is spent by the various levels of government. Governments buy almost every kind of product. They run schools, police departments, and military organizations. They also run supermarkets, public utilities, research laboratories, offices, hospitals, and liquor stores. Government buying cannot be ignored by an aggressive marketing manager.

Bid buying is common

Many government customers buy by description—using a required bidding procedure which is open to public review. Often the government buyer is forced to accept the lowest bid. His biggest job—after deciding generally what is wanted—is to correctly describe the need so that the description is clear and complete. Otherwise, the buyer may find sellers bidding on a product he doesn't even want. By law, the buyer might have to accept the low bid—for an unwanted product!

Negotiated contracts are common, too

Bargaining is often necessary when products are not standardized. Unfortunately, this is exactly where "favoritism" and "influence" can slip in. Nevertheless, bargaining (negotiating) is an important buying method in government sales. Here, a marketing mix must emphasize more than just low price.

Learning what government wants

Since most government contracts are advertised, marketers should focus on the government agencies they want to sell to—and learn their bidding procedures. The Canadian government offers a purchasing directory that explains its procedures. Various provincial and local governments also offer help. There are trade magazines—and trade associations—providing information on how to reach schools, hospitals, highway departments, park departments, and so on. These are unique target markets. They must be treated as such when developing marketing strategies.

CONCLUSION

In this chapter we have considered the number, size, location, and buying habits of organizational customers. We tried to identify logical dimensions for potential target markets. We saw that the nature and size of the buyer—as well as the buying situation—are important. We saw that the problem-solving models of buyer behavior introduced in Chapter 7 can be used here—with modifications.

The chapter emphasized buying in the industrial market—because more is known about manufacturers' buying behavior. Some specific differences in buying by retailers and wholesalers were discussed. The trend toward fewer, larger, more productive farms with better-informed and more progressive farmers was emphasized. The government market was described as an extremely large, complex set of markets—which requires much market analysis.

A clear understanding of organizational customer buying behavior can make marketing strategy planning easier. And since there are fewer intermediate customers than final customers, it may even be possible to develop a special marketing mix for each potential customer.

QUESTIONS FOR DISCUSSION

1. Discuss the importance of thinking "target marketing" when analyzing organizational customer markets. How easy is it to isolate homogeneous market segments in these markets?

2. Explain how SIC codes might be helpful in evaluating and understanding industrial markets.

3. Compare and contrast the problem-solving approaches used by final consumers and by industrial buyers.

4. Describe the situations which would lead to the use of the three different buying processes for a particular product, such as computer tapes.

5. Compare and contrast the buying processes of final consumers and industrial buyers.

6. Distinguish among the four methods of evaluating and buying (inspection, sampling, etc.) and indicate which would probably be most suitable for furniture, baseball gloves, coal, and pencils, assuming that some intermediate customer is the buyer.

7. Discuss the advantages and disadvantages of reciprocity from the industrial buyer's point of view. Are the advantages and disadvantages merely reversed from the seller's point of view?

8. Is it always advisable to buy the highest quality product?

9. Discuss how much latitude an industrial buyer has in selecting the specific brand and the specific source of supply for that product, once a product has been requisitioned by some production department. Consider this question with specific reference to pencils, paint for the offices, plastic materials for the production line, a new factory, and a large printing press. How should the buyer's attitudes affect the seller's marketing mix?

10. How does the kind of industrial good affect manufacturer's buying habits and practices? Consider lumber for furniture, a lathe, nails for a box factory, and a sweeping compound.

11. Considering the nature of retail buying, outline the basic ingredients of promotion to retail buyers. Does it make any difference what kinds of products are involved? Are any other factors relevant?

12. Discuss the impact of the decline in the number of commercial farmers on the marketing mixes of manufacturers and middlemen supplying this market. Also consider the impact on rural trading communities which have been meeting the needs of farmers.

13. The government market is obviously an extremely large one, yet it is often slighted or even ignored by many firms. "Red tape" is certainly one reason, but there are others. Discuss the situation and be sure to include the possibility of segmenting in your analysis.

SUGGESTED CASES

3. Kemek Manufacturing Company

5. Laurentian Steel Company

When you finish this chapter, you should:

1. Know what market segmentation is.

2. Understand the three approaches to target marketing.

3. Know the dimensions which have been useful for segmenting markets.

4. Know a seven-step approach to segmenting which you can do yourself.

5. Understand several forecasting approaches which extend past behavior.

6. Understand several forecasting approaches which do not rely on extending past behavior.

7. Recognize the important new terms (shown in red).

SEGMENTING MARKETS AND FORECASTING SALES

9

You have to aim at somebody—not just everybody—to make a profit.

Aiming at "somebody" is the big difference between production-oriented managers and target marketers. Production-oriented managers think of their markets in terms of *products*—and aim at everybody. They think of the "women's clothing" market or the "car" market. Target marketers think of their markets in terms of *customers' needs.* They segment (split up) such markets into sub-markets as they look for attractive opportunities.

In this chapter, we'll talk about segmenting markets—and forecasting sales in these markets. It's important to see that segmenting markets is not just a classroom exercise. If a product isn't aimed at a specific target market, all the effort may be wasted.

TARGET MARKETING REQUIRES EFFECTIVE MARKET SEGMENTATION

What is market segmentation?

We have been casually referring to how target marketers segment markets, but now let's take a close look at what segmenting involves. **Market segmentation** is the process of identifying more homogeneous sub-markets or segments within a market—in order to select target markets and develop suitable marketing mixes. You can see that market segmentation—

181

or "segmenting"—is *not* planning marketing strategies. Segmenting is concerned only with identifying markets or sub-markets which might become parts of marketing strategies.[1]

The basic idea underlying market segmentation is that any market is likely to consist of sub-markets—which might need separate marketing mixes. (In the extreme, we are all unique individuals—so each of us might be considered a separate target market within many product–markets.) So target marketers segment markets into smaller, more homogeneous markets—which they may be able to satisfy better than if they treat everybody alike.

MARKET SEGMENTATION LEADS TO THREE APPROACHES TO TARGET MARKETING

Target marketers aim at specific targets

There are three basic ways of developing market-oriented strategies for a product–market:

1. The **single target market approach**—segmenting the market and picking one of the homogeneous sub-markets as the target market.
2. The **multiple target market approach**—segmenting the market and choosing two or more homogeneous sub-markets—each of which will be treated as a separate target market needing a different marketing mix (as Procter & Gamble does with Crest, Gleem, and so on).
3. The **combined target market approach**—combining two or more homogeneous sub-markets into one larger target market as a basis for one strategy.

Note, all three approaches involve target marketing—they are all aiming at specific—and clearly defined—target markets. See Figure 9–1. For con-

Figure 9–1: Target marketers have specific aims

In a general market area

A segmenter		A combiner
Using single target market approach— can aim at one sub-market with one marketing mix	Using multiple target market approach— can aim at two or more sub-markets with different marketing mixes	Using combined target market approach— aims at two or more sub-markets with the same marketing mix

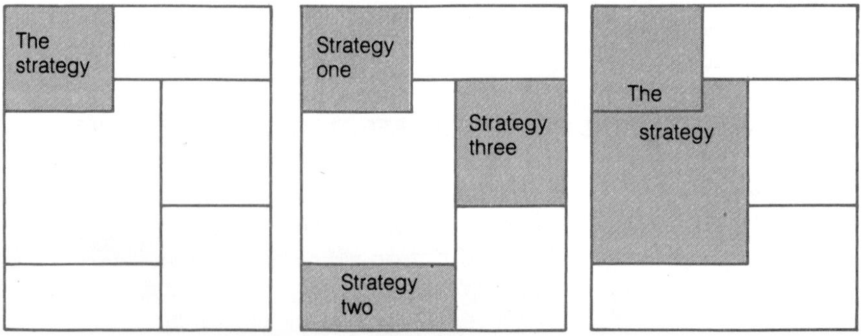

Figure 9–2: There may be different demand curves in different market segments

A. Mass marketer sees one demand curve for its target market

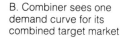
B. Combiner sees one demand curve for its combined target market

C. Segmenter sees one demand curve for each sub-market

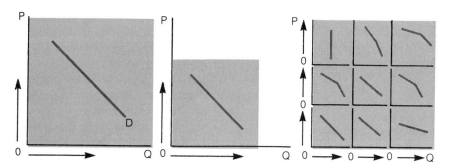

Note: A familiarity with economic analysis, and especially demand curves and demand elasticity, is assumed in this text. Those desiring a review of these materials should see Appendix C at the end of Chapter 2.

venience, we will call people who follow the first two approaches the "segmenters," and the people who use the third approach "combiners."

Combiners try to satisfy "pretty well"

Combiners try to increase the size of their target markets by combining two or more sub-markets—perhaps to gain some economies of scale, to minimize their risk, or just because they don't have enough resources to develop more than one marketing mix. Combiners look at various sub-markets for similarities—rather than differences. Then they try to extend or modify their basic offering to appeal to these "combined" customers—with just one marketing mix. See Figure 9–2. For example, combiners may try a new package, a new brand, or new flavors. But even if physical changes are made, their aim is *not* at smaller sub-markets. Instead, combiners try to improve the general appeal of their marketing mix—to appeal to a bigger "combined" target market.

Combiners often rely heavily on promotion—to convince the different sub-markets that a single product or marketing mix satisfies each segment's needs. Relying more on promotion is also necessary because there are probably fewer product differences from competition. And the differences may be quite small. But these little differences—in color, texture, or ease of use—may be *very* important to some customers. Also, the many different customers combined into one target market may be interested in different features of the same product. In the cosmetics market, the same product may have different meanings—and fill different needs—for each customer. For example, some women may be concerned with cleanliness, others with beauty, and others with glamour. One advertisement for one cosmetic product might appeal to all of them—but for different reasons. A combiner might see that the firm could serve *all* these needs at the same time. If the needs aren't too different, this may not only be possible—but will make economic sense for the firm.

Segmenters try to satisfy "very well"

Segmenters, on the other hand, aim at one or more homogeneous sub-markets and try to develop a different marketing mix for each sub-market—one that will satisfy each sub-market very well.

Segmenters may make more basic changes in marketing mixes—perhaps in the physical product itself—because they are aiming at smaller, more homogeneous target markets—each needing a separate marketing mix. A segmenter would worry that trying to appeal to *several* sub-markets at the same time—with the same mix—might confuse the customers. For example, some of the early entries in the "instant breakfast" market failed with combination appeals to dieters (as a low-calorie meal), harried commuters (as a breakfast substitute), working mothers (for a quick, complete, nutritious breakfast for kids), and housewives (as a nutritious snack between meals). Now, some segmenters have aimed at the "nutritious-snack" market—and succeeded with "crunchy granola" bars. It is interesting to note that while they aimed at the snack market, they are also getting some of the "quick-lunch" and "fast-breakfast" customers.

Segmenters see each sub-market's demand curve

Segmenters see different demand curves in different parts of a market area. Instead of assuming that the whole market consists of a fairly homogeneous set of customers—as the mass marketer does—or merging various sub-markets together—as the combiner does—the segmenter sees sub-markets with their own demand curves—as shown in Figure 9–2. Segmenters believe that aiming at one—or some—of these smaller markets will provide greater satisfaction to the target customers—and greater profit potential and security for the segmenter.

Segmenting may produce bigger sales

It is very important to understand that a segmenter is not settling for a smaller sales potential. Instead, by aiming the firm's efforts at only a part of a larger market, the segmenter expects to get a much larger share

A segmenter trys to find sub-markets within larger markets and satisfy them very well.

of his target market(s). In the process, total sales may be larger. The segmenter may even get almost a monopoly in "his" market(s).

A segmenter may be able to avoid extremely competitive market conditions. For example, the Wolverine World Wide Company came out with Hush Puppies—a casual, split-pigskin shoe that moved the firm into the very competitive shoe market with spectacular success—while conventional small shoe manufacturers were offering just "shoes" and facing tough competition.

Should you segment or combine?

Which approach should be used? This depends on many things, including the firm's resources, the nature of competition, and—most important—the similarity of customer needs, attitudes, and buying behavior.

It is tempting to aim at larger combined markets—instead of smaller segmented markets. If successful, such a strategy could result in economies of scale. Also, offering one marketing mix to two or more segments usually requires less investment—and may appear to involve less risk—than offering different marketing mixes to different market segments.

However, combiners face the continual risk of segmenters "chipping away" at the various sub-markets of their combined target markets—especially if the combined markets are quite heterogeneous. In the extreme, a combiner may create a fairly attractive marketing mix, but then watch segmenters capture one after another of its sub-markets with more targeted marketing mixes—until finally the combiner is left with no market at all!

The single or multiple target market approaches may be better

In general, it's safer to be a segmenter—that is, to try to satisfy customers *very* well—instead of only *fairly* well. That's why many firms use the single or multiple target market approach—instead of the combined target market approach. Procter & Gamble, for example, markets many products which—on the surface—may appear to be directly competitive with each other (e.g., Tide versus Cheer or Crest versus Gleem). However, P&G follows a strategy of offering "tailor-made" marketing mixes (including products) to each sub-market that is large enough and profitable enough to deserve a separate marketing mix. This approach can be extremely effective—but it may not be possible for a smaller firm with more limited resources. It may have to use the single target market approach—aiming at the one sub-market which looks "best" for it.

WHAT DIMENSIONS ARE USED TO SEGMENT MARKETS?

Segmenting forces the marketing manager to decide which dimensions might be useful for planning marketing mixes. Ideally, of course, the dimensions should help guide marketing mix planning. Table 9–1 shows some of the kinds of dimensions we have been talking about in the last several chapters—and their probable effect on the four Ps. Ideally, we would like to describe any potential market in terms of all three types of dimensions— because these dimensions will help us develop better marketing mixes.

Table 9–1: **Relation of potential target market dimensions to marketing mix decision areas**

Potential target market dimensions	Effects on decision areas
1. Geographic location and other demographic characteristics of potential customers	Affects size of *Target Markets* (economic potential) and *Place* (where products should be made available) and *Promotion* (where and to whom to advertise)
2. Behavioral needs, attitudes, and how present and potential goods or services fit into customers' consumption patterns	Affects *Product* (design, packaging, length or width of product line) and *Promotion* (what potential customers need and want to know about the product offering, and what appeals should be used)
3. Urgency to get need satisfied and desire and willingness to compare and shop	Affects *Place* (how directly products are distributed from producer to consumer, how extensively they are made available, and the level of service needed) and *Price* (how much potential customers are willing to pay)

Consumers have many dimensions—and several may be useful for segmenting a market. Table 9–2 shows some geographic and demographic segmenting dimensions—and their typical breakdowns.

Figure 9–3 shows the major segmenting dimensions that have been used for final consumer markets. As the figure shows, there are customer-related dimensions and situation-related factors—which are more important in some markets. When all competitors in a market are imitating each other, for example, then some product feature may be *the most important dimension*. Or the degree of brand loyalty—or even whether the brand is in a store when it is wanted (that is, the buying situation)—may decide which product is purchased. Let's look at these potential dimensions now—to see which ones will be the most useful.

Geographic dimensions can be useful

Geographic dimensions are a good basis for segmenting—because consumers in different areas do have different life-styles and needs. Further, customers in different areas may have to be served by different middlemen—and reached with different media. In fact, this is such a basic segmenting dimension that it may be more practical to use it in the title of a market—rather than as a segmenting dimension—for example, the "British Columbia market for high-priced status symbols."

Using geographic dimensions usually leads to a quick split of a market—but it does not give the detail needed for planning a marketing strategy. So more segmenting of each geographic market is usually necessary.

Other demographic dimensions are useful, too

Demographic variables (such as age, sex, family size, income) have been popular segmenting dimensions—because they are easy to measure—and data is easy to get. These however, are not good reasons

Table 9–2: **Some segmenting dimensions and typical breakdowns**[2]

Dimensions	Typical breakdowns
Geographic	
Region	Atlantic Provinces, Quebec, Ontario, Prairie Provinces, and British Columbia
City, county, or CMA size	Under 5,000; 5,000–19,999; 20,000–49,999; 50,000–99,999; 100,000–249,999; 250,000–499,999; 500,000–999,999; 1,000,000–3,999,999; 4,000,000 or over
Demographic	
Age	Infant, under 6; 6–11; 12–17; 18–24; 25–34; 35–49; 50–64; 65 and over
Sex	Male, female
Marital status	Single, married, divorced, widowed
Family size	1, 2, 3, 4, 5, 6, or more
Family life cycle	Young, single; young, married, no children; young, married, youngest child under 6; young, married, youngest child 6 or older; older, married, with children; older, married, no children under 18; older, single; other
Income	Under $8,000; $8,000–$11,999; $12,000–$15,999; $16,000–$19,999; $20,000–$24,999; $25,000 or more
Occupation	Professional and technical; managers, officials, and proprietors; clerical, sales; crafters, supervisors; operatives; farmers; retired; students; homemakers; unemployed
Education	Grade school or less, some high school, graduated high school, some college, college graduate
Mobility	Same residence for 2 years; changed residence in past 2 years
Home ownership	Owned or rented
Religion	Catholic, Protestant, Jewish, Moslem, Hindu, other
Race	White, black, oriental, other
Nationality	Canadian, British, American, German, etc.
Social class	Lower-lower, upper-lower, lower-middle, upper-middle, lower-upper, upper-upper

for using demographics. Often, product choice—and especially brand choice—are only slightly related to demographics. Higher-income consumers may be able to afford more expensive items—but that doesn't mean they'll buy them. Luxury cars aren't bought only by the wealthy. So, mechanically segmenting with demographics should be avoided.

Needs, attitudes, activities, interests, and opinions affect buying

Because demographics don't give very good answers, behavioral dimensions have been getting increasing attention. Sometimes two or three need or attitude dimensions can help segment a market. But generally, life-style specialists work with many variables at the same time (maybe 25 to 100). And different sets of variables are found useful in different markets.

Figure 9–3: **Types of segmenting dimensions**

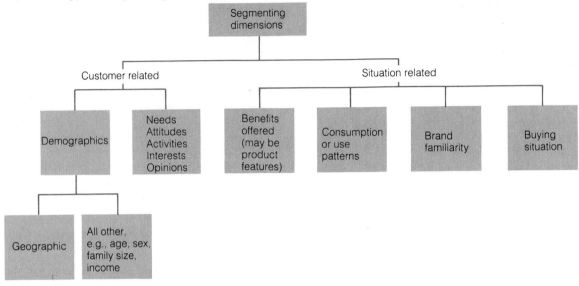

Benefits are why some people buy

Customers buy goods or services to satisfy needs. So it is sometimes useful to segment a market based on the benefits sought—or being offered. These dimensions will obviously be specific to a market—the benefits from buying skis are quite different from buying snack foods. Segmenting based on benefits can be tricky. Not everyone may be interested in the same benefits. Nevertheless, product features or benefits can help explain how customers see a market. For example, "high-performance" athletic equipment—such as some snow skis—may give status to those who can really use them, but make fools of beginners who buy them to impress others.[3]

Consumption or use patterns—related to how much is bought

Segmenting by whether people are current product users and at what rate—heavy, medium, light—has helped some target marketers. Research often shows, for example, that a small group of "heavy users" accounts for a large part of sales. The firm may want to aim at these heavy users—to make sure they keep on buying. Or, the present nonusers or light users might be attractive target markets.

Brand familiarity affects brand choice

Some firms segment their markets by how well present customers know the various brands. This approach can be interesting—especially if a brand has reached the stage where customers demand it. This may suggest that competitors should change their focus—to people less attached to a particular brand.

Buying situation—is the product in the store?

Some people have segmented markets based on how consumers behave in different buying situations. In a small convenience food store, for example, consumers may do less brand and price comparison than when on their weekly shopping trip to a supermarket. They may be willing to pay higher prices for convenience. Of course, this affects marketing strategy planning.

Possible buying-situation dimensions include the kind of store, its depth of assortment, whether it is leisurely or rushed buying, or whether it is a "serious" or a "browsing" shopping trip. Obviously, using these dimensions requires real knowledge of the market.

MARKET SEGMENTATION IS EASIER SAID THAN DONE

Segmenting does not mean "breakdown"

Some first-time segmenting efforts are very disappointing—because beginners often start with the whole "mass market." Then they try to find one or two demographic characteristics to explain differences in customer buying behavior. Typically, they get little—because they are trying to work with too few or the wrong dimensions.

Sometimes many different dimensions are needed to describe the different sub-markets. This was the case in the home decorating market example we used in Chapter 2. Recall that the British paint manufacturer finally settled on the Cost Conscious Couple as its target market. In that case, four possible target markets with *very different* dimensions were placed in the four corners of a market diagram. This is the kind of segmenting we want to do.

Segmenting is a gathering process

Target marketers think of **segmenting** as a gathering process. They start with the idea that each person is "one of a kind"—and can be described by a special set of dimensions. Using these sets of dimensions, the segmenter tries to gather similar customers together.

Gathering loses detail

Once the gathering is started, some details of each individual are ignored—as we look for similarities. This can be seen in Figure 9–4—where the many dots show each person's position in a market with respect to two dimensions: status and dependability. To get three (a convenient number) fairly homogeneous groups, the segmenter might gather these people into three groups—A, B, and C. Group A might be called "status oriented" and group C "dependability oriented." Members of group B want both—and might be called the "demanders."

Each group should represent a homogeneous set of people—a market segment. The larger the group is made, the less homogeneous it becomes. At some point, the segmenter has to decide: "This is the limit of this group."

One of the difficult things about segmenting is that some potential customers just don't fit neatly into market segments. Not everyone in Figure 9–4 was put into one of the three groups. They could be *forced* into one of the groups—but this wouldn't really be segmenting. Additional segments

Figure 9–4: **Every individual has his or her own unique position in the market— those with similar positions can be gathered into potential target markets**

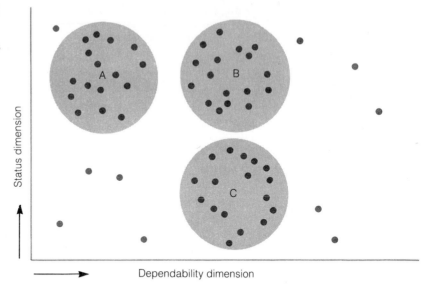

Status dimension

Dependability dimension

could be created—but they might be small and hard to describe. Some people may be too "special." It may not be possible to group them with anyone else.

HOW FAR SHOULD THE GATHERING GO?

There is no point in treating each individual in a market as a separate market segment if they all are basically the same. Usually, however, there are some important differences—and segmenting is helpful. In fact, in very competitive markets, even small variations can make a big difference in how well a firm does against tough competitors.

Basically, profit-oriented firms would probably want to continue gather-

Some people are too "unique" to fit easily into reasonable sized sub-markets.

ing potential customers into a larger market as long as a marketing mix could satisfy those customers—at a profit.

Standards for segmenting markets

Ideally, "good" market segments would meet the following standards:

1. Homogeneous (similar) within—the people in a market segment should be as homogeneous as possible with respect to their needs and attitudes—and their likely responses to the marketing mix variables.
2. Heterogeneous (different) between—buying behavior, not just customer characteristics, should be different from segment to segment.
3. Substantial—be big enough to be profitable.
4. Operational—their dimensions should be useful for deciding on marketing mix variables. There is no point in having a dimension that isn't usable.

Number 4 is especially important—because it is possible to find dimensions which are useless—even though they are related to past buying behavior. A personality trait like moodiness, for example, might be found among the traits of heavy buyers of a product—but how could you use it? Personal salespeople would have to give a personality test to each buyer—an impossible task. Similarly, advertising media buyers or copywriters could not make much use of this information. So, although moodiness might be related in some way to previous purchases, it would not be a useful dimension for segmenting.

Profit is the balancing point

Target marketers do not segment markets without thinking of what could be done for the markets. Even how the market is segmented should be affected by these practical business matters. Target marketers develop whole strategies—they don't just segment markets. As a practical matter, this means that *more gathering probably would be encouraged by cost considerations—to obtain economies of scale—while demand considerations would suggest less gathering—to satisfy needs more exactly.*

Profit would be the balancing point—determining how unique a marketing mix the firm can afford to offer to a particular group.

Too much gathering is risky

Segmenters must be careful about trying to gather too far—in search of profit. As sub-markets are made larger, they become less homogeneous—and individual differences within each sub-market may even begin to outweigh the similarities. This makes it harder to develop marketing mixes which can do an effective job of satisfying potential customers within each of the sub-markets. This leaves the firm more open to competitive efforts—especially from innovative segmenters who are offering more attractive marketing mixes to more homogeneous sub-markets.

A SEVEN-STEP APPROACH TO SEGMENTING MARKETS

We have discussed the ideas behind segmenting—and some dimensions which are often used. Now let's look at a seven-step approach which can be used without expensive marketing research—or computer analysis. More complicated methods are discussed later—but this approach works and has led to successful strategies.

So that you can understand this approach better, we will list each step separately, explain its importance, and use a common example to show how each step works. The example we will use is rental housing—in particular, the apartment market in a big urban area.

① **1. Select the product-market area to be considered.**   After the firm has defined its objectives, it must decide what market it wants to serve. If it is already in some market, this might be a good starting point. If it is just starting out, then many more choices are open—although the available resources, both human and financial, will limit the possibilities.

Example: The firm might be building small utility apartments for low-income families—basically just satisfying physiological needs. A narrow view of the market—that is, considering only products now being produced—might lead the firm to thinking only in terms of more low-income families. A bigger view—considering more market needs—might see these compact apartments as only a small part of the total apartment—or total rental housing—or even the total housing market in the firm's area. Taking an even bigger view, the firm could consider expanding to other geographic areas—or moving out of housing into other construction markets.

Of course, there has to be some balance between defining the market too narrowly (same old product, same old market) and defining it too broadly (the whole world and all its needs is our market). Here, the firm looked at the whole apartment market in one urban area—because this is where the firm had some experience and wanted to work.

② **2. List all the needs that all potential customers may have in this product-market area.**   This is an "idea-gathering" step. We want to write down as many needs as we can—as quickly as possible. The list doesn't have to be complete. The idea here is to get enough ideas to stimulate thinking in the next several steps. Some need dimension which

When segmenting the apartment dweller market, managers should consider variables such as party areas, cost and convenience.

is just "thrown in" now may be the most important dimension for a market segment. If that need were not included at this time, it is possible that this market segment would be missed.

Possible need dimensions can be identified by starting with the PSSP hierarchy of basic needs—see Chapter 7—to be sure that all potential dimensions are being considered. Expanding these four basic needs into more specific needs can be done by thinking about why some people buy the present offerings in this market.

Example: In the rental apartment market, it is fairly easy to list the following needs—which start with but move beyond the basic needs: basic shelter, parking, play space, safety and security, distinctiveness, economy, privacy, convenience (to something), enough living area, attractive interiors, and good supervision and maintenance to assure trouble-free and comfortable living.

3. Form possible market segments. Assuming that some market segments will have different needs than others, select out of the above list the most important ones for yourself, then for a friend, then for several acquaintances from widely different demographic groups. Form one segment around yourself or an obvious user—and then go on gathering others into other segments until three or more market segments emerge. Be sure you know the customer-related characteristics of the segments—so it will be possible to name them later.

There is obviously some guesswork here—but you should have some thoughts about how you behave. Given that you are "one-of-a-kind," you can see that others have different needs and attitudes. Once this is accepted, it is surprising how good your judgment becomes about how others behave. We all may have different preferences—but well-informed observers do tend to agree at least roughly on how and why people behave. Market-related experience and judgment are needed to screen all the possible dimensions. But at the least, the geographic, demographic, and behavioral topics discussed in earlier chapters should be considered when forming these market segments.

Example: A college student living off campus would probably want an apartment to provide basic shelter, parking, economy, convenience to school and work, and enough room somewhere to have parties. An older married couple, on the other hand, might have quite different needs—perhaps for basic shelter and parking, but also privacy and good supervision so they would not have to put up with rowdy parties—which might appeal to the student. Someone with a family would also be interested in shelter and parking—but might not have much money. So they would want economy—while getting enough room for the children.

4. Look for segmenting dimensions. Review the lists of dimensions in each market segment and remove any that appear in each segment. They may be important dimensions, but they are not the segmenting dimensions which we are seeking now.

A potential dimension—such as low price or good value—may be important for *all* potential customers. It may be an extremely important dimension which will have to be satisfied in *any* marketing mix. But for segmenting purposes, it should be removed at this stage.

Example: With our "apartment hunters," the needs for basic shelter, parking, and safety and security appear to be common. Therefore, in this step, we will remove them from our list of potential segmenting dimensions.

5. Name the possible product-market segments. Review the remaining dimensions—segment by segment—and give each segment a name—based on the dominant segmenting dimension(s). Then, draw a picture of the market area and put these segments in it.

Here is where creativity and judgment are needed—to compare the relative importance of the remaining dimensions. This should lead to giving each market segment a people-related name—or even a nickname.

Example: We can identify the following apartment segments at this time: swingers, sophisticates, family, job-centered, home-centered, and urban-centered. Each segment wants a different set of product features—which follow directly from the people types and the needs they have. See the legend at the bottom of Figure 9–5.

6. Seek better understanding of possible market segments. After naming the segments as we did in Step 5, more thought about what is already known about each segment is needed—to help you understand how and why these markets behave the way they do. This can explain why some present offerings are more successful than others. It also can lead to splitting and renaming some segments.

Example: Newly married couples might have been treated as swingers in Step 5 if the married dimension was ignored. But, with more thought, we see that while some newly married couples are still swingers at heart, others have shifted their focus to buying a home. For these newly marrieds, the apartment is only a temporary place. Further, they are not like the sophisticates (as shown at the bottom of Figure 9–5)—and probably should be treated as a separate segment. The point here is that these market differences might only be discovered in Step 6. It would be at this point that the "newly married" segment would be named.

7. Tie each segment to demographic and other customer-related characteristics, if possible, and then draw a new "picture" of the whole market to show their relative sizes. Remember, we are looking for profitable opportunities. So now we must try to tie our market segments to demographic data—to make it easier to estimate the sizes of the segments. We aren't trying to estimate market potential here. Now we only want to provide the basis for later forecasting—and marketing mix planning. The more we know about different target markets, the easier those jobs will be.

Fortunately, much demographic data is available. And bringing in demographics adds a note of economic reality. It is possible that some market segments will have almost no market potential. Without some hard facts, the risks of aiming at such markets are great.

Finally, to help understand the whole market and explain it to others, it is useful to draw a picture of the market with boxes that give some

Figure 9–5: **Market for apartment dwellers in a metropolitan area**[4]

Swingers	Family
	Job centered
Sophisticates	Home centered
Newly married	Urban centered

Name of market segment	People types and needs characteristics	Determining benefits sought (Product features)
Swingers	Young, unmarried, active, fun-loving, party-going	Economy Common facilities Close-in location
Sophisticates	Young, but older than swingers, more mature than swingers, more income and education than swingers, more desire for comfort and individuality	Distinctive design Privacy Interior variety Strong management
Newly married	No longer swingers, want a home but do not yet have enough money, wife works so economy not necessary	Privacy Strong management
Job centered	Single adults, widows, or divorcees, not much discretionary income and want to be near job	Economy Close-in location Strong management
Family	Young families with children and not enough income to afford own home	Economy Common facilities Room size
Home centered	Former homeowners who still want some aspects of suburban life	Privacy Room size Interior variety
Urban centered	Former homeowners in the suburbs, who now want to be close to attractions of city	Distinctive design Close-in location Strong management

idea of the size of the various market segments. This will help the company aim toward larger—and perhaps more attractive markets.

Example: It is possible to tie the swingers to demographic data. Most of them are young—in their 20s. And the Statistics Canada has very detailed information about age. Given age data—and an estimate of what percentage are swingers—it would be easy to estimate the number of swingers in an urban area.

Market dimensions suggest a good mix

Once we have followed all seven steps, we should be able to see the outlines (at least) of the marketing mixes which would appeal to the various market segments. Let's take a look.

We know that swingers are active, young, unmarried, fun-loving, and party-going. The housing needs shown at the bottom of Figure 9–5 show what the swingers want in an apartment. (It is interesting to note what they do *not* want—strong management. Most college students will probably understand why!)

A very successful appeal to the swingers in Vancouver, British Columbia, includes an apartment complex with a swimming pool, a putting green, a night club that offers jazz and other entertainment, poolside parties, receptions for new tenants, and so on. To maintain their image, management insists that tenants who get married move out shortly—so that new swingers can move in.

As a result, apartment occupancy rates were extremely high. At the same time, other builders were having trouble filling their apartments—mostly because their units were just "little boxes" with few uniquely appealing features.

COMPUTER-AIDED MARKETING RESEARCH CAN HELP IN SEGMENTING

The seven-step approach is logical, practical—and it works. But a marketing manager is no longer limited to this approach. Some computer-aided methods can help.

Market judgment is still needed

The basic aim of these methods is to try to find similar patterns within sets of data. This data could include such things as demographics, attitudes toward the product or life in general, and past buying behavior. The computer searches among all the data for homogeneous groups of people. When they are found, the dimensions of the people in the groups must be studied to find why the computer grouped them together. If the results make some sense, they may suggest new—and perhaps better—marketing strategies.

A computer analysis of the toothpaste market, for example, might show that some people buy toothpaste because it tastes good (the sensory segment), while others are concerned with the effect of clean teeth on their social image (the sociables). Others are worried about decay (the worriers), and some are just interested in the best value for their money (the economic men). Each of these market segments calls for a different marketing mix—although some of the four Ps may be similar. Finally, a marketing manager would have to decide which one (or more) of these segments would be the firm's target market(s).

You can see that computer-aided methods are only a help to the manager. Judgment is still needed to develop an original list of possible dimensions—and then to name the resulting groups.[5]

Segmenting applies to services, too

These computer methods can be used for both goods and services—and consumer goods and industrial goods.

In a study of the commercial banking market, for example, six different groups were found. These groups were called the "non-borrowers," "value

Computers can help segment markets.

seekers," "non-saving convenience seekers," "loan seekers," "one-stop bankers," and an "other" group (which was not particularly different on any dimension). Because of this study, changes were made in the bank's whole program—aiming at each of the markets—and treating them as the basis for separate strategies. Instead of the old—"we are friendly people"—advertising campaign, the bank focused on its various products and services—to try to appeal to the different markets. The non-borrowers were appealed to with messages about the bank's checking account, bank charge card, insurance, and investment counseling. For the convenience seekers, on the other hand, the bank talked about its teller service, express drive-in windows, overnight drop boxes, and deposit-by-mail accounts. To try to reach the loan seekers, the promotion stressed auto-loan checking accounts, mail-loan request forms, and loan programs through automobile dealers.[6]

FORECASTING TARGET MARKET POTENTIAL AND SALES

Estimates of target market potential and likely sales volumes are necessary for effective strategy planning. But a manager can't forecast *sales* without some possible plans. Sales are *not* just "out there for the taking." Market opportunities may be there—but whether a firm can change these opportunities into sales depends on the strategy it selects. Much of our discussion in this chapter, therefore, will be concerned with estimating **market potential**—what a whole market segment might buy—rather than a sales forecast. A **sales forecast** is an estimate of how much an industry or firm hopes to sell to a market segment. We may have to estimate the potential before we can talk about what share of that potential a firm *may* be able to win. In other cases—say when economic conditions are steady and no strategy changes are planned—sales may be forecasted directly.

TWO APPROACHES TO FORECASTING

Many methods are used in forecasting potential and sales—but they can be grouped under two basic approaches: (1) extending past behavior and (2) predicting future behavior. The large number of methods may seem confusing at first—but this variety is an advantage. Forecasts are so important that management often prefers to develop forecasts in two or three different ways—and then compare the differences before preparing a final forecast.

Extending past behavior

Trend extension can miss important turning points

When we forecast for existing products, we usually have some past data to go on. The basic approach—called **trend extension**—extends past experience into the future. See Figure 9–6.

Ideally—when extending past sales behavior—one should decide why sales vary. This is a difficult and time-consuming part of sales forecasting. Usually we can gather a lot of data about the product or market—or about the economic environment. But unless the *reason* for past sales variations is known, it's hard to predict in what direction—and by how much—sales will move. Graphing the data and statistical techniques—including correlation and regression analysis—can be useful here. These techniques are beyond our scope. They are discussed in beginning statistics courses.

Once we know why sales vary, we usually can develop a specific forecast. Sales may be moving directly up as population grows, for example. So we can just get an estimate of how population is expected to grow and project the impact on sales.

The weakness of the trend-extension method is that it assumes past conditions will continue unchanged into the future. In fact, the future is not always like the past. And, unfortunately, trend-extension will be wrong whenever there are important variations. For this reason—although they may extend past behavior for one estimate—most managers look for another way to help them forecast sharp economic changes.

Predicting future behavior takes judgment

When we try to predict what will happen in the future—instead of just extending the past—we have to use other methods and add a bit more

Figure 9–6: Straight-line trend projection—extends past sales into the future

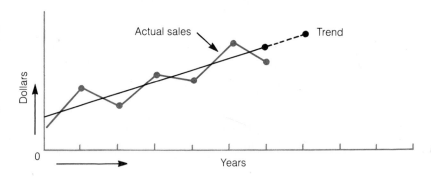

judgment. Some of these methods—to be discussed later—include juries of executive opinion, salespeople's estimates, surveys, panels, and market tests.

THREE LEVELS OF FORECAST ARE USEFUL

We are interested in forecasting the potential in specific market segments. To do this, it helps to make several kinds of forecasts.

Some economic conditions affect the entire economy. Others may influence only one industry. And some may affect only one company or one product's sales potential. For this reason, a common approach to sales forecasting is to:

1. Develop a *national income forecast* and use this to:
2. Develop an *industry sales forecast,* which then is used to:
3. Develop *specific company* and *product forecasts.*

Generally, a marketing manager does not have to make forecasts for the national economy or his industry. This kind of forecasting—basically trend projecting—is a specialty in itself. Fortunately, these forecasts are available in business and government publications. So managers can simply use one source's forecast—or combine several together. Unfortunately, however, the more targeted the marketing managers' previous segmenting efforts were, the less likely that available industry data will fit the firms' target markets. So the managers will have to try to estimate potential for their own company and specific products. This topic is discussed next.

FORECASTING COMPANY AND PRODUCT SALES BY EXTENDING PAST BEHAVIOR

Past sales can be extended

At the very least, a marketing manager ought to know what the firm's markets look like—and what it has sold to them in the past. A detailed

Managers use related variables to help forecast sales—such as building starts for lumber sales

sales analysis—for products and geographic areas—helps in projecting future results.

Simply extending past sales into the future may not seem like much of a forecasting method. But it is better than just assuming that next year's *total* sales will be the same as this year's.

Factor method includes more than time

Simple extension of past sales gives one forecast. But it usually is desirable to tie future sales to something more than the passage of time. The factor method tries to do this.

The **factor method** tries to forecast sales by finding a relation between the company's sales and some other factor (or factors). The basic formula is: something (past sales, industry sales, etc.) *times* some factor *equals* sales forecast. A **factor** is a variable which shows the relation of some variable to the item to be forecasted.

An example for bread

The following example for a bread manufacturer shows how forecasts can be made for many geographic market segments using the factor method and available data. This general approach can be useful for any firm—manufacturer, wholesaler, or retailer.

Analysis of past sales relationships showed that a particular bread manufacturer regularly sold one half of 1 percent (0.005) of the total retail food sales in its various target markets—this is a single factor. By using this single factor, estimates of the manufacturer's sales for the coming period could be obtained by multiplying a forecast of expected retail food sales by 0.005.

Retail food sales estimates are made each year by *Sales & Marketing Management* magazine. Figure 9–7 shows the kind of geographically detailed data available each year in its "Survey of Buying Power" issues.

Let's carry this bread illustration further, using the data in Figure 9–7 for Victoria, British Columbia. Victoria's food sales were $208,528,000 for the previous year. Start by simply accepting last year's food sales as an estimate of current year's sales. Then multiply the food sales estimate for Victoria by the 0.005 factor, (the firm's usual share in such markets). The manager would now have an estimate of current year's bread sales in Victoria. That is, last year's food sales estimate ($208,528,000) times 0.005 equals this year's bread sales estimate of $1,042,640.

The factor method is not limited to using just one factor—like in the food example. Several factors can be used together. For example, *Sales & Marketing Management* regularly gives a "buying power index" as a measure of the potential in different geographic areas. See Figure 9–7. This index combines the population in a market with the income and retail sales in that market. But whether one or several factors are included, the same basic approach is used with the factor method.

Figure 9–7: Sample of pages from *Sales & Marketing Management's* "Survey of Buying Power"[7]

PROVINCE Census Metropolitan Area	Total Pop. (thousands)	% Of Canada	Households (thousands)	% Of Canada	Total Retail Sales ($000)	% Of Canada	Food ($000)	Eating & Drinking Places ($000)	General Mdse. ($000)	Apparel & Accessories ($000)	Furniture/ Furnish./ Appliance ($000)	Auto-motive ($000)	Gas Stations ($000)	Hard-ware ($000)	Drug ($000)	Sales Activity	Buying Power	Quality
ALBERTA																		
Calgary	603.7	2.4687	216.7	2.5795	3,681,427	3.5512	733,379	321,786	636,894	215,215	173,545	870,745	226,226	7,443	83,749	144	3.0283	123
Edmonton	665.5	2.7214	237.9	2.8318	3,640,586	3.5118	691,399	300,821	822,695	188,339	150,295	550,204	191,183	16,224	141,117	129	3.0932	114
BRITISH COLUMBIA																		
Vancouver	1,270.2	5.1945	481.2	5.7282	6,386,760	6.1608	1,229,476	623,842	1,278,086	255,879	269,949	1,239,577	332,197	25,747	269,938	119	5.8714	113
Victoria	233.6	.9552	96.2	1.1448	1,090,846	1.0523	208,528	87,461	248,253	43,270	49,821	165,867	55,565	4,102	34,990	110	1.0141	106
MANITOBA																		
Winnipeg	587.4	2.4021	220.7	2.6277	2,564,686	2.4741	624,087	236,673	517,387	98,890	76,997	440,307	116,076	5,521	72,658	103	2.3759	99
TOTAL ABOVE AREAS	13,721.2	56.1105	4,923.6	58.6026	62,603,458	60.3886	15,038,121	5,962,498	9,501,525	3,375,256	2,369,743	11,361,712	4,033,318	404,827	2,023,384	108	59.7360	106

SMM ESTIMATES — $$ EFFECTIVE BUYING INCOME—1981 — % of Households by EBI Group: (A) $0–$4,999 (B) $5,000–$7,999 (C) $8,000–$9,999 (D) $10,000–$14,999 (E) $15,000 & Over

PROVINCE Census Metropolitan Area	Total EBI ($000)	% Of Canada	Per Capita EBI	Average Hsld EBI	A	B	C	D	E
ALBERTA									
Calgary	6,243,402	2.9384	10,342	28,811	3.4	5.8	5.3	25.9	59.6
Edmonton	6,354,675	2.9908	9,549	26,712	2.8	4.7	4.4	20.7	67.4
BRITISH COLUMBIA									
Vancouver	12,681,946	5.9687	9,984	26,355	4.6	4.2	3.4	19.5	68.3
Victoria	2,155,416	1.0144	9,227	22,406	5.2	5.2	4.5	19.4	65.7
MANITOBA									
Winnipeg	4,900,489	2.3063	8,343	22,204	5.4	6.1	5.4	33.6	49.5

PROVINCE Census Metropolitan Area	Total EBI ($000)	% Of Canada	Per Capita EBI	Average Hsld EBI	A	B	C	D	E
ONTARIO									
Hamilton	5,214,596	2.4543	9,607	27,174	4.8	3.1	2.5	18.2	71.4
Kitchener	3,125,570	1.4710	10,815	30,855	3.5	5.3	5.3	27.9	58.0
London	3,166,295	1.4902	11,125	29,454	4.9	4.8	4.0	30.9	55.4
Oshawa	1,513,901	.7125	9,692	29,170	3.2	3.0	2.8	16.7	74.3
Ottawa-Hull	8,037,228	3.7828	11,163	30,759	3.3	4.4	4.2	21.6	66.5
St. Catharines-Niagara	2,625,481	1.2357	8,619	24,514	5.2	4.7	3.7	17.8	68.6
Sudbury	1,188,840	.5596	7,979	24,361	2.3	2.1	1.9	8.5	85.2
Thunder Bay	1,137,114	.5351	9,359	26,819	3.4	2.4	2.2	10.0	82.0
Toronto	29,778,274	14.0150	9,870	28,156	3.3	3.3	3.5	21.5	68.4
Windsor	2,278,068	1.0722	9,260	26,005	5.0	3.9	3.3	11.1	76.7
TOTAL ABOVE AREAS	129,173,257	60.7952	9,414	26,236	3.9	4.8	4.6	23.4	63.3

PREDICTING FUTURE BEHAVIOR CALLS FOR MORE JUDGMENT AND SOME OPINIONS

The methods discussed above make use of quantitative data—projecting past experience and assuming that the future will be somewhat like the past. But this may be risky in competitive markets. Usually, it is desirable to add judgment to hard data to obtain other forecasts—before making the final forecast.

Jury of executive opinion adds judgment

One of the oldest and simplest methods of forecasting—the **jury of executive opinion**—combines the opinions of experienced executives—perhaps from marketing, production, finance, purchasing, and top management. Basically, each executive is asked to estimate market potential and sales for the coming years.

The main advantage of the jury approach is that it can be done quickly and easily. On the other hand, the results may not be very good. There may be too much extending of the past. Some of the executives may have little contact with outside market influences. At the best, however, it could alert the forecasters to important changes in customer demand or competition.

Estimates from salespeople can help, too

Using salespeople's estimates to forecast is like the jury approach. But salespeople are more likely than home office managers to be familiar with customer reactions—and what competitors are doing. Their estimates are especially useful in industrial markets—where a limited number of customers may be well known to the salespeople. But this approach is useful in any type of market. Good retail clerks have a "feel" for the market—their opinions should not be ignored.

Three limitations concerning the use of salespeople's estimates should be kept in mind.

First, salespeople usually don't know about possible changes in the national economic climate—or even about changes in the company's marketing mix.

Second, salespeople may have little to offer if they change jobs often. Finally, care is needed if the estimates are used for other purposes. If bonuses are based on these sales estimates, for example, the estimates may be low to make it easier to go over the estimate. But, if the promotion money given to each territory is based on sales prospects, the estimates may be high. In both cases, it is only human for salespeople to suit their forecasts to their own advantage.

With these limitations in mind, salespeople's estimates can provide another forecast for comparison before the final forecast is made.

Surveys, panels, and market tests

Special marketing research surveys of final buyers, retailers, and wholesalers can be useful. Some firms use panels of stores or final consum-

Salespeople's estimates can be useful in forcasting because they are in the field and know the market.

ers to keep track of buying behavior. This helps them decide just when extending past behavior is not enough.

Survey methods are sometimes combined with market tests—when the company wants to estimate the reaction of customers to possible changes in the marketing mix. A market test might show that a product increases its share of the market by 10 percent when its price is dropped 1 cent below competition. But this extra business might be quickly lost if the price were increased 1 cent above competition.

Such market experiments can help the marketing manager make good estimates of future sales when one or more of the four Ps are changed.

ACCURACY OF FORECASTS

The accuracy of forecasts varies a lot. Annual forecasts of national income may be accurate within 5 percent. Industry sales forecasts are usually accurate within 10 percent.

When estimates are made for individual products, there is even more chance for errors. Where style and new ideas are involved, forecast errors of 10 to 20 percent for established products are common. The accuracy of specific new-product forecasts is even lower! Many new products fail completely.[8]

CONCLUSION

This chapter discusses the process of segmenting markets—to find potentially attractive target markets. Some people try to segment markets by breaking them down into smaller submarkets. But this can lead to poor results. Instead, segmenting should be seen as a gathering process. The more similar customers' needs, the larger the market segments can be. Four standards for evaluating market segments were presented.

Ways of developing better strategies—the single, multiple, and combined target market approaches—basically segmenting and combining—were discussed. Segmenting aims the firm's efforts at smaller, more homogeneous target markets. Combining, on the other hand, builds up the size of a firm's target market by combining smaller, homogeneous sub-markets into one larger target market.

We also talked about several approaches to forecasting market potential and sales. The most common approach is to extend past behavior into the future. Reasonably good results can be obtained if market conditions are fairly stable. Methods here include extension of past sales data and the factor method. We saw that projecting the past into the future is risky when big market changes are likely. To make up for this possible weakness, marketers must use their own experience and judgment. They also may be able to bring in the judgment of others—using the jury of executive opinion method and salespeople's estimates. They may also use surveys, panels, and market tests.

We saw that the accuracy of forecasts depends on how general a forecast is being made—with the most error when specific forecasts for products, and especially for new products, are made.

Even though forecasts are subject to error, they are still necessary to help the firm choose among alternative strategic plans. Sloppy forecasting could lead to poor strategies. No forecasting at all is stupid!

QUESTIONS FOR DISCUSSION

1. Explain what market segmentation is.

2. Explain the three approaches to developing market-oriented strategies for product-markets.

3. Distinguish between segmenters and combiners. Further, explain which approach is being followed if cold cream is offered in a new, more distinctively shaped jar. Which approach is being followed if only the label is changed to gold foil for distinctiveness?

4. List three products that seem to be offered by segmenters and three that seem to be offered by combiners. Do any of these products have anything in common?

5. List the types of potential segmenting dimensions and explain which you would try to apply first, second, and third in a particular situation. If the nature of the situation would affect your answer, explain how.

6. Explain why "first-time" segmentation efforts may be very disappointing.

7. Illustrate the concept that segmenting is a gathering process by referring to the apparent admissions policies of your own college and a nearby college or university.

8. (a) Evaluate how "good" the seven markets identified in the market for apartments (Figure 9–5) are with respect to the four standards for selecting good market segments. (b) Same as (a) but evaluate the four corner markets in the British home decorating market (Figure 2–10).

9. Review the types of segmenting dimensions listed in Figure 9–3 and Table 9–2 and select the ones you feel should be combined to fully explain the market you, personally, would be in if you were planning to buy a new automobile today. Do not hesitate to list several dimensions, but when you have done so, then attempt to develop a shorthand name, like "swinger," to describe your own personal market. Try to estimate what proportion of the total automobile market would be accounted for by your market.

10. Apply the seven-step approach to segmenting consumer markets to the college-age market for off-campus recreation, which can include eating and drinking. Then, evaluate how well the needs in these market segments are being met in your geographic area. Is there an obvious breakthrough opportunity waiting for someone?

11. Apply the seven-step approach to segmenting industrial markets for a new "super glue" which can be useful for basic production processes as well as almost any kind of repair job, because it can bond together almost any kinds of surfaces.

12. Explain the difference between a forecast of market opportunities and a sales forecast.

13. Suggest a plausible explanation for sales fluctuations for (a) bicycles, (b) baby food, (c) motor boats, (d) baseball gloves, (e) wheat, (f) woodworking tools, and (g) latex for rubber-based paint.

14. Discuss the relative accuracy of the various forecasting techniques. Explain why some are more accurate than others.

15. Explain (in your own words) what the factor method is and how to use it.

16. Given the following annual sales data for a company that is not planning any spectacular marketing strategy changes, forecast sales for the coming year (7) and explain your method and reasoning.

	(a)		(b)
Year	Sales (in 000s)	Year	Sales (in 000s)
1	$200	1	$160
2	230	2	155
3	210	3	165
4	220	4	160
5	200	5	170
6	220	6	165

17. Discuss the relative market potential of Oshawa and Sudbury, Ontario, for: (a) prepared cereals, (b) automobiles, and (c) furniture.

18. Discuss how a General Motors market analyst might analyze the potential for an electric car which might be suitable for salespeople, commuters, homemakers, farmers, and perhaps other groups. The analyst is trying to consider the potential in terms of possible price levels—$2,000, $4,000, $6,000, $8,000, and $10,000—and driving ranges—10 miles, 20 miles, 50 miles, 100 miles, and 200 miles—which would typically be desired or needed before recharging. He is assuming that gasoline-powered vehicles would become illegal for use within the major urban cities. Further, it is expected that while personal gasoline-driven cars still would be used in rural and suburban areas, they would not be permitted within some suburban areas, especially around the major metropolitan areas.

SUGGESTED CASES

4. Redi, Limited
6. The Capri
17. New Start Furniture

When you finish this chapter, you should:

1. Understand what "Product" really means.

2. Know the differences among the various consumer and industrial goods classes.

3. Understand how the goods classes can help a marketing manager plan marketing strategies.

4. Understand the stragtegic importance of packaging.

5. Understand what branding is—and how it can be used in strategy planning.

6. Recognize the important new terms (shown in red).

ELEMENTS OF PRODUCT PLANNING

10

The product must satisfy customers—what they want is what they'll get.

Developing the "right" product isn't easy—because customer needs and attitudes keep changing. Further, *most customers want some combination of goods and services in their product.* We'll talk about this first.

Then, to help you understand marketing strategy planning better, we'll talk about some goods classes. The consumer goods and industrial goods classes introduced in this chapter should be studied carefully. They can speed your development as a marketing strategy planner.

We will also talk about packaging and branding. Most products need some packaging. And both physical goods and services should be branded. A successful marketer wants to be sure that satisfied customers will know what to ask for the next time.

In summary, we will talk about the strategic decisions of manufacturers—or middlemen—who must make these product, packaging, and branding decisions. These strategic decisions are shown in Figure 10–1.

WHAT IS A PRODUCT?

Customers buy satisfaction, not parts

First, we have to decide what we mean by a "product."

If we sell an automobile, are we selling a certain number of nuts and bolts, some sheet metal, an engine, and four wheels?

Figure 10–1: Strategy planning for Product

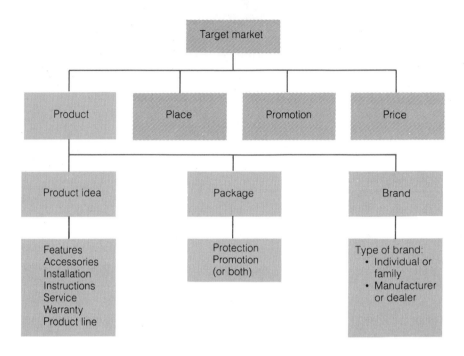

If we sell a detergent to be used in a washing machine, are we selling several chemical raw materials?

If we sell a delivery service, are we selling so much wear and tear on a delivery truck—and so much operator fatigue?

The answer to all these questions is *no.* Instead, what we are really selling is the satisfaction, use, or profit the customer wants.

All the customers ask is that their cars look good—and keep running. They don't care how they were made. Further, they want to clean with detergent—not analyze it. And when they order something, they don't really care how much out of the way the driver had to go—or where he has been. They just want their package.

Similarly, when producers and middlemen buy products, they are interested in the profit they will make from their purchase—through its use and resale—not how the products were made.

Product means the needs-satisfying offering of a firm. The idea of product as potential customer satisfactions or benefits is very important. Many business managers—trained in the production side of business—get wrapped up in the number of nuts and bolts, the fertilizer application per acre, and other technical problems. Middlemen, too, are often concerned with technical details. But while these are important *to them,* they have little effect on the way most customers view the product. What matters to customers is how *they* see what is being offered. And these two views may be far apart.

Product is more than just a physical thing

The Product is more than just a physical good with its related features. It includes accessories, installation, instruction on use, the package, perhaps a brand name which fills some psychological needs, a warranty, and confidence that service will be available after the purchase.

Product may only be a service

Product may not include a physical good at all! The product of a barber or hair stylist is the trimming or styling of your hair. A medical doctor may just look at you—neither taking anything away nor giving you anything physical. Nevertheless, each satisfies needs—and provides a product in the sense we will use "product" in this book. Figure 10–2 emphasizes this point by showing that a Product could range from 100 percent physical good—such as commodities like common nails or dried beans—to 100 percent service. Most products are a blend of physical goods *and* services.[1] This shows why it is so important to fully understand the needs and attitudes of target customers—and then to develop a *complete* product to satisfy their needs.

Need satisfaction comes from the whole "product"

This bigger view of a product must be understood completely—it's too easy to slip into a *physical good* point of view. In fact, marketing has usually focused on physical goods—almost ignoring services. Actually, however, services are a very important—and growing—share of total national income. We certainly can't ignore services. But we don't want to just focus on services either.

Instead, we want to think of a product in terms of the *needs it satisfies.* If the objective of a firm is to satisfy customer needs, it must see that service may be part of or may be *the* product—and has to be provided as part of the marketing mix. An automobile without any repair service, for example, is not a very useful product.

Whole product lines must be developed too

We have been talking about a single product. But customer needs cannot always be satisfied by one product. Manufacturers, wholesalers and retailers may have to offer complete lines of products to satisfy their customers. This makes the job of product planning harder. But if this is what customers want, then complete lines have to be offered.

For convenience, we will focus mainly on developing one marketing strategy at a time. But you should remember that several physical goods and/or services might have to be planned—to develop an effective marketing program for a whole company.

Figure 10–2: Possible blends of goods and services in a product

100% Good	50/50	100% Service
Common nails Dried beans	Auto rustproofing Restaurant meal	Medical exam Radio program

GOODS CLASSES AFFECT MARKETING STRATEGY PLANNING

To avoid trying to treat *every* product as unique when planning strategies, it would help to have some goods classes which are related to marketing mixes. Luckily, products can be classified this way. These goods classes will be a useful starting point for developing marketing mixes for new products—and evaluating present mixes.

Goods class depends on who will use the product

Whether a product should be treated as a consumer or industrial good depends on who will use it. **Consumer goods** are products meant for final consumers. **Industrial goods** are products meant for use in producing other products. All goods fit into one of these two groups. Customer research supports the idea that these goods classes are useful in marketing mix planning.[2]

CONSUMER GOODS CLASSES

Based on customer buying behavior

Workable consumer goods classes are based on the way people buy products. Consumer goods can be divided into four groups: (1) convenience goods, (2) shopping goods, (3) specialty goods, and (4) unsought goods. See Figure 10–3 for a summary of how these goods classes are related to a marketing mix.

CONVENIENCE GOODS—USUALLY PURCHASED QUICKLY

Convenience goods are products the customer needs but isn't willing to spend much time shopping for. Examples are: cigarettes, soap, drugs, newspapers, magazines, chewing gum, candy, and most grocery products. These products are bought often, require little service or selling, don't cost much, and may even be bought by habit.

Figure 10–3: Consumer goods classes and marketing mix planning

1. *Convenience goods.*
   a. Staples—need maximum exposure—need widespread distribution at low cost.
   b. Impulse goods—need maximum exposure—need widespread distribution but with assurance of preferred display or counter position.
   c. Emergency goods—need widespread distribution near probable point of use.
2. *Shopping goods.*
   a. Homogeneous—need enough exposure to facilitate price comparison.
   b. Heterogeneous—need adequate representation, in major shopping districts or large shopping centers near other, similar shopping goods.
3. *Specialty goods*—can have limited availability, but in general should be treated as a convenience or shopping good (in whichever category product would normally be included), to reach persons not yet sold on its specialty-goods status.
4. *Unsought goods*—need attention directed to product and aggressive promotion in outlets, or must be available in places where similar products would be sought.

Convenience goods are of three types—staples, impulse goods, and emergency goods—again based on *how customers think about products*—not the features of the products themselves.

Staples—purchased and used regularly

Staples are goods which are bought often and routinely—without much thought. Examples include food and drug items used regularly in every household. Here, branding can become important—to help customers cut shopping effort.

Staples are sold in convenient places like food stores, drugstores, discount and hardware stores, and vending machines. Some customers want convenience so much that they have milk, bread, and newspapers delivered directly to their homes.

Shopping for staples may not even be planned. Many shoppers plan meals in the store—and modern supermarkets are laid out to make this easier. "Go-togethers" like strawberries and sponge cake—or ice cream and chocolate sauce—are placed next to each other to encourage unplanned buying.

Impulse goods—bought immediately on sight

Impulse goods are goods which are bought quickly—as unplanned purchases—because of a strongly felt need. True impulse goods are items that the customer decides to buy on sight, may have bought the same way many times before, and wants "right now."

If a shopper passes a street corner vendor, for example, and gets a sudden urge for ice cream, that ice cream bar is an impulse good. But if the same shopper bought a box of ice cream bars in the supermarket as a family dessert, the bars would be staples—because the shopper was looking for a dessert.

There is an important difference between buying something to satisfy a current need and buying for later use. If the customer doesn't buy an impulse good immediately, the need may disappear—and no purchase will be made. But if the customer needs a dessert, a purchase will be made sometime.

This difference is important because it affects Place—and the whole marketing mix. Place is very important for impulse goods. If the buyer doesn't see them at the "right" time, the sale may be lost. As a result, special methods are developed for selling impulse goods. They are put where they'll be seen and bought—near front doors, near the checkout counters, or on display shelves in front of the store.

Emergency goods— purchased only when urgently needed

Emergency goods are goods which are purchased only when the need is great. Little shopping is done. The customer needs the product immediately. Price isn't important. Examples are ambulance services, umbrellas or raincoats during a rainstorm, and tire chains during a snowstorm.

Some retailers carry emergency goods to meet such needs. They know that many potential customers will face certain kinds of emergencies. And they set up their operations to serve them. Small gasoline stations in rural areas—and service stations on toll-roads and thruways—carry tires to

Emergency goods are purchased with little or no shopping because the need is immediate.

meet emergency needs. The buyer probably could get a tire at a lower price back home—but with a blowout, any price is right.

Some small, neighborhood grocery stores meet the ''fill-in'' needs of customers who need a few items between weekly supermarket trips. Usually these stores charge higher prices. But customers will pay it because they think of these goods as ''emergencies.'' One study found that almost 80 percent of households use such a fill-in store.[3] In the last 20 years, chains of such convenience food stores have been spreading. They provide emergency service—staying open ''7 till 11'' and stocking items that are needed in a hurry.

SHOPPING GOODS

Shopping goods are those products a customer feels are worth the time and effort to compare with competing products.

Shopping goods can be divided into two types—depending on what customers are comparing: (1) homogeneous and (2) heterogeneous shopping goods.

Homogeneous shopping goods—the price must be right

Homogeneous shopping goods are shopping goods that the customer sees as basically the same—and wants at the lowest price. Some consumers feel that certain sizes and types of refrigerators, television sets, washing machines, and even automobiles are basically similar. They are shopping for the best price.

In one study of automobile purchasing behavior, about half of the people wanted the ''best price'' or ''best deal'' and did shop at more than one dealership.[4] Three out of four supermarket shoppers shop for advertised specials every week.[5]

This buyer interest in price helps explain why some retailers emphasize "low prices" and "price cuts."

Low-price items are seen this way, too

Even some inexpensive items like butter and coffee may be thought of as homogeneous shopping goods. Some customers carefully read food store advertising for the lowest prices. Then they go from store to store getting the items. (This is called "cherry picking" in the food business.)

Heterogeneous shopping goods—the product must be right

Heterogeneous shopping goods are shopping goods that the customer sees as different—and wants to inspect for quality and suitability. Examples are furniture, dishes, some cameras, and clothing. Style and/or features are more important than price.

Even if an item costs only $5 or $10, consumers may look in three or four stores to be sure they have done a good job of shopping.

Price isn't ignored. But for nonstandardized goods, it is harder to compare price. Once the customer has found the right product, price may not matter—providing it is "reasonable."

Branding may be less important for heterogeneous shopping goods. The more consumers want to make their own comparisons, the less they depend on brand names and labels.

Often the buyer of heterogeneous shopping goods not only wants—but expects—some kind of help in buying. And, if the product is expensive, the buyer may want extra service—such as alteration of clothing or installation of appliances.

SPECIALTY GOODS

Specialty goods are consumer goods that the customer really wants—and will make a special effort to buy. Shopping for a specialty good doesn't

People are willing to search for their specialty goods.

mean comparing—the buyer wants that special product and is willing to search for it. It is not the extent of searching, but the customer's *willingness* to search that makes it a specialty good.

Don't want substitutes!   Specialty goods don't have to be expensive, once-in-a-lifetime purchases. *Any* branded item that develops a strong "customer franchise" may win specialty goods status. Consumers have been observed asking for a drug product by its brand name and—when offered a chemically identical substitute—actually leaving the store in anger.

UNSOUGHT GOODS

Unsought goods are consumer goods that potential customers do not yet want—or know they can buy. Therefore, they don't search for them at all. In fact, consumers probably wouldn't buy these goods if they saw them—unless Promotion could show their value.

There are two types of unsought goods: new unsought and regularly unsought.

New unsought goods are products offering really new ideas that potential customers don't know about yet. Informative promotion can help convince consumers to accept or even seek out the products—ending their unsought status.

Regularly unsought goods are products—like gravestones, life insurance, and encyclopedias—that may stay unsought but not unbought forever. These products may be some of the biggest purchases a family ever makes—but few people would even drive around the block to find them. There may be a need—but the potential customers are not motivated to satisfy it. And there probably is little hope that they will move out of the unsought category for most consumers. For this kind of product, Promotion is *very* important.

ONE PRODUCT MAY BE SEEN AS SEVERAL CONSUMER GOODS

We have been looking at one good at a time. But the same product might be seen in different ways by different target markets *at the same time.*

The marketing manager might find that the market consists of several groups of people—each of which has similar attitudes toward the product. This is shown in Figure 10–4. This diagram groups people in terms of their willingness to shop, and by brand familiarity. It is a simple way of summarizing our discussion of consumer goods. Each of these groups might need a different marketing mix.

A tale of four motels   Motels are a good example of a service that can be seen as *four different* kinds of goods. Some tired motorists are satisfied with the first motel they come to—a convenience good. Other travelers shop for the kind of facilities they want at a fair price—a heterogeneous shopping good. Others

Figure 10–4: How potential customers might view some product[6]

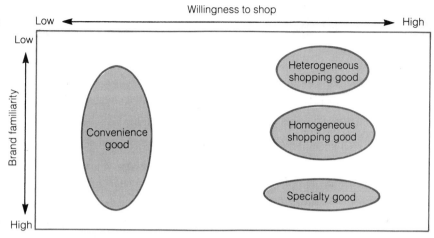

Note: The number of people holding each view is indicated roughly by the size of the cluster.

shop for just basic facilities at the lowest price—a homogeneous shopping good. And others study tourist guides, talk with traveling friends, and phone ahead to reserve a place in a recommended motel—a specialty good.

Perhaps one motel could satisfy all potential customers. But it would be hard to produce a marketing mix attractive to everyone—easy access for convenience, good facilities at the right price for shopping goods buyers, and qualities special enough to attract the specialty goods travelers. As a result, we see very different kinds of motels—seemingly (but not really) competing with each other.

Anyone planning new strategies can improve their understanding of what is needed by studying potential target markets in terms of these goods classes. Of course, strategy planners would like to know more about potential customers than the consumer goods classes can tell them. But they are good place to start.

INDUSTRIAL GOODS CLASSES

Industrial goods buyers do little shopping—especially compared to consumer goods buyers. Usually the seller comes to the buyer. This means that product classes based on shopping behavior are not useful for industrial goods.

Industrial goods classes are based on how buyers see products—and how the products are to be used. Expensive and/or long-lasting products are treated differently than inexpensive items. Products that become a part of a firm's own product are seen differently from those which only aid production. Finally, the size of a particular purchase can make a difference. An air compressor may not be very important to a buyer for General Motors, but it might be very important for a small garage owner.

The classes of industrial goods are: (1) installations, (2) accessory

Figure 10–5: Industrial goods and marketing mix planning

1. *Installations.*
   a. Buildings (used) and land rights—need widespread and/or knowledgeable contacts, depending upon specialized nature of product.
   b. Buildings (new)—*need technical and experienced personal contact, probably at top management level (multiple buying influence).*
   c. Major equipment.
      i. *Custom-made*—need technical (design) contacts by person able to visualize and design applications, and present to high-level and technical management.
      ii. Standard—need experienced (not necessarily highly technical) contacts by person able to visualize applications and present to high-level and technical management.
2. *Accessory equipment*—need fairly widespread and numerous contacts by experienced and sometimes technically trained personnel.
3. *Raw materials.*
   a. Farm products—need contacts with many small farmer producers and fairly widespread contact with users.
   b. Natural products—need fairly widespread contacts with users.
4. *Component parts and materials*—need technical contacts to determine specifications required—widespread contacts usually not necessary.
5. *Supplies.*
   a. Maintenance—need very widespread distribution for prompt delivery.
   b. Repairs—need widespread distribution for some, and prompt service from factory for others (depends on customers' preferences).
   c. Operating supplies—need fair to widespread distribution for prompt delivery.
6. *Services*—most need very widespread availability.

equipment, (3) raw materials, (4) component parts and materials, (5) supplies, and (6) services. See Figure 10–5 for a summary of how these goods classes are related to what is needed in a marketing mix.

INSTALLATIONS—MAJOR CAPITAL ITEMS

Installations are important long-lasting capital items—durable goods which are depreciated over many years. They include buildings and land rights, custom-made equipment, and standard equipment. Buildings and custom-made equipment generally require special negotiations for each individual product—because they are one of a kind. Standard major equipment is more homogeneous—and is treated more routinely. All installations, however, are important enough to require high-level—and even top-management—consideration.

Size of market small at any time

Installations are long-lasting goods—so they are not bought very often. The number of potential buyers at any particular time usually is small. For custom-made machines, there may be only a half-dozen potential customers—compared to a thousand or more potential buyers for similar standard machines.

Potential customers are generally in the same industry. Their plants are likely to be near to each other—which makes Promotion easier. A unique situation exists in Canada, with the majority of all manufacturing located in the "megalopolis" between Quebec City and Windsor, Ontario, a stretch some 750 miles long and 100 miles wide. Various industries are concentrated in areas within this stretch—oil refining in east-end Montreal and steel in Hamilton are two examples. However, mining and forestry are located well outside the megalopolis, in Canada's far north.

Buying needs basically economic

Buying needs are basically economic and concerned with the performance of the installation over its expected life. After comparing expected performance to present costs and figuring interest, the expected return on capital can be determined. Yet emotional needs—such as a desire for industry leadership and status—also may be involved.

Installations may have to be leased or rented

Since installations are expensive, the producer often will lease or rent the product—rather than sell it. Examples are buildings and land rights and some special equipment—including computers.

Specialized services are needed as part of the product

Since the expected return on an installation is based on efficient operation, the sales contract may require regular service visits. Service people may even be permanently attached to the company. Computer manufacturers sometimes station service people with the machines. The cost is included in the price—or rent.

ACCESSORY EQUIPMENT—IMPORTANT BUT SHORT-LIVED CAPITAL ITEMS

Accessory equipment are short-lived capital items. They are the tools and equipment used in production or office activities. Examples include portable drills, sanding machines, electric lift trucks, typewriters, filing cases, accounting machines, wheelbarrows, hand trucks, and small lathes.

Since these products cost less and last a shorter time than installations, the multiple buying influence is less important. Operating people and purchasing managers—rather than top-level managers—may do the buying.

Installations are expensive and involve multiple buying influence.

*More target markets
requiring different
marketing mixes*

Accessories are more standardized than installations. And they are usually needed by more customers! A large, special-purpose belt sanding machine, for example, might be produced as a custom-made installation for woodworking firms. But small portable sanding machines would be considered accessory equipment. Since there are many more possible customers and less geographic concentration, different marketing mixes would be needed for accessory equipment than for installations.

*Might prefer to lease or
rent*

Leasing or renting accessories is attractive to some target markets because the costs can be treated as expenses. A manufacturer of electric lift trucks, for instance, was able to expand its sales by selling the basic truck outright—but charging for the expensive battery system by the amount of time it was used. This increased sales because, as one of the company managers said: "Nobody worries about costs which are buried as an operating expense."[7]

RAW MATERIALS—FARM PRODUCTS AND NATURAL PRODUCTS ARE EXPENSE ITEMS

*Become part of a
physical good*

Raw materials are unprocessed industrial goods—such as logs, iron ore, sand, and freshly caught fish—that are handled as little as is needed to move them to the next step in the production process. Unlike installations and accessories, raw materials become part of a physical product—and are expense items.

We can break raw materials into two categories: (1) farm products, and (2) natural products. **Farm products** are grown by farmers—examples are cotton, wheat, strawberries, sugar cane, cattle, hogs, poultry, eggs, and milk. **Natural products** are products which occur in nature—such as fish and game, lumber and maple syrup, and copper, zinc, iron ore, oil, and coal.

FARM PRODUCTS ARE VARIABLE IN QUALITY AND QUANTITY

*Involve grading, storage,
and/or transportation*

The need for grading is one of the important differences between farm products and other industrial goods. Nature produces what it will—and someone must sort and grade farm products to satisfy various market segments. Some of the top grades of fruits and vegetables find their way into the consumer goods market. The lower grades are treated as industrial goods—and used in juices, sauces, and frozen pies.

Most farm products are produced seasonally—yet the demand for them is fairly constant all year. As a result, storage and transportation are important in their marketing process.

As noted, buyers of industrial goods usually don't seek suppliers. This complicates the marketing of farm products. The many small farms usually are widely scattered—sometimes far from potential buyers. Selling direct to final users would be difficult. So Place and Promotion are important in marketing mixes for these products.

Natural product production can be varied from year to year to meet demand.

NATURAL PRODUCTS—QUANTITIES ARE MORE ADJUSTABLE

In contrast to the farm products market with its many producers, natural products are produced by fewer and larger companies. There are some exceptions—such as the coal and lumber industries—but oligopoly conditions are common.

Typically, the total supply of natural products is limited—and can't be expanded easily. But the supply harvested or mined in any one year is adjustable.

Most of the products are bulky and have transportation problems. But storage is less important—since few are perishable. And some can be produced year-round. Major exceptions are fish and game—which have "runs" or seasons—and are more like farm products than forest or mineral products in their marketing patterns.

As with farm products, buyers of natural products usually need specific grades and dependable supply sources—to be sure of continued production in their own plants. Large buyers, therefore, often try to buy—or at least control—their sources of supply. This is easier than with farm products—because fewer and larger production facilities are involved.

One way to control supply sources is **vertical integration**—here meaning ownership of the natural product source by the user. Examples are paper manufacturers who control timber resources, oil refiners who control crude oil sources, and tire manufacturers who control rubber plantations.

Sellers who do not integrate with users usually find that their customers want to be sure of dependable sources of supply. This is often done through contracts—perhaps negotiated by top-level managers—using standard grades or specifications.

COMPONENT PARTS AND MATERIALS—IMPORTANT EXPENSE ITEMS

The sum is no better than . . .

Component parts and materials are expense items which have had more processing than raw materials. They require different marketing mixes

Component parts need only minor processing and/or assembly to complete a finished product.

than raw materials—even though they both become part of a finished product.

Component *parts* include those items that are (1) finished and ready for assembly or (2) nearly finished—requiring only minor processing (such as grinding or polishing) before being assembled into the final product. Examples are automobile batteries, small motors, and tires—all of which go directly into a finished product.

Component *materials* are items such as wire, paper, textiles, or cement. They have already been processed but must be processed further before becoming part of the final product.

Multiple buying influences

Component parts are often custom-made. Much negotiation may be necessary between the engineering staffs of both buyer and seller to arrive at the proper specifications. If the price of the item is high—or if it is extremely important in the final product—top-level managers may become involved.

Other components are produced to commonly accepted standards or specifications—and produced in quantity. Production people in the buying firm may specify quality—but the purchasing manager will do the buying. And he will want several dependable sources of supply.

Since components go into the firm's own product, quality is important. The buyer's own name—and whole marketing mix—are at stake. Quality may be less important for component parts that are well branded (such as a tire or spark plug). The blame for a defective product can fall upon the component supplier. Generally, however, a buyer will try to buy from component sources that help assure a good product.

SUPPLIES—EVERYBODY WANTS THESE EXPENSE ITEMS, BUT HOW MUCH?

Supplies are expense items that do not become a part of the final product. They may be treated less seriously by buyers.

They are called MRO items

Supplies can be divided into three categories: (1) maintenance, (2) repair, and (3) operating supplies—giving them their common name: "MRO items."

Maintenance items include such things as paint, nails, light bulbs, sweeping compounds, brooms, and window-cleaning equipment. Repair items are nuts and bolts or parts needed to repair existing equipment. Operating supplies include lubricating oils and greases, grinding compounds, coal, typing paper, ink, pencils, and paper clips.

Important operating supplies

Some operating supplies are needed regularly—and in large amounts. They receive special treatment from buyers. Some companies buy coal and fuel oil in carload quantities. Usually there are several sources for such homogeneous products—and large volumes may be purchased in highly competitive markets. Or contracts may be negotiated, perhaps by high-level managers.

Maintenance and most operating supplies

These items are like convenience goods. They are so numerous that a buyer can't possibly be an expert in buying all of them.

Each requisition for maintenance and small operating supplies may be for relatively few items. The purchase requisitions can amount to only $1 to $2. Although the cost of handling a purchase order may be from $5 to $10, the item will be ordered—because it is needed. But not much time will be spent on it.

Branding can become important for such products. It makes product identification and buying easier for such "nuisance" items. The width of assortment and the dependability of the seller are important when buying supplies. Middlemen usually handle the many supply items.

Repair items

The original supplier of installations or accessory equipment may be the only source of supply for repairs and parts. The cost of repairs in relation to the cost of a production break-down may be so small that buyers are willing to pay the price charged—whatever it is.

SERVICES—YOU EXPENSE THEM

Services are expense items which support the operations of a firm. Engineering or management consulting services can improve the plant layout or the operation of the company. Design services can supply designs for the physical plant, products, and graphic materials. Maintenance services can handle window-cleaning, painting, or general housekeeping. Other companies can supply in-plant lunches and piped-in music—to improve employee morale and production.

The cost of buying services outside the firm is compared with the cost of having company people do them. For special skills needed only occasionally, an outsider can be the best source. And service specialists are growing in number in our complex economy.

Good packaging can cut costs by protecting products and making handling easier.

May improve or create a "new" product

A new package can make *the* important difference in a new marketing strategy—by improving the total product. A better box, wrapper, can, or bottle may even let a relatively small, unknown firm compete successfully with the established competitors. Carter Products Co.—new to the men's toiletries field—introduced its first product, Rise shaving cream, in aerosol cans and was able to compete effectively. The usual tube and carton might not have been so successful.

A package change often creates a "new" product by giving customers a more desirable quantity. Packaging frozen vegetables in 1-pound packages—instead of 10-ounce packages—served larger families better. The smaller packages held too little for them—while two packages held too much.

Multiple packs can be the basis of a new marketing strategy, too. Consumer surveys showed that some customers were buying several units at a time of products like soft drinks, beer, and frozen orange juice. This suggested a "new" market. Manufacturers tried packaging in 4-, 6-, and 8-packs—and have been very successful.

May lower total distribution costs

Better protective packaging is especially important to manufacturers and wholesalers. They often have to pay the cost of goods damaged in shipment. There are also costs for settling such claims—and getting them settled is a nuisance. Goods damaged in shipment also may delay production—or cause lost sales.

Retailers need good packaging too. Packaging which provides better protection can reduce stores' costs—by cutting breakage, preventing discoloration, and stopping theft. Packages that are easier to handle can cut costs by speeding price marking, improving handling and display, and saving space.

May be "better" than advertising

Packaged goods are regularly seen in retail stores. They may actually be seen by many more potential customers than the company's advertising. A good package sometimes gives a firm more promotion effect than it could possibly afford with advertising.

Promotion-oriented packaging also may reduce total distribution costs. An attractive package may speed turnover so much that total costs will drop as a percentage of sales. Rapid turnover is one of the reasons for the success of self-service retailing. Without packages that "sell themselves," self-service retailing would not be possible.

Or . . . may raise total costs

In other cases, total distribution costs may rise because of packaging. But customers may be satisfied because the packaging improves the product—perhaps by offering much greater convenience or reducing waste.

Packaging costs as a percentage of a manufacturer's selling price vary widely—ranging from 1 to 70 percent. Let's look at sugar as an example. In 100-pound bags, the cost of packaging sugar is only 1 percent of the selling price. In 2- and 5-pound cartons, it is 25–30 percent. And for individual serving packages, it is 50 percent. Most customers don't want to haul a 100-pound bag home—and are quite willing to pay for more convenient packages. Restaurants use one-serving envelopes of sugar—finding that they reduce the cost of filling and washing sugar bowls, and that customers prefer the more sanitary little packages. In both cases, packaging adds value to the product—actually creating new products and new marketing strategies.

The right packaging is just enough packaging

Experience shows that a specific package must be designed for each product. The package must safely transport its contents, serve in a specific climate (especially if the product is to be exported), and last for a specific time. To provide such packaging, the manufacturer must know the product, the target customers, and how the product will be delivered to them. Underpackaging costs money for damage claims or poor sales. But overpackaging also costs money—because dollars are spent for no benefit. Glassware, for example, needs to be protected from even relatively light blows that might smash it. Heavy-duty machinery doesn't need protection from blows—but may need protection from moisture.

WHAT IS SOCIALLY RESPONSIBLE PACKAGING?

Some consumers say that some package designs are misleading—perhaps on purpose. They feel that the great variety of package designs makes it hard to compare values.

Federal law tries to help

The **Hazardous Products Act** gives Consumer and Corporate Affairs Canada, the authority either to ban or to regulate the sale, distribution, and labelling of hazardous products.

Since 1971, all products considered potentially hazardous—such as cleaning substances, chemicals, and aerosol products—have had to carry on their labels an appropriate symbol which reveals both the possible danger and the necessary precautions. Figure 10–6 shows the symbols used to indicate whether the product is poisonous, flammable, corrosive, or explosive.

The **Consumer Packaging and Labelling Act** calls for bilingual labels as well as the standardization of package sizes and shapes. It also required that all food products be labelled in metric terms as well as in traditional Canadian measures by March 1976. When reference is made on a label or package to the number of servings being provided, the average size of these servings must also be indicated. The term *best before* must appear in both official languages along with a date reflecting the durability of the product.

Labelling requirements for certain specified products are also set forth in the National Trademark and True Labelling Act, the Textile Labelling Act, and the Precious Metals Marking Act. Other federal initiatives include the Textile Care Labelling Program that provides for all garments and other textiles being labelled with washing or dry cleaning instructions. Similarly, the CANTAG program now being introduced will provide customers with performance, capacity, and energy consumption data on major appliances.

Figure 10–6

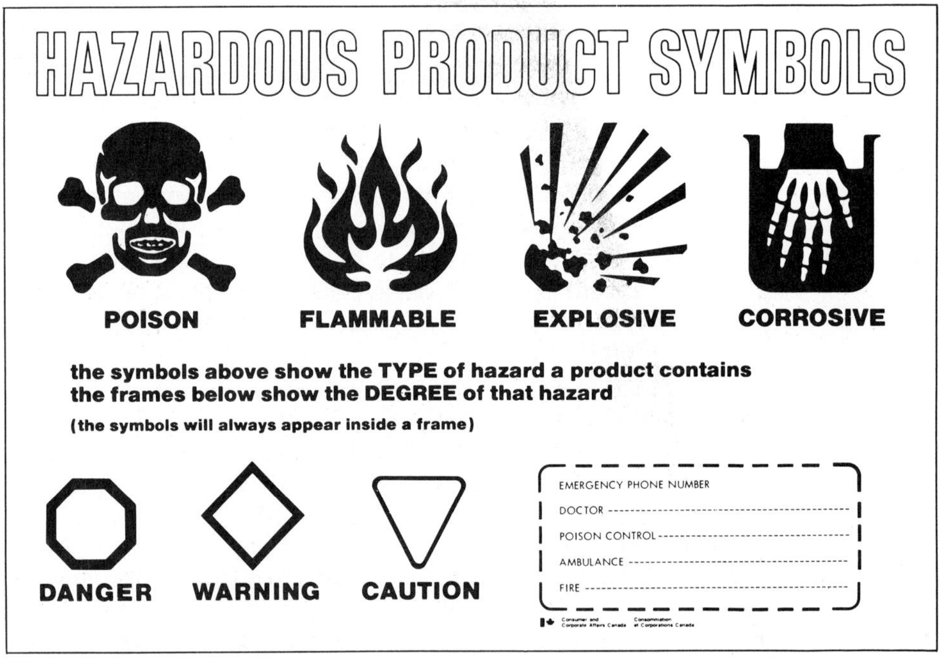

HAZARDOUS PRODUCT SYMBOLS

POISON   FLAMMABLE   EXPLOSIVE   CORROSIVE

the symbols above show the TYPE of hazard a product contains
the frames below show the DEGREE of that hazard

(the symbols will always appear inside a frame)

DANGER   WARNING   CAUTION

EMERGENCY PHONE NUMBER
DOCTOR
POISON CONTROL
AMBULANCE
FIRE

Unit-pricing—a possible help

There is growing interest in unit-pricing, which aids comparison shopping—using weight and volume. **Unit-pricing** involves placing the price per ounce (or some other standard measure) on or near the product. Some supermarket chains offer unit-pricing. And many consumers do appreciate this service.[8]

Universal product codes may lead to less price information

To "automate" the handling of foods and drugs, government and industry representatives have developed a **universal product code** —which identifies each product with marks that can be read by electronic scanners and related to prices by computers. Figure 10–7 shows a universal product code mark.

Large supermarket chains have been eager to use these codes. They would speed the checkout process—and get rid of the need for marking the price on every item in the store. Prices would still be shown near the product—but not on each individual item.

Some customers don't like the codes, however, because they can't compare prices later—either in the store or at home. These complaints have made the code idea less attractive. But probably more electronic checkout systems will be installed—whether the prices are marked on each item or not—because it does speed the checkout process and also improves inventory control.

Figure 10–7: An illustration of a universal product code for a ballpoint pen

BRANDING HAS STRATEGIC IMPORTANCE, TOO

There are so many brands—and we're so used to seeing them—that we take them for granted. In the grocery products area alone, there are about 38,000 brands. Many of these brands are of real value to their owners—because they help identify the company's marketing mix—and help consumers recognize the firm's products and advertising. This is an important area which is ignored by many business people. So we will treat it in some depth.

What is branding, brand name, and trademark?

Branding means the use of a name, term, symbol, or design—or a combination of these—to identify a product. It includes the use of brand names, trademarks, and practically all other means of product identification.

Brand name has a narrower meaning. A **brand name** is a word, letter, or a group of words or letters.

Trademark is a legal term. A **trademark** includes only those words, symbols, or marks that the law says are trademarks.

The word *Buick* can be used to explain these differences. The Buick car is *branded* under the *brand name* "Buick" (whether it is spoken or printed in any manner). When "Buick" is printed in a certain kind of script, however, it becomes a *trademark*. A trademark need not be attached to the product. It need not even be a word. A symbol can be used.

These differences may seem technical. But they are very important to business firms that spend much money to protect their brands.

BRANDING—WHY IT DEVELOPED

Brands meet needs

Branding started during the Middle Ages when craft guilds (similar to labor unions) and merchant guilds formed to control the quantity and quality of production. Each producer had to mark his goods—so output could be cut back when necessary. This also meant that poor quality—which might reflect unfavorably on other guild products and discourage future trade—could be traced back to the guilty producer. Early trademarks were also a protection to the buyer—who could now know the source of the product.

Not restriction but identification

More recently, brands have been used mainly for identification.

The earliest and most aggressive brand promoters in America were the patent medicine companies. They were joined by the food manufacturers—who grew in size after the Civil War. Some of the brands started in the 1860s and 1870s (and still going strong) are Borden's Condensed Milk, Quaker Oats, Vaseline, Pillsbury's Best Flour, and Ivory Soap.[9]

Customers are willing to buy by brand without inspection when they can be sure of quality. In many countries, however, the consumer doesn't feel so sure. In India, for example, inspecting the product is common—because there is little faith in packaged goods and brands. There is good reason for this. Foods are often mixed with sawdust, husks, and colored earth—which may be 10–50 percent of the weight of packaged or prepared foods. And an Indian car battery manufacturer has had great success with its brand by correctly advertising "the battery you don't have to test."

CONDITIONS FAVORABLE TO BRANDING

Most marketing managers accept branding and are concerned with seeing that their brand succeeds.

Branding speeds shopping by assuring consistent quality.

The following conditions would be favorable to successful branding:

1. The demand for the general product class should be large.
2. The demand should be strong enough so that the market price can be high enough to make the effort profitable.
3. There should be economies of scale. If the branding were really successful, the cost of production would drop—and profits would increase.
4. The product quality should be the best for the price. And the quality should be easy to maintain.
5. The product should be easy to identify by brand or trademark.
6. Dependable and widespread availability should be possible. When customers start using a brand, they want to be able to continue finding it in their stores.
7. Favorable positioning in stores will help.

ACHIEVING BRAND FAMILIARITY IS NOT EASY

Brand familiarity means how well customers recognize and accept a company's brand.

The brand familiarity earned by the brander (and competitors) obviously affects the planning for the rest of the marketing mix—especially where the product should be offered and what promotion is needed.

There are five levels of brand familiarity

Five levels of brand familiarity are useful for strategic planning: (1) rejection, (2) nonrecognition, (3) recognition, (4) preference, and (5) insistence.

Some brands have been tried and found wanting. **Brand rejection** means the potential customers won't buy a brand—unless its image is changed. Brand rejection may suggest a change in the product—or perhaps only a shift to target customers who have a better image of the brand. Overcoming negative images is difficult—and can be very expensive.

Some products are seen as basically the same. **Brand nonrecognition** means a brand is not recognized by final consumers at all—even though middlemen may use the brand name for identification and inventory control. Examples here are: school supplies, novelties, inexpensive dinnerware, and similar goods found in discount stores.

Brand recognition means that customers remember the brand. This can be a big advantage if there are many "nothing" brands on the market.

Most branders would like to win **brand preference**—which means target customers will choose the brand over other brands—perhaps out of habit or past experience.

Brand insistence means customers insist upon a product and would be willing to search for it. This is the goal of many target marketers.

Knowing how well you're known may take research

While the level of brand familiarity will affect the development of a marketing mix, marketing research may be needed to find out exactly how well the firm is known—and in which target markets. Sometimes, managers

When a product reaches the brand preference or insistence stage, a customer buys it with little thought.

feel their products have a higher level of brand familiarity than they really do—and they develop their marketing mixes accordingly. This mistake puts too much stress on the other Ps in their marketing mixes. Studies show that some brands don't reach even the brand recognition level. One study, for example, showed that two out of every five homemakers couldn't name the brand of furniture they owned.[10]

CHOOSING A BRAND NAME

Brand name selection is still an art. It's hard to say what is a good brand name. Some successful brand names seem to break all the rules. Many of these names, however, got started when there was less competition.

A good brand name can make a difference—helping to tell something important about the company or its product. Just using the company's name or a family member's name is no longer enough. See Figure 10–8 for the characteristics of a good brand name.

Figure 10–8: Characteristics of a good brand name

Short and simple.
Easy to spell and read.
Easy to recognize and remember.
Pleasing when read or heard—and easy to pronounce.
Pronounceable in only one way.
Pronounceable in all languages (for goods to be exported).
Always timely (does not get out of date).
Adaptable to packaging or labeling needs.
Legally available for use (not in use by another firm).
Not offensive, obscene, or negative.
Suggestive of product benefits.
Adaptable to any advertising medium (especially billboards and television).

PROTECTING CANADIAN TRADEMARKS

Benefits of trademark registration

Common law protects the owners of trademarks and brand names. Ownership of brand names and trademarks is established by continued usage without abandonment.

Since the basic right is found in "use," a Canadian firm need not register its trademarks under the **Trade Marks Act.** But when a trademark is so registered, the registering firm is legally protected against any other company using a trademark that might be confused with its own. In contrast, the holder of an unregistered trademark could not sue a firm merely for using a similar trademark. The owner of the unregistered trademark would have to prove that the defendant was deliberately trying to create confusion in the minds of consumers.

Canadian and U.S. legislation differ in the types of trademark protection they provide. In Canada, a firm producing a substantially different product may use the same trade name as another product used for some other purpose. This is not so in the United States. On the other hand, there is less likelihood of a Canadian trade name being ruled "generic" or a common descriptive term and therefore no longer protectable by its original owner. For example, Bayer's Aspirin is still a protected trademark in Canada, even though "aspirin" has become a generic term in the United States. Since a protected trademark can be a real asset, every effort should be made to keep such trademarks from becoming the generic name for a whole category of products.[11]

You must protect your own

A brand or trademark can be a real asset to a company. So each firm should try to see that it doesn't become a common descriptive term for its kind of product. When this happens, the brand name or trademark becomes public property—the owner loses all rights to it. This happened in the U.S. with cellophane, aspirin, shredded wheat, and kerosene. There was concern that Teflon and Scotch Tape might become public property— and Miller Brewing Company tried unsuccessfully to protect its Lite beer by suing brewers who wanted to use the word *light.*[12]

WHAT KIND OF BRAND TO USE?

Keep it in the family

Branders who manufacture or handle more than one item must decide whether they are going to use a **family brand**—the same brand name for several products—or individual brands for each product.

The use of the same brand for many products makes sense if all are about the same in nature and quality. The goodwill attached to one or two products may help the others. This cuts promotion costs. It tends to build customer loyalty for the family brand—and makes it easier to introduce new products.

Examples of family brands are the Heinz 57 food products, three A&P

brands (Ann Page, Sultana, and Iona), and Sears' Craftsman tools and Kenmore appliances.

Individual brands for outside and inside competition

Individual brands—separate brand names for each product—are used by a brander when its products are of varying quality or type. If the products are distinctly different—such as meat products and glue—individual brands are better.

Sometimes firms use individual brands to encourage competition within the organization. Each brand is managed by a different group. Management feels that internal competition keeps everyone alert. The theory is that—if anyone is going to take business away from them—it ought to be their own brand. This kind of competition is found among General Motors' brands. Chevrolet, Pontiac, Oldsmobile, Buick, and even Cadillac compete with each other in some markets.

Generic brands at lower prices

Products which are seen by consumers as "commodities" may be difficult to brand. Recently, some manufacturers and middlemen have faced up to this problem and come out with **generic products**—products which have no brand other than the identification of their contents. For example, some supermarkets offer the following generic products: corn flakes, macaroni, beans, noodles, and dog food. Typically, these are offered in plain packages at lower prices. Some have been well accepted by consumers—because the quality compares well with the "commodities" which are offered at higher prices in fancier packages.

Producers and advertisers of "me-too" products should worry about this development—if it continues to spread.[13]

WHO SHOULD DO THE BRANDING?

Manufacturer brands versus dealer brands

Manufacturer brands are brands which are created by manufacturers. These are sometimes called "national brands"—because manufacturers often promote these brands all across the country or in large regions.

Generic brands may be promoted less and sold for less than well-promoted brands.

Such brands include Kellogg's, Stokely, Whirlpool, International Harvester, and IBM.

Dealer brands are brands created by middlemen. These are sometimes called "private brands." Examples of dealer brands include the brands of Eatons, Sears, and The Bay. Some of these are advertised and distributed more widely than many national brands.

Middlemen have been moving into branding their own products. They see the big sales volumes involved—and the profit possibilities of controlling their own brands—especially when they know that they control the end of the distribution channel.

THE BATTLE OF THE BRANDS—WHO'S WINNING?

The **battle of the brands** is the competition between dealer brands and manufacturer brands. The "battle" is just a question of whose brands are to be more popular—and who is to be in control.

Some research suggests (for food products at least) that manufacturers' brands may be losing the fight. In 1951, manufacturers' brands were preferred by 2 or 3 to 1. Even higher prices were accepted. This strong preference has continued to go down. By 1970, almost half of the consumers had shifted to dealer brands. Younger households may be leading here.[14]

One of the reasons for this shift is that some of the manufacturers' brands have come to be thought of as luxuries—while the dealer-branded chain store products are seen as necessities.[15] Then, too, the chains' dealer-branded products are more likely to be in stock—because the chains control the channel of distribution.

Another reason for the growth of dealer branding is that some stores needed a competitive weapon against retail price cutters—who promoted discounts on well-known manufacturer brands. Department stores, supermarkets, service stations, clothing stores, and drugstores are all doing more dealer branding.

Manufacturers may become only manufacturers

The battle of the brands certainly isn't over. But the former dominance of manufacturers' brands may have ended. If the trend continues, manufacturers could become just that—only production departments for middlemen. Retailers and wholesalers might become the leaders in marketing. Certainly, they are closer to final consumers—and can have more control of the final sale.[16]

WARRANTIES ARE IMPORTANT TOO

Warranty should mean something

Common law says that producers should stand behind—i.e., provide a **warranty** for—their products. And both present and proposed warranty legislation tries to see that such warranties or guarantees are neither deceptive nor unfair. Warranties—are a major source of consumer complaint and dissatisfaction.

Both provincial and federal legislation attempts to see that any warranty offered is fair to the consumer, easy to understand, and precise as to what is and what is not covered. Prior to this increased government concern, some firms simply said their products were "fully warranted" or "absolutely guaranteed" without either specifying a time period or spelling out the meaning of the guarantee.

On the federal level, protection against misleading warranties is provided by one of the Stage I amendments to the Combines Investigation Act. Specifically prohibited are warranties that seem unlikely to be carried out, warranties where excessive labor or handling charges are used to cover the manufacturer's cost of allegedly replacing defective parts "free of charge," and warranties that reduce a purchaser's usual rights under common law.[17]

Provincial legislation designed to make warranties more meaningful was greatly influenced by the recommendations of a 1972 study of warranties and guarantees made by the Ontario Law Reform Commission.[18] However changes have not occurred all that quickly! Ten years after the Law Reform study, only Saskatchewan had its new legislation in force.

Customers might like a strong warranty—but it can be very expensive. It might even be economically impossible for small producers. Some customers abuse products and demand a lot of service on warranties. Backing up warranties can be a problem too. Although manufacturers may be responsible, they may have to depend upon reluctant middlemen to do

A warranty explains what the seller guarantees about its product.

LIMITED WARRANTY
SHEPARD'S SHOES, INC. GUARANTEE

Except as specifically otherwise provided below, we will repair or replace for no charge any part of any leather shoe that wears out during the guarantee period according to the following schedule:
Children: (age 15 or under) — 3 months from date of purchase.
Women: (age 16 and over) — 4 months from date of purchase.
Men: (age 16 and over) — 6 months from date of purchase.

SPECIFICALLY EXCLUDED FROM THIS GUARANTEE OF REPAIR OR REPLACEMENT ARE THE FOLLOWING:
1. This guarantee does not cover any part of a patent leather shoe.
2. This guarantee does not cover any damage caused by water.
3. This guarantee does not cover more than a single repair or replacement to each part of a leather shoe.

This guarantee will be honored in all cases where the condition of the shoe is such that repair or replacement of any part is required in order to render it fit for the normal use required of it.

To receive the free repair or replacement, this guarantee must be presented at any Shepard's Shoes location before expiration of the guarantee period. Shepard's Shoe Stores are located at Downtown Lansing, East Lansing, Frandor and Lansing Mall.

Category *Women's Bass*   Authorization *Laurie Froh*

Stock No. *2501*   Size *8 h*   *Marie Johnson*
                                                    Name

Date *12-27-81*   *6948 Uhinta*
                                                    Address

Marie Johnson   *Houston*
        Signature   City

the job—or set up their own service companies. This can make it hard for a small firm to compete with larger firms that have many service centers. Foreign auto producers and small domestic auto producers, for example, can't match the number of Chevrolet or Ford service locations.

Deciding on the warranty is a strategic matter. Specific decisions should be made about what the warranty will cover—and then it must be communicated clearly to the target customers. In some cases, the warranty may make the difference between success and failure for a whole strategy.

CONCLUSION

In this chapter, we looked at Product very broadly. A Product may not be a physical good at all. It may be a service. Or it may be some combination—like a meal at a restaurant.

A firm's product is what satisfies the needs of its target market. This *may* be a physical good, but also could include a package, brand, installation, repair service, and so on—whatever is needed to satisfy target customers.

Consumer goods and industrial goods classes were introduced to simplify your study of marketing—and help in planning marketing mixes. The consumer goods classes are based on consumers' buying behavior. Industrial goods classes are based on how buyers see the products—and how they are used.

Knowing these goods classes—and learning how marketers handle specific products within these classes—will speed the development of your "marketing sense."

The fact that different people may view the same product differently helps explain why firms may use very different marketing mixes—quite successfully.

Packaging and branding can create a new and more satisfying product. Variations in packaging can make a product salable in various target markets. A specific package must be developed for each product. Both under-packaging and over-packaging can be expensive.

To customers, the main value of brands is as a guarantee of quality. This leads to repeat purchasing. For marketers, such "routine" buying means lower promotion costs and higher sales.

Should brands be stressed? The decision depends on whether the costs of brand promotion and honoring the brand guarantee can be more than covered by a higher price or more rapid turnover—or both. The cost of branding may reduce other costs—by reducing pressure on the other three Ps.

In recent years, the strength of manufacturers' brands has declined—and dealer brands have become more important. The dealer-labeled products may win in the battle of the brands—because dealers are closer to customers and can emphasize their own brands.

Branding gives marketing managers choice. They can add brands—and use individual or family brands. In the end, however, customers express their approval or disapproval of the whole product (including the brand). The degree of brand familiarity is a measure of management's ability to carve out a separate market—and affects Place, Price, and Promotion decisions.

Warranties are also important strategic matters. A warranty need not be strong—it just has to be clearly stated. But some customers like strong warranties.

So, it should be clear that Product is concerned with much more than a physical good or service. The marketing manager must also be concerned about packaging, branding, and warranties—if he is to help his firm succeed in our increasingly competitive marketplaces.

QUESTIONS FOR DISCUSSION

1. Define, in your own words, what a Product is.

2. Explain how the addition of guarantees, service, and credit can improve a "product." Cite a specific case where this has been done and explain how customers viewed this new "product."

3. What "products" are being offered by an exclusive men's shop? By a nightclub? By a soda fountain? By a supermarket?

4. What kinds of consumer goods are the following: (a) fountain pens, (b) men's shirts, (c) cosmetics? Explain your reasoning and draw a picture of the market in each case to help illustrate your thinking.

5. Some goods seem to be treated perpetually as unsought goods by their producers. Give an example and explain why.

6. How would the marketing mix for a staple convenience good differ from the one for a homogeneous shopping good? How would the mix for a specialty good differ from the mix for a heterogeneous shopping good? Use examples.

7. Which of the Ps would receive the greatest emphasis in the marketing mix for a new unsought good? Explain why, using an example.

8. In what types of stores would you expect to find: (a) convenience goods, (b) shopping goods, (c) specialty goods, and (d) unsought goods?

9. Cite two examples of industrial goods which require a lot of service in order to make them useful "products."

10. Would you expect to find any wholesalers selling the various types of industrial goods? Are retail stores required (or something like retail stores)?

11. What kinds of industrial goods are the following?
    a. Nails and screws.
    b. Paint.
    c. Dust-collecting and ventilating systems.
    d. An electric lift truck.
    Explain your reasoning.

12. What impact does the fact that demand for industrial goods is derived and fairly inelastic have upon the development of industrial goods marketing mixes? Use examples.

13. How do farm product raw materials differ from other raw materials or other industrial goods? Do the differences have any impact on their marketing mixes? If so, what, specifically?

14. For the kinds of industrial goods described in this chapter, complete the table at the top of the next column (use one or a few *well-chosen* words).

Goods	1	2	3
Installations: Buildings and land rights			
Major equipment: Standard			
Custom made			
Accessory equipment			
Raw materials: Farm products			
Natural products			
Components: Parts			
Materials			
Supplies: Operating supplies			
Maintenance and small operating supplies			
Services			

1—Kind of distribution facility(ies) needed and functions they will provide.
2—Caliber of salespeople required.
3—Kind of advertising required.

15. Explain the increasing interest in packaging, not only for consumer goods but also for industrial goods. Is this likely to continue?

16. Suggest an example where packaging costs probably: (a) lower total distribution costs, and (b) raise total distribution costs.

17. Is there any difference between a brand name and a trademark? If so, why is this difference important?

18. Is a well-known brand valuable only to the owner of the brand?

19. Would it be profitable for a firm to expend large sums of money to establish a brand for any type product in any competitive situation? Why, or why not? If the answer is no, suggest examples.

20. Evaluate the suitability of the following brand names: (a) Star (sausage), (b) Pleasing (books), (c) Rugged (shoes), (d) Shiny (shoe polish), (e) Lord Jim (ties).

21. Explain family brands. Sears and A&P use family brands but they have several different family brands. If the idea is a good one, why don't they have just one brand?

22. What is the "battle of the brands"? Who do you think will win and why?

23. What does the degree of brand familiarity imply about previous promotion efforts and the future promotion task? Also, how does the degree of brand familiarity affect the Place and Price variables?

24. If you have been operating a small supermarket with emphasis on manufacturers' brands and have barely been breaking even, how should you evaluate the proposal of a large wholesaler who offers a full line of dealer-branded groceries at substantially lower prices? Specify any assumptions necessary to obtain a definite answer.

25. Explain the strategic decisions a manufacturer's marketing manager must make about Product. Illustrate.

SUGGESTED CASES

9. Annie's Floral
10. Byron Pharmaceutical Company
12. Ski Haus Sports Shop

When you finish this chapter, you should:

1. *Understand how product life cycles should affect strategy planning.*

2. *Understand product positioning.*

3. *Know what is involved in designing new products—and what "new products" really are.*

4. *Understand new-product development as a total company effort.*

5. *Understand the need for product or brand managers.*

6. *Recognize the important new terms (shown in red).*

PRODUCT MANAGEMENT AND NEW-PRODUCT DEVELOPMENT

11

Product management is an exciting, full-time job for product managers.

In this chapter, we will talk about product management and new-product planning. Developing a good new product isn't easy. Not only are customer needs and attitudes changing, but competition continually makes current products obsolete. In some lines of business, new-product development is so rapid that 50 percent or more of the products made by a firm were not even in the planning stages 5 to 10 years earlier!

Products go through product life cycles. So we'll talk about managing products over their cycles. We will also discuss (1) some analytical aids to product management, (2) the importance of an organized new-product development effort to ensure that the company continues to produce successful products, and (3) the role of product managers.

MANAGEMENT OF PRODUCTS OVER THEIR LIFE CYCLES

Industry sales and profits don't move together

Products—like consumers—have life cycles. So product and marketing mix planning are important. Competitors are always developing and copying ideas and products—making existing products out-of-date more quickly than ever.

237

The **product life cycle** is the stages a new product goes through from beginning to end. It is divided into four major stages: (1) market introduction, (2) market growth, (3) market maturity, and (4) sales decline.

A particular firm's marketing mix for a product should change during these stages—for several reasons. Customers' attitudes and needs may change through the course of the product's life cycle. Entirely different target markets may be appealed to at different stages in the life cycle. The nature of competition moves toward pure competition or oligopoly.

Further, the total sales of the product—by all competitors in the industry—varies in each of its four stages. And more importantly, the profit picture changes. It is important to see that the two do not move together. Profits decline while sales are still rising. Their general relationships can be seen in Figure 11–1.

*Market introduction—
investing in the future*

The **market introduction** stage occurs while a new idea is being introduced to a market. Customers aren't looking for the product—they don't even know about it. Promotion is needed to tell potential customers about the new product—its advantages and uses.

Even though a firm promotes its new product, it takes time for customers to learn about it. The introductory stage usually is marked by losses—with much money spent for Promotion and Product and Place development. Money is being invested in the hope of future profits.

*Market growth—many
competing products and
best profits*

The **market growth** stage occurs when industry sales start growing fast—but profits rise and then start falling. The innovator begins to make big profits. Competitors start coming into the market—each trying to develop a better product design. There is much product variety. But some competitors copy the most successful products.

During this stage, the sales of the industry are rising fairly fast as more and more customers buy. This second stage may last from several days to several years—depending on whether the product is hula hoops, credit card service, or color television sets. This is the time of biggest profits—for the industry. *But* it is *also the beginning of the decline of industry profits*—as competition increases. Some *firms* even lose money in this stage.

**Figure 11–1: Life cycle of a
typical product**

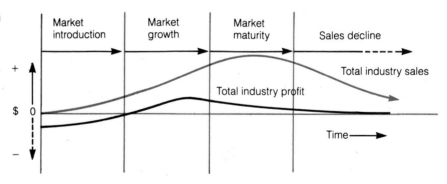

Market maturity—sales level off, profits down

The **market maturity** stage occurs when industry sales level out—and competition gets tougher. Many competitors have entered the race for profits—except in oligopolies. Industry profits go down throughout the market maturity stage—because promotion costs climb. Some competitors begin to cut prices to attract business. Even in oligopoly situations, there is a long-run downward pressure on prices.

New firms may enter the market at this stage—increasing competition even more. Note that late entries do skip the early stages—including the profitable market growth stage!

Promotion becomes more important during the market maturity stage. Products differ only slightly—if at all. Most competitors have discovered the most effective appeals—or copied the leaders.

In monopolistic competition, we see increasing competition on Product, Price, and Promotion. Although each firm may still have its own demand curve, the curves are becoming more elastic—as the various products become almost the same in the minds of potential consumers.

In Canada as well as in the United States, the markets for most automobiles, boats, many household appliances, most groceries, television sets, and tobacco products are in market maturity.[1] This period may continue for many years—until a basically new product idea comes along. This is true although different brands or models may come and go. Gasoline-powered automobiles, for example, replaced horse-drawn carriages. Eventually they may be replaced by some other method of transportation—electric autos and high-speed mass transit, for example.

Sales decline—a time of replacement

The **sales decline** stage occurs when new products replace the old. Price competition from dying products may increase—but products with strong brands may make profits almost till the end. These firms will have down-sloping demand curves—because they have been able to differentiate their products.

As the new products go through their introductory stage, the old ones may keep some sales—by appealing to the most loyal target customers.

Our earlier discussion of customer buying behavior showed that some customers accept new ideas more easily than others. The former would "discover" the new product. More conservative buyers might switch later—smoothing the sales decline.

Product life cycles are getting shorter

The total length of the cycle may vary from 90 days—in the case of hula hoops—to possibly 90 years for automobiles. In general, however, product life cycles are shortening.

In the highly competitive grocery products industry, they are down to 12–18 months for really new ideas. Simple variations of such a new idea may have even shorter life cycles. Competitors may copy flavor or packaging changes in a matter of weeks or months.

Large manufacturers—even in the industrial goods area—face product life cycles. A top Du Pont manager said: "Lead time is gone . . . there's no company so outstanding technically today that it can expect a long

Product imitation has cut product life cycles—especially for grocery items.

lead time in a new discovery.''[2] Du Pont had nylon to itself for 15 years. But in just two years a major competitor—Celanese Corporation—came out with something very competitive to Delrin—another synthetic fiber discovery that Du Pont hoped would be as important as nylon. Similarly, six months after U.S. Steel came out with a new ''thin tin'' plate, competitors were out with even better products.

Even copying products is not uncommon. And this speeds up the cycle. Westinghouse found a company copying its new hair dryer and instruction book almost exactly.[3] Patents may not be much protection—the product life may be over before a case would get through the courts. The copier might be out of business by then.

The early bird makes the profits

The increasing speed of the product life cycle means that the modern firm must be developing new products all the time. It must try to have marketing mixes that will make the most of the market growth stage—when profits are highest.

PRODUCT LIFE CYCLES SHOULD BE RELATED TO MARKET AREAS

Each market area should be carefully defined

To fully understand the *why* of a product life cycle, we should carefully define the market area we are considering. The way we define a market makes a difference in the way we see product life cycles—and who the competitors are. If a market is defined very generally, then there may be many competitors—and the market may appear to be in market maturity. On the other hand, if we look at a narrow area—and a particular way of satisfying specific needs—then we might see much shorter product life cycles—as improved products come along to replace the old. For example, there may be an ongoing general market demand for copies of letters, term papers, and book pages. If we add the annual sales of all the copying machines which have come on the market during the last few decades and treat them as the sales of one ''product,'' the industry seems to be in the market growth stage. On the other hand, if we think of the individual kinds of machines as not being substitutes for each other—because they are applying quite different technical principles—we see several shorter life cycles—as new types of machines come along.[4] In this case, "wet-copy" machines have already gone through their sales decline stage and disappeared from the market—while some "dry-copy" machines are still fighting it out.

Each market segment has its own product life cycle

Too narrow a view of a market may lead to misreading the nature of competition—and the speed of the relevant product life cycle. A firm producing exercise machines, for example, could focus only on the "exercise machine" market. But this narrow view may lead it to compete only with other exercise machine producers—when it might be more sensible to compete in the "fitness" market. Of course it can't ignore competitors' machines, but even tougher competition may come from health clubs—and suppliers of jogging suits, athletic shoes, and other fitness-related goods. Perhaps there should be one strategy for the people who are already interested in exercise machines—and a different strategy for potential customers who still don't think of exercise machines as a way of satisfying their fitness needs. In other words, there may be two markets and life cycles to work with—the exercise machine market and the fitness market. It is important to see that aiming only at the exercise machine market might cause the managers to feel they are in the market maturity-stage—especially if some panicky competitor starts cutting prices—when actually there is much potential in the fitness market. If all the exercise machine firms start cutting prices, however, there may be little money left for developing the fitness market. And this could lead to retailers dropping the product—and an untimely shortening of the product's life.[5]

Individual products don't have product life cycles

Notice that product life cycles describe *industry* sales and profits within a particular product-market—*not* the sales and profits of an *individual* product or brand. Individual products or brands may be introduced—or withdrawn—during any stage of the product life cycle. Further, their sales and profits may vary up and down throughout the life cycle—sometimes moving in the opposite direction of industry sales and profits.

A "me-too" product introduced during the market growth stage, for example, might reach its peak and start to decline even before the market maturity stage begins. Or it may never get any sales at all—and suffer a quick death. Other "me-too" products may enter the market in the market maturity stage—and have a difficult time trying to capture a share of the market from established competitors. Market leaders may earn high profits during the market maturity stage—even though industry profits are declining. Weaker products, on the other hand, may not earn a profit during any stage of the product life cycle.

What this discussion suggests, therefore, is that the sales of *individual* products do not follow any general pattern—and studying past sales patterns can be misleading for strategy planning purposes. It's the life cycle for the whole product-market—including all current or potential competi-

Figure 11–2: **Typical changes in marketing variables over the course of the product life cycle**

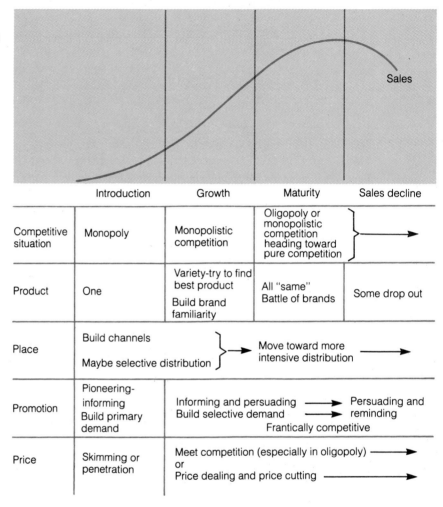

		Introduction	Growth	Maturity	Sales decline
Competitive situation		Monopoly	Monopolistic competition	Oligopoly or monopolistic competition heading toward pure competition	→
Product		One	Variety-try to find best product Build brand familiarity	All "same" Battle of brands	Some drop out
Place		Build channels Maybe selective distribution	→ Move toward more intensive distribution		→
Promotion		Pioneering-informing Build primary demand	Informing and persuading → Persuading and Build selective demand → reminding Frantically competitive		
Price		Skimming or penetration	Meet competition (especially in oligopoly) → or Price dealing and price cutting →		

tors—that marketing managers must study when planning their strategies. In fact, it might be more sensible to think in terms of "market life cycles" or "product-market life cycles" rather than product life cycles—but we will use the term *product life cycle* because it is commonly accepted and widely used.

PLANNING FOR DIFFERENT STAGES OF THE PRODUCT LIFE CYCLE

Length of cycle affects strategy planning

The probable length of the cycle affects strategy planning—realistic plans must be made for the later stages. In fact, where a product is in its life cycle—and how fast it's moving to the next stage—should affect strategy planning. Figure 11–2 shows the relation of the product life cycle to various marketing variables. The "technical" terms in this figure are discussed later in the book.

Introducing new products

Figure 11–2 shows that a marketer has a tough job introducing a really new product. The product may be unique—but this doesn't mean that everyone will immediately come running to the producer's door. The firm will have to build channels of distribution—perhaps offering special incentives to win cooperation. Promotion will have to build demand for the whole idea—not just try to sell a specific brand. All of this is expensive—and losses can be expected in the market introduction stage of the product life cycle. This may lead the marketer to try to "skim" the market—charge a relatively high price to help pay for the introductory costs.

What is the best strategy, however, depends on how fast the product life cycle is likely to move—that is, how quickly the new idea will be accepted by customers—and how quickly competitors will follow with their own version of the product. Also relevant is how quickly the firm can change its strategy as the life cycle moves on. Some firms are very flexible—and may be able to compete effectively with larger, less flexible competitors.

Managing maturing products

Product life cycles keep moving—but a company doesn't have to sit by and watch its products go through a complete product life cycle. It has choices. It can improve the product—for the same or a different market—and let it start off on a different cycle. Or it can withdraw the product before it completes the cycle. These two choices are shown in Figure 11–3. Of importance here is whether the firm has developed some competitive advantage. As we move into market maturity, even small differences can matter—and some firms do very well by careful management of maturing products. They may be able to make a slightly better product—or perhaps lower production and/or marketing costs. Or they may simply be more successful at promotion—enabling them to successfully differentiate their more or less homogeneous product.

Figure 11–3

A. Significantly improved product starts a new cycle, but maybe with short introductory stage

B. Profit-oriented firm dropping out of market during market maturity stage

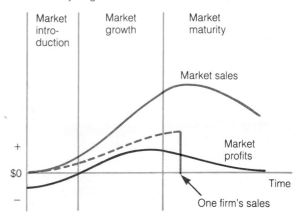

Something to remember here, however, is that industry profits are dropping in market maturity. Financially oriented top management has to be aware of this—or they will continue to expect the attractive profits of the market growth stage. This is simply not possible here. Everyone must understand the situation, or impossible burdens will be placed on the marketing department—causing marketing managers to begin to think about collusion with competitors, deceptive advertising, or some other desperate way of reaching impossible objectives.

Top management must see that there is an upper limit in any product-market. The product life cycle concept has been very useful in communicating this unhappy message. It is one of the powerful tools of marketing which is turning up in the finance and top management literature—because it does affect overall corporate planning and objective setting.

Product life cycles can be extended

When a product wins the position of *"the* product that meets my needs,"   its life may last as long as it continues to meet the needs of those customers. If the needs change, the product may have to change—but the consumers will continue to buy if it does meet their needs. An outstanding example is Procter & Gamble's Tide. Introduced in 1947, this synthetic detergent gave consumers a cleaner wash than they were able to get before—by eliminating the soap film which was common with the soaps made from animal fats. Tide led to a whole new generation of laundry products and made the modern automatic washing machine possible—it produced better cleaning with fewer suds. Since 1947, washing machines and fabrics have changed, so the Tide sold today is much different than that sold in 1947. In fact, there were 55 technical changes during its first 29 years of life. But the product continues to sell well—because it continues to meet consumers' needs.[6]

Do the kinds of product changes made on Tide create a new product which should have its own product life cycle—or are they just changes in the original product concept? We will take the second position—focusing on the idea of "product as need satisfier." Detergents did permit a new standard of cleaning. And people who wanted cleanliness did shift quite rapidly to detergent products—causing sales decline for the traditional soaps. As detergents were gaining acceptance, they went through the early stages of the product life cycle. Now they will continue, in market maturity—with various technical changes—until a new idea—perhaps, ultrasonic cleaning—comes along.

Phasing out dying products

Not all strategies have to be growth strategies. If prospects are poor in some product-market, then a "phase-out" strategy may be needed. The need for phasing out may become more obvious as the sales decline stage arrives. But even in market maturity, it may be clear that a particular product is not going to be profitable enough to reach the company's objectives. Then, the right move is to develop a strategy which helps the firm get out of the product-market as quickly as possible—even before the sales decline stage sets in—while minimizing possible losses.

Strategic plans are carried out as "ongoing" strategies—with salespeople making calls, inventory moving in the channel, advertising planned for several months into the future, and so on. So usually it isn't possible to abruptly end a plan without some losses. It may be better to phase out the product. This might involve selective materials ordering—so that production can end with a minimum of unused inventory. Salespeople might be shifted to other jobs (or laid off). The advertising and other promotion efforts might be canceled or phased out as quickly as possible— since there is no point in promoting for the long run anymore. These various actions will affect morale within the company—and may cause channel members to pull back also. So it may be necessary to reassure employees—and to offer price incentives in the channels.

There are some difficult problems here. But it should be clear that a phase-out strategy is also a *strategy*—and it should be market-oriented, to cut losses. In fact, it may even be possible to "milk" a dying product for some time if competitors move out more quickly. There still is ongoing demand—although it is declining—and some customers may be willing to pay attractive prices to obtain their "old favorite." Further, there may be an ongoing need for repair parts and service—which may add to the overall profitability of the phase-out strategy. Or a new strategy could handle just the repairs and service—even as the basic product is being phased out. You can see that whole product life cycles should be planned— for each strategy.

PRODUCT POSITIONING AIDS PRODUCT MANAGEMENT

Product positioning may see new possibilities

A new aid to product planning—**product positioning**—shows where proposed and/or present brands are located in a market—as seen by customers. It requires some formal marketing research. The results are usually plotted on graphs to help see where the products are "positioned" in relation to competitors. Usually, the products' positions are related to two product features which are important to the target customers.

We won't discuss product positioning techniques here, but the results of one such analysis—for the beer industry—shows the possibilities. In this case—besides plotting the customers' view of several beers in relation to two product features—the respondents were also asked about their "ideal" beer.

Figure 11–4 shows the product space for various beers, using two dimensions—price and lightness. This data was obtained by asking beer drinkers to rate several beers. Then computer routines analyzed these ratings—and plotted the results as shown. Note that the "name" brands are seen as high priced—as the "premium" beers. But not all the premium beers are direct competitors with respect to lightness.

Figure 11–4: **Product space for the Chicago beer market**[7]

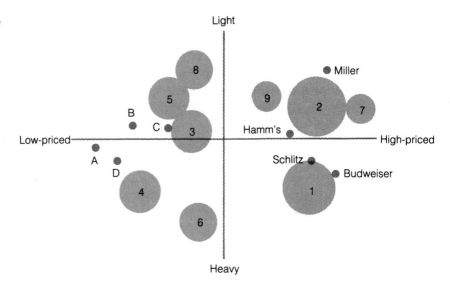

The circles on Figure 11–4 show consumers clustered near their ideal beer preferences. These clusters were obtained by asking the consumers to rate their ideal beer, plotting the results, and then drawing circles around concentrations of consumers.

Note that there are several ideal clusters which aren't near any of the present brands. This might be a chance to introduce new products—both heavier and lighter beers at lower prices. You can see that product positioning can help show how customers see markets.

NEW-PRODUCT PLANNING

Competition is so fierce in most markets that a firm has to keep developing new products—as well as modifying its current products—to meet changing customer needs and competitors' actions. Not having an active product development process means that consciously—or subconsciously—the firm has decided to "milk" its current products and go out of business. New-product planning has to be done—just to survive in our dynamic marketplaces.

What is a new product— lemons?

A **new product** is one that is new *in any way* for the company concerned. A "new product" can become "new" in many ways. A new idea can be turned into a new item or service. Small changes in an existing product also can make it "new." Or an existing product may be offered to new markets as a "new" product. Lemons are a good example.

In the marketing of lemons by one company, no physical changes were made—but much promotion created many "new" products. The same old lemons were promoted successfully for lemonade, mixed drinks, diet supplements, cold remedies, lemon cream pies, a salad dressing, sauce

Physical changes aren't always necessary to create new products.

More, perhaps, than you care to know about Sunkist lemons.

for fish, and many other uses. For each of these markets, the product had to go through the early stages of the product life cycle.[8]

A product can be called "new" for only a limited time. Twelve months is the longest time that a product should be called new—according to Consumer and Corporate Affairs Canada. To be called new a product must be entirely new or changed in "a functionally significant or substantial respect."[9] While 12 months may seem a short time for production-oriented managers, it may be reasonable, given the length of product life cycles.

Find out what the customers and middlemen want

Everyone who handles, sells, or uses a product must be considered when developing a new product. Of course, the product should reflect the needs and attitudes of the target customers. But the product designers must not only think about final customers—but intermediate customers too. There may be special packaging or handling needs. The shelf height in supermarkets, for example, might limit package size. Shipping or handling problems in the warehouse—or on carriers—might call for different types of packaging or package sizes—to keep damage down or make the package easier to handle.

Design long-term "goodness" into products if possible

Socially responsible firms are becoming aware that they must consider consumers' long-term interests when designing products. Consumer groups are helping to force this awareness on more firms.

The firm's final choice in product design should fit with the company's overall objectives—and make good use of the firm's resources. But it would also be desirable to create a need-satisfying product which will appeal to consumers—not only in the short run but also in the long run. These kinds of new product opportunities are shown in Figure 11–5. Obviously, a socially responsible firm would try to find "desirable" opportunities—rather than "deficient" ones. This may not be as easy as it sounds, however. Consumers may want "pleasing products" instead of "desirable products." And some competitors may be very willing to offer what consumers want. Being "socially responsible" will challenge new-product planners.

Safety should also be considered in product design

Real acceptance of the marketing concept would lead to the design of safety into products. But some inherently risky products may be purchased because they do provide thrills and excitement, e.g. bicycles and skis. Even so, safety features can usually be added, and they are desired by some potential customers.

The **Hazardous Products Act** passed by the Canadian Parliament in June 1969, gives the Department of Consumer and Corporate Affairs the authority either to ban outright or to regulate the sale, distribution, labeling, and advertising of potentially dangerous products. This act reemphasizes the need for businesspeople to become more safety-oriented.

Product liability must be taken seriously

Another factor must be considered regarding safety—product liability. **Product liability** means the legal obligation of sellers to pay damages to individuals who are injured by defective products—or unsafely designed products. Businesses are responsible for what they sell—and so they usually buy insurance to protect against large claims. Now some firms are

Figure 11–5: Types of new-product opportunities[10]

	Immediate satisfaction	
	High	Low
Long-run consumer welfare — High	Desirable products	Salutary products
Long-run consumer welfare — Low	Pleasing products	Deficient products

finding their product liability insurance costs rising rapidly, to the point where they have to "self-insure"—take the risk themselves—or go out of business. The potential for more suits is great. Recently, a paper-making machinery manufacturer was notified of claims by users of two of its presses for damages due to industrial accidents. One of the presses was built in 1895—and the other in 1897.[11]

The uncontrollable environment has changed—especially where safety is concerned. Safety is one of the four basic needs—and people feel strongly about it. So it is more important than ever to take new product planning—and especially product safety—seriously. Production-oriented managers will have to become more market-oriented—or they may be forced out of business.

NEW-PRODUCT DEVELOPMENT: A TOTAL COMPANY EFFORT

Some organization helps

A new-product development group helps make sure that new ideas for products are carefully studied—and good ones marketed profitably. Delays can lead to late introductions and give competition a head start in the product life cycle. A delay of even six months may make the difference between a product's success or failure in a competitive market.

A well-organized development procedure might even help a firm copy good ideas quickly and profitably. This shouldn't be overlooked. No one company can hope to be first always—with the best.[12]

Top-level support is needed

New-product development must have the support of top management. New products tend to upset the old routines. So someone has to be in charge of new-product development. The organization arrangement may not be too important—as long as new-product development has top-level support.[13]

A total company effort is needed

Developing new products should be a total company effort—as Figure 11–6 shows. Here, we see that the whole process involves people in management, research, production, promotion, packaging, and branding. The process moves from exploration of ideas to development of the product and product-related ideas. Technical development of the product itself is *not* the first step in new-product development. Evaluating the idea comes first. Many "odd-ball" items can be produced—but who wants them?

After the product has been developed, the total marketing mix is developed and matched against the company's resources to see whether the product looks profitable.

If the answer is yes, then management must make another decision: Does it want to test-market before the real market introduction? This is an important decision. Although test marketing can check ideas, it also alerts competitors. After seeing the speed of product life cycles, you can see why some firms avoid test marketing.

Figure 11–6: New-product development sequence[14]

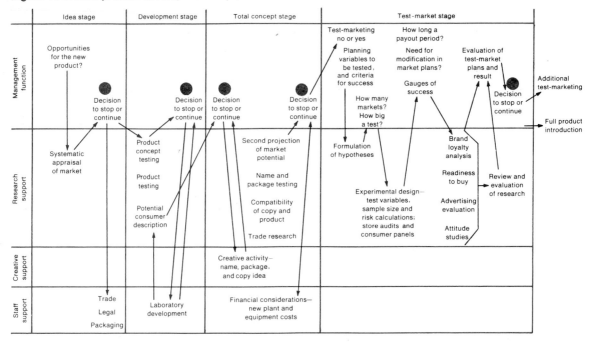

Rejection and failure rates are high

The role of marketing management and top management in product development is shown in Figure 11–6. Management has the power to push or reject development. Developing new ideas costs money. As a result, the rejection rate for new ideas during this process is high. One study of 80 companies found that only 1 out of 40 new ideas survive this kind of organized development process.[15]

As the development process moves along, the decisions become more difficult. The costs and risks increase. And managers know that even with careful work, as many as half of new products do fail.[16]

The failure rate for new products is high, so managers should study their markets carefully to reduce their costs and risks.

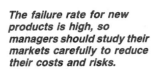

NEED FOR PRODUCT MANAGERS

Product variety leads to product managers

When a company has only one or a few related products, the whole firm is interested in them. But when *new* products are being developed, someone should be in charge of new-product planning—to be sure it isn't neglected. Also, when a firm has several different kinds of products, it may decide to put someone in charge of each one (or even each brand) to be sure they are not lost in the rush of business. **Product managers** or **brand managers** manage specific products—often taking over the jobs once handled by an advertising manager.

Experience is vital

Product managers are common in large companies that produce many kinds of products. There may be several product managers working under a marketing manager. Sometimes a product manager is responsible for the profitable operation of the whole marketing effort for a particular product. In other situations, he may be basically a "product champion"—concerned with planning and getting the promotion effort done.

The activities of product managers vary considerably—depending on their experience and aggressiveness. But now more emphasis is being placed on marketing experience—as it becomes clear that this important job takes more than academic training and enthusiasm.[17]

A CANADIAN PERSPECTIVE ON PRODUCT PLANNING

The efforts of Canada's industrial marketers to launch new products have been extensively studied.[18] Particular attention has been paid to why some of these products succeeded and others failed. One major difference appears to be the amount of time, effort, and money devoted to researching the market at various stages of development and commercialization. New product failures were characterized by an almost complete neglect of marketing research and a corresponding overemphasis on technical considerations and on spending for R&D.[19] In contrast, marketing considerations had received far more attention in successful new product launches.[20] Actually, there is no reason to believe Canada's manufacturers of industrial goods are any more guilty of being production-oriented than their counterparts elsewhere. These Canadian findings have also shown to apply in other industrialized countries.[21]

CONCLUSION

Product planning is an increasingly important activity in a modern economy—because it is no longer very profitable to sell just commodities. Product positioning was described as an aid to product planning—helping to see where products and brands are positioned in a market.

The product life cycle concept is especially important to marketing strategy planning. It shows that different marketing mixes—and even strategies—are needed as a product moves through its cycle. This is an important point, because profits change during the life cycle—with most of the profits going to the innovators or fast copiers.

We pointed out that a new product is not limited to physical newness. We will call a product "new" if it is new in any way—to any target market.

New products are so important to the survival of firms in our competitive economy that some organized method for developing them is needed. A general approach was discussed. But it is obvious that it must be a total company effort to be successful.

The failure rate of new products is high, but it is lower for better-managed firms that have recognized the importance of product planning and management. It is so important that some firms have product managers to manage individual products. Also, some have new-product committees to assure that the process is carried out successfully.

QUESTIONS FOR DISCUSSION

1. Explain how market sales and market profits behave over the product life cycle.

2. Cite two examples of products which you feel are currently in each of the product life-cycle stages.

3. Explain how different conclusions might be reached with respect to the correct product life-cycle stage(s) in the automobile market, especially if different views of the market are held.

4. Can product life cycles be extended? Illustrate your answer for a specific product.

5. Discuss the life cycle of a product in terms of its probable impact on a manufacturer's marketing mix. Illustrate using battery-operated toothbrushes.

6. Explain how product positioning differs from segmenting markets. Is target marketing involved in product positioning?

7. What is a new product? Illustrate your answer.

8. Explain the importance of an organized new-product development process and illustrate how it might be used for: (a) an improved phonograph, (b) new frozen-food items, (c) a new children's toy.

9. Explain the role of product or brand managers. Are they usually put in charge of new-product development work?

10. Discuss the social value of new-product development activities which seem to encourage people to discard products which are not "all worn out." Is this an economic waste? How worn out is "all worn out?" Must a shirt have holes in it? How big?

SUGGESTED CASES

8. Woodwards' Department Stores; Holiday Travel
11. Bing Corporation
18. Billing Sports Company
35. Bramalea Realty Ltd.

When you finish this chapter, you should:

1. Understand how and why marketing specialists adjust discrepancies of quantity and assortment.

2. Know why physical distribution is such an important part of Place and *marketing*.

3. Know about the transporting and storing possibilities a marketing manager can use.

4. Know about the different kinds of channel systems.

5. Understand how much market exposure would be "ideal."

6. Recognize the important new terms (shown in red).

PLACE AND PHYSICAL DISTRIBUTION

12

You may build a "better mousetrap" but if it's not in the right place at the right time, it won't do anyone any good.

In the next three chapters, we will look at some of the activities and specialists needed to provide "Place"—and build channels of distribution.

Place is concerned with the selection and use of marketing specialists—middlemen and transportation and storage agencies—to provide target customers with time, place, and possession utilities. A marketing manager's decisions on Place have long-run effects. They are harder to change than Product, Price, and Promotion decisions. It's hard to move retail stores and wholesale facilities. And good working arrangements among middlemen may take several years—and a good deal of money—to develop.

Place decisions are important strategic decisions. See Figure 12–1 for a picture of the strategic areas we will discuss in the next three chapters.

"IDEAL" PLACE OBJECTIVES SUGGESTED BY GOODS CLASSES

Obviously, the needs and attitudes of potential target markets have to be considered when developing Place. People in a particular target market should have similar attitudes and, therefore, should be satisfied with a similar Place system. Their attitudes about urgency to have needs satisfied—and willingness to shop—have already been summarized in the

Figure 12–1: Strategy planning for Place

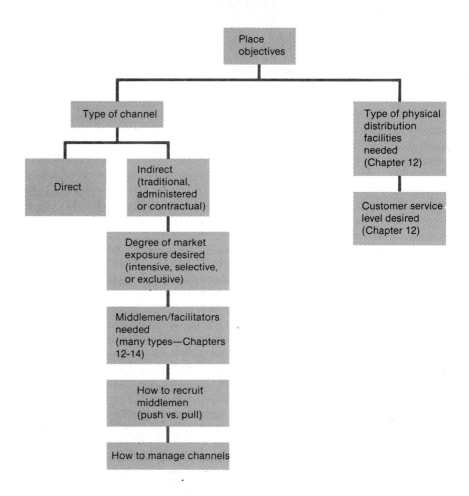

goods classes. Now we should be able to use these goods classes to suggest how Place should be handled.

The relationship between goods classes and *ideal place objective* was shown in Figure 10–3 for consumer goods and Figure 10–5 for industrial goods. These figures should be studied carefully—since they set the framework for solving the whole Place problem.

Place system is not automatic

Just as goods classes are not automatic, we cannot automatically decide on the one best Place arrangement. If there are two or three market segments with different views of the Product, then different Place arrangements may be needed as well. Further, Place depends on both (1) what customers would like best and (2) what channel members can provide profitably.

DIRECT CHANNEL SYSTEMS MAY BE BEST, SOMETIMES

Many producers like to handle the whole distribution job themselves. There are advantages in selling directly to the final user or consumer.

Marketing research is easier, because the producer's sales reps are in direct contact with the target customers. If any special selling effort or technical services are needed, the marketing manager can be sure that the sales force will receive the necessary training and motivation.

Some products typically have short channels of distribution—and a *direct-to-user channel* is not uncommon. It is not always necessary to use middlemen. On the other hand, it is not always best to "go direct" either.

SPECIALISTS AND CHANNEL SYSTEMS DEVELOP TO ADJUST DISCREPANCIES

Discrepancies require channel specialists

All producers want to be sure that their products reach the final customer. But the assortment and quantity of goods wanted by customers may be different than the assortment and quantity of goods normally produced. Specialists have developed to adjust these discrepancies.

Discrepancy of quantity means the difference between the quantity of goods it is economical for a producer to make and the quantity normally wanted by final users or consumers. For example, most manufacturers of golf balls produce large quantities—such as 200,000 to 500,000 in a given time period. The average golfer, however, wants only a few balls at a time. Adjusting for this discrepancy usually requires middlemen— wholesalers and retailers.

Producers typically specialize by product—and therefore another discrepancy develops. **Discrepancy of assortment** means the difference between the lines the typical producer makes and the assortment wanted by final consumers or users. Most golfers, for example, need more than golf balls. They want golf shoes, gloves, clubs, a bag, and so forth. And probably they would prefer not to shop around for each item. So, again, there is a need for middlemen to adjust these discrepancies.

Retailers and wholesalers adjust discrepancies of assortment.

Channel specialists adjust discrepancies with regrouping activities

Regrouping activities involve adjusting the quantities and/or assortments of goods handled at each level in a channel of distribution.

There are four regrouping activities: accumulation, allocation, sorting-out, and assorting. When one or more of these activities is required, a marketing specialist might develop to fill this need.

Adjusting quantity discrepancies by accumulating and allocating

The **accumulation process** involves collecting products from many small producers. This is common for agricultural products. It is a way of obtaining the lowest transportation rate—by putting together small quantities which then can be shipped in truckload or carload quantities.

The **allocation process** involves breaking bulk—breaking up the carload or truckload shipments into smaller quantities as the goods get closer to the final market. This may involve several middlemen. Wholesalers may sell smaller quantities to other wholesalers—or directly to retailers. Retailers continue the allocation process as they "break bulk" to their customers.

Adjusting assortment discrepancies by sorting-out and assorting

Different types of specialists are needed to adjust assortment discrepancies. Two types of regrouping activities may be needed: sorting-out and assorting.

The **sorting-out process** means grading or sorting products. This is a common process for agricultural products. Nature produces what it wants—and then these products must be sorted into the grades and qualities desired by different target markets.

The **assorting process** means putting together a variety of products to give a target market what it wants. Here, instead of nature producing a mixed assortment which must be sorted out, marketing specialists put together an assortment to satisfy some target market. This usually is done by those close to the final cosumer or user—retailers or wholesalers who try to supply a wide assortment of products for the convenience of their customers. An electrical goods wholesaler, for example, may take on a line of lawnmowers or garden products for the convenience of hardware retailer-customers.

Channel systems can be complex

Adjusting discrepancies can lead to complex channels of distribution. The possibility for competition between different channels is shown in Figure 12–2. This figure shows the many channels used by manufacturers of paperback books. These can be both consumer goods and industrial goods. This helps explain why some channels would develop. But note that the books go through wholesalers and retailers—independent and chain bookstores, schools, drugstores, supermarkets, and convenience stores. This can cause problems—because these wholesalers supply retailers who are used to different markups. Among such channels, there is

Figure 12–2: Sales of paperback books are made through many kinds of wholesalers and retailers[1]

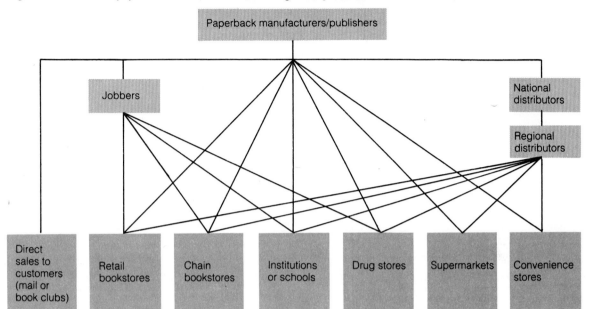

a lot of competition—including price competition. And the different markups may lead to open price wars—especially on well-known and branded products.

Dual distribution occurs when a manufacturer uses several competing channels to reach the same target market—perhaps using several middlemen and selling directly himself. This is resented by some established middlemen because they do not appreciate *any* competition—especially competition set up by their own suppliers. But manufacturers often are forced to use dual distribution—because their present channels are doing a poor job or aren't reaching some potential customers.

Sometimes there's not much choice

The paperback example seems to suggest that there are plenty of middlemen around to form almost any kind of channel system. But this isn't true. Sometimes there is only one key middleman serving a market. To reach this market, producers may have no choice but to use this one middleman.

In other cases, there are no middlemen at all! Then a producer may try to go directly to target customers. If this isn't possible, the product may die because it can't be economically distributed. Some products are not wanted in big enough volume and/or at high enough prices to justify any middlemen providing the regrouping activities needed to reach the potential customers.

PHYSICAL DISTRIBUTION IS AN IMPORTANT PART OF PLACE PLANNING

Physical distribution (PD) is the transporting and storing of physical goods within individual firms and along channel systems. Nearly half of the costs of marketing are spent on physical distribution. These PD activities are very important to a firm and the macro-marketing system. Goods that remain in the factory or on the farm really have no "use" at all. And possession utility is not possible until time and place utility have been provided. This requires the transporting and storing functions that are a part of physical distribution.

A marketing manager must decide how the transporting and storing functions should be divided within a channel. Physical distribution can be varied endlessly in a marketing mix and in a channel system. *But these decisions will affect the other three Ps—especially Price.*

THE TRANSPORTING FUNCTION

Modern transporting facilities—including railroads, pipelines, trucks, barges and ships, and airplanes—have changed marketing. Without these transporting facilities, there could be no mass distribution—with its regrouping activities—or any urban life as we know it today. Producers in small towns and rural areas can now reach customers all over the world.

Ton-miles carried is the most common method of measuring the importance of various methods of transportation. A ton-mile represents the movement of a ton of goods one mile. If, for example, 10 tons of sand were carried 10 miles, the total movement would be 100 ton-miles.

Using this measure makes it obvious that railways are the backbone of the Canadian transportation system. Rail accounts for more than five times as many ton-miles as highway. Discussions of ton miles, however, do not tell the whole story. By 1968, trucks were carrying as many tons of freight as the railroads, but not for as many miles.[2]

Can you afford to hit the target?

The cost of shipping an average product by rail is about 5 percent of wholesale cost.[3] For many bulky and low-value products, however, the percentage is much higher. Transporting sand and gravel, for example, costs about 55 percent of its value. At the other extreme, lighter or more valuable commodities—such as copper or office machines—are transported for less than 1 percent of wholesale cost.[4]

Different transporters charge different rates

Common carriers—such as the railroads and major truck lines—are transporters which maintain regular schedules and accept goods from any shipper. They charge rates which are fixed for all users by government regulators. **Contract carriers** are transporters who are willing to work for anyone for an agreed sum—and for any length of time. They are less strictly regulated. **Private carriers** are company-owned transportation facilities. Do-it-yourself transporting is always a possibility, but it often isn't

Contract carriers are less strictly regulated and will take a cargo anywhere.

economical because the contract or common carriers can make fuller use of their facilities and, therefore, charge less.

Common carriers provide a dependable transportation service for the many producers and middlemen who make small shipments in various directions. Contract carriers, on the other hand, are a more free-wheeling group—going wherever goods have to be moved.

Marketing manager can affect rates

There is nothing final about the present common carrier rate structure. Carriers can and do propose changes—and if no one objects—the new rates usually go into effect. Rate changes can be made relatively quickly (1 to 30 days) and easily. Each year, about 150,000 changes are made in rail rates alone. And with the government encouraging deregulation we probably will see more and faster changes.

Creative marketing managers—by bargaining for rate changes—can help their channel system members with the transporting function. In fact, some manufacturers and middlemen maintain traffic departments to deal with carriers. These departments can be a great help—not only to their own firms but also to their suppliers and customers—finding the best route at the lowest rates.

Which transportation alternative is best?

The best transportation choice should not only be as low in cost as possible, but also provide the level of service (e.g., speed and dependability) required. Sometimes this would mean using one of the special services offered by railroads. In other cases, air freight might be the best choice. Or it might be best to "do it yourself" if the transporting specialists don't have any advantage.

Piggyback service can cut costs and provide flexibility for shippers.

Railroads

The railroads have been the workhorses of Canadian transportation—carrying heavy, bulky freight such as coal, sand, and steel. By handling large quantities of such goods, the railroads are able to charge relatively low rates. But railroads have had profit difficulties in recent years, in part because trucks have set their rates low enough to get some of the more profitable business that railroads were counting on to make up for the low rates on the bulky products.

Truck competition has forced the railroads to offer faster and more flexible services. A "fast freight" service for perishable or high-value items, for example, can be competitive with trucks if the shippers and receivers are located near rail lines. And a **piggy-back service** loads truck trailers on rail cars to provide both speed and flexibility. On some routes it may even cost less.

Trucks

The flexibility of trucks makes them especially good for moving small loads for short distances. They can travel on almost any road. They can give extremely fast service. Also, trucks cause less breakage and handling than rails—an important factor because it may allow lower packaging costs. For short distances and for higher-value products, trucks may charge rates that are the same as (or lower than) railroad rates—yet provide much faster service.

Ships and barges

Waterways play an important role in Canada's transportation network, particularly in two areas of the country. These are the eastern Great Lakes–St. Lawrence coastal system and the British Columbia coastal system.

Air freight is the most expensive transporting alternative, but it may reduce the total distribution cost.

The availability of ocean transport to the vast industrial and agricultural hinterlands of Canada and the United States, as well as easier movement of traffic in the Great Lakes–St. Lawrence River area, was made possible in 1959 by the completion of the St. Lawrence Waterway System. This 2,342-mile-long waterway opened the Great Lakes to 80 percent of all ocean vessels. Only the very largest ships are excluded. **Lakers** on these internal waterways are used chiefly for bulky, nonperishable products, such as iron ore, grain, steel, petroleum products, cement, gravel, sand, coal, and coke.

Bulk movement of a few commodities (particularly forest products) also dominates the British Columbia coastal system. But in contrast to the communities along the eastern waterways, the British Columbia communities are almost entirely dependent upon ships for receipt of supplies from the Lower Mainland. No other form of transport is available for shipment of freight. The barge and tug are the predominant type of shipping used.

Airplanes

The most expensive means of cargo transportation is air freight—but it also is fast! Air freight rates normally are at least twice as high as trucking rates—but the greater speed may be worth the added cost. Most air freight so far has been fashions, perishable commodities, and high-value industrial parts for the electronics and metal-working industries. California's strawberries, for example, are flown to distant markets all through the year.

A big advantage of air transport is that the cost of packing, unpacking, and preparing goods for sale may be reduced or eliminated when goods are shipped by air. Some women's fashions are shipped on racks which eventually are moved right into the store!

Air freight can help a producer reduce inventory costs by eliminating outlying warehouses. The greater speed may also reduce spoilage, theft, and damage. So, although the *transportation cost* may be higher, the *total cost of distribution* for a firm using air freight may be lower.

STORING MAY BE NEEDED IN SOME CHANNELS

Storing is the marketing function of holding goods. It provides time utility. Storing is necessary because production does not always match consumption. Some products—such as farm produce—are produced seasonally although they are in demand year-round. And some products—such as car antifreeze—have a big demand for short periods.

Storing can be done by both manufacturers and middlemen. It can balance supply and demand—keeping stocks at convenient locations, ready to meet customers' needs. Storing is one of the major activities of some middlemen.

Specialized storage facilities can be very helpful

Private warehouses are storing facilities owned by companies for their own use. Most manufacturers, wholesalers, and retailers have some storing facilities in their own main buildings or in a warehouse district.

Private warehouses are used when a large volume of goods must be stored regularly. Owning warehouse space can be expensive, however. If the need changes, the extra space may be hard—or impossible—to rent to others.

Public warehouses are independent storing facilities. They can provide all the services that could be obtained in a company's own warehouse. A company might choose to use a public warehouse if it did not have a regular need for warehouse space. With a public warehouse, the customer pays only for space used—and may purchase a variety of additional services. Public warehouses are useful to manufacturers who must maintain stocks in many locations—including foreign countries. Public warehouses are found in all major urban areas—and many smaller cities. Rural towns also have public warehouses for locally produced agricultural commodities.

General merchandise warehouses are public warehouses which store almost any kind of manufactured goods. **Bonded warehouses** are public warehouses which specialize in imported goods or other goods (such as liquors or cigarettes) on which a tax must be paid before the goods are released for sale. **Commodity warehouses** and **cold-storage warehouses** are public warehouses that are designed specifically for storing perishable products—such as grain, apples, butter, and furs. Grain, for example, is stored in big elevators which move the grain around to keep it cool.

Modernized warehousing facilities have developed

The cost of physical handling is a major storing cost. The goods must be handled once when put into storage and again when removed to be sold. Further, in the typical old "downtown" warehouse districts, traffic congestion, crowded storage areas, and slow freight elevators slow the process. This increases the cost.

Today, modern one-story buildings are replacing the old multistory buildings. They are located away from downtown traffic. They use power-oper-

Distribution centers can speed service while lowering costs.

ated lift trucks, battery-operated motor scooters, roller-skating order-pickers, electric hoists for heavy items, and hydraulic ramps to aid loading and unloading.

Distribution center is a different kind of warehouse

A **distribution center** is a special kind of warehouse designed to speed the flow of goods—and avoid unnecessary storage. Basically, it is a breaking-bulk operation. Turnover is increased—and the cost of carrying inventory is reduced. This is important because these costs may run as high as 35 percent of the value of the average inventory each year.

The idea behind the distribution center is that reducing costs and increasing turnover will lead to bigger profits. Storing is sensible only if it helps obtain time utility.

Some large food manufacturers and supermarket operators run their own distribution centers. For example, the Pillsbury Company—a large manufacturer of baking mixes and flour—ships products in rail carloads from its various manufacturing plants (which each specialize in a few product lines) directly to distribution centers. Almost no goods are stored at the factories. These distribution centers are able to quickly ship any combination of goods by the most economical transportation route. This lets Pillsbury offer faster service at lower cost.

PHYSICAL DISTRIBUTION CONCEPT FOCUSES ON WHOLE DISTRIBUTION SYSTEM

We have been looking at the transporting and storing functions as separate activities—partly because this simplifies discussion but also because it is the usual approach. Recently, however, attention has turned to the *whole* physical distribution function—not just storing and transporting. Focusing only on one function at a time may actually increase a firm's and channel's total distribution costs. "Physical distribution" people usually study the total cost of possible PD systems because there may be attractive trade-offs. For example, higher transporting costs may be more than offset by lower storing costs—as with air freight.

**Total cost approach
helps**

The **total cost approach**—to selecting a PD system—evaluates *all* the costs of possible PD systems. This means that all costs—including some which are sometimes ignored—should be considered. Inventory costs, for example, are often ignored in marketing decisions—because these costs are buried in "overhead costs." But inventory costs may be very high. In fact, including them may lead to a different decision. See Figure 12–3 for a picture of the typical relation of physical distribution costs.

**Physical distribution not
just cost-oriented**

Early physical distribution efforts focused attention on lowering costs. Now, there is more emphasis on making physical distribution planning a part of the company's strategy planning. Sometimes, by increasing physical distribution cost somewhat, the customer service level can be increased so much that, in effect, a new and better marketing mix is created.

Customer service level is a measure of how rapidly and dependably a firm can deliver what customers want. Figure 12–3 shows the typical relation between physical distribution costs and customer service level. When a firm decides to minimize total cost, it may also be settling for a lower customer service level. By increasing the number of distribution points, the firm might be able to serve more customers within a specified time period. Transporting costs would be reduced—but warehousing and inventory costs would be increased. The higher service level, however, might greatly improve the company's strategy. Increased sales might more than make up for increased costs. Clearly, the marketing manager has a strategic decision to make about what service level to offer. Minimizing cost is not always the right answer.

**Figure 12–3: Higher
customer service levels are
obtained at a cost**

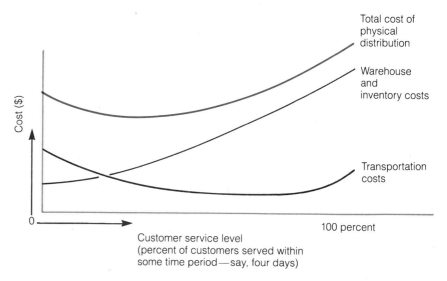

INDIRECT CHANNELS MAY BE BEST, SOMETIMES

Although a producer might prefer to handle the whole distribution job himself, this is just not economical for many kinds of goods—unless the firm integrates and forms its own "vertical marketing system." But typically, producers have to use middlemen—like it or not. They may join vertical marketing systems—or simply traditional channel systems. The survival of the firm may depend on what type it joins—or develops. The kinds of systems—and their characteristics—are summarized in Figure 12–4 and discussed below.

Traditional channel systems are common

In a **traditional channel system**—the various channel members make little or no effort to cooperate with each other. They buy and sell from each other—and that's all. In some very independent channels, buyers may even prefer to wait until sellers desperately need to sell—hoping to force the price down. This leads to erratic production, inventory, and employment patterns that can only increase total costs. Traditional channel members may have their independence—but they may pay for it too. As we will see, such channels are declining in importance—with good reason. But they are still typical in some industries.

Corporate channel systems—shorten channels

Some corporations develop their own vertically integrated channel systems. With corporate ownership all along the channel, we can say that the firm is "going direct"—but actually it may be handling manufacturing, wholesaling, *and* retailing—and it is more meaningful to think of it as running a vertical marketing system.

Figure 12–4: **Types of channel systems**

| | Traditional | Vertical marketing systems | | |
		Administered	Contractual	Corporate
Amount of cooperation	Little or none	Some to good	Fairly good to good	Complete
Control maintained by	None	Economic power and leadership	Contracts	Ownership by one company
Examples	Typical channel of "independents"	General Electric, Miller's Beer, O.M. Scott & Sons (lawn products)	McDonald's, Holiday Inn, IGA, Ace Hardware, Super Valu, Coca-Cola, Chevrolet	Florsheim Shoes, Firestone Tire

Vertical integration is at different levels

In **vertical integration,** control is expanded to two or more successive stages of production or distribution. A retailer might go into wholesaling and perhaps even manufacturing. Some companies are integrated both horizontally and vertically. A&P, Steinberg, Bata, and Florsheim Shoes are wholesalers or manufacturers as well as retailers. A&P, for example, has fish-canning plants. Bata and Florsheim make their own shoes, and Steinberg has its own bakeries.

There are many possible advantages to vertical integration—stability of operations, assurance of materials and supplies, better control of distribution, better quality control, larger research facilities, greater buying power, and lower executive overhead. Provided that the discrepancies of quantity and assortment are not too great at each level in a channel—that is, the firms fit together well—vertical integration may be very efficient and profitable.[5]

Vertical integration may benefit the consumer, too—through lower prices and better products. Vertical integration brings smooth, routine operation—and can cut costs. Business transactions that once required negotiations between separate firms are now routine requisitions, acknowledgements, and internal accounting transactions.

Administered and contractual systems may work well

The natural advantages of an integrated system have been understood by some progressive marketers. But instead of integrating corporately, they have developed administered or contractual channel systems. In **administered channel systems**—the various channel members informally agree to cooperate with each other. This could include agreements to routinize ordering, standardize accounting, and coordinate promotion efforts. In **contractual channel systems**—the various channel members agree by contract to cooperate with each other. With both of these systems, the members get some of the advantages of corporate integration—while retaining some of the flexibility of a traditional channel system.

Norge Division of Borg-Warner Corporation, a large U.S. appliance manufacturer, developed an informal arrangement—with its independent wholesalers—to provide them automatically and continually with a six weeks' inventory of appliances—based on current inventory and sales, plus projected sales. Every week, Norge makes a thorough item-by-item analysis of 125,000–130,000 major appliance units valued at around $18 million. These units are located in many warehouses operated by 87 wholesalers throughout the country. Each week, all this data is analyzed by the president and the managers of distribution, sales, and marketing research (as well as the manufacturing heads)—and plans for production and sales activities for the following weeks are set.

Similar systems have been developed and coordinated by middlemen in the grocery, hardware, and drug industries. In fact, a retailer in these lines almost has to be a member of such a system to survive.

Channel captains should organize the whole channel so it works as a unit instead of many independent firms.

Vertical marketing systems—new wave in the marketplace

The advantages of a coordinated channel system have been understood by progressive marketers. Some corporations integrate vertically to link production with wholesaling and/or retailing. Others are simply developing contractual or informal (administered) relationships with others in their channel system. See Figure 12–4. These more smoothly operating channel systems appear to be competively better than the traditional channel systems which do not cooperate.

CHANNEL CAPTAIN NEEDED TO GUIDE CHANNEL PLANNING

Until now, we have considered an individual marketing manager as the strategy planner. But now we see that there may be several firms and managers in a single distribution channel. It is logical that each channel have a **channel captain**—a manager who would help direct the activities of the whole channel. The question is: which marketing manager should be the captain?

The idea of a single channel captain makes sense—but some channels do not have such a captain. The various firms may not be acting as a system because of lack of leadership. Or, the members of a system may not understand that they are part of a channel.

But, even if they don't know it, firms *are* connected by their policies. It makes sense to try to avoid channel conflicts by planning for channel relationships.

Manufacturer or middlemen?

In North America manufacturers frequently are the leaders in channel relations. Middlemen wait and see what the manufacturer intends to do and what it wants done. Then they decide whether their roles will be profitable—and whether they want to join in the manufacturer's plans.

Some middlemen do take the lead—especially in foreign markets where there are fewer large manufacturers. Such middlemen may decide what their customers want and seek out manufacturers—perhaps small ones—who can provide these products at reasonable prices.

Large middlemen are closer to the final user or consumer—and in an ideal position to assume the channel captain role. It is even possible that middlemen—especially retailers—may dominate the marketing systems of the future.

Middlemen are especially likely to serve as channel captains when a limited number of companies make most of the retail sales. This is often the case in Canada and especially true in the grocery trade. Five Canadian chains account for about 40 percent of all grocery outlet sales![6] Few manufacturers can afford to argue with these chains on pricing or merchandising matters for fear that their products will no longer be carried.[7]

Our captain the producer—for convenience only

For convenience, let's assume that the channel captain is a producer. (Remember, though, that a middleman may play this role too.)[8]

The job of the channel captain is to arrange for the necessary marketing activities in the best way. This might be done as shown in Figure 12–5 in a manufacturer-dominated channel system. Here, the manufacturer has selected a target market and developed a product, set the price structure, done some promotion, and developed the place setup. Middlemen are then expected to finish the promotion job—at their own places.

If a middleman is the channel captain, we would see quite a different diagram. In the extreme—in a channel like that dominated by Eaton's—the middleman circle would be almost completely shaded for some products. Manufacturers would be mainly concerned with manufacturing the product to meet Eaton's requirements.

A coordinated channel system may help everyone

A channel system in which the members have accepted the leadership of a channel captain can work very well—even though not everyone in the channel system is strongly market-oriented. As long as the channel

Figure 12–5: How channel strategy might be handled in a manufacturer-dominated system[9]

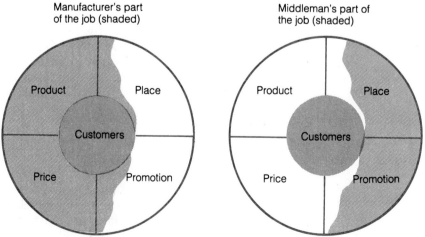

Manufacturer's part of the job (shaded)

Middleman's part of the job (shaded)

captain is market-oriented, it should be possible to win the confidence and support of production-oriented firms—and make the whole channel work well. Small production-oriented producers in Japan or Hong Kong, for example, may become part of an effective channel reaching the Canadian market—if there is a middleman who correctly understands market needs and explains them clearly to the producers. The producers may not even know where their products are going—but the system still can compete with other systems and be profitable for the members.

THE BEST CHANNEL SYSTEM SHOULD ACHIEVE IDEAL MARKET EXPOSURE

The best channel system does not just happen. Someone must plan the system. And someone must make specific decisions about how much market exposure will be needed in each geographic area. Although it might seem that all marketing managers would want their products to have maximum exposure to potential customers, this is not the case. Some products require much less market exposure than others.

The **ideal market exposure** should make a product widely enough available to satisfy target customers' needs—but not exceed them. Too much exposure would only increase the total marketing cost.

Three degrees of market exposure may be ideal

Intensive distribution is selling a product through all responsible and suitable wholesalers or retailers who will stock and/or sell the product. **Selective distribution** is selling through only those middlemen who will give the product special attention. **Exclusive distribution** is selling through only one middleman in each geographic area.

In practice, this means that cigarettes are handled—through intensive distribution—by at least 90,000 Canadian outlets, while Rolls Royces are handled—through exclusive distribution—by only a limited number of middlemen across the country.

Intensive distribution— sell it where they buy it

Intensive distribution is commonly needed by convenience goods and for industrial supplies (such as pencils, paper clips, and typing paper) used by all plants or offices. Customers want such goods nearby.

The seller's *intent* is important here. Intensive distribution refers to the *desire* to sell through all responsible and suitable outlets. What this means depends on customer habits and preferences. If the target customers normally buy a certain product in a certain type of outlet, then ideally we would specify this type of outlet in our Place policy. If customers prefer to buy hardware items only at hardware stores, for example, then an intensive distribution policy would mean selling through all hardware stores. If, however—as it seems today—many customers will buy certain hardware items at any convenient outlet—including drugstores and food stores—then an intensive distribution policy would require use of these outlets—and probably more than one channel of distribution.

**Selective distribution—
sell it where it sells best**

Selective distribution covers the area between intensive and exclusive distribution. It can be suitable for any kind of product. Only the better middlemen are used here. The usual purpose is to get some of the advantages of exclusive distribution—while still getting fairly widespread coverage.

A selective distribution policy might be used to avoid selling to wholesalers or retailers who: (1) have a poor credit rating, (2) have a reputation for making too many returns or requesting too much service, (3) place orders that are too small to justify making calls or providing service, or (4) are not in a position—for any other reason—to do a satisfactory marketing job.

Selective distribution is growing in popularity as marketers decide it is not necessary to get 100 percent coverage of a market. Some perfume manufacturers, for example, use selective distribution because they want good display and sales help for their products.

**Exclusive distribution
sometimes makes sense**

Exclusive distribution means that one (only) middleman is selected in each geographic area. Besides the various advantages of selective distribution, manufacturers might want to use exclusive distribution to help control prices and the service offered in a channel.

**But is limiting market
exposure legal?**

Exclusive distribution is not specifically illegal in the antimonopoly laws. But current interpretation of these laws by the courts gives the impression that almost any exclusive distribution arrangement *could* be interpreted as an injury to some competitor somewhere.

Any consideration of Place raises the question of the legality of limiting market exposure.

Exclusive distribution, as such, is not illegal in Canada. "Horizontal" agreements among competing retailers, wholesalers, and/or manufacturers would almost certainly be judged a violation of section 32 of the Combines Act. However, it would have to be proven that such agreements had "unduly lessened competition."

**Using selective distribution
can obtain better displays
and sales help.**

Stage I amendments to the Combines Act allows the Restrictive Trade Practices Commission to act against vertical agreements judged as having an adverse effect upon competition. This legislation (Bill C–2) also specified that "unduly lessening competition" meant lessening it to any extent judged detrimental to the public interest. (Previously, it had to be shown that competition would be completely or virtually eliminated).

Obviously, considerable caution must be exercised before firms enter into any exclusive dealing arrangement. The same probably holds true for selective distribution. Here, however, less formal and binding arrangements are typical and the chance of an adverse impact on competition being proven is more remote.

PUSHING OR PULLING THROUGH AN INDIRECT CHANNEL SYSTEM

A producer has a special challenge with respect to channel systems: How to win channel cooperation to make sure that the product reaches the target market.

The two basic methods of achieving channel cooperation are pushing and pulling.

Pushing policy—get a hand from the firm in the channel

Pushing a product through the channels means using normal promotion effort—personal selling and advertising—to help sell the whole marketing mix to possible channel members. This approach emphasizes the importance of building a channel and getting the cooperation of channel members. The producer, in effect, tries to develop a team that will work together to get the product to the user.

Pulling policy—make them reach for it out there

By contrast, **pulling** means getting consumers to ask middlemen for the product. This usually involves very aggressive promotion to final consumers—perhaps using coupons or samples. If the promotion works, the middlemen are forced to carry the product to satisfy their customers. Of course, the middlemen should be told about the promotion—so they can be ready if it is successful.

A pulling policy depends on consumers asking for an advertised product.

This method—common in the soap industry—may be necessary if many products are already competing in all desired outlets.

Sell the whole mix to channel members

However channel cooperation is won, potential channel members must be convinced that the producer knows what he's trying to do and why. The marketing manager's sales reps must be able to tell prospective channel members what is expected of them—and how much competition they may get from other channels. It may be a good idea to spell out how the firm and channels will react to probable competitive marketing mixes. In other words, Place policies must be tied in with the rest of the marketing mix if the whole mix is going to work.

CONCLUSION

This chapter has discussed the role of Place—and noted that Place decisions are especially important because they may be difficult to change.

Marketing specialists and channel systems develop to adjust discrepancies of quantity and assortment. Their regrouping activities are basic in any economic system, and adjusting discrepancies provides opportunities for creative marketers.

Physical distribution functions—basically transporting and storing—were discussed. These activities are needed to provide time, place, and possession utility. And by using the total cost approach, the lowest cost PD alternative or the cost of various customer service levels can be found.

The importance of planning channel systems was discussed—along with the role of a channel captain. It was stressed that channel systems compete with each other—and that smoothly operating vertical marketing systems seem to be winning out in the marketplace.

Channel planning also requires deciding on the degree of market exposure desired. The legality of limiting market exposure should also be considered—to avoid jail or having to undo an expensively developed channel system.

Finally, it was emphasized that producers aren't necessarily channel captains. Often, middlemen control or even dominate channels of distribution. The degree of this control must be considered by producers when they decide whether they should try to push or pull their product through a channel system.

QUESTIONS FOR DISCUSSION

1. Explain "discrepancies of quantity and assortment" using the clothing business as an example. How does the application of the concept of discrepancies change when coal for sale to the steel industry is considered rather than clothing? What impact does this have on the number and kinds of marketing specialists required?

2. Explain the four steps in the regrouping process with an example from the building supply industry (nails, paint, flooring, plumbing fixtures, etc.). Would you expect many specialists to develop in this industry or would the manufacturers handle the job themselves? What kind of marketing channels would you expect to find in this industry and what functions would be provided by various channel members?

3. If a manufacturer has five different markets to reach, how many channels is he likely to use? If only one, why? If more than one, what sort of problems will this raise?

4. Discuss the relative advantages and disadvantages of railroads, trucks, and airlines as transporting methods.

5. Distinguish between common carriers and contract carriers. What role do the contract carriers

play in our economic system? How would our economy be different if there were no common carriers?

6. Explain which transportation method would probably be most suitable for shipment of goods to a large Toronto department store:
   a. A 10,000-lb. shipment of dishes from Japan.
   b. 15 lbs. of screwdrivers from Quebec.
   c. Three couches from High Point, N.C.
   d. 500 high-fashion dresses from the garment district in New York City.
   e. 300 lbs. of Pacific Coast lobsters.
   f. 60,000 lbs. of various appliances from Montreal.
   How would your answers change if this department store were the only one in a large factory town in Ontario?

7. Indicate the nearest location where you would expect to find substantial storage facilities. What kinds of products would be stored there, and why are they stored there instead of some other place?

8. Indicate when a producer or middleman would find it desirable to use a public warehouse rather than a private warehouse. Illustrate, using a specific product or situation.

9. Discuss the distribution center concept. Is this likely to eliminate the storing function of conventional wholesalers? Is it applicable to all products? If not, cite several examples.

10. Clearly differentiate between a warehouse and a distribution center. Explain how a specific product would be handled differently by these marketing institutions.

11. Explain total cost approach and customer service level in your own words. Explain why raising customer service levels might increase the total cost.

12. Explain how a "channel captain" could help independent firms compete with integrated ones.

13. Relate the nature of the product to the degree of market exposure desired.

14. Why would middlemen seek to be exclusive distributors for a product? Why would producers seek exclusive distributors? Would middlemen be equally anxious to obtain exclusive distribution for any type of product? Why or why not? Explain with reference to the following products: cornflakes, razor blades, golf clubs, golfballs, steak knives, hi-fi equipment, and industrial woodworking machinery.

15. Explain the present legal status of exclusive distribution.

16. Discuss the promotion a grocery products manufacturer would need in order to develop appropriate channels and move goods through these channels. Would the nature of this job change at all for a dress manufacturer? How about for a small producer of installations?

17. Discuss the advantages and disadvantages of either a pushing or pulling policy for a very small manufacturer who is just getting into the candy business with a line of inexpensive candy bars. Which policy would probably be most appropriate? State any assumptions you need to obtain a definite answer.

18. Explain the strategic decisions a manufacturer's marketing manager must make about Place. Illustrate.

SUGGESTED CASES

When you finish this chapter, you should:

1. Understand about retailers planning their own marketing strategies.

2. Know about the many kinds of retailers which might become members of producers' or wholesalers' channel systems.

3. Understand the differences among the conventional retailers and the nonconventional retailers—including those who have accepted the mass merchandising concept.

4. Understand scrambled merchandising and the "wheel of retailing."

5. Recognize the important new terms (shown in red).

RETAILING

13

If the products aren't sold, nobody makes any money.

Retailing is a very important activity. It is concerned with satisfying *final* consumers. It is *not* concerned with industrial goods—or the sale of consumer goods in the channels.

Retailing covers all of the activities involved in the sale of goods and/or services to final consumers. The retailer must (1) put together an assortment of products to satisfy some target market, (2) make these products available at a reasonable price, and (3) convince customers that these products will satisfy their needs. The term *merchandising* is often used to cover all these activities.

RETAILERS MUST PLAN MARKETING STRATEGIES, TOO

A retailer should plan a marketing strategy just like any other marketing manager. In fact, retailers are so close to final consumers that their strategy *has* to work if they are to survive. Unlike some manufacturers or wholesalers, they can't "unload" their mistakes on middlemen. Because they are so aware that they must satisfy consumers, retailers make *buying* an important activity. Successful retailers are well aware of an old rule: "Goods well bought are half sold."

Figure 13–1 shows some of the strategic decision areas for a retailer. Usually, a particular retailer may appeal to more than one target market at the same time. Further, they usually sell whole assortments (or combina-

Figure 13–1: Strategic decision areas for a retailer

Target market

Product | Place | Promotion | Price

Assortment
Customer service
Hours
Credit

Location
Facilities
Size
Layout

tions) of goods and services—not just individual products. So, it is useful to think of a retailer's whole offering as a "product." Then, most of what we said in the Product area can be applied here, too.

Goods classes help understand store types

Retail strategy planning can be simplified by recalling our earlier discussion of consumer behavior and the consumer goods classes—convenience goods, shopping goods, and specialty goods.

We can define three types of stores: *convenience* stores, *shopping* stores, and *specialty* stores. But it is very important to see that these classes refer to the *customer's* image of the store.

A **convenience store** is a convenient place to shop—either centrally located "downtown" or "in the neighborhood." Such stores attract customers because they are so handy.

Shopping stores attract customers from greater distances because of the width and depth of their assortments. Stores selling clothing, furniture, or household appliances are usually thought of as shopping stores.

Specialty stores are those for which customers have developed a strong attraction. For whatever reasons—service, selection, or reputation—some customes will consistently buy convenience, shopping, and specialty goods at these stores.

Store type sets strategy guidelines

A retailer's strategy planning should consider potential customers' attitudes toward both the product and the store. Classifying stores by type of goods—as shown in Figure 13–2—helps you understand a retailer's possibilities. By identifying which competitors are satisfying various market segments, a retailer may see new opportunities. In some cases, the manager may find that he and his competitors are all concentrating on only certain customers and completely missing others. Or he may see an opportunity for building a new strategy—as Liz Gray did.

Liz Gray opens a convenience store for shopping goods

Liz Gray—a buyer in a local department store—is considering opening her own women's clothing shop. She knows that most of her competitors

Figure 13–2: **How customers view store goods classes**[1]

Product type / Store type	Convenience	Shopping	Specialty
Convenience	Will buy any brand at most accessible store	Shop around to find better service and/or lower prices	Prefer store. Brand may be important
Shopping	Want some selection but will settle for assortment at most accessible store	Want to compare both products and store mixes	Prefer store but insist on adequate assortment
Specialty	Prefer particular product but like place convenience too	Prefer particular product but still seeking best total product and mix	Prefer both store and product

are shopping or specialty stores—carrying the kinds of shopping goods Liz would like to offer. Checking further, she finds that the convenience store–shopping goods market has been overlooked by her competitors. Liz rents a store in a small shopping center where no competitors are located. She decides to avoid competing directly in the other markets. Instead, Liz plans to offer a reasonable selection of *shopping* goods items at her *convenient* location. She knows prices will have to be reasonable because customers do shop around. But since she will have no direct competition, a ''sale'' atmosphere won't be necessary. And, she won't have to carry deep assortments of high-fashion items. Liz feels that a selection of smart but not ''faddy'' blouses, skirts, sweaters, and accessories will meet the needs of this market segment. Of course, she plans to study the special needs and attitudes of the people in the nearby area when selecting her stock, but the store-goods class helped Liz set the guidelines for her strategy.

EVOLUTION OF CONVENTIONAL RETAILERS

Many different kinds of retailers have developed over the years—to meet changing customer needs. In the following sections, you will learn why these retailers have developed and why there are so many stores—especially so many small stores.

Actually, there is constant change in retailing. So a good understanding of the *why* of various kinds of retailing facilities will help you plan better marketing strategies now—and in the future.

Figure 13–3 shows some types of retailers who have survived by finding a place in a very competitive market.

Figure 13–3: **Types of retailers and the nature of their offerings**

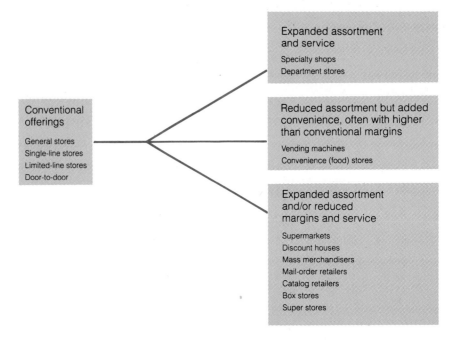

Conventional offerings

General stores
Single-line stores
Limited-line stores
Door-to-door

Expanded assortment and service

Specialty shops
Department stores

Reduced assortment but added convenience, often with higher than conventional margins

Vending machines
Convenience (food) stores

Expanded assortment and/or reduced margins and service

Supermarkets
Discount houses
Mass merchandisers
Mail-order retailers
Catalog retailers
Box stores
Super stores

Conventional retailers are durable

Conventional retailers have been around for a long time. It is clear that they satisfy some consumers' needs. Usually conventional retailers start with one person or family running the store. Their assortment is limited by how much money (capital) they have—and how well they can manage the whole operation by themselves. They may handle a single or limited line of merchandise—so they can carry the minimum assortment which will satisfy their potential customers. If they face much competition, however, they may increase their assortment or specialize further. At the same time, they try to keep costs down and prices up—by avoiding competition on the same products. Let's take a closer look at these conventional retailers.

Door-to-door retailers— effective for "unsought goods"

Door-to-door selling means going directly to the consumer's home. This can be a good method for introducing a new product or for selling unsought goods. But it is an expensive method—markups range from 30 to 50 percent, and often higher.

Door-to-door selling can be very successful—although it accounts for just over 1 percent of retail sales. Electrolux sells vacuum cleaners this way and claims the top position in the vacuum cleaner business—selling all its cleaners at list price! Fuller Brush, Avon, and most encyclopedia companies also use this approach successfully.

General stores were popular

General stores sell anything the local consumers will buy in enough volume to justify carrying it. In the early days of our country, they were the main type of retail outlet. And they served as more than just a retail store. They were also a social center, perhaps the post office, and a collecting point for agricultural products.

Today such stores are usually located in rural communities. They are defined by Statistics Canada as retail outlets selling dry goods or apparel plus at least one other subsidiary line (such as hardware, appliances, paint, and so forth) with groceries accounting for between one third and two thirds of sales. In 1980, they represented only 1.8 percent of total retail sales.[2]

Single-line, limited-line stores are being squeezed

Single-line or limited-line stores specialize in certain lines rather than the broad assortment carried by general stores. These kinds of stores became common in the late 19th century. The increasing output and variety of consumer goods made it impossible for the general store to carry large assortments in all its traditional lines. Some stores began specializing in clothing, furniture, or groceries. Some specialized even within a single line—like butcher shops, bakeries, or fish stores.

Most conventional retailers are single-line or limited-line stores. And this probably will be true as long as customers demand a wide choice of products. These stores can satisfy *some* target markets very well. Their major disadvantage is that they are usually small—and their expenses are high in relation to sales. This leads them to adopt the conventional retailer's philosophy of "buy low and sell high." It is this attitude which is causing some of them to be squeezed out by newer types of retailers.

Convenience stores must have the right assortment

Convenience (food) stores are a variation of the conventional limited-line food stores. Instead of carrying a big variety, they limit their stock to "fill-in" items—like bread, milk, ice cream, or beer. Stores such as 7–Eleven or Mac's fill needs between major shopping trips. They are offering *convenience*—not assortment—and often charge prices 10–20 percent higher than prices at nearby supermarkets.

The number of such stores has increased steadily and is expected to continue increasing in the 1980s. Interestingly enough, two major Quebec food chains, Provigo and Steinberg's, have recently entered this segment of retailing by establishing their own convenience store franchise systems.

Specialty shops usually sell shopping goods

A **specialty shop**—a type of limited-line store—usually is small, with a distinct personality. It aims at a carefully defined market segment with a unique product assortment, good service, and salespeople who know their products. For example, a small chain of specialty shops has developed to satisfy the growing market of joggers. The clerks are runners themselves. They know the sport and are eager to explain the advantages of different styles of running shoes to their customers. These stores also carry a selection of books on running, as well as clothes for the jogger. They even offer a discount to customers who are members of local track teams.

A specialty shop's major advantage is that it caters to certain types of customers whom the management and salespeople come to know well. This is important because specialty shops usually offer special types of

Specialty shops cater to well-defined markets with unique product assortments and knowledgeable salespeople.

shopping goods. Knowing their market simplifies buying, speeds turnover, and cuts cost.

Specialty shops probably will continue to be a part of the retailing scene as long as customers have varied tastes and the money to satisfy them.

Do not confuse specialty *shops* with specialty *stores*. A specialty *store* is a store that for some reason (service, quality, etc.) has become THE store for some customers. For example, a large number of customers buy all their appliances, tools, hardware, and paint supplies at Sears. For this group of consumers, Sears is a specialty store *for those items*. They do not plan to "shop around" in other stores first—they always "shop Sears."

Department stores are many limited-line stores and specialty shops

Department stores are larger stores—organized into separate departments. Each of these departments is really a limited-line store or specialty shop. In this way, the department store can get some economies of scale. Department stores handle a wide variety of goods—such as women's ready-to-wear and accessories, men's and boy's wear, fabrics, housewares, and house furnishings.

Department stores generally try to cater to customers seeking shopping goods. Originally they were located in downtown districts close to other department stores and convenient to many potential customers. Historically, this close grouping developed to facilitate shopping at the junctions of major transportation facilities. Since the early 1950s, many downtown department stores have opened suburban branches in shopping centers to serve the middle and higher income groups who moved to the suburbs.

By 1978 these suburban outlets accounted for 68.4 percent of total department store sales.[3] Consequently, downtown main store sales have suffered.

Some department stores are now making plans to renew the appeal of their traditional downtown locations by (1) carrying wide lines in the major shopping goods items for which they have long been famous, (2) attracting the trade of conventioneers and tourists, and (3) appealing to low-income groups remaining in the residential neighborhoods near the downtown area. New urban trends, including downtown apartment units, urban redevelopment, and improved mass transit, may save some of the big downtown stores.[4]

Department stores are often looked to as the retailing leaders in a community. Leaders, first, because they seem to be so generous with customer services, including credit, merchandise return, delivery, fashion shows, and Christmas displays. And leaders also because of their size. In 1979, there were in total some 713 Canadian department store locations (315 major and 398 junior) with sales of $8.5 billion, accounting for 11.1 percent of total retail trade.[5]

Certain department stores have a strong grip on local markets. Across Canada, the department store sector is dominated by three giant chains, each with sales in excess of $1 billion. These include the Hudson's Bay Company, now the number-one retailer in Canada, Simpsons-Sears, and Eaton's. In 1980 the Hudson's Bay Company and Sears together accounted for more than half (54.5 percent) of all the sales made by department stores and general merchandise stores in Canada. This is in marked contrast to the situation in the United States, where there are many large department store operations with branches across the country, as well as several regional department store groups. No one group has achieved the share of market enjoyed by their Canadian counterparts.

Mail-order retailing reaches out

Mail-order retailing allows customers to "shop by mail"—using mail-order catalogs to "see" the offerings—and delivers the purchases by mail or truck. This method can be very useful for reaching widely scattered markets. Some mail-order houses aim at narrow target markets—selling

Automatic vendors have to charge higher prices but customers are willing to pay for the convenience.

only electronic components, phonograph records, or health foods. Large mail-order houses offer both convenience goods and shopping goods.

According to Statistics Canada, mail-order selling reached 328 million dollars in 1980, a figure that represents less than one half of 1 percent of total retail sales.[6]

The early mail-order houses were extremely successful—because of their low prices and wide variety. But today, mail-order selling has changed. The emphasis isn't only on low price anymore. Many mail-order retailers now offer high-fashion clothes and luxury gift items. Some companies have catalog stores, telephone service, convenient pick-up stations—even delivery service—to make it easier to buy from their catalogs. Even some department stores and limited-line stores are selling by mail.

Vending machines are convenient

Automatic vending is selling and delivering goods with vending machines. Vending machine sales have increased—but still are only 0.5 percent of total Canadian retail sales.

In 1980 a total of 584 businesses were classified as vending machine operators. They had sales of about $372 million, made through some 119,316 vending machines. The majority of machines were located in industrial plants. The largest part of vending machine sales (38 percent) was in cigarettes, followed by coffee and soft drinks (36 percent).[7] Marketers of certain product lines clearly cannot ignore this nonstore retailing method.

The major problem with automatic vending is the high cost. Marketers of similar, nonvended products can operate profitably on a margin of about 20 percent—while the vending industry requires about 41 percent. So they must charge higher prices.[8] But where consumers want convenience, vending machines can be *the* right method for delivering the goods.

Planned shopping centers—not just a group of stores

Planned shopping centers are a group of stores planned as a unit—to satisfy some market needs. Usually, free parking facilities are provided. Many centers are enclosed to make shopping more pleasant. The centers are made up of several independent merchants—who sometimes act together for Promotion purposes.

Neighborhood shopping centers consist of several convenience stores. These centers usually include a supermarket, drugstore, hardware store, beauty shop, laundry, dry cleaner, gas station, and perhaps others, such as a bakery or appliance shop. They normally must serve 7,500 to 40,000 people living within 6 to 10 minutes driving distance.

Community shopping centers are larger and offer some shopping stores as well as the convenience stores found in neighborhood shopping centers. They usually include a small department store which carries shopping goods (clothing and home furnishings). But the bulk of sales in these centers are convenience goods. These centers must serve 40,000 to 150,000 people within 3–4 miles.

Regional shopping centers are the largest centers and emphasize shopping stores and shopping goods. They include one or two large department stores—and as many as 200 smaller stores. Stores that feature convenience goods are often placed at the edge of the center—so they won't get in the way of customers primarily interested in shopping.

Regional centers must serve 150,000 or more persons within 5–6 miles. They are like downtown shopping districts of larger cities. Regional centers usually are found near suburban areas.

EVOLUTION OF MASS MERCHANDISING

Mass merchandising is different than conventional retailing

Supermarkets started the move to mass merchandising

So far we have been describing retailers mainly in terms of the *number of lines carried* and their *physical facilities*. This is the conventional way to think about retailing. We could talk about supermarkets and discount houses in these terms, too. But then we would miss an important difference. Many conventional retailers made that mistake when supermarkets and discount houses first appeared.

Conventional retailers follow a policy of "buy low and sell high." Some modern retailers, however, have accepted the **mass merchandising concept**—which says that retailers should offer low prices to get faster turnover and greater sales—by appealing to larger markets. To better understand what mass merchandising is, let's look at the way it has developed from supermarkets and discount houses to the modern mass merchandisers like K mart.

A **supermarket** is a large store specializing in groceries—with self-service and wide assortments. As late as 1930, most food stores were small single-line or limited-line stores. In the early Depression years, some creative people felt that they could increase their sales by charging lower prices. Their early experiments—in large warehouses—were an instant success. Independent and chain food stores quickly copied this new idea—emphasizing low prices and self-service.

In 1976, supermarkets accounted for almost 74 percent of all dollars spent on groceries. Supermarket chains predominated, making almost 52 percent of total Canadian grocery sales. And the same high degree of concentration that exists among Canadian department stores also holds true for supermarkets. The five dominant corporate supermarket chains—Loblaws, Dominion, Safeway, Steinberg's, and A&P—control 75 to 80 percent of the grocery chain market, or some 40 percent of total grocery sales! This is in marked contrast to the United States, where the five largest chains have less than 20 percent of the grocery market.[9]

Supermarkets sell convenience goods—but in *quantity*. These stores are planned so goods can easily be loaded on the shelves. The store layout makes it easy for customers to shop quickly. Some stores carefully study the sales and profits of each item—and allow more shelf space for the faster moving and higher profit items. This approach helps sell more in less time, reduces the investment in inventory, makes stocking easier, and lowers the cost of handling goods. Such efficiency is very

Box stores offer little variety but much lower prices.

important because there is so much competition. Net profits in grocery supermarkets usually run a thin 1 percent of sales *or less*.

Box stores reduce assortment and prices

A new development in the food industry is the **box store**—a small supermarket-sized store which carries a reduced assortment of staples—selling them out of shipping boxes—at much lower prices. These are relatively bare, plain stores—catering to the price-conscious. They don't offer a full assortment of groceries or all the popular brands. In fact, they may have few or no nationally known brands. Usually the products are fast-moving canned and boxed commodities which some supermarkets are now offering as generic brands.

The box stores do not carry perishable merchandise, fresh fruits and vegetables, meats, milk or any other items which require special facilities or care. In other words, this is a "bare-bones," low-overhead type of operation. The early supermarkets started this way during the Great Depression of the 1930s. But they soon expanded beyond basic canned and boxed goods. Now, the box store seems to be a well-planned attempt to take *some* of their "commodity" business—moving large volumes at low prices.[10]

Mass merchandisers' customers get less personal service and lower prices.

*Catalog showroom
retailers preceded
discount houses*

Catalog showroom retailers sell several lines out of a catalog and display showroom—with backup inventories. Before 1940, these retailers were usually wholesalers who also sold at retail to friends and members of groups—such as labor unions or church groups. In the 1970s, however, these operations expanded rapidly—offering significant price savings on jewelry, gifts, luggage, and small appliances.

The conventional retailers weren't worried about the early catalog retailers. They were not well publicized—and accounted for only a small part of total retail sales. If these pioneer catalog retailers had moved ahead aggressively—as the current catalog retailers are doing—the retailing scene might be quite different. But instead, discount houses developed.

*Discount houses upset
some conventional
retailers*

Right after World War II, some retailers moved beyond offering discounts to selected customers. These **discount houses** offered "hard goods" (cameras, TVs, appliances) at substantial price cuts—to customers who would go to the discounter's low-rent store, pay cash, and take care of any service or repair problems. They cut prices to obtain fast turnover. And when, in the early 1950s, well-known brands became more plentiful, discount houses began to offer full assortments. They also tried to improve their image by moving to better locations—and offering more services and guarantees. They began to act more like conventional retailers—*but still kept their prices lower to keep turnover high.*

*Mass merchandisers are
more than discounters*

The **mass merchandisers** are large, self-service stores with many departments—which emphasize "soft goods" (housewares, clothing, and fabrics) but still follow the discount house's emphasis on lower margins to get faster turnover. Mass merchandisers—for example, K mart and Woolco—have checkout counters in the front of the store and little or no sales help on the floor. This is in contrast to more conventional retailers—such as Sears and Penney's—who still offer some service and have sales stations and cash registers in each department.

Recently, some of the mass merchandisers have moved into groceries. These "discount" stores are a real threat to their competitors. They are selling more food—among other things—per store than the chain supermarkets!

*Scrambled merchandising
means selling whatever
products can be sold
profitably.*

Four important mass-merchandise competitors in Canada include K mart, owned by S. S. Kresge Co.; Woolco, owned by F. W. Woolworth; Miracle Mart, operated by Steinberg's, Ltd. and Towers Department Stores, Ltd., run by the Oshawa Group, Ltd. The K marts are 100,000-square-foot, full-line department stores that sell top-quality manufacturers' and dealer brands at moderate prices.

The mass merchandisers may have reached the market maturity stage of their life cycle. Profits are declining—and some have gone bankrupt. The number of stores grew so rapidly in some areas that they were no longer taking customers from conventional retailers, but from each other.[11]

Super-stores meet all routine needs

Super-stores are very large stores that try to carry not only foods, but all goods and services which the consumer purchases *routinely*. Such a store or "hyper market" may *look* like a mass merchandiser, but it is different. The super-store is attempting to meet *all* the customer's routine needs—at a low price.

Some supermarkets and mass merchandisers have moved toward becoming super-stores—but the super-store idea is big. It requires the retailer to carry not only foods, but also personal care products, alcoholic beverages, some apparel products, some lawn and garden products, gasoline, and household services—such as laundry, dry cleaning, shoe repair, check cashing, and bill paying. If the trend to super-stores continues, the "groceries-only" supermarkets may suffer badly. Their present buildings and parking lots are not large enough to become super-stores. Super-stores could put 50 percent of the existing supermarkets out of business in the near future.[12]

WILL SCRAMBLED MERCHANDISING CONTINUE?

Who's selling what to whom?

Conventional retailers tend to specialize by product line. But current retailing can be called **scrambled merchandising**—retailers carrying *any* product lines which they feel they can sell profitably. Mass merchandisers are selling groceries—while supermarkets are selling anything they can move in volume.

The wheel of retailing keeps rolling

What is behind this scrambled merchandising? The **wheel of retailing** theory says that new types of retailers enter the market as low-status, low-margin, low-price operators and then—if they are successful—evolve into more conventional stores offering more services—with higher operating costs and higher prices. Then they must compete with new low-status, low-margin, low-price outlets—and the wheel turns again.

Early department stores began this way. Then they became higher priced and built "bargain basement" departments to serve the more cost-conscious customers. The mail-order house was developed on a price basis. So were the food chains, economy apparel chains, drug chains, and the automobile accessory chains which developed during the 1920s.

Some innovators start with high margins

The wheel of retailing theory, however, does not explain all major retailing developments. Vending machines entered retailing as high-cost, high-margin operations. Convenience food stores are high priced. The development of suburban shopping centers has not had a low-price emphasis.

The probable cause of these exceptions has been summarized very well by Hollander:

> . . . retailers are constantly probing the empty sectors of competitive strategy with many failures until someone uses exactly the right technique at the right time. In at least a few cases, the merchant prince's skill may have been in judging opportunities rather than in originating techniques.[13]

Customers' needs and preferences help explain scrambled retailing

A clear view of current retailing can be seen in Figure 13–4—which gives a simplified view of the consumer market. It suggests that three consumer-oriented dimensions affect the types of retailers customers choose. These dimensions are: (1) width of assortment desired: (2) depth of assortment desired; and (3) price/service combination desired. It is possible to position most current retailers within this three-dimensional market.

Figure 13–4, for example, suggests the *why* of vending machines. Some people—in the front upper left-hand corner—have an urgent need for a specific item and are not interested in width of assortment, depth of assortment, *or* price.

Some customers, however, have very specific needs and want a deep assortment *and* a range of prices. Various kinds of specialty shops have developed to fill these needs. This market can be seen in the lower left front corner of Figure 13–4.

Figure 13–4: A three-dimensional view of the market for retail facilities and the probable position of some present offerings

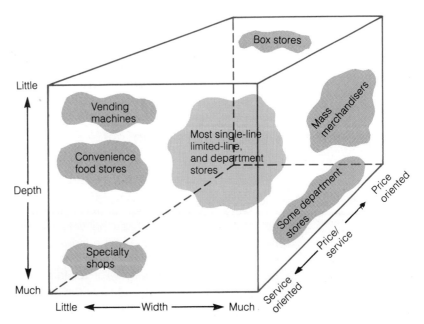

Figure 13–5: Retailer
life-cycle positions[14]

Retailers	Early growth	Maturity	Approximate time required to reach maturity
Department stores	Mid-1860s	Mid-1960s	100 years
Variety stores	Early 1900s	Early 1960s	60 years
Supermarkets	Mid-1930s	Mid-1960s	30 years
Discount department stores	Mid-1950s	Mid-1970s	20 years
Fast-food outlets	Early 1960s	Mid-1970s	15 years
Home improvement centers	Mid-1960s	Late 1970s	15 years
Furniture warehouse showrooms .	Late 1960s	Late 1970s	10 years
Catalog showrooms	Late 1960s	Late 1970s	10 years

Product life-cycle concept helps, too

People's needs help explain why the various kinds of retailers developed. But we need to apply the product life-cycle concept to understand this evolutionary process better. A "merchant prince" may take big profits on a new idea—for a while—but if it's really a good idea, he can count on fairly speedy imitation and a squeeze on his profits.

Some conventional retailers are far along in their cycle. And some have already declined—while current innovators are still in the market growth stage. See Figure 13–5.

Some retailers are confused by the scrambling going on around them. They don't see this evolutionary process. They don't understand that some of their more successful competitors are aiming at the needs of different market segments—instead of just selling products.

It is not surprising to find that some modern success stories in retailing are among firms which moved into a new market and started another "product life cycle"—by aiming at needs along the edges of the market shown in Figure 13–4. The convenience food store chains, for example, don't just sell food. They deliberately sell a particular assortment-service combination to meet a different need. This is also true of specialty shops—and some of the mass merchandisers and department store chains.[15]

GAINING ECONOMIES OF SCALE IN RETAILING

Some retailers have expanded to try to achieve economies of scale. Let's see why such growth may be desirable.

Small size may be expensive

A small independent retailer may satisfy some emotional needs by being his own boss. Also, he can be very helpful to some target customers because of his flexibility. But the store may only *seem* profitable because some of the costs of doing business are ignored. The owner may not be allowing for depreciation—or for family members clerking or keeping books without pay. Sometimes he can keep the doors open only because he has a full-time job elsewhere.

Many retail stores are too small to enjoy the economies associated with size. An annual sales volume of $300,000 is not very impressive given the fact that net profits as a percentage of sales range from about 1 to 5 percent. To get a better idea about size, remember that a supermarket sells more than $1 million per year!

The disadvantage of small size may even apply to the many departments within a large department store. It consists of many specialty shops and limited-line stores which may not be any larger than independent limited-line stores. So there may be little or no possibility for volume buying.

Being in a chain may help

The disadvantage of small size—even in department stores—has led to the growth of chains—to achieve the benefits of large-scale operations. A (corporate) **chain store** is one of several stores owned and managed by the same corporation. Chains grew slowly until after World War I, then spurted ahead during the 1920s. In some lines, chain stores are dominant.

In 1979 chains with annual sales volumes in excess of 5 million (245 organizations) accounted for 95.9 percent of total chain store sales. More significantly, those few chain organizations (32) which enjoyed annual sales of over $100 million accounted for 64.6 percent of all chain store sales. Although only 41 of the 842 chains operated more than 100 stores, their sales amounted to slightly over 60 percent of total chain sales.[16]

The importance of chains varies by kind of business. Table 13–1 shows the percentage of total retail sales accounted for by chain store operations. The chain store concept is particularly strong in the foods and general merchandise groups. It has had far less impact in the automotive or hardware and home furnishings fields.

Independents form chains, too

The growth of corporate chains has encouraged the development of both cooperative chains and voluntary chains.

Cooperative chains are retailer-sponsored groups—formed by independent retailers—to run their own buying organizations and conduct joint promotion efforts. Sales of cooperative chains have been rising as they have learned how to meet the corporate chain competition. Examples include Associated Grocers and Certified Grocers.

Voluntary chains are wholesaler-sponsored groups which work with independent retailers. Some are linked by contracts stating common operating procedures—and the use of common store front designs, store name, and joint promotion efforts. Examples include IGA and Super Valu in groceries and Canadian Tire in auto supplies.

Franchising is similar

Franchise operations are like voluntary chains—with the franchiser developing a good marketing strategy and the franchise holders carrying out the strategy in their own units. Examples include McDonald's, Burger King, Wendy's, and automobile (new) dealerships. The voluntary chains have tended to work with existing retailers, while some franchisers like to work with newcomers—whom they train and get started. Sometimes

Table 13–1: Chain stores' share of retail trade by kind of business[17]	1974	1977	1980
All stores*	42.0	42.0	42.3
Combination stores	69.5	71.5	68.5
Grocery, confectionery, and sundries	17.4	15.0	22.0
All other food stores	10.2	9.5	8.4
Department stores	100.0	100.0	100.0
General merchandise stores	79.8	76.6	79.9
General stores	19.2	28.0	34.4
Variety stores	75.7	76.2	77.7
Motor vehicle dealers	1.2	1.2	1.2
Used car dealers	—	—	—
Service stations	19.2	20.0	18.8
Garages	—	—	—
Automotive parts, and accessories	17.0	13.5	9.1
Men's clothing stores	24.4	33.2	34.5
Women's clothing stores	46.6	53.4	55.2
Family clothing stores	40.4	46.3	53.4
Specialty shoe stores	42.4	42.2	45.0
Family shoe stores	54.4	59.1	69.3
Hardware stores	15.7	16.2	—
Household furniture stores	19.6	15.5	18.7
Household appliance stores	20.2	17.2	—
Furniture, TV, radio, and appliance	28.6	25.3	24.5
Pharmacies, patent medicine, and cosmetics	20.1	22.4	22.2
Book and stationery stores	35.5	41.8	51.1
Florists	5.7	4.8	4.7
Jewelry stores	41.6	41.8	49.1
Sporting goods and accessories	5.0	9.6	—
Personal accessory stores	20.7	25.0	28.1
All other stores	53.6	52.7	52.2

they will locate the site, as well as supervise building and the initial promotion and opening.[18]

Co-ops try—but usually in vain

Cooperative and voluntary chains should not be confused with **consumer cooperatives**—which are groups of *consumers* who buy together. These groups usually operate on a nonprofit basis with voluntary or poorly

Consumer co-ops don't have much impact in the U.S. because traditional retailers have competed vigorously for customers.

paid management. Consumer cooperatives have never made much of an impact in Canada.

Consumer cooperatives have been more successful in Europe—where most retailers have been high priced and inefficient. Most Canadian markets, on the other hand, have been so competitive that customers have not been willing to go to the typically out-of-the-way location for the (sometimes) unknown or co-op dealer brand—which may or may not be offered at lower prices.

FUTURE POSSIBILITIES IN RETAILING

Retailing has changed rapidly in the last 30 years. Scrambled merchandising may become more scrambled. Some people are forecasting larger stores. Others are predicting smaller ones. What is behind these different predictions?

More customer-oriented retailing may be coming

Forecasting trends is risky, but our three dimensional picture of the retailing market (Figure 13–4) can be helpful. Those who suggest larger stores may be primarily concerned with the mass market. Those who expect more small stores and specialty shops may be anticipating more small but increasingly wealthy target markets able to afford higher prices for different products.

To serve small but wealthy markets, convenience food stores continue to spread. Sales by vending machines—even with their higher operating costs and prices—may grow. Certainly, some customers are getting tired of the large supermarkets that take so much of their time. Logically, convenience goods should be offered at the customer's, rather than the retailer's convenience. Some retailers still fight night and weekend hours, for example, although it is convenient for most working people to shop then.

In-home shopping will become more popular

Telephone shopping may become more popular also. The mail-order houses and department stores already find phone business attractive. Telephone supermarkets—now a reality—sell only by phone and deliver all orders. Linking the phone to closed-circuit TV would let the customer see the products at home—while hearing well-prepared sales presentations. The customer could place an order through a small computer system—which would also handle the billing and delivery.

Retailers who don't satisfy their markets may fail.

We now have far greater electronic capabilities than we are using. There seems to be no reason why the customer couldn't shop in the home—saving time and gasoline. Such automated retailing could take over a large share of the convenience goods and homogeneous shopping goods business.[19]

Retailers becoming manufacturers and vice versa

We also may see more horizontally and vertically administered channel systems. This would have a major impact on present manufacturers. Some retailers are developing their own brands—using manufacturers mainly as production arms.

The large manufacturers themselves may go into retailing—for self-protection. Various drug, paint, tire, and shoe manufacturers already control their own retail outlets.

Retailing certainly will continue to be needed. But the role of individual retailers—and even the concept of a retail store—may have to change. Customers will always have needs—and they will probably want to satisfy those needs with combinations of goods and services. But retail stores may not be the only way of doing this.

Retailers must face the challenge

One thing is certain—retailing will change. For years, traditional retailers' profits have gone down. Even some of the newer discounters and shopping centers haven't done well. Department stores and food and drug chains have had profit declines. The old variety stores are even worse. Some are shifting into mass merchandising, and—as we saw—even some mass merchandisers are in trouble as well.

A few firms—especially K mart—have avoided this general profit squeeze. But the future looks grim for retailers who can't change their old ways.

In fact, it seems that there isn't an easy way to big profits any more. Instead, careful strategy planning—and great care in carrying out the plan—will be needed for success in the future. This means more careful market segmenting to find unsatisfied needs which (1) have a long life expectancy and (2) can be satisfied with low levels of investment. This won't be easy. But you can be sure that the imaginative marketing planner will find more profitable opportunities than a conventional retailer—who doesn't know that a product life cycle is moving along and who is just "hoping for the best."[20]

CONCLUSION

Modern retailing is scrambled. And we will probably see more changes in the future. A producer's marketing manager must choose among the available retailers very carefully. Retailers must plan the kind of store they are going to run with their target customers' needs in mind.

We described a wide variety of retailers and saw that each has its advantages—and disadvantages. We also saw that some modern retailers have left conventional ways behind. The old "buy low and sell high" idea is no longer an effective rule. Fast turnover with lower margins is the new idea—as retailers move from discounting into mass merchandising. Even this is no guarantee of success as retailers' product life cycles move on.

Scrambled merchandising will probably continue as the "wheel of retailing" continues to roll. But important breakthroughs are possible—because consumers may want different retail facilities. Convenience goods, for example, may be made more easily available by some combination of electronic ordering and home delivery or vending. Our society needs a retailing function, but it is not clear that *all* the present facilities are needed. The future retail scene will offer the marketing manager new challenges and opportunities.

QUESTIONS FOR DISCUSSION

1. Identify a specialty store selling convenience goods in your city. Explain why you feel it is that kind of a store and why an awareness of this status would be important to a manufacturer. Does it give the retailer any particular advantage? If so, with whom?

2. What sort of a "product" are specialty shops offering? What are the prospects for organizing a chain of specialty shops?

3. A department store consists of many departments. Is this horizontal integration? Are all of the advantages of horizontal integration achieved in a department store operation?

4. Many department stores have a bargain basement. Does the basement represent just another department, like the hat department or the luggage department, for example, or is some whole new concept involved?

5. Distinguish among discount houses, discount selling, and mass merchandising. Forecast the future of low-price selling in food, clothing, and appliances.

6. Suggest what the supermarket or scrambled merchandising outlet of the future may be like.

7. List five products that seem suitable for automatic vending and yet are not normally sold in this manner. Generally, what characteristics are required?

8. Apply the "Wheel of Retailing" theory to your local community. What changes seem likely? Does it seem likely that established retailers will see the need for change, or will entirely new firms have to develop?

9. Discuss the kinds of markets served by the three types of shopping centers. Are they directly competitive? Do they contain the same kinds of stores? Is the long-run outlook for all of them similar?

10. Explain the growth and decline of various retailers and shopping centers in your own community. Use the text's three-dimensional drawing (Figure 13–4) and the product life-cycle concept. Also, treat each retailer's whole offering as a "product."

11. Many retailers are expanding their operations by selling by mail. Some catalogs cost from $1 to $2.50 each, and they go out by the millions. Department stores have also become more interested in this method of selling. Most have found that there are no really "hot" items. But sales have been good for food processors, microwave oven cookware, soft-sided luggage, and "cold weather-oriented" articles like shawls, warm sleepwear, and electric blankets. Although there have been no outstanding winners, it is clear that the department stores are avoiding some items, such as children's clothing, toys, and "brown" goods—like television sets, because they do not view them as department-store items. Instead, the department stores seem to be concentrating on softer-looking clothing, accessories for both men and women, and currently popular home goods such as linens, glassware, and small appliances. As more department stores enter the competition, the costs are rising; so are the costs of errors. Evaluate the department stores' current product offerings. Suggest what you would offer and explain why.

12. Explain the strategic decisions a retailer's marketing manager must make. Illustrate.

SUGGESTED CASES

13. Andrews Photo Limited
16. The Donell Company

When you finish this chapter, you should:

1. Understand what wholesalers are—and the wholesaling functions they may provide for others in channel systems.

2. Know the various kinds of merchant wholesalers and agent middlemen.

3. Understand when and where the various kinds of merchant wholesalers and agent middlemen would be most useful to channel planners.

4. Understand why wholesalers have lasted.

5. Recognize the important new terms (shown in red).

WHOLESALING

14

"I can get it for you wholesale," the man said. But could he? Would it be a good deal?

Wholesaling is an important activity in the marketing process. To understand the wholesalers' role better, think of them as members of channels of distribution. Although they are individual firms, they help link many producers and final consumers.

WHAT IS A WHOLESALER?

It is not easy to define what a wholesaler is—because there are so many different kinds of wholesalers doing different jobs. Some of their activities may even seem like manufacturing. As a result, we find some "wholesalers" calling themselves "manufacturer and dealer." Others like to identify themselves with such general terms as *merchant, dealer,* or *distributor*—because they do various jobs. Others just use the name which is commonly used in their trade—without really thinking about what it means.

To avoid a long technical discussion on the nature of wholesaling, we will use the Statistics Canada definition. This is basically:

Wholesalers are primarily engaged in buying merchandise for resale to retailers; to industrial, commercial, institutional, and professional users; to other wholesalers; for export; to farmers for use in farm production; or acting as agents in such transactions.

Mixed activity business (such as firms engaged in both wholesaling and retailing, contracting, service trades, manufacturing, etc.) are considered to be in wholesale trade whenever they derive the largest portion of their gross margin from their wholesaling activity.[1]

Wholesalers are firms whose main function is providing wholesaling activities.

It should be noted that producers who take over wholesaling activities are not considered wholesalers. However, if separate "middlemen facilities"—such as branch warehouses—are set up, some of these facilities are counted as wholesalers by Statistics Canada as explained later.

Wholesaling must be understood as a middleman activity. Let's look at these wholesaling functions.

POSSIBLE WHOLESALING FUNCTIONS

Wholesalers *may* perform certain functions for both their own customers and their suppliers. Remember—these functions are provided by *some*—but *not all*—wholesalers.

What a wholesaler might do for customers

1. *Anticipate needs*—forecast customers' demands and buy for them.
2. *Regroup goods*—provide the assortment wanted by customers at the lowest possible cost.
3. *Carry stocks*—carry inventory so customers don't have to store a large inventory.
4. *Deliver goods*—provide prompt delivery at low cost.
5. *Grant credit*—give credit to customers—perhaps supplying their working capital. (Note: This financing function may be very important to small customers. It is sometimes the major reason why they use wholesalers rather than buying directly from manufacturers.)
6. *Provide information and advisory service*—supply price and technical information as well as suggestions on how to install and sell products. (Note: The wholesaler's sales force may be experts in the products they sell.)
7. *Provide part of buying function*—offer products to potential customers so they do not have to hunt for supply sources.
8. *Own and transfer title to goods*—to permit completing a sale without the need for other middlemen—speeding the whole buying and selling process.

What a wholesaler might do for producer-suppliers

1. *Provide part of producer's selling function*—by going to producer-suppliers, instead of waiting for their sales reps to call.

2. *Store inventory*—this reduces a producer's need to carry large stocks—and cuts his warehousing expenses.
3. *Supply capital*—producer's need for working capital is reduced by buying his output—and carrying it in inventory until it is sold.
4. *Reduce credit risks*—by selling to customers the wholesaler knows—and taking the loss if these customers do not pay.
5. *Provide market information*—as an informed buyer and seller closer to the market, the wholesaler reduces the producer's need for market research.

KINDS AND COSTS OF AVAILABLE WHOLESALERS

Table 14–1 lists the types, numbers, sales volume, and operating expenses of wholesalers. The differences in operating expenses show that each of these wholesaler types performs different wholesaling functions. But which ones and why?

Why do manufacturers use merchant wholesalers costing about 20 percent of sales instead of using their own sales branches?

Why use either when brokers cost only about 3 percent?

To answer these questions we must understand what these wholesalers do—and do not do. Figure 14–1 gives a big-picture view of the wholesalers described in more detail below. Note that a major difference is whether they *own* the goods they sell.

Table 14–1: **Wholesale merchants, agents and brokers, principal statistics by geographic location, Canada, 1979**[2]

	Number of establishments		Percentage distribution		Volume of trade ($000)		Percentage distribution	
	Whole-sale mer-chants	Agents and brokers	Whole-sale mer-chants	Agents and brokers	Wholesale merchants	Agents and brokers	Whole-sale mer-chants	Agents and brokers
Total all trades	27,526	4,557	100	100	$109,633,724	$16,285,418	100%	100%
Newfoundland	400	104	1.5	2.3	846,147	133,954	0.8	1.8
Prince Edward Island	124	24	0.5	0.5	181,949	14,836	0.2	0.3
Nova Scotia	687	192	2.5	4.2	1,282,435	236,179	1.2	3.0
New Brunswick	566	158	2.1	3.4	2,847,588	148,360	2.6	2.2
Quebec	7,958	937	28.8	20.6	25,241,335	2,183,349	23.0	24.9
Ontario	10,092	1,288	36.6	28.3	42,748,031	5,533,663	39.0	29.1
Manitoba	1,178	382	4.3	8.4	11,533,652	4,168,714	10.5	6.7
Saskatchewan	1,147	371	4.2	8.1	3,657,051	831,396	3.3	5.3
Alberta	2,257	528	8.2	11.6	9,103,177	1,461,960	8.3	12.1
British Columbia*	3,117	573	11.3	12.6	12,192,359	1,573,007	11.1	14.6

* Includes Yukon and Northwest Territories.

Figure 14–1: **Types of wholesalers**

	Merchant wholesalers (own the goods)		Agent middlemen (don't own the goods, emphasize selling)
	Service (all the functions)	Limited function (some of the functions)	
	General merchandise wholesalers (or mill supply houses) Single-line or general-line wholesalers Specialty wholesalers	Cash-and-carry wholesalers Drop-shippers Truck wholesalers Mail-order wholesalers Producers' cooperatives Rack jobbers	Auction companies Brokers Commission merchants Manufacturers' agents Food brokers Selling agents

MERCHANT WHOLESALERS ARE THE MOST NUMEROUS

Merchant wholesalers own (take title to) the goods they sell. They also provide some—or all—of the wholesaling functions. There are two basic kinds of merchant wholesalers: (1) service—sometimes called full-service—wholesalers, and (2) limited-function or limited-service wholesalers. Their names explain their difference.

More than three fourths of all wholesaling establishments are merchant wholesalers, but they handle only about half of wholesale sales. Understanding *why* is important to understanding wholesaling. Basically, it's because other kinds of wholesalers play an important role, too.

Service wholesalers provide all the functions

Service wholesalers provide all the wholesaling functions. Within this basic group are three subtypes: (1) general merchandise, (2) single-line, and (3) specialty.

General merchandise wholesalers carry a wide variety of nonperishable items—such as hardware, electrical supplies, plumbing supplies, furniture, drugs, cosmetics, and automobile equipment. With this broad line of convenience and shopping goods, they can serve many kinds of retail stores. In the industrial goods field, the "mill supply house" operates in the same way. Somewhat like a retail hardware store, the mill supply house carries a wide variety of accessories and supplies for industrial customers.

Single-line (or general-line) wholesalers carry a narrower line of merchandise than general merchandise wholesalers. For example, they might carry only groceries, or wearing apparel, or paint, or certain types of industrial accessories or supplies.

Specialty wholesalers carry a very narrow range of products. A *consumer goods* specialty wholesaler might carry only health foods or Oriental foods—instead of a full line of groceries. For industrial goods, a specialty wholesaler might limit itself to fields requiring technical knowledge or service—perhaps electronics or plastics.

Specialty wholesalers carry a narrow range of products.

The specialty wholesaler tries to become an expert in selling the product lines it carries. Where there is need for this kind of technical service, the specialty wholesaler's salespeople usually have little difficulty taking business away from less specialized wholesalers.

The Cadillac Plastic & Chemical Co. in Detroit, for example, became a specialty wholesaler serving the needs of plastics makers *and* users. Neither the large plastics manufacturers nor the merchant wholesalers with wide lines were able to give individual advice to the many users (who often could not judge which product would be best for them). Cadillac carries 10,000 items and sells to 25,000 customers—ranging in size from very small firms to General Motors.

Limited-function wholesalers provide certain functions

Limited-function wholesalers provide only *some* wholesaling functions. Table 14–2 shows the functions typically provided—and not provided. In the following paragraphs, the main features of these wholesalers will be discussed. Some are not very numerous. In fact, they are not counted separately by Statistics Canada. Nevertheless, these wholesalers are very important for some products.

Cash-and-carry wholesaler wants cash

Cash-and-carry wholesalers operate like service wholesalers—except that the customer must pay cash. Many small retailers—especially small grocers and garages—are too small to be served profitably by a service wholesaler. To handle these markets, service wholesalers often set up cash-and-carry operations—to serve these small retailers for cash on the counter. The cash-and-carry wholesaler can operate at lower cost because the retailer takes over many wholesaling functions.

Drop-shipper does not handle the goods

Drop-shippers own the goods they sell—but do not actually handle, stock, or deliver them. These wholesalers are mainly involved in selling.

Table 14–2: Functions provided by limited-function merchant wholesalers

Functions	Cash-and-carry	Drop-shipper	Truck	Mail-order	Cooperatives	Rack-jobbers
For customer:						
Anticipates needs	X		X	X	X	X
"Regroups" goods (one or more of four steps)	X		X	X	X	X
Carries stocks	X		X	X	X	X
Delivers goods			X		X	X
Grants credit		X	Maybe	Maybe	Maybe	Consignment (in some cases)
Provides information and advisory services		X	Some	Some	X	
Provides buying function		X	X	X	Some	X
Owns and transfers title to goods	X	X	X	X	X	X
For producers:						
Provides producer's selling function	X	X	X	X	X	X
Stores inventory	X		X	X	X	X
Helps finance by owning stocks	X		X	X	X	X
Reduces credit risk	X	X	X	X	X	X
Provides market information	X	X	Some	X	X	Some

They get orders—from wholesalers, retailers, or industrial users—and pass these orders on to producers. Then the orders are shipped directly to the customers. Because drop-shippers do not have to handle the goods, their operating costs are lower.

Drop-shippers commonly sell products which are so bulky that additional

Bulky products are usually handled by drop-shippers who never handle the actual products.

handling would be expensive—and possibly damaging. Also, the quantities they usually sell are so large that there is little need for regrouping—for example, rail carload shipments of coal, lumber, oil, or chemical products.

Truck wholesalers deliver—at a cost

Truck wholesalers specialize in delivering goods which they stock in their own trucks. When handling perishable products in general demand—tobacco products, candy, potato chips, and salad dressings—truck wholesalers may provide almost the same functions as full-service wholesalers. Their big advantage is that they deliver perishable products that regular wholesalers prefer not to carry. Others call on the many small service stations and "back-alley" garages—providing local delivery of the many small items these customers often forget to pick up from a service wholesaler. Truck wholesalers' operating costs are relatively high—because they provide a lot of service for the little they sell.

Mail-order wholesalers reach outlying stores

Mail-order wholesalers sell out of a catalog which may be distributed widely to industrial customers or retailers. These wholesalers operate in the hardware, jewelry, sporting goods, and general merchandise lines. Their best markets are small industrial or retailer customers who might not be called on by other middlemen.

Producers' cooperative does sorting-out

Producers' cooperatives operate almost as full-service wholesalers—with the "profits" going to the cooperative's customer-members.

The successful producers' cooperatives have emphasized the sorting-out process—to improve the quality of farm products offered to the market. Some have also branded their products—and promoted these brands. Farmers' cooperatives have sometimes had success limiting production and then increasing price—by taking advantage of the normal inelastic demand for agricultural goods.

Examples of producers' cooperatives are the California Fruit Growers Exchange (citrus fruits), Sunmaid Raisin Growers Association, the California Almond Exchange, and Land-O-Lakes Creameries, Inc.

Rack-jobber sells hard-to-handle assortments

Rack-jobbers specialize in nonfood items which are sold through grocery stores and supermarkets—and they often display them on their own wire racks. Many grocers don't want to bother with nonfood items (housewares, hardware items, and health and beauty aids) because they sell small quantities of so many different kinds of goods. So the rack-jobber specializes in these items.

Rack jobbers handle many different kinds of products which sell in small amounts and are hard for retailers to handle economically.

Rack-jobbers are almost service wholesalers, except that they usually are paid cash for the stock sold or delivered. This is a relatively expensive service—with operating costs of about 18 percent of sales. The large volume of nonfood sales from these racks has encouraged some large food chains to try to handle these items themselves. But they often find that rack-jobbers can provide this service as well as—or better than—they can.

MANUFACTURERS' SALES BRANCHES PROVIDE WHOLESALING FUNCTIONS, TOO

Many manufacturers have set up their own sales branches whenever the sales volume—or the nature of their products—justified it. These branches may also sell products produced by others.

Manufacturers' sales branches are separate businesses which manufacturers set up away from their factories. For example, computer manufacturers such as IBM set up local branches to provide service, display equipment, and handle sales. Since these branches are usually placed in the biggest markets, many of them do a considerable volume of business. This also helps explain why their operating costs are often lower. But cost comparisons between various channels can be misleading. Sometimes the cost of selling is not charged to the branch. If all the expenses of the manufacturers' sales branches were charged to them, they probably would turn out to be more costly than they seem now.

AGENT MIDDLEMEN ARE STRONG ON SELLING

They don't own the goods

Agent middlemen *do not* own the goods they sell. Their main purpose is to help in buying and selling. They usually provide even fewer functions than the limited-function wholesalers. In certain trades, however, they are extremely valuable. They may operate at relatively low cost too—sometimes 2–6 percent of selling price.

Table 14–3: Functions provided by agent middlemen

Functions	Auction companies	Brokers	Commission merchants	Manufacturers' agents and food brokers	Selling agents
For customers:					
Anticipates needs		Some		Sometimes	
"Regroups" goods (one or more of four steps)	X		X	Some	
Carries stocks	Sometimes		X	Sometimes	
Delivers goods			X	Sometimes	
Grants credit	Some		Sometimes		X
Provides information and advisory services		X	X	X	X
Provides buying function	X	Some	X	X	X
Owns and transfers title to goods	Transfers only		Transfers only		
For producer:					
Provides selling function	X	Some	X	X	X
Stores inventory	X		X	Sometimes	
Helps finance by owning stocks					
Reduces credit risk	Some				X
Provides market information		X	X	X	X

In the following paragraphs, only the most important points about each type will be mentioned. See Table 14–3 for details on the functions provided by each. It is obvious from the number of empty spaces in Table 14–3 that agent middlemen provide fewer functions than merchant wholesalers.

Auction companies— display the goods

Auction companies provide a place where buyers and sellers can come together and complete a transaction. There aren't many of these middlemen (see Table 14–3), but they are very important in certain lines—

Auction companies provide a place for buyers and sellers to come together for products that need inspection.

such as fruit, livestock, fur, tobacco, and used cars. For these products, demand and supply conditions change rapidly. Also, these goods must be looked at. The auction company allows buyers and sellers to come together and set the price while the goods are being inspected.

Facilities can be simple—keeping overhead low. Often, auction companies are close to transportation so that the products can be reshipped quickly. The auction company just charges a set fee or commission for the use of its facilities and services.

Brokers—provide information

Brokers bring buyers and sellers together. Unlike the auction company, a broker does not need any physical facilities. Brokers may not even have a separate office. They may work out of their homes—perhaps with the aid of an answering service. Their "product" is information about what buyers need and what supplies are available. They aid in buyer-seller negotiations. When a deal is completed, they earn a commission from whoever hired them.

Brokers are especially useful for selling seasonal products—like fruits and vegetables. They also sell used machinery, real estate, and even ships. These products are not similar—but the needed marketing functions *are*. In each case, buyers don't come into the market often. Someone with knowledge of the available products is needed—to help both buyers and sellers complete the sale quickly and at a reasonable cost.

Commission merchants handle and sell the goods in distant markets

Commission merchants handle goods shipped to them by sellers, complete the sale, and send the money—minus their commission—to each seller.

Commission merchants are common in agricultural markets where farmers must ship to big-city central markets. They need someone to handle the goods there as well as to sell them—since the farmer cannot go with each shipment. Although commission merchants do not own the goods, they generally are allowed to sell them at the market price—or the best price above some stated minimum. Prices in these markets usually are published in newspapers, so the producer-seller has a check on the commission merchant. Usually costs are low—because commission merchants handle large volumes of goods and buyers usually come to them.

Commission merchants are sometimes used in other trades, too—such as textiles. Here, many small producers wish to reach buyers in a central market—without having to maintain their own sales forces.

Manufacturers' agents— free wheeling sales reps

A **manufacturers' agent** sells similar products for several noncompeting manufacturers—for a commission on what is actually sold. Such agents work almost as members of each company's sales force—but they are really independent middlemen. They may cover one city or several provinces.

Their big "plus" is that they already call on a group of customers and can add another product line at relatively low cost. If the sales potential in an area is low, a manufacturers' agent may be used instead of a compa-

Manufacturers' agents handle products from non-competing firms.

ny's own sales rep—because he can do the job at lower cost. A small producer often has to use agents—because its sales volume is too small to support a sales force anywhere.

Manufacturers' agents are very useful in fields where there are many small manufacturers who need to call on customers. These agents are often used in the sale of machinery and equipment, electrical goods, automobile products, clothing and apparel accessories, and some food products.

The agent's main job is selling. The agent—or his customer—sends the orders to the producer. The agent, of course, gets credit for the sale. Agents seldom have any part in setting prices or deciding on the producer's policies. Basically, they are independent, aggressive salespeople.

Agents can be especially useful in introducing new products. For this service, they may earn 10 to 15 percent commission. (By contrast, their commission on large-volume established goods may be quite low—perhaps only 2 percent.) The higher rates for new products often come to be the agent's major disadvantage for the manufacturer. The 10 to 15 percent commission rate may have seemed small when the product was new—and sales volume was low. Once the product is selling well, the rate seems high. At about this time, the producer often begins using his own sales reps—and the manufacturers' agent must look for other new products to develop. Agents are well aware of this possibility. They try to work for many manufacturers—so they are not dependent on only one or a few lines.

Food brokers—fill a gap

Food brokers are manufacturers' agents who specialize in grocery distribution. More than half of the processed goods handled by grocery stores is sold by these brokers.

Food brokers call on grocery wholesalers and large retailers for their manufacturer clients. Because they know their own territory so well, some aggressive food brokers have become involved with their client's strategy

Good food brokers are respected because they know their territory and customers well.

planning. They may even work closely with the producers' advertising agency.[3]

For the usual commission of 5 percent of sales, food brokers may take over the entire selling function for a manufacturer. Some even suggest what prices and advertising allowances should be offered to particular retailers. For a small manufacturer—or even large firms with many small divisions—food brokers can be a great help.

Food brokers specialize by geographic area. A manufacturer could achieve national distribution with a small number of food brokers.

The food broker fills a need for manufacturers. Brokers hire very capable salespeople—and pay them well. So their sales reps stay on the job longer—and they develop greater understanding of their markets. In contrast, manufacturers often use their sales territories as training grounds. They move good salespeople to larger territories or home offices as soon as—and sometimes before—they have really become effective in their sales areas.

Selling agents—almost marketing managers

Selling agents take over the whole marketing job of manufacturers—not just the selling function. A selling agent may handle the entire output of one or more producers—even competing producers—with almost complete control of pricing, selling, and advertising. In effect, the agent becomes each producer's marketing manager.

Financial trouble is the main reason a producer calls in a selling agent. The selling agent may provide working capital—while taking over the affairs of the business.

Selling agents have been common in highly competitive fields such as fabrics or coal. They also have been used for marketing lumber and some food, clothing, and metal products. In these industries, marketing is much more important than production for survival. The selling agent provides the necessary financial assistance and marketing know-how.

A selling agent may be asked to handle the whole marketing effort for a company with financial problems.

International marketing is not so different

We find agent middlemen in international trade, too. Most operate much like the ones we just discussed. **Export or import agents** are basically manufacturers' agents. **Export or import commission houses** and **export or import brokers** are really brokers. A **combination export manager** is a blend of a manufacturers' agent and a selling agent—handling the entire export function for several manufacturers of noncompeting lines.

Agent middlemen are more common in international trade. Financing is usually needed, and yet many markets include only a few well-financed merchant wholesalers. The best that many manufacturers can do is obtain local representation through agent middlemen and arrange financing through banks which specialize in international trade.

COMEBACK AND FUTURE OF WHOLESALERS

Necessary—and lasting

In the 1800s, wholesalers dominated marketing. The many small producers and retailers needed their services. But as producers became larger, some bypassed the wholesalers. When retailers also began to grow larger—especially during the 1920s when the chain stores began to spread rapidly—many predicted the end of wholesalers. Some people felt this would be desirable because many wholesalers apparently had grown "fat and lazy"—contributing little more than breaking bulk. Their salespeople often were only order-takers. The selling function was neglected. High-quality management was not attracted to wholesaling.

Our review here, however, has shown that wholesaling functions are necessary. And wholesalers have not been eliminated. The traditional merchant-wholesaler did go through a critical period in the late 1940s and early 1950s but seems to have adjusted to new market conditions.[4] The manufacturer's agent has also successfully adapted to changing market conditions, particularly those brought about by the increasing size of the Canadian market.[5]

Producing profits, not chasing orders

Wholesalers have lasted, in part, because of new management and new techniques. Many are still operating in the old ways. But progressive wholesalers have become more concerned with their customers—and with channel systems. Some are offering more services. Others are developing voluntary chains that bind them more closely to their customers. Some of this ordering is done routinely by mail, telephone, or directly by telephone to computer.

Some modern wholesalers no longer make all customers pay for services simply because some customers use them. This traditional practice had the effect of encouraging limited-function wholesalers and direct channels. Now, some wholesalers are making a basic service available at a minimum cost—then charging additional fees for any special services required. In the grocery field, for instance, the basic servicing of a store might cost 3 to 4 percent of wholesale sales. Promotion assistance and other aids are offered at extra cost.

Modern wholesalers also are becoming more selective in picking customers—as cost analysis shows that many of their small customers are unprofitable. By cutting out these customers, wholesalers can give more attention to their better customers. In this way, they are helping to promote healthy retailers who are able to compete in any market.

Today's *progressive* wholesaler is no longer just an order-taker. Some wholesalers have renamed their salespeople "store advisors" or "supervisors"—to reflect their new roles. They may provide management advisory services, including site selection and store design. They may offer legal assistance on new leases or adjustment in old leases. They may even provide store-opening services, sales training and merchandising assistance, and advertising help.

Some wholesalers are using electronic data processing systems to control inventory. Others are modernizing their warehouses and physical handling facilities, and offering central bookkeeping facilities. Modern wholesalers realize that their own survival is tied to their customers' survival. Now, instead of overloading their retailer's shelves, they try to clear the merchandise *off* the retailer's shelves. They know the old line is true: "Nothing is really sold until it is sold at retail."[6]

Good-bye to some wholesalers

Not all wholesalers are progressive, however. Some of the smaller, less efficient ones may fail. While the average operating expense ratio is 20 percent for merchant wholesalers, some small wholesalers have expense ratios of 20–30 percent.

Low cost, however, is not the only thing required for success. The higher operating expenses of some wholesalers may be caused by the special services they offer to *some* customers. Truck wholesalers, for example, are usually small and have high operating expenses—yet *some* customers are willing to pay the higher cost of this service. And although full-service wholesalers can seem expensive, *some* will continue operating because they offer the wholesale functions and sales contacts needed by *some* small manufacturers.

It is clear that if they are going to survive, wholesalers must each carve out a specific market. Profit margins are not large in wholesaling—typically ranging from less than 1 percent to 2 percent—and they have been declining in recent years as the competitive squeeze has tightened.

The function of wholesaling certainly will last, but weaker, less aggressive wholesalers may not.

CONCLUSION

Wholesalers can provide wholesaling functions for those both above and below them in a channel of distribution. These functions are closely related to the basic marketing functions.

There are many types of wholesalers. Some provide all the wholesaling functions, while others specialize in only a few. Eliminating wholesalers would not eliminate the need for the functions they provide. And we cannot assume that direct channels will be more efficient.

Merchant wholesalers are the most numerous, and account for just over half of wholesale sales.

They take title to—and often possession of—goods. Agent middlemen, on the other hand, act more like sales representatives. And usually they *do not* take title or possession.

Despite predictions of the end of wholesalers, they're still around. The more progressive ones have adapted to a changing environment. No such revolutions as we saw in retailing have yet taken place in wholesaling—and none seems likely. But it is probable that some smaller—and less progressive—wholesalers will fail in the future.

QUESTIONS FOR DISCUSSION

1. Discuss the evolution of wholesaling in relation to the evolution of retailing.

2. What risks do merchant wholesalers assume by taking title to goods? Is the size of this risk about constant for all merchant wholesalers?

3. Why would a manufacturer set up its own sales branches if established wholesalers were already available?

4. What is an agent middleman's marketing mix? Why don't manufacturers use their own sales people instead of agent middlemen?

5. Discuss the future growth and nature of wholesaling if low-margin retailing and scrambled merchandising become more important. How will wholesalers have to adjust their mixes if retail establishments become larger and the retail managers more professional? Might the wholesalers be eliminated? If not, what wholesaling functions would be most important? Are there any particular lines of trade where wholesalers may have increasing difficulty?

6. Which types of wholesalers would be most appropriate for the following products? If more than one type of wholesaler could be used, provide the specifications for the situation in each case. For example, if size or financial strength of a company has a bearing, then so indicate. If several wholesalers could be used in this same channel, explain this also.
   a. Fresh tomatoes.
   b. Paper-stapling machines.
   c. Auto mechanics' tools.
   d. Canned tomatoes.
   e. Men's shoes.
   f. An industrial accessory machine.
   g. Ballpoint pens.
   h. Shoelaces.

7. Would a drop-shipper be desirable for the following products: coal, lumber, iron ore, sand and gravel, steel, furniture, tractors? Why, or why not? What channels might be used for each of these products if drop-shippers were not used?

8. Which types of wholesalers are likely to become more important in the next 25 years? Why?

SUGGESTED CASES

14. Deller Company
15. Watson Sales Company

When you finish this chapter, you should:

1. Know the advantages and disadvantages of the promotion methods which a marketing manager can use in strategy planning.

2. Understand the importance of promotion objectives.

3. Know how the communication process should affect promotion planning.

4. Know how the adoption processes can guide promotion planning.

5. Understand how promotion blends may have to change along the adoption curve.

6. Know how typical promotion budgets are blended.

7. Know who plans and manages promotion blends.

8. Recognize the important new terms (shown in red).

PROMOTION-INTRODUCTION

15

People won't buy your product if they've never heard of it.

Promotion is communicating information between seller and buyer—to influence attitudes and behavior. The marketing manager's promotion job is to tell target customers that the right Product is available at the right Place at the right Price.

What the marketing manager communicates is pretty well set when the target customers' needs and attitudes are known.

How the messages are delivered depends on what promotion methods are chosen.

SEVERAL PROMOTION METHODS ARE AVAILABLE

The marketing manager can choose from three promotion methods. These are: personal selling, mass selling, and sales promotion. See Figure 15–1.

Personal selling—flexibility is its biggest asset

Personal selling involves direct face-to-face communication between sellers and potential customers. It lets the salesperson see the customer's reactions immediately. This allows the salespeople to adapt the company's marketing mix to the needs of each target market.

Figure 15-1: Basic promotion methods and strategy planning

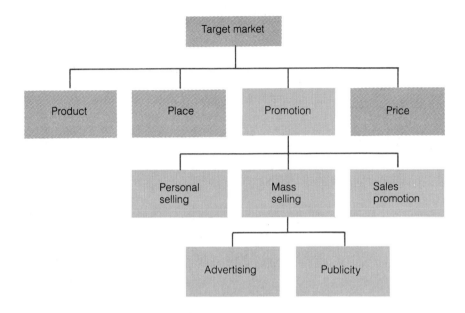

Salespeople are included in most marketing mixes. Personal selling can be very expensive, however. It is often necessary to combine personal selling with mass selling and sales promotion.

Mass selling—reaches millions at a price or even free

Mass selling is communicating with large numbers of customers at the same time. It is less flexible than personal selling. But when the target market is large and spread out, mass selling may be less expensive.

Advertising is the main form of mass selling. **Advertising** is any *paid* form of nonpersonal presentation of ideas, goods, or services by an identified sponsor. It uses such media as magazines, newspapers, radio and TV, signs, and direct mail. While advertising must be paid for, another form of mass selling—publicity—is "free."

Publicity is "free"

Publicity is any *unpaid* form of nonpersonal presentation of ideas, goods, or services. Although, of course, publicity people get paid, they try to attract attention to the firm and its offerings *without having to pay media costs.*

If a firm has a "new" message, publicity may be more effective than advertising. Trade magazines, for example, may carry articles featuring the newsworthy products of regular advertisers—in part because they *are* regular advertisers. This publicity may raise more interest than the company's paid advertising. The publicity people probably would write the basic copy—and then "sell" its use to the magazine editors.

Large firms have specialists to handle this job. Usually though, it is treated as just another kind of advertising. And often it isn't used as effectively as it could be. Much more attention needs to be paid to publicity in the future.[1]

Sales promotion tries to complement

Sales promotion refers to those promotion activities which complement personal selling and mass selling. It may use displays, shows and exhibitions, or demonstrations.

Sales promotion people develop—and may install—point-of-purchase materials. They may invent contests. They may also prepare training materials for the company's own sales force. They may even design the sales materials for the company's own sales force to use during sales calls.

THREE TYPES OF SALES PROMOTION

There are three types of sales promotion—those aimed at: (1) final consumers or users, (2) middlemen, and (3) the company's own sales force. The three types make it clear that sales promotion complements the other promotion methods. Sales promotion specialists are needed because the personal selling and mass selling people may be too busy with their own functions to have the time to develop the skill to handle the "fill-in" activities which are usually handled by sales promotion. Sales promotion specialists must be flexible—working in areas that most need improvement.

Sales promotion for final consumers or users

Sales promotion aimed at final consumers or users usually is trying to increase demand—or speed up the time of purchase. Such promotion might involve developing materials to be displayed in retailers' stores—including banners and streamers, sample packages, calendars, and various point-of-purchase materials. The sales promotion people might also develop the aisle displays for supermarkets. They might be responsible for "jackpot" and "sweepstakes" contests—as well as coupons designed

Sales promotion can get immediate, measurable results and is gaining in popularity.

to get customers to try a product. All of these efforts would be aimed at specific promotion objectives.

Sales promotion directed at industrial goods customers might use some of the ideas we just mentioned. In addition, the sales promotion people might set up and staff trade show exhibits. These activities would be especially important in international marketing. Here, attractive models are often used to try to encourage economically oriented buyers to look over a particular firm's product—especially when it is displayed near other similar products in a circus-like atmosphere.

Sales promotion for middlemen

Sales promotion aimed at middlemen—sometimes called *trade promotion*—stresses price-related matters—because the objective assigned to sales promotion may be to encourage stocking new items, or buying larger quantities, or buying early. The tools used here are price and/or merchandise allowances, promotion allowances, and perhaps sales contests—to encourage retailers or wholesalers to sell specific items—or the company's whole line. Offering to send contest winners to Hawaii, for example, may increase sales greatly.

Sales promotion for own sales force

Sales promotion aimed at the company's own sales force might try to encourage getting new customers, selling a new product, or generally stimulating sales of the company's whole line. Depending on the objectives, the tools might be contests, bonuses on sales or number of new accounts, and holding sales meetings at fancy resorts to raise everyone's spirits.

Ongoing sales promotion work might also be aimed at the sales force—to help sales management. Sales promotion might be responsible for preparing sales portfolios, displays, and other sales aids. They might develop the sales training material which the salespeople could use in working with customers—and other channel members. They might develop special racks for product displays—which the sales rep could sell or give to retailers. Rather than expecting each individual salesperson—or the sales manager—to develop these sales aids, sales promotion might be given this responsibility.

Sales promotion—like publicity—is a weak spot in marketing. Sales promotion includes a wide variety of activities—each of which may be custom-designed and used only once. Few companies develop their own experts in sales promotion. Many companies—even large ones—do not have a separate budget for sales promotion. Few even know what it costs in total.

This neglected method is bigger than advertising

This neglect of sales promotion is a mistake however. In total, sales promotion costs much more than is spent on advertising. This means it deserves more attention—and perhaps separate status within the marketing organization.[2]

The spending on sales promotion is large and growing—sometimes at the expense of other promotion methods. There are several reasons for this growth. Sales promotion has proved successful in an increasingly competitive market. Sales promotion can usually be implemented quickly—and get results sooner than advertising. Sales promotion activities may help the product manager win support from an already overworked sales force. Salespeople welcome sales promotion—including promotion in the channels—because it makes their job easier.[3]

Creative sales promotion can be very effective, but making it work is a learned skill—not a sideline for amateurs. It isn't something that should be delegated to a sales trainee. In fact, specialists in sales promotion have developed—both inside firms and as outside consultants. Some are extremely creative—and might be willing to take over the whole promotion job. But it's the marketing manager's job to set promotion objectives and policies which will fit in with the rest of the marketing strategy.[4]

WHICH METHOD TO USE DEPENDS ON PROMOTION OBJECTIVES

Marketers want to affect buying decisions

Good marketers don't want to just "communicate." They want to communicate information so that target customers choose their product. Therefore, they are interested in (1) reinforcing present attitudes that can lead to favorable behavior, and (2) actually changing the attitudes and behavior of the firm's target market.

Informing, persuading, and reminding are promotion objectives

For a firm's promotion to work, it's necessary to clearly define the firm's promotion objectives. This is because the right promotion blend depends on what the firm wants to accomplish.

The three general **promotion objectives** are to *inform, persuade,* and *remind* target customers about the company and its marketing mix. All three aim at providing more information.

A specific set of promotion objectives—that states exactly *who* the firm would want to inform, persuade, or remind to do *what*—would be desirable in a specific case. But this is unique to each company strategy—and too detailed to discuss here. Instead, we will focus on these three general promotion objectives—and how we might reach them.

Informing is educating

An informing objective would be used when the manager just wants to tell customers about a firm's product. Potential customers have to know about product offerings before they buy at all.

Persuading usually necessary

A persuading objective would be necessary when competitors are offering similar products. The firm must not only inform target customers that its products are available—it must also persuade them to buy. The company might try to develop or reinforce a favorable set of attitudes—hoping to affect buying behavior. Here, comparative information could be supplied.

Reminding may be enough, sometimes

A reminding objective might be used if the firm's target customers already have positive attitudes about the firm's offering. This objective can be extremely important. Even though customers had been attracted and sold once, they are still targets for competitors' promotion. Reminding them of their past satisfaction may keep them from shifting to a competitor.

PROMOTION REQUIRES EFFECTIVE COMMUNICATION

Promotion obviously must get the attention of the target market—or it is wasted. What is obvious, however, isn't always easy to do. Much promotion doesn't really communicate. Behavioral science studies show that the communication process may be more complicated than we thought.

The same message may be interpreted differently

Different people see the same message in different ways. They may interpret the same words differently. Such differences are common in international marketing where translation is a problem. Parker Pen Co., for example, once blanketed Latin America with an ad campaign that, unfortunately, suggested that its new ink would help prevent unwanted pregnancies. General Motors had trouble in Puerto Rico with its Nova automobile. Then it was discovered that while Nova means "star" in Spanish, when it is spoken it sounds like "no va," which means "it doesn't go." The company quickly changed the car's name to "Caribe" and it sold well.[5]

Such problems in the same language may not be so obvious. But they must be recognized and solved to avoid offending customers. This is an especially sensitive matter now—to make sure that advertising does not offend any minority groups. Blacks and women have been especially vocal—but other minorities are becoming more sensitive. These may seem like small differences, but they can make a target market tune out a message—wasting the whole promotion effort.

The communication process needs feedback

The **communication process** shows how a source tries to reach a receiver with a message. Figure 15–2 illustrates this. Here we see that a **source**—the sender of a message—is trying to deliver a message to a **receiver**—a potential customer. A source can deliver a message by many message channels. A personal salesperson does it with voice and actions.

Figure 15–2: The communication process

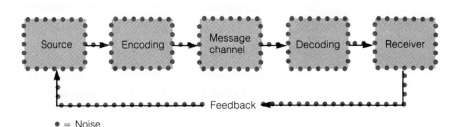

● = Noise

Figure 15–3: Encoding and decoding depend on common frame of reference

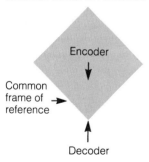

Encoder

Common frame of reference →

Decoder

Advertising must do it with mass media—such as magazines, newspapers, radio, and TV.

A major advantage of personal selling is that the source—the seller—can receive immediate feedback from the receiver. The source can judge how the message is being received—and change it if necessary. This is a real advantage to personal selling. Mass sellers must depend on marketing research or total sales figures to measure success.

The **noise**—shown in Figure 15–2—is any factor which reduces the effectiveness of the communication process. Perhaps the source can't agree on what should be said and how—and settles for a general message. Or the receiver—perhaps a parent—may be distracted by children when the message comes out of the radio. Or other advertisers or salespeople may be saying the same things—and the receiver may become confused and ignore everyone.

Encoding and decoding depend on common frames of reference

The basic difficulty in the communication process occurs during encoding and decoding. **Encoding** is the source deciding what it wants to say and translating it into a message that will have the same meaning to the receiver. **Decoding** is the receiver translating the message. The whole process can be very tricky—because the meanings of various words and symbols may differ depending on the attitudes and experiences of the two groups. This can be seen in Figure 15–3.

Average car drivers, for example, might think of the Ford Mustang as a sports car. If they are the target market, they want to hear about ease of handling, acceleration, and racing symbols—such as wide tires. Auto engineers and sports car fanatics, however, don't consider the Mustang a real sports car. So, if they were writing or approving copy, they might encode the message in regular "small-car" terms.

Noise in the channel can block the communication process.

Message channel is important, too

The communication process is complicated even more because the receiver is aware that the message is not only coming from a source but also coming through some **message channel**—the carrier of the message. The receiver may attach more value to a product if its message comes in a well-respected newspaper or magazine. Similarly, information from the president of a company might be more impressive than from a junior sales representative.

ADOPTION PROCESSES CAN GUIDE PROMOTION PLANNING

The adoption process discussed in Chapter 7 is related to effective communication and promotion planning. You learned that there are six steps in the adoption process: awareness, interest, evaluation, trial, decision, and confirmation. Further, in Chapter 7 we saw consumer buying as a problem-solving process in which buyers go through these several steps on the way to adopting (or rejecting) an idea or product. Now we will see that the basic promotion objectives can be related to these various steps—to show what is needed to achieve the objectives. See Figure 15–4.

Informing and persuading may be needed to affect the potential customer's knowledge and attitudes about a product—and then bring about its adoption. Later, promotion can simply remind the customers about that favorable experience—aiming to confirm the adoption decision.

The AIDA model is a practical approach

The basic adoption process fits very neatly with another action-oriented model—called AIDA—which we will use in this and the next two chapters to guide some of our discussion.

The **AIDA model** consists of four promotion jobs—(1) to get *Attention,* (2) to hold *Interest,* (3) to arouse *Desire,* and (4) to obtain *Action.*[6] (As a memory aid, note that the first letters of the four key words spell AIDA—the well-known opera.)

The relation of the adoption process to the AIDA tasks can be seen in Figure 15–4.

Getting attention is necessary if the potential customer is to become aware of the company's offering. Holding interest gives the communication

Figure 15–4: Relation of promotion objectives, adoption process, and AIDA model

Promotion objectives	Adoption process (Chapter 6)	AIDA model
Informing	Awareness	Attention
	Interest	Interest
	Evaluation	Desire
Persuading	Trial	
	Decision	Action
Reminding	Confirmation	

Promotion has to get and hold interest before customers will buy.

a chance to really build the prospect's interest in the product. Arousing desire affects the evaluation process—perhaps building preference. And obtaining action includes obtaining trial—which may lead to a purchase decision. Continuing promotion is needed to confirm the decision—and encourage continuing action.

GOOD COMMUNICATION VARIES PROMOTION BLENDS ALONG ADOPTION CURVE

The communication and adoption processes discussed above look at individuals. This emphasis on individuals helps us understand how people behave. But it also is useful to look at markets as a whole. Different customers within a market may behave differently—with some taking the lead in accepting products and, in turn, influencing others.

Adoption curve focuses on market segments, not individuals

Research on how markets accept new ideas has led to the adoption-curve concept. The **adoption curve** shows when different groups accept ideas. It shows the need to change the promotion effort as time passes. It also emphasizes the relations among groups. It shows that some groups act as leaders in accepting a new idea.

Promotion for innovators leaves laggards behind

The adoption curve for a typical successful product is shown in Figure 15–5. Some of the important characteristics of each of these customer groups are discussed below. Which one are you?

Innovators—3 to 5 percent of the market

The **innovators** are the first to adopt. They tend to be young and—at the same time—high in social and economic status. They have many contacts outside their own social group and community. They are also mobile and creative.

An important characteristic of innovators is that they rely on impersonal

Figure 15–5: The adoption curve[7]

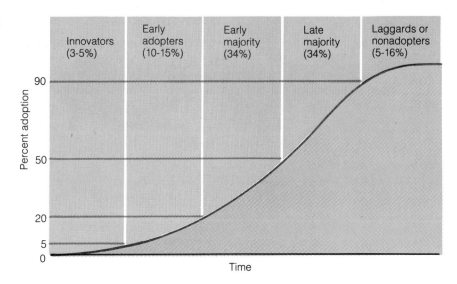

and scientific information sources or other innovators—instead of personal salespeople. They often read articles in technical publications or informative advertisements in "respectable" publications.

Early adopters—10 to 15 percent of the market

Early adopters are relatively high in social status—and probably opinion leaders. They are younger, more mobile, and more creative than later adopters. But they have few contacts outside their own social group or community. Of all the groups, this one tends to have the greatest contact with salespeople. Mass media are important information sources, too.

Early majority—about 34 percent of the market

The **early majority** are those with above average social status. They usually will not consider a new idea until many early adopters have tried it. There may be a long time between trial and adoption.

The early majority have a lot of contact with mass media, salespeople, *and early adopters.*

Late majority—34 percent of the market

The **late majority** tend to be below average in social status and income. They are less likely to follow opinion leaders and early adopters. In fact, some social pressure from their own group may be needed before they try the product. Then adoption may follow quickly.

The late majority make little use of mass media or salespeople. They are influenced more by other late adopters than by outside sources of information.

Laggards or nonadopters—5 to 16 percent of the market

The **laggards** or **nonadopters** tend to be low in social status and income. They prefer to stay with their traditional ideas.

The main source of information for laggards is other laggards. This certainly is bad news for marketers who want to reach a whole market quickly—or use only one promotion method. In fact, it may not pay to bother with this group![8]

Opinion leaders help spread the word

Adoption curve research supports our earlier discussion (in Chapter 7) on opinion leaders. It shows the importance of the early adopters. They influence the early majority—and help spread the word to many others.

Marketers recognize the importance of these personal conversations and recommendations by opinion leaders. If early groups reject the product, it may never get off the ground. But if the early groups accept it, then what the opinion leaders in each social group say about it may be very important. The "web-of-word-of-mouth" may do the real selling job—long before the customer ever walks into the retail store. This shows the importance of trying to reach the opinion leaders in various social groups. But because they are hard to identify—recall from Chapter 7 that different kinds of people may be opinion leaders for different products—mass media can play an important role in getting the message to them.

May need a different blend for each market segment

Each market segment needs a separate marketing mix—and each may require a different promotion blend. This is mentioned here because some mass selling specialists have missed this point. They think mainly in "mass marketing"—rather than target marketing—terms. Aiming at large markets may be all right in some situations, but unfortunately, promotion aimed at everyone can end up hitting no one. In the promotion area, we should be especially careful about using a "shotgun" approach when what is really needed is a "rifle" approach—with careful aiming.

Opinion leaders get the web-of-word-of-mouth going.

SUCCESSFUL PROMOTION MAY BE AN ECONOMICAL BLEND

Once promotion objectives have been set, a marketing manager may decide to use a blend of promotion methods. Certain jobs can be done more cheaply one way than another. This can be seen most clearly in the industrial goods market.

A personal sales call can be expensive

While personal selling dominates most industrial goods promotion budgets, mass selling is necessary, too. Personal salespeople nearly always have to complete the sale. But it is usually too expensive for them to do the whole promotion job. The cost of each sales call is over $100.[9] This relatively high cost comes from the fact that salespeople have only limited time during the "business day" and much of that time is spent on nonselling activities—traveling, paperwork, sales meetings, and service calls. Only 42 percent of their time is available for face-to-face selling.

The job of reaching all the possible customers is made more costly and difficult by the constant turnover of buyers and influences. An industrial salesperson may be responsible for several hundred customers and prospects—with about four "buying influences" per company. They don't have enough time to get the company's whole message across to every possible contact. The problem is shown in the classic McGraw-Hill advertisement in Figure 15–6. As the ad suggests, too much has been invested in a salesperson to use his time and skill to answer questions that could be handled better by mass selling. Mass selling can do the general ground work. The salesperson should concentrate on answering specific questions—and closing the sale. These mass selling "sales calls" can be made at a small fraction of the cost of a personal call. One McGraw-Hill study found a mass selling "call" costing 1/645th the cost of a personal call.[10]

HOW TYPICAL PROMOTION BUDGETS ARE BLENDED

There is no one right blend

There is no one right promotion blend. Each must be developed as part of a marketing mix. But to sum up our discussion of promotion blends, we can make some general statements about how manufacturers have divided their promotion budgets. They do vary a lot. Retailers' blends also vary widely. Wholesalers' blends, on the other hand, use personal selling almost exclusively.

Figure 15–7 shows how manufacturers have divided their promotion budgets. It shows the relationship of advertising expenditures to personal selling which might be expected in various situations.

Figure 15–7 shows that manufacturers of well-branded consumer goods—such as cars, breakfast cereals, and nonprescription drugs—tend to favor advertising. This is especially true of those trying to build brand familiarity. And the emphasis on advertising might be even stronger if the firm had already established its channel relationships.

At the other extreme, smaller companies with new consumer goods would tend to use more personal selling. The same thing applies for most

Figure 15–6

"I don't know who you are.
I don't know your company.
I don't know your company's product.
I don't know what your company stands for.
I don't know your company's customers.
I don't know your company's record.
I don't know your company's reputation.
Now—what was it you wanted to sell me?"

MORAL: Sales start **before** your salesman calls—with business publication advertising.

McGRAW-HILL MAGAZINES
BUSINESS•PROFESSIONAL•TECHNICAL

"That guy's probably been asking the same questions
for fifty years.
Man, am I glad to hear he's retiring."

"I don't know who you are.
I don't know your company.
I don't know your company's product.
I don't know what your company stands for.
I don't know your company's customers.
I don't know your company's record.
I don't know your company's reputation.
Now—what was it you wanted to sell me?"

MORAL: Sales start **before** your salesman calls—with business publication advertising.

McGRAW-HILL MAGAZINES
BUSINESS•PROFESSIONAL•TECHNICAL

"Oh, no!"

One generation passeth away,
and another generation cometh ...
There is no new thing under the sun.
(Ecclesiastes)

Figure 15–7: Typical promotion blends of manufacturers (ratio of advertising to personal selling)

10:1	5:1 *Advertising emphasis*	1:1	1:5 *Personal selling emphasis*	1:10
	Firms with well-branded consumer goods (with established channels)	Blend of consumer and industrial goods	Smaller companies and any firms offering relatively undifferentiated consumer goods or industrial goods	

industrial goods. Because buyers want several sources of supply, personal selling is quite important—to be sure that the seller continues to satisfy and remain on the supplier list.[11]

Personal selling usually is dominant

The relatively heavier emphasis on personal selling which you might have assumed from the figure is correct. The many advertisements you see in magazines and newspapers and on television are impressive and expensive. But this shouldn't make you forget that most retail sales are completed by salesclerks. Further—behind the scenes—much personal selling is going on in the channels.

PROMOTION BLEND—SOMEONE HAS TO PLAN IT—AND MAKE IT WORK

Good blending calls for a marketing manager

Choosing a promotion blend is a difficult strategic decision which should fit in with the rest of the marketing strategy.

Deciding on the right promotion blend is a job for the marketing manager.

Sales managers are concerned with managing personal selling. The sales manager may also be responsible for building good distribution channels.

Advertising managers manage their company's mass selling effort—

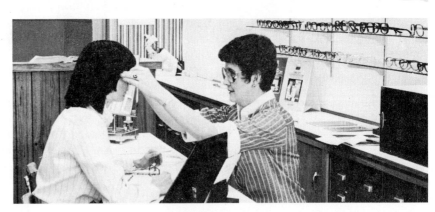

Personal selling includes all sales people and accounts for the largest share of promotion.

in television, newspapers, magazines, and other media. Their job is choosing the right media for each purpose—and developing the ads. They may use an advertising department within their own firms—especially if they are in retailing—or work through outside advertising agencies. They may also handle publicity.

Sales promotion managers manage their company's sales promotion effort. Nearly everything the sales promotion department does *could* be done by the sales or advertising departments. But sales promotion activities are so varied that specialists often develop. In some companies, the sales promotion managers work for the sales managers. In others, they report directly to the marketing manager.

Marketing manager puts the parts together

Because of differences in outlook and experience, the advertising, sales, and sales promotion managers may have a hard time working together. It is the marketing manager's job to decide the value of the various approaches. Then he has to develop an effective promotion blend—fitting the various departments and personalities into it and tying their efforts together.

CONCLUSION

Promotion is an important part of any marketing mix. Most consumers and organizational customers can choose from among many products. To be successful, a producer must do more than offer a good product at a reasonable price. It must also tell potential customers about the product—and where they can buy it. Producers must also tell wholesalers and retailers in the channel about their product—and their marketing mix. These middlemen, in turn, must use promotion to reach *their* customers.

The promotion effort should fit into the strategy which is being developed to satisfy the needs of some target market. *What* should be communicated to them and *how* should be stated as part of the strategy planning.

Basically, promotion is concerned with affecting buying behavior. But three general promotion objectives were discussed—informing, persuading, and reminding.

Various promotion methods can be used to reach these objectives. How the promotion methods are combined for successful communication can be guided by behavioral science findings.

In particular, we know something about the communications process—how individuals adopt new ideas—and the adoption curve—how groups react.

An action-oriented framework—called AIDA—will help guide strategic planning of promotion blends. But finally, the marketing manager is responsible for blending the alternative promotion methods into one promotion effort—for each marketing mix.

In this chapter, we have studied some basic ideas. In the next two chapters we will treat personal and mass selling (advertising) in more detail. We won't discuss sales promotion again here—because it is difficult to generalize about all the possibilities. Further, the fact that most sales promotion activities are short-run "tactical" efforts—which must be specially tailored—means that sales promotion will probably continue to be a "stepchild"—even though sales promotion costs more than advertising. Marketers must find a better way of handling this important decision area.

QUESTIONS FOR DISCUSSION

1. Briefly explain the nature of the three basic promotion methods which are available to a marketing manager. Explain why sales promotion is currently a "weak spot" in marketing and suggest what might be done about it.

2. Relate the three basic promotion objectives to the four tasks (AIDA) of the promotion job, using a specific example.

3. Discuss the communication process in relation to a manufacturer's promotion of an accessory good, say, a portable air hammer used for breaking up concrete pavement.

4. Explain how an understanding of the way individuals adopt new ideas or products (the adoption process) would be helpful in developing a promotion blend. In particular, explain how it might be desirable to change a promotion blend during the course of the adoption process. To make this more concrete, discuss it in relation to the acceptance of a new men's sportcoat style.

5. Discuss how our understanding of the adoption curve should be applied to planning the promotion blend(s) for a new, small (personal) electric car.

6. Discuss the nature of the promotion job in relation to the life cycle of a product. Illustrate, using household dishwashing machines.

7. Promotion has been the target of much criticism. What specific types of promotion are probably the object of this criticism?

8. Might promotion be successful in expanding the general demand for: *(a)* oranges, *(b)* automobiles, *(c)* tennis rackets, *(d)* cashmere sweaters, *(e)* iron ore, *(f)* steel, *(g)* cement? Explain why or why not in each case.

9. Indicate the promotion blend that might be most appropriate for manufacturers of the following established products (assume average- to large-sized firms in each case) and support your answer:
   a. Candy bars.
   b. Men's T-shirts.
   c. Castings for automobile engines.
   d. Car batteries.
   e. Industrial fire insurance.
   f. Inexpensive plastic raincoats.
   g. A camera that has achieved a specialty-goods status.

10. Discuss the potential conflict among the various promotion managers. How might this be reduced?

SUGGESTED CASES

18. Billing Sports Company
37. Mayfair Detergent Co.

When you finish this chapter, you should:

1. Understand the importance and nature of personal selling.

2. Know the three basic sales tasks—and what the various kinds of salespeople can be expected to do.

3. Understand when and where the three types of sales presentations should be used.

4. Know what a sales manager must do to carry out the job assigned to personal selling.

5. Recognize the important new terms (shown in red).

PERSONAL SELLING

16

Today, many salespeople are problem-solving professionals.

A seller needs to communicate with possible customers. Personal selling is often the best way to do it.

Sales managers and marketing managers must decide how much and what kind of personal selling effort will be needed in each marketing mix. As part of their strategy planning, they must decide: (1) how many salespeople will be needed, (2) what kind of salespeople are needed, (3) what kind of sales presentation is desired, (4) how salespeople should be selected, and (5) how they should be motivated. These strategic decisions can be seen more clearly in Figure 16–1.

In this chapter, we'll talk about the importance and nature of personal selling—so you will be able to understand the strategic decisions which face sales managers and marketing managers.

THE IMPORTANCE OF PERSONAL SELLING

About 10.5 percent of the total Canadian labor force in 1981, or some 1,195,000 persons were in sales positions. Employment in selling has more than doubled since 1971. More Canadians are now employed in

Figure 16–1: **Strategy planning for personal selling**

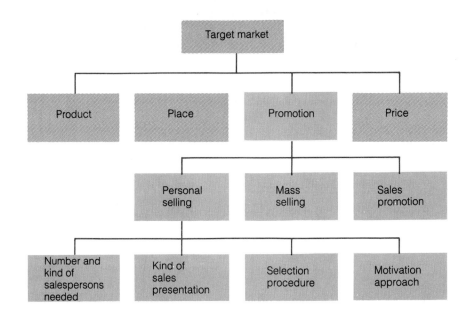

sales than in agriculture and in all forms of teaching combined.[1] Any activity that involves so many people and is so important to the economy deserves study.

Death of a salesman?

In spite of its importance, personal selling is often criticized. The too-aggressive and sometimes dishonest practices of some salespeople—especially door-to-door peddlers and the "hucksters" involved in county or street fairs—have discouraged some from entering the sales field. There also have been doubts about the effectiveness of personal selling—especially at the retail level. Everyone has had experiences with indifferent retail clerks who couldn't care less about customers—or their needs.

The poor image of personal selling—along with the incompetence of many salespeople—led some to predict that personal selling would die out. This has happened in some parts of retailing—resulting in more self-service stores.

Rebirth of salespeople

Personal salespeople are far from dead. Their role is just being redefined and upgraded—as different types of sales jobs are needed. Modern sales and marketing management have gone far in redefining what needs to be done—then selecting, training, and motivating salespeople to perform effectively—while also providing them with personal satisfaction. In some cases, selling is becoming a profession. Most high-level salespeople believe in the importance and value of personal selling. Some follow codes of ethics.

It's more than "get rid of the product"

While discussing selling—within marketing strategy planning—we will assume that the product the salespeople are to sell is reasonably good.

But in fairness to salespeople, this is not always the case. Production-oriented managers often feel that it is the salesperson's job to "get rid of the product"—whether it's any good or not. If the salespeople know that they don't have much to sell, you can see why their morale would slip—and the whole promotion job might suffer.

Helping to buy is good selling

Increasingly, good salespeople don't try to "sell" the customer. Rather, they try to help him buy—by presenting both the advantages and disadvantages of their product and showing how it will satisfy needs. They find that this helpfulness results in satisfied customers and long-term relationships.

The old-time salesman with the funny story and the big smile is being replaced by salespeople who have something real to contribute. The smiling "bag of wind" with the big expense account is on the way out.

Salespeople represent the whole company

Increasingly, the salesperson is recognized as a representative of the whole company—responsible for explaining its total effort to target customers—rather than just moving products. As evidence of this change in thinking, some companies now give their salespeople such titles as field manager, market specialist, sales representative, or sales engineer.

A salesperson is both transmitter and receiver

A salesperson is expected to do much more than just bring in new business—though this certainly is an important part of the job. At the same time, the salesperson should gather feedback to help the company to do a better job in its future planning.

The modern salesperson, in other words, not only communicates the company's story to customers, but also feeds back customer reaction to the company. He is an important link in both the communication and marketing processes.

Good sales people try to determine a company's needs and only sell what is best for them.

Salespeople can be strategy planners, too

Some sales representatives are expected to be marketing managers in their geographic territories. Some may become marketing managers by default—because their own managers have not provided clear guidelines. In this case, the salesperson must develop his own marketing mix or even his own strategy. He may be given a geographic territory, but it may be unclear exactly who his customers are. He may have to start from scratch in his strategy planning. The only limits may be the product line he is expected to sell and probably a price structure. He may have his own choice about (1) who he aims at, (2) which particular products in the line he will push aggressively, (3) which middlemen he will try to work with, (4) how he will spend any promotion money that he controls, and (5) how he will adjust prices within company limits.

A salesperson who can put together profitable strategies—and make them work—can rise very rapidly. If a strategy will work in his territory, it may work elsewhere. And it is very likely that he will become responsible for larger territories. The opportunity is there for those who are prepared and willing to work.

And even the starting selling job may offer great opportunities. Some beginning salespeople—especially those working for manufacturers or wholesalers—are responsible for larger sales volumes than are achieved by average or even large-sized retail stores. This is a responsibility which must be taken seriously—and should be planned for.

Further, the sales job is often used as an entry-level position—to find out what a new employee can do. Success in this job can lead to rapid promotion to higher-level sales and marketing jobs—and more money and job security.

BASIC SALES TASKS MAY BE SPLIT

One of the difficulties of discussing selling is that every sales job is different. While the engineer or accountant can look forward to fairly specific duties, the salesperson's job is constantly changing.

Selling is divided into three parts

There are three basic sales tasks which a sales representative might have to perform. These tasks are (1) order getting, (2) order taking, and (3) supporting. For convenience, we will describe salespeople by these terms—referring to their main task—although one person might have to do all three jobs in some situations.

As the names imply, order-getters and order-takers are interested in obtaining orders for their companies. In contrast, supporting salespeople are not directly interested in orders. Their job is to help the order-oriented salespeople. With this variety, you can see that there is a place in personal selling for almost everyone.

Order-getters develop new business

Order-getters are concerned with getting new business. **Order getting** means aggressively seeking out possible buyers with a well-organized sales presentation designed to sell a product or idea.

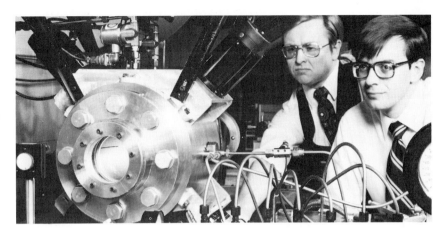

Industrial goods order getters often have more technical-market knowledge about their product than their customers do.

Order-getting salespeople work for manufacturers, wholesalers, and retailers. They normally are well paid—many earning more than $25,000 per year.

Manufacturers' order-getters—find new opportunities

Manufacturers of all kinds of goods—but especially industrial goods—have a great need for order-getters. They are needed to locate new prospects, open new accounts, see new opportunities, and help establish and build channel relationships.

Industrial goods order-getters need the "know-how" to help solve their customers' problems. To be sure of technically competent order-getters, producers often give special training to business-trained college graduates. Such salespeople are a real help to their customers. In fact, they may be more technically able—in their narrow specialty—than anyone in the customer's firm. They can provide a unique service.

Wholesalers' order-getters—hand it to the customer, almost

Progressive wholesalers are developing into counselors and store advisors—rather than just order-takers. Such order-getters are almost "partners" of retailers in the job of moving goods from the wholesale warehouse through the retail store to consumers. These order-getters almost become a part of the retailer's staff—helping to check stock, write orders, conduct demonstrations, and plan advertising, special promotions, and other retailing activities.

Retail order-getters—visionaries at the storm window

Order-getters are necessary for unsought goods and desirable for some shopping goods.

Unsought goods need order-getters

Convincing customers of the value of products they have not seriously considered takes a high degree of personal sales ability. Order-getters have to be able to see how a new product might satisfy needs now being filled by something else. Early order-getters for aluminum storm windows and other aluminum and plastic home improvements faced a difficult task—convincing skeptical customers that these materials were not only durable but also would save money and require less maintenance in the long run. Similar problems were faced by early refrigerator salespeople in the 1920s—and air-conditioning salespeople in the 1930s.

Without order-getters, many of the products we now accept as part of our standard of living—such as refrigerators and window air-conditioners—might have died in the introductory stage. It is the order-getter who sells enough customers to get the web-of-word-of-mouth going. Without sales and profits in the early stages, the product may fail—and never be offered again.

They help sell shopping goods

Order-getters are desirable for selling heterogeneous shopping goods. Consumers shop for many of these items on the basis of price and quality. They welcome useful information. Automobiles, furniture and furnishings, cameras and photographic supplies, and fashion items can be sold effectively by an order-getter. Helpful advice—based on knowledge of the product and its alternatives—may help consumers make a choice and bring profits to the salesperson and the retailers.

Order-takers—keep the business coming

Order-takers sell the regular or typical customers. Order-takers complete most sales transactions. After the customer becomes interested in the products of a specific firm—from an order-getter or a supporting salesperson or through advertising or sales promotion—an order-taker usually is necessary to answer any final questions and complete the sale. **Order taking** is the routine completion of sales made regularly to the target customers.

Sometimes sales managers or customers will use the term *order-taker* as a "put-down" when referring to unaggressive salespeople. While a particular salesperson may perform so poorly that criticism of him is justified, it is a mistake to downgrade the function of order taking. Order taking is extremely important—whether handled by human hands or machines.

Manufacturers' order-takers—train and explain

After order-getters open up industrial, wholesale, or retail accounts, regular follow-up is necessary. Someone has to explain details, make adjustments, handle complaints, and keep customers informed about new developments. The customers' employees may need training to use machines or products. In sales to middlemen, it may be necessary to train the wholesalers' or retailers' salespeople. These activities are part of the order-taker's job.

Usually these salespeople have a regular route with many calls. To handle these calls well, they must have physical energy, persistence, enthusiasm, and a friendly personality.

Sometimes jobs that are basically order taking are used to train potential order-getters and managers—since they may offer some order-getting possibilities. This can be seen in the following description of his job by a young Colgate salesman—who moved rapidly into the ranks of sales management.

> Over many months, I worked carefully with Gromer's Super Market. It was an aggressive young store. After a few calls, I felt I had built up a warm friendship with the store personnel. They came to trust me and, more frequently than not, after I straightened shelves, checked out-of-stocks, and did the usual dusting and rearranging, I gave them an order blank already filled in.
>
> It got to be a joke with big, husky Paul Gromer, the owner, and his hard-working manager-brother. They kept asking, "Well, what did we buy today?" and they signed the order book without checking.
>
> Naturally, I worked at the order like it was my own business, making certain that they were never stuck with dead stock or over-orders. They were making continual progress, though nothing sensational.
>
> Finally, Colgate came out with a good deal. I knew it was right for Gromer's and I thought the store ought to double its weekly order to 400 cases. I talked to Paul Gromer about it and, without any reason that I'm able to think of today, I said, "Paul, this is a hot deal and I think you're ready for a carload order."
>
> He looked at me for just a moment. I braced myself for an argument. Then he said, "Sure, why not? You've always been right before. Just ship it."
>
> It was the biggest order of soap Gromer's had ever taken—and the store soon became a regular carload buyer.[2]

Wholesalers' order-takers—not getting orders but keeping them

While manufacturers' order-takers handle relatively few items—and sometimes only a single item—wholesalers' order-takers may handle 125,000 items or more. Most of these order-takers just sell out of their catalog. They have so many items that they can't possibly give aggressive sales effort to many—except perhaps the newer or more profitable items. The strength of this type of order-taker is his wide assortment—rather than detailed knowledge of individual products.

Manufacturers' order takers get to know their customers well and understand their needs.

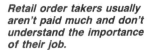
Retail order takers usually aren't paid much and don't understand the importance of their job.

The wholesale order-taker's main function is to keep in close contact with his customers—perhaps once a week—and fill any needs that have developed. Some retailers let him take inventory and write up his own order. Obviously, this position of trust can't be abused. After writing up the order, the order-taker normally checks to be sure his company fills the order promptly and accurately. He also handles any adjustments or complaints—and generally acts as a link between his company and customers.

Such salespeople are usually of the low-pressure type, friendly and easy going. Usually these jobs are not as high paying as the order-getting ones—but are attractive to many because they aren't as demanding. Relatively little traveling is required. And there is little or no pressure to develop new accounts.

Retail order-takers—often they are poor salesclerks

Order taking may be almost mechanical at the retail level—say at the supermarket checkout counter. Sometimes, retail clerks seem to be annoyed by having to complete sales. This is too bad—because order taking is important. They may be poor order-takers, however, because they are not paid very well—often at the minimum wage. But they may be paid little because they do little. In any case, order taking at the retail level appears to be declining in quality. Probably there will be far fewer such jobs in the future—as more and more marketers turn to self-service selling.

Supporting sales force—informs and promotes in the channel

Supporting salespeople help the order-oriented salespeople—but don't try to get order themselves. Their activities are directed toward obtaining sales in the long run. For the short run, however, they are ambassadors of goodwill who provide specialized services. Almost all supporting salespeople work for manufacturers—or middlemen who do this supporting work for manufacturers. There are two types of supporting salespeople: missionary salespeople and technical specialists.

Missionary salespeople

Missionary salespeople work for manufacturers—calling on their middlemen and their customers. The usual puposes are to develop goodwill and stimulate demand, help the middlemen train their salespeople, and often take orders for delivery by the middlemen.

Missionary salespeople are sometimes called *merchandisers* or *detailers.*[3] They may be absolutely vital if a manufacturer uses the typical merchant wholesalers to obtain widespread distribution—but knows that the retailers will need promotion help which won't come from the merchant wholesalers. Merchandisers or detailers may be able to give an occasional "shot in the arm" to the company's regular wholesalers and retailers. Or, they may work regularly with these middlemen—setting up displays, arranging promotions, and, in general, supplying what the company's sales promotion specialists have developed.

Technical specialists

Technical specialists provide technical assistance to order-oriented salespeople. They are usually scientists or engineers who have little interest in sales. Instead, they have technical know-how—plus the ability to explain the advantages of the company's product. Since they usually talk to the customer's technical people, there is little need for much sales ability. Before the specialist's visit, an order-getter probably has stimulated interest. The technical specialist provides the details. Some of these technical specialists eventually become fine order-getters. But most are more interested in proving the technical excellence of their product than in actual sales work.

Most selling requires a blend of all three sales tasks

We have described three sales tasks—order getting, order taking, and supporting. Remember, however, that a particular salesperson might have to do any or all of these jobs. Ten percent of a particular job may be order getting, 80 percent order taking, and the remaining 10 percent supporting.

The kind of person needed for a given sales position—and the level of compensation—will depend largely on which sales tasks are required and in what combination. This is why job descriptions are so important.

Job descriptions are needed

A **job description** shows what a salesperson is expected to do. It might list 10 to 20 specific tasks—as well as the routine prospecting and sales report writing. Each company must write its own job specifications—but when they are written, they should provide clear guidelines to what kind of salespeople should be selected and how they should be motivated. These strategic matters are discussed later in the chapter.

NATURE OF THE PERSONAL SELLING JOB

Good salespeople are taught, not born

The idea that good salespeople are born has some truth in it—but it is far from the whole story. Experiments have shown that it is possible to train any alert person to be a good salesperson. This training includes basic steps which each salesperson should follow. These include: prospecting, planning sales presentations, making sales presentations, and following up after the sale. See Figure 16–2 for a diagram which shows that a personal salesperson is just carrying out the communications process discussed in the last chapter.

While these basic steps may seem logical, managers don't always follow them. New salespeople often are hired and sent out on the road or retail selling floor with no training in the basic steps and no information about the product or the customer—just a price list and a pat on the back. This isn't enough!

It is up to sales and marketing management to be sure that the salespeople know what they are supposed to do and how to do it.

Finding prospects—the big buyer who wasn't there

Finding "live" prospects is not as easy as it sounds. Although the marketing strategy should specify the target market, we have already seen that some people within a target market may be very interested in change, while others are late adopters.

Basically, **prospecting** involves following down all the "leads" in the target market. But which ones are currently "live" and will help make the buying decision? In the industrial goods area, for example, about two thirds of industrial calls are made on the wrong person—because of multiple buying influences and the fact that companies often change their organizational structures and buying responsibilities. This means that constant and detailed customer analysis is needed. This requires lots of personal calls and telephone calls.

How long to spend with whom?

Another part of prospecting is deciding how much time to spend developing each prospect. Here, the potential sales volume as well as the proba-

Figure 16–2: **Personal selling is a communication process**

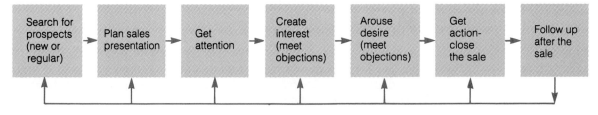

bility of actually making a sale must be considered. This obviously requires judgment. But well-organized salespeople usually develop some system to guide prospecting—because most of them have too many potential customers. They can't afford to "wine and dine" all of them. Some prospects deserve only a phone call—taking them to lunch would be a waste of the salesperson's time. There are only a few hours in each business day for personal sales calls. This time must be used carefully if the salesperson is to succeed. So it is clear that effective prospecting is important to success. In fact, it may be more important than making a good sales presentation—especially if the company's marketing mix is basically strong.

Three kinds of sales presentations may be useful

Once a promising prospect has been found, it is necessary to make a **sales presentation**—a salesperson's effort to make a sale. Someone has to plan what kind of sales presentation is to be made. This is a strategic matter. The kind of presentation should be set *before* the salesperson is sent prospecting. Or, in situations where the customer comes to the salesperson—for example, in a retail store—the planners have to make sure that prospects are brought together with salespeople. Then, the planned sales presentation must be made.

The marketing manager can choose among three basically different sales presentations: the black-box approach, the selling formula approach, and the need-satisfaction approach.[4] Each of these has its place.

The black-box approach

The **black-box approach** uses a "canned" or prepared sales presentation—building on the black-box (stimulus–response) model discussed in Chapter 7. This model says that a customer faced with a particular stimulus will give the desired response—say, a yes answer to the salesperson's request for an order.

The use of these prepared sales presentations is shown in Figure

Salespeople have to analyze their customers constantly to avoid wasted calls.

Figure 16–3: Black-box approach to sales presentations

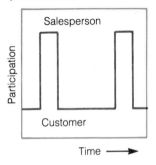

Figure 16–3: Black-box approach to sales presentations

16–3. Basically, the salesperson does most of the talking—see the shaded area in Figure 16–3—only occasionally letting the customer talk when the salesperson attempts to close. If one closing attempt does not work, he goes on until he makes another try at closing. This procedure can go on until either the salesperson runs out of material—or the customer buys or decides to leave.

This approach can be effective and practical when the possible sale is low in value and the time that can be spent on selling is short. This is true, for example, for many convenience goods in food stores, drug stores, and department stores. The presentation might be as simple as: "That's very nice, should I wrap it up?" or "Would you like to try it on?" or "Would you like a carton instead of a package?" or "Should I fill'er up?"

The black-box approach treats all potential customers the same. It may work for some and not for others—and the salespeople probably won't know why. They don't improve their performance as a result of this experience, because they are just mechanically trying a standardized presentation. This method can be suitable for simple order taking. It is no longer considered good selling for complicated situations.

Selling-formula approach

The **selling-formula approach** uses a prepared outline—also building on the black box (stimulus–response) model—taking the customers through some logical steps to a final close. The steps are logical because we assume that we know something about the target customers' needs and attitudes.

Figure 16–4: Selling-formula approach to sales presentations

The selling-formula approach is illustrated in Figure 16–4. A salesperson does most of the talking at the beginning of the presentation, because he knows exactly what he wants to say—it even may have been prepared for him as part of the marketing strategy. Then he brings the customer into the discussion to see what special needs this customer has. Next, the salesperson tries to show how his product satisfies those needs. Finally, he goes on to close the sale.

This approach can be useful for both order-getting and order-taking situations—where potential customers are similar and relatively untrained salespeople must be used. This is a little like using advertising—where only one general presentation must be tailored to a large audience—only, here, several preplanned presentations are possible. Some of the office equipment and computer manufacturers, for example, have used this approach. They know the kinds of situations that their salespeople will meet—and roughly what they want them to say. Using the selling-formula approach speeds the training process—and makes the sales force productive sooner.

Need-satisfaction approach

The **need-satisfaction approach** involves developing a good understanding of the prospective customer's needs before trying to close the sale. Here, the salesperson leads the customer to do most of the talking at first—to help the salesperson pinpoint the customer's needs. See Figure 16–5. When he feels that he understands the customer's needs, the sales rep begins to do more in the sales presentation—trying to help the customer

Figure 16–5: Need-satisfaction approach to sales presentations

understand his own needs better. Once they agree, the seller tries to show how his product fills the customer's special needs—and then closes the sale.

The need-satisfaction approach can be useful if there are many differences among the various customers in a target market. The salesperson has to discover which of the many potentially relevant dimensions describe a particular person—and then help that customer understand what his needs are. This kind of sales presentation obviously takes more skill—and also more time. This approach is more practical when the sale is large.

With this approach, the salesperson is much more on his own. He should have a good understanding of the company's products and policies. Some knowledge of the behavioral science theories we have discussed would also be useful—especially a good understanding of the "hierarchy of needs."

Using AIDA to plan sales presentations

AIDA—Attention, Interest, Desire, Action. Each presentation—except some simple black-box types—follows this AIDA sequence. The "how-to-do-it" might even be spelled out as part of the marketing strategy. The time spent with each of the steps might vary, depending on the situation and the selling approach being applied. But it is still necessary to begin a presentation by getting the prospect's attention and, hopefully, moving him to action at the close. The ways in which these steps might work are discussed in the following paragraphs.

Attention

There is no sure way to get a prospect's attention. Much depends on the salesperson's instincts and originality—as well as knowledge of his customers. If a salesperson calls on the same people frequently, he will want to use a new approach each time. If each call is on a new prospect, a few successful attention getters will do.

At the first stage of a meeting with a customer, the salesperson's main purpose is to distract the potential customer from his current thoughts and begin a conversation. The seller might do this by just introducing himself or saying, "Hello, can I help you?" as a retail clerk might. Or a statement about the plans of the prospect's competitors might get attention.

Whatever method is used, the attention getter should be casual, so the presentation can move quickly, naturally, and logically into the next step—creating interest.

Interest

Creating interest takes more time. The best way is to look for the prospect's basic needs or problems—especially those which the salesperson might be able to solve. A furniture store salesclerk should not make a

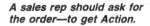
*A sales rep should ask for
the order—to get Action.*

prepared speech about rugs every time a customer comes in—some might want lamps, chairs, and so on. Getting the customer to talk helps the salesperson get the all-important feedback which guides further effort. Of course, the sales rep should understand his target market. By choosing prospects from this group, he can know roughly what they want—and have a marketing mix that has been designed specifically for them.

Desire

Arousing desire requires an even more persuasive effort. At this stage, the salesperson definitely has to determine exactly what the prospect's specific needs are. This lets the seller show how his product fits the needs, answer objections, and prepare to close the sale. This feedback is vital to the sales presentation—and is an important "plus" of personal selling.

Action

Finally, the salesperson will try to summarize the important points, suiting arguments to the customer's needs and attitudes, and try to close the sale—i.e., affect the prospect's behavior. It is interesting to note that one of the most frequent reasons for losing a sale is that the salesperson *never asks for the order!* Perhaps this is because he's afraid that a direct request for the order is too easily answered with a "no."

The experienced salesperson knows how to avoid this awful word. Without asking for a direct yes or no, he may just assume that "of course" the customer will buy. He may begin to write up the order—or ask which of various delivery dates would be better. He may ask what quantity the customer would like to try in a new display. This may lead the customer into taking action without consciously having to make a direct decision— a difficult step for some people.

SALES MANAGEMENT MUST BE PLANNED, TOO

Marketing strategy planning must include some sales management guidelines—about how the personal selling job will be carried out—including selecting and motivating salespeople.

Besides helping the marketing manager set these guidelines, the sales manager must (1) organize and train a sales force, (2) assign territories, (3) set quotas, and (4) evaluate and control the whole process. We can't cover all the details of sales management here, but it is important to see that they are done within the guidelines set by the marketing strategy. The more that is known about the needs and attitudes of the target market, the easier it will be for the sales manager to set his own plan.

Selecting good salespeople takes judgment, plus

It is very important to obtain good, competent salespeople. A careful job description—related to the whole marketing strategy—should be the basis for choosing a sales force.

Unfortunately, the selection of salespeople in most companies is a hit-or-miss affair. They are often hired without any job description or serious thought about exactly what kind of person is needed. This approach has led to poor sales and high personnel turnover for many companies.

Progressive companies have tried to use more scientific procedures in hiring—including interviews with various managers as well as psychological tests. Unfortunately, these techniques do not guarantee success. But experiments have shown that using *some* kind of selection method brings in better people than using no selection aids at all.

Compensating and motivating

While it is true that public recognition, sales contests, or just personal recognition for a job well done may be effective in stimulating greater sales effort, most companies also use cash incentives to encourage salespeople. Let's take a look at some ways this can be done.

Two basic decisions must be made in developing a compensation plan: (1) the level of compensation and (2) the method of payment.

Level of compensation

To attract and keep good people, most companies must at least pay the going market level for the different kinds of salespeople. Order-getters are paid more than order-takers, for example.

The job description explains the salesperson's role in the marketing mix. It should show whether any special skills or responsibilities are required—perhaps suggesting higher pay levels. To make sure that it can afford a given type of salesperson, the company should estimate—at the time this description is being written—how valuable such a salesperson will be. A good order-getter might be worth over $50,000 a year to one company, but only $5,000 to another—simply because the second one doesn't have enough to sell. In such a case, the second company will have to rethink its job specification or completely change its promotion

The amount of travel needed and type of customer called on can affect a salesrep's compensation.

plans—because the going rate for good order-getters is much higher than $5,000 a year.

If a job will require a lot of traveling, aggressive pioneering, or contacts with difficult customers, the pay may have to be increased. The salespersons' compensation level should compare at least roughly with the pay scale of the rest of the firm. They are normally paid more than the office or production force, but usually less than the managers who supervise them.

Method of payment

Once the general level of compensation has been determined, then the method of payment must be set. There are three basic methods of payment: (1) straight salary, (2) straight commission, or (3) a combination plan.

Straight salary gives the salesperson the most security—and straight commission, the most incentive. Most companies want to offer some balance between incentive and security. Therefore, the most popular method of payment is a combination plan—which includes some salary and some commission. Bonuses and other goal-directed incentives are becoming more popular, too. Pensions, insurance, and other fringe benefits may be included—but salary and/or commission are basic to most combination plans.

A sales manager's control over a sales rep depends on the compensation plan. The straight salary plan permits the greatest amount of supervision. The person on commission tends to be his own boss.

The marketing manager should probably try to avoid very complicated compensation plans—or plans that change frequently. Complicated plans are hard for salespeople to understand—and costly for the accounting department to handle. Also, low morale may result if salespeople can't see a direct relationship between their effort and their income.

Simplicity is probably best achieved with straight commission. But, in practice, it is usually better to give up some simplicity to have some control over salespeople—while still providing flexibility and incentive.[5]

Sales management must work with marketing management

There are, unfortunately, no easy answers to the compensation problem. It is up to the sales manager—working with the marketing manager—to develop a good compensation plan. The sales manager's efforts have to be part of the whole marketing plan, because he can't accomplish his goals if enough funds aren't included for this job.

It is the marketing manager's job to balance the promotion blend. The expected cost and performance of the sales force are only two things he must consider. To make these judgments, the marketing manager must know what kind of sales force is needed, what its goals should be, and how much it will cost.

When the marketing manager has OK'd the sales manager's basic plan and budget, the sales manager must carry out the plan. This includes directing and controlling the sales force, determining and assigning sales territories, and evaluating performance. You can see that a sales manager is really concerned with the basic management tasks of planning and control—as well as implementing the personal selling effort.

CONCLUSION

In this chapter, we have discussed the importance and nature of personal selling. Selling is much more than just "getting rid of the product." In fact, a salesperson who is not provided with strategic guidelines may have to become his own strategic planner. Ideally, however, the sales manager and marketing manager should work together to decide some strategic matters: the number and kind of salespersons needed, the kind of sales presentation, and selection and motivation approaches.

Three basic kinds of sales tasks were described: (1) order getting, (2) order taking, and (3) supporting. Most sales jobs are a combination of at least two of these three tasks. The level and method of compensation depend—in large part—on the blend of these tasks. A job description should be developed for each sales job. This provides the guidelines for selecting and compensating salespeople.

Three kinds of sales presentations were discussed. Each has its place, but the need-satisfaction approach seems best for higher-level sales jobs. It is in these kinds of jobs that personal selling is achieving a new, professional status—because of the ability and amount of personal responsibility needed by the salesperson. The grinning "back slapper" is being replaced by the specialist who is creative, hard-working, persuasive, highly trained, and therefore able to help the buyer. This type of salesperson probably will always be in short supply. And the demand for such high-level salespeople is growing.

QUESTIONS FOR DISCUSSION

1. Identify the strategic planning decisions needed in the personal selling area and explain why they should be treated as strategic decisions to be made by the marketing manager.

2. What kind of salesperson (or what blend of the basic sales tasks) is required to sell the following products? If there are several selling jobs in the channel for each product, then indicate the kinds of salespeople required. (Specify any assumptions necessary to give definite answers.)

a. Soya bean oil.
b. Costume jewelry.
c. Nuts and bolts.
d. Handkerchiefs.
e. Mattresses.
f. Corn.
g. Cigarettes.

3. Distinguish among the jobs of manufacturers', wholesalers', and retailers' order-getting salespeople. If one order getter is needed, must all the salespeople in a channel be order getters? Illustrate.

4. Discuss the role of the manufacturers' agent in the marketing manager's promotion plans. What kind of salesperson is he?

5. Discuss the future of the specialty shop if manufacturers place greater emphasis on mass selling because of the inadequacy of retail order taking.

6. Explain the sequential nature of the personal selling job.

7. Cite an actual local example of each of the three kinds of sales presentations discussed in the chapter. Explain for each situation whether a different type of presentation would have been better.

8. Describe a need-satisfaction sales presentation which you have experienced recently and explain how it might have been improved by fuller use of the AIDA framework.

9. Explain how a straight commission system might provide flexibility in the sale of a line of women's clothing products which continually vary in profitability.

10. Explain how a compensation system could be developed to provide incentives for older salespeople and yet make some provision for trainees who have not yet learned their job.

11. Describe the operation of our economy if personal salespeople were outlawed. Could the economy work? If so, how; if not, what is the minimum personal selling effort necessary? Could this minimum personal selling effort be controlled effectively by law?

SUGGESTED CASES

19. Debmar Corporation
20. Bayer Furniture Company
27. Lewis Tool Company

When you finish this chapter, you should:

1. Understand when the various kinds of advertising are needed.

2. Understand how to go about choosing the "best" medium.

3. Understand how to plan the "best" message—that is, the copy thrust.

4. Understand what advertising agencies do—and how they are paid.

5. Understand how to advertise legally.

6. Recognize the important new terms (shown in red).

ADVERTISING

17

To reach a lot of people quickly and cheaply, advertising may be the answer.

Advertising makes widespread distribution easier. Although a marketing manager might prefer to use only personal selling, it is very expensive. Advertising can be much cheaper. It is not as flexible as personal selling, but it can reach large numbers of potential customers at the same time. Today, most promotion blends contain both personal selling and advertising.

Marketing managers have strategic decisions to make about advertising. Working with advertising managers, they must decide: (1) who is the target, (2) what kind of advertising to use, (3) how customers are to be reached (through which types of media), (4) what is to be said to them (the copy thrust), and (5) by whom (the firm's own advertising department or outside advertising agencies). See Figure 17–1.

THE IMPORTANCE OF CANADIAN ADVERTISING

Canadian versus U.S. expenditure

Expenditures in Canada for advertising continue to rise, and no end is in sight. Table 17–1 shows the amount spent on advertising between 1962 and 1980 in Canada and the United States, both in total and as a

Figure 17–1: Strategy planning for advertising

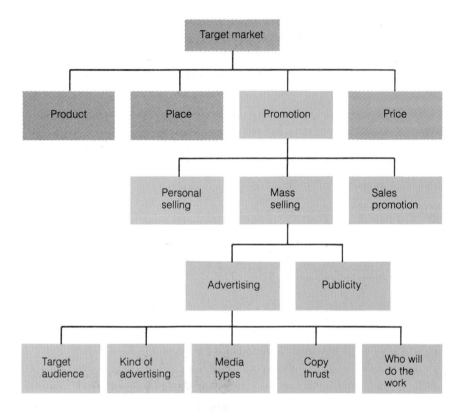

Table 17–1: Advertising expenditures, United States and Canada, 1962–1980[1]

	Total advertising expenditures ($ millions)		Per capita expenditures		Advertising expenditures, percent of GNP	
	United States	Canada	United States	Canada	United States	Canada
1962	$12,430	$ 643	$ 66	$ 35	2.21%	1.52%
1964	14,150	724	74	38	2.23	1.45
1966	16,630	873	85	44	2.22	1.42
1968	18,090	982	90	47	2.09	1.38
1970	19,550	1,138	95	53	2.00	1.33
1972	23,300	1,391	110	64	1.99	1.32
1974	26,820	1,830	127	82	1.90	1.24
1976	33,690	2,387	157	104	1.97	1.25
1978	43,840	2,973	201	127	2.06	1.29
1980[p]	54,600	3,853	246	161	2.08	1.33

[p] = preliminary.
Note: Expenditures quoted in national currencies.

percentage of each country's GNP. That table also reveals annual per capita advertising expenditures in both nations.

These figures clearly indicate that Canadian advertising expenditures are substantial in their own right. They reached almost $4 billion dollars in 1980, more than doubling in the relatively brief period since 1974. However, both per capita advertising and aggregate expenditures on advertising, expressed as a percentage of GNP, are generally about 50 percent greater for the United States than the corresponding Canadian figures.

Relative importance of media

Table 17–2 shows the changes over time in how Canadian advertising revenues have been divided up among the different media. Not surprisingly, television's share of the media dollar has kept on climbing as the percentage of Canadian homes with television sets steadily increased. But our figures do not always reveal the obvious. Would you have guessed in 1956 that radio would more than hold its own over the next two decades? Would you have predicted the continuing importance of catalogue selling and direct mail as a Canadian advertising medium? Aren't you surprised even now to find advertiser expenditures in this category somewhat greater than what is spent on television?

Some spend more than others

Canadian firms and industries differ in the percentage of their sales spent on advertising. This reflects the relative importance of advertising to the firm's or the industry's marketing mix. The last Canadian study of advertising as a percentage of industry sales showed that soap and related products manufacturers spent 10.9 percent of industry sales on advertising. Drug manufacturers spent 8.65 percent, and toilet article manufacturers 15.2 percent. At the other extreme, artificial ice manufacturers, pulp and paper mills, and sugar refineries all spent less than one fourth of 1 percent of their sales on advertising.[2]

Table 17–3 lists Canada's top 50 advertisers in print radio and TV during

Table 17–2: Net advertising revenues percent share by media, 1956–1981[3]

	1956	1960	1964	1968	1972	1976	1980*
Radio	9.0%	9.2%	9.7%	10.4%	11.1%	10.8%	10.8%
TV	6.3	9.1	12.0	12.6	12.7	14.4	16.9
Dailies	32.9	30.9	29.0	28.4	28.7	29.5	24.7
Weekend supplements	3.4	3.1	2.7	1.9	2.0	1.1	0.5
Weekly semi-tri	4.5	4.3	4.0	5.5	4.9	4.9	5.8
General magazines	4.1	3.8	2.6	2.6	2.4	3.0	4.2
Business papers	4.8	4.7	3.9	3.1	2.5	3.2	2.7
Farm papers	1.5	1.2	0.8	0.6	0.6	0.4	0.4
Directories, phone, city	3.7	5.2	5.1	4.7	5.5	6.1	6.5
Religious, school, and other	0.6	0.4	0.3	0.4	0.4	0.4	0.4
Catalogues, direct mail	23.4	21.4	22.2	20.4	20.8	19.4	20.6
Billboards, car cards, signs	5.8	6.7	7.7	9.4	8.4	6.8	6.5

* Maclean Hunter Research Bureau Estimates.

1.	Government of Canada	$53,723,698
2.	Procter & Gamble	27,336,275
3.	John Labatt	24,557,465
4.	General Foods	24,444,038
5.	Rothmans of Canada	20,953,868
6.	Ontario Government	18,614,603
7.	Dart and Kraft	18,580,402
8.	General Motors of Canada	15,478,937
9.	Standard Brands	15,181,097
10.	The Molson Companies	14,974,750
11.	American Home Products	13,466,497
12.	Kellogg Salada	12,613,915
13.	Unilever	12,492,065
14.	Imasco	12,189,096
15.	Quebec Government	12,047,581
16.	CP Enterprises	11,888,614
17.	Ford Motor of Canada	10,973,001
18.	Warner-Lambert Canada	10,837,205
19.	Bristol-Myers Canada	10,418,489
20.	Canada Packers	8,876,667
21.	Dairy Bureau of Canada	8,805,604
22.	Hudsons Bay	8,592,950
23.	Coca-Cola	8,179,982
24.	Union Carbide Canada	7,965,157
25.	The Seagram Co.	7,925,170
26.	Nestle Canada	7,835,714
27.	Colgate-Palmolive Canada	7,824,507
28.	McDonalds Restaurants Canada	7,611,281
29.	Dominion Stores	7,535,459
30.	Imperial Oil	7,518,206
31.	Chrysler Canada	7,499,489
32.	S. C. Johnson and Son	7,488,608
33.	Nabisco	7,485,698
34.	Gillette Canada	7,161,002
35.	Ralston Purina Canada	6,732,857
36.	General Mills Canada	6,712,339
37.	RJR	6,543,826
38.	Hiram Walker Resources	6,535,372
39.	Bank of Montreal	6,459,249
40.	Royal Bank of Canada	6,445,751
41.	Cadbury, Schweppes, Powell	6,304,446
42.	George Weston	6,123,452
43.	Johnson & Johnson	6,035,215
44.	Toyota Canada	5,371,333
45.	Canadian Imperial Bank of Commerce	5,316,824
46.	Gulf Canada	5,149,258
47.	Simpsons-Sears	4,864,314
48.	Canadian Honda Motor	4,848,132
49.	Benson & Hedges Canada	4,839,050
50.	Gilbey Canada	4,732,730

Note: The above expenditures are for space and time only in the following media: Daily newspapers, consumer magazines (does not include "Special Interest"), farm papers, radio, television. Radio and TV do not include direct buys.

1977. Advertising expenditures are concentrated in a limited number of consumer product categories (food and food products—19 percent, drugs and cosmetics—10 percent, automotives—8.5 percent, brewers and distillers—8 percent, financial and insurance—6 percent, household supplies—4 percent).[5] Table 17–3 also shows that the federal, the Quebec, and the Ontario governments are among Canada's largest advertisers. These totals tell us how much was spent in Canada by different governmental departments. They do not include substantial outlays for tourist advertising in other countries.

Less costly than personal selling

Clearly, advertising is an important factor in certain markets. Nevertheless, in total, much less is spent on advertising than on personal selling. And although total advertising expenditures are large, the advertising industry itself employs relatively few people. Probably less than 30,000 individuals work directly in Canadian advertising. This figure includes everyone who helps create or sell advertising for the different advertising media as well as those in advertising agencies. It also includes those working for retailers, wholesalers, and manufacturers who either create their own advertising or at least manage that activity.

ADVERTISING OBJECTIVES ARE SET BY MARKETING STRATEGY

Every advertisement—and every advertising campaign—should have clearly defined objectives. These should flow from the overall marketing strategy—and the jobs assigned to advertising. But it is not enough for the marketing manager to say just—"Promote the product."

If you want half the market, say so!

A marketing manager should spell out exactly what is wanted. A general objective: "To assist in the expansion of market share," could be stated more specifically: "To increase traffic in our cooperating retail outlets by 25 percent during the next three months."

Such specific objectives would obviously affect promotion methods. Advertising that might be right for building a good image among opinion leaders might be all wrong for getting customers into the retailers' stores.

Advertising objectives should be very specific—much more so than personal selling objectives. One of the advantages of personal selling is that the salespeople can change their presentations to meet customers' needs. Each advertisement, however, is a specific communication that must be effective—not just for one customer—but for thousands or millions of target customers. This means that definite objectives should be set for each advertisement—as well as a whole advertising campaign. If this isn't done, a creative advertising staff may just set some general objective like "selling the product." Then it will plan ads that will win artistic awards within the advertising industry—but fail to do the advertising job management hoped for.

OBJECTIVES DETERMINE THE KINDS OF ADVERTISING NEEDED

The advertising objectives will determine which of two basic types of advertising to use—product or institutional.

Product advertising tries to sell a product. It may be aimed at final users or channel members.

Institutional advertising tries to develop goodwill for a company or even an industry—instead of a specific product.

Product advertising— meet us, like us, remember us

Pioneering advertising—builds primary demand

Pioneering advertising tries to develop **primary demand**—demand for a product category rather than a specific brand. Its basic job is to inform—not persuade. It is needed in the early stages of the adoption process—to inform potential customers about a new product. It is also needed in the introductory stage of the product life cycle.

Pioneering advertising doesn't have to mention a brand or specific company at all. The California olive industry promoted olives as olives—not certain brands. This was so successful that after only five years of promotion, the industry's surpluses became shortages. Then it shifted promotion funds to product research—to increase production.

Competitive advertising—emphasizes selective demand

Competitive advertising tries to develop **selective demand**—demand for a specific brand rather than a product category. A firm can be forced into competitive advertising—as the product life cycle moves along—to hold its own against competitors. The United Fruit Company gave up a 20-year pioneering effort to promote bananas—in favor of advertising its own Chiquita brand. The reason was simple. While United Fruit was promoting "bananas," it slowly lost market share to competitors. The competitive advertising campaign tried to stop these losses.

Competitive advertising may be either direct or indirect. The **direct type** aims for immediate buying action. The **indirect type** points out product advantages—to affect future buying decisions.

Airline advertising uses both types of competitive advertising. Direct-action ads use prices, timetables, and phone numbers to call for reservations. Indirect-action ads suggest that you mention the airline name when talking to your travel agent.

Comparative advertising is even rougher. **Comparative advertising** is competitive advertising which makes specific brand comparisons—using actual product names. Although certain government agencies have encouraged this kind of advertising, some ad agencies are backing away from it. They feel this approach has raised legal as well as ethical problems. Research is supposed to support superiority claims, but the rules aren't clear. Some firms just keep running small tests until they get the results they want. Others focus on minor differences that do not reflect the overall

Comparative advertising makes specific brand comparisons and lets the customers decide.

IS MORE EFFECTIVE THAN

In fact, Ban Roll-On is more effective at stopping wetness than all leading aerosols.

benefits of a product. This may make consumers less—rather than more—informed. Some comparative ads leave consumers confused—or even angry—if the product they are using has been criticized. And, in at least one instance, comparative ads seem to have helped the competitive product (Tylenol) more than the advertisers' products (Datril, Anacin, and Bayer aspirin).[6]

Many advertisers don't like comparative advertising. But it is likely that the approach will be continued by some advertisers—and encouraged by the government—as long as the ad copy is not obviously false.[7]

Reminder advertising—reinforces early promotion

Reminder advertising tries to keep the product's name before the public. The advertiser may use "soft-sell" ads that just mention the name— as a reminder. Much Coca-Cola advertising has been of this type. Reminder advertising may be useful when the product has achieved brand preference or insistence—perhaps in the market maturity or sales decline stages of the product life cycle.

Institutional advertising—remember our name in Vancouver, Toronto, Montreal

Institutional advertising emphasizes the name and prestige of a company or industry. It tries to inform, persuade, or remind. General Motors, for example, does institutional advertising of the GM name—emphasizing the quality and research behind *all* GM products. See Figure 17–2.

COOPERATIVE ADVERTISING MAY BUY MORE

Vertical cooperation— advertising allowances, cooperative advertising

The discussion above might suggest that only producers do advertising. This isn't true, of course. But producers can affect the advertising done by others. Sometimes a manufacturer knows what he wants advertising to do—but finds that it can be done better or cheaper by someone further along in the channel. In this case, he may offer **advertising allowances**— price reductions to firms further along in the channel to encourage them to advertise or otherwise promote the firms locally.

Cooperative advertising may get more cooperation

Cooperative advertising involves middlemen and producers sharing in the cost of ads.

It helps a manufacturer get more promotion for the advertising dollar. Media rate structures usually give local advertisers lower rates than national firms. Also, a retailer is more likely to follow through when he is paying part of the cost.

Cooperative advertising and advertising allowances can be abused. Allowances can be given to retailers without really expecting that they will be used for ad purposes. This may become a hidden price cut— and even price discrimination. To avoid charges of discrimination and to be certain they have received advertising support in return for their allowance, intelligent producers insist on advertising tearsheets and other proof of use.

THE "BEST" MEDIUM—HOW TO DELIVER THE MESSAGE

For effective promotion, ads have to reach specific target customers. Unfortunately, not all potential customers read all newspapers or maga-

Figure 17–2: An example of institutional advertising

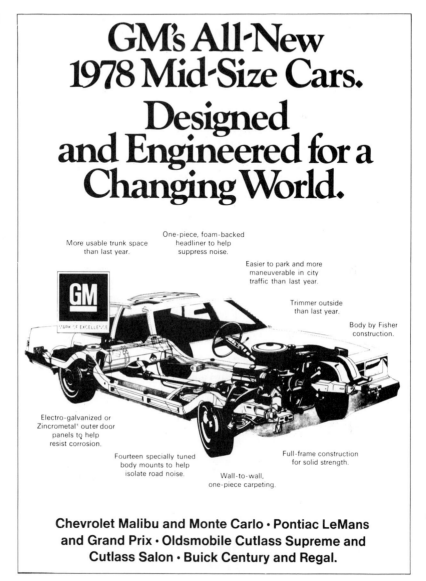

GM's All-New 1978 Mid-Size Cars. Designed and Engineered for a Changing World.

More usable trunk space than last year.

One-piece, foam-backed headliner to help suppress noise.

Easier to park and more maneuverable in city traffic than last year.

Trimmer outside than last year.

Body by Fisher construction.

Electro-galvanized or Zincrometal' outer door panels to help resist corrosion.

Fourteen specially tuned body mounts to help isolate road noise.

Wall-to-wall, one-piece carpeting.

Full-frame construction for solid strength.

Chevrolet Malibu and Monte Carlo • Pontiac LeMans and Grand Prix • Oldsmobile Cutlass Supreme and Cutlass Salon • Buick Century and Regal.

zines—or listen to every radio and television program. So not all media are equally effective.

There is no simple answer to the question: What is the best medium? Effectiveness depends on how well it fits with the rest of a particular marketing strategy. It depends on (1) your promotion objectives, (2) your target markets, (3) the funds available for advertising, and (4) the nature of the media—including who they *reach,* with what *frequency,* with what *impact,* and at what *cost.*

Specify promotion objectives

Before a firm can choose the best medium, it must decide on its promotion objectives. They can affect which media are practical. For example, if the objective is to inform—telling a long story with a lot of detail and pictures—then magazines or newspapers may be best. Jockey switched its annual budget of more than $1 million from TV to magazines when it decided to show the variety of colors, patterns, and styles that Jockey briefs offer. They felt that it was too hard to show this in a 30-second TV spot. Jockey ads were run in men's magazines such as *Sports Illustrated, Outdoor Life, Field and Stream, Esquire,* and *Playboy.* But, aware that women buy over 80 percent of men's ordinary underwear—and 50 percent of fashion styles—they also placed ads in *TV Guide, New Yorker, People, Money, Time,* and *Newsweek.* And a page of scantily clad males was run in *Cosmopolitan.*[8]

Specify target markets and match with media

To guarantee good media selection, the advertiser must specify its target market—a step necessary for all marketing strategy planning. Then, media can be chosen that will reach these target customers.

Matching target customers and media is the hardest part of effective media selection. It's hard to be sure who sees or hears what. Most of the major media use marketing research to develop profiles of the people who buy their publications—or live in their broadcasting area. But they can't be as definite about who actually reads each page—or sees or hears each show.

The difficulty of evaluating alternative media has led some media buyers to select media based on the lowest "cost per 1,000 people" figures. This concern with "bodies" can lead to ignoring the target market's dimensions—and slipping into "mass marketing." The media buyer may look only at the relatively low-cost (per 1,000 persons) "mass media" such as national network radio or TV, when a more specialized medium—aimed at the buyer's target market—might be a much better buy.

Specialized media help zero in on target markets

Media are now trying to reach smaller, more defined target markets. National media may offer regional editions. Major magazines such as

Market profiles are available for some media, but there is no guarantee that the target customers will receive the message.

Chatelaine, MacLean's and *Reader's Digest* all offer regional or even metropolitan editions.

Many magazines serve only special-interest groups—such as fishermen, radio and television fans, homemakers, religious groups, and professional groups. In fact, the most profitable magazines seem to be the ones aiming at clearly defined markets—*Playboy, Car Craft, Skiing,* and *Bride's Magazine* have been doing well.

Radio was hit hard at first by TV competition. But now—like some magazines and newspapers—it has become more specialized. Some stations aim at particular nationality, racial, and religious groups—such as Puerto Ricans, blacks, and Catholics—while others feature country, rock, or classical music.

Perhaps the most specific medium is **direct-mail advertising**—selling directly to the customer via his mailbox. The method is to send a specific message to a carefully selected list of names. Some firms specialize in providing mailing lists—ranging in number from hundreds to millions of names. The variety of these lists is shown in Table 17–4—and shows the importance of knowing your target market.[9]

Specifying the copy thrust

Once it has been decided *how* the messages are to reach the target audience, then it is necessary to decide on the **copy thrust**—*what* is to be communicated by the copy and illustrations. This should flow from the promotion objectives—and the specific tasks assigned to advertising.

Carrying out the copy thrust is the job of advertising specialists. But the advertising manager and the marketing manager should have an understanding of the process—to be sure that the job is done well.

Table 17–4: Examples of available Canadian mailing lists

Approximate quantity of names available	Name of list
12,000	Amateur radio enthusiasts
25,000	Canadian college faculty
30,000	Mail-order buyers of woolens
12,000	Campers in Canada
420,000	Farmers and grain growers
7,000	Dentists
20,000	French Canadian outdoorsmen
54,000	Snowmobile owners
58,000	Senior business executives
15,000	Buyers of art prints
2,076,000	Rural Canada file
235,000	University students
14,000	Canadian churches
46,000	Vitamin buyers
	Canadian Amateur Hockey Association
20,000	Coaches, trainers, and managers
310,000	Players, age 11 to over 20
44,000	Canadian architects and engineers

*Let AIDA help guide
message planning*

There are few tried-and-true rules in message planning. It is clear that the overall marketing strategy should determine *what* should be said in the message. Then management judgment—with the help of marketing research—can decide how this message can be encoded so it will be decoded as intended.

As a guide to message planning, we can make use of the communication process and the AIDA concept: getting Attention, holding Interest, arousing Desire, and obtaining Action.

Getting attention

Getting attention is the first job of an advertisement. If this is not done, the whole effort is wasted. Many readers page through magazines or news-

*Getting attention is the first
job of an ad.*

It's one third of your life. Live a little.

Now. The Calvin Klein bed.

Stainless Steel bed by Brueton.

Good news! Life is just a bed of roses. Indulge yourself in Wamsutta sheets.
Calvin Klein has designed "Checkered Rose" just for the occasion.
Crisp tattersall combined with a touch of femininity make this the freshest look for a bed today.
The feeling is rich. Because these sheets are a soft no-iron blend of cotton and Fortrel® polyester.
And the quality is distinctly Wamsutta. But then it's to be expected. Over 130 years of crafting bed linens has taught us a thing or two.
Besides, we're involved in one third of your life.
We want it to be sensational **Wamsutta**®

Div. M. Lowenstein & Sons, 111 West 40th St., N.Y.

papers without paying attention to any of the advertisements. Many listeners or viewers run errands—or get snacks—during commercials on radio and TV.

There are many ways to catch the customer's attention. A large headline, newsy or shocking statements, pictures of pretty girls, babies, cartoon characters—anything that is "different" or eye catching—may work. But . . . the attention-getting device must not take away from the next step—holding interest.

Holding interest

Holding interest is another matter. A pretty girl may get attention. But once you've seen her, then what? A man may pause to appreciate her. Women may evaluate her. But if there is no relation between the girl and the product, observers of both sexes will move on.

More is known about holding interest than getting attention. The tone and language of the advertisement must fit in with the experience and attitudes of target customers. A food advertisement featuring fox hunters in riding costumes, for example, might not communicate with many potential customers who do not "ride to the hounds."

Further, the advertising layouts should look right to the customer. Print illustrations and copy should be arranged so that the reader's eye is encouraged to move smoothly through the ad.

Arousing desire

Arousing desire for a particular product is one of the most difficult jobs. It requires that the advertiser communicate effectively with the target customers. This means that the advertiser should understand how these customers think, behave, and make decisions—and then give them a reason to buy.

To be successful, an advertisement must convince customers that the product can meet their needs. Pioneering advertising may be useful to develop primary demand for the whole product class. Later—in the market growth and market maturity stages—competitive advertising can show how a particular brand satisfies particular wants.

Obtaining action

Getting action is the final requirement—and not an easy one. The potential customer should be encouraged to try the product. He should go beyond considering how the product might fit into his life to actually trying it—or letting the company's sales rep come in and show how it works.

Strongly felt customers' needs might be featured in the ads—to communicate better. Careful research on the attitudes in the target market may help uncover such strongly felt—but unsatisfied—needs.

Appealing to these needs can get more action—and also provide the kind of information the buyer needs to confirm his decision. Postpurchase doubts may set in after the purchase. So providing reassurance may be one of the important roles of advertising. Some customers seem to read more advertising *after* the purchase than before. What is communicated to them may be very important if satisfied customers are to start—or keep—the web-of-word-of-mouth going. The ad may reassure them about the correctness of their decision. It may also supply the words they use to tell others about the product.

ADVERTISING MANAGER DIRECTS MASS SELLING

An advertising manager manages a company's mass selling effort. Many advertising managers—especially those working for retailers—have their own advertising departments that plan the specific advertising campaigns—and carry out the details. Others use advertising agencies.

ADVERTISING AGENCIES OFTEN DO THE WORK

Ad agencies are specialists

Advertising agencies are specialists in planning and handling mass selling (advertising) details for advertisers. Agencies play a useful role—because they are independent of the advertiser—and have an outside viewpoint. They bring experience to the individual client's problems, because they work for many other clients. Further, as specialists they often can do the job more economically than a company's own department.

Are they paid too much?

The major users of advertising agencies are manufacturers or national middlemen—because of the media rate structure. Normally, media have two prices: one for national advertisers and a lower rate for local advertisers, such as retailers. The advertising agency gets a 15 percent commission on national rates—only. The national advertiser would have to pay this higher media rate even if it places its own ads. This makes it worthwhile for national advertisers to use agencies. It makes sense to let the agency experts do the work—and earn their commission. Local retailers—allowed the lower media rate—seldom use agencies.

There is a growing resistance to the traditional method of paying agencies. The chief complaints are (1) that the agencies receive the flat 15 percent commission—regardless of work performed, and (2) that the commission system makes it hard for the agencies to be completely objective about low-cost media—or promotion campaigns that use little space or time.

Not all agencies are satisfied with the present arrangement either. Some would like to charge additional fees—as they see costs rising and advertisers demanding more services.

The fixed commission system is most favored by accounts—such as producers of industrial goods—that need a lot of service but buy relatively little advertising. These are the firms the agencies would like to—and sometimes do—charge additional fees.

Ad agencies are specialists in mass selling.

The fixed commission system is generally opposed by very large consumer goods advertisers who do much of their own advertising research and planning. They need only basic services from their agencies. Some of these accounts can be very profitable for agencies. Naturally, these agencies would prefer the fixed-commission system.

Fee for service commonly used

Canadian advertising budgets are, on the average, much smaller than American ones. The rates charged by Canadian media serving a more limited audience are, on a per-page or per-minute basis, far less than U.S. rates. On the other hand, the same tasks must be performed by Canadian agencies planning campaigns and preparing effective advertisements. Also, the salaries they must pay are not that much lower. These factors have resulted in the fee-for-service basis of agency compensation being well established and widely used in Canada.

MEASURING ADVERTISING EFFECTIVENESS IS NOT EASY

Success depends on the total marketing mix

It would be convenient if we could measure advertising results by a simple analysis of sales. Unfortunately, this isn't possible—although the advertising literature is filled with success stories that "prove" advertising has increased sales. The total marketing mix—not just promotion—is responsible for the sales result. The one exception to this rule is direct-mail advertising. If it doesn't produce immediate results, it is considered a failure.

Research and testing can improve the odds

Ideally, advertisers should test advertising. They shouldn't depend only on the judgment of creative people or advertising "experts."

Some progressive advertisers now demand laboratory or market tests to evaluate the effectiveness of ads. Sometimes, opinion and attitude re-

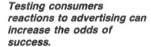
Testing consumers reactions to advertising can increase the odds of success.

search is used before ads are run generally. Or researchers may try to evaluate consumers' reactions to particular advertisements with devices which measure skin moisture or eye reaction.

While advertising research techniques are far from foolproof, they are probably much better than depending only on the judgment of advertising experts. Until better advertising research tools are developed, the present methods seem safest. This means carefully defining specific advertising objectives, choosing media and messages to accomplish these objectives, testing plans, and then evaluating the results of actual advertisements.

GOVERNMENT REGULATION OF CANADIAN ADVERTISING

Advertising abuses have been a favorite target of Canadian consumerists. Their efforts, along with those of Consumer and Corporate Affairs Canada, have led to stricter enforcement of existing laws and to new legislation. A number of Canadian firms have been brought to court for use of misleading advertising. For up-to-date information on enforcement efforts, take a look at the *Misleading Advertising Bulletin,* published quarterly by Consumer and Corporate Affairs Canada.

The Stage I amendments to the Combines Act, strengthened that law by extending its coverage to services as well as to products. All forms of misrepresentations (including not only published advertisements, but also the package) are now covered. In addition, not only the literal meaning of an advertisement, but also the general impression it conveys are considered in assessing misrepresentation. Untrue or misleading warranties, bait-and-switch advertising, and contests which mislead the public as to its chances of success are also specifically prohibited.[10]

The provinces are also active

The stricter federal controls on advertising have their provincial counterparts. Almost all the provinces are now regulating advertising far more aggressively than was previously the case. Such regulation is an especially prominent feature of the new "trade practices" laws recently passed by many Canadian provinces.

Conflicting provincial legislation can make it impossible for national advertisers to use the same campaign across Canada. Provincial differences are greatest in the advertising of liquor, beer, and wine. Some provinces ban it outright, others place restrictions on what can be said, and still others limit the advertiser to specific media. Complying with all this legislation is no easy task.

The Canadian Radio-Television and Telecommunications Commission (CRTC) controls the content of all radio and television commercials. The CRTC lets the Health Protection Branch of the Department of National Health and Welfare regulate the advertising of drugs, cosmetics, and birth-control devices. Similarly, the CRTC allows other types of advertising to Consumer and Corporate Affairs Canada. Firms using radio and television must obtain approval in advance for every food and drug commercial.

These government agencies do not have the same kind of advance veto power over print advertising. However, they can and do insist that print advertisements which violate existing regulations be corrected. Also, both advertisers and their agencies have been brought to court for violating the false advertising provisions of the Combines Act or comparable provincial legislation.[11]

Self-regulation also a factor

Additional forms of regulation are imposed by the media themselves and by industry associations. The CBC and CTV networks also have their own codes of advertising acceptability. The Canadian Advertising Advisory Board has a self-regulating arm, the Advertising Standards Council. The council which includes public representatives, administers both a Code of Advertising Standards and more specific codes governing advertisements directed toward children and the advertising of nonprescription drug items.

CONCLUSION

It may seem simple to develop an advertising effort. Simply pick the media and develop a message. It's not that easy. Effectiveness depends upon using the "best" medium and the "best" message—considering: (1) promotion objectives, (2) the target market, and (3) the funds available for advertising.

Specific advertising objectives will determine what kind of advertising to use—product or institutional. If product advertising is needed, then the particular type must be decided—pioneering, competitive (direct or indirect action, and comparative) or reminder. And advertising allowances and cooperative advertising may be helpful.

There are many technical details involved in advertising. Specialists—advertising agencies—have evolved to handle some of these tasks. But they need to have specific objectives set for them—or their advertising may have little direction and be almost impossible to evaluate.

Effective advertising should affect sales. But the whole marketing mix affects sales. The results of advertising cannot be measured by sales changes alone. Advertising is only a part of promotion. And promotion is only a part of the total marketing mix that the marketing manager must develop to satisfy target customers.

QUESTIONS FOR DISCUSSION

1. Identify the strategic decisions a marketing manager must make about advertising.

2. Discuss the relation of advertising objectives to marketing strategy planning and the kinds of advertising actually needed. Illustrate.

3. Present three examples where advertising to middlemen might be necessary. What would be the objective(s) of such moves?

4. What does it mean to say that "money is invested in advertising"? Is all advertising an investment? Illustrate.

5. Find advertisements to final consumers which illustrate the following types of advertising: *(a)* institutional, *(b)* pioneering, *(c)* competitive, *(d)* reminder. What objective(s) does each of these ads have? List the needs used in each of these advertisements.

6. Describe the type of media that might be most suitable for promoting: *(a)* tomato soup, *(b)* greeting cards, *(c)* an industrial component material, *(d)* playground equipment. Specify any assumptions necessary to obtain a definite answer.

7. Discuss the use of testimonials in advertising. Which of the four AIDA steps might testimonials accomplish? Would they be suitable for all types of products? If not, for which types would they be most suitable?

8. Find an advertisement that seeks to accomplish all four AIDA steps and explain how you feel this advertisement is accomplishing each of these steps.

9. Discuss the future of independent advertising agencies now that the 15 percent commission system is not required.

10. How would retailing promotion be affected if all local advertising via mass media such as radio, television, and newspapers were prohibited? Would there be any impact on total sales? If so, would it probably affect all goods and stores equally?

11. Is it "unfair" to advertise to children? Is it "unfair" to advertise to less educated or less experienced people of any age? Is it "unfair" to advertise for "unnecessary" products?

SUGGESTED CASES

17. Spears National Bank
18. Billing Sports Company
37. Mayfair Detergent Company

When you finish this chapter, you should:

1. Understand how pricing objectives should affect pricing.

2. Understand the choices the marketing manager must make about— price flexibility, price level, and pricing over the product life cycle.

3. Understand the legality of price level and price flexibility policies.

4. Understand the many possible variables of a price structure— including discounts, allowances, and who pays the transportation costs.

5. Recognize the important new terms (shown in red).

PRICING OBJECTIVES
AND POLICIES

18

Deciding what price to charge can be agonizing.

Price is one of the four major variables that the marketing manager controls. Price decisions affect both the firm's sales and profits. So they must be taken seriously.

Guided by the company's objectives, marketing managers must develop a set of pricing objectives—and then pricing policies. These policies should state: (1) how flexible prices will be, (2) what price level will be set, (3) how pricing will be handled during the course of the product life cycle, (4) how transportation costs will be handled, and (5) to whom and when discounts and allowances will be given. These pricing decisions areas are illustrated in Figure 18–1.

PRICE HAS MANY DIMENSIONS

While economists casually refer to "market price," it is not so easy to define price in real-life situations. Price has many dimensions. For example, if you were offered a current-model Ford station wagon for $2,000, would this be a good price for a car that normally sells for over $6,000? Or, if you were offered a 21-inch television set for $200 that normally sells for $400, would this be a good buy?

Figure 18–1: **Strategy
planning for Price**

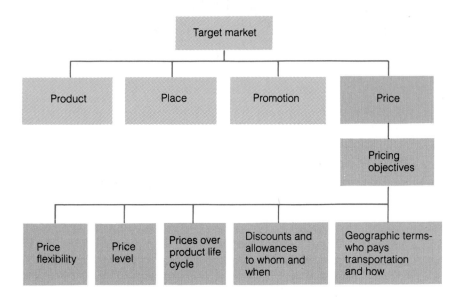

In each case, the first reaction might be an eager "yes." But wait a minute! It might be wise to look further. The $2,000 for the Ford station wagon might be the price of a wreck worth only a few hundred dollars at the junk yard. And the $200 for the TV set might be a reasonable price for all its components in parts bins at the factory. If you wanted these assembled, you would have to pay $50 extra. If you wanted a cabinet, it might be an additional $50. And if you wanted a quality guarantee, there might be an added charge of $100.

The price equation: Price equals Something

These examples show that a price should be related to some assortment of goods and/or services. So, **price** is what is charged for "something." Any business transaction can be thought of as an exchange of money—the money being the price—for Something.

This Something can be a physical good in various stages of completion—with or without the services usually provided, with or without quality guarantees, and so on.

The Something may not be a physical product at all. It may be a play in a theater, a medical checkup, or a suit being dry-cleaned. And, this "product" may or may not be conveniently available.

How much money is charged for this Something will depend on what is included. Some consumers may pay list price—while others may get discounts or allowances because some service is not included. The possible variations are shown in Figure 18–2 for consumers or users—and in Figure 18–3 for channel members. Some of these variations will be discussed more fully below—but here it should be clear that Price has many dimensions.

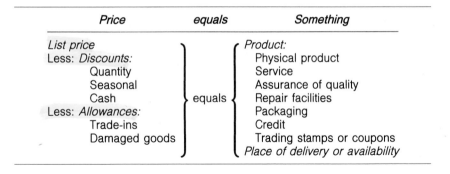

Figure 18–2: **Price as seen by consumers or users**

Price	equals	Something
List price Less: *Discounts:* 　　Quantity 　　Seasonal 　　Cash Less: *Allowances:* 　　Trade-ins 　　Damaged goods	} equals {	*Product:* 　Physical product 　Service 　Assurance of quality 　Repair facilities 　Packaging 　Credit 　Trading stamps or coupons *Place of delivery or availability*

Figure 18–3: **Price as seen by channel members**

Price	equals	Something
List price Less: *Discounts:* 　　Quantity 　　Seasonal 　　Cash 　　Trade or functional Less: *Allowances:* 　　Damaged goods 　　Advertising 　　Push money	} equals {	*Product:* 　Branded—well known 　Guaranteed 　Warranted 　Service—repair facilities 　Convenient packaging for handling *Place:* 　Availability—when and where *Price:* 　Price-level guarantee 　Sufficient margin to allow chance for 　　profit *Promotion:* 　Promotion aimed at customers

PRICING OBJECTIVES SHOULD GUIDE PRICING

Pricing objectives should flow from company-level objectives. They should be clearly stated—because they have a direct effect on pricing policies and the price setting method used.

Possible pricing objectives are shown in Figure 18–4.

Profit-oriented objectives

Target returns provide specific guidelines

A **target return objective** sets a specific profit-related goal. Seeking a target return is a common profit-oriented objective. The firm's target may be a certain percentage return on sales—perhaps a 1 percent return on sales, as in the supermarket industry. Or a large producer might aim for a 25 percent return on investment. Or a small family-run firm might want a fixed dollar amount of profit—to cover living expenses.

A target return objective has advantages for a large company. It makes it easier for everyone to know what they are supposed to do. And it makes it easier to control the various divisions. Some companies will cut out divisions—or drop products—that don't earn a set target return on investment. Naturally, therefore, managers try to hit this target.

Figure 18–4: Possible pricing objectives

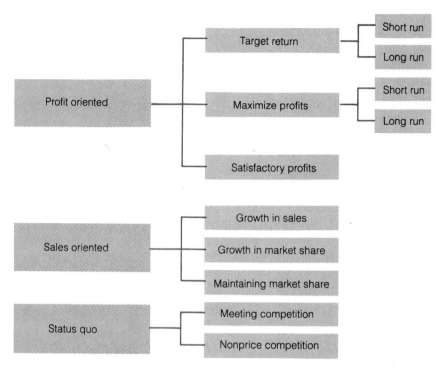

Profit maximization can be socially responsible

A **profit maximization objective** states that the firm seeks to get as much profit as it can. It might be stated as a desire for a rapid return on investment. Or—more bluntly—to earn "all the traffic will bear."

Profit maximization objectives seem to be more common among small firms—small retailers and manufacturers—who are out of the public eye.[1] Large firms, on the other hand, might avoid a profit maximization objective.

The public—and many business executives—link a profit maximization objective with high prices and monopolies. They feel that anyone trying to maximize profits is not operating in the public interest.

Economic theory does not support this idea. Profit maximization doesn't always lead to high prices. True, demand and supply *may* bring extremely high prices—if competition can't offer good substitutes. But this happens *if and only if* demand is highly inelastic (i.e., if higher prices will not reduce the quantity demanded very much). If demand is very elastic, it might be in a monopolist's interest to charge relatively low prices—so sales will increase.

Some just want satisfactory profits

Some businesses aim for only "satisfactory" profits. They may work for profits—but they aren't nearly as aggressive as they might be if they were trying to maximize profits. They want to convince stockholders of their competence. And they also want to be sure of the firm's survival. As long as profits are "good enough," they feel that they have reached their objective.[2]

Sales-oriented objectives

A **sales-oriented objective** states that the firm seeks to get some level of sales or share of market—without referring to profit.

Sales growth does not mean big profits

Some managers seem more concerned about sales growth than profits. This is probably because many feel sales growth always means big profits. This belief is dying, however. Major corporations have faced a continuing profit squeeze over the last 20 years—while sales have grown. More attention is now being paid to profits—along with sales.[3]

Another reason for the popularity of sales growth–oriented objectives is that a manager's salary may be more closely tied to sales than to profits.[4] Here, compensation systems may have affected the selection of objectives—rather than vice versa!

Maintaining market share may be enough

Just maintaining market share—the percentage of the market you are "entitled to" because of your size and reputation—seems to be very important to some managers. This is partly because market share is easier to measure than whether profits are being maximized. It is fairly easy to measure whether a company has maintained its percentage of a market. So, as long as some profit is earned, the managers may prefer stressing market share instead—especially if job promotions are based on market share.

How about increasing market share?

Aggressive companies often aim to increase market share—or even to control a market. In some businesses, economies of scale logically encourage a firm to seek increased market share—and probably greater profits. Sometimes, however, firms blindly follow the market growth goal. This leads to pricing almost at cost to get more of the market. Sales growth objectives sometimes lead to profitless prosperity—where slight errors lead to bankruptcy.

Status-quo objectives

Don't rock the boat objectives

Status-quo objectives are "don't-rock-the-*pricing*-boat" objectives—and are fairly common. They may be stated as "meeting competition" or "avoiding competition" or "stabilizing prices."

Often, a status-quo objective is held by conservative managers who

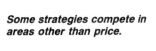

Some strategies compete in areas other than price.

want to reduce the risk of loss. They prefer instead a comfortable way of life and some assurance of profit. Maintaining stable prices may discourage price competition—and remove the need for hard decisions. The managers may have more time for golf!

Or stress nonprice competition instead

On the other hand, a status-quo *pricing* objective can be part of an extremely aggressive marketing strategy. The pricing objective may seem conservative, but the aim could be to avoid price competition in favor of **nonprice competition**—aggressive action on one or more of the Ps *other than Price.*

MOST FIRMS SET SPECIFIC PRICING POLICIES

Specific pricing policies are important for any firm. Otherwise, the marketing manager must rethink his strategy every time a customer asks for a price.

Price policies usually lead to **administered prices**—consciously set prices. In other words, instead of letting daily market forces decide their prices, most firms set their own prices. Some firms do their pricing mechanically—and without much thought—just "meeting competition." Actually, however, they do have many choices. And they should consider price setting carefully. If the customers won't pay the price—the whole marketing mix fails. In the rest of this chapter, we will talk about the pricing policies a marketing manager must set to do an effective job of administering Price.

Prices start with a list price

Most price structures are built around list prices. How these list prices are set is discussed in the next chapter. For now, however, we must see that there may be several list prices. Then, we will go on to see the many variations from list.

Basic list prices—are "list prices"

Basic list prices are the prices that final consumers or users are normally asked to pay for products. Unless noted otherwise, "list price" refers to "basic list price" in this book.

Unchanging list prices—an administrative convenience

Unchanging list prices are published prices that remain the same for long periods of time—perhaps years—but the actual price is adjusted upward or downward by "add-ons" or discounts. This method of changing prices is often used where frequent price changes are necessary. It avoids many catalog price revisions. Rather than printing a complete new catalog, the seller can just publish a new list of add-ons or discounts.

Phony list prices for "bargain hunters"

Phony list prices are prices that customers can be shown to suggest that the price they are to pay has been discounted from "list." Some customers seem more interested in the size of the supposed discount than the list price itself. And they can end up paying more than the competitive market price!

Most businesses, Better Business Bureaus, and government agencies frown on phony prices. We shall soon review the section of the Combines Act that allows legal action to be taken against deceptive pricing. This area is one of the relatively few now being actively implemented by the Canadian courts.

Oldsmobile suggests list prices from which adjustments are made.

TORONADO BROUGHAM
Coupe Model . . . Z57 $13,029.56
Prices do not include destination charges

STANDARD EQUIPMENT

- Air Conditioner, Four-Season
- Armrest, Front with Power Controls
- Armrests, Front Seat Center
- Armrests, Rear Seat Center
- Ashtrays, Instrument Panel and Dual Rear
- Automatic Level Control
- Brakes, Power Front Disc and Rear Drum
- Bumper Guards, Front and Rear
- Cigar Lighter, Instrument Panel
- Clock, Electric Digital
- Defogger, Side Window Glass
- Delcotron
- Door Locks, Power
- Door-Pull Handles
- Deluxe Luggage Compartment, Trim and Spare Tire Cover
- Electronic Ignition System, High-Energy
- Engine, 4.1-liter V6, 4-bbl
- Floor Carpeting, Wall-to-Wall Cut-Pile with Carpeted Lower Door Panels
- Frame, Torque-Beam
- Headlamps, Tungsten Halogen (High Beams)
- Hood Release, Interior Operated
- Impact Strips, Front and Rear Bumper
- Instrument Panel, Temperature Gage and Trip Odometer
- Instrument Panel Trim, Simulated Butterfly Walnut Grained
- Lamps, Courtesy/Warning Door
- Lamps, Cornering
- Lamps, Instrument Panel Courtesy Glove Box

FACTORY-INSTALLED OPTIONAL EQUIPMENT

AC1 Seat Adjuster, 6-Way Power Bucket – Passenger Side. Available with XSC Sport Package (Y78) only	$183.00
AG2 Seat Adjuster, 6-Way Power Divided Front – Passenger Side	$183.00
AT6 Reclining Seat Back, Passenger Side Manual (N A with LF9)	$ 71.00
A79 Reclining Seat Back, Driver Side Manual	$ 71.00
A81 Reclining Seat Back, Passenger Side Power (N A with AT6 or Y78)	$130.00
A90 Trunk-Lid Lock Release, Power	$ 29.00
B34 Floor Mats, Auxiliary Front with Carpet Inserts	$ 35.00
B35 Floor Mats, Auxiliary Rear with Carpet Inserts	$ 20.00
B36 Floor Mat, Luggage Compartment	$ 12.00
B84 Moldings, Body Side – Color-Coordinated with Lower Body except when Vinyl Rooftop ordered, then Color-Keyed to Vinyl Rooftop	$ 48.00
B93 Moldings, Bright Door-Edge Guard	$ 14.00
***CA1 Sunroof**, Electric Sliding Metal Panel	$915.00
CD4 Wiper System, Pulse	$ 44.00
***CF5 Sunroof**, Electric Sliding Tempered Glass Panel in silver tint	$1055.00
C04 Landau Roof Covering, Vinyl padded	$210.00
C49 Defogger, Electric Rear Window	$115.00
C65 Air Conditioner, Tempomatic	$ 53.00
C93 Lamps, Opera Exterior	$ 72.00
C95 Lamp, Combination Dome and Dual Lens Reading	$ 12.00
C96 Lamps, Reading – Sail-Panel Mounted	$ 45.00

P42 Tires, Puncture-Sealing – QXW required	$ 99.20
QXW Tires, P195/75R14 Steel-Belted Radial-Ply White-Stripe. Required with P42	$ 56.00
QXY Tires, P205/75R14 Steel-Belted Radial-Ply White-Stripe	$ 86.60
QYC Tires, P205/70R14 Steel-Belted Radial-Ply Black-wall with Raised White Letters	$130.08
UA1 Battery, High-Capacity	
With LD5/LV8	$ 34.00
With LF9	$ 44.00
UE8 Clock, Electric Digital (N A with UM7)	$ 57.00
U35 Clock, Electric (N A with UM7)	$ 25.00
U46 Monitor, External Lamps, Front and Rear	$ 68.00
VJ9 California Emission Equipment and Test, Required for California (Out-of-State Dealers must order on New Vehicles that are intended for registration or leasing in California) (N A with LF9)	$ 46.00
V2D California Diesel Engine Emission Requirements, Required for California (Out-of-State Dealers must order on New Vehicles that are intended for registration or leasing in California with LF9)	$182.00
Y55 Reminder Group Package – Includes Headlamp-On and Low Fuel Indicator	$ 42.00
Y60 Convenience Group, Includes Visor Vanity Mirror and Luggage Compartment Underhood Glove Box and Courtesy/Map Lights	$ 33.00
Y71 Paint Scheme, This consists of a Compatible Accent Color applied to the Body Side in the following Lower Body Upper Body and Paint Scheme Color Code Combinations 22-22-4, 22-22-0, 22-22-1, 29-29-5, 29-F4/S, 36-36-W, 36-X4/W, 45-45-A, 45-J4/A, 47-47-J, 68-68-S, 69-69-N, 72-72-T, 77-77-P, 77-M4/P, 77-S, 77-M4/S (N A with D90)	$202.00

SPECIAL USE EQUIPMENT

A02 Windshield, Soft-Ray Tinted (Fleet Sales only)	$ 57.00

U89 Wiring Harness, Trailer Electrical – 5-Wire (NE7 or N85 required)	$ 25.00
VO2 Cooling System, High-Capacity Radiator Recommended for normal driving in high temperature areas (C60 or C65 required – N A with LF9 or V08)	$ 22.00
V08 Cooling System, High-Capacity Recommended for trailer towing. Required with optional axles (N A with VO2)	
With C60 or C65	$ 34.00
Without C60 or C65	$ 78.00
With LF9 and C60 or C65	$ 25.00
With LF9 and without C60 or C65	$ 53.00

AVAILABLE RADIO EQUIPMENT

UM2 Radio, AM-FM Stereo Pushbutton with Stereo Tape Player – Includes Dual Rear Speakers	$252.00
UM7 Radio, Electronically Tuned AM-FM Stereo Pushbutton with Electronic Digital Display Clock – Includes Dual Rear Speakers with extended range (UQ1) (N A with UE8 or U35)	$402.00
UN3 Radio, AM-FM Stereo Pushbutton with Cassette Tape Player – Includes Dual Rear Speakers	$264.00
UN9 Radio Accommodation Package, Includes Windshield Antenna and Suppression Equipment – Included in all Radios unless U73, U75 or U83 is ordered (N A with UP6, U73, U75 or U83)	$ 27.00
UP6 Radio, AM-FM Stereo Pushbutton with 40 Channel CB – Includes Power Front Fender Tri-Band Antenna (U83) and Dual Rear Speakers	$491.00
UQ1 Radio Speakers, Dual Rear with extended range. Included in UM7 (N A with U80)	
With UM2, UN3, UP6 or U58	$ 25.00
With U63, U69 or without a Radio	$ 53.00
U58 Radio, AM-FM Stereo Pushbutton – Includes Dual Rear Speakers	$178.00
U63 Radio, AM Pushbutton	$ 90.00
U69 Radio, AM-FM Stereo Pushbutton – Includes Dual Rear Speakers	$142.00
U73 Antenna, Fixed Mast (N A with UN9, UP6, U75 or U83) UM2, UM7, UN3, U58, U63 or U69 required	$ 11.00

There is also some question whether customers are really deceived by "high" list prices from which they bargain. Do the list prices from which "discounts" are offered on cars fool anyone? The government officials think so. But auto industry executives feel that consumers understand the meaning of the sticker price—as a starting point from which to begin bargaining about price and trade-in allowance. What do you think?

PRICE FLEXIBILITY POLICIES

One of the first decisions any marketing manager has to make is about price flexibility. Shall he have a one-price—or a flexible-price—policy.

One-price policy—the same price for everyone

A **one-price policy** means offering the same price to all customers who buy goods under basically the same conditions—and in the same quantities. Most Canadian firms use a one-price policy. This is mainly for convenience—and to maintain goodwill among customers.

A one-price policy makes pricing easier—but the marketing manager must be careful not to be inflexible about it. This could amount to broadcasting a price which competitors could undercut—especially if the price is somewhat high. One reason for the growth of discount houses is that conventional retailers used traditional margins—and stuck to them.

Flexible-price policy— different prices for different customers

A **flexible-price policy** means the same products and quantities are offered to different customers at different prices.[5]

Flexible pricing was most common when businesses were small, products were not standardized, and bargaining was expected. These conditions still exist in most foreign countries.

Flexible pricing does have advantages, however—and is often used in the channels, in direct sales of industrial goods, and at retail for more expensive items. It allows a sales rep to make adjustments for market conditions—instead of having to turn down an order.

It has disadvantages, too. If customers know that prices are flexible, they may want to bargain. The cost of selling may rise—as buyers become aware that bargaining could save them money. Also, some sales reps may let price cutting become a habit. This could make price useless as a competitive tool and lead, instead, to a lower price level.

PRICE-LEVEL POLICIES

When marketing managers administer prices—as most do—they must decide on a price-level policy: Will the price be set below the market, at the same level as competition, or above the market?

Is it below, at, or above the market?

Some firms seem to emphasize below-the-market prices in their marketing mixes. Retail discounters and mass merchandisers offer goods below

Some firms use below-the-market prices in their strategies.

the prices charged by conventional retailers. And some manufacturers—such as Honda—regularly sell products which appear to be offered below the market. At the other extreme, manufacturers such as Zenith Radio Corporation proudly claimed that their prices started well above those of competing models. They felt that one of the reasons for many successful sales years was that Zenith regularly maintained high quality—and prices—while other companies cut prices and skimped on quality.

The question is: Do these various strategies contain prices which are above or below the market? Or are they just different prices in different markets? Perhaps some target customers do see important differences in the physical product or in the whole marketing mix. Then what we are really talking about are different marketing strategies—not different price levels. Lower prices are just *part* of different marketing strategies. The retail discounters, for example, may have lower prices than conventional retailers, but they may not be direct competitors—for *some* customers. Economic shoppers may be comparing prices only between discounters—a fact which some discounters are beginning to discover to their dismay!

Obviously, target marketing applies here. If some market segment was not previously satisfied, a more attractive marketing mix might be offered with a higher price. That price should not be thought of as "above the market," but as a new price which is part of a new marketing mix. Similarly, a "lower" price may not automatically cause the firm to be "below the market." It may be the price needed to make a good mix and compete with similar "low-price" mixes—i.e., it is "at the market" against these mixes.[6]

Meeting competition may be best in oligopoly

In highly competitive markets—and especially in oligopoly situations—pricing "at the market"—i.e., meeting competition—may be the only sensible policy. To raise prices might lead to a substantial loss in sales. And cutting the price would probably cause competitors to cut price too. This can only lead to a drop in total revenue for the industry—and probably for each firm. Therefore, a meeting-competition policy may make sense for each firm. And price stability may develop without any price fixing in the industry.

PRICING OVER THE PRODUCT LIFE CYCLE

The product life cycle should be considered when the original price level for a new product is set. The price will affect how fast the product moves through the cycle. A high price, for example, may lead to attractive profits—but also to competition and a faster cycle. With this in mind, should a firm's original price be a skimming or a penetration price?

Skimming pricing—feeling out demand at a good price

A **skimming pricing policy** tries to get the "cream" of a market (the top of a demand curve) at a high price before aiming at the more price-sensitive segments of that market.

Skimming is useful for feeling out demand—for getting a better understanding of the shape of the demand curve. It is easier to start with a high price and lower it, than to start with a low price and then try to raise it.

Penetration pricing—get the business at a low price

A **penetration pricing policy** tries to sell the whole market at one low price. This policy might be used where there is no "elite" market—where the whole demand curve is fairly elastic—even in the early stages of the product life cycle.

A penetration policy will be even more attractive if—as volume expands—economies of scale reduce costs. And it may be wise if the firm expects strong competition very soon after introduction. A *low* penetration price is a "stay-out" price. It is intended to discourage competitors from entering the market.

Introductory price dealing—temporary price cuts

Price cuts do attract customers. Therefore, marketers often use **introductory price dealing**—temporary price cuts—to speed new products into a market. These temporary price cuts should not be confused with low penetration prices, however. The plan here is to raise prices as soon as the introductory offer is over.

Established competitors often choose not to meet introductory price dealing—as long as the introductory period is not too long or too successful.[7]

DISCOUNTS POLICIES—OFF LIST PRICES

Discounts are reductions from list price that are given by a seller to a buyer who either gives up some marketing function or provides the function for himself. Discounts can be useful tools in marketing strategy planning.

In the following discussion, think about what function the buyers are giving up or providing when they get each of these discounts.

Quantity discounts encourage volume buying

Quantity discounts are discounts offered to encourage customers to buy in larger amounts. This lets the seller get more of a buyer's business, shifts some of the storing function to the buyer, reduces shipping and selling costs—or all of these. These discounts are of two kinds: cumulative and noncumulative.

Cumulative quantity discounts apply to purchases over a given period—such as a year—and normally increase as the quantity purchased increases. Cumulative discounts are intended to encourage buying from a single company—by reducing the price for additional purchases.

Noncumulative quantity discounts apply only to individual orders. Such discounts encourage larger orders—but do not tie a buyer to the seller after that one purchase.

Quantity discounts may be based on the dollar value of the entire order, or on the number of units purchased, or on the size of the package purchased. While quantity discounts are usually given as price cuts, sometimes they are given as "free" or "bonus" goods. Customers may receive one or more units "free" with the purchase of some quantity.

Quantity discounts can be a very useful tool for the marketing manager. Some customers are eager to get them. But marketing managers must use quantity discounts carefully—to avoid price discrimination.

Seasonal discounts— buy sooner and store

Seasonal discounts are discounts offered to encourage buyers to stock earlier than present demand requires. If used by producers, this discount tends to shift the storing function further along in the channel. It also tends to smooth out sales during the year and, therefore, permit year-round operation. If seasonal discounts are large, channel members may pass them along to their customers. In coal sales, for example, seasonal discounts are given in the spring and summer all the way through the channel to final consumers and users.

Payment terms and cash discounts set payment dates

Most sales to channel members and final users are made on credit. The seller issues a bill (invoice)—and the buyer sends it through the accounting department for payment. Many channel members come to depend on other members for temporary working capital. Therefore, it is very important for both sides to clearly state the terms of payment—including the availability of cash discounts. The following terms of payment commonly are used.

Net means that payment for the face value of the invoice is due immediately. These terms are sometimes changed to "net 10" or "net 30"—which mean payment is due within 10 or 30 days of the date on the invoice.

1/10 net 30 means that a 1 percent discount off the face value of

Servco, Ltd.

1475 Lake Lansing Road
Port Moody , B.C.
(604)291-3708

N⁰ 1522

An invoice shows the terms of sale.

			DATE
			10-20-80

Sold To	JONES SUPPLY COMPANY		CUSTOMER'S ORDER
			#179642
	220 COMMERCIAL DRIVE		SALESMAN
			Miller
	BURNABY, B.C. V5G 3H2		TERMS
			Net 30
Shipped To	JONES SUPPLY CO., 623 KENSINGTON.		F.O.B.
			Port Moody
	VANCOUVER, B.C. V5K 2P9		SHIPPED VIA
			Truck

200	Smoke Alarms, #263 - A	12.	00	2400.	00
	Thank you.				

the invoice is allowed if the invoice is paid within 10 days. Otherwise, the full face value is due within 30 days. And it usually is understood that an interest charge will be made after the 30-day free credit period.

Why cash discounts are given and should be taken

Cash discounts are reductions in the price to encourage buyers to pay their bills quickly. Smart buyers take advantage of them. A discount of say 2/10, net 30 may not look like very much, but any company that passes it up is missing a good chance to save money. In this case, a 2 percent discount would be earned just for paying 20 days before the full amount is due anyway. This would amount to an annual interest rate of about 36 percent. The company would be better off to borrow at a bank—if necessary—to pay such invoices on time.

While the marketing manager can often use cash discounts as a marketing variable, a specific cash discount may be so firmly established in his industry that he can't change it. He must give the usual terms—even if he has no need for cash. Purchasing agents are aware of the value of cash discounts and will insist that the marketing manager offer the same terms offered by competitors. In fact, some buyers automatically deduct the accepted cash discount from their invoices—regardless of the seller's invoice terms.

Trade-in allowances are a bargaining point for both buyer and seller.

Trade discounts often are set by tradition

A **trade (functional) discount** is a list price reduction given to channel members for the job they are going to do.

A manufacturer, for example, might allow retailers a 30 percent trade discount from the suggested retail list price—to cover the cost of the retailing function and their profit. Similarly, the manufacturer might allow wholesalers a chain discount of 30 percent and 10 percent off the retail price. In this case, the wholesalers would be expected to pass the 30 percent discount on to retailers. But while such discounts are legal and widely offered in the United States, they violate the price discrimination provisions of the Combines Act. A Canadian wholesaler cannot legally be offered a larger discount than a retailer purchasing the same quantity of merchandise.

ALLOWANCE POLICIES—OFF LIST PRICES

Allowances—like discounts—are given to final consumers, customers, or channel members for doing Something or accepting less of Something.

Bring in the old, ring up the new—with trade-ins

A **trade-in allowance** is a price reduction given for used goods when similar new goods are bought.

Trade-ins give the marketing manager an easy way to lower the price without reducing list price. Proper handling of trade-ins is important when selling durable goods. Customers buying machinery or buildings, for example, buy long-term satisfaction—in terms of more manufacturing capacity. If the list price less the trade-in allowance does not offer greater satisfaction—as the customer sees it—then no sales will be made.

Many firms replace machinery slowly—perhaps too slowly—because they value their old equipment above market value. This also applies to new cars. Customers often want higher trade-ins for their old cars than the current market value. This encourages the use of high—perhaps "phony"—list prices so that high trade-in allowances can be given.

Advertising allowances—Something for Something

Advertising allowances are price reductions given to firms further along in a channel to encourage them to advertise or otherwise promote the firm's products locally. Channel system thinking is involved here. General Electric has given a 1.5 percent allowance to its wholesalers of housewares and radios. They, in turn, are expected to provide something—in this case, local advertising.

PMs—push for cash

Push Money (or Prize Money) allowances are given to retailers by manufacturers or wholesalers to pass on to the retailers' salesclerks—for aggressively selling particular items. PM allowances are used for new merchandise, slower moving items, or higher margin items. They are especially common in the furniture and clothing industries. A salesclerk, for example, might earn an additional $5 for each mattress of a new type sold.

SOME CUSTOMERS GET EXTRA SOMETHINGS

Trading stamps—Something for nothing?

Trading stamps are free stamps (like "Green Stamps") given by some retailers with every purchase.

Retailers can buy trading stamps from trading-stamp companies—or set up their own plans. In either case, customers can trade stamps for merchandise premiums, or cash, or goods at the merchant's own store, or at stamp redemption centers.

Some retailers offer trading stamps to their customers to differentiate their offering. Some customers seem to be attracted by trading stamps. They feel they are getting something for nothing. And, sometimes they are—if competitive pressures don't allow the retailers to pass the cost of the stamps (2 to 3 percent of sales) along to customers. Also, lower promotion costs—or a large increase in sales—may make up for the increased cost of the stamps.[8]

The early users of stamps in a community seem to gain a competitive advantage. But when competitors start offering stamps, the advantage can disappear. This is similar to competition in the product life cycle—where new ideas are copied and profits are squeezed.

There was much interest in trading stamps in the 1950s and 1960s. Then their use declined—especially in grocery retailing. There, food discounters cut into the attractiveness of seemingly "higher cost" stamp givers. Now that some of the enthusiasm for stamp plans is dying down, perhaps they can be seen for what they really are. They are a potential addition to a marketing mix—perhaps instead of a price reduction. In some situations, stamp plans may be very effective—especially if half of a market wants stamps.[9] So we may see them used more in the future.

Clipping coupons brings other extras

Many manufacturers and retailers are offering discounts—or free items—through the use of coupons found in packages, mailings, newspapers and magazine advertising—or at the store. By presenting a coupon

Couponing is popular with consumers.

to a retailer, the consumer is given "10 cents off" or may be given the product at no charge. This plan is especially effective in the food business. Supermarkets are filled with customers clutching handfuls of coupons.[10]

LIST PRICE MAY DEPEND ON GEOGRAPHIC PRICING POLICIES

Retail list prices often include free delivery—because the cost may be small. But producers and middlemen must take the matter of who pays for transportation more seriously. Much more money may be involved. Usually, purchase orders spell out these matters—because transportation cost might be as much as half of the delivered cost of goods! There are many possible variations here for a creative marketing manager. Some special terms have developed. A few are discussed in the following paragraphs.

FOB pricing is easy

A commonly used transportation term is *FOB*. **FOB** means "free on board" some vehicle at some place. Typically, it is used with the place named, that is, the location of the seller's factory or warehouse—as in "FOB Hamilton," "FOB Montreal," or "FOB mill." It means that the seller pays the cost of loading the merchandise onto some vehicle—usually a common carrier such as a truck, railroad car, or ship. At the point of loading, title to the goods passes to the buyer. Then the buyer pays the freight and takes responsibility for damage in transit—except as covered by the transportation company.

Variations are made easily—by changing the place part of the term. If the marketing manager wanted to pay the freight for the convenience of customers, he could use: "FOB delivered" or "FOB buyer's factory" (or warehouse). In this case, title would not pass until the goods were delivered. If he did want title to pass immediately—but still wanted to pay the freight

386

(and then include it in the invoice)—he could use "FOB seller's factory-freight prepaid."

FOB "shipping point" pricing simplifies the seller's pricing—but it may narrow his market. Since the delivered cost of goods will vary depending on the buyer's location, a customer located farther from the seller must pay more—and might buy from closer suppliers.

Zone pricing smoothes delivered prices

Zone pricing means making an average freight charge to all buyers within specified geographic areas. The seller pays the actual freight charges and then bills the customer for an average charge. Canada might be divided into five zones, for example—and all buyers within each zone would pay the same freight charge.

Zone pricing reduces the wide variation in delivered prices which result from an FOB shipping point pricing policy. It also simplifies charging for transportation.

This approach often is used by manufacturers of hardware and food items—both to lower the possibility of price competition in the channels and to simplify figuring transportation charges for the thousands of whole-salers and retailers they serve.

Uniform delivered pricing—one price to all

Uniform delivered pricing means making an average freight charge to all buyers. It is an extension of zone pricing. An entire country may be considered as one zone—and the average cost of delivery is included in the price. It is most often used when transportation costs are relatively low and the seller wishes to sell in all geographic areas at one price—perhaps a nationally advertised price.

Freight-absorption pricing—competing on equal grounds in another territory

When all the firms in an industry use FOB shipping point pricing, a firm usually does well near its shipping point—but not so well farther away. As sales reps look for business farther away, delivered prices rise. They find themselves priced out of the market. This problem can be solved with frieght absorption.

Freight-absorption pricing means absorbing freight cost so that a firm's delivered price meets the nearest competitor's. This amounts to cutting list price to appeal to new market segments.

With freight absorption pricing, the only limit on the size of a firm's territory is the amount of freight cost it is willing to absorb. These absorbed costs cut net return on each sale—but the new business may raise total profit.

LEGALITY OF PRICING POLICIES

Even very high prices may be OK—if they are not fixed

From our general discussion of legislation in Chapter 3, you might think that companies have little freedom in pricing—or may even need government approval for their prices. Generally speaking, this is *not* true. They can charge what they want—even "outrageously high" prices—if they are not fixed with competitors.

But they should be legal—to avoid fines or jail

There are some restrictions on pricing, however. Difficulties with pricing—and perhaps violation of price legislation—usually occur only when competing marketing mixes are quite similar. When the success of an entire marketing strategy depends upon price, there is pressure (and temptation) to make agreements (conspire) with competitors. And **price fixing**—competitors getting together to raise, lower, or stabilize prices—is common and relatively easy. But it is also completely illegal. It is a "conspiracy" under the antimonopoly laws. And fixing prices can be dangerous. Some business managers have already gone to jail! And governments are getting tougher on price fixing—especially by smaller companies.

The first step to understanding pricing legislation is to know the thinking of legislators and the courts. Ideally, they try to help the economy perform more effectively in the consumers' interest. In practice, this doesn't always work out as neatly as planned. But generally their intentions are good. And if we take this view, we get a better idea of the "why" of legislation. This helps us to anticipate future rulings. We will look at Canadian legislation here, but other countries have similar laws on pricing.[11] More specifically we will discuss the kinds of pricing action the Combines Act made illegal, past difficulties in enforcing that law, and recent efforts to make enforcement easier.

Price discrimination as a violation of the Combines Act

Prior to its amendment by Bill C–2, section 34a of the Combines Act made it illegal for a supplier to discriminate in price between competitors purchasing like quantities of goods or for a buyer knowingly to benefit from such discrimination. However, it was not easy to prove price discrimination had actually occurred.

1. There must have been two or more sales that could be compared.
2. There must have been a discount, rebate, allowance, price concession,

Many of Borden's products have "recognized consumer appeal."

Courtesy Borden, Inc.

or other advantage granted to one purchaser that was not available to another.

3. The persons between whom there was discrimination must have been purchasers in competition with each other.
4. The discriminatory prices must have applied to articles of like quality and like quantity.
5. The discriminatory transaction must have been part of a practice of discrimination.

Section 34a was obviously intended to make price discrimination illegal. But because of difficulties in enforcement, no Canadian manufacturer was ever convicted of price discrimination.[12]

Amendments contained in Bill C–2 dealt with some but not all of these barriers to enforcement. Discrimination in the pricing of services as well as of articles is now banned. The provision that requires "a practice" of discrimination has been deleted from the legislation. But defining what constitutes "competing customers" and "like quality" continues to pose enforcement problems. Also, differences in the amount purchased, even relatively small differences, still justify whatever quantity discount structure a manufacturer chooses to introduce.[13]

Legal barriers to predatory pricing

Section 34b of the Combines Act outlaws regional price differentials that limit competition. This provision forbids a company making profits in one area from pricing at an unreasonably low level in another area in order to eliminate local competition. But for an offense to have been committed, (1) a policy of selling the articles in one area of Canada at prices lower than those charged elsewhere in Canada was required; and (2) this policy must have had the effect, tendency, or intent of substantially lessening competition or eliminating a competitor. Section 34c of the same act contained a more general bar to predatory pricing. Very few Canadian firms have been brought to court under either of these two predatory price-cutting provisions. Whether Bill C–2, which less strictly defines a substantial lessening of competition, will lead to more aggressive enforcement remains to be seen.

Discriminatory promotional allowances and the law

Section 35 of the Combines Act makes it an offense, either for a seller to offer or for a customer to seek, any form of promotional allowance (including discounts, rebates, and price concessions) not offered on proportionate terms to all other competing customers. A small customer purchasing half as much as a larger competitor must receive a promotional allowance equal to half of what was offered to this competitor. In fact, this means that promotional allowances must be granted on a "per case" or "per dozen" basis. The cost of promotional services required from customers in return for promotional allowances must also be approximately proportionate to their purchases.

This section of the Combines Act resembles the Robinson-Patman Act, which requires American manufacturers to offer competing customers "proportionately equal" promotional allowances. However, remember that in Canada, unlike in the United States, functional discounts are illegal. Wholesalers and retailers are considered to be directly competing customers who must receive proportionately equal promotional allowances.

Legislation against misleading price advertising

The section designed to prevent deceptive price advertising has been actively policed in the courts. More aggressive prosecution may be due to the fact that misleading price advertising is a lesser offense under the Criminal Code and one easier to establish. Although the publicity surrounding a conviction may do great harm to the offender's public image, violations have customarily been punished by relatively modest fines.

Additional restrictions on misleading price advertising were introduced by Bill C–2. One such section was directed against "bait-and-switch" advertising. This practice involves the customer being lured to a store by advertising that stresses the low price of an article which the retailer does not stock at all or only in token quantities. Under the new provision, an advertiser must have available for sale reasonable quantities of any product so advertised. However, a merchant would be exempt from prosecution if he offered, in place of an advertised but unavailable item, "rain checks" which could be used for that item within a reasonable period of time.

Legislation against resale price maintenance

Resale price maintenance is the marketing practice whereby a producer or brander of an article requires subsequent resellers to offer it at a stipulated (or not below a stated minimum) price. But although such a practice has been illegal in Canada since 1951, has that law been enforced? Some have argued that efforts at resale price maintenance are few and far between. Others have maintained that the restoration has been relatively ignored.[14]

Section 38 of Bill C–2 was intended to correct one apparent weakness in the existing legislation, its inability to deal with general exhortations by a supplier to "get your price up." Any effort to influence upward or to discourage the reduction of "a price" is now illegal. A number of other Stage I changes were also designed to tighten up the price discrimination rules.

Provincial pricing legislation

British Columbia, Alberta, and Manitoba have provincial legislation that prevents firms from selling below "landed" invoice cost plus a minimum markup, such as 5 percent. Such legislation outlaws predatory pricing, but the real intent would appear to involve protecting limited-line retailers from "ruinous" competition were full-line stores to sell milk below cost as a loss leader. But although such legislation may be on the books, it has not been vigorously enforced.

More recently, newly enacted Provincial Trade Practices Legislation has focused on protecting consumers from misleading price advertising and the deceptive pricing practices of door-to-door salespeople. Particular attention has been paid to seeing that any comparison of a sale price with a so-called regular price is valid.

CONCLUSION

The Price variable offers an alert marketing manager many possibilities for varying marketing mixes. What pricing policies will be used depends on pricing objectives. We looked at profit-oriented, sales-oriented, and status-quo–oriented objectives.

A marketing manager must set policies about price flexibility, price level, who will pay the freight, and who will get discounts and allowances. Also, the manager should be aware of pricing legislation affecting these policies.

In most cases, a marketing manager must set prices—that is, administer prices. Starting with a list price, a variety of discounts and allowances may be offered—to adjust for the Something being offered in the marketing mix.

Throughout this chapter, we have assumed that a list price had already been set. We have emphasized what may be included (or specifically excluded) in the Something—and what objectives a firm might set to guide its pricing policies. Price setting itself was not discussed. We will cover this in the next chapter—showing ways of carrying out the various pricing objectives.

QUESTIONS FOR DISCUSSION

1. Identify the strategic decisions a marketing manager must make in the Price area. Illustrate your answer for a local retailer.

2. How should the acceptance of a profit-oriented, a sales-oriented, or a status quo-oriented pricing objective affect the development of a company's marketing strategy? Illustrate for each.

3. Distinguish between one-price and flexible-price policies. Which would be most appropriate for a supermarket? Why?

4. Cite two examples of continuously selling above the market price. Describe the situations.

5. Explain the types of competitive situations which might lead to a "meeting competition" pricing policy.

6. What pricing objective(s) would a skimming pricing policy most likely be implementing? Could the same be true for a penetration pricing policy? Which policy would probably be most appropriate for each of the following products: (a) a new type of home lawn-sprinkling system, (b) a new low-cost meat substitute, (c) a new type of children's toy, (d) a faster computer.

7. Indicate what the final consumer really obtains when paying the list price for the following "products": (a) an automobile, (b) a portable radio, (c) a package of frozen peas, and (d) a lipstick in a jeweled case.

8. Are seasonal discounts appropriate in agricultural businesses (which are certainly seasonal)?

9. What are the "effective" annual interest rates for the following cash discount terms: (a) 1/10 net 60, (b) 1/5 net 10, (c) net 30?

10. Explain how a marketing manager might change his FOB terms to make his otherwise competitive marketing mix more attractive.

11. What type of geographic pricing policy would seem most appropriate for the following products (specify any assumptions necessary to obtain a definite answer): (a) a chemical by-product, (b) nationally advertised candy bars, (c) rebuilt auto parts, (d) tricycles?

12. Explain how the prohibition of freight absorption (that is, requiring FOB factory pricing) might affect a producer with substantial economies of scale in production.

13. Discuss unfair trade practices acts. To whom are they "unfair"?

14. How would our marketing structure be changed if manufacturers were required to specify retail prices on all products sold at retail and all retailers were required to use these prices? Would this place greater or lesser importance on the development of the manufacturer's marketing mix? What kind of an operation would retailing be? Would consumers get more or less service?

15. Would price discrimination be involved if a large oil company sold gasoline to taxicab associations for resale to individual taxi cab operators for 2½ cents a gallon less than charged to retail service stations? What happens if the cab associations resell gasoline not only to taxicab operators, but to the general public as well?

SUGGESTED CASES

23. Ace Photofinishing Company

24. The Schmidt Manufacturing Company

36. Beaver Spirits Ltd.

MARKETING ARITHMETIC

When you finish this appendix, you should:

1. *Understand the components of an operating statement (profit and loss statement).*
2. *Know how to compute the stockturn rate.*
3. *Understand how operating ratios can help analyze a business.*
4. *Understand how to calculate markups and markdowns.*
5. *Understand how to calculate return on investment (ROI) and return on assets (ROA).*
6. *Recognize the important new terms (shown in red).*

A beginning business student ought to know the basics of the "language of business." Business people commonly use accounting terms when discussing costs, prices, and profit. It is important for you to understand these terms—if the use of accounting data is to be a practical tool in analyzing marketing problems.

THE OPERATING STATEMENT

An operating statement—commonly referred to as a profit and loss statement—is shown in Figure B–1 for a wholesale or retail business. A complete and detailed statement is shown so you will see the framework during our discussion. But the amount of detail on an operating statement is not fixed. Many companies use a much less detailed statement. They emphasize readability—rather than detail. To really understand an operating statement, however, you must know about its parts.

An **operating statement** is a simple summary of the financial results of the operation of a company over a specified period of time. Some beginning students may feel the operating statement is not simple—but,

393

Figure B–1

XYZ COMPANY
Operating Statement
For the Year Ended December 31, 198X

Gross sales			$54,000
Less: Returns and allowances			4,000
Net sales			50,000
Cost of goods sold			
Beginning inventory at cost		$ 8,000	
Purchases at billed cost	$31,000		
Less: Purchase discounts	4,000		
Purchases at net cost	27,000		
Plus freight-in	2,000		
Net cost of delivered purchases		29,000	
Cost of goods available for sale		37,000	
Less: Ending inventory at cost		7,000	
Cost of goods sold			30,000
Gross margin (gross profit)			20,000
Expenses			
Selling expenses			
Sales salaries	6,000		
Advertising expense	2,000		
Delivery expense	2,000		
Total selling expense		10,000	
Administrative expense			
Office salaries	3,000		
Office supplies	1,000		
Miscellaneous administrative expense	500		
Total administrative expense		4,500	
General expense			
Rent expense	1,000		
Miscellaneous general expenses	500		
Total general expense		1,500	
Total expenses			16,000
Net profit from operation			$ 4,000

as we shall see—this isn't true. The main purpose of an operating statement is to determine the net profit figure—and show data to support that figure.

Only three basic components

The basic components of an operating statement are sales—which come from the sale of goods or services; costs—which come from the making and selling process; and the balance (called profit or loss)—which is merely the difference between sales and costs. So there are only three basic components in the statement: *sales, costs,* and *profit.*

Time period covered may vary

There is no one time period which an operating statement covers. Rather, statements are prepared to satisfy the needs of a particular business. This could be at the end of each day or at the end of each week. Usually, however, an operating statement summarizes the results of one month, three months, six months, or a full year. Since this time period does vary with the company preparing the statement, this information is included in the heading of the statement as follows:

XYZ COMPANY
Operating Statement
For the (Period) Ended (Date)

Management uses of operating statements

Before going on to a more detailed discussion of the components of our operating statement, note some of the uses for such a statement. A glance at Figure B–1 shows that a wealth of information is shown in a clear and brief manner. With this information, management can easily figure the relation of its net sales to its cost of goods sold, gross margin, expenses, and net profit. Opening and closing inventory figures are available. So is the amount spent for the purchase of goods for resale. The total expenses are listed to make it easier to compare them with previous statements— to help control these expenses.

All of this information is of vital interest to the management of a company. Assume that a particular company prepared monthly operating statements. By comparing results from one month to the next, management can uncover disappointing trends in the sales, expense, or profit areas of the business— and take the needed action.

A skeleton statement gets down to essential details

Let's refer to Figure B–1 and begin to analyze this seemingly detailed statement. The aim at this point is to get first-hand knowledge of what makes up an operating statement.

As a first step, suppose we take all the items that have dollar amounts extended to the third (right-hand) column. Using these items alone, the operating statement looks like this:

Gross sales	$54,000
Less: Returns and allowances	4,000
Net sales	50,000
Less: Cost of goods sold	30,000
Gross margin	20,000
Less: Total expenses	16,000
Net profit (loss)	$ 4,000

Is this a complete operating statement? The answer is yes. The skeleton statement differs from Figure B–1 only in supporting detail. All of the basic components are included. In fact, the only items required to have a complete operating statement are:

Net sales	$50,000
Less: Costs	46,000
Net profit (loss)	$ 4,000

These three items are the heart of an operating statement. All other subdivisions or details are merely helpful additions.

Meaning of "sales"

Now let's define the meaning of the terms that are used in the skeleton statement.

The first item is "sales." What do we mean by sales? **Gross sales** is the total amount charged to all customers. It is certain, however, that there will be some customer dissatisfaction—or just plain errors in ordering and shipping goods. This results in returns and allowances which reduce gross sales.

A **return** occurs when a customer sends back purchased goods. The company either refunds the purchase price or allows the customer dollar credit on other goods.

An **allowance** occurs when a customer is not satisfied with the purchased goods for some reason. The company gives a price reduction on the original invoice (bill)—but the customer keeps the goods.

These refunds and reductions must be considered when the sales figure for the period is computed. Really, we are only interested in the amount which the company manages to keep. This is **net sales**—the actual sales dollars the company will receive. Therefore, all reductions, refunds, and so forth—made because of returns and allowances—are deducted from the gross sales to get net sales. This is shown below:

Gross sales	$54,000
Less: Returns and allowances	4,000
Net sales	$50,000

Meaning of "cost of goods sold"

The next item in the operating statement—**cost of goods sold**—is the total value (at cost) of all the goods *sold* during the period of the statement. We will discuss its calculation later. Meanwhile, merely note that after the cost-of-goods-sold figure is obtained, it is subtracted from net sales to get the gross margin.

Meaning of "gross margin" and "expenses"

Gross margin (gross profit) is the money left to cover the cost of selling the goods and managing the business. It is hoped, of course, that a profit will be left—after subtracting the cost of goods sold.

Selling expense is usually the major expense below the gross margin. Note that in Figure B–1, all **expenses** are subtracted from the gross margin to get the net profit. The expenses in this case are the selling, administrative, and general expenses. (Note that the cost of goods sold is not included in this total expense figure—it was subtracted from net sales earlier to get the gross margin.)

Net profit—at the bottom of the statement—is what the company has earned from its operations during a particular period. It is the amount left after the cost of goods sold and the expenses have been subtracted from net sales.

DETAILED ANALYSIS OF SECTIONS OF THE OPERATING STATEMENT

Cost of goods sold for a wholesale or retail company

The cost-of-goods sold section includes details which are used to determine the "cost of goods sold" ($30,000 in our example).

In Figure B–1, it is obvious that beginning and ending inventory, purchases, purchase discounts, and freight-in are all necessary in calculating cost of goods sold. If we take the cost of goods sold section from the operating statement, it appears as follows:

Cost of goods sold

Beginning inventory at cost		$8,000
Purchases at billed cost	$31,000	
Less: Purchase discounts	4,000	
Purchases at net cost	27,000	
Plus: Freight-in	2,000	
Net cost of delivered purchases		29,000
Cost of goods available for sale		37,000
Less: Ending inventory at cost		7,000
Cost of goods sold		$30,000

The inventory figures merely show the cost of merchandise on hand at the beginning and end of the period the statement covers. These figures may be obtained by an actual count of the merchandise on hand on these dates. Or they may be estimated with inventory records which show the inventory balance at any time.

The net cost of delivered purchases must include freight charges and purchase discounts received. This is because these items affect the cash actually spent to buy the goods and bring them to the place of business. A **purchase discount** is a reduction of the original invoice amount for some business reason. For example, a cash discount can be given for prompt cash payment of the amount due. The total of such discounts is subtracted from the original invoice cost of purchases to find the net cost of purchases. Then we add the freight charges for bringing the goods to the place of business. This gives the net cost of *delivered* purchases. When the net cost of delivered purchases is added to the beginning inventory at cost, we have the total cost of goods available for sale during the period. When we subtract the ending inventory at cost from the cost of the goods available for sale, we finally obtain the cost of goods sold.

Cost of goods sold for a manufacturing company

Figure B–1 shows the way the manager of a wholesale or retail business would arrive at the cost of goods sold. Such a business would buy finished goods and resell them. In a manufacturing firm, the "purchases" section of this operating statement would be replaced by a section called "cost of goods manufactured." This section would include purchases of raw materials and parts, and direct and indirect labor costs. It would also list factory overhead charges (such as heat, light, and power) which are necessary to produce finished goods. The cost of goods manufactured is added to the beginning finished-goods inventory to arrive at the cost of goods available for sale. Frequently, a separate "cost of goods manufactured" statement is prepared, and only the total cost of production is shown in the operating statement. See Figure B–2 for an illustration of the "cost of goods sold" section of an operating statement for a manufacturing company.

Figure B–2: Cost-of-goods-sold section of an operating statement for a manufacturing firm

Cost of goods sold		
Finished goods inventory (beginning)	$ 20,000	
Cost of goods manufactured (Schedule 1)	100,000	
Total cost of finished goods available for sale......................	120,000	
Less: Finished goods inventory (ending)	30,000	
Cost of goods sold		$ 90,000

Schedule 1, Schedule of cost of goods manufactured

Beginning work in process inventory			15,000
Raw materials			
Beginning raw materials inventory		$ 10,000	
Net cost of delivered purchases		80,000	
Total cost of materials available for use		90,000	
Less: Ending raw materials inventory		15,000	
Cost of materials placed in production		75,000	
Direct labor		20,000	
Manufacturing expenses			
Indirect labor	$4,000		
Maintenance and repairs	3,000		
Factory supplies	1,000		
Heat, light, and power	2,000		
Total manufacturing expenses		10,000	
Total manufacturing costs			105,000
Total work in process during period			120,000
Less: Ending work in process inventory			20,000
Cost of goods manufactured			$100,000

Note: The last item, cost of goods manufactured, is used in the operating statement to determine the cost of goods sold, as above.

Expenses

Expenses typically appear below the gross margin. They usually include the costs of selling, and running the business. They do not include the cost of goods—either purchased or produced.

There is no "right" way of classifying the expense accounts or arranging them on an operating statement. They might just as easily have been arranged alphabetically—or according to amount, with the largest placed at the top, and so on down the line. In a business of any size, though, it is desirable to group the expenses in some way and to use subtotals by groups for analysis and control purposes. This was done in Figure B–1.

Summary on operating statements

The operating statement presented in Figure B–1 contains all the basic components in an operating statement—together with a normal amount of supporting detail. Further detail could be added to the statement under any of the headings without changing the nature of the statement. The amount of detail usually depends on how the statement will be used. A stockholder may be presented with a simplified operating statement, while the one prepared for internal company use may include much detail.

We have already seen that leaving out some of the detail in Figure B–1 did not affect the basic components of the statement—net sales, costs, and net profit. Whatever further detail is added to the statement aims to help the reader to see how these three figures have been determined. A very detailed statement might easily run to several single-spaced pages— yet the nature of the operating statement would be the same.

COMPUTING THE STOCKTURN RATE

A detailed operating statement can provide the data needed to determine the **stockturn rate**—a measure of the number of times the average inventory is sold during a year. Note, the stockturn rate is concerned with the turnover *during a year, not* the time covered by a particular operating statement.

The stockturn rate is a very important measure because it shows how fast the firm's inventory is moving. Some lines of trade have slower turnover than others. But a drop in the turnover rate in a particular business can be a warning sign. For one thing, it may mean that the firm's assortment of goods is no longer as attractive as it was. Also, it may mean that more working capital will be needed to handle the same volume of sales. Most businesses pay close attention to the stockturn rate—trying to get faster turnover.

Three methods—all basically similar—can be used to figure the stockturn rate. Which method is used depends on the data which are available. These three methods are shown below and usually give approximately the same results.*

$$\frac{\text{Cost of goods sold}}{\text{Average inventory at cost}} \qquad (1)$$

$$\frac{\text{Net sales}}{\text{Average inventory at selling price}} \qquad (2)$$

$$\frac{\text{Sales in units}}{\text{Average inventory in units}} \qquad (3)$$

Computing the stockturn rate will be illustrated for formula (1)—since all are similar. The only difference is that the cost figures used in formula (1) are changed to a selling price or numerical count basis in formulas (2) and (3). It is necessary—regardless of the method used—to have both items of the formula in the same terms.

Using formula (1), the average inventory at cost is figured by adding the beginning and ending inventories at cost and dividing by 2. This average inventory figure is then divided into the cost of goods sold (in cost terms) to get the stockturn rate.

For example, suppose that the cost of goods sold for one year was $100,000. Beginning inventory was $25,000 and ending inventory $15,000.

---

* Differences will occur because of varied markups and different product assortments. In an assortment of tires, for example, those with high markups might have sold much better than those with small markups, but with formula (3) all tires would be treated equally.

Adding the two inventory figures and dividing by 2, we obtain an average inventory of $20,000. We next divide the cost of goods sold by the average inventory ($100,000 divided by $20,000) and get a stockturn rate of 5.

Further discussion of the use of the stockturn rate is found in Chapter 19.

OPERATING RATIOS HELP ANALYZE THE BUSINESS

The operating statement is also used for a number of other purposes. In particular, many business people calculate **operating ratios**—the ratio of items on the operating statement to net sales—and compare these ratios from one time period to another. They also can compare their own operating ratios with those of competitors. Such competitive data is often available through trade associations. Each firm may report its results to the trade association—then summary results are distributed to the members. These ratios help management control its operations. If some expense ratios are rising, for example, those particular costs are singled out for special attention.

Operating ratios are figured by dividing net sales into the various operating statement items appearing below the net sales level in the statement. Net sales is used as the denominator in the operating ratio, because this figure most concerns a business manager. It is the dollar amount actually received by the business.

We can see the relation of operating ratios to the operating statement if we think of there being another column to the right of the dollar figures in an operating statement. This additional column would list percentage figures—using net sales as 100 percent. This can be seen below:

Gross sales	$540	
Less: Returns and allowances	40	
Net sales	500	100%
Cost of goods sold	350	70
Gross margin	150	30%
Expenses	100	20
Net profit	$ 50	10%

The 30 percent ratio of gross margin to net sales in the above illustration means that 30 percent of the net sales dollar is available to cover sales expenses, run the business, and provide a profit. Note that the ratio of expenses to sales plus the ratio of profit to sales equals the 30 percent gross margin ratio. The net profit ratio of 10 percent shows that 10 percent of the net sales dollar is left for profit.

The usefulness of percentage ratios should be obvious. Percentages are easily figured. And they are much easier to work with than large dollar figures. With net sales as the base figure, they provide a useful means of comparison and control.

Note that because of the relation between these various items and their ratios, only a few pieces of information are necessary and the others can be figured easily. In this case, for example, knowing the gross margin percent and net profit percent makes it possible to figure expense and cost-of-goods-sold percentages. Further, knowing a single dollar amount would let you figure all the other dollar amounts.

MARKUPS

A **markup** is the dollar amount added to the cost of goods to get the selling price. The markup is similar to the gross margin. Gross margin and the idea of markup are related because the amount added onto the unit cost of a product by a retailer (or wholesaler) is expected to cover all the costs of selling and running the business—and to provide a profit.

The markup approach to pricing is discussed in Chapter 19—so it will not be discussed at length here. A simple example will illustrate the idea, however. If a retailer bought an article which cost $1 when delivered to his store, then obviously he must sell it for more than this cost if he hopes to make a profit. He might add 50 cents to the cost of the article to cover his selling and other costs with the hope of providing a profit. The 50 cents would be the "markup."

It would also be the gross margin (or gross profit) on that item if it is sold. But note that it is *not* the net profit. His selling expenses might amount to 35 cents, 45 cents, or even 55 cents. In other words, there is no guarantee that the markup will cover his costs. Also, there is no guarantee that the customers will buy at the marked-up price. This may require markdowns. They are discussed later in this appendix.

Markup conversions

Sometimes it is convenient to talk in terms of *markups on cost,* while at other times *markups on selling prices* are useful. To have some agreement, **markup** (without any explanation) will mean percentage of selling price. By this definition, the 50-cent markup part of the $1.50 selling price is a markup of 33⅓ percent [i.e., $(50/1.50) \times 100 = 33\frac{1}{3}$].

Some retailers and wholesalers have developed markup conversion tables so they can easily convert from cost to selling price—depending on the markup they want. To see the interrelation, look at the two formulas below. They can be used to convert either type of markup to the other.

$$\frac{\text{Percentage markup}}{\text{on selling price}} = \frac{\text{Percentage markup on cost}}{100\% + \text{percentage markup on cost}} \quad (4)$$

$$\frac{\text{Percentage markup}}{\text{on cost}} = \frac{\text{Percentage markup on selling price}}{100\% - \text{Percentage markup on selling price}} \quad (5)$$

In the previous example, we had a cost of $1, a markup of 50 cents, and a selling price of $1.50. We saw that the markup on selling price was 33⅓ percent. On cost, it was 50 percent. Let us substitute these percentage figures into Formulas (4) and (5) to see how to convert markups from one basis to another. First, assume that we only know the markup on selling price and want to convert to markup on cost. Using Formula (5) we have:

$$\text{Percentage markup on cost} = \frac{33 \ 1/3\%}{100\% - 33 \ 1/3\%} = \frac{33 \ 1/3\%}{66 \ 2/3\%} = 50\%$$

If we know, on the other hand, only the percentage markup on cost, we could convert to markup on selling price as follows:

$$\text{Percentage markup on selling price} = \frac{50\%}{100\% + 50\%} = \frac{50\%}{150\%} = 33 \ 1/3\%$$

These results can be proved and summarized as follows:

Markup	$0.50 =	50% of cost or 33 1/3% of selling price
plus cost	$1.00 =	100% of cost or 66 2/3% of selling price
Selling price	$1.50 =	150% of cost or 100% of selling price

It is important to see that only the percentage figures changed—while the money amounts for cost, markup, and selling price stayed the same. Notice, too, that when the selling price is used as the base figure (100 percent), then the cost percentage plus the markup percentage equals 100 percent. But when the cost of the product is used as the base figure (100 percent), it is obvious that the selling price percentage must exceed 100 percent—by the markup on cost.

MARKDOWN RATIOS HELP CONTROL RETAIL OPERATIONS

The ratios we discussed above were concerned with numbers on the operating statement. Another important ratio—the **markdown ratio**—is a tool used by many retailers to measure the efficiency of various departments and their whole business. But note—it is not related to the operating statement. It requires special calculations.

A **markdown** is a retail price reduction which is required because the customers will not buy some item at the originally marked-up price. This refusal to buy may be due to a variety of "business errors"—soiling, style changes, fading, damage caused by handling—or an original markup which was too high. To get rid of these goods, the retailer offers them at a lower price.

Markdowns are similar to allowances because price reductions are made. So, in computing a markdown ratio, markdowns and allowances are added together and then divided by net sales. This markdown ratio is computed as follows:

$$\text{Markdown \%} = \frac{\$ \ \text{markdowns} + \$ \ \text{allowances}}{\$ \ \text{net sales}} \times 100$$

The 100 is multiplied by the fraction to get rid of decimal points.

Returns are not included when figuring the markdown ratio. Returns are considered as "consumer errors"—not "business errors"—and therefore are not included in this measure of business efficiency.

Retailers who use markdown ratios keep a record of the amount of markdowns and allowances in each department and then divide the total by the net sales in each department. Over a period of time, these ratios give management a measure of the efficiency of the buyers and salespersons in the various departments.

It should be stressed again that the markdown ratio has nothing to do with the operating statement. It is not figured directly from data on the operating statement—since the markdowns take place before the goods are sold. In fact, some goods may be marked down and still not sold. Even if the marked-down items are not sold, the markdowns are included in the calculations in the time period when they are taken.

The markdown ratio would be calculated for a whole department (or profit center)—not individual items. What we want is a measure of the effectiveness of a whole department—not how well the department did on individual items.

RETURN ON INVESTMENT (ROI) REFLECTS ASSET USE

Another "off the operating statement" ratio is **return on investment (ROI)**—the ratio of net profit (after taxes) to the investment used to make the net profit—multiplied by 100 to get rid of decimals. "Investment" is not shown on the operating statement—but it would be on the **balance sheet** (statement of financial condition)—another accounting statement—which shows the assets, liabilities, and net worth of a company. It might take some "digging" or special analysis, however.

"Investment" means the dollar resources the firm has "invested" in a project or business. For example, a new product might require $400,000 in new money—for inventory, accounts receivable, promotion, and so on—and its attractiveness might be judged by its likely ROI. If the net profit (after taxes) for this new product was expected to be $100,000 in the first year, then the ROI would be 25%—that is ($100,000 ÷ $400,000) × 100.

There are two ways to figure ROI. The *direct* way is:

$$\text{ROI (in \%)} = \frac{\text{Net profit (after taxes)}}{\text{Investment}} \times 100$$

The *indirect* way is:

$$\text{ROI (in \%)} = \frac{\text{Net profit (after taxes)}}{\text{Sales}} \times \frac{\text{Sales}}{\text{Investment}} \times 100$$

This way is concerned with net profit margin and turnover—that is:

$$\text{ROI (in \%)} = \text{Net profit margin} \times \text{Turnover} \times 100$$

This indirect way makes it clearer how to *increase* ROI. There are three ways:

1. Increase profit margin.
2. Increase sales.
3. Decrease investment.

Effective marketing strategy planning and implementation are ways of increasing profit margin and/or sales. And careful asset management can decrease investment.

ROI is a revealing measure of managerial effectiveness. Most companies have alternative uses for their funds. If the returns in the business aren't at least as high as outside uses, then the money probably should be shifted to the more profitable uses. Further, many companies must borrow to finance some of their operation. So the ROI should be higher than the cost of money—or the company should cut back until it can operate more profitably.

Some firms borrow more than others to make "investments." In other words, they invest less of their own money to acquire assets—what we have called "investments." If ROI calculations use only the firm's own "investment," this gives higher ROI figures to those who borrow a lot—which is called leveraging. To adjust for different borrowing proportions—to make comparisons among projects, departments, divisions, and companies easier—another ratio (ROA) has come into use. **Return on assets (ROA)** is the ratio of net profit (after taxes) to the assets used to make the net profit—times 100.

Both ROI and ROA measures are trying to get at the same thing—how effectively is the company using resources. These measures have become increasingly popular recently—as profit rates have dropped and it becomes more obvious that increasing sales does not necessarily lead to higher profits—or ROI—or ROA. Further, inflation and higher costs for borrowed funds force more concern for ROI and ROA. Marketers must include these measures in their thinking—or top managers are likely to ignore their plans and requests for financial resources.

QUESTIONS FOR DISCUSSION

1. Distinguish between the following pairs of items which appear on operating statements:

   a. Gross sales and net sales.
   b. Purchases at billed cost and purchases at net cost.
   c. Cost of goods available for sale and cost of goods sold.

2. How does gross margin differ from gross profit? From net profit?

3. Explain the similarity between markups and gross margin. What connection do markdowns have with the operating statement?

4. Compute the net profit for a company with the following data:

Beginning inventory (cost)	$ 15,000
Purchases at billed cost	33,000
Sales returns and allowances	25,000
Rent	6,000
Salaries	40,000
Heat and light	18,000
Ending inventory (cost)	25,000
Freight cost (inbound)	9,000
Gross sales	130,000

5. Construct an operating statement from the following data:

Returns and allowances	$ 15,000
Expenses	20%
Closing inventory at cost	60,000
Markdowns	2%

Inward transportation	3,000
Purchases	100,000
Net profit (5%)	30,000

6. Data given:

Markdowns	$ 10,000
Gross sales	100,000
Returns	8,000
Allowances	12,000

Compute net sales and percent of markdowns.

7. *(a)* What percentage markups on cost are equivalent to the following percentage markups on selling price: 20, 37½, 50, and 66⅔? *(b)* What percentage markups on selling price are equivalent to the following percentage markups on cost: 33⅓, 20, 40, and 50?

8. What net sales volume is required to secure a stockturn rate of 20 times a year on an average inventory at cost of $100,000, with a gross margin of 30 percent?

9. Explain how the general manager of a department store might use the markdown ratios computed for his various departments? Would this be a fair measure? Of what?

10. Compare and contrast return on investment (ROI) and return on assets (ROA) measures. Which would be best for a retailer with no bank borrowing or other outside sources of funds (i.e., the retailer has put up all the money that is needed in the business)?

letter code	album price	8-track price	cassette price	letter code
A	4.99	4.99	4.99	A
C	5.49	5.49	5.49	C
D	7.49	7.49	7.49	D
E	7.99	7.99	7.99	E
F	8.49	8.49	8.49	F
G	8.99	8.99	8.99	G
I	9.49	9.49	9.49	I
L	11.49	11.49	11.49	L
M	12.49	12.49	12.49	M
N	13.49	13.49	13.49	N

When you finish this chapter, you should:

1. *Understand how most wholesalers and retailers set their prices—using markups.*

2. *Understand why turnover is so important in pricing.*

3. *Understand the advantages and disadvantages of average cost pricing.*

4. *Know how to find the most profitable price and quantity.*

5. *Know the many ways that price setters use demand estimates in their pricing.*

6. *Recognize the important new terms (shown in red).*

PRICE SETTING IN THE REAL WORLD

19

"How should I price this product?" is a common problem facing marketing managers.

In the last chapter, we talked about variations from a list price. Now let's see how the list price might be set in the first place.

Cost-oriented pricing is typical in business. As we will see, however, cost-oriented pricing is not as easy—or foolproof—as some people think. Ideally, a marketing manager should consider potential customers' demand—as well as his own costs—when setting prices. We will start, however, by looking at how most firms—including wholesalers and retailers—set cost-oriented prices.

PRICING BY WHOLESALERS AND RETAILERS

Why use traditional markups?

Most retail and wholesale prices are set by using the markups which are commonly used in a particular line of business. The **markup** is the dollar amount added to the cost of goods to get the selling price. For example, retailers usually add a markup to their cost of goods to get their own selling price.

407

The markup is usually large enough to cover the middleman's cost of doing business—and to provide some profit. So these traditional markups are often applied automatically. Some middlemen, in fact, use the same markup for all of their goods. This makes pricing easier for them!

When you think of the large number of items the average retailer and wholesaler carries—and the small sales volume of any one item—this cost-oriented approach makes sense. Spending the time to find the "best" price to charge on every item in stock (day-to-day or week-to-week) probably wouldn't pay.

Should you markup on cost or selling price?

Suppose that a retailer buys an article for $1. To make a profit, the retailer obviously must sell this article for more than $1. If the retailer adds 50 cents to cover operating costs and provide a profit—we say that he is marking up the item 50 cents.

Markups, however, usually are stated as percentages rather than dollar amounts. And this is where the difficulty begins. Is a markup of 50 cents on a cost of $1 a markup of 50 percent? Or should the markup be figured as a percentage of the selling price—$1.50—and therefore be 33⅓ percent? A clear definition is necessary.

Markup on selling price is a convenient rule

We will use the following definition: Unless otherwise stated: **markup (percent)** means "percentage of selling price." So, the 50-cent markup on the $1.50 selling price is a markup of 33⅓ percent.

Markups are related to selling price for convenience. For one thing, the markup on selling price is roughly equal to the gross margin. Most business managers understand the idea of gross margin—because they always see gross margin data on their profit and loss statement. (See Appendix B, on Marketing Arithmetic, if you are unfamiliar with these ideas.) They know that unless there is a large enough gross margin, there won't be any profit. For this reason, they accept traditional markups that are close to their usual gross margins.

Relating markups to the selling price also agrees with our emphasis on the customer. There is nothing wrong, however, with the idea of markup on cost. The important thing is to state clearly which markup we are using—to avoid confusion.

Retailers often need to change a markup on cost to one based on selling price—or vice versa. Conversion tables are available for this purpose. But they aren't really necessary—because the calculations are simple. (See the section on "Markup Conversion" in Appendix B.)

Markup chain may be used in channel pricing

A markup chain can set the price structure in a whole channel. A markup is figured on the selling price at each level of the channel. The producer's selling price becomes the wholesaler's cost—the wholesaler's selling price becomes the retailer's cost—and this cost plus a retail markup becomes the retail selling price. Each markup should cover the costs of selling, running the business—and leave a profit. Figure 19–1 shows how a markup might be used at each level of a channel system.

Figure 19–1: Example of a markup chain and channel pricing

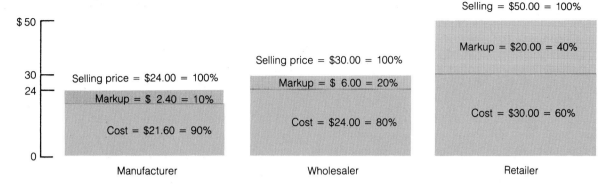

Figure 19–1 starts with a production cost (factory cost) of $21.60. In this case, the producer is taking a 10 percent markup and sells the goods for $24. The markup is 10 percent of $24 or $2.40. The producer's selling price now becomes the wholesaler's cost—$24. If the wholesaler is used to taking a 20 percent markup on selling price, the markup is $6—and the selling price becomes $30. The wholesaler's selling price of $30 now becomes the retailer's cost. And if the retailer is used to a 40 percent markup, he adds $20 and the retail selling price becomes $50.

High markups don't always mean big profits

Some people—including many retailers—link high markups with high profits. But this is often not true. Some kinds of business just have high operating costs—and need high markups. In other cases, high markups may lower sales and lead to low profits—or even losses.

The problem with trying to get high profits with high markups can be seen by an extreme example. A 90 percent markup on selling price may not be nearly as profitable as a 10 percent markup on selling price! This is easy to understand if we assume that no units are sold at the high markup, but a very large number are sold at the low one. The key is *turnover.* You can't earn much if you don't sell much—no matter how high your markup. But many retailers and wholesalers seem more concerned with the size of their markup than total profit.

Lower markups can speed turnover—and the stockturn rate

Some retailers and wholesalers, however, are trying to speed turnover to increase profit—even if this means reducing the markup. They see themselves in a business that is running up costs over time. If they can sell a much greater amount in the same time period, they may be able to take a lower markup and still have a higher profit at the end of the period.

An important idea here is the **stockturn rate**—the number of times the average inventory is sold in a year. Various methods of figuring stockturn rates are used—but they all measure how many times the average inventory is sold in a year. (See the section "Computing the Stockturn

Rate" in Appendix B.) If the stockturn rate is low, this may be bad for profits.

At the very least, a low stockturn will increase cost by tying up working capital. If the stockturn were 1 (once per year) instead of 5, selling goods costing $100,000 would require $100,000 rather than $20,000 in working capital—just to carry the necessary inventory.

Whether stockturn is high or low depends on the industry. An annual rate of 1 or 2 might be expected in the retail jewelry industry—while 40 to 50 would be typical for fresh fruits and vegetables.

Grocers run in fast company

Supermarket operators know the importance of fast turnover. They put only small markups on fast-selling items like sugar, shortening, soaps and detergents, canned milk, soups, desserts, beverages, baby foods, pet foods, bleaches, flour, and canned vegetables. Sugar, for example, may carry a markup of 9 percent—coffee 10 percent—canned and dry milk 13 percent.

Since supermarket expenses are 16–18 percent of sales, it looks like many of these items are carried at a loss! But since such figures are storewide averages, this need not be true.

Fast-moving goods usually are less expensive to stock and sell. They take up valuable space for shorter periods, are damaged less, and tie up less working capital. Lower markups will cover the costs of these items—and make a profit too. With lower markups, the goods may sell even faster—and a small profit per unit will be earned more often.

These fast-moving goods may be more profitable per item—in spite of the low margins—because of the higher turnover. The average turnover in one study was 14 times a year. Yet sugar turned over 31 times, beverages 28 times, shortening 23 times, and soups 21 times.

Faster selling items may carry a lower markup.

Note that high-margin items are not necessarily unprofitable. They simply may not be as profitable *per item* as some of the low-margin items.[1]

Discounters are running faster

The modern food discounters and mass merchandisers carry the fast turnover idea of the supermarket even further. By pricing food even lower—and attracting customers from wider areas who purchase in large quantities—they are able to operate profitably on even smaller margins.

PRICING BY PRODUCERS

It's up to the producer to set the list price

Some markups eventually become customary in a trade. Most of the channel members will tend to follow a similar process—adding a certain percentage to the previous price. Who sets price in the first place?

The basic list price usually is decided by the producer and/or brander of the product—a large retailer, a large wholesaler, or most often the producer. From here on, we'll look at the pricing approaches of such firms. For convenience, we will call them "producers."

AVERAGE-COST PRICING IS COMMON AND DANGEROUS

Average-cost pricing is adding a "reasonable" markup to the average cost of an item. The average cost per unit is usually found by studying past records. The total cost for the last year is divided by all the units

Figure 19–2: Results of average-cost pricing

Calculation of planned profit if *10,000 items are sold*	Calculation of actual profit if *only 5,000 items are sold*
Calculation of costs:	Calculation of costs:
Fixed overhead expenses .... $ 5,000	Fixed overhead expenses $5,000
Labor and materials 5,000	Labor and materials 2,500
Total costs $10,000	Total costs $7,500
"Reasonable" profit 1,000	
Total costs and planned profit ... $11,000	

Calculation of "reasonable" price for both possibilities:

$$\frac{\text{Total costs and planned profit}}{\text{Planned number of items to be sold}} = \frac{\$11,000}{10,000} = \$1.10 = \text{"Reasonable" price}$$

Calculation of profit or (loss):	Calculation of profit or (loss):
Actual unit sales (10,000) times price	Actual unit sales (5,000) times price
($1.10) = ... $11,000	($1.10) = ... $5,500
Minus: Total costs 10,000	Minus: Total costs $7,500
Profit (loss) 1,000	Profit (loss) .... (2,000)
Therefore: Planned ("reasonable") profit of $1,000 is earned if 10,000 items are sold at $1.10 each.	Therefore: Planned ("reasonable") profit of $1,000 is not earned. Instead, $2,000 loss results if 5,000 items are sold at $1.10 each.

produced and sold in that period—to get the average cost per unit. If the total cost were $5,000 for labor and materials and $5,000 for fixed overhead expenses—such as selling expenses, rent, and manager salaries—then total cost would be $10,000. If the company produced 10,000 items in that time period, the average cost would be $1 a unit. To get the price, the producer would decide how much profit per unit seems "reasonable." This would be added to the cost per unit. If 10 cents were considered a reasonable profit for each unit, then the new price would be set at $1.10. See Figure 19–2.

It does not make allowances for cost variations as output changes

This approach is simple. But it also can be dangerous. It's easy to lose money with average-cost pricing. To see why, let's follow this example further.

If, in the next year only 5,000 units are produced and sold, the firm may be in trouble. Five thousand units sold at $1.10 each would yield a total revenue of $5,500. The overhead would still be fixed at $5,000. And the variable material and labor cost would drop in half to $2,500—for a total of $7,500. This would mean a loss of $2,000 or 40 cents a unit. The method that was supposed to allow a profit of 10 cents a unit actually causes a loss of 40 cents a unit! See Figure 19–2.

The basic problem is that this method did not allow for cost variations at different levels of output. In a typical situation, average costs per unit are high when only a few units are produced. Average costs continually drop as the quantity produced increases. This is shown in Figure 19–3. This typical decline in the average cost curve occurs because of "economies of scale." This is why mass production and mass distribution often make sense. And this behavior of cost must be considered when setting prices.

Figure 19–3: Typical shape of average cost curve

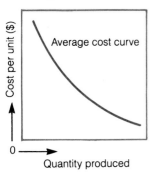

MARKETING MANAGER MUST CONSIDER VARIOUS KINDS OF COST

Average-cost pricing may fail because total cost includes a variety of costs. And each of these costs changes in a different way as output changes. Any pricing method that uses cost must consider these changes. To understand why, however, we need to define six types of costs. Differences among these costs help explain why many companies have problems with pricing.

There are three kinds of total cost

Total fixed cost is the sum of those costs that are fixed in total—no matter how much is produced. Among these fixed costs are rent, depreciation, managers' salaries, property taxes, and insurance. Such costs must be paid even if production stops temporarily.

Total variable cost, on the other hand, is the sum of those changing expenses that are closely related to output—expenses for parts, wages, packaging materials, outgoing freight, and sales commissions.

At zero output, total variable cost is zero. As output increases, so do variable costs. If a dress manufacturer doubles the output of dresses in a year, the total cost of cloth would also roughly double.

Total cost is the sum of total fixed and total variable costs. The growth of total cost depends upon the increase in total variable cost—since total fixed cost is already set.

There are three kinds of average cost

The pricing manager usually is more interested in cost per unit than total cost—because prices are usually quoted per unit. Costs per unit are called "average costs."

Average cost is obtained by dividing total cost by the related quantity (i.e., the total quantity which causes the total costs). See Table 19–1.

Average fixed cost is obtained by dividing total fixed cost by the related quantity. See Table 19–1.

Average variable cost is obtained by dividing total variable cost by the related quantity. See Table 19–1.

An example illustrates cost relations

Table 19–1 shows typical cost data for one firm. Here we assume that average variable cost is the same for each unit. Notice how average fixed cost goes down steadily as the quantity increases. Notice also how total variable cost increases when quantity increases, although the average variable cost remains the same. Average cost decreases continually too. This is because average variable cost is the same—and average fixed cost is decreasing. Figure 19–4 graphs the three average-cost curves.

Table 19–1: **Cost structure of a firm**

Quantity (Q)	Total fixed costs (TFC)	Average fixed costs (AFC)	Average variable costs (AVC)	Total variable costs (TVC)	Total cost (TC)	Average cost (AC)
0	$30,000	$	$	$ 0	$ 30,000	$
10,000	30,000	3.00	0.80	8,000	38,000	3.80
20,000	30,000	1.50	0.80	16,000	46,000	2.30
30,000	30,000	1.00	0.80	24,000	54,000	1.80
40,000	30,000	0.75	0.80	32,000	62,000	1.51
50,000	30,000	0.60	0.80	40,000	70,000	1.40
60,000	30,000	0.50	0.80	48,000	78,000	1.30
70,000	30,000	0.43	0.80	56,000	86,000	1.23
80,000	30,000	0.38	0.80	64,000	94,000	1.18
90,000	30,000	0.33	0.80	72,000	102,000	1.13
100,000	30,000	0.30	0.80	80,000	110,000	1.10

$$
\begin{bmatrix} 110,000 \ (TC) \\ -80,000 \ (TVC) \\ \hline 30,000 \ (TFC) \end{bmatrix}
\quad
\begin{array}{l} 0.30 \ (AFC) \\ (Q)\ 100,000\overline{)30,000}\ (TFC) \\[4pt] 0.80 \ (AVC) \\ (Q)\ 100,000\overline{)80,000}\ (TVC) \end{array}
\quad
\begin{bmatrix} 100,000 \ (Q) \\ \times 0.80 \ (AVC) \\ \hline 80,000 \ (TVC) \end{bmatrix}
\quad
\begin{bmatrix} 30,000 \ (TFC) \\ +80,000 \ (TVC) \\ \hline 110,000 \ (TC) \end{bmatrix}
\quad
\begin{array}{l} 1.10 \ (AC) \\ (Q)\ 100,000\overline{)110,000}\ (TC) \end{array}
$$

Figure 19–4: Typical shape of cost (per unit) curves when AVC is assumed constant per unit

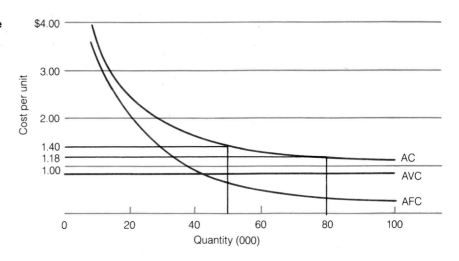

Ignoring demand is major weakness of average-cost pricing

Average-cost pricing works well if the firm actually sells the quantity which was used in setting the average cost price. Losses may result, however, if actual sales are *much lower* than were expected. On the other hand, if sales are much higher than expected, then profits may be very good. But this will only be by accident—because the firm's demand is much larger than expected.

To use average-cost pricing, a marketing manager must make some estimate of the quantity to be sold in the coming period. But unless this quantity is related to price—that is, unless the firm's demand curve is considered—the marketing manager may set a price that doesn't even cover a firm's total cost! This can be seen in a simple illustration for a firm with the cost curves shown in Figure 19–4. This firm's demand curve is shown in Figure 19–5. It is important to see that customers' demands (and their demand curve) are still important—whether management takes time to analyze the demand curve or not.

In this example, whether management sets the price at a high $3—or a low $1.25—it will have a loss. At $3, only 10,000 units will be sold for a total revenue of $30,000. But total costs will be $38,000—for a loss of $8,000. At the $1.25 price, 50,000 units will be sold—for a loss of $7,500. If management tried to estimate the demand curve—however roughly—the price probably would be set in the middle of the range—say at $2, where a profit of $6,000 would result. See Figure 19–5.

In short, average cost pricing is simple in theory—but often fails in practice. In stable situations, prices set by this method may yield profits—but not necessarily maximum profits. And interestingly, such cost-based prices might be higher than a price that would be more profitable for a firm—as shown in Figure 19–5. When demand conditions are changing, average-cost pricing may be even more risky.

Figure 19–5: Evaluation of various prices along a firm's demand curve

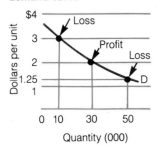

FINDING THE MOST PROFITABLE PRICE AND QUANTITY TO PRODUCE

A marketing manager facing the typical down-sloping demand curve must pick *one* price (for a time period). His problem is which price to choose. This price, of course, will set the quantity that will be sold.

To maximize profit, the marketing manager should choose the price which will lead to the greatest difference between total revenue and total cost. Finding this best price and quantity requires an estimate of the firm's demand curve. This should be seen as an "iffy" curve—*if* price A is set then quantity A will be sold—*if* price B is set then quantity B will be sold—and so on. By multiplying all these possible prices by their related quantities, you can figure the possible total revenues. Then, by estimating the firm's likely costs at various quantities it is possible to figure a total cost curve. The differences between these two curves show possible total profits. Clearly, the best price would be the one which has the greatest distance between the total revenue and total cost curves. These ideas are shown in Table 19–2—and in Figure 19–6, where these data are plotted in a graph. In this example, you can see that the best price is $79—and the best quantity is six units.

A profit range is reassuring

Estimating demand curves is not easy. But some estimate of demand is needed to set prices. This is just one of the tough jobs facing marketing managers. Ignoring demand curves does not make them go away! So some estimates must be made. This points up again how important it is to understand the needs and attitudes of your target market.

Notice that the demand estimates do not have to be exact. Figure 19–7 shows that there is a *range* of profitable prices. The strategy would be profitable all the way from a price of $53 to $117. $79 is just the "best" price.

Table 19–2: Revenue, cost, and profit for an individual firm

(1) Quantity Q	(2) Price P	(3) Total revenue TR	(4) Total cost TC	(5) Profit TR–TC
0	$150	$ 0	$200	$−200
1	140	140	296	−156
2	130	260	316	− 56
3	117	351	331	+ 20
4	105	420	344	+ 76
5	92	460	355	+105
6	79	474	368	+106
7	66	462	383	+ 79
8	53	424	423	+ 1
9	42	378	507	−129
10	31	310	710	−400

Figure 19–6: Graphic determination of the output giving the greatest total profit for a firm

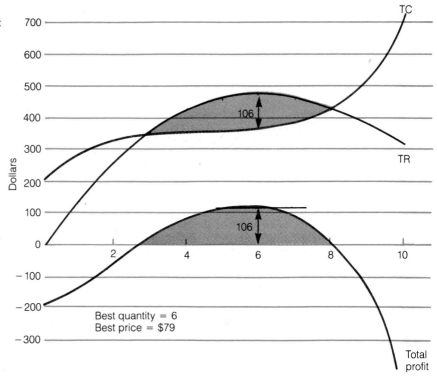

Best quantity = 6
Best price = $79

Figure 19–7: Range of profitable prices for illustrative data in Table 19–2 and Figure 19–6

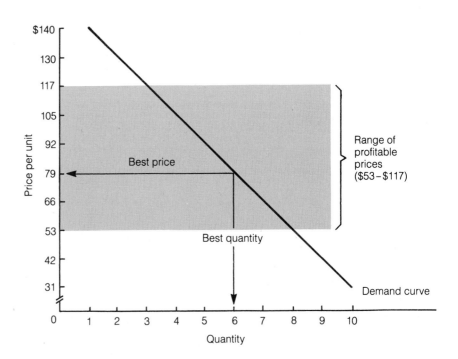

The marketing manager probably would want to try to estimate the price which would lead to the middle of the profit range. But a slight "miss" would not mean failure. And at least trying to estimate demand would probably lead to being some place in the profitable range. In contrast, mechanical use of average-cost pricing might lead to much too high or much too low prices—as you saw earlier in the chapter. This is why estimating demand is not only desirable—but necessary.

SOME PRICE SETTERS DO ESTIMATE DEMAND

Full use of demand curves is not very common in business. But we do find marketers setting prices as though they believe certain types of demand curves are there. (And pricing research indicates they are.)

The following section discusses various examples of demand-related pricing. Some may be only instinctive adjustments of cost-based prices—but you can see that demand is being considered.

Prestige pricing—make it high and not too low

Prestige pricing is setting a rather high price to suggest high quality or high status. Some target customers seem to want the "best." If prices are dropped a little below this "high" level, they may see a bargain. But if the prices begin to appear "cheap," they may become worried about quality and stop buying.[2]

Target customers who respond to prestige pricing give the marketing manager an unusual demand curve. Instead of a normal down-slope, the curve goes down for a while and then bends back to the left again. See Figure 19–8. Marketing managers faced with this kind of demand—such as jewelry and fur retailers and night club owners—typically set high prices.

Figure 19–8: Demand curve showing a prestige price situation

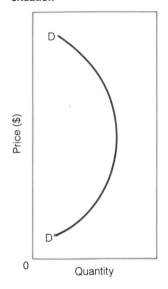

Figure 19–9: Demand curve when odd-even pricing is appropriate

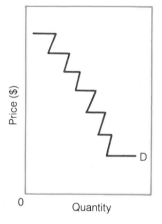

Figure 19–10: Demand curve when psychological pricing is appropriate

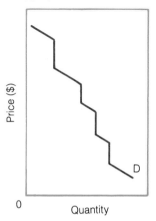

Leader pricing—make it low to attract customers

Leader pricing is setting some very low prices—real bargains—to get customers into retail stores. Certain products are picked for their promotion value and priced low—but above cost. In food stores, the leader prices are the ''specials'' that are advertised regularly—to give an image of low prices.

Leader pricing usually is limited to well-known, widely used items which customers don't stock heavily—milk, butter, eggs, or coffee—but on which they will recognize a real price cut. The idea is to attract customers—not to sell large quantities of the leaders. To avoid hurting the firm's own profits, items may be used that are not directly competitive with major lines—as when bargain-priced cigarettes are sold at a gasoline station.

Bait pricing—offer a ''steal,'' but sell under protest

Bait pricing is setting some very low prices to attract customers—but not to sell products. It's something like leader pricing. But here the seller *doesn't* plan to sell much at the low price.

This approach is used by some furniture retailers. To attract customers, a store will offer an extremely low price on an item. Once customers are in the store, the salespeople are expected to point out the disadvantages of the lower-quality item and sell customers higher-quality, more expensive products instead. Customers can buy the bait items—but only with great difficulty.

This policy tries to attract bargain hunters—or customers on the very low end of the demand curve who are not usually part of the market. If bait pricing is successful, customers may be ''traded up''—and the demand for higher-quality products will expand. But extremely aggressive—and sometimes dishonest—bait-pricing advertising has given this method a bad reputation. In fact, all throughout Canada, bait pricing is illegal, either specifically, or indirectly.

Odd-even pricing

Odd-even pricing is setting prices which end in certain numbers. Some marketers do this because they feel that consumers react better to these prices.

For goods selling under $50, prices ending with 95—such as $5.95, $6.95, and so on—are common. In general, prices ending in nine are most popular, followed by prices ending in five and three. For products selling over $50, prices that are $1 or $2 below the even-dollar figures are the most popular.[3]

Marketers using these prices seem to assume that they have a rather jagged demand curve—that consumers will buy less for a while as prices are lowered and then more as each ''magic'' price is reached. This kind of demand curve is shown in Figure 19–9.

Odd-even prices were used long ago by some retailers to force their clerks to make change. Then they had to record the sale and could not pocket the money. Today, however, it is not always clear why these prices are used—and whether they really work. Perhaps consumers have learned

Shop
Woolworth
for
Value
$1 89
Woolworth

to expect better buys at certain prices and they do work. Or perhaps it is done simply because "everyone else does it."

Psychological pricing—some prices just seem right

Psychological pricing is setting prices which have special appeal to target customers. Some people feel there are whole ranges of prices which potential customers see as the same. Price cuts in these ranges would not increase the quantity sold. But just below this range, customers may buy more. Then, at even lower prices the quantity demanded would stay the same again. And so on.

The kind of demand curve that fits psychological pricing is shown in Figure 19–10. Vertical drops mark the price ranges which customers see as the same. Pricing research shows that there are such demand curves.[4]

PRICING A FULL LINE OR A TOTAL PRODUCT

Our emphasis has been—and will continue to be—on the problem of pricing a single item, mainly because this makes our discussion easier. But most marketing managers are responsible for more than one product. In fact, their "product" may be the whole company line!

Full-line pricing—market or firm oriented?

Full-line pricing is setting prices for a whole line of products. How to do this depends on which of two basic strategies a firm is using. In one case, all products in the company's line are aimed at the same general target market—which makes it important for all prices to be related to one another.

In other cases, the different products in the line are aimed at entirely different target markets. Here, there doesn't have to be any relation between the various prices. A chemical manufacturer of a wide variety of products with several target markets, for example, probably should price each product separately.

Examples of a full line being offered to the same target market are a TV manufacturer selling a whole line to retailers, or a forklift truck producer offering various sizes to large manufacturers, or a grocery retailer with thousands of items. Here the firm has to think of the customers' reaction to its full line of prices.

Cost is not much help in full-line pricing

The marketing manager must try to recover all costs on the whole line—perhaps by pricing quite low on competitive items and much higher on less competitive items. But costs are not much help to the marketing manager in full-line pricing. There is no one "right" way to assign a company's fixed costs to each of the products. And if any method is carried through without considering demand, it may lead to very unrealistic prices. The marketing manager should judge demand for the whole line—as well as demand for each individual product in each target market—to avoid mistakes.

Price lining can simplify buying and selling.

Price lining—a few prices cover the field

Price lining is like full-line pricing—but here the focus is on how prices look at the retail level.

Price lining is setting a few price levels for a product class and then marking all items at these prices.

Most customers will pay between $5 and $15 for a necktie. In price lining, there will not be many prices in this range. There will be only a few. Ties will not be priced at $5.50, $5.65, $5.75, and so on. They might be priced at three levels—$5, $10 and $15.

The main advantage of price lining is simplicity—for both clerks and customers. It is less confusing than a big variety of prices. Some customers may consider goods in only one price class. Their big decision then is which items to choose at that price. Price is no longer a question—unless the goods at that price are not satisfactory. Then, perhaps the customer can be "traded up" to the next price level.

For retailers, price lining has several advantages. Sales may increase because (1) they can offer a bigger variety in each price line and (2) it is easier to get customers to make decisions within one price line. Stock planning is simpler—because demand is larger at the relatively few prices. Price lining also can reduce costs—because inventory needs are lower even though large stocks are carried in each line. In summary, price lining results in faster turnover, fewer markdowns, quicker sales, and simplified buying.

Demand-backward pricing aids price lining

Demand-backward pricing starts with an acceptable final consumer price and works backward to what a producer can charge. It is commonly used by producers of final consumer goods—especially shopping goods, such as women's and children's clothing and shoes. It is also used for toys or other gifts—for which customers will spend a specific amount

All costs and the likely competition have to be figured in a good bid.

because they are seeking a five-dollar or a ten-dollar gift. Here, a reverse cost-plus pricing process is used. This method has been called "market-minus" pricing.

The producer starts with the retail price for a particular item and then works backward—subtracting the typical margins which channel members expect. This gives the approximate price that he can charge. Then, he subtracts from this price the average or planned marketing expenses—to determine how much can be spent producing the item.

Demand estimates are necessary if demand-backward pricing is to be successful. The quantity which will be demanded affects production costs—i.e., where the firm will be on its average cost curve. Also, since competitors can be expected to make the best product possible, it is important to know customer needs—to set the best amount to be spent on manufacturing costs. By increasing costs a little, the product might be so improved in consumers' eyes that the firm would sell many more units. But if consumers only want novelty—additional quality might not increase the quantity demanded—and shouldn't be offered.

BID PRICING DEPENDS HEAVILY ON COSTS

A new price for every job   **Bid pricing** is offering a specific price for each possible job—rather than setting a price that applies for all potential customers. Building contractors, for example, must bid on possible projects. And many companies selling services (such as cleaning or data processing) must submit bids for jobs they would like to have.

The big problem in bid pricing is collecting all the costs that apply to each job. This may sound easy, but thousands of cost components may have to go into a complicated bid. Further, management must include an overhead charge—and a charge for profit.

Demand must be considered too

It is when adding in overhead and profit that demand and competition must be considered. Usually, the customer will get several bids and accept the lowest one. So mechanical rules for adding in overhead and profit should be avoided. Some bidders use the same overhead and profit rates on all jobs—regardless of competition—and then are surprised when they don't get some jobs.

Bidding can be expensive. So a firm should be selective about which jobs it will bid on—hopefully selecting those where they feel they have the greatest chance of success.[5] Thousands or even millions of dollars have been spent just developing cost-oriented bids for large industrial or government orders.

Sometimes bids are bargained

Some buying situations (including much government buying) require the use of bids—and the purchasing agent must take the lowest bid. In other cases, however, bids may be called for and then the company submitting the most attractive bid—not necessarily the lowest—will be singled out for further bargaining. This may include price adjustments—but it also may be concerned with how additions to the job will be priced, what guarantees will be provided, and the quality of labor and supervisors who will do the job. Some projects—such as construction projects—are hard to define exactly. So it is important that the buyer be satisfied about the whole marketing mix—not just the price. Obviously, effective personal selling can be important here.

CONCLUSION

In this chapter, we discussed various approaches to price setting. Generally, retailers and wholesalers use traditional markups. Some use the same markups for all their items. Others have found that varying the markups may increase turnover and profit. In other words, demand is considered!

Cost-oriented pricing seems to make sense for middlemen—because they handle small quantities of many items. Producers must take price setting more seriously. They are the ones that set the "list price" to which others apply markups.

Producers commonly use average cost curves to help set their prices. But this approach sometimes ignores demand completely. A more realistic approach requires a sales forecast. This may just mean assuming that sales in the next period will be roughly the same as in the last period.

This *will* enable the marketing manager to set a price—but this price *may or may not* cover all costs and earn the desired profit.

We discussed how demand could be brought into pricing. This could help a marketing manager maximize profits—if this were his objective. It appears that some marketers do consider demand in their pricing. We saw this with prestige pricing, leader pricing, bait pricing, odd-even pricing, psychological pricing, full-line pricing, and even bid pricing.

We have stressed throughout this book that the customer must be considered before anything is done. This certainly applies to pricing. It means that when managers are setting a price, they have to consider what customers will be willing to pay. This isn't always easy—but it is nice to know that there is a profit range around the "best" price. Therefore, even "guesstimates" about what potential customers will buy at various prices will probably lead to a better price than just mechanical use of traditional markups or cost-oriented formulas.

QUESTIONS FOR DISCUSSION

1. Why do department stores seek a markup of about 40 percent when some discount houses operate on a 20 percent markup?

2. A manufacturer of household appliances distributed its products through wholesalers and retailers. The retail selling price was $250, and the manufacturing cost to the company was $100. The retail markup was 40 percent and the wholesale markup 25 percent.
   a. What was the cost to the wholesaler? To the retailer?
   b. What percentage markup did the manufacturer take?

3. Relate the concept of stock turnover to the rise of discounters. Use a simple example in your answer.

4. If total fixed costs are $100,000 and total variable costs are $200,000 at an output of 10,000 units, what are the probable total fixed costs and total variable costs at an output of 20,000 units? What are the average fixed costs, average variable costs, and the average costs at these two output levels? Determine the price that should be charged. (Make any simplifying assumptions necessary to obtain a definite answer.)

5. Explain how target return pricing differs from average cost pricing.

6. Construct an example showing that mechanical use of a very large or very small markup might still lead to unprofitable operation, while some in-between price would be profitable.

7. How would a prestige pricing policy fit into a marketing mix? Would exclusive distribution be necessary?

8. Cite a local example of the use of odd-even pricing and then evaluate whether you feel it makes sense.

9. Cite a local example of the use of psychological pricing and then evaluate whether you feel it makes sense.

10. Distinguish between leader pricing and bait pricing. What do they have in common? How can their use affect a marketing mix?

11. Is a full-line pricing policy available only to producers? Cite local examples of full-line pricing. Why is full-line pricing important?

SUGGESTED CASES

22. A–A Fabricators Ltd.
26. Demmer Manufacturing Company

When you finish this chapter, you should:

1. Understand the various ways that businesses can get into international marketing.

2. Understand what multinational corporations are.

3. Understand the kinds of opportunities in international markets.

4. Understand the market dimensions which may be useful in segmenting international markets.

5. Recognize the important new terms (shown in red).

MARKETING STRATEGY PLANNING FOR INTERNATIONAL MARKETS

20

Did you know that more packaged spaghetti is eaten in Germany than in Italy?

Planning strategies for international markets can be even harder than for domestic markets. Now, cultural differences are more important. Each foreign market must be treated as a separate market—with its own submarkets. Lumping together all people outside Canada as "foreigners"—or assuming that they are just like Canadian customers—is almost a guarantee of failure.

There has been too much narrow thinking about international marketing. This chapter aims to get rid of some of these ideas—and to suggest how strategy planning has to be changed when a firm enters international markets. We will see that a marketing planner must make several strategic decisions about international marketing: (1) whether the firm even wants to work in international markets and, if so, its degree of involvement, and (2) which markets. See Figure 20–1.

Figure 20–1: Strategic decisions about international marketing

Degree of involvement	Which markets

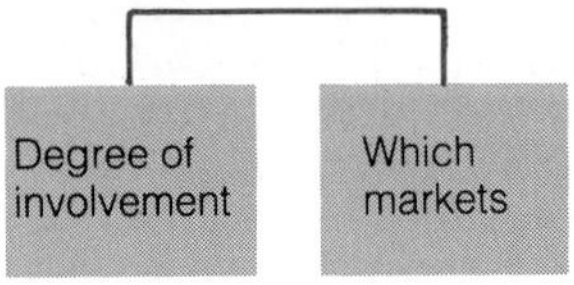

CANADA'S FOREIGN TRADE

Foreign trade accounts for about 20 percent of Canada's Gross National Product (GNP). This makes foreign trade as important a component of Canada's GNP as it is in Germany and the United Kingdom. The corresponding figure for the United States is less than 15 percent.

United States the major trading partner

Table 20–1 reveals that Canada does most of its foreign trading with the United States. Although the proportions differ somewhat from year to year, Canada's trade with the United States is many times more important than with any other nation or trading group. Canada is also the major trading partner of the United States, but it accounts for only 20–22 percent of total U.S. foreign trade.

The United Kingdom became a member of the European Economic Community (EEC) on January 1, 1973. In a sense, Canada's second and third largest trading partners merged at that time as the U.K. gradually adopted EEC economic policies. As Table 20–1 indicates, a significant volume of Canadian trade takes place with an expanded EEC and with Japan, now our third most important partner. However, its value is nowhere close to the level of our trade with the United States.

What Canada buys and sells

Canada has remained basically an exporter of natural resources and an importer of finished products. On the other hand, our large trading partners are big importers of primary products and large exporters of

Table 20–1: Canadian import-export patterns[1]

	What gets exported (percent)		What gets imported (percent)	
	1979	1981	1979	1981
Live animals	.4%	.3%	.2%	.3%
Food, feed, beverages, tobacco	9.4	11.3	6.6	6.3
Crude materials	19.5	18.8	12.7	15.4
Fabricated materials	37.9	37.7	19.1	18.5
End products	32.5	31.1	60.5	58.2
Special transactions	.3	.8	.9	1.3

	Where it goes (percent)		Where it comes from (percent)	
	1979	1981	1979	1981
United States	67.7%	66.3%	72.5%	68.8%
United Kingdom	4.0	4.1	3.1	2.8
Other EEC	7.3	6.7	5.9	5.2
Japan	6.3	5.6	3.4	5.1
Other OECD	2.7	2.8	2.9	2.8
Other America	4.5	4.7	4.6	6.4
Other countries	7.5	9.8	7.6	8.9

manufactured goods. (Far more detailed information is available on the quantity of specific products exported from or imported into Canada.[2] The United Nations also reports on each country's exports and imports from every other nation. But our present concern is with Canada's overall trade patterns.) In 1977 raw materials and semifinished products accounted for 56.8 percent of all Canadian exports to the United States, 88.2 percent of our EEC exports, and 97.8 percent of our exports to Japan. The proportion of *finished products* in our imports from these three regions amounted to 70.3 percent (United States), 59.2 percent (EEC), and 74.9 percent (Japan).[3]

Motor vehicles and parts now account for about two thirds of Canada's exports of manufactured end products. All other sales of end products have averaged between 10 percent and 12 percent of total exports. This pattern is due to the fact that a duty-free market in automotive and related products was created by the Canada-U.S. Automotive Agreement of 1965. There has been some Canadian interest in expanding Canada's free-trading arrangements with the United States. However, political considerations makes such action unlikely in the foreseeable future.[4]

Government services available to exporters

Foreign trade and an acceptable balance-of-payments position is important to the nation's economic health. For this reason, the Canadian government provides a number of services to would-be exporters. Most of this assistance comes from the Department of Industry, Trade and Commerce. Its Fairs and Mission Branch arranges trade fair exhibits in foreign countries, trade missions to and from Canada, and visits by foreign buyers to Canadian sources of supply. The Market Development Group brings together Canadian manufacturers so that they may collectively bid on foreign projects too large for any one firm. The Canadian Trade Commissioners posted abroad act as export marketing consultants to interested sellers. They also serve as liaison officers between foreign buyers and Canadian exporters.[5]

Additional types of assistance are made available to present and prospective exporters by other federal agencies. For example, the Export Development Corporation provides insurance to exporters, guarantees payment, and provides other types of interim financing. The Canadian Commercial Corporation, also wholly owned by the Government of Canada, helps other governments and international agencies wishing to purchase Canadian goods and services. The Canadian International Development Agency encourages exports by making foreign aid recipients "buy Canadian" when such action is possible and appropriate.

Many of the provinces have somewhat similar programs designed to encourage exports. The provinces have been especially active in promoting large-scale trade missions to various parts of the world. There has also been considerable interest, at both the provincial and federal level, in the establishment of an "official" or "state" trading company. This type of firm would cultivate foreign markets for large numbers of Canadian manufacturers otherwise unable to pursue export opportunities.

DEGREES OF INVOLVEMENT IN INTERNATIONAL MARKETING

Opportunities in foreign countries have led many companies into world-wide operations. The marketing concept is less understood in some foreign markets. So there are great opportunities for those who want to apply it abroad—from just exporting, to joint ventures, to investment in foreign operations. See Figure 20–2. Many companies are very interested in foreign market prospects—because they find their foreign operations becoming more profitable than domestic activities.

Exporting often comes first

Some companies enter international marketing by selling the products they already are producing. Sometimes this is just a way of "getting rid of" surplus output. Other times, it comes from a real effort to look for new opportunities.

Exporting is selling some of what the firm is producing to foreign markets. Often this is tried without changing the physical goods—or the services or instruction manuals! As a result, some of these early efforts are not very satisfying—to buyers or sellers.

Exporting gets a firm involved in a lot of government "red tape." Beginning exporters may build their own staffs—or depend on specialized middlemen to handle these details. Export agents can handle the paperwork as the goods are shipped outside the country. Then agents or merchant wholesalers can handle the importing details. Even large manufacturers with many foreign operations may use international middlemen for some products or markets. They know how to handle the sometimes confusing formalities and specialized functions. Even a small mistake can tie goods up at national borders for days—or months.

Some relationships get a firm more involved

Exporting doesn't have to involve permanent relationships. Of course, channel relationships take time to build—and shouldn't be treated lightly. Sales reps' contacts in foreign countries are "investments." Nevertheless, it is relatively easy to cut back on these relationships—or even drop them.

Some firms, on the other hand, form more formal and permanent relationships with nationals in foreign countries—including licensing, contract manufacturing, management contracting, and joint venturing.[6]

Licensing is an easy way

Licensing is a relatively easy way to enter foreign markets. **Licensing** means selling the right to use some process, trademark, patent, or other

Figure 20–2: Kinds of involvement in international marketing that a marketing manager can choose

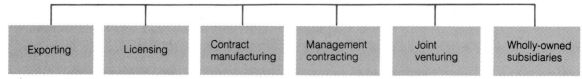

Gerber entered the Japanese market through licensing.

right—for a fee or royalty. The licensee takes most of the risk because it must invest some capital to use the right.

This can be an effective way of entering a market if good partners are available. Gerber entered the Japanese baby food market in this way. But Gerber still exports to other countries.

Contract manufacturing takes care of the production problems

Contract manufacturing means turning over production to others while retaining the marketing process. Sears, Roebuck used this approach as it opened stores in Latin America and Spain.

This approach can be especially good where there are difficult labor relations—or problems obtaining supplies and "buying" government cooperation. Growing nationalistic feelings may make this approach more attractive in the future.

Management contracting sells know-how

Management contracting means the seller provides only management skills—the production facilities are owned by others. Some mines and oil refineries are operated this way—and Hilton operates hotels all over the world for local owners. This is a relatively low-risk approach to international marketing. No commitment is made to fixed facilities—which can be taken over or damaged in riots or wars. If conditions get too bad, the key management people can fly off on the next plane—and leave the nationals to manage the operation.

Joint venturing is more involved

Joint venturing means a domestic firm entering into a partnership with a foreign firm. As with any partnership, there can be honest disagreements over objectives—for example, about how much profit is desired and how fast it should be paid out—and operating policies. Where a close working relationship can be developed—perhaps based on a Canadian firm's technical and marketing know-how, and the foreign partner's knowledge of the market and political connections—this approach can be very attractive to both parties. At its worst, it can be a nightmare—and cause the Canadian firm to want to go into a wholly owned operation. But the terms of the joint venture may block this for years. Or the foreign partners may acquire enough know-how to be tough competitors.

When production costs less in a foreign country, it may be profitable for a company to import its own products.

Wholly owned subsidiaries give more control

When a firm feels that a foreign market looks really promising, it may want to go the final step. A **wholly owned subsidiary** is a separate firm—owned by a parent company. This gives complete control—and helps a foreign branch work more easily with the rest of the company.

Some multinational companies have gone this way. It gives them a great deal of freedom to move goods from one country to another. If it has too much capacity in a country with low production costs, for example, some production may be moved there from other plants—and then exported to countries with higher production costs. This is the same way that large firms in Canada ship goods from one area to another—depending on costs and local needs.

MULTINATIONAL CORPORATIONS EVOLVE TO MEET INTERNATIONAL CHALLENGE

Multinational corporations have a direct investment in several countries and run their businesses depending on the choices available anywhere in the world. Well known U.S.-based multinational firms include Eastman Kodak, Warner-Lambert, Pfizer, Anaconda, Goodyear, Ford, IBM, ITT, Corn Products, 3M, National Cash Register, H. J. Heinz, and Gillette. They regularly earn over 30 percent of their total sales or profits abroad. And Coca-Cola recently moved past the half-way point—more than half of its profits come from international operations! Coca-Cola sees a day coming when as much as 75 percent of its earnings will be from abroad—because there will be more young people with money there than in aging America.[7]

Most multinational companies are American. But there are some well-known companies based in other countries—for example, Nestle's, Shell (Royal Dutile Shell), and Lever Brothers (Unilever). They have well-accepted ''foreign'' brands—not only in Canada, but around the world. And

Japanese firms producing Sony, Honda, Panasonic, and other well-known brands are operating around the globe.

Such Canadian organizations as Alcan, Canron, CIL, Consolidated Bathurst, Massey-Ferguson, and Seagrams have a controlling or complete interest in U.S. firms.

Indeed, Canadian-owned firms are far more multinational than most of us realize. Some 22 Canadian-controlled firms appear in *Fortune* magazine's 1981 list of "500 Largest Non-U.S. Industrial Corporations." (Another 10 Canadian-based but foreign-owned firms—the largest being General Motors of Canada—also appear on that list).

Multinational operations make sense to more firms

As firms move more deeply into international marketing, some reach the point where the firm sees itself as a worldwide business. As a chief executive of Abbott Laboratories—a pharmaceutical company with plants in 22 countries—said, "We are no longer just a U.S. company with interests abroad. Abbott is a worldwide enterprise and many major fundamental decisions must be made on a global basis."

A Texas Instruments executive had a similar view: "When we consider new opportunities and one is abroad and the other domestic, we can't afford to look upon the alternative here as an inherently superior business opportunity simply because it is in the United States. We view an overseas market just as we do our market, say, in Arizona, as one more market in the world."

A General Motors executive sees this trend as ". . . the emergence of the modern industrial corporation as an institution that is transcending national boundaries."[8]

Much of the multinational activity of the 1960s and early 1970s was U.S.-based firms expanding to other countries. As these opportunities became less attractive in the mid-1970s—due to the energy crisis, inflation, currency devaluations, labor unrest, and unstable governments—foreign multinational companies have been moving into North America.

Foreign firms are beginning to see that it may be attractive to operate

Multinational marketers view the world as many possible markets instead of U.S. and "foreign" markets.

in this large—if competitive—market. The Japanese "invasion" with all kinds of electronic products is well known. And they are building plants, too. For example, Sony has a TV assembly plant and a TV tube plant in southern California. And French firms (including the producers of Michelin tires) are setting up or buying facilities in the United States.[9]

Multinational companies overcome national boundaries

From an international view, multinational firms do—as the GM executive said—"transcend national boundaries." They see world market opportunities and locate their production and distribution facilities for greatest effectiveness. This has upset some nationalistic business managers and politicians. But these multinational operations may be difficult to stop. They are no longer just exporting or importing. They hire local residents and build plants. And they have business relationships with local business managers and politicians. These are powerful organizations which have learned to deal with nationalistic feelings and typical border barriers—treating them simply as uncontrollable variables.

We do not have "one world" politically as yet—but business is moving in that direction. We may have to develop new kinds of corporations and laws to govern multinational operations. The limitations of national boundaries on business and politics will make less and less sense in the future.[10]

CANADA AND THE FOREIGN OWNERSHIP ISSUE

Multinational operations may be necessary for corporate health. They may also contribute to the economic growth of the nation in which subsidiaries are established. However, **foreign ownership** is on the other side of the multinational coin. Many Canadians object to the fact that so large a proportion of this nation's industry is controlled by foreign firms. As Figure 20–3 shows, foreign direct investment in Canada is high. The degree of foreign ownership has remained stable over the past several years. It may now be declining in size relative to the Canadian economy as a whole.[11]

Concern over foreign ownership led to passage of the Foreign Investment Review Act in December 1973. This legislation gives the Canadian Cabinet the final say in determining whether foreigners will be allowed (1) to acquire control of existing businesses, (2) to expand into areas unrelated to those businesses they are already carrying on in Canada, or (3) to establish new businesses. However, proposed foreign investments are actually evaluated by FIRA, the Foreign Investment Review Agency. FIRA then advises the Minister of Industry, Trade & Commerce whether or not he should recommend cabinet approval.

The criteria used by FIRA and the Cabinet in either sanctioning or preventing any proposed "takeover" or expansion all relate to the proposed impact on Canada's economic interests. These factors include:

> The effect of the proposed investment on the level of economic activity and on such specifics as employment, resource processing, utilization of Canadian components, and exports.

Figure 20–3: Degree of foreign ownership, 1974 (as measured by assets)[12]

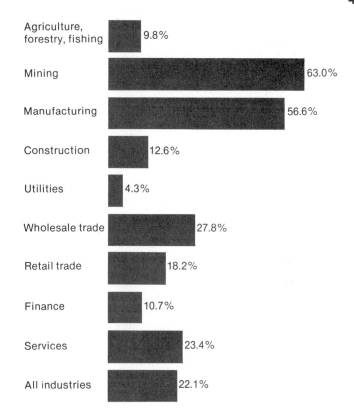

Agriculture, forestry, fishing	9.8%
Mining	63.0%
Manufacturing	56.6%
Construction	12.6%
Utilities	4.3%
Wholesale trade	27.8%
Retail trade	18.2%
Finance	10.7%
Services	23.4%
All industries	22.1%

The degree and significance of participation by Canadians in the enterprise or new business.

How productivity, industrial efficiency, technological development product innovation, and product variety will be affected.

The effect of the investment on competition within specific Canadian industries.

The compatibility of the investment with national and stated provincial industrial and economic objectives.[13]

IDENTIFYING DIFFERENT KINDS OF OPPORTUNITIES

Firms usually start from where they are

A really multinational firm which has accepted the marketing concept will look for opportunities in the same way that we have been discussing throughout the text, i.e., looking for unsatisfied needs—anywhere—that it might be able to satisfy—given its resources and objectives.

The typical approach, however, is to start with the firm's current products and the needs it knows how to satisfy, and try to find new markets—wherever they may be—with the same or similar unsatisfied needs. Next, the firm adapts the product, and perhaps its promotion. Later, the firm may think about developing new products and new promotion policies.

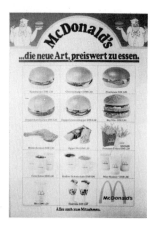

Some of these possibilities are shown in Figure 20–4. Here we only look at Product and Promotion—because Place would obviously have to be changed in new markets, and Price adjustments probably would be needed also.

The "Same-Same" box in Figure 20–4 can be illustrated with McDonald's (fast-food chain) entry into European markets. Its Director of International Marketing says, "Ronald McDonald speaks eight languages. Our target audience is the same worldwide—young families with children— and our advertising is designed to appeal to them." The basic promotion messages must be translated, of course, but the same strategy decisions which were made for the U.S. market apply. McDonald's has adapted its Product in Germany, however, by adding beer to appeal to adults who prefer beer to soft drinks. Its efforts have been extremely successful so far. Some stores are selling over $1 million per year—something that took many more years to do in the United States.[14]

McDonald's and other firms expanding into international markets usually move first into markets with good economic potential—such as Western Europe and Japan. But if McDonald's or some other fast-food company wanted to move into much lower-income areas, it might have to develop a whole new Product—perhaps a traveling street vendor with "hamburgers" made out of soy products. This kind of opportunity is in the upper right-hand corner of Figure 20–4.

The lower left-hand box in this figure is illustrated by the different kind of promotion that is needed for just a simple bicycle. In some parts of the world, a bicycle provides basic transportation—while in Canada, it is

Figure 20–4: International marketing opportunities as seen by a U.S. firm from the viewpoint of its usual product-market.[15]

		Product		
		Same	Adaptation	New
Promotion	Same	Same needs and use conditions (McDonald's usual strategy)	Basically same needs and use conditions (McDonald's strategy with beer in Germany)	Basically same needs, but different incomes and/or applications (street vendor with low-cost hamburgers)
	Adaptation	Different needs but same use conditions (bicycles)	Different needs and use conditions (clothing)	Different needs and different incomes and/or applications (hand-powered washing machines)

mainly a recreation vehicle. So a different promotion emphasis is needed in these different target markets.

Both product and promotion changes will be needed as one moves to the right along the bottom row in Figure 20–4. Such moves would obviously require more market knowledge—and may increase the risk.

The risk of opportunities varies by environmental sensitivity

International marketing means going into unfamiliar markets. This can increase risks. The farther one is from familiar territory, the greater the likelihood of making big mistakes. But not all products offer the same risk. It is useful to think of the risks running along a "range of environmental sensitivity." See Figure 20–5. Some products are relatively insensitive to the economic or cultural environment in which they are placed. These products may be accepted "as is." Or they may require relatively little adaption to make them suitable for local use. Most industrial goods would tend to be near the insensitive end of this range.

At the other end of the range, we find highly sensitive products which may be difficult or impossible to adapt to all international situations. At this end we would find "faddy" or high-style consumer goods. It is sometimes difficult to understand why a particular product is well accepted in a home market—which makes it even more difficult to know how it might be received in a different environment.

This range of sensitivity helps explain why many of the early successes in international marketing involved basic commodities—such as gasoline, soap, transportation vehicles, mining equipment, and agricultural machinery. It also suggests that firms producing and/or selling highly sensitive products should carefully study how their products will be seen and used in the new environment.[16]

Evaluating opportunities in alternative international markets

Judging opportunities in international markets uses the same principles we have been discussing. Basically, each opportunity must be evaluated within the uncontrollable variables. But there may be more of these varia-

Figure 20–5: Range of environmental sensitivity

Continuum of environmental sensitivity

Insensitive   *Sensitive*

Industrial goods

Basic commodity-type consumer goods

Faddy or high-style consumer goods

Exporting commodities and industrial goods involves less risk than faddy or high-style consumer products.

bles—and they may be more difficult to evaluate in international markets. Estimating the risk involved in particular opportunities may be very difficult. Some countries are not as politically stable. Their governments and constitutions come and go. An investment that was safe under one government might become the target for a takeover under another. Further, the possibility of foreign exchange controls and tax rate changes can reduce the chance of getting profits and capital back to the home country.

Because the risks are hard to judge, it may be wise to enter international marketing by exporting first—building know-how and confidence over time. Experience and judgment are needed even more in unfamiliar areas. Allowing time to develop these skills among a firm's top management—as well as its international managers—makes sense. Then the firm will be in a better position to estimate the prospects—and risks—of going further into international markets.

INTERNATIONAL MARKETING REQUIRES EVEN MORE SEGMENTING

Success in international marketing requires even more attention to segmenting. There are over 140 nations—each with its own unique differences! There can be big differences in language, customs, beliefs, religion, race, and even income distribution patterns from one country to another. This obviously complicates the segmenting process. But what makes it even worse is that there is less good data as one moves into international markets. While the number of variables increases, the quantity and quality of data go down. This is one reason why some multinational firms insist that local operations be handled by natives. They at least have a "feel" for their markets.

There are more dimensions—but there is a way

Segmenting international markets may require more dimensions. But a practical method adds just one step before the seven-step approach discussed in Chapter 9. See Figure 20–6. First, segment by country or

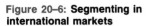

Figure 20–6: **Segmenting in
international markets**

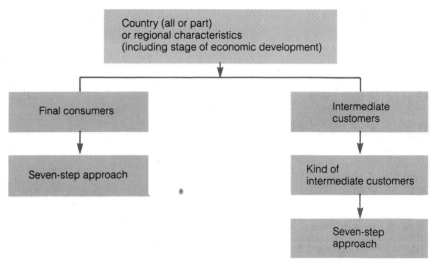

region—looking at demographic, cultural, and other characteristics—including stage of economic development. This may help find reasonably similar sub-markets. Then, depending upon whether the firm is aiming at final consumers or organizational customers, it could apply the seven-step approach discussed earlier.

Most of the discussion in the rest of this chapter will emphasize final consumer differences—because they are likely to be greater than organizational customer differences. Also, we will consider regional groupings and stages of economic development which can aid your segmentation efforts. Basically, our objective is to broaden your view of international markets.

REGIONAL GROUPINGS MAY MEAN MORE THAN NATIONAL BOUNDARIES

While national boundaries are a common and logical dimension for segmenting markets, sometimes it makes more sense to treat several nearby countries with similar cultures as one region. Or, if several nations have banded together to have common economic boundaries, then these nations may be treated as a unit. The outstanding example is the European Economic Community (EEC)—or Common Market. They have dared to abandon old ideas and nationalistic prejudices—in favor of cooperative efforts to reduce tariffs and other controls usually applied at national boundaries.

These cooperative arrangements are very important—because the taxes and restrictions at national borders can be not only annoying but may greatly reduce marketing opportunities. **Tariffs**—taxes on incoming goods—vary, depending on whether the country is trying to raise revenue or limit trade. Restrictive tariffs cause red-tape and discourage free movement of goods. Quotas act like restrictive tariffs. **Quotas** set the specific quantities of goods which can move in or out of a country. There might

Pre-industrial countries produce raw materials with outside technological help.

be great market opportunities abroad, but import quotas (or export controls applied against a specific country) may discourage outsiders from entering.

STAGES OF ECONOMIC DEVELOPMENT HELP DEFINE MARKETS

International markets are so varied that we can't make general rules for all of them. Some markets are more advanced and/or growing more rapidly than others. And some countries—or parts of a country—are at different stages of economic development. This means their demands—and even their marketing systems—will vary.

To get some idea of the many possible differences in potential markets, let's discuss six stages of economic development. These stages are over-simplified, of course. But they are helpful in understanding economic development—and how it affects marketing.[17]

Stage 1—agricultural self-supporting

In this stage, most people are subsistence farmers. There may be a simple marketing system—perhaps weekly markets—but most of the people are not even in a money economy. Some parts of Africa and New Guinea are in this stage. In a practical marketing sense, these people are not a market—they have no money to buy goods.

Stage 2–preindustrial or commercial

Some countries in Sub-Sahara Africa and the Middle East are in this second stage. During this stage, we see more market-oriented activity. Raw materials such as oil, tin, and copper are extracted and exported. Agricultural and forest crops such as sugar, rubber, and timber are grown and exported. Often this is done with the help of foreign technical skills and capital. A commercial economy may develop along with—but unrelated to—the subsistence economy. These activities may require the beginning of a transportation system—to open the extracting or growing areas to shipping points. A money economy operates at this stage.

In this stage, industrial machinery and equipment are imported. And huge construction projects may need many special supplies. Buying for these needs may be handled by purchasing agents in industrial countries. There is also the need for imports—including luxury goods—to meet the living standards of technical and supervisory people. These may be handled by company stores—rather than local retailers.

The relatively few large landowners and those who benefit by this business activity may develop expensive tastes. The few natives employed by these larger firms—and the small business managers who serve them—may develop into a small, middle-income class. But most of the population are still in the first stage—for practical purposes they are not in the market. This total market may be so small that local importers can easily handle the demand. There is little reason for local manufacturers to try to supply it.

Stage 3—primary manufacturing

In the third stage, there is some processing of metal ores or the agricultural products that once were shipped out of the country in raw form. Sugar and rubber, for example, are both produced and processed in Indonesia. The same is true for oil on the Persian Gulf. Multinational companies may set up factories to take advantage of low-cost labor. They may export most of the output—but they do stimulate local development. More local labor becomes involved at this stage. A domestic market develops. Small local businesses start to handle some of the raw material processing.

Even though the local market expands in this third stage, a large part of the population is still at the subsistence level—almost entirely outside the money economy. There may still be a large foreign population of professionals and technicians needed for the expanding agricultural-industrial complex. The demands of this group—and of the growing number of wealthy natives—are still quite different from the needs of the lower class and the growing middle class. A domestic market among the local people begins to develop. But there may not be enough demand to keep local manufacturers in business.

Stage 4—nondurable and semidurable consumer goods manufacturing

At this stage, small local manufacturing begins—especially in those lines that need only a small investment to get started. Often, these industries grow out of small firms that developed to supply the primary manufacturers dominating the last stage. For example, plants making sulfuric acid and explosives for extracting mineral resources might expand into soap manufacturing. And recently, multinational firms have speeded development of countries at this stage by investing in promising opportunities.

Paint, drug, food and beverage, and textile industries develop now. The textile industry is usually one of the first to develop. Clothing is a necessity. This early emphasis on the textile industry in developing nations is one reason the world textile market is so competitive.

Some of the small manufacturers become members of the middle- or even upper-income class. They help to expand the demand for imported goods. As this market grows, local manufacturers begin to see enough

Stage 6 countries have a large middle class and much purchasing power.

volume to operate profitably. So the need for imports to supply nondurable and semidurable goods is less. But consumer durables and capital goods are still imported.

Stage 5—capital goods and consumer durable goods manufacturing

In this stage, the production of capital goods and consumer durable goods begins. This includes automobiles, refrigerators, and machinery for local industries. Such manufacturing creates other demands—raw materials for the local factories, and food and fibers for clothing for the rural population entering the industrial labor force.

Industrialization has begun. But the economy still depends on exports of raw materials—either unprocessed or slightly processed.

It still may be necessary to import special heavy machinery and equipment at this stage. Imports of consumer durable goods may still compete with local products. The foreign community and the status-conscious wealthy may prefer these imports.

Stage 6—exporting manufactured products

Countries that have not gone beyond the fifth stage are mainly exporters of raw materials. They import manufactured goods and equipment—to build their industrial base. In the sixth stage, exporting manufactured goods becomes most important. The country may specialize in certain types of manufactured goods—such as iron and steel, watches, cameras, electronic equipment, or processed food.

There are many opportunities for importing and exporting at this stage. These countries have grown richer and have needs—and the purchasing power—for a great variety of products. In fact, countries in this stage often carry on a great deal of trade with each other. Each trades those goods in which it has production advantages. In this stage, almost all consumers are in the money economy. There may be a large middle-income class. North America, most of the Western European countries, and Japan are at this last stage.[18]

It is important to see that it is not necessary to label a whole country or geographic region as being in one stage. Certainly, different parts of

Stage 6 countries are attractive markets so there are many competitors.

Canada have developed differently—and could be placed in different stages.

HOW THESE STAGES CAN BE USEFUL IN FINDING MARKET OPPORTUNITIES

A good starting point for estimating present and future market potentials in a country—or part of a country—is to estimate its present stage of economic development and how fast it is moving to another stage. Actually, the speed of movement, if any, and the possibility that stages may be skipped may suggest whether market opportunities are there—or are likely to open. But just naming the present stage can be very useful in deciding what to look at—and whether there are prospects for the firm's products.

Fitting the firm to market needs

Manufacturers of automobiles, expensive cameras, or other consumer durable goods, for example, should not plan to set up a mass distribution system in a market that is in stage 2 (the preindustrial) or even in Stage 3 (the primary manufacturing stage). One or a few middlemen may be all that are needed. Even the market for Canadian "necessities"—items such as canned foods or drug products—may not yet be large. Large-scale selling of these consumer items requires a large base of cash or credit customers—but as yet too few are part of the money economy.

On the other hand, a market in the nondurable goods manufacturing stage has more potential—especially for durable goods producers. Incomes and the number of potential customers are growing. There is no local competition yet.

Opportunities might still be there for durable goods imports in the fifth stage—even though domestic producers are trying to get started. But more likely, the local government would raise some controls to aid local industry. Then the foreign producer might have to start licensing local producers—or building a local plant.

Pursuing that tempting inverted pyramid

Areas or countries in the final stage often are the biggest and most profitable markets. While there may be more competition, there are many more customers with higher incomes. We have already seen how income distribution shifted in Canada from a pyramid to more families with middle and upper incomes. This can be expected during the latter stages—when a "mass market" develops.

OTHER MARKET DIMENSIONS MAY SUGGEST OPPORTUNITIES, TOO

Considering country or regional differences—including stages of economic development—can be useful as a first step in segmenting international markets. After finding some possible areas (and eliminating less attractive ones) we must look at more specific market characteristics.

We discussed many potential dimensions in the Canadian market. It is impossible to cover all possible dimensions in all world markets. But, some of the ideas discussed for Canada certainly apply in other countries. So here, we will just outline some dimensions of international markets—and show some examples to emphasize that depending on half-truths about "foreigners" won't work in increasingly competitive international markets.[19]

The number of people in our world is staggering

Although our cities may seem crowded with people, the over 220 million population of the United States is less than 5 percent of the world's population—which is over 4 billion.

Numbers are important

Instead of a boring breakdown of population statistics, let's look at a map showing area in proportion to population. Figure 20–7 makes Canada

Figure 20–7: Map of the world showing area in proportion to population[20]

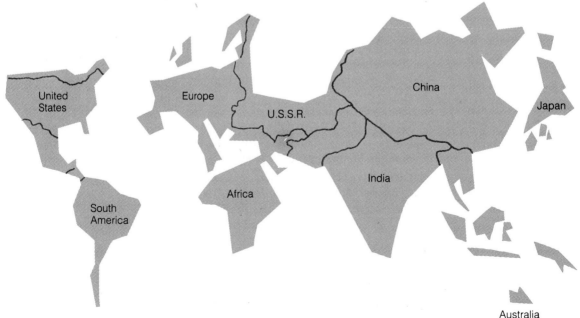

look unimportant because of our small population in relation to land area. This is also true of Latin America and Africa. In contrast, Western Europe is much larger—and the Far Eastern countries are even bigger.

But people are not spread out evenly

People everywhere are moving off the farm into industrial and urban areas. Shifts in population—combined with already dense populations—have led to extreme crowding in some parts of the world.

Figure 20–8 shows a map of the world emphasizing density of population. The darkest shading shows areas with more than 250 persons per square mile.

Developing interurbias in Canada show up clearly as densely populated areas. Similar areas are found in Western Europe, along the Nile River Valley in Egypt, and in many parts of Asia. In contrast, many parts of the world (like our western plains and mountain provinces) have few people.

Population densities are likely to increase in the near future. Birth rates in most parts of the world are high—higher in Africa, Latin America, Asia, and Oceania than in Canada and the United States—and death rates are declining as modern medicine is more widely accepted. Generally, population growth is expected in most countries. But the big questions are: How rapidly? *and* Will output increase faster than population? This is important to marketers because it affects how rapidly some economies move to

Figure 20–8: Map of the world emphasizing density of population[21]

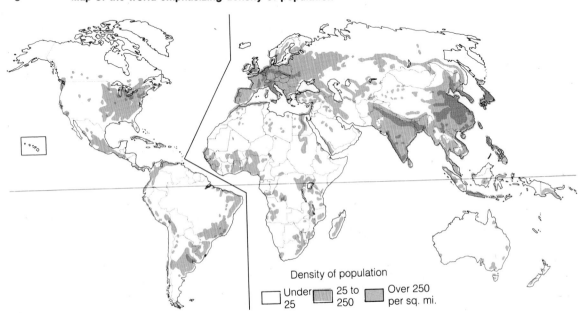

Density of population

Under 25 | 25 to 250 | Over 250 per sq. mi.

higher stages of development and become new markets for different kinds of products.

You must sell where the income is

Profitable markets require income as well as people. The best available measure of income in most countries is **gross national product (GNP)**—the total market value of goods and services produced in a year. Unfortunately, this may not give a true picture of consumer well-being in many countries—because the methods commonly used for figuring GNP may not be comparable for very different cultures and economies. For instance, do-it-yourself activities, household services, and the growing of produce or meat by family members for their own use are not usually figured as part of GNP. Since the activities of self-sufficient family units are not included, GNP can give a false picture of economic well-being in less-developed countries.

Gross national product, though, is a useful and sometimes the only available measure of market potential in many countries. Table 20–2 shows the population and GNP of major regions of the world—except the USSR and mainland China. You can see that the more developed industrial regions have the biggest share of the world's GNP. This is why so much trade takes place between these countries—and why many companies see them as the more important markets.

Income per person— useful to a point

GNP per person is a commonly available figure—but it can give a mistaken view of market potential. When GNP per person is used for comparison, we assume that the wealth of each country is distributed evenly among all consumers. However, this is seldom true. In a developing economy, 75 percent of the population may be on farms and receive 25 percent or less of the income.[22] And there may be unequal distribution along class or racial lines. In South Africa, for example, the average family income in 1970 for whites was $5,830, for Asians $2,352, for mulattos $1,411, and for blacks $538.[23]

To provide some examples, the GNP per person for several countries is shown in Table 20–3. The range is wide, from $95 (in U.S. dollars) per person per year in Ethiopia to $20,945 in the United Arab Emirates.

Table 20–2: Population and gross national product of major geographic regions of the world[24]

Region	Population (millions)	GNP ($ billions)
North America	240	2,089
Latin America	342	429
Europe*	478	2,024
Africa	431	242
South and East Asia†	1,505	1,277
Oceania	22	120
Totals	3,017	6,181

* Except USSR.
† Except China.

Table 20–3: Gross national product per capita for major regions of the world and selected countries (in 1977 U.S. dollars)[25]

	GNP/capita for countries	GNP/capita for regions		GNP/capita for countries	GNP/capita for regions
North America		$8,720	Africa		560
United States	$ 8,731		Algeria	1,102	
Canada	8,573		Egypt	485	
Latin America		1,320	Ethiopia	95	
Argentina	1,351		Kenya	320	
Brazil	1,463		Nigeria	479	
Haiti	284		South Africa	1,427	
Mexico	1,172		Rwanda	176	
Europe		5,850	South and East Asia		780
United Kingdom	4,430		India	163	
France	7,191		Pakistan	232	
West Germany	8,396		Japan	6,094	
Italy	3,813		Indonesia	318	
Sweden	9,490		Oceania		5,470
Portugal	1,671		Australia	7,132	
Near East		2,170	New Zealand	4,781	
Israel	4,073				
United Arab Emirates	20,945				

A business, and a human opportunity

You can see that much of the world's population lives in extreme poverty. Many of these countries are in the early stages of economic development. Large parts of their population work on farms—and live barely within the money economy.

These people, however, have needs. And many are eager to improve themselves. But they may not be able to raise their living standards without outside help. This presents a challenge—and an opportunity—to the developed nations—and to their business firms.

Some companies—including Canadian firms—are trying to help the people of developing countries. Corporations such as Pillsbury, Corn Products, Monsanto, and Coca-Cola have developed nutritious foods that can be sold cheaply—but still profitably—in poorer countries. One firm sells a milk-based drink (Samson)—with 10 grams of protein—to the Middle East and the Caribbean areas. Such a drink can make an important addition to diets. Poor people in developing lands usually get only 8–12 grams of protein per day in their normal diet. Sixty to 75 grams are considered necessary for an adult.[26]

Reading, writing, and marketing problems

The ability of a country's people to read and write has a direct influence on the development of the economy—and on marketing strategy planning. Certainly, the degree of literacy affects the way information is delivered—which in marketing means promotion.

Literacy studies show that only about two thirds of the world's population can read and write.[27]

Low literacy sometimes causes difficulties with product labels and with instructions—for which we normally use words. In highly illiterate countries, some manufacturers have found that placing a baby's picture on food packages is unwise. Illiterate natives believe that the product is just that—a ground-up baby! Singer Sewing Machine Co. met this lack of literacy with an instruction book that used no words.[28]

Even in Latin America—which has generally higher literacy rates than Africa or Asia—a large number of people cannot read and write. Marketers have to use symbols, colors, and other nonverbal means of communication if they want to reach the masses.

CAREFUL MARKET ANALYSIS IS BASIC

The opportunities in international marketing are exciting. But market differences present a real challenge to target marketers. Careful market analysis is especially important since there often are fine points that are easy to miss.

What are you drinking?

Tastes do differ across national boundaries. French Burgundy wine going to Belgium must have a higher sugar content than the Burgundy staying in France. Burgundy going to Sweden must have still another sugar content to be sold successfully there.

Milk-drinking habits also differ greatly. Scandinavians consider milk a daily staple—while Latins feel that milk is only for children. A former French premier was able to get his picture on the front page of every Paris newspaper simply by drinking a glass of milk in public.

Who wears the makeup in France?

The great variety of international markets almost demands marketing research to learn the habits and attitudes of the many possible target markets.

The need for research to avoid common stereotypes is emphasized by the following results from a large-scale survey of European Common Market adults:

> The average Frenchman uses almost twice as many cosmetics and beauty aids as his wife.
> The Germans and the French buy more packaged spaghetti than the Italians.
> French and Italian housewives are not as interested in cooking as their counterparts in Luxembourg and Belgium.[29]

CONCLUSION

The international market is large—and keeps growing in population and income. Many North American companies are becoming aware of the enormous opportunities open to alert and aggressive businesses.

The great variations in stages of economic development, income, population, literacy, and other factors, however, mean that foreign markets must be treated as many separate target markets—and studied carefully. Lumping foreign nations together under the vague heading of "foreigners"—or, at the other extreme, assuming that they are just like Canadian customers—is almost a guarantee of failure. So is treating them like common Hollywood stereotypes.

Involvement in international marketing usually begins with exporting. Then a firm may become involved in joint ventures or wholly owned subsidiaries in several countries. Companies that become this involved are called multinational corporations. Some of these corporations have a global outlook—and are willing to move across national boundaries as easily as our national firms move across state boundaries.

Much of what we have said about strategy planning throughout the text applies directly in international marketing. Sometimes Product adaptions or changes are needed. Promotion messages must be translated into the local languages. And, of course, new Place arrangements and Prices are needed. But blending the four Ps still requires a knowledge of the all-important customer.

The major "roadblock" to success in international marketing is an unwillingness to learn about—and adjust to—different people and cultures. To those who are willing to make these adjustments, the returns can be great.

QUESTIONS FOR DISCUSSION

1. Discuss the "typical" evolution of corporate involvement in international marketing. What impact would a wholehearted acceptance of the marketing concept have on this evolutionary process?

2. Distinguish between licensing and contract manufacturing in a foreign country.

3. Distinguish between joint ventures and wholly owned subsidiaries.

4. Discuss the long-run prospects for (a) multinational marketing by Canadian firms producing in Canada only, and (b) multinational firms willing to operate anywhere.

5. Discuss how a manufacturer interested in finding new international marketing opportunities might organize its search process. What kinds of opportunities would it look for first, second, and so on?

6. Discuss how the approaches to market segmenting (which were described in Chapter 9) might have to be modified when one moves into international markets.

7. Discuss the prospects for a Latin American entrepreneur who is considering building a factory to produce machines that would manufacture cans for the food industry. His country happens to be in stage 4—the nondurable and semidurable consumer goods manufacturing stage. The country's population is approximately 20 million and there is some possibility of establishing sales contacts in a few nearby countries.

8. Discuss the value of gross national product per capita as a measure of market potential. Refer to specific data in your answer.

9. Discuss the possibility of a multinational marketer using essentially the same promotion campaign in Canada and in many international markets.

10. Discuss the kinds of products you feel may become popular in Europe in the near future. Does the material on Canadian consumption behavior, discussed earlier in the text, have any relevance here?

11. Discuss the importance of careful target marketing within the European Common Market.

SUGGESTED CASES

30. Canadian Foods, Limited

31. Modern Homes, Ltd.

32. The Adanac Manufacturing Company

When you finish this chapter, you should:

1. Understand why marketing must be evaluated differently at the micro and macro levels.

2. Understand why the text argues that micro-marketing costs too much.

3. Understand why the text argues that macro-marketing does not cost too much.

4. Know some of the challenges facing marketers in the future.

MARKETING IN A CONSUMER-ORIENTED SOCIETY: APPRAISAL AND CHALLENGES

21

Does marketing cost too much?

Does marketing cost too much? This is a basic question. Many people feel strongly that marketing *does* cost too much—that it is a waste of resources which would be better used elsewhere.

Your answer to this basic question is important. Your own business career—and the economy in which you will live—will be affected by your answer.

While we have talked about what marketing is, we also have mentioned criticisms of marketing—and the possible effects of business practices on consumer welfare. But we have *not* tried to answer this basic question of whether marketing costs too much. We felt you needed background before you could answer that question. Now let's talk about it—and then go on to discuss challenges facing marketers.

MARKETING MUST BE EVALUATED AT TWO LEVELS

As we saw in Chapter 1, it is useful to talk about marketing at two levels: the micro level (how individual firms run) and the macro level (how the whole system works). Some complaints against marketing are aimed

Customer satisfaction is the objective of the Canadian macro-marketing system.

at only one of these levels. In other cases, the criticism *seems* to be directed at one level, but actually it is aimed at the other. Some critics of specific ads, for example, probably would not be satisfied with *any* advertising. When evaluating marketing, we have to treat each of these levels separately.

HOW SHOULD MARKETING BE EVALUATED?

Different nations have different social and economic objectives. Dictatorships, for example, may be concerned mainly with satisfying the needs of the people at the top. In a socialist state, the objective is to satisfy the needs of the people—as defined by social planners.

Therefore, the effectiveness of any nation's marketing system can only be judged in terms of that nation's objectives.

Consumer satisfaction is basic in Canada

The aim of our economic system has been to satisfy consumer needs as they—the consumers—see them. This is no place for a long discussion of the value of this objective. Our democratic political process is where such matters get settled.

Therefore, we will be concerned with evaluating marketing in the Canadian economy where the objective is to satisfy consumer needs—*as consumers see them.* This is the base of our system—and the business firm that ignores this fact is in for trouble.

CAN CONSUMER SATISFACTION BE MEASURED?

Since satisfaction of consumers is our goal, marketing must be measured by how *well* it satisfies them. Unfortunately, however, consumer satisfaction is hard to define—and harder to measure.

Measuring macro-marketing isn't easy

Economists believe that consumer satisfaction comes from economic utility—remember form, time, place, and possession utility. However, no practical method of measuring utility has yet been developed. This is in part because satisfaction seems to depend upon each person's own view of things. Further, products that were satisfactory one day may be unsatisfactory the next day—and vice versa. Thus, consumer satisfaction is a very personal concept which does not provide a very good standard for evaluating marketing effectiveness. The final measure, probably, is whether the macro-marketing system satisfies enough individual consumer/citizens so that they vote—at the ballot box—to keep it running. So far, we have done so in Canada.

There are ways to measure micro-marketing

Measuring micro-marketing effectiveness is also difficult. But there are ways that individual business firms can measure how well their products satisfy their customers. These methods include attitude studies, analysis of consumer complaints, opinions of middlemen and salespeople, market test results, and profits.[1]

Since every company uses slightly different marketing strategies, it is up to each customer to decide how well individual firms satisfy his or her needs. Generally speaking, customers are willing to pay higher prices to buy more of those goods which satisfy them. So, profits can be used as a rough measure of a firm's success in satisfying customers. In this sense, a firm's own interests and society's interests are the same.

Evaluating marketing effectiveness is difficult—but not impossible

In view of the difficulty of measuring consumer satisfaction—and, therefore, the effectiveness of marketing—it is easy to see why there are different views on the subject. If the objective of the economy is clearly defined, however, the question of marketing effectiveness probably *can* be answered.

In this chapter, we will argue that micro-marketing (how *individual* firms and channels operate) often *does* cost too much. But we will argue, too, that macro-marketing (how the *whole* marketing system operates) does *not* cost too much—given the present objective of the Canadian economy—consumer satisfaction. In the end, you will have to make your own decision.[2]

MICRO-MARKETING OFTEN *DOES* COST TOO MUCH

Throughout the text we have talked about what marketing managers could or should do to help their firms do a better job of satisfying customers—and achieving company objectives. While many firms carry out very successful marketing programs, many more firms are still too production-oriented and inefficient. It is plain that many consumers are not happy with the marketing efforts of some firms. A recent study showed that "helping consumers get a fair deal when shopping" ranked very high among public concerns. Only inflation, unemployment, government spending, welfare, and taxes were ranked higher.[3]

Companies are likely to fail if they ignore their customers' needs or the environment they sell in.

The failure rate is high

Further evidence that most firms are too production-oriented—and not nearly as efficient as they could be—is the fact that most new products fail. New and old businesses fail regularly, too. These failures are caused by one or more of three reasons:

1. Lack of interest in—or understanding of—the customer.
2. Improper blending of the four Ps—because of a lack of a customer orientation.
3. Lack of understanding of—or adjustment to—uncontrollable variables.[4]

The company can get in the way of the customer

Serving the customer should be the goal of business—but some producers seem to feel that customers are eagerly waiting for any product they turn out. They don't understand a business as a "total system" responsible for satisfying customer needs.

Middlemen, too, often get tied up in their own internal problems. Goods may be stocked where it is convenient for the retailer to handle them—rather than for consumers to find them. And fast-moving, hard-to-handle goods may not be stocked at all—because "they are too much trouble" or "we're always running out."

In the same way, accounting or financial departments in all kinds of businesses may try to cut costs by encouraging the production of standardized products—even though this may not be what customers want.

Company objectives may force higher-cost operation

Top management decisions on company objectives may increase the cost of marketing. A decision to aim for growth for growth's sake, for example, might mean too much spending for Promotion. Or diversification for diversification's sake could require the development of expensive new Place arrangements.

For these reasons, the marketing manager should take a big part in shaping the firm's objectives. Recognizing the importance of marketing, progessive firms have given marketing management more control in determining company objectives. Unfortunately, though, in many more firms, marketing is still looked upon as the department that "gets rid of" the product.

Micro-marketing does cost too much—but things are changing

Marketing *does* cost too much in many firms. The marketing concept has not really been applied in very many places. Sometimes, sales managers are renamed "marketing managers," and vice presidents of sales are called "vice presidents of marketing"—but nothing else changes. Marketing mixes are still put together by production-oriented people in the same old ways. The customer is considered last—if at all.

But not all business firms are so old-fashioned. More firms are becoming customer-oriented. And some are paying more attention to strategic planning—to better carry out the marketing concept.

One hopeful sign is the end of the idea that practically anybody can run a business successfully. This never was true. And today the growing complexity of business is drawing more and more professionals into business. This includes not only professional business managers, but psychologists, sociologists, statisticians, and economists.

Managers who adopt the marketing concept as a way of business life do a better job. As more of these professionals enter business, micro-marketing costs will go down.

MACRO-MARKETING DOES *NOT* COST TOO MUCH

Many critics of marketing take aim at the operation of the macro-marketing system. They suggest that advertising—and promotion in general—are socially undesirable. They feel that the macro-marketing system causes a poor distribution of resources, limits income and employment, and leads to an unfair distribution of income. Most of these complaints imply that

As more marketing professionals enter business, micro-marketing costs should come down.

some micro-marketing activities should not be allowed—and because of them our macro-marketing system does a poor job.

Many of these critics have their own version of the ideal way to run an economy. Some of the most severe critics of our marketing system are economists who use pure competition as their ideal. They would give consumers free choice in the market, but are critical of the way the present market operates. Meanwhile, other critics would scrap our market-directed system and substitute the decisions of central planners for those of individual producers and consumers—reducing freedom of choice in the marketplace. These viewpoints should be kept in mind when evaluating criticisms of marketing.

Is pure competition the ideal?

One criticism of our macro-marketing system is that it permits—or even encourages—the use of too many resources for marketing activities—and that this may actually reduce consumer "welfare." This argument is concerned with how the economy's resources (land, labor, and capital) are used for producing and distributing goods. These critics usually argue that scarce resources should be spent on *producing* goods—not on marketing them. The basis for this view is the idea that marketing activities are unnecessary—and don't provide any value. These critics feel that pure competition would result in the greatest consumer benefits.

In pure competition, you remember, we assume that consumers are "economic men," i.e., that they know all about available offerings—and will make "wise" choices. Economic analysis can be made to prove that pure competition will provide greater consumer welfare than monopolistic competition—*if all the conditions of pure competition are met.* But are they?

Our marketing system tries to satisfy different people's needs.

Different people want different things

First of all, we can say that our present knowledge of consumer behavior—and people's desire for different products—pretty well destroys the economists' "economic man" idea—and therefore, the pure competition ideal.[5] People, in fact, are different—and do want different products. With this type of demand (down-sloping demand curves), monopoly elements naturally develop. A pioneer in this kind of analysis concluded that "monopoly is necessarily a part of the welfare ideal."[6]

Once we admit that not all consumers know everything—and that they have many different demands—the need for a variety of micro-marketing activities becomes clear.

New ideas help the economy grow

Some critics feel that marketing helps create monopolistic competition—and that this leads to higher prices, limits production, and reduces national income and employment.

It is true that firms in a market-directed economy try to carve out separate markets for themselves with new products. But customers don't have to buy the new product unless they feel it is a better value. The old products are still available. The prices may even be lower on the old products—to meet the new competition.

Over several years, the profits of the innovator may rise—but the rising profits also encourage new ideas by competitors. This leads to new investments—which contribute to economic growth—raising the level of national income and employment.

Does marketing make people buy things they don't need?

It would seem that the individual firm's efforts to satisfy consumer needs would lead to a better division of national income. Giving customers what they want, after all, is the purpose of our market-directed economic system. However, some critics feel that most firms—especially large corporations—do not really try to satisfy the consumer. Instead, these critics argue, they use clever ads to persuade consumers to buy whatever the firms want to sell.

Historian Arnold Toynbee, for example, felt that American consumers have been manipulated into buying products which aren't necessary to satisfy "the minimum material requirements of life." Toynbee saw American firms as mainly trying to fulfill *unwanted demand*—demand created by advertising—rather than "genuine wants." He defined *genuine wants* as "wants that we become aware of spontaneously, without having to be told by Madison Avenue that we want something that we should never have thought of wanting if we had been left in peace to find out our wants for ourselves.[7]

What are the minimum requirements of life?

One problem with this kind of thinking is how to decide what *are* "the minimum material requirements of life." Which products that we use today

Consumers are problem-solvers and only buy what they want and/or need.

are unnecessary—and should be taken off the market? One writer has suggested, for example, that North Americans could and should do without items such as pets, newspaper comic strips, second family automobiles, motorcycles, snowmobiles, campers, recreational boats and planes, cigarettes, aerosol products, pop and beer cans, and hats.[8] You may agree with some of those, but who should decide "minimum material requirements of life" if not the consumers themselves?

Consumers are not puppets

The idea that firms can persuade consumers to buy anything the company decides to produce simply isn't true. A consumer who buys a can of soda pop that tastes terrible won't buy another can of that brand no matter how much it's advertised. In fact, *most* new products fail the test of the marketplace. Not even large corporations can be sure of success everytime they market a new product. Consider, for example, the dismal fate of products such as Ford's Edsel, DuPont's Corfam, Campbell's Red Kettle Soups, the "midi-skirts'" that the fashion industry tried to persuade women to wear back in the 1960s, or more recently, "light whisky."[9]

Needs and wants change

Consumer needs and wants are constantly changing. Few of us would care to live like our grandparents lived—let alone like the pioneers who traveled the rugged journey west in covered wagons. Marketing's job is not to satisfy consumer wants just for today. Rather, marketing must always *keep* looking for new—and better—ways to serve customers.[10]

Does marketing make people materialistic?

There is no doubt that our marketing system caters to materialistic values. But there is a lot of disagreement as to whether marketing creates these values—or just appeals to values that are already there.

Anthropologists tell us that—even in the most primitive societies—people decorate themselves with trinkets and want to accumulate possessions. In fact, in some tribal villages social status is measured in terms of how many goats or sheep a person owns. Surely the desire of ancient pharaohs and kings to surround themselves with wealth and treasures can hardly be blamed on the persuasive powers of the advertising agencies!

The idea that marketers create and serve *false tastes*—as defined by individual critics—has been rebutted by a well-known economist, George Stigler, who said:

> The marketplace responds to the tastes of consumers with the goods and services that are salable, whether the tastes are elevated or depraved. It is unfair to criticize the marketplace for fulfilling these desires, when clearly the defects lie in the popular tastes themselves. I consider it a cowardly concession to a false extension of the idea of democracy to make sub rosa attacks on public tastes by denouncing the people who serve them. It is like blaming the waiters in restaurants for obesity.[11]

Marketing reflects our own values

The various experts who have studied the issue of materialism seem to agree that—in the short run—marketing reflects social values—while in the long run—it reinforces them. One expert pointed out that consumers vote for what they want in the marketplace *and* in the polling place. To say that what they want is *wrong* is to criticize the basic idea of free choice and democracy![12]

Products do improve the quality of life

More is not always better. The quality of life can't be measured only in terms of quantities of products. But when goods and services are seen as the means to an end—rather than the end itself—we can see that products do make it possible to achieve higher-level needs. Modern appliances, for example, have greatly reduced the amount of time and effort that must be spent on household duties—leaving homemakers with more time for other interests.

Consumers ask for it, consumers pay for it

The monopolistic competition typical of our economy is the result of customer demands—not control of markets by business. Monopolistic competition may seem expensive at times—when we look at individual firms—but it seems to work fairly well at the macro level, in serving the many needs and wants of consumers.

All these demands add to the cost of satisfying consumers. Certainly, the total cost is larger than it would be if simple, homogeneous products were offered at the factory door on a take-it-or-leave-it basis to long lines of customers.

If the role of the marketing system is to serve the consumer, however, then the cost of whatever services he demands can't be considered too expensive. It is just the cost of serving the consumer the way he wants to be served.[13]

Does macro-marketing cost enough?

The question, "Does marketing cost too much?" has been answered by one well-known financial expert with another question, "Does distribution cost enough?"[14] What he meant was that marketing is such an important part of our economic system that perhaps even more should be spent on it since "distribution is the delivery of a standard of living"—that is, the satisfaction of consumers' basic needs and wants. In this sense, then, macro-marketing does not cost too much. If these micro-level activities are improved, the performance of the macro system probably will improve. But, regardless, our macro-marketing system performs a vital role in our economic system—and _does not cost too much_.

CHALLENGES FACING MARKETERS

We have said that our macro-marketing system does _not_ cost too much—given the present objective of our economy—while admitting that the performance of many business firms leaves a lot to be desired. This presents a challenge to serious-minded students and marketers. What needs to be done—if anything?

We need better performance at the micro level

Some business managers seem to feel that in a market-directed economy they should be completely "free." They don't understand the idea that our system is a market-directed system—and that the needs of consumer/citizens must be met. Instead, they focus on their own internal problems—without satisfying consumers very well.

We need better planning

Most firms are still production-oriented. Some hardly plan at all. Others just extend this year's plans into next year. Progressive firms are beginning

Micro-marketers need to study consumers' needs more carefully.

Figure 21–1: Typical changes in marketing variables over the course of the product life cycle

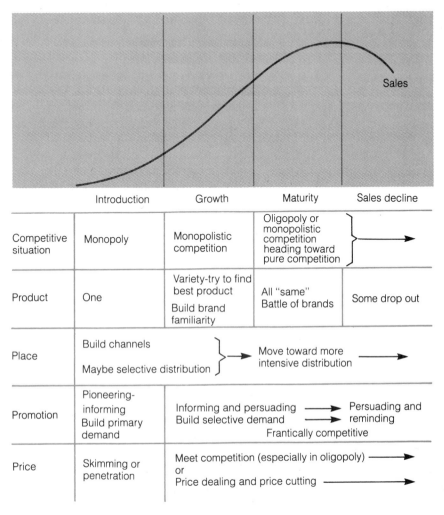

	Introduction	Growth	Maturity	Sales decline
Competitive situation	Monopoly	Monopolistic competition	Oligopoly or monopolistic competition heading toward pure competition } →	
Product	One	Variety-try to find best product Build brand familiarity	All "same" Battle of brands	Some drop out
Place	Build channels Maybe selective distribution } →		Move toward more intensive distribution →	
Promotion	Pioneering-informing Build primary demand	Informing and persuading → Persuading and Build selective demand → reminding Frantically competitive		
Price	Skimming or penetration	Meet competition (especially in oligopoly) → or Price dealing and price cutting →		

to realize that this doesn't work in our changing marketplaces. Strategy planning is becoming more important in many companies. More attention is being given to the product life cycle—because marketing variables should change through the product's life cycle.[15]

Figure 21–1 shows some of the typical changes in marketing variables which might be needed over the course of a product life cycle. This figure should be a good review—but it also should emphasize why much better planning is needed. As the product life cycle moves on, the marketing manager should *expect* to find more products entering "his" market—and pushing the market closer to pure competition or oligopoly. This means that as the cycle moves along, he might want to shift from a selective to an intensive distribution policy *and* move from a skimming to a penetration pricing policy. And the original strategic plan might include these adjustments—and the probable timing.

May need more social responsiveness

A smart business manager would put himself in the consumer's place. This would mean developing more satisfying marketing mixes for specific target markets. This may mean building in more quality or safety. And the consumers' long-run satisfaction should be considered, too. How will the product hold up in use? How will it be kept operating?

It seems doubtful that production-oriented methods will work in the future. Tougher competition—and more watchful government agencies—may force the typical production-oriented business manager to change. Many of the concerns of the consumerism movement are caused by the failure of businesses to put the marketing concept into practice. This has to change.

May need more environmental concern

Besides satisfying consumers' needs, marketers have to be aware of environmental problems. A lack of understanding of uncontrollable variables—and a failure to recognize new environmental trends—could be major causes of marketing failure in the future. Conditions around the world are changing rapidly. Marketing managers must try to anticipate the economic opportunities that every new human problem offers—while at the same time trying to see the social-political problems which are part of every new opportunity.[16] An understanding of new developments may help the firm avoid expensive mistakes—and see new opportunities.

We need better performance at the macro level

One of the advantages of a market-directed economic system is that its operation is relatively automatic. But in our version of this system, consumer/citizens provide limits (laws). These laws can be strengthened—or modified—at any time.

Need tougher enforcement of present laws

Before piling on too many new laws, however, it probably would be wise to really enforce the ones we have. The antimonopoly laws, for exam-

Marketing managers must be aware of environmental concerns.

ple, have often been used to protect competitors from each other—when they really were intended to protect competition.

Laws should affect top management

The results of strict enforcement of present laws could be far-reaching if more price fixers, dishonest advertisers, and others who are obviously breaking the laws were sent to jail—or given heavy fines. A quick change in attitudes might occur if top managers—who plan overall business strategy—were prosecuted, rather than the salespersons or advertisers who are expected to "deliver" on weak strategies.

In other words, if the government made it clear that it was serious about improving the performance of our economic system, a lot could be achieved within the present system—without adding new laws or trying to "patch up" the present ones.

Need better-informed consumers

We may need some changes to help customers become better informed about the many goods and services on the market. Laws to assure consumers that they will have ways for comparing products—for example, life expectancy of light bulbs and appliances—would be helpful. Consumer education programs designed to teach people how to buy more wisely could be helpful too.

Need socially responsible consumers

We have been stressing the obligation of producers to act responsibly, but consumers have responsibilities too. Some consumers abuse returned-goods policies, change price tags in self-service stores, expect attractive surroundings and courteous sales and service people, but want discount prices. Others think nothing of "ripping off" businesses.

Canadians tend to perform their dual role of consumer/citizens with something of a split personality. We often behave one way as consumers—and then take the opposite stand at the ballot box. For example, while our beaches and parks are covered with litter, we call for stiff action to curb pollution. We protest sex and violence in the media—and then flock to see R- or X-rated movies. We complain about high energy costs—and then purchase low-efficiency appliances.

Consumer advocates have stressed the need for business firms to use social responsibility in the marketplace. They have said almost nothing, however, about the need for consumers to behave responsibly.[17]

Let's face it. There is a lot of information already available to improve consumer decision making. The consumerism movement has encouraged nutritional labeling, unit pricing, truth-in-lending, plain language contracts and warranties, and so on. And, government agencies publish many consumer buying guides—as do groups like The Consumers' Association of Canada. But most consumers continue to ignore this information!

We may need to modify our macro-marketing system

Our macro-marketing system is built on the idea that we are trying to satisfy consumers. But with resource shortages and rising energy costs, how far should the marketing concept be allowed to go? Should consumers be treated as kings and queens?

Should marketing managers limit consumers' freedom of choice?

A "better" macro-marketing system is certainly a good idea, but an important question is what should marketers do—in their roles as producers? Should they, for example, deliberately refuse to produce "energy-gobbling" appliances or cars that consumers demand? Or should they be expected to install devices which will increase costs—and which are very definitely *not* wanted by potential customers—like seat belts with buzzer systems?

Consumer/citizens should vote on the changes

Marketing managers should be expected to improve and expand the range of goods and services they make available to consumers—always trying to satisfy the needs and wants of potential customers. This is the job which has been assigned to business.

If this objective makes "excessive" demands on scarce resources—or causes an "intolerable" level of ecological damage—then consumer/citizens have every right to vote for laws to limit individual firms. These firms can't be expected to fully understand the impact of all their actions.

Consumers are not consistent in what they say they want and what they buy.

This is the role which we as consumers have assigned to the government—to make sure that the macro-marketing system works effectively.

It is important to see that some critics of marketing are really interested in *basic* changes in our macro-marketing system. And, some major changes might be accomplished by what seem like minor modifications in our present system. Allowing some government agency, such as Consumer and Corporate Affairs Canada, to ban the sale of products for seemingly good reasons may severely limit our choices in ways we never intended. (Bicycles, for example, are very dangerous consumer products—perhaps they should not be sold!) Clearly, such government actions could seriously reduce consumers' present right to freedom of choice—including "bad" choices.[18]

Consumer/citizens have to be careful to see the difference between changes designed just to modify our system and those designed to change it—perhaps completely. In either case, the consumer/citizen should make the decision (through elected representatives). This decision should not be left in the hands of a few well-placed producers' representatives—even if they are marketing managers—or government planners.

Marketing people may be even more necessary in the future

No matter what changes might be voted by consumer/citizens, some kind of a marketing system will be needed. And market-oriented business managers probably would be needed to help define and satisfy any "new needs." In fact, if satisfying more subtle needs—such as the "good life"—becomes the goal, it could be even more necessary to have market-oriented firms. It may be necessary, for example, not only to define individuals' needs, but also society's needs—for a "better neighborhood" or "more enriching social experiences," and so on. As one goes beyond physical goods into more sophisticated need-satisfying blends of goods and services, the trial-and-error approach of the typical production-oriented manager will be even less acceptable.

CONCLUSION

Macro-marketing does not cost too much. Business firms have been assigned the role—by consumers—of satisfying their needs. Customers find it satisfactory—even desirable—to permit businesses to cater to them. As long as consumers are satisfied, macro-marketing will not cost too much—and business firms will be allowed to continue as profit-making groups. It must always be remembered that business exists at the consumers' approval. It is only by satisfying the consumer that a particular business firm—and our economic system—can justify their existence and hope to keep operating.

In carrying out this role granted by consumers, the activities of business firms are not always as effective as they might be. Many business managers do not understand the marketing concept—or the role that marketing plays in our way of life. They seem to feel that business has a God-given right to operate as it chooses. And they proceed in their typical production-oriented ways. Further, many managers have had little or no training in business management—and are not as competent as they should be. In this sense, micro-marketing does cost too much. The situation is being improved, however, as training for business expands—and as more competent people are attracted to marketing and business generally. Clearly, *you* have a role to play in improving marketing in the future.

Marketing has new challenges to face in the future. All consumers may have to settle for a lower standard of living. Resource shortages, rising energy costs, and slowing population growth may all combine to reduce income growth. This may force consumers to shift their consumption patterns—and politicians to change some of the rules governing business. Even our present market-directed system may be threatened.

To keep our system working effectively, individual business firms should try to be more efficient and socially responsible—as they carry out the marketing concept. At the same time, individual consumers have the responsibility to use goods and services in an intelligent and socially responsible manner. Further, they have the responsibility to vote—to make sure that they get the kind of macro-marketing system they want. What kind do you want? What can and should you do to see that fellow consumer/citizens will vote for your system? Is your system likely to satisfy you, personally, as well as another macro-marketing system? You don't have to answer these questions right now, but your answers will affect the future in which you will live—as well as how satisfied you will be.

QUESTIONS FOR DISCUSSION

1. Explain why marketing must be evaluated at two levels. Also, explain what criteria you feel should be used for evaluating each level of marketing, and defend your answer. Explain why your criteria are "better" than alternative criteria.

2. Discuss the merits of various economic system objectives. Is the objective of the Canadian economic system sensible? Do you feel more consumer satisfaction might be achieved by permitting some sociologists or some public officials to determine how the needs of the lower-income or less-educated members of the society should be satisfied? If you approve of this latter suggestion, what education or income level should be required before an individual is granted free choice by the social planners?

3. Should the goal of our economy be maximum efficiency? If your answer is yes, efficiency in what? If not, what should the goal be?

4. Cite an example of a critic using his own value system when evaluating marketing.

5. Discuss the conflict of interests among production, finance, accounting, and marketing executives. How does this conflict contribute to the operation of an individual business? Of the economic system? Why does this conflict exist?

6. Why does the text indicate that the adoption of the marketing concept will encourage more efficient operation of an individual business? Be specific about the impact of the marketing concept on the various departments of a firm.

7. It appears that competition sometimes leads to inefficiency in the operation of the economic system in the short run. Many people argue for monopoly in order to eliminate this inefficiency. Discuss this solution to the problem of inefficiency.

8. How would officially granted monopolies affect the operation of our economic system? Specifically, consider the effect on allocation of resources, the level of income and employment, and the distribution of income. Is the effect any different than if a monopoly were obtained through winning out in a competitive market?

9. Is there any possibility of a pure-competition economy evolving naturally? Could legislation force a pure-competition economy?

10. Comment on the following statement: "Ultimately, the high cost of marketing is due only to consumers."

11. Should the consumer be king or queen? How should we decide this issue?

12. Should marketing managers, or business managers in general, be expected to refrain from producing profitable products that some target customers want but may not be in their long-run interest? Contrariwise, should firms be expected to produce "good" products that offer a lower rate of profitability than usual? What if only a break-even level were obtainable? What if the products were likely to be unprofitable, but the company was also producing other products which were profitable so that on balance it would still make some profit? What criteria are you using for each of your answers?

13. Should a marketing manager or a business refuse to produce an "energy-gobbling" appliance that some consumers are demanding? Similarly, should it install an expensive safety device that does not appear to be desired by potential customers and inevitably will increase costs? Are the same principles involved in both of these questions? Explain.

14. Discuss how much slower economic growth or even no economic growth would affect your college community, and in particular its marketing institutions.

SUGGESTED CASES

CASES

Guide to the use of these cases:

Cases can be used in many ways. And the same case may be fruitfully considered several times for different purposes.

"Suggested cases" are listed at the end of most chapters, but these cases could also be used later in the text. The main criterion for the order of these cases is the amount of technical vocabulary or text principles which are needed to read the case meaningfully. The first cases are "easiest" in this regard. This shows why an early case could easily be used two or three times—for different purposes. Some early cases might require some consideration of Price, for example, and might be used twice, say in regard to product planning and, later, pricing. But later cases which focus more on Price might be treated more effectively *after* the Price chapters have been covered.

1. Quenton, Limited

It is now 1973, and Mr. Donald Elsworth, newly elected president of Quenton, Ltd., is faced with some serious problems. Quenton, Ltd., is a 105-year-old Toronto-based food processor. Its multiproduct lines are widely accepted under the "Quenton" brand. The company and subsidiaries prepare, can, package, and sell canned and frozen foods. Beginning with beef, the company expanded to include fruits, vegetables, pickles and condiments, British Columbia salmon, and can manufacturing. Operating more than 27 processing plants in Canada, Quenton became one of the largest Canadian food processors—with annual sales (in 1972) of $348,065,000.

Until 1971, Quenton was a subsidiary of a major prairie meat-packing company, and many of the present managers came up through the meat-packing industry. Quenton's last president recently said: "Almeat's (the meat-packing firm) influence is still with us. Quenton has always been run like a meat-packer. As long as new products show a potential for an increase in the company's sales volume, they are produced. Traditionally there has been little, if any, attention paid to margins. We are well aware that profits will come through good products."

Warren Austin, a 25-year Quenton employee and now production manager, is in full agreement with the multiproduct-line policy. Mr. Austin said: "Volume comes from satisfying needs. We at Quenton will can, pack, or freeze any meat, vegetable, or fruit we think the consumer might want." He also admitted that much of the expansion in product lines was encouraged by economics. The typical plants in the industry are not fully used. By adding new products to use this excess capacity, costs are spread over greater volume. So the production department is always looking for new ways to make more effective use of its present facilities.

The wide expansion of product lines coupled with Quenton's line-forcing policy has resulted in 85 percent of Quenton's sales coming from supermarket chain stores—such as Dominion and Loblaws. Smaller stores are generally not willing to accept the Quenton policy—which requires that any store wanting to carry its brand name must be willing to carry the whole line of 68 varieties of fruits, vegetables, and meats. Mr. Austin explains, "We know that only large stores can afford to invest the amount of money in inventory that it would take to be adequately supplied with our products. But, the large stores are the volume! We give

consumers the choice of any Quenton product they want, and the result is maximum sales." Many small retailers have complained about Quenton's policy, but they have been considered to be too small in potential sales volume per store to be of any significance.

In 1973, a stockholders' revolt over low profits (in 1972, they were only $5,769) resulted in Quenton's president and two of its five directors being removed. Donald Elsworth, a lawyer who had been a staff assistant to the chairman of the board, was elected president. One of the first things he decided to focus on was the variable and low level of profits earned in the past several years. A comparison of Quenton's results with those of Canada Packers and some other large competitors supported Mr. Elsworth's concern. In the past ten years, Canada Packers had an average profit return on shareholder's investment of 10.8 percent, H. J. Heinz averaged 9 percent, Hunt Food 6 percent, and Quenton 3.8 percent. Further, Quenton's sales volume, $348,065,000 in 1972, had not increased much from the 1956 level of $325 million—while operating costs have soared upward. Profits for the firm were about $8 million in 1956. The closest they have come since then is about $6 million—in 1964.

In his last report to the Quenton board of directors, the outgoing president blamed his failure on an inefficient marketing department. He wrote, "Our marketing department has deteriorated. I can't exactly put my finger on it, but the overall quality of marketing people has dropped and morale is bad. The team just didn't perform." When Mr. Elsworth confronted Jack Grey—the vice president of marketing—with the previous statement, his reply was, "It's not our fault. I think the company made a key mistake after World War II. It expanded horizontally—by increasing its number of product offerings—while competitors like Canada Packers were expanding vertically, growing their own raw materials and making all of their packing materials. They can control quality and make profits in manufacturing which can be used in marketing. I lost some of my best people from frustration. We just aren't competitive enough to reach the market to the extent we should with a comparable product and price."

In further conversation with Grey, Mr. Elsworth learned more about the nature of Quenton's market. Although all the firms in the food-processing industry advertise widely to the consumer market, there has been no real increase in the size of the market for processed foods. Further, consumers aren't very selective. If they can't find the brand of food they are looking for, they'll pick up another brand rather than go without a basic part of their diet. No company in the industry has much effect on the price at which its products are sold. Chain store buyers are used to paying about the same price per case for any competitor's product—and won't exceed it. They will, however, charge any price they wish on a given brand sold at retail (i.e., a 48-can case of sweet peas might be purchased from any supplier for $6.83, no matter whose product it is. Generally, the shelf price for each is no more than a few pennies different, but chain stores occasionally attract customers by placing a well-known brand on "sale.")

At this point Mr. Elsworth is wondering why Quenton is not as profitable as it once was. Also, he is puzzled as to why the competition is putting products on the market with low potential sales volume. For example, one major competitor recently introduced a small line of dietary fruits and vegetables—with a potential sales volume so small that almost every nationally known food processor had previously avoided such specialization.

Discuss Quenton's policies and what it might do to improve its situation.

2. Tom's Cleaning Company

Tom Wills is a 26-year-old ex-Army man and a life-long resident of Brockville, Ontario—a beautiful summer resort area situated on the St. Lawrence in the Thousand Island region. The permanent population is about 20,000—and this more than trebles in the summer months.

Tom spent seven years in the Canadian Armed Forces after high school graduation, returning home in June 1977. Tom decided to go into business for himself, because he couldn't find a good job in the Brockville area. He set up Tom's Cleaning Company. Tom felt that his savings would allow him to start the business without borrowing any money. His estimates of required expenditures were: $3,900 for a used panel truck, $475 for a steam-cleaning machine adaptable to carpets and furniture, $330 for a heavy-duty commercial vacuum cleaner, $50 for special brushes and attachments, $75 for the initial supply of cleaning fluids and compounds, and $200 for insurance and other incidental expenses. This total of $5,030 still left Tom with about $2,800 in savings to cover living expenses while getting started.

One of the reasons Tom chose this line of work is his previous work experience. From the time he was 16, Tom had worked part time for Joel Bidwell. Mr. Bidwell operated the only other successful carpet-cleaning company in Brockville. (One other company was in Brockville, but rumors suggest it is near bankruptcy.)

Mr. Bidwell prides himself on quality work and has gained a loyal clientele. Specializing in residential carpet cleaning, Bidwell has been able to build a strong customer franchise. For 35 years, Bidwell's major source of new business has been retailer recommendations and satisfied customers who tell friends about the quality service received from Mr. Bidwell. He is so highly thought of that the leading carpet and furniture stores in Brockville always recommend Bidwell's for preventive maintenance in quality carpet and furniture care. Often Bidwell is trusted with the keys to Brockville's finest homes for months at a time—when owners are out of town and want his services. Bidwell's customers are so loyal, in fact, that a national household carpet-cleaning franchise found it next to impossible to compete with him. Even price cutting was not an effective weapon against Mr. Bidwell.

Tom Wills felt that he knew the business as well as Mr. Bidwell—having worked for him many years. Tom was anxious to reach his $20,000-per-year sales goal because he thought this would provide him with a comfortable living in Brockville. While aware of opportunities for carpet cleaning in businesses, office buildings, motels, and so on, Tom felt that the sales volume available there was only about $8,000 because most businesses had their own cleaning staffs. As he saw it, his only opportunity was direct competition with Bidwell.

To get started, he allocated $600 to advertise his business in the local newspaper. With this money he was able to purchase two half-page ads and have enough left over to buy daily three-line ads in the classified section, listed under Miscellaneous Residential

Services, for 52 weeks. All that was left was to paint a sign on his truck and wait for business to "catch on."

Tom had a few customers and was able to gross about $100 a week. He had, of course, expected much more. These customers were usually Bidwell regulars who, for one reason or another (usually stains, spills, or house guests), weren't able to wait the two weeks required until Bidwell could work them in. While these people did admit that Tom's work was of the same quality as Mr. Bidwell's, they preferred Bidwell's "quality-care" image. Sometimes, Tom did get more work than he could handle. This happened during April and May—when resort owners were preparing for summer openings and owners of summer homes were ready to "open the cottage." The same rush occurred in September and October—as resorts and homes were being closed for the winter. During these months, Tom was able to gross about $100–$120 a day—working ten hours.

Toward the end of his first year in business, Tom Wills began to have thoughts about quitting. While he hated to think of having to leave Brockville, he couldn't see any way of making a living in the carpet- and furniture-cleaning business in Brockville. Mr. Bidwell had the whole residential market sewed up—except in the rush seasons and for people who needed fast cleaning.

Why wasn't Tom able to reach his goal of $20,000? Is there any way Tom can stay in business?

---

3. Kemek Manufacturing Company

Kemek Manufacturing Co. is a large manufacturer of basic chemicals and polymer resins, located in Alberta.

John Gorman, a bright young engineer, has been working for Kemek as a research engineer in the polymer resins laboratory. His job is to do research on established resins—to find new, more profitable applications for resin products.

During the last five years, John has been under heavy pressure from top management to come up with an idea that would open up new markets for the company's foamed polystyrene.

Two years ago, John developed the "spiral-dome concept," a method of using the foamed polystyrene to make dome-shaped roofs and other structures. He described the procedure for making domes as follows:

The construction of a spiral dome involves the use of a specially designed machine which bends, places, and bonds pieces of plastic foam together into a predetermined dome shape. In forming a dome, the machine head is mounted on a boom, which swings around a pivot like the hands of a clock, laying and bonding layer upon layer of foam board in a rising spherical form.

According to John, polystyrene foamed boards have several advantages:

1. Foam board is stiff—but capable of controlled deformation—and can be bonded to itself by heat alone.

2. Foam board is extremely lightweight and easy to handle. It has good structural rigidity.

3. Foam board has excellent and permanent insulating characteristics. (In fact, the major use for foamed board is as an insulator.)

4. Foam board provides an excellent base on which to apply a variety of surface finishes.

With his fine speaking and reasoning abilities, John had little trouble convincing top management of the soundness of the idea.

According to a preliminary study by the marketing department, the following were areas of construction that could be served by the domes:

1. Bulk storage.
2. Cold storage.
3. Educational construction.
4. Industrial tanks (covers for).
5. Light commercial construction.
6. Planetariums.
7. Recreational construction (such as a golf-course starter house).

The study focused on uses for existing dome structures. Most of the existing domes are made of concrete or some cement base material. It was estimated that large savings would result from using foam boards—due to the reduction of construction time.

Because of the new technology involved, the company decided to do its own contracting (at least for the first four to five years after starting the sales program). It felt this was necessary to make sure that no mistakes were made by inexperienced contractor crews. For example, if not applied properly, the plastic may burn.

After building a few domes to demonstrate the concept, the company contacted some leading architects across the country. Reactions were as follows:

It is very interesting, but you know that the Fire Inspector of Toronto will never give his OK.

Your tests show that foamed domes can be protected against fires, but there are no *good* tests for unconventional building materials as far as I am concerned.

I like the idea, but foam board does not have the impact resistance of cement.

We design a lot of recreational facilities and kids will find a way of sawing holes into the foam.

Building codes around Vancouver are written for wood and cement structures. Maybe when the codes change.

After this unexpected reaction, management did not know what to do. John still thinks the company should go ahead. He feels that a few reports of well-constructed domes in leading newspapers would go a long way toward selling the idea.

What should Kemek do? Why did it get into the present situation?

---

4. Redi, Limited

Mr. Bob Wilson is the president and only stockholder of Redi, Limited, a small, successful firm in the restaurant and recreation business in the small town of Mackenzie—the site of a university (population 7,000 plus 20,000 students). Mr. Wilson attended the university in the 1930s—and paid most of his college expenses by selling refreshments at all of the school's athletic events. As he expanded his business, he hired local high school students to help him. The business became so profitable that Mr. Wilson decided to stay in Mackenzie after graduation—renting a small building near the campus and opening a restaurant.

Over the years, his restaurant business was fairly successful. Mr. Wilson earned a $36,000 profit on sales of $1,462,500 in 1975. The restaurant now consists of an attractive 40-table dining room, a large drive-in facility, and free delivery of orders to any point on the campus. The only thing that hasn't changed much is Mr. Wilson's customers. He estimates that his restaurant business is still over 90 percent students—and that over three fourths of his sales are made between 6 P.M. and 1 A.M. There are several other restaurants with comparable facilities near to the campus, but none of these is as popular with the university students as his "Papa Bob's."

As a result of the restaurant's success with the student market, Mr. Wilson has aimed his whole promotion effort in that direction—by advertising only through the campus newspaper and over the campus and local rock music radio stations. In an attempt to increase his daytime business, from time to time Mr. Wilson has used such devices as coupon mealbooks priced at 85 percent of face value. And he features daily "lunch special" plates. Nevertheless, he admits that he has been unable to compete with the university cafeterias for daytime business.

In 1972, when Mr. Wilson was seeking a new investment opportunity, he contacted a national manufacturer of bowling equipment and supplies about the feasibility of opening a bowling lanes operation. Mackenzie didn't have such a facility at the time, and Mr. Wilson felt that both the local and university communities would provide a good market. He already owned a large tract of land which would be suitable for construction of the bowling lanes. The land was next to the restaurant—and he felt that this would result in each business stimulating the other.

The decision was made to go ahead with the venture, and to date the results have been nothing short of outstanding. Several local and university groups have formed bowling leagues. The university's men's and women's physical education departments schedule several bowling classes at Mr. Wilson's bowling lanes each term. And the casual bowling in the late afternoons and evenings is such that at least 12 of the 16 lanes are almost always in use. Some local radio advertising is done for the bowling lanes, but Mr. Wilson doesn't feel that much is necessary. The success of the bowling lanes has encouraged the developer of a small shopping center in the residential part of town to make plans to include a similar facility in his new development. But Mr. Wilson believes that competition won't hurt his business, because he has more to offer in his recreation center—a restaurant and bowling.

Pleased with the profitability of his latest investment, Mr. Wilson decided to expand his recreational center even further. He noted that both students and local citizens patronized his bowling lanes and concluded that the addition of an attractive, modern billiard parlor would also have a common appeal. There were already two poolrooms in Mackenzie. One was modern—about two miles from campus. The other one was considered to be a "hangout" and was avoided by townspeople and students. Mr. Wilson decided that distance and atmosphere were the factors which resulted in both operations being only marginally successful. Further, he felt that by offering a billiard parlor operation, he would be able to supply yet another recreational demand of his market. He obtained a loan from a local bank and began to build a third building at the back of his land. The billiard parlor was outfitted with 12 tables, a snack bar, wall-to-wall carpeting, and a soft-music background system.

Today, eight months later, Mr. Wilson is extremely disappointed with the billiard parlor operation. After the first two or three weeks, business steadily dropped off until now usually one or two tables are in use—even during the evening hours when business at the bowling lanes is at its peak. Promotion for the billiard

parlor has been combined with promotions for the other facilities—which are still doing very well.

In an effort to discover what went wrong, Mr. Wilson interviewed several of his restaurant and bowling customers. Some typical responses were:

—a coed: "I had enough trouble learning how to bowl—but at least it's sociable. Pool looks hard and everyone is so serious."
—a fraternity man: "My idea of a good date is dinner at Papa Bob's, then the movies or an evening of bowling. You just can't make a good impression by taking a girl to play pool."
—a Mackenzie citizen: "I've never allowed my children to enter the local pool halls. What's more, as a kid I wasn't allowed either, and so I've never learned the game. It's too late to teach an old dog new tricks!"

Mr. Wilson is thinking about selling the billiard equipment and installing some pinball machines—because he has heard they can be very profitable.

Evaluate Mr. Wilson's overall position and suggest what should be done.

5. Laurentian Steel Company

Laurentian Steel Company is one of the two major producers of wide-flange beams in the Montreal area. The other major producer in the area is Quebec Steel Limited (QSL)—which is several times larger than Laurentian, as far as production capacity on this particular product is concerned.

Wide-flange beams are one of the principal steel products used in construction. They are the modern version of what are commonly known as "I-beams." QSL rolls a full range of wide flanges from 6 to 36 inches. Laurentian entered the field about 15 years ago—when it converted an existing mill to produce this product. This mill is limited to flanges up to 24 inches, however. At the time of the conversion, it was estimated that customer usage of sizes over 24 inches was likely to be small. In the past few years, however, there has been a definite trend toward the larger and heavier sections.

The beams produced by the various competitors are almost identical—since customers buy according to standard dimensional and physical-property specifications. In the smaller size range, there are a number of competitors, but above 14 inches only QSL and

Laurentian compete in the Montreal area. Above 24 inches, QSL has had no competition.

All the steel companies sell these beams through their own sales forces. The customer for these beams is called a "structural fabricator." This fabricator typically buys unshaped beams and other steel products from the mills and shapes them according to the specifications of his customer. The fabricator's customer is the contractor or owner of a particular building or structure which is being built.

The structural fabricator usually sells his product and services on a competitive-bid basis. The bidding is done on the basis of plans and specifications which are prepared by an architectural or structural engineering firm—and forwarded to him by the contractor wanting the bid. Although several hundred structural fabricators compete in the region, relatively few account for the majority of wide-flange tonnage. Since the price is the same from all producers, they typically buy beams on the basis of availability (i.e., availability to meet production schedules) and performance (reliability in meeting the promised delivery schedule).

Several years ago, Laurentian production schedulers saw that they were going to have an excess of hot-rolled plate capacity in the near future. At the same time, a new production technique was developed which would enable a steel company to weld three plates together into a section with the same dimensional and physical properties and almost the same cross section as a rolled wide-flange beam. This technical development appeared to offer two advantages to Laurentian: (1) it would enable Laurentian to use some of the excess plate capacity, and (2) larger sizes of wide-flange beams could be offered. Cost analysts showed that by using a fully depreciated plate mill and the new welding process it would be possible to produce and sell larger wide-flange beams at competitive prices, i.e., at the same price charged by QSL.

Laurentian's managers were excited about the possibilities—because customers usually appreciate having a second source of supply. Also, the new approach would allow the production of up to a 60-inch depth of section and an almost 30-inch width of flange. With a little imagination, these larger sizes could offer a significant breakthrough for the construction industry.

Laurentian decided to go ahead with the new project. As the production capacity was being converted, the salespeople were kept well informed of the progress. They, in turn, promoted this new capability—emphasizing that soon they would be able to offer a full range of beam products. Several general information letters were sent to the trade, but no advertising was used. Moreover, the market development section of the sales department was very busy explaining the new possibilities of the process—particularly to fabricators at engineering trade associations and shows.

When the new line was finally ready to go, the reaction was disappointing. In general, the customers were wary of the new product. The structural fabricators felt they could not use it without the approval of their customers—because it would involve deviating from the specified rolled sections. And, as long as they could still get the rolled section, why make the extra effort for something unfamiliar—especially with no price advantage. The salespeople were also bothered with a very common question: "How can you take plate which you sell for about $121 per ton and make a product which you can sell for $122?" This question came up frequently and tended to divert the whole discussion to the cost of production—rather than to the way the new product might be used.

Evaluate Laurentian's situation. What should it do to gain greater acceptance for its new product?

---

6. The Capri

The Capri is a fairly large restaurant—covering about 20,000 square feet of floor space—located in the center of a small shopping center which was completed early in 1971. In addition to this restaurant, other businesses in the shopping center include a bakery, a beauty shop, a liquor store, and a meat market. There is parking space for several cars in front of each of the stores.

The shopping center is located in a residential section of a growing suburb in Ontario—along a heavily traveled major traffic artery. The nearby population is middle-income families, and although the ethnic background of the residents is fairly heterogeneous, a large proportion are Italians.

The Capri—which sells mostly full-course dinners (no bar)—is operated by Lu DeLuca, a neat-appearing man who was born in the community in 1920, of Italian parentage. He graduated from a local high school and a nearby university and has been living in this town with his wife and two children for many years. He has been in the restaurant business (self-employed) since his graduation from college in 1945. His most recent venture—before opening this restaurant—was a large restaurant which he operated successfully with his brother from 1961 to 1967. In 1967, he sold out because of illness. Following his recovery, he was anxious for something to do and opened the present restaurant in April 1971.

Lu felt that his plans for the business and his opening were well thought out. He had even designed his very attractive sign three years before. When he was ready to go into this business, he looked at several possible locations before finally deciding on the present one. He said: "I looked everywhere, and this is one of the areas I inspected. I particularly noticed the heavy traffic when I first looked at it. This is the crossroads from north to south for practically every main artery province-wide. So obviously the potential is here."

Having decided upon the location, Lu attacked the problem of the new building with enthusiasm. He tiled the floor; put in walls of surfwood; installed new plumbing and electrical fixtures and an extra wash-room; and purchased the necessary restaurant equip-ment—all brand new. All this cost $32,000—which came from his own cash savings. He then spent an additional $600 for glassware, $1,500 for his initial food stock, and $675 to advertise his opening in the local newspaper. The local newspaper covered the whole metro area, so the $675 purchased only three quarter-page ads. These expenditures also came from his own personal savings. Next, he hired five waitresses, at $50 a week and one chef at $150 a week. Then, with $6,000 cash reserve for the business, he was ready to open. Reflecting his "sound business sense," Lu realized he would need a substantial cash reserve to fall back on until the business got on its own feet. He expected this to take about one year. He did not have any expectations about "getting rich overnight."

The business opened in April and by August had a weekly gross revenue of only $1,200. Lu was a little discouraged with this, but he was still able to meet all his operating expenses without investing any "new money" in the business. However, he was concerned that he might have to do so if business didn't pick up in the next couple of months. It had not by Septem-ber, and Lu did have to invest an additional $1,200 in the business "for survival purposes."

Business had not improved in November and Lu was still insisting that it would take at least a year to build up a business of this type. In view of the failure to "catch on rapidly," Lu stepped up his advertising to see if this would help the business any. In the last few weeks, he had spent $250 of his own cash for radio advertising—ten late evening spots on a news program at a station which aims at "middle-income America." Moreover, he was planning to spend even more during the next several weeks for some newspa-per ads.

By February 1972, business had picked up very slightly—about a $50 increase in the average weekly gross.

By April 1972, the situation had begun to improve and by June his weekly gross was up to between $1,700 and $1,800. By March in the following year, the weekly gross had risen to about $2,100. Lu in-creased the working hours of his staff six to seven hours a week—and added another cook to handle the increasing number of customers. Lu was more optimis-tic for the future because he was finally doing a little better than "breaking even." His full-time involvement seemed to be paying off. He had not put any new money into the business since the summer of 1972 and expected business to continue to rise. He had not yet taken any salary for himself, even though he had built up a small "surplus." Instead, he planned to put in an air-conditioning system at a cost of $5,-000—and was also planning to use what salary he would have taken for himself to hire two new wait-resses to handle his growing volume of business. And he saw that if business increased much more he would have to add another cook.

In explaining the successful survival and growth of his business, Lu said: "I had a lot of cash on hand, a well-planned program, and the patience to wait it out."

Evaluate Lu's marketing strategy. How might he have improved his chances for success and achieved more rapid growth?

7. Sleep-Inn Motel

After several years as a partner responsible for sales in a medium-sized manufacturing concern, in 1975 Phil Barnes sold his interest at a nice profit. Then, looking for an interesting opportunity that would be less demanding, he spent considerable time studying alternatives. He decided to purchase the Sleep-Inn—a recently completed 60-room motel at the edge of a small town in a relatively exclusive but rapidly ex-panding resort area. He saw a strong market potential for public accommodations. The location was also within one-half mile of an interstate highway. Fifteen miles away in the center of the tourist area were sev-eral nationally franchised full-service resort motels suitable for longer vacations.

He was able to hire the necessary staff—which ini-tially consisted of four maids and a handyman—to care for general maintenance. Mr. Barnes looked after reg-istration and office duties—assisted by his wife. Since he had traveled a lot himself and had stayed at many different hotels and motels, he had some definite ideas about what vacationers wanted in accommodations. He felt that a relatively plain but modern room with a comfortable bed, standard bath facilities, and air con-ditioning would appeal to most people.

He did not consider a swimming pool or any other nonrevenue-producing additions to be worthwhile—and considered a restaurant to be a greater management problem than the benefits it would offer. However, after many customers commented, he arranged to serve a continental breakfast of coffee and rolls from a service counter in a room next to the registration desk.

During the first year after opening, occupancy began to stabilize around 50–60 percent of capacity. According to figures which Mr. Barnes obtained from *Motel-Hotel Lodging,* published by the MacLean Hunter Ltd., his occupancy rate ranked much below the average for his classification—motels without restaurants.

Comparison of these results after two years of operation began to disturb Mr. Barnes. He decided to evaluate his operation and look for a way of increasing both occupancy rate and profitability. He did not want to give up his independence—and was trying not to compete directly with the resort areas offering much more complete services. Mr. Barnes stressed a price appeal in his signs and brochures. He was quite proud of the fact that he had been able to avoid all the "unnecessary expenses" of the resorts and was able to offer lodging at a very modest price—much below that

of even the lowest-priced resort. The customers who stayed at his motel said they found it quite acceptable, but he was troubled by what seemed to be a large number of cars driving into his parking lot, looking around, but not coming in to register.

Mr. Barnes was particularly interested in the results of a recent study by the regional tourist bureau. This study revealed the following information about area vacationers:

1. 68 percent of the visitors to the area are young couples and older couples without children.
2. 40 percent of the visitors plan their vacations and reserve rooms more than 60 days in advance.
3. 66 percent of the visitors stay more than three days in the area and at the same location.
4. 78 percent of the visitors indicated that recreational facilities were important in their choice of accommodations.
5. 13 percent of the visitors had family incomes of less than $7,500 per year.
6. 38 percent of the visitors indicated that it was their first visit to the area.

Evaluate Mr. Barnes' strategy. What should he do to improve the profitability of the motel?

---

8. Woodwards' Department Stores: Holiday Travel*

During the summer of 1977, executives of Woodwards, a multi-unit western Canadian department store chain with headquarters in Vancouver, had to decide about their involvement in the travel agency business. The decision boiled down to a choice between accepting an offer from Maple Leaf Travel Ltd. to operate agencies within Woodwards' stores as a licencee, or developing agencies owned and operated by the department store.

Woodwards had been founded in Vancouver in 1892 by Mr. C. W. Woodward. By 1977 the company had sales of over $653 million and profits of $8.3 million from 21 stores in British Columbia and Alberta. Woodwards served a wide cross section of the consumer population and, although there was variation from store to store, tended to be most attractive to the middle socioeconomic market.

Holiday Carousels Ltd., which had operated travel

agencies in eight Woodwards Stores, went out of business in the early summer of 1977. The Holiday Carousels organization had created a unique physical unit to house their agencies. Called carousels, they were semicircular in design, attractively decorated, and occupied about 300 square feet of floor space.

Woodwards' management considered the sales growth of Holiday Carousels promising, with average sales of approximately $700,000–$80,000 per unit per month in the spring of 1977. Each unit employed the equivalent of four full-time agents. (Industry rules of thumb suggest that an experienced agent should sell about $300,000 of travel per month.)

Woodwards' executives determined to continue to offer travel agency service to their customers for the following reasons:

a. The results of the Holiday Carousel experience were promising.
b. Increasing disposable incomes, smaller families, and larger numbers of senior citizens suggested a growing travel market.

---

* This case was written by Dr. Robert G. Wyckham, who at the time of its preparation was associated with the Faculty of Business Administration at Simon Fraser University.

c. Travel was seen as a natural complement to a full-line department store image and to the existing level of customer traffic.

d. That level of customer traffic, plus customer confidence and loyalty to Woodwards, provided an excellent opportunity for travel sales.

e. There was a high potential profit per square foot of space occupied.

f. A travel agency service was necessary in order to remain competitive with other department store chains who were in the travel business.

After receiving proposals from a number of travel agencies, Woodwards' management decided to compare the Maple Leaf offer with the alternative of setting up their own travel agencies.

Maple Leaf Travel Ltd. was a Vancouver-based travel agency with all national and international accreditations. It was owned, in part, by the credit unions of the province, which had more than 600,000 members. Total revenue of the travel agency in 1976 exceeded $2 million, the bulk of which was developed by direct mail to credit union members.

The Maple Leaf proposal was based on an immediate reopening of the Park Royal, West Vancouver travel office. Other offices would be opened when, by mutual agreement, a sufficiently smooth operating system had been achieved. Additional openings would occur first on the Lower Mainland of British Columbia and later in Alberta.

Maple Leaf required about 300 square feet of space for an initial staff of two. Hours would be 9:30 A.M. to 5:30 P.M., Monday to Friday. Experiments with evening and Saturday openings were also to be carried out. Location of the travel office within each store was to be based on a trade-off between the need for traffic flow and visibility, the consumers' need for privacy, and the travel agents' need for relative quiet.

The lease agreement requested by Maple Leaf was as follows:

1. Five years with a five-year renewal clause.
2. 300 sq.ft. of space initially; option to increase to 600 sq.ft. as business warrants.
3. Rent formula:
   1.0% of net sales of less than $250.000.
   1.5% of net sales of $250,000 to $499,999.
   2.0% of net sales of $500,000 to $999,999.
   1.5% of net sales of $1,000,000 to $1,500,000.
   1.0% of net sales of more than $1,500,000.

Assuming an average commission rate of 9 percent,

Maple Leaf Travel estimated a break-even point of sales of $411,000 in the first year. Pro forma contribution for the first year was estimated conservatively at $4,000 and optimistically at $16,000.

Three markets were identified for potential development: credit union members in the Woodwards' trading areas, current Woodwards' customers, and the general public. Cooperative direct-mail and newspaper advertising were suggested as the most productive forms of promotion.

In analyzing the alternate possibility, the creation of wholly owned and operated units, Woodwards' executives outlined some financial and other advantages:

1. The contribution to overhead and profit of travel outlets owned by Woodwards was estimated to be 2.6 percent on annual sales of $1 million compared to 1.625 percent from Maple Leaf Travel.
2. Because of the fixed nature of many expenses, it was thought that the contribution rate from owned agencies would increase as sales grew.
3. Advantageous advertising rates and in-house advertising expertise could be extended to a travel business operated directly by Woodwards.
4. Having control over an important service to Woodwards' customers was felt to be an advantage. Ownership was also seen as leading to greater flexibility in promotion, rate of growth, and operating characteristics.
5. Through various merchandising and promotional activities Woodwards already was generating customer traffic; owned travel agencies would result in greater benefits to Woodwards from this traffic.
6. Woodwards had a "built-in" market, the corporate travel of executives, and direct access to a large number of employees.
7. Individuals expert in the travel business were available and accounting services with travel agency experience could be retained.

A number of disadvantages of ownership were pointed out. In any new business the first weeks and months are difficult. A large amount of executive time would likely have to be allocated to the travel business, a business in which Woodward executives lacked any great degree of prior experience. There would also likely be some fairly substantial losses in the initial period before accreditations were received and business was built up.

A number of advantages would also be forgone if the Maple Leaf proposal was not accepted. The major potential loss was the opportunity to have more direct exposure to hundreds of thousands of credit union members. Also, Woodwards rather than Maple Leaf Travel would have to absorb any losses incurred in the start-up period. Any lease arrangements with Maple Leaf in contrast, would be based on that firm's sales. There would, therefore, always be a positive contribution to Woodwards even if the travel agencies did not make a profit. Finally, Maple Leaf had marketing and operating systems already in place. Hence the amount of time Woodwards executives would have to apply to the travel business would be greatly reduced.

Which of these two alternatives should Woodwards select? How would you support that recommendation?

9. Annie's Floral

Annie's Floral is a florist shop owned and operated by Harold and Anne Clark (a husband-and-wife team). Offering hundreds of varieties and arrangements of flowers, Annie's also carries small gift items to complement a floral arrangement. Mr. Clark serves as manager and sales clerk, while Mrs. Clark uses her artistic talents to select and arrange flowers. Since opening in 1974, sales have been good. Mr. Clark, however, is concerned about the failure of a recent addition to the gift line.

The Clarks bought the present operation in 1974 from Jack Boyd—who had been in the location for 20 years. Called Boyd's Florists, the shop was then grossing about $100,000 a year. Harold and Anne were confident that their previous 12 years' experience owning a smaller floral shop in a tiny (population 6,500) resort town less than 20 miles south would help them become a success in their new location.

Harold Clark feels their new store is in an excellent location. Located in a residential area of a northwestern Ontario community of 130,000 population, the new Annie's Floral is somewhat isolated from other neighborhood stores. It is eight blocks to the nearest store—a drugstore—and three and one-half miles to the closest shopping center. But it is near the intersection of the major north-south and east-west streets.

Mr. Clark understood his primary customers' characteristics. This helped him to direct his efforts more efficiently. As a result, sales increased steadily from $150,000 at the end of 1974 to $300,000 in 1980. Most of the regular customers were women—from medium- to high-income families living in the local middle-class residential areas. Also, Mr. Clark was pleased to see that some of his old customers from the resort town come to Annie's—probably because a strong customer acceptance had been built on friendly service and quality floral arrangements. Those customers who stopped in less frequently were assumed to be similar to the "regulars."

The largest part of the shop's business consists of weddings, funerals, parties, dances, and other big, one-time events which need flowers. However, about 25 percent of the purchases are by casual buyers who like to browse and chat with the Clarks. Approximately 60 percent of the sales are telephone orders, while the remaining 40 percent are made in the shop. Almost all of the telephone orders are for special, one-time events, while the walk-in traffic is divided equally between special events and spur-of-the-moment purchases. Almost no one buys flowers on a daily or regular basis. There is some FTD (Florist Telegraph Delivery) business, but Mr. Clark considers this to be an added service. It is only about 5 percent of his volume.

Mr. Clark feels that flowers are fairly homogeneous, unbranded products. Therefore, he feels that he must charge competitive prices to meet those of his 14 competitors throughout the community.

The shop was remodeled in 1976—and selling space was doubled. To fill in the increased display area, it was decided to add several complementary gift items—such as a famous brand of candies, high-quality flowerpots and vases, a quality line of leather vests for men and woman, pen-and-pencil sets, and candles. All the new lines—except the vests—have taken hold and have increased in sales each month since the items were added. Sales of vests have been very disappointing. In fact, they haven't paid their way on the basis of display area allotted (about 1/50 of the total display area).

When the busiest store traffic occurs (during a three- to four-day period before traditional flower-giving days), additional help is used. When available, Mary and Will Clark—the high-school-aged children of the owners—fill these jobs. (It was the children who suggested that the market for leather vests was growing in their high school during the last school year.) At other times, only one of the owners and a full-time sales clerk handle store traffic.

Samples of everything the shop has for sale are on display. The main activity of the sales clerk is to show customers various selections which could be used for a particular occasion—and then ring up the sale. Other than store display, advertising consists only of what is printed on the delivery truck, an ad in the Yellow Pages of the local telephone directory, and an occasional ad (five or six times per year) in the daily newspaper. None of the advertising mentions anything but flowers—because the Clarks wish to maintain their identity as florists.

Mr. Clark is wondering if more display area, a lower price, or extra promotion by the sales clerks might move more vests. Further, he is thinking of disposing of them, but isn't sure what should replace them if he did.

Evaluate the present operation and why leather vests don't sell. What strategy should the shop follow?

10. Byron Pharmaceutical Company

The Byron Pharmaceutical Company is a well-known manufacturer of high-quality cosmetics and ointments. A little over a year ago, Mr. Alcott, the president of Byron, was scanning the income statements for the last three quarters and did not like what he saw. At the next board meeting he stated that Byron should be showing a larger profit. It was generally agreed that the reason for the profit decline was that the firm had not added any new products to its line during the last two years.

Management was directed to investigate this problem—and remedy it if possible.

Mr. Alcott immediately asked for a report from the product planning group and found that it had been working on a new formula for a toothpaste that might be put into production immediately if a new product were needed. Mr. Emerson, the head of the research department, assured Mr. Alcott that the new ingredients in this toothpaste had remarkable qualities. Clinical tests had consistently shown that the new, as yet unnamed, dentifrice cleaned teeth better than the many toothpastes furiously battling for market share. Based on these tests, Mr. Alcott concluded that perhaps this product was what was needed and ordered work to proceed quickly to bring it to the market.

The marketing research department was asked to come up with a pleasing name and a tube and carton design. The results were reported back within two months. The product was to be called "Pearly" and the package would emphasize eye-catching colors.

The marketing department decided to offer Pearly along with its other "prestige" products in the drugstores which were carrying the rest of Byron's better-quality, higher-priced products. Byron's success had been built on moving quality products through these outlets, and management felt that quality-oriented customers would be willing to pay a bit more for a better toothpaste. Byron was already well established with the wholesalers selling to these retailers and had little difficulty obtaining distribution for Pearly.

It is now six months after the introduction of Pearly, and the sales results have not been good. The regular wholesalers and retailers carried the product, but relatively little was purchased by final customers. And now many retailers are asking that Byron accept returns of Pearly. They feel it is obvious that it is not going to catch on with consumers—despite the extremely large (matching that of competitors) amounts of advertising which have supported Pearly.

Mr. Alcott has asked the marketing research department to analyze the situation and explain the disappointing results thus far. An outside survey agency interviewed several hundred consumers and has tabulated its results. These are pretty well summarized in the following quotes:

> The stuff I'm using now tastes good. Pearly tastes terrible!
>
> I never saw that brand at the supermarket I shop at.
>
> I like what I'm using . . . why change?
>
> I'm not going to pay that much for any toothpaste . . . it couldn't be *that* much better!

What recommendation would you make to Mr. Alcott? Why?

11. Bing Corporation

Bing Corporation is one of the larger chemical companies in Canada—making a wide line of organic and inorganic chemicals, plastics, bio-products, and metals. Technical research has played a vital role in the company's growth.

Recently, Bing's research laboratories developed a new product in the antifreeze line—Pro Tek 20. Much research was devoted to the technical phase, involving various experiments concerned with the quality of the new product.

The antifreeze commonly used now is ethylene glycol. If it leaks into the crankcase oil, it forms a thick, pasty sludge that can produce bearing damage, cylinder scoring, or a dozen other costly and time-consuming troubles for both the operator and the owner of heavy-duty equipment.

Bing Corporation believed that Pro Tek 20 would be very valuable to the owners of heavy-duty diesel and gasoline trucks—as well as other heavy-equipment owners. Chemically, Pro Tek 20 uses methoxy propanol—instead of the conventional glycol and alcohol products. It cannot prevent leakage, but if it does get into the crankcase, it will not cause any problems.

At first, Bing thought it had two attractive markets for this product: (1) the manufacturers of heavy-duty equipment, and (2) the users of heavy-duty equipment. Bing sales reps have made numerous calls and so far neither type of customer has been very interested. The manufacturers are reluctant to show interest in the product until it has been proven in actual use. The buyers for construction companies and other firms using heavy-duty equipment have also been hesitant. Some felt the price was far too high for the advantages offered. Others didn't understand what was wrong with the present antifreeze—and dismissed the idea of paying extra for "just another" antifreeze.

The price of Pro Tek 20 is $14.98 per gallon—which is more than twice the price of regular antifreeze. The higher price is the result of higher costs in producing the product and an increment for making a better type of antifreeze.

Explain what has happened so far. What would you do if you were responsible for this product?

12. Ski Haus Sports Shop

Tom and Ida Cory graduated from a university in Alberta in 1977. Then, with some family help, they were planning to open a small ski equipment shop in Banff, Alberta. They were sure that by offering friendly, personal service they would have something unique and be able to compete with the many other ski shops in town. They were well aware that there were already many competitors, because many "ski bums" choose Banff as a place to live—and then try to find a way to earn a living there. By keeping the shop small, however, the Corys hoped to be able to manage most of the activities themselves—thereby keeping costs down and also being sure the service is good.

Now they are trying to decide which line or lines of skis they should carry. Almost all the major manufacturers' skis are offered in the competing shops, so Tom and Ida are seriously considering specializing in the Hoffwurtz brand—which is not now carried by any local shops. In fact, the Hoffwurtz sales rep has assured them that if they are willing to carry the line exclusively, then Hoffwurtz will not sell its skis to any other retailers in Banff. This idea appeals to Tom and Ida because it would give them something unique—a full line of German-made skis which have just been introduced into the Canadian market with supporting full-page ads in skiing magazines. The skis have an injected foam core that is anchored to the glass layers above and below by a patented process which causes the glass fibers to penetrate the foam. This process is used in a full line of skis, so the Corys would have a unique story to sell for skis which could satisfy everyone's needs. Further, the suggested retail prices and markups were similar to other manufacturers, so the Ski Haus could emphasize the unique features of the Hoffwurtz skis while feeling confident that their prices were competitive.

Besides the exclusive fiber-penetrative construction offered by Hoffwurtz—for strength and durability—the German company had developed a special recreational ski for women—with the help of Olympic triple-medal-winner Heidi Schmidt. The Corys felt that this might be a special selling point for the Hoffwurtz line. Many women need and want recreational skis (skis that are easier to use) and a ski designed specifically for them might be appealing and very profitable.

The only thing that worries the Corys about committing so completely to the Hoffwurtz line is that there are many other manufacturers—both domestic and foreign—which offer full lines and claim to offer unique features. In fact, most ski manufacturers regularly come out with new models and features and the Corys realize that most consumers are confused about the relative merits of all of the offerings. In the past, Tom, himself, has been reluctant to buy "off-brand" skis—preferring instead to stay with major names such as Hart, Head, K2, and Rossignol. So he is wondering whether a complete commitment to the Hoffwurtz line is wise. On the other hand, the Corys want to offer something unique. They don't want to open just another ski shop carrying lines which are available "everywhere." The Hoffwurtz line isn't their only possibility, of course. There are other off-brands which are not yet carried in Banff. But the Corys like the idea that Hoffwurtz is planning to give national promotional support to the skis during the introductory campaign in Canadian markets. They feel that this might make a big difference in how rapidly the new skis are accepted. And if they provide friendly sales assistance and quick binding-mounting service, perhaps their chances for success will improve. Another reason for committing to the Hoffwurtz line is that they like the sales rep, Kurt Basse, and they feel he would be a big help in their initial stocking and set-up efforts. They talked briefly with some other firms' salespeople at the major trade shows, but had not gotten along nearly so well with any of them. In fact, most of the sales reps didn't seem too interested in helping a newcomer—preferring instead to talk with and entertain buyers from established stores. The major ski shows are over, so any more contacts with manufacturers will require the Corys to take the initiative. But from their past experience, this does not sound too appealing. Therefore, they seem to be drifting fast toward having the Ski Haus specialize in selling the Hoffwurtz line.

Evaluate the Corys' thinking. What would you suggest they do?

13. Andrews Photo, Ltd.

Andrews Photo, Ltd., is located in a residential area along a major street about two miles from the downtown of a metropolitan area of 450,000. It is also near a big university. It sells high-quality still and movie cameras, accessories, and projection equipment—including 8mm and 16mm movie projectors, 35mm slide projectors, opaque and overhead projectors, and a large assortment of projection screens. Most of the sales of this specialized equipment are made to area school boards for classroom use, to industry for use in research and sales, and to the university for use in research and instruction.

Andrews Photo offers a wide selection of film and a specialized film-processing service. Instead of processing film on a mass production basis, Andrews gives each roll of film individual attention—to bring out the particular features requested by the customer. This service is used extensively by local industries who need high-quality pictures of lab or manufacturing processes for analytical and sales work.

To encourage the school and industrial trade, Andrews Photo offers a graphics consultation service. If a customer wants to build a display—whether large or small—professional advice is readily available. Along with this free service, Andrews carries a full line of graphic arts supplies.

Andrews Photo employs four full-time store clerks and two outside sales reps. These sales reps make calls on industry, attend trade shows, make presentations for schools, and help both present and potential customers in their use and choice of visual aids.

The people who make most of the over-the-counter purchases are (1) serious amateur photographers and (2) some professional photographers who buy in small quantities. Price discounts of up to 25 percent of the suggested retail price are given to customers who buy more than $500 worth of goods per year. Most regular customers qualify for the discount.

In the last few years, many more "amateurs" have been taking 35mm slide pictures. Because of this, Kevin Arnold, the manager of Andrews Photo, felt that there ought to be a good demand for some way of viewing them. Therefore, he planned a special pre-Christmas sale of inexpensive slide projectors, viewers, and home-sized projection screens. Hoping that most of these would be purchased as Christmas gifts, Arnold selected some products which offered good value and discounted the price to competitive levels—

for example, projectors at $99.50, viewers at $9.95, and screens at $29.95. To promote the sale, large signs were posted in the store windows—and ads were run in a Christmas-gift-suggestion edition of the local newspaper. This edition appeared each Wednesday during the four weeks before Christmas. At these prices and with this promotion, Arnold hoped to sell at least 150 projectors, 150 screens, and 200 viewers. When the Christmas returns were in, total sales were 22 projectors, 15 screens, and 48 viewers. He was most disappointed with these results—especially because trade estimates suggested that sales of projection equipment in this price and quality range were up 300 percent over last year.

Evaluate what happened. What should Mr. Arnold do in the future?

14. Deller Company

Jim Deller graduated in business from a large university in 1977. After a year as a car salesman, he decided to go into business for himself. In an effort to locate new opportunities, Jim placed several ads in his local newspaper—in Calgary, Alberta—explaining that he was interested in becoming a sales representative in the local area. He was quite pleased to receive a number of responses. Eventually, he became the sales representative in the Calgary area for three local manufacturers: the Caldwell Drill and Press Co., which manufactured portable drills; the T. R. Rolf Co., a manufacturer of portable sanding machines; and the Bettman Lathe Co., which manufactured small lathes. All of these companies were relatively small and were represented in other areas by other sales representatives like Jim Deller.

Deller's main job was to call on industrial customers. Once he made a sale, he would send the order to the respective manufacturer, who would in turn ship the goods directly to the particular customer. The manufacturer would bill the customer, and Deller would receive a commission varying from 5 percent to 10 percent of the dollar value of the sale. Deller was expected to pay his own expenses.

Deller called on anyone in the Calgary area who might use the products he was handling. At first, his job was relatively easy, and sales came quickly because there was little sales competition. There are many national companies making similar products, but at that time they were not well represented in the Calgary area.

In 1979, Deller sold $150,000 worth of drills, earning a 10 percent commission; $100,000 worth of sanding machines, also earning a 10 percent commission; and $75,000 worth of small lathes, earning a 5 percent commission. He was encouraged with his progress and was looking forward to expanding sales in the future. He was especially optimistic because he had achieved these sales volumes without overtaxing himself. In fact, he felt he was operating at about 70 percent of his capacity.

Early in 1980, however, a local manufacturer with a very good reputation—the Bonner Electrical Equipment Company—started making a line of portable drills. It had a good reputation locally, and by April 1980 Bonner had captured approximately one half on Caldwell's Calgary drill market by charging a substantially lower price. Bonner was using its own sales force locally, and it was likely that it would continue to do so.

The Caldwell Company assured Deller that Bonner couldn't afford to continue to sell at such a low price and that shortly Caldwell's price would be competitive with Bonner's. Jim Deller was not nearly as optimistic about the short-run prospects, however. He began looking for other products he could handle in the Calgary area. A manufacturer of hand trucks had recently approached him, but he wasn't too enthusiastic about this offer because the commission was only 2 percent on potential annual sales of $150,000.

Now Jim Deller is faced with another decision. The Phillips Paint Company in Edmonton, Alberta, has made what looks like an attractive offer. They heard what a fine job he was doing in the Calgary area and felt that he could help them solve their present problem. Phillips is having trouble with its whole marketing effort and would like Jim Deller to take over.

The Phillips Paint Company has been selling primarily to industrial customers in the Edmonton area and is faced with many competitors selling essentially the same product and charging the same low prices. Phillips Paint is a small manufacturer. Last year's sales were $140,000. They would like to increase this sales volume and could handle at least double this sales volume with ease. They have offered Deller a 12 percent commission on sales if he will take charge of their pricing, advertising, and sales efforts in the Edmonton area. Jim was flattered by their offer, but he is a little worried because there would be a great deal more traveling than he is doing at present. For one thing, he would have to spend a couple of days each week in the Edmonton area, which is 110 miles away.

Further, he realizes that he is being asked to do more than just sell. But he did have some marketing courses in college and thinks the new opportunity might be challenging.

What should Jim Deller do? Why?

---

15. Watson Sales Company

Bill Watson—now 55 years old—has been a salesman for over 30 years. He started selling in a department store, but gave it up after ten years to work in a lumberyard because the future looked much better in the building materials industry. After drifting from one job to another, he finally settled down and worked his way up to manager of a large wholesale building materials distribution warehouse in Hamilton, Ontario. In 1958 he decided to go into business for himself, selling carload lots of lumber to large retail yards in the Niagara Peninsula area.

He made arrangements to work with several large lumber mills in British Columbia. They would notify him when a carload of lumber was available to be shipped, specifying the grade, condition, and number of each size board in the shipment. Bill wasn't the only person selling for these mills, but he was the only one in his area. He was not obligated to take any particular number of carloads per month—but once he told the mill he wanted a particular shipment, title passed to him and he had to sell it to someone. Bill's main function was to buy the lumber from the mill as it was being shipped, find a buyer, and have the railroad divert the car to the buyer.

Bill has been in this business for 20 years, so he knows all of the lumberyard buyers in his area very well—and is on good working terms with them. Most of his business is done over the telephone from his small office, but he tries to see each of the buyers about once a month. He has been marking up the lumber between 4 and 6 percent—the standard markup, depending on the grade—and has been able to make a good living for himself and his family.

In the last few years, however, interest rates have been rising for home loans and the building boom slowed down. Bill's profits did, too, but he decided to stick it out—figuring that people still needed housing, and business would pick up again.

Six months ago, an aggressive salesman—much younger than Bill—set up in the same business, covering about the same area but representing different mills. This new salesman charged about the same prices as Bill, but would undersell him once or twice a week in order to get the sale. Many lumber buyers—knowing that they were dealing with a homogeneous product—seemed to be willing to buy from the lowest-cost source. This has hurt Bill financially and personally—because even some of his "old friends" are willing to buy from the new man if the price is lower. The near-term outlook seems dark, since Bill doubts if there is enough business to support two firms like his, especially if the markup gets shaved any more.

One week ago, Bill was contacted by Mr. Talbott, representing the Talbott and White particleboard manufacturing plant. Mr. Talbott knew that Bill was well acquainted with the local building supply dealers and wanted to know if he would like to be the sole distributor for Talbott and White in that area—selling carload lots, just as he did lumber. Mr. Talbott gave Bill several brochures on particleboard, a product introduced about 20 years ago, describing how it can be used as a cheaper and better subflooring than the standard lumber usually used. The particleboard is also made with a wood veneer so that it can be used as paneling in homes and offices. He told Bill that the lumberyards could specify the types and grades of particleboard they wanted. Therefore, they could get exactly what they needed, unlike lumber where they choose from carloads that are already made up. Bill knew that a carload of particleboard cost about 30 percent more than a carload of lumber and that sales would be less frequent. In fact, he knew that this product has not been as well accepted in his area as many others, because no one has done much promotion in his area. But the 20 percent average markup looks very tempting—and the particleboard market is expanding.

Bill has three choices:

1. Take Mr. Talbott's offer and sell both products.
2. Take the offer and drop lumber sales.

3. Stay strictly with lumber and forget the offer.

Mr. Talbott is expecting an answer within another week, so Bill has to decide soon.

Evaluate what Bill Watson has been doing. What should he do now? Why?

16. Partitions Canada Ltd.*

Mr. Colin Dennis, the president of Partitions Canada, called Bruce Laine, the firm's controller, into his office. "Most of our branch centers may appear to be making a good profit, but the overall profit picture of the company is pretty poor. All of our unit costs seem reasonable and our selling prices are in line with the competitors. Your idea of decentralizing everything by making each branch an individual profit center and each department in the plant accountable for its expenses may have been a good one but it hasn't improved anything. We still can't tell why we're not making much profit."

"A friend at the club was telling me that he increased his overall profits by 6 percent by centralizing the management of his distribution. He not only reduced his distribution costs by 20 percent but improved the level of service being provided to customers. He also thinks sales have gone up 7 percent or 8 percent because of better service. Distribution may be where our problem lies. I think that we've got distribution costs that are spread across both the sales and production departments. Nobody's really keeping track of these expenses and nobody's coordinating our distribution activities. I'm thinking of hiring a manager of physical distribution to make recommendations and carry out the necessary changes."

Partitions Canada Ltd. is a branch of a U.S. firm, with manufacturing facilities in Cambridge, Ontario. The firm was established in Canada in 1961. It has enjoyed rapid growth, at least partly due to the continuing surge in the construction of large buildings. The growth was also due to an aggressive sales program which included a massive distribution network stimulated by an environment of competition within the firm itself.

The company manufactures semi-permanent but movable partitions and portable dividers used in office buildings, hospitals, schools, small shopping centers, and other institutions. Distribution is through branch centers in 18 Canadian cities. Sales are made to build-ing owners and large tenants both directly and through architects, interior designers, consulting engineers, and contractors. Smaller office installations are sold through large stationery retailers, stationery wholesalers, and office furniture and equipment suppliers.

The branch centers are located in Victoria, Vancouver, Calgary, Edmonton, Regina, Winnipeg, Thunder Bay, Sudbury, Windsor, London, Hamilton, Toronto, Kingston, Cornwall, Ottawa, Montreal, Quebec City, and St. John, N.B. Each branch consists of a small office, warehouse, and light manufacturing area where panels can be cut and painted or coated to customers' requirements. A small staff is maintained for this purpose as well as for installation if required.

This distribution structure was originally regarded as being an ideal arrangement in a market that stretched across Canada for 5,000 miles in a belt that was scarcely 200 miles wide. Transportation over the two national railroads could be very economical, although somewhat slow, if carload lots were shipped. Although communications might be expensive, autonomous management and the fact that each branch was a profit center meant that most decisions could be made without clearing with Head Office. Actually, individual managers often competed against each other for contracts in adjacent territories. The sales volume and profit performance of successful branch managers was flaunted monthly in the faces of the others to stimulate aggressive selling and cost cutting.

The company's policy provided for freight to distribution centers, warehousing and packing costs to be averaged and incorporated into a uniform base price charged to the local distribution centers. They could also compete fairly and uniformly with each other regardless of where in Canada they were located. These centers could then compete effectively against smaller local manufacturers who would otherwise have underbid the company due to transportation differentials.

Rather than maintain large inventories, the managers were inclined to place specific orders with the warehouse at Cambridge for whatever was required for each job. They also usually requested that each order be packed completely in a separate unit and that it be shipped directly to the job site. Such practices

---

* This case was written by Mr. Gerry Byers, who at the time of its preparation was associated with the Business Division at Humber College.

meant that branches were saved the costs associated with maintaining a large inventory, "picking" an individual order, custom cutting and finishing panels, packing and loading, and providing local transportation for orders to the job site.

Orders, in all their detail, were phoned in to Cambridge collect—in order to speed up delivery. The back-up paperwork followed by mail. Invariably, orders were accompanied by special instructions requesting shipments to be sent out by the following day. Although the actual installation at the job site might not be required for another month, the managers had experienced erratic deliveries by rail and therefore wanted to allow lots of time so as to protect their reputation with customers.

The effects of these practices and policies were felt by the Production Department at Head Office. Transportation, warehousing, custom cutting, and packing came under the jurisdiction of the production manager, Mr. Bill Prouse. He was constantly harassed by Mr. Dennis to fulfill every request by the branch managers. Errors in order filling and delayed shipments were continually brought to his attention.

Mike Alberts, the warehouse and shipping manager, who was also responsible for the finished-goods inventory, found it very difficult to maintain adequate stocks of all sizes in all finishes. He constantly had to order up special runs from the manufacturing department. Robbie Dixon, who was in charge of manufacturing, complained that he could never get a large enough

production run to effect any economies of scale. He often had to pay overtime in order to meet the demands of the sales department.

Although the railroads had created special incentive-rate tariffs for large shipments, Sergio Cericola, the traffic manager, found that he could rarely ship even a carload at a time. Individually packed job orders were so irregular in shape that there was generally a lot of wasted volume in the railway cars. When Sergio tried to hold back orders so as to consolidate shipments, he got complaints from the field about these delays.

Branch managers would often order shipments on flat cars instead of in box cars so that unloading at scattered job-sites could be done more easily with fork-lift trucks where no receiving dock was available. However, flat cars cost more to ship on than box cars; requests for such flat cars were also filled more slowly by the railroads. Flat car shipments also had to have extra protection so that merchandise would arrive in usable condition.

Mr. Dennis eventually hired a Physical Distribution Manager to review the situation and to recommend whatever changes were necessary to deal with existing problems.

What changes should that physical distribution manager be recommending? What special studies, if any, might he have to conduct?

17. New Start Furniture*

Sam Jones was dissatisfied with his current job with the Department of Transport at the Calgary Airport. He wanted a position or career with more challenge and personal responsibility. One of the alternatives he was considering was opening a store in the town of Cochrane, Alberta.

Sam had joined the Canadian Airforce after his graduation from high school. He performed various duties including aircrew member on submarine spotters during his ten years in the Airforce. Upon leaving the Airforce he earned an economics degree from the University of Victoria. After graduating from university, Sam went to work for the Canadian Department of

Transport. His first assignment was to develop plans for leasing the retail space in the new $136 million airport then under construction in Calgary.

Both Sam and his wife liked the idea of living in a small town. Upon getting the assignment in Calgary, they had explored the small towns surrounding the city. Eventually, they decided to locate in Cochrane, a small but fast growing town situated in the valley of the Bow river, some 20 kilometers northwest of Calgary. The population of the town had increased from some 500 people in 1970 to 2,000 in 1978. A major developer had plans to build an additional 400 to 500 new homes in Cochrane over the next three years.

The area surrounding Cochrane was changing rapidly from farming and ranching to small hobby farms and acreages. Most of the people living on the acre-

---

* This case was written by Dr. James B. Graham, who at the time of its preparation was associated with the Faculty of Management at the University of Calgary.

ages worked in Calgary. Their homes varied, but most were large and expensive. As a result of increased building in the area, the district's school population had grown from 300 students in the mid-1960s to over 1,750 students in 1978.

Industrial employment in the Cochrane district had also increased in the last few years. In 1977 Canron opened a plant to produce reinforced concrete pipe that employed between 50 and 75 people. Spray Lake Saw Mills and Domtar Construction Products had plants in Cochrane employing a total of 150 people. Three natural gas processing plants, each with approximately 50 employees, were also operating in the area. With the exception of the Domtar Plant, all these industries had located in the Cochrane district within the last ten years. Over half the people working in these plants commuted from Calgary.

Prior to the period of industrial expansion and subdivision of the surrounding land, Cochrane's merchants had served the large ranches and farms located in the area. A good variety of services including a hotel, a lumberyard, a hardware store, four garages offering repair services, three bulk gasoline distribution centers, a dry goods store, a drugstore, a bank, a barber shop, two restaurants, a supermarket, a medical clinic, and a veterinary clinic had been available in Cochrane.

The services offered had expanded in the last five years. A number of small construction and oil well servicing firms located in Cochrane. In 1977 two new shopping centers had opened. These centers were small but greatly expanded the retail space available in the town. A new supermarket, several arts and crafts shops, a bakery, a delicatessen, a pool room, a sporting goods shop, two dress shops, a convenience store, a second drugstore, a dry-cleaning shop, a paint and interior decorating shop, a jewelry store, a laundromat, a dentist office, a second lumberyard, and other service establishments such as a bookkeeping agency and real estate firms had quickly rented the space. A new provincial building containing a liquor store, new medical clinic, and a Fish and Wildlife office had also opened in the last year. Mr. Jones was not sure how well these new stores were doing. He had heard rumors that several were not achieving the sales volumes they had expected.

Mr. Jones observed that most of the older businesses had well established clientele. The store owners were relaxed, friendly, and had good relationships with their customers. They always seemed to have time to discuss the weather, town politics, or family happenings with their customers. Casual conversations revealed that the reaction of the newer residents of Cochrane to the local merchants' way of doing business varied. Some people enjoyed the relaxed, unhurried atmosphere of the small town. Others were extremely impatient with the "poor service and high prices." These people tended to shop in the nearby Calgary stores where prices were slightly lower and variety somewhat greater.

Mr. Jones believed that Cochrane's growth might make it possible for him to operate a furniture store in that community. He felt that he could offer a friendly, reassuring environment that would attract customers. He hoped to be able to sell good quality, stylish, attractive furniture to people living or moving into the area.

Sam realized that people often bought new furniture when their life situation changed. They bought new furniture as their families expanded or became smaller. Also, people liked to buy new furniture when they moved. The newer, large warehouse-type furniture stores located in the southern section of Calgary were farther away from the rapidly expanding northwestern part of that city than was Sam's proposed Cochrane location. He wondered, therefore, if he could attract not only local residents but also people moving into northwestern Calgary to his local store.

He was particularly intrigued by the success of MacKay's Ice Cream Parlour in attracting Calgarians. Each evening and Sunday afternoon in the spring, summer, and fall, large numbers of Calgarians drove to Cochrane for "homemade" ice cream. At times the line of people waiting to be served stretched for half a block down main street. Obviously people would travel for some kinds of products so why not for an important purchase like furniture?

Mr. Jones realized the marketing mix offered by his store would be critical to its success or failure. He wondered about the size of store, the price range, the furniture to carry, the advertising strategy, the level and type of salesperson to hire. And, of course, he could not be certain that a furniture store would be successful.

How should Mr. Jones decide whether or not to go ahead with his plans? If he does, what marketing mix would be appropriate?

18. Billing Sports Company

Two years ago, Tom Billings bought the inventory, supplies, equipment, and business of Western Sport Sales—which was located in one of the suburbs of Saskatoon. The business was in an older building along a major highway leading out of town, but it was several miles from any body of water. The previous owner had achieved sales volumes of about $200,000 a year—just breaking even. For this reason—plus the desire to retire to Vancouver—the owner had been willing to sell to Tom for roughly the value of the inventory. Western Sport Sales had been selling two well-known brands of small pleasure boats, a leading outboard motor, two brands of snowmobiles, and a line of trailer and pickup-truck campers. The total inventory was valued at about $78,000 and Tom used all of his own savings and borrowed some from two friends to buy the inventory. At the same time, he took over the lease on the building—so he was able to begin operations immediately.

Tom had never operated a business of his own before, but he was sure that he would be able to do well. He had worked in a variety of jobs as an auto repair man, service man, and generally a jack-of-all-trades in the maintenance departments of several local businesses.

Soon after opening his business, Tom hired a friend who had had a similar background. Together, they handled all selling and set-up work on new sales, and performed maintenance work as necessary. Sometimes they were extremely busy—at the peaks of each sport season. Then, both sales and maintenance kept them going up to 16 hours a day. At these times it was difficult to have both new and repaired equipment available as soon as desired by customers. At other times, however, Tom and his friend, Bud, had almost nothing to do.

Tom usually charged the prices suggested by the various manufacturers, except at the end of a weather season when he was willing to make deals to minimize his inventory. Tom was a little annoyed that some of his competitors sold mainly on a price basis, offering 10 to 20 percent off the manufacturer's suggested list prices. Tom did not feel he wanted to get into that kind of business, however, because he wanted to build a loyal following based on friendship and personal service. He didn't feel he really had to cut price, because all of the lines he carried were "exclusive" for him in the area. No stores within a ten-mile radius carried any of his brands.

To try to build a favorable image for his company,

Tom occasionally placed advertisements in local papers and purchased some radio spots. The basic theme of this advertising was that the Billing Sports Company was a good place to buy the equipment needed for that season of the year. Sometimes he mentioned the brand names he carried, but generally he was trying to build his own image. He decided in favor of this approach because, although he had exclusives on the brands he carried, there generally were 10 to 15 different manufacturers' goods being sold in each product category at any one time—and most of the products were quite similar. Tom felt that this similarity among competing products almost forced him to try to differentiate himself on the basis of his own store's services.

The first year's operation was not profitable. In fact, after paying minimal salaries to Bud and himself, the business just about broke even. And this was without making any provision for return on his investment. In hopes of improving his profitability, Tom jumped at a chance to add a line of lawn tractors and attachments as he was starting into his second year of business. This line was offered by a well-known equipment manufacturer who was expanding into Tom's market. The equipment was similar to that offered by other lawn equipment manufacturers, but had a number of unique features and specialized attachments. The manufacturer's willingness to do some local advertising on his own and to provide some point-of-purchase displays appealed to Tom. And he also liked the idea that customers probably would be wanting this equipment sometime earlier than they would become interested in boats and other summer items. So, he would be able to handle this business without interfering with his other peak selling seasons.

Now it is two years after Tom started the Billing Sports Company and he is still only breaking even. Sales have increased a little, but he has had to hire some part-time help. The lawn-equipment line did help to expand sales as he had expected, but unfortunately it did not appear to increase profits. The part-time helpers were needed to service this business—in part because the manufacturer's advertising had generated a lot of sales inquiries. Relatively few of these resulted in sales, however, and so it is possible that Tom may have even lost money handling the new line. He hesitates to give up this line, however, because he has no other attractive choices right now and he doesn't want to give up that sales volume. Further, the manufacturer's sales rep has been most encouraging—assuring Tom that things will get better and that they will be glad to continue their promotion support for Tom's business during the coming year.

Evaluate Tom's overall strategy. What should he do in the future, especially regarding the lawn-tractor line?

19. Debmar Corporation

The Debmar Corporation produces wire rope and cable ranging from one-half inch to four inches in diameter. The Montreal-based company sells on a national basis. Principal users of the products are manufacturing firms using cranes and various other overhead lifts in their operations. Ski resorts, for example, are customers because cables are used in the various lifts. The main customers, however, are still cement plants, railroad and boat yards, heavy-equipment manufacturers, mining operations, construction companies, and steel manufacturers.

Debmar employs its own sales specialists to call on the purchasing agents of potential users. All the sales reps are engineers who go through an extensive training program covering the different applications, strengths, and other technical details concerning rope and cable. Then they are assigned a region or district—the size depending on the number of customers.

Phil Larimer went to work for Debmar in 1952, immediately after receiving a civil engineering degree from McGill University. After going through the training program, he was assigned, along with one other representative, to the Quebec Maritimes region. His job was to service and give technical help to present customers of rope and cable. He was expected to call on new customers when inquiries came in. But his primary duties were to: (1) supply the technical assistance needed to use rope or cable in the most efficient and safe manner, (2) handle complaints, and (3) provide evaluation reports to customers' management regarding their use of cabling.

Phil Larimer became one of Debmar's most successful representatives. His exceptional ability to handle customer complaints and provide technical assistance was noted by many of the firm's customers. He also brought in a great deal of new business—mostly from the automobile manufacturers and ski resorts in Quebec.

Larimer's success established Quebec as Debmar's largest-volume state. As a result, Quebec be-

came a separate district, and Phil Larimer was assigned as the representative for the district in 1959.

Although the company's sales in Quebec have not continued to grow in the past few years, the replacement market has been steady and profitable. This fact is mainly due to the ability and reputation of Phil Larimer. As one of the purchasing agents for a large automobile manufacturer mentioned, "When Phil Larimer makes a recommendation regarding use of our equipment and cabling, even if it is a competitor's cable we are using, we are sure it is for the best for our company. Last week, for example, a cable of one of his competitors broke and we were going to give him a contract. He told us it was not a defective cable that caused the break, but rather the way we were using it. He told us how it should be used and what we needed to do to correct our operation. We took his advice and gave him the contract as well!"

Four years ago, Debmar introduced an expensive wire sling device for holding cable groupings together. The sling makes operations around the cable much safer—and its use could reduce hospital and lost-time costs due to accidents. The profit margin for the sling is high, and Debmar urged all its representatives to push the sling.

The only sales rep to sell the sling with any success was Phil Larimer. Eighty percent of his customers are currently using the wire sling. In other areas, sling sales are disappointing.

As a result of his success, Debmar is now considering forming a separate department for sling sales and putting Phil Larimer in charge. His duties would include traveling to the various sales districts and training other representatives in how to sell the sling. The Quebec district would be handled by a new person.

The question Debmar's management faces now is: should they gamble on losing profitable customers in Quebec in hopes that sling sales will increase?

What would you advise? Why?

20. Bayer Furniture Company

Mrs. Carol Raines has been operating the Bayer Furniture Co. for ten years and has slowly built the sales to $575,000 a year. Her store is located in the downtown shopping area of a city of 150,000 population. This is basically a factory town, and she has deliberately selected "blue-collar" workers as her target market. She carries some higher-priced furniture lines, but puts great emphasis on budget combinations and easy credit terms.

Mrs. Raines is most concerned because she feels she has reached the limit of her sales potential—because sales have not been increasing during the last two years. Her newspaper advertising seems to attract her target customers, but many of these people come in, shop around, and then leave. Some of them come back, but most do not. She feels her product selections are very suitable for her target market and is concerned that her salespeople do not close more sales with potential customers. She has discussed this matter several times with her salespeople. They respond that they feel they ought to treat all customers alike, the way they personally would want to be treated—that is, they feel their role is just to answer questions when asked, not to make suggestions or help customers arrive at their selections. They feel that this would be too "hard sell."

Mrs. Raines argues that this behavior is interpreted as indifference by the customers who are attracted

Table 1

In shopping for furniture I found (find) that:	Demographic groups				Marital status	
	Group A	Group B	Group C	Group D	Newly-weds	Married 3–10 yrs.
I looked at furniture in many stores before I made a purchase	78%	57%	52%	50%	66%	71%
I went (am going) to only one store and bought (buy) what I found (find) there	2	9	10	11	9	12
To make my purchase I went (am going) back to one of the stores I shopped in previously	48	45	39	34	51	49
I looked (am looking) at furniture in no more than three stores and made (will make) my purchase in one of these	20	25	24	45	37	30
No answer	10	18	27	27	6	4

Table 2
The sample design

Demographic status

Upper class (group A); 13% of sample
  This group consisted of managers, proprietors, or executives of large businesses. Professionals, including doctors, lawyers, engineers, college professors and school administrators, research personnel. Sales personnel, including managers, executives, and upper-income sales people above level of clerks.
  Family income over $20,000.
Middle class (group B); 37% of sample
  Group B consists of white-collar workers including clerical, secretarial, sales clerks, bookkeepers, etc.
  It also includes school teachers, social workers, semiprofessionals, proprietors or managers of small businesses; industrial foremen and other supervisory personnel.
  Family income between $10,000 and $20,000.
Lower middle class (group C); 36% of sample
  Skilled workers and semiskilled technicians were in this category along with custodians, elevator operators, telephone linemen, factory operatives, construction workers, and some domestic and personal service employees.
  Family income between $10,000 and $20,000.
  No one in this group had above a high school education.
Lower class (group D); 14% of sample
  Nonskilled employees, day laborers. It also includes some factory operatives, domestic and service people.
  Family income under $10,000.
  None had completed high school; some had only grade school education.

to the store by her advertising. She feels that customers must be treated on an individual basis—and that some customers need more encouragement and suggestion than others. Moreover, she feels that some customers will actually appreciate more help and suggestion than the salespeople themselves might. To support her views, she showed her salespeople the data from a study about furniture store customers (Tables 1 and 2). She tried to explain to them about the differences in demographic groups and pointed out that her store was definitely trying to aim at specific groups. She argued that they (the salespeople) should cater to the needs and attitudes of their customers and think less about how they would like to be treated themselves.

Evaluate Mrs. Raines' thinking and suggest implications for her promotion.

---

21. The Niagara Peninsula Rehabilitation Centre*

The Niagara Peninsula Rehabilitation Centre, founded in 1970, is located in St. Catherines, Ontario. The center is a community resource which acts as an outpatient service fully equipped to provide rehabilitative care. There is normally no cost to patients since their expenses are covered by the Ontario Health Insurance Programme. The center is financed in part by the Ontario Ministry of Health as well as from community funds.

In the past five years, the center has treated more than 4,000 patients from across the Niagara Peninsula. These patients suffer from such disabilities as stroke, arthritic and cardiac disorders, respiratory ailments, industrial and home accidents, and hearing or speech disorders. A medical referral is needed for treatment at the center. The center has a staff of approximately 40, two thirds of whom are directly involved in the treatment process.

The objective of the center is to provide each patient with a controlled treatment program that deals with the patient's disability and facilitates a return to home or occupational environment. On the initial visit to the center, both patient and family are seen by the medical director and a social worker. The emphasis is on assessment of the emotional, social, and family situations as they relate to the physical disability. If required, a number of services, including counseling and referral to community resources, are provided. The center is divided into four departments—physiotherapy, occupational therapy, speech pathology/audiology, and advisory services (social work).

Although the center is located at the southern boundary of the city of St. Catherines (with a total population in 1976 of approximately 125,000), it has a mandate to serve the entire Niagara Peninsula (total population approximately 300,000). Its assigned territory includes the communities of Dunnville, Fort Erie, Grimsby, Niagara Falls, Niagara-on-the-Lake, Port Colborne, Welland, and of course, the city of St. Catherines. Patients who, because of their disability or the inadequacy of public transportation, would otherwise be unable to be present for treatment may use the center's own transport system. Those who conveyed are able to pay for all or some of their transportation costs are expected to do so.

Physiotherapy and occupational therapy are generally available in some regional hospitals when a patient is hospitalized. The Niagara Rehabilitation Centre is able to treat such patients once they are discharged from hospital but still need rehabilitation care. In addition, the center is unique in providing speech therapy and audiology services. It is the only institution in the peninsula which brings all these services together under one roof. The center has been successful in its mission. It has grown steadily to the point where it was operating at almost full utilization of capacity in 1978, having dealt with over 1,500 cases in the 1977 calendar year.

In January of 1978, Dr. Allan Kroll, director of speech pathology and audiology at the Niagara Peninsula Rehabilitation Centre, casually asked Dr. Ronald Rotenberg of the Brock University business program whether marketing might be applicable to a situation which had developed at the rehabilitation center. While he wasn't sure any problem existed, Dr. Kroll indicated that the director of the center, Evelyn Tipson, had expressed some concern over the fact that a relatively high proportion of the patients treated at the center came from the city of St. Catherines. The number of patients from areas other than St. Catherines were not fully represented at the center. Dr. Kroll wondered whether "marketing" could aid in the analysis and per-

---

* This case was written by Dr. Ronald Rotenberg who, at the time of its preparation, was associated with the School of Administrative Studies at Brock University.

haps solution of the situation. On the other hand, he expressed some doubts as to the applicability and appropriateness of advertising. Furthermore, he felt that Miss Tipson probably had even stronger feelings about the appropriateness of utilizing commercial promotion to advance the goals of a rehabilitation center. Nevertheless, it was decided that a meeting between Miss Tipson, Dr. Kroll, and Dr. Rotenberg could prove to be of some benefit to the center.

Such a meeting took place the following week. It began with Miss Tipson expressing concern over the fact that patients from the communities outside of St. Catherines were underrepresented at the center. There was *no immediate urgency* to resolve the situation, since the center was already operating at near capacity. However, she felt it would be better in the long run if the patient mix at the center more closely reflected the actual population distribution of the Niagara Peninsula at large. (Exhibit 1 compares the geographic mix of patients treated at the center for 1974 to 1977 inclusive with the actual geographic distribution of population in 1976 of the Niagara Peninsula.)

A number of other issues and concerns were reviewed at the same meeting. First, the possibility existed of some kind of rivalry between the medical facilities (hospitals and doctors) in Niagara Falls and those in St. Catherines. Perhaps doctors in the Falls would not normally refer their patients to a St. Catherines-based rehabilitation center even if that center were the only one of its kind in the peninsula. It was also felt that doctors in the communities of Dunnville and Grimsby were more likely to refer their patients to the

Chedoke Hospital in Hamilton because that institution was closer. There had been no formal studies of former patients to determine their degree of satisfaction with the center. While patients could only come to the center on a doctor's referral, it was not really known whether patients generally asked a physician for a referral, or whether the doctor, or possibly a nurse, initiated most referrals. Although Miss Tipson believed that most of the 300 doctors in a position to refer patients knew of the center's existence, she felt some of them might not be aware of the full range of its available facilities and services. In addition, there was no information as to physicians' images of, and attitudes toward, the center. Finally, nothing was known either of the general public's degree of awareness of the rehabilitation center or of the center's image among those who know of its existence.

After some discussion, Miss Tipson reiterated that there was no urgency in dealing with the situation. Nevertheless, she felt it would be desirable to have a more proportionate representation of area residents as patients at the center. While acknowledging "marketing" could be applicable in helping to analyze and correct the situation, she felt advertising of any kind would not be appropriate. Such advertising could give the impression that the rehabilitation center is in desperate need of patients. It could also contravene an unwritten code of ethics or practice which states that hospitals (or other such public institutions) "don't advertise." In the past, the rehabilitation center had used audio visual tapes/displays for the public and letters to doctors. Although she considered displays an ac-

Exhibit 1
Breakdown of patients by geographic locations in Niagara region

Geographic distribution of patients	Percent of total region population	1977		1976		1975		1974	
		Number	Percent	Number	Percent	Number	Percent	Number	Percent
Dunnville	3.1%	1	.1%	2	.2%	2	.2%	6	.7%
Fort Erie	6.3	34	2.2	23	1.9	26	2.8	28	3.4
Grimsby	4.3	10	.6	4	.3	12	1.3	16	1.9
Lincoln	3.9	55	3.5	30	2.4	23	2.4	28	3.4
Niagara Falls	18.3	98	6.3	115	9.3	104	11.1	69	8.2
Niagara-on-the-Lake	3.4	43	2.8	22	1.8	22	2.4	26	3.1
Pelham	2.7	33	2.1	46	3.7	32	3.4	35	4.2
Port Colborne	5.6	49	3.2	21	1.8	23	2.4	16	1.9
St. Catherines	32.1	994	64.0	732	59.5	525	56.0	425	50.7
Thorold	4.0	81	5.2	68	5.5	45	4.8	33	3.9
Wainfleet	1.6	4	.3	2	.2	1	.1	5	.6
Welland	12.5	140	9.0	154	12.5	117	12.5	146	17.4
West Lincoln	2.5	4	.3	9	.7	5	.5	3	.4
Other		6	.4	2	.2	1	.1	2	.2
Total referred		1,522	100.0	1,230	100.0	938	100.0	838	100.0

ceptable method of communication, there had never been any formal evaluation of their effectiveness. Miss Tipson wondered whether use of tapes and displays should be continued, or even expanded through the utilization of (temporary) displays in shopping malls throughout the Niagara region.

Regardless of the additional or intensified method of communication (if any), ultimately chosen, Miss Tipson felt that there had to be some reasonable justification. The center's operating grant did not provide for any extensive promotional program. In order to implement any such program, the center would have to apply for additional funding either to the Ministry of Health or some other granting agency. Miss Tipson did, however, mention that volunteers from the community might be available to aid in gathering the data required before any decision regarding promotion was made.

What marketing problem, if any, does the rehabilitation center face? If you believe a marketing problem exists, what information is needed before any marketing decisions can be taken or any marketing plan prepared? What marketing action could be taken with a limited budget of $2,000–$3,000 a year?

22. A–A Fabricators, Ltd.

A–A Fabricators, Ltd.—located in Winnipeg, Manitoba—is a custom producer of industrial wire products. The company has a great deal of experience bending wire into many shapes—and also has the facilities to chrome- or gold-plate finished products. The company was started ten years ago, and has slowly built its sales volume to $1 million a year. Just one year ago, Frank Josephs was appointed sales manager of the consumer products division. It was his responsibility to develop this division as a producer and marketer of the company's own branded products—as distinguished from custom orders which the industrial division produces for others.

Mr. Josephs has been working on a number of different product ideas for almost a year now, and has developed several unique designs for letter holders, flowerpot holders, key and pencil holders, and other novelties. His most promising product is a letter holder in the shape of a dog. It is very similar to one which the industrial division produced for a number of years for another company. In fact, it was experience with the seemingly amazing sales volume of this product which interested the company in the consumer market—and led to the development of the consumer products division.

Mr. Josephs has sold hundreds of units of his various products to local chain stores and wholesalers on a trial basis, but each time the price has been negotiated and no firm policy has been set. Now he is faced with the decision of what price to set on the dog-shaped letter holder which he plans to push aggressively wherever he can. Actually, he hasn't decided on exactly which channels of distribution he will use—but the trials in the local area have been encouraging, and, as noted above, the experience in the industrial division suggests that there is a large market for the product.

The manufacturing cost on this product is approximately 10 cents if it is painted black, and 20 cents if it is chromed or gold-plated. Similar products have been selling at retail in the 75 cents to $2.50 range. The sales and administrative overhead to be charged to the division would amount to $35,000 a year. This would include Mr. Joseph's salary and some office expenses. It is expected that a number of other products will be developed in the near future, but for the coming year it is hoped that this letter holder will account for about half the consumer products division's sales volume.

Evaluate Mr. Josephs' marketing strategy. What price should he set?

23. Ace Photofinishing Company

Organized in 1948, the Ace Photofinishing Company soon became one of the four major Ontario-based photofinishers—each with annual sales of about $2.5 million.

Ace was started by three people who had a lot of experience in the photofinishing industry—working in Kodak's photofinishing division in Rochester, New York. Ace started in a small rented warehouse in Hamilton, Ontario. Today it has seven company-owned plants in five cities.

The two color-processing plants are located in Toronto and London. Black-and-white-processing plants are located in Toronto and London as well as Kingston, Hamilton, and Windsor.

Ace does all of its own processing of black-and-white films, slides, prints, and movies. While they do own color-processing capability, Ace has found it more economical to have most color film processed by the regional Kodak processing plant. The color film processed by Ace is of the "off-brand" variety—or is special work done for professional photographers. Despite this limitation in color finishing, the company has always given its customers fast, quality service. All pictures—including those processed by Kodak—can be returned within three days of receipt by Ace.

Ace started as a wholesale photofinisher—and later developed its own processing plants in a drive for greater profit. Its customers are drugstores, camera stores, department stores, photographic studios, and any other retail outlets where photofinishing is offered to consumers. These retailers insert film rolls, cartridges, negatives, and so on, into separate bags—marking on the outside the kind of work to be done. The customer is handed a receipt, but seldom sees the bag into which the film has been placed. The bag has the retailer's name on it—not Ace's.

Each processing plant is fronted by a small retail outlet for drop-in customers who live near the plant. This is a minor part of Ace's business.

The company is also engaged in direct-mail photofinishing. Each processing plant in Ontario is capable of receiving direct-mail orders from consumers. All film received is handled in the same way as the other retail business.

A breakdown of the dollar volume by type of business is shown in Table 1.

All processing is priced at the level established by local competition. Ace sets a retail list price, and each retailer then is offered a trade discount based on the volume of business generated for Ace. The pricing

Table 1

Type of business	Percent of dollar volume
Sales to retail outlets	80
Direct-mail sales	17
Retail walk-in sales	3
	100

schedule used by each of the major competitors in the Ontario market is shown in Table 2. All direct-mail processing for final consumers is priced at the 33⅓ percent discount off retail price—but this is done under a disguised name so that retailer customers are not antagonized. Retail walk-in accounts are charged the full list price for all services performed.

Retail stores offering photofinishing are served by Ace's own sales force. Each processing plant has at least three people servicing accounts. Their duties include daily visits to all accounts to pick up and deliver all photofinishing work. These sales reps also make daily trips to the bus terminal nearby to pick up and drop off color film to be processed by Kodak.

Since the consumer does not come in contact with Ace, the firm has not found it necessary to advertise its retail business. To reach retailers, Ace is listed in the Yellow Pages of all telephone books in cities and towns served by its seven plants. There has been no attempt to make the consumer aware of Ace's service—since all consumers are served through retail stores.

The direct-mail portion of Ace's business is generated by regular advertisements in the pictorial supplements of weekend newspapers. These advertisements usually stress the low-price service, two-week turn-around, and fine quality. Ace does not use its own name for these markets. Mailers are provided for the consumer to send in to the plant. Some people in the company felt this part of the business might have great potential if pursued more aggressively.

Recently, Ace's president, Mr. Randall, has become

Table 2

Monthly dollar volume (12-month average)	Discount (2/10 net 30)
$ 0–$ 100	33⅓%
$ 101–$ 500	40
$ 501–$1,000	45
$1,001–above	50

worried over the loss of several retail accounts in the $500–$1,000 discount range. He has been with the company since its beginning—and has always stressed quality and rapid delivery of the finished product. Demanding that all plants produce the finest quality, Mr. Randall personally conducts periodic quality tests of each plant through its direct-mail service. Plant managers are called on the carpet for any slips in quality.

To find out what is causing the loss in retail accounts, Mr. Randall is reviewing sales rep's reports and talking to various employees. In their weekly reports, Ace's sales reps have reported a possible trend toward higher trade discounts being offered to retailer customers. Fast-Film—a competitor of equal size that offers the same services as Ace—is offering an additional 5 percent discount in each sales volume category. This really makes a difference at some stores—because these retailers feel that all the major pro-

cessors can do an equally good job. Further, they note, consumers apparently feel that the quality is acceptable, because there have been no complaints so far.

Ace has faced price cutting before—but never by an equally well-established company. Mr. Randall cannot understand why these retailer customers would leave Ace, because Ace is offering higher quality and the price difference is not that large. He is considering a direct-mail and newspaper campaign to consumers to persuade them to demand Ace's quality service from their favorite retailer. Mr. Randall feels that consumers demanding quality will force retailers to stay with—or return to—Ace. He says: "If we can't get the business by convincing the retailer of our fine quality, we'll get it by convincing the consumer."

Evaluate Ace's strategies and Mr. Randall's present thinking. What would you do?

---

24. The Schmidt Manufacturing Company

The Schmidt Manufacturing Company—of Vancouver—is a leading manufacturer in the wire machinery industry. It has patents covering over 200 machine variations, but it is rare for Schmidt's customers to buy more than 30 different types in a year. Its machines are sold to wire and small-tubing manufacturers—when they are increasing production capacity or replacing outdated equipment.

Established in 1865, the company has enjoyed a steady growth to its present position with annual sales of $27 million.

About ten firms compete in the wire machinery market. Each is about the same size and manufactures basically similar machinery. Each of the competitors has tended to specialize in its own geographic area. Four of the competitors are in eastern Canada, and two—including Schmidt—in the West. All of the competitors offer similar prices and sell F.O.B. their factories. Demand has been fairly strong in recent years. As a result, all of the competitors have been satisfied to sell in their geographic areas and avoid price cutting. In fact, price cutting is not a popular idea, because about 20 years ago one firm tried to win additional business and found that others immediately met the price cut but industry sales (in units) did not increase at all. Within a few years prices had returned to their earlier level, and since then competition has tended to focus on promotion.

Schmidt's promotion has depended largely on company sales reps who cover British Columbia and the Prairies. They usually are supported by sales engineers when the company is close to making a sale. Some advertising is done in trade journals. And direct mailings are used occasionally, but the main promotion emphasis is on personal selling. Personal contact outside of western Canada, however, is through manufacturers' agents.

Errol Lang, president of Schmidt Manufacturing Co., is not satisfied with the present situation. Industry sales have begun to level off and so have Schmidt's sales—although the firm has continued to hold its share of the market. Lang would like to find a way to compete more effectively in the other regions, because he sees that there is great potential outside of western Canada, if he can only find a better way of reaching it.

Schmidt has been acknowledged by competitors and buyers as one of the top-quality producers in the industry. Its machines have generally been somewhat superior to others in terms of reliability, durability, and productive capacity. The difference, however, has not been great enough to justify a higher price—because the others are able to do the necessary job. In short, if a buyer had a choice between Schmidt's and another's machines at the same price, Schmidt would probably get the business. But it seems clear that Schmidt's price must be at least competitive.

The average wire machine sold by Schmidt (or any of its competitors) sells for about $115,000, F.O.B. shipping point. Shipping costs within any of three major regions averages about $1,500—but another $1,000 must be added on shipments from western Canada to Ontario and Quebec (either way) and another $1,000 from there to the Atlantic Provinces.

Mr. Lang is thinking about expanding his market by being willing to absorb the extra freight costs which would be incurred if a customer in eastern Canada were to buy from his western Canada location. In other words, he would absorb the additional $1,000–$2,000 in transportation costs. By so doing, he would not be cutting price in those markets, but rather reducing his net return. He feels that his competitors would not see this as price competition and therefore would not resort to cutting prices themselves. Further, he thinks such a move would be legal—because all the customers in each major region would be offered the same price.

The sales manager, Robert Dixon, felt that the proposed freight absorption plan might actually stimulate price competition in the eastern markets and perhaps in western Canada as well. He proposed instead, that Schmidt hire some sales reps to work the eastern markets—rather than relying on the manufacturers' agents. He felt that an additional three sales reps would not increase costs too much—and could greatly increase the sales from these markets over that brought in by the agents. With this plan, there would be no need to absorb the freight and risk disrupting the status quo with respect to competitive methods. He felt this was especially important, because competition in the East was somewhat "hotter" than in the West due to the number of competitors in these regions. The situation had been rather quiet in the West—because only two firms were sharing this market.

Mr. Lang agrees that Mr. Dixon has a point, but in view of the leveling off of industry sales, he feels that the competitive situation might change drastically in the near future and that he would rather be a leader in anything that is likely to happen rather than a follower. He is impressed with Mr. Dixon's comments about the greater competitiveness in the other markets, however, and therefore is unsure about what should be done—if anything.

Evaluate Schmidt's strategy planning in the light of its market situation, and explain what it should do now.

25. Valley View Company

The Valley View Company is a well-established manufacturer in the highly seasonal vegetable canning industry. It packs and sells canned beans, peas, carrots, corn, peas and carrots mixed, and kidney beans. Sales are made mainly through food brokers to merchant wholesalers, supermarket chains (such as Dominion, Loblaws, A&P, and so forth), cooperatives, and other outlets—mostly in the Toronto area. Of secondary importance, by volume, are sales in the immediate local market to institutions, grocery stores, and supermarkets—and sales of dented canned goods at low prices to walk-in customers.

Valley View is the second-largest vegetable canner in the Niagara Peninsula of Ontario—with sales in excess of $10 million annually (exact sales data is not published by the closely held corporation). Plants are located throughout the crop growing areas of Ontario, with main offices in Waterside. The Valley View brand is used only on canned goods sold in the immediate local market. In most other cases, the goods are sold and shipped under the retailer's label, or the broker's/wholesaler's label.

Operating since 1905, Valley View has an excellent reputation for the consistent quality of its product offerings. And it is always willing to offer competitive prices. Strong channel rapport was built by Valley View's former chairman of the board and chief executive officer, E. J. McWirter. Mr. McWirter—who owns controlling interest in the firm—had "worked" the Toronto area as an aggressive company salesman in the firm's earlier years—before he took over from his father as president in 1931. He was an ambitious and hardworking executive, active in community affairs, and the firm prospered under his direction. He became well known within the canned food processing industry for technical/product innovations. During World War II, he was appointed to a position in Ottawa—on the board which helped set wartime food rationing policies.

During the off-canning season, Mr. McWirter traveled widely. In the course of his travels, he arranged several important business deals. His 1968 and 1970 trips resulted in the following two events: (1) inexpensive pineapple was imported from Formosa and marketed in central Canada through Valley View—primarily to expand the product line; and (2) a technically advanced continuous process cooker (65 feet high) was imported from England and installed at the Waterside plant in February/March 1975. It was the first of its kind in Canada and cut process time sharply.

Mr. McWirter retired in 1975 and named his son-in-law, the 35-year-old Mr. King, as his successor. Mr. King is intelligent and hard-working. He had been concerned primarily with the company's financial matters, and only recently with marketing problems. During his seven-year tenure as financial director, the firm had received its highest credit rating ever—and was able to borrow working capital ($3 million to meet seasonal seed, fertilizer, can stockage, and wage requirements) at the lowest rate ever received by the company.

The fact that the firm isn't unionized allows some competitive advantage. However, minimum wage law changes have increased costs. And these and other rising costs have caused profit margins to narrow. The narrowed profit margins led to the recent closing of two plants as they became comparatively less efficient to operate. The remaining two plants were considerably expanded in capacity (especially warehouse facilities), so that they could operate more profitably due to maximum use of existing processing equipment.

Shortly after Mr. McWirter's retirement, Mr. King reviewed the company's current situation with his executives. He pointed out narrowing profit margins, debts contracted for new plant and equipment, and an increasingly competitive environment. Even considering the temporary labor-saving competitive advantage of the new cooker system, there seemed to be no way to improve the "status quo" unless the firm could sell direct—as they do in the local market—absorbing the food brokers' 5 percent commission on sales. This was the plan of action decided upon, and Mr. Freds was directed to test the new method for six months.

Mr. Freds is the only full-time salesman for the firm. Other top executives do some selling—but not much. Being a relative of Mr. McWirter's, Freds is also a member of the board of directors. He is well qualified in technical matters—he has a college degree in food chemistry. Although Mr. Freds formerly did call on some important customers with the brokers' sales reps, he is not well known in the industry or even by Valley View's usual customers.

Five months later, after Mr. Freds has made several selling trips and hundreds of telephone calls, he is unwilling to continue sales efforts on his own. He insists that a sales staff be formed if the present operation is to continue. Orders are down in comparison both to expectations and to the previous year's operating results. And sales of the new pineapple products are very disappointing. Even in regular channels, Mr. Freds sensed a reluctance to buy—though basic consumer demand had not changed. Further, some potential customers have demanded quantity guarantees considerably larger than the firm can supply. Expanding supply would be difficult in the short run—because the firm typically must contract with farmers for production acreage, to assure supplies of the type and quality they normally offer.

Mr. McWirter, still the controlling stockholder, has scheduled a meeting in two weeks to discuss the status of Valley View's current operations.

Evaluate Mr. King's strategy planning. What should he tell Mr. McWirter? What should be done next?

26. Demmer Mfg. Company

Bill Carson is currently employed as a sales representative for a plastics goods manufacturer. He calls mostly on large industrial accounts—such as refrigerator manufacturers—who might need large quantities of custom-made products. He is on a straight salary of $20,000 per year, plus expenses and a company car. He expects some salary increases, but does not see much long-run opportunity with this company. As a result, he is seriously considering changing jobs and investing $20,000 in the Demmer Mgf. Co.—an established thermoplastic molder and manufacturer. Carl Weiss, the present owner, is nearing retirement age and has not developed anyone to run the business. He has agreed to sell the business to Robert Watson, a lawyer-entrepreneur, who has invited Bill Carson to invest and become the sales manager. Mr. Watson has agreed to give Carson his current salary plus expenses, plus a bonus of 1 percent of profits. However, Bill must invest to become part of the new company. He will obtain a 5 percent interest in the business for his $20,000 investment.

The Demmer Mfg. Co. is well established—and last year had sales of $1.5 million, but no profits. In terms of sales, cost of materials was 46 percent; direct labor,

13 percent; indirect factory labor, 15 percent; factory overhead, 13 percent; and sales overhead and general expenses, 13 percent. The company has not been making any profit for several years—but has been continually adding new machines to replace those made obsolete by technological developments. The machinery is well maintained and modern, but most of it is similar to that owned by its many competitors. Most of the machines in the industry are standard. Special products are then made by using specially made dies with these machines.

Sales have been split about two-thirds custom-molded products (that is, made to order for other producers or merchandising concerns) and the balance proprietary items (such as housewares and game items, like poker chips and cribbage sets). The housewares are copies of articles developed by others—and indicate neither originality nor style. Carl Weiss is in charge of the proprietary items distributed through any available wholesale channels. The custom-molded products are sold through three full-time sales engineers who receive a 5 percent commission on sales up to $10,000 and then 3 percent above that level, as well as by three manufacturers' reps getting the same commissions.

Financially, the company seems to be in fairly good condition—at least as far as book value is concerned. The $20,000 investment would buy approximately $30,000 in assets.

Mr. Watson feels that—with new management—the company has a real opportunity for profit. He expects to make some economies in the production process and hold custom-molding sales to approximately the present $1 million level. The other major expectation is that he will be able to develop the proprietary line from a sales volume of about $500,000 to $2 million a year. Bill Carson is expected to be a real asset here because of his sales experience. This will bring the firm up to about capacity level—but of course it will mean adding additional employees. The major advantage of expanding sales would be spreading overhead. Some of the products proposed by the lawyer for the expansion of the proprietary line are listed below.

New products for consideration:

Women's tool kit—molded housewares.

Six-bottle soft drink case.

Laminating printed film on housewares—molded.

Short legs for furniture—molded, $0.5 million minimum market.

Home storage box for milk bottles, $0.5 million minimum market.

Step-on garbage can without liner.

Importing and distributing foreign housewares.

Black-nylon-handled table utensils.

Extruded and embossed or formed wall coverings.

Extruded and formed wall decorations—nursery-rhyme figures, etc.

Formed butyrate outside house shutters.

Formed inside shutters in lieu of venetian blinds.

School and toy blackboards.

Translucent bird houses.

Formed holder for vacuum cleaner attachments.

Formed household door liners.

Formed "train terrain" table topography for model trains.

Formed skylights.

There is heavy competition in these markets from many other companies like Demmer. Further, most retailers expect a wide margin, sometimes 40 to 50 percent. Even so, manufacturing costs are low enough so some money can be spent for promotion, while still keeping the price competitive. Apparently many customers are willing to pay for the novelty of new products—if they see them in their stores.

How would you advise Bill Carson? Explain your reasoning.

---

27. Lewis Tool Company

Lewis Tool Co. is a manufacturer of industrial cutting tools. These tools include such items as lathe blades, drill press bits, and various other cutting edges used in the operation of large metal cutting, boring, or stamping machines. The president of the company, Chuck Taylor, takes great pride in the fact that his company—whose $1,759,000 sales in 1979 is small by industry standards—is recognized as a producer of the highest-quality line of cutting tools to be found.

Competition in the cutting-tool industry is intense. Lewis Tool faces competition not only from the original manufacturers of the machines, but also from many other relatively powerful companies offering cutting tools as one of many diverse product lines. This situation has had the effect, over the years, of standardizing the price, specifications, and in turn, the quality, of the competing products of all manufacturers.

About a year ago, Mr. Taylor was tiring of the tremendous financial pressure of competing with companies enjoying economies of scale. At the same time, he noted that more and more potential cutting-tool customers were turning to small custom tool-and-die shops because of specialized needs that could not be met by the mass production firms. Mr. Taylor considered a basic change in strategy. Although he was unwilling to become strictly a custom producer, Mr. Taylor felt that the recent trend toward buying customized cutting edges might be a good indication of the development of new markets which would be too small for the large, multiproduct-line companies to serve profitably. He thought that the new markets might be large enough for a flexible company of Lewis Tool's size to make a good profit.

An outside company, Ampex Research Associates, was hired to study the feasibility of serving this potential new market. The initial results were encouraging. It was estimated that Lewis Tool could increase sales by 50 percent and double profits by servicing the emerging market.

The next step taken by Lewis Tool was to develop a team of technical specialists to maintain continuous contact with potential cutting-tool customers. They were supposed to identify any present or future needs which might exist in enough cases to make it possible to profitably produce a specialized product. The technical specialists were not to take orders or "sell" Lewis Tool to the potential customers. Mr. Taylor felt that only through this policy could these representatives easily gain access to the right persons.

The initial feedback from the technical specialists was most encouraging. The company, therefore, decided to continually adapt its high-quality products to the ever-changing, specialized needs of users of cutting tools and edges.

The potential customers of Lewis Tool's specialized tools are widely scattered. The average sale per customer is not expected to exceed $250 at a time, but the sale will be repeated several times within a year. Because of the widely dispersed market and low sales volume per customer, Mr. Taylor doesn't feel that selling the products direct—as is done by small custom shops—is practical. At the present time, the Lewis Tool Company distributes 90 percent of its regular output through an industrial supply wholesaler which serves the entire area east of the Manitoba-Ontario border. This wholesaler, although very large and well known, is having trouble moving cutting tools. It is losing sales of cutting tools in some cities to newer wholesalers specializing in the cutting-tool industry. The new wholesalers are able to give more technical help to potential customers, and therefore better service. The Lewis Tool wholesaler's chief executive is convinced that the newer, less-experienced concerns will either realize that a substantial profit margin can't be maintained along with their aggressive tactics, or they will eventually go broke trying to "overspecialize."

From Mr. Taylor's standpoint, the present wholesaler has an established reputation and has served Lewis Tool well in the past. The traditional wholesaler has been of great help to Lewis Tool in holding down the firm's inventory costs—by increasing the amount of inventory maintained in the 34 branch wholesale locations operated by the wholesaler. Although he has received several complaints about the lack of technical assistance given by the wholesaler's sales reps, Mr. Taylor feels that the present wholesaler is providing the best service it can. He explains the complaints as "the usual trouble you get into from just doing business."

Mr. Taylor feels that there are more urgent problems than a few complaints—profits are declining. Sales of the new cutting-tool line are not nearly as high as forecasted—even though all indications are that the company's new products should serve the intended market perfectly. The high costs involved in the high-quality product line and the technical specialist research team—together with lower-than-expected sales—have significantly reduced the firm's profits. Mr. Taylor is wondering whether it is wise to continue to try to cater to the needs of specific target markets when the results are this discouraging. He also is considering increasing advertising expenditures in the hope that customers will "pull" the new products through the channel.

Evaluate Lewis Tool's strategy. What should Mr. Taylor do now?

28. Cando, Ltd.

Jerry Bullard and Joel Flynn are partners in several small businesses—operated under the name of Cando, Ltd. They are now seriously considering whether they should take on the local franchise for "Save-A-Life" products. Jerry saw an advertisement in The *Financial Post* and called for more information about the product and the franchise possibility. Now he and Joel are considering whether they should take on the local franchise and hire two more people to do the direct selling which is required. Joel is sure that he could hire and supervise the right kind of sales people without taxing his available time. In fact, the partners are looking for something more for Joel to do because his current responsibilities to the partnership do not fully use his time. So supervision and personnel aren't the problem. What is bothering the partners is whether this particular franchise is the right thing for them to do. Even more, Joel is worried that there is an ethical problem. Is it "right" to send sales people with a "good story" to call on "vulnerable" people?

The main Save-A-Life product involves a small radio transmitter which a person can carry around the house and a larger receiving unit which can be placed anywhere in the house. Just a push of a button on the transmitter will cause the receiver to dial up to four telephone numbers and play a prerecorded message. Depending on the situation, these calls could be to the police, fire department, or an emergency service, the person's doctor, and/or relatives. An obvious market is older people who live alone and are worried about what happens to them if they get sick, have an accident, or are bothered by intruders. Further, women of all ages might be interested in the product if they are concerned about their personal safety. It seems likely that there would be more potential customers in urban areas where there is great concern about crime.

The national distributor of the franchise has found that it is possible to get leads for prospective customers by running advertisements in local newspapers—with pictures stressing emergency situations. Then, personal sales follow-up is necessary. Sometimes several calls are needed. The system sells for $600. Jerry and Joel would have to pay $300 for each system—leaving $300 to cover the cost of sales, advertising, and general overhead. The national organization indicates that some franchise holders pay direct salespeople a commission of $100–$150 per unit sold. In addition, paying about $25 per installation seems to be adequate for proper installation by "handymen" who are willing to make the necessary connections to the telephone system. The national organization is willing and able to train technical people and salespeople in all the necessary functions as part of the original franchise fee. To get started, a franchise fee of $7,000 is required to cover the purchase of 15 systems, all necessary sales and promotion aids, and the right to unlimited home-office training of sales and technical personnel.

Jerry and Joel operate in a metropolitan area of about 450,000 people with a higher-than-average percentage of upper-income people. So they feel the economic potential may be adequate—although it is quite clear that an aggressive sales effort is required. The national distributor's sales rep feels that Jerry and Joel's salespeople (they are thinking of hiring two) ought to be able to sell at least 20 units each per month after a two-month break-in period—but, of course, no guarantee can be made.

Clearly, aggressive salespeople will be necessary. That is why the relatively "generous" return to the salespeople is suggested by the national distributor. But Joel wonders if it is really fair to appeal to sickly old people—or those who are worried about their safety. Further, is it right to take such a big markup? Joel realizes that without the $300 markup, there may not be any profit in it for the partners—but he still has nagging doubts about the whole idea.

Evaluate the Save-A-Life possibility for Jerry and Joel. Is this a good economic opportunity? Would it be "socially responsible" for them to take on this line?

29. Rundle Manufacturing Company

Rundle Manufacturing Company is a supplier of malleable iron castings for several automobile and aircraft manufacturers—and a variety of other users of castings. Last year's sales of castings amounted to over $50 million.

In addition to the foundry operations which produce the iron castings, Rundle also produces roughly 50 percent of all the original equipment bumper jacks installed in new automobiles each year. This is a very price-competitive business, but Rundle has been able to obtain this large share of the market by relying on close personal contact between the company's sales executives and its customers—supported by very close cooperation between the company's engineering department and its customers' buyers. This has been extremely important because the wide variety of models and model changes frequently requires alterations in the specifications of the bumper jacks. All of Rundle's bumper jacks are sold directly to the automobile manufacturers. No attempt has been made to sell bumper jacks to final consumers through hardware and automotive channels—although they are available through the manufacturers' automobile dealers.

Mr. Karns, Rundle's production manager, would now like to begin producing hydraulic jacks for sale through automotive-parts wholesalers to garages, body shops, and (in the case of one specialized design with some extra accessories) to fire and police departments—to aid in rescuing accident victims in cases where risks of fire prevent the use of cutting torches. Mr. Karns saw a variety of hydraulic jacks at a recent automotive show, and saw immediately that his plant could produce these products. This especially interested him because of the possibility of using excess capacity. Further, he feels that "jacks are jacks," and

that the company would merely be broadening its product line by introducing hydraulic jacks. As he became more enthusiastic about the idea, he found that his engineering department already had a design which appeared to be technically superior to the products now offered on the market. Further, he says that the company would be able to produce a product which is better-made than the competition (i.e., smoother castings, etc.) although he agrees that customers probably wouldn't notice the differences. The production department's costs for producing products comparable to those currently offered by competitors would be about one half the current retail prices.

Mr. Phil Wolf, the sales manager, has just received a memo from William Harrison, the president of the company, explaining about the production department's enthusiasm for broadening its jack line into hydraulic jacks. He seems enthusiastic about the idea, too, noting that it may be a way to make fuller use of the company's resources and increase its sales. Recognizing this enthusiasm, Phil Wolf wants to develop a well-thought-out explanation of why he can't get very excited about the proposal. He knows he is already overworked and could not possibly promote this new line himself—and he is the only salesman the company has. But more basically, he feels that the proposed hydraulic-jack line is not very closely related to the company's present emphasis. He has already indicated his lack of enthusiasm to Mr. Karns, but this has made little difference in Karns' thinking. Now, it is clear that Phil will have to convince the president or he will soon be responsible for selling hydraulic jacks.

What would you advise Phil to say and do?

---

30. Canadian Foods Limited*

Stan Roberts has been the marketing director of Canadian Foods Limited for the last two years. Canadian Foods—headquartered in Toronto—is a subsidiary of a large U.S.-based consumer packaged-food company with worldwide sales of more than $2 billion in 1979. Its Canadian sales were just under $250 mil-

lion—with the Quebec and Ontario markets accounting for 65 percent of the company's Canadian sales.

The company's product line includes such items as cake mixes, puddings, pie fillings, pancakes, and prepared foods. The company has successfully introduced at least six new products every year for the last five years. Its most recent new product was a line of frozen dinners successfully launched last year. Products from Canadian Foods are known for their

* This case was written by Professor Robert Tamilia, who at the time of its preparation was associated with the Faculty of Business Administration at the University of Quebec at Montreal.

Exhibit 1
Sales, Quebec and Canada (1973 = 100)

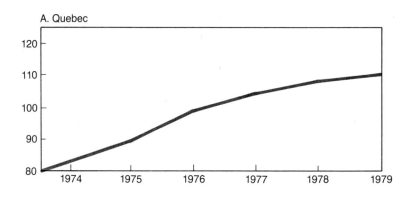

A. Quebec

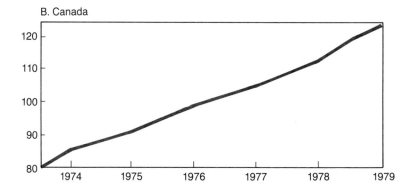

B. Canada

high quality and enjoy considerable brand appeal throughout Canada—including the Province of Quebec.

Sales of the company's products have risen every year since Mr. Roberts has taken over as marketing director. In fact, the company's market share has increased steadily in each of the product categories in which it competes. The Quebec market has closely followed the national trend except that, in the past two years, sales growth in that market began to lag (Exhibit 1).

According to Mr. Roberts, a big advantage of Canadian Foods over its competitors is the ability to coordinate all phases of the food business from Toronto. For this reason, Mr. Roberts meets at least once a month with his product managers—to discuss developments in local markets that might affect marketing plans. While each manager is free to make suggestions—and even to suggest major departures from cur-

rent marketing practices—Mr. Roberts has the final say.

One of the product managers, Claude Aylmer, expressed great concern at the last monthly meeting about the weak performance of the company's products in the Quebec market. While a broad range of possible reasons—ranging from inflation to politics—were reviewed to try to explain the situation, Mr. Aylmer maintained it was due to a basic lack of understanding of that market. Not enough managerial time and money had been spent studying the Quebec market. As a result, Aylmer felt that the current marketing approach to that market needed to be reevaluated. An inappropriate marketing plan may well be responsible for the sales slowdown. After all, "80 percent of the market is French-speaking. It's in the best interest of the company to treat that market as being separate and distinct from the rest of Canada."

Mr. Aylmer supported his position by showing that

per capita consumption in Quebec of many product categories in which the firm competes is above the national average (Exhibit 2). Research projects conducted by Canadian Foods also supports the "separate and distinct" argument. The firm has found—over the years—many French-English differences in brand attitudes, lifestyles, usage rates, and so on.

Mr. Aylmer argued that the company should develop a unique Quebec marketing plan for some or all of its brands. He specifically suggested that the French-language advertising plan for a particular brand be developed independently of the plan for English Canada. Currently, the agency assigned to the brand adapts its English-language plan to meet the perceived needs of the French Market. Mr. Roberts pointed out that the existing advertising approach assured Canadian Foods of a uniform brand image across Canada. However, the discussion that followed suggested that a different brand image might be needed in the French market if the company wanted to stop the brand's decline in sales.

The food distribution system in Quebec was then discussed. The major chains have their lowest market share of the food business in that province. Independents are strongest there. Specifically, the "mom-and-pop" food stores fast disappearing outside Quebec remain alive and well in the province. Traditionally, these stores have stocked a higher proportion (than supermarkets) of their shelf space with national brands—a point of some interest to Canadian Foods.

Finally, various issues related to discount policies, pricing structure, sales promotion, and cooperative advertising were discussed. All of this suggested that things were different in Quebec—and that future marketing plans for the firm's brands should reflect these differences to a greater extent than they do now.

After the meeting, Mr. Roberts stayed in his office to think about what had been said. Although he agreed with the basic idea that the Quebec market was in

Exhibit 2
Per capita consumption index, Province of Quebec
(Canada = 100)

Cake mixes	103	Pie fillings	115
Pancakes	91	Frozen dinners	84
Puddings	111	Prepared packaged	
Salad dressings	87	foods	89
Molasses	129	Cookies	119
Soft drinks	122		

many ways different, he was unsure as to how far his company should go in recognizing this fact. He knew that regional differences in food tastes and brand purchases existed not only in Quebec, but in other parts of Canada as well. People were people, on the other hand, with far more similarities between them than differences.

Mr. Roberts was afraid that giving special status to one region might conflict with top management's goal of trying to establish a uniform marketing program whenever possible. Management philosophy was that such a goal not only facilitated the administration and control of the marketing program but also encouraged the flow of information between markets. He was also worried about the long-term effect of such a policy change on costs, organizational structure, and on brand image. Still, enough product managers had expressed their concern over the years about the Quebec market to make him wonder if he shouldn't order a reevaluation of the company's current approach.

What would you tell Mr. Roberts? What are the future implications of your recommendations? In what way can marketing research help Mr. Roberts in this situation? How can per capita consumption differences between markets be explained?

31. Modern Homes, Ltd.*

Michael Good—marketing manager of Modern Homes, Ltd.—is finding it difficult to get his fellow executives interested in exporting. He has been impressed by reports of the buying power of the newly wealthy Middle East nations. His own company's receipt of an export inquiry from a customer in Saudi Arabia has further confirmed his feeling.

Modern Homes, Inc., is a New Brunswick producer of wooden factory-built homes. The company was formed in the 1960s, when industrial house production methods began to be accepted. One of the major attractions of such housing is the 20–30 percent price advantage that it offers over contractor-built homes. Modern Homes produces modular homes in two or three sections, which are shipped to the site, placed on a foundation, assembled, and finished.[1] From its beginning, Modern Homes, Ltd., has actively competed with other Maritime producers of factory-built homes. The plant capacity is about 600 units a year. While sales have been improving over the last few years, the current year's sales are estimated to be about 400 units. The underutilized capacity is a big concern to the company's management—and one for which they have no easy solution. Domestic sales were hard to expand since a troubled economy held back many prospective home purchasers. Expansion of sales westward into central Canada is not considered practical since transportation costs would make Modern's homes more expensive than those of Western competitors. Good's feeling, however, is that export sales might help solve the capacity problem—and provide longer-term growth prospects. There is no illusion on his part that exporting is easy. He had some experience with exporting to Iran in the past, and understands some of the problems.

It was in this climate that management began to more seriously consider export marketing. While there was agreement within the company that the Middle East presented good opportunities, there was uncertainty about the type of home that Modern Homes might export. While modular homes are reasonably priced in the Canadian domestic market, a major problem with exporting is transportation costs. Modular

homes are essentially big empty boxes. Since shipping costs are based on volume, shipping such homes is very costly. For example, the cost of shipping four homes to Iran was $80,000—with the homes themselves only valued in total at $100,000. Exporting panelized homes might be more sensible since the shipping costs of such homes were roughly one quarter those for modular homes. This results from the possibility of knocking down the walls of the home and folding everything into a smaller "box."

Attention also had to be paid, however, to the different assembly skills each type of home required in the

Exhibit 1
Notes from an industry, trade, and commerce seminar on manufactured homes industry—December 1978

1. The Oil Crisis and aftermath has changed picture for Middle East as export markets for many goods, including manufactured homes.

Market ratings:		Saudi Arabia	+3
		Iran	+3
Markets range in rating from +5		Iraq	+2
to −5, based on a number of crite-		Kuwait/Trucial	
ria, with plus ratings showing areas		States	+2
of best potential.		Syria	+1

Israel and Lebanon ratings have deteriorated such that both are rated negatively. However, the long-term prospects for both countries are good. Currently, there is an embargo on imports of house components in Israel, and income levels are being squeezed. In Lebanon, it was the opinion of ITC officials that it would be at least one year after peace before rebuilding would start.

2. Attitudes toward wood as a building material have improved, mainly because it is available and can be brought into the market quickly.

3. Two types of Canadian involvement have prevailed, mainly in Iran and Saudi Arabia:

   a. Demonstration homes—2–3 units for individual buyers—testing consumer acceptability.

   b. Contractual erections of 100–300 units on planned development sites.

4. Sales have almost exclusively been on the panelized variety. Modular homes have been erected for camp use, but most modular designs are either too small, or if they are large enough, transportation costs make them costly.

5. Four Canadian companies are active in the area. Competition is stiff involving U.S., U.K., Romanian and Scandinavian companies.

6. Price is not the only important factor, perhaps more critical are quality, reliability and delivery.

7. ITC review of most would-be exporters reveals:

   a. Little experience.

   b. Little assessment of company capabilities or goals.

   c. Little knowledge of what is involved.

   ITC suggests companies *first* review what units they want to sell, when they want to sell them, and what level of involvement they desire, and then to review markets with the objective of making a compatible fit.

---

* This case was written by Prof. Philip Rosson, who at the time of its preparation was associated with the Centre for International Business Studies at Dalhousie University.

[1] In contrast, *panelized* construction is a knocked-down form of building, where completely finished panels are placed in position on the site; *precut* construction implies that all components are precut and then assembled on the site.

export market. A panelized home could take about three to four weeks to erect, whereas a modular home could be completed in four to five days. Given the relative wealth of some Middle East consumers, a modular home might be worth its high transportation charges. Good had been told that Modern's houses would sell in the range of $80,000 to $100,000 in Saudi Arabia. A typical modular home with a delivered cost of $45,000 would offer quite a profit margin to a would-be Saudi middleman.

While there was agreement on the potential of export markets, contrasting points of view were expressed by individual executives. The general manager recognized the potential of the Middle East, but was uncertain about how to proceed, what the operation would cost, and how exports could best be handled. On this latter point, there were three main alternatives:

1. Modern Homes to export directly and to handle the overseas sales operation themselves.
2. Modern Homes to appoint overseas sales agents.
3. Modern Homes to seek out other interested parties and to "go in on their coattails."

Michael Good and the sales manager, Bill Comeau, felt that an overseas trip should be made to investigate the markets in depth. As Comeau said, "No one in the company knows what is wanted in the various export markets." Comeau felt that once a market had been selected by the company, Modern would probably need to develop a strong relationship with a local company. Overall, he felt that while there were good long-term prospects in the Middle East, the company shouldn't rush into exporting. A great deal of money has been made and *lost* by exporters in this area. Good agreed but was turned down when he asked the controller whether he would approve $50,000 to investigate and develop Middle East markets. The controller argued that the company knew that a market existed. What was required was to put together the right package, i.e., a product that shipped easily. He pointed to the requests for sales literature as strong enough indication that Modern Homes had a "hot" product.

In December 1980, the Modern Homes management was planning through 1983. Part of the company plan could involve export marketing if some agreement could be reached on the matter. The only additional information on hand (Exhibit 1) had been obtained at an Industry, Trade, and Commerce seminar held just a few days earlier.

What action should Modern Homes now take regarding the Middle East market?

---

32. The Adanac Manufacturing Company*

William Johnson is president of the Adanac Manufacturing Company—located in Cambridge, Ontario. The firm manufactures high-quality, hot-air oil furnaces. Prior to 1956, Mr. Johnson worked for a large furnace manufacturer in Toronto—first as production manager, and later as general manager of the firm. With $200,000 his aunt left him in her estate, Mr. Johnson established the Adanac Manufacturing Company in 1956.

In 1977, the Adanac Manufacturing Company had gross sales of $8 million (all in Canada). At this time, the firm was operating at 65 percent of capacity and was barely profitable—in part because it had to compete with many other furnace manufacturers, some of whom were much larger and well established.

On Saturday, June 24, 1978, Adanac's vice president of marketing, Grant Oxley, was married. At a party for the couple, Mr. Oxley met Ian Smyth, a Canadian Trade Commissioner stationed in London.

Upon learning of the kind of products Adanac manufactured, Mr. Smyth suggested that Mr. Oxley give serious consideration to exporting some of his firm's production to Britain. That country, Mr. Smyth believed, was badly in need of better heating equipment. Mr. Oxley promised to take the matter up with his company's president. Upon further inquiry, Mr. Oxley discovered that, since the United Kingdom had joined the European Economic Community, the duty on oil furnaces imported from abroad (including Canada) was 18 percent. He also learned that the term used in the United Kingdom for furnaces in the home was *central heating units* or *domestic boilers*.

By consulting various publications during his honeymoon in England, Mr. Oxley found some data about the furnace industry in Britain. In 1974 there were nine manufacturers of central heating units in the United Kingdom—using various types of fuel. Of the over 20

---

* This case was written by Dr. Herman Overgaard, who at the time of its preparation was associated with the School of Business and Economics at Wilfrid Laurier University.

million dwellings in the United Kingdom, 78 percent of the households occupied the entire house, 21 percent of the households occupied apartments and flats, and the remaining 1 percent occupied mobile homes.

Mr. Oxley also discovered from the 1973 General Household Survey that 34.9 percent of the households in the United Kingdom had central heating units installed. Also in 1974, 91 percent of all new dwellings in England and Wales were constructed with central heating units. Permanent new dwellings completed in

the United Kingdom in 1974 numbered 278,363. Mr. Oxley also learned that about 8.5 million homes had been built in the United Kingdom since 1945. Some 24,923 central heating units were imported in 1974 at a total value of 1,864,529 pounds sterling.

What should Mr. Oxley do next? Explain what you would suggest if the company decided to compete in the U.K. market.

33. Metro Nurses Association

The Metro Nurses Association is a nonprofit organization which has been operating—with varying degrees of success—for 20 years. Some of its funding comes from the local "community chest"—to provide emergency nursing services for those who can't afford to pay. The balance of the revenues—about 80 percent of the $1 million annual budget—comes from the provincial governments concerned, in the form of a Medicare payment and to a much lesser degree, from private insurance companies.

Jane Burns has been director of the association for two years now—and has developed a well-functioning organization—able to meet the requests for service which come to it from some local doctors and from the discharge officers at local hospitals. Some business also comes to the association by self-referral—the client finding the name of the association in the Yellow Pages of the local telephone directory.

The last two years have been a rebuilding time—because the previous director had had personnel problems. This led to a weakening of the association's image with the local referring agencies. Now, the image is more positive. But Jane is not completely satisfied with the situation. By definition, the Metro Nurses Association is a nonprofit organization—but it still has to cover all its costs in order to meet the payroll, rent payments, telephone expenses, and so on—including her own salary. She can see that while the association is growing slightly and now breaking even, it doesn't have much of a cushion to fall back on if (1) people stop needing as many nursing services, (2) the government changes its rules about paying for the association's kind of nursing services—either cutting back on what would be paid or reducing the amount that would be paid—or (3) if new competitors enter the market. In fact, the latter possibility is of great concern to her. Some for-profit organizations are developing around

the country—to provide home health care services—including nursing services of the kind offered by Metro Nurses Association. Reports from the industry indicate that these for-profit organizations are efficiently run—offering good service at competitive—and sometimes even lower—prices than some nonprofit organizations. And seemingly they are doing this at a profit—which suggests that it would be possible for them to lower their prices if the nonprofit organizations tried to compete on price.

Jane is trying to decide whether she should ask her board of directors to let her begin to expand the association's activities by moving into the home health care market.

Now, the association is primarily concerned with providing professional nursing care in the home. But her nurses are much too expensive for routine health-care activities—such as helping fix meals, bathing and dressing patients, and so on. A registered nurse is not needed for these jobs. All that is required is an ability to get along with all kinds of people—and a willingness to do this kind of work. Generally, any mature person can be fairly quickly trained to do the job—following the instructions and under the general supervision of a physician, a nurse, or family members. There seems to be a growing demand for home health-care services as more women have joined the work force and can't take over home health care when the need arises—either due to emergencies or long-term disabilities. And with older people living longer, there are more single-survivor family situations where there is no one nearby to take care of their needs. Often, however, there are family members—or third-party payers such as the government or insurers—who would be willing to pay for such services. Now, Jane sometimes assigns nurses to this work—because the association is not in a position to send home health-care aides. Sometimes she recommends other agencies, or suggests one or another of three people who have been doing this work on their own—part-time. But with growing demand—she is wondering if the association should get into this business—hiring aides as needed.

Jane is concerned that a new, competitive, full-service home health-care organization—which would provide both nursing services *and* less-skilled home health-care services—might be very appealing to the local hospitals and other referers. So she can see the possibility of losing nursing service business if the Metro Nurses Association does not begin to offer a more complete service. This would cause real problems for the association—because there are overhead costs which are more or less fixed. A loss in revenue of as little as 10 or 20 percent could require laying off some nurses—or perhaps laying off some secretaries, giving up part of the office, and so on.

Another reason for seriously considering expanding beyond nursing services—using paraprofessionals and relatively unskilled personnel—is to offer a better service to present customers *and* make more effective use of the organization structure which has been developed over the last two years. Jane estimates that the administrative and office capabilities could handle 50 to 100 percent more clients without straining the system. It would be necessary to add some clerical help—if the expansion were quite large—as well as expanding the hours when the switchboard was open. But these increases in overhead would be minor compared to the present proportions of total revenues which go to covering overhead. In other words, additional clients could increase revenue and assure the survival of the association—providing a cushion to cover the normal fluctuations in demand—and providing some security for the administrative personnel. Further, she feels that if the association were successful in expanding its services—and therefore could generate some surplus—it would be in a position to extend services to those who are not now able to pay. One of the least attractive parts of her job is cutting off service to clients whose third-party benefits have run

out—or for whatever reason can no longer afford to pay the association. Jane is uncomfortable about having to cut off service, but must schedule her nurses to provide revenue-producing services if she's going to be able to meet the payroll every two weeks. By expanding to provide more services, she might be able to keep serving more of these nonpaying clients. This possibility excites her because her nurse's training has instilled a deep desire to serve people—whether they can pay or not. This continual need to cut off service—because people can't pay—has been at the root of many disagreements—and even arguments—between the nurses serving the clients and Jane, as director and representative of the board of directors.

Expanding into home health-care services will not be easy, however. It may even require convincing the nurses' union that the nurses should be available on a 24-hour schedule—rather than the eight-to-five schedule six days a week, which is typical now. It would also require some decisions about relative pay levels for nurses, paraprofessionals, and home health-care aides. It would also require setting prices for these different services and telling the present customers and referers about the expanding service.

These problems aren't bothering Jane, however, because she thinks she could handle them. She is sure that the services are in demand and could be supplied at competitive prices.

Her primary concern is whether this is the right thing for a nurses' association to do. The name of her group is the Metro Nurses Association and its whole history has been oriented to supplying nurses' services. Nurses are dedicated professionals who bring high standards to any job they undertake. The question is whether the Metro Nurses Association should offer less "professional" services. Inevitably, some of the home health-care aides will not be as dedicated as the nurses might like them to be. And this might reflect unfavorably on the nurse image. At the same time, however, Jane is concerned about the future of the Metro Nurses Association and her own future.

What should Jane Burns do? Why?

34. West City's Committee on Fitness*

The members of the Mayor's Committee on Fitness listened attentively while Professor Henry Morgan, chairman of its research subcommittee, presented the findings of a research study the committee had authorized. The committee had been formed 12 months earlier when the mayor of West City had invited each of a number of clubs and organizations concerned with fitness and health—the YMCA, the medical association, the parks and recreation commission, sports clubs, and so forth—to appoint a representative to the committee. In his invitation, the mayor suggested the following objectives for the Committee on Fitness to consider:

1. To indicate to the people of West City the opportunities existing within the community for living more fully through personal involvement.
2. To suggest ways in which every member of the community can be encouraged to take part in his or her own way in fun-associated activity on a regular basis.
3. To involve the citizens of West City in physical activity—particularly of a vigorous nature, over an extended period of time.

Committee representatives subsequently discussed the reason for the formation of the committee. They generally agreed that there was a genuine need to develop programs designed to meet the objectives given in the mayor's invitation. The sedentary lifestyles of the people, developed over the last century as industrialization and urbanization increased, had led to some serious problems. A large proportion of the community's heath costs, existing inefficiencies in labor productivity and even low enjoyment or satisfaction with life itself could be attributed to inappropriate lifestyles. Lack of physical activity and fitness, poor eating habits, and excessive use of alcohol, tobacco, and drugs could all be viewed as contributing factors. The level of physical fitness was considered especially important since it was known that people with high physical activity levels also ate better and made far less use of alcohol, tobacco, and drugs.

The members of the committee agreed that the objectives of the committee should go well beyond the first and second points mentioned by the mayor. It would not be enough "to indicate" or "to suggest."

Rather, the committee should strive to bring about increased participation of the citizens of West City in physical activities of a "vigorous nature" over an "extended period of time." Since there was no well-known method of creating the major shift in lifestyles and behavior that achievement of their objective would require, the committee decided to seek the cooperation of several experts in physiology, human kinetics, recreation, and applied behavioral science on the staff of the local university. Accordingly, a research subcommittee was formed with the assistance of various faculty members. Professor Henry Morgan was chosen as that subcommittee's chairman.

After meeting several times, the research committee approved the following statement of its objectives:

To describe the current physical activities, fitness capabilities, and predispositions toward physical activity of West City residents in a manner which will:

a. Provide measures for use in future evaluations of the impact and effectiveness of programs implemented by the mayor's committee.
b. Help to identify target markets and objectives suitable for program development.
c. Provide information which is useful in designing and implementing programs.

Given these objectives, the research committee then designed a research project to measure three main classes of variables: (1) attitudes related to fitness; (2) rates of participation in physical activities; and (3) attitudes toward fitness and health. Using volunteer university and high school students as interviewers, 354 interviews were conducted in West City homes. A significant response bias was experienced in this interviewing as students reported that people who were overweight or negative in their attitudes toward physical activities were less likely to agree to be interviewed.

Striking findings were revealed when two activity indices were calculated. In the week prior to the study, 55 percent of the sample had an activity index number of 2.3 or less. To achieve an index number of 2.3, the individual need only move his or her body for 14 hours out of a 168 hour week. In other words, two hours or less per day of movement was the norm for 55 percent of the sample. Even given a sample which was biased toward those who are more fit—very little physical activity took place in the week prior to the study!

In terms of the index for the previous year's activity,

* This case was prepared by Dr. John Liefeld, who at the time of its preparation was associated with the Department of Consumer Studies at the University of Guelph.

Exhibit 1
Attitude responses—physical activity

Statement	Disagree	Disagree somewhat	Agree somewhat	Agree
1. In our modern society there is no need for strenuous physical activity	69.4%	11.6%	9.3%	9.6%
2. I would participate more in physical activities if my doctor advised me to be more active	15.3	4.3	18.8	61.6
3. My athletic skills and capabilities are below average	34.7	21.9	22.2	21.3
4. I don't know enough about the role of exercise in health and fitness	43.3	16.5	21.1	19.1
5. I enjoy being a spectator of sports and physical activities more than being a participant	33.6	15.4	21.7	29.3
6. The companionship and socializing I get when participating in physical activities are more important to me than the health benefits of physical activities	35.0	23.9	27.1	14.0
7. I would participate more in physical activities and sports but I am embarrassed about my lack of physical skills	55.1	17.3	14.8	12.8
8. The health benefits of physical activities and sports are more important to me than the companionship and socializing I get from such activities	14.0	22.3	25.5	38.1
9. Medical science can keep us healthy and fit; exercise is not necessary	84.4	6.8	5.1	3.7
10. I prefer active recreations such as skating, swimming, or other physical activities to passive recreations such as reading, watching TV, or doing crafts	14.8	22.5	19.7	43.0
11. I would participate more in physical activities but my job is too tiring	43.6	14.0	23.5	18.9
12. I like my body the way it is	34.8	27.9	16.8	20.5
13. I want to know more about exercise, health, and fitness	11.4	11.4	31.1	46.0
14. In the summer it is too hot for me to participate in physical activities	66.0	16.7	9.6	7.6
15. I am personally committed to participation in active physical activities	45.5	13.9	15.9	24.7
16. I would participate more in physical activities and sports but there are not enough facilities in West City (i.e., fields, gyms, pools, courts, etc.)	57.9	16.6	13.8	11.7
17. In our modern society there is a real need for strenuous physical activity	15.1	14.2	21.7	49.0
18. It is important to me to be physically fit in order to manage my daily life and make my work and leisure more meaningful	5.9	10.5	20.4	63.2
19. I am too busy to participate in physical activities	45.0	17.6	27.8	9.6
20. I would participate in more physical activities if more of my friends would also participate	37.6	13.1	29.3	19.0
21. When I start some form of physical activity I always continue it	28.2	26.7	21.3	23.9
22. In the past year, I would have participated more in physical activities and sports but the programs cost too much money	54.7	12.9	18.6	13.8
23. A nutritious diet by itself will guarantee health and fitness	63.7	19.0	12.5	4.8
24. I would participate more in physical activities and sports but I don't have the time	34.0	14.7	32.9	18.4
25. Other people think I am fit	21.5	21.8	33.5	23.2

Exhibit 2
Physical activities during the past year

	Number of respondents			Number of respondents
Walking to, or at, work	236		Gardening	213
Walking for recreation	180		Snow shovelling	186
Jogging	64		Social dancing	129
Competitive running	7		Dancing classes	11
Calisthenic exercises	79		Yoga	22
Recreational bicycling	97		Horseback riding	9
Bicycling to work	32		Boxing, judo, karate	7
Bicycle racing	3		Tennis	41
Recreational swimming	171		Table tennis	30
Competitive swimming	3		Badminton	27
Platform diving	5		Handball or squash	8
Skin diving	4		Volleyball	21
Scuba diving	1		Curling	20
Recreational sailing	15		Bowling	50
Sailboat racing	3		Golfing	44
Recreational skating	45		Touch football	17
Figure skating	2		Soccer	9
Competitive skating	2		Hardball	7
Downhill skiing	23		Softball	20
Cross-country skiing	29		Ice hockey	16
Snow shoeing	6		Floor hockey	10
Repairs around the house	209		Basketball	20

similar results were reported. Seventy one percent of the sample had an index score of 200 or less. To achieve this index number, the individual need only move his or her body for one and a quarter hours a day every day of the year. This means that they spent less than 5.2 percent of the year in any kind of movement. That a very large majority of the residents of West City are extremely sedentary was an inevitable conclusion.

The responses of the subjects to the survey's probing as to attitudes are summarized in Exhibit 1. The physical activities of respondents during the previous year are presented in Exhibit 2 and the reasons given for so participating are shown in Exhibit 3.

After Professor Morgan's presentation, the committee discussed the implications of the research findings for the programs which the mayor's committee might introduce. Some members of the committee advocated programs which would increase the number of organized fitness-related activities people could select. Others argued for an educational program to make people more knowledgeable about the relationship between fitness and health. A third group maintained

Exhibit 3
Reasons for participating in physical activity
(multiple responses possible)

		Percent of subjects
1.	It makes me feel good	85.6
2.	To maintain health and fitness	80.7
3.	To help control weight	63.7
4.	For social contacts	56.9
5.	For excitement	42.4
6.	Advised to do so by doctor	16.1
7.	To get recognition and admiration from friends	12.5

that fitness motivation was the central problem. They insisted that programs designed either to educate or to offer more activities were doomed to failure until people could be motivated to change their way of life.

Given the data presented, what are the problems confronting the committee? What, if anything, can marketing contribute to their solution?

35. Bramalea Realty Ltd.*

Bramalea Realty Ltd. is a small independent real estate firm located in Lethbridge, Alberta. Because of its success the company has recently decided to expand operations from residential real estate to office development. The decision to move into this area was felt by management to be sound because of the buoyant economy Alberta was experiencing in the seventies and the fact that all projections for business, population, and construction were very positive for the next decade. Although most of this activity was centered in Calgary, Edmonton, and points north, it was felt that considerable spillover was affecting Lethbridge, which is located in the southwest corner of the province and has a population of 50,000.

Bramalea's accountant had indicated that he noticed some figures in the *Financial Post Survey of Markets* indicating that Lethbridge's growth rate per decade was 35 percent—significantly higher than the Canadian average of 10 percent and even 1 percent higher than the Alberta average. In the same publication he found Lethbridge to have a market rating of 86 percent above the national average and also higher than Edmonton and Calgary. This, he surmised, was a result of high retail expenditures per capita and a large retail drawing from the smaller communities surrounding Lethbridge. Although Bramalea's management was a bit hesitant to move so quickly they were aware that the demand for office space increased in proportion to population, income, and retail expenditures and these variables were all rapidly increasing. The accountant pointed to the fact that construction in Lethbridge was going ahead strongly and that it would be an ideal time for Bramalea to enter this area of office development.

As a result, Bramalea purchased a site one block from the central business district—with plans to construct an office building. Although the site contained an old building, it was planned that it would be replaced with a four-story office building of about 40,000 square feet.

Before going ahead with construction Bramalea decided to do some research on the type of facilities which prospective tenants would prefer (e.g., underground parking, recreation facilities, restaurant, etc.). They felt that acting on the results of this research would increase their chances for a high early occupancy rate of at least 90 percent, which they were going to require to make the project financially feasible. Results of their investigation revealed the following in addition to revealing tenant preferences regarding amenities desired.

1. Confirmation that the population of Lethbridge was growing at a rate of 35 percent per decade *(FP Survey of Markets),* whereas Canadian average is 10 percent.
2. Confirmation that the market rating index of Lethbridge was 86 percent above the national average in 1979 *(FP Survey of Markets).*
3. Per capita retail sales for Lethbridge in 1979 was $5,924—considerably above the Canadian average of $3,190.
4. Population projections for Lethbridge:

1979	50,000
1984	58,000
1989	66,000

5. Present supply of office space in Lethbridge (1979) was estimated at 425,000 sq. ft., with a vacancy rate of 20 percent.
6. Averages for other cities in Canada show an average of about 6.5 to 7 sq. ft. per capita in office space at 90 percent occupancy.
7. There did not appear to be a great demand for restaurant, recreation facilities, because the major preference was to be close to downtown.

In view of this information Bramalea is still planning to proceed with construction of the building, but they are now a bit worried.

Should Bramalea be concerned about the results of their most recent research? How should Bramalea have gone about assessing the market potential for their new office building? What additional information, if any, is required at this point? What would you advise Bramalea to do at this time?

---

* This case was written by Professor D. W. Balderson, who at the time of its preparation was associated with the University of Lethbridge.

36. Beaver Spirits Ltd.*

Beaver Spirits Limited President, Pat Brendan, had asked Tim McLaughlin, his marketing manager, to prepare a report on the status of the liquor market in Canada at year-end, 1977. In that report, McLaughlin stated that the time was right to add a new brand to Beaver's line. The two men agreed that a rye should be added. They disagreed, however, as to the price category in which they should compete.

Beaver Spirits had originally been a subsidiary of one of the bigger Canadian liquor corporations. When the parent company decided to make some major policy changes, Brendan obtained the financing required to buy Beaver and its brands. He also negotiated an agreement whereby Beaver would receive product from the former parent's several distilleries. He had received permission to go after McLaughlin, then a top sales representative with the same corporation.

The two men had worked for ten years to put together a solid organization. They had built sales on hard work, good product, and a price positioning policy. When they saw an opportunity for a brand, they negotiated to get product, making sure the brand could be differentiated via packaging, taste, or advertising.

Beaver had a good product mix: several ryes, three rums (light, dark, gold), two vodkas, and a gin. They imported and sold a quality scotch and three liqueurs. Most of their brands held somewhere between a 1 percent and 3 percent share of the markets in which they competed. They would have liked larger shares but felt hindered by selling only in four provinces.

Their main effort was usually getting the provincial Liquor Boards to list a new product. This normally consisted of a board consenting to take a quantity of the new product into a number of key retail outlets. If the brand sold at or above a predetermined rate, the board would then expand the quantity ordered and the number of outlets "listing" the product. It was easier to get a brand listed if the selling company were willing to delist an existing brand. Beaver had a successful record of marketing a limited number of brands.

When Beaver was reorganized the company had no French-language representative. Ten years later, this situation had not changed. Brendan believed he needed someone in Quebec who spoke the language but he had never actively recruited there. Neither had the company done anything about the large and growing British Columbia market. He justified staying out of the Atlantic Provinces, citing the higher cost of transportation to a smaller population. And the Atlantic Provinces, like Quebec, had "local" brand favorites. He ignored the fact that many brands selling well in the Prairie markets were, for the most part, also "local." Beaver operated only in Ontario, Manitoba, Saskatchewan, and Alberta.

Since Beaver tried to buy most of its product from the ex-parent, it had developed few alternate sources of supply. The company maintained a price policy of positioning brands at or near the bottom of the price categories set by the provinces. They were usually 15 or 30 cents lower than the top brand in the price category. The firm had built a reputation for good quality and inexpensive brands. Beaver also had stayed out of head-to-head competition with the ex-parent which was a price leader in virtually all the categories in which it competed.

After reading McLaughlin's report, Brendan knew he agreed with his marketing manager that the rye market was the one to go after. Rye accounted for about 40 percent of the total liquor market, with a continuous increase in national case sales. Beaver had no "winning" rye brand in the four-province territory. The ryes it did have had no better than a 1 percent share of the market. The firm could use an existing brand in bargaining with the Boards and, if necessary, a poor-selling rye could be delisted.

The two men differed on the price category of rye to select. McLaughlin favored the higher-priced "B" ryes; Brendan was inclined to go after the lowest-priced "F" category. Neither man cared to take on the best-selling (over 50 percent) "E" category with its more than 25 brands, including 5 strong leaders.

Brendan pointed out that a Beaver brand in the "B"s would be competing against the traditionally strong Canadian Club and V.O. brands. These two brands together held slightly over 75 percent of the "B" sales. If Beaver introduced a "B" brand, it would be bucking its old organization for customers. McLaughlin was aware of this fact but saw only the strong growth record of the "B" category. As Exhibit 1 indicates, "B" was the second largest seller of all rye price categories with case sales in 1977 close to 1.9 million. Only the low-price "E"s accounted for a larger proportion of total rye sales.

"B" had gained 190,500 cases out of 1976's total 341,000 case increase for all ryes. Brendan, on the other hand, backed his argument for an "F" category

* This case was prepared by Mr. William Kalaher, who at the time of its preparation was associated with the Marketing Department, Lakeshore Campus, Humber College.

Exhibit 1
Rye whiskey sales, 1977, by price category (00's cases, twelve 25-ounce bottles per case)

	A		B		C		D		E		F		Total	
	Cases	Percent	Cases	Percent	Cases	Percent	Cases	Percent	Cases	Percent	Cases	Percent	Cases	Percent
Atlantic	2.9	2.1%	96.4	5.0%	1.6	0.7%	94.5	7.5%	254.6	6.3%	88.4	7.4%	538.5	6.1%
Quebec	9.3	6.8	174.9	9.2	9.8	4.1	54.0	4.3	95.0	2.3	53.3	4.5	396.5	4.5
Ontario	66.0	47.4	944.6	49.8	150.9	63.2	758.1	60.0	2,247.0	55.5	*	*	4,170.2	47.5
Manitoba	6.6	4.7	79.1	4.2	9.9	4.2	37.0	2.9	239.9	5.9	270.3	22.7	643.1	7.3
Saskatchewan	3.8	2.7	126.7	6.7	5.2	2.2	22.6	1.8	433.6	10.7	45.7	3.8	637.9	7.3
Alberta.............	30.6	22.0	240.5	12.7	35.5	14.9	169.2	13.4	345.0	8.5	350.2	29.3	1,171.2	13.3
British Columbia	19.8	14.3	235.8	12.4	25.6	10.7	126.0	10.1	433.9	10.8	385.3	32.3	1,226.5	14.0
	139.2	100.0	1,898.2	100.0	238.7	100.0	1,261.7	100.0	4,049.2	100.0	1,193.4	100.0	8,784.0	100.0

* = Province has no "F" category.
A = Highest-priced rye.
F = Lowest-priced rye.

brand, citing the case increase "Fs" had scored (see Exhibit 2) and their strong 1977 sales record. The competition in "F," Brendan said, consisted of new, not-yet-firmly-established names plus a few older ones. "It's a price market, Tim, and we know how to go after customers in that area," Brendan argued.

Other points brought out in discussion involved the number of brands in the two price categories being considered. Five brands had a little over 90 percent share in the "B" category, with another five sharing the remaining 10 percent of sales. Canadian Club held a 50 percent plus share, followed by a strong V.O. franchise. In "F," the brand names and share leaders differed in each province. About 20 brands competed in each of the three Prairie Provinces, with no one brand holding more than a 10 percent share.

The new brand, McLaughlin said, was to serve as an incentive for Beaver sales people. It would give them something new to talk about plus the status that comes with an entry in the prestigious "B" category. He also reminded Brendan that Ontario had no "F"

category. A decision to enter "F" rather than "B" would shut Beaver out of close to 50 percent of the national sales total of rye which Ontario traditionally maintained.

"If we go after the 'F' market," McLaughlin said, "we will have to get our sales in the three Prairie provinces or think about going into British Columbia or Quebec. We'll have to do mostly local advertising and there is no advertising allowed in Saskatchewan." He reminded Brendan that Beaver's media policy had always been to advertise in local media, such as daily newspapers or regional editions of national magazines.

While Brendan saw the wisdom of his marketing manager's recommendations, he was hesitant about competing against the organization from which Beaver purchased most of its existing product supply. He also remained concerned about the tougher competition in the "B" market.

In what price category should Beaver compete? Why do you feel this way?

Exhibit 2
Canadian Rye whiskey case sales, 1976 versus 1977 (intra-category changes)

Category	1976	1977	+/−cases	+/−percent	1977 market share
A	108,889	139,206	+ 30,317	27.8%	1.6%
B	1,707,655	1,898,251	+190,596	11.1	21.6
C	250,887	238,796	− 12,092	−4.8	2.7
D	1,226,866	1,261,789	+ 34,923	2.8	14.4
E	4,017,480	4,049,284	− 31,804	0.8	46.1
F	1,127,509	1,193,497	+ 65,988	5.9	13.6
Total	8,439,288	8,780,823	+341,535	4.1	100.0

37. Mayfair Detergent Company*

Mike Powell is product manager on Protect Deodorant Soap. He is working on developing and securing management approval of next year's marketing plan for Protect. His first step involves submitting a draft marketing plan to Gerry Holden who has recently been appointed group product manager.

Mike's marketing plan is the single most important document he will produce on his brand assignment. Written annually, the marketing plan does three main things:

1. It reviews the brand's performance in the past year, assesses the competitive situation, and highlights problems and opportunities for the brand.
2. It spells out marketing, advertising, and sales promotion strategies and plans for the coming year.
3. Finally, and most importantly, the marketing plan sets out the brand's sales objectives and advertising/promotion budget requirements.

In preparing this marketing plan Mike gathered the information in Exhibit 1.

Mike was aware of the regional disparities in the bar soap market and recognized the significant regional skews:

a. The underdevelopment of the deodorant bar segment in Quebec with a corresponding overdevel-

opment of the beauty bar segment. Research showed this was due to cultural factors. An identical pattern is evident in most European countries where the adoption of deodorant soaps has been slower than in North America. For similar reasons, the development of perfumed soaps is highest in Quebec.

b. The overdevelopment of synthetic bars in the Prairies. These bars, primarily in the deodorant segment, lather better in the hard water of the Prairies. Nonsynthetic bars lather very poorly in hard-water areas and leave a soap film.

c. The overdevelopment of the "all-other" segment in Quebec. This segment, consisting of smaller brands fares better in Quebec, where 40 percent of the grocery trade is done by independent stores. Conversely, large chain grocery stores predominate in Ontario and the Prairies.

Mike's brand, Protect, is a highly perfumed, deodorant bar. His business is relatively weak in the key Ontario market. To confirm this share data, Mike calculated consumption of Protect per thousand people in each region (see Exhibit 2).

These differences are especially interesting since per capita sales of total bar soap products are roughly equal in all provinces.

A consumer attitude and usage research study had been conducted approximately a year ago. This study

---

* This case was prepared by Mr. Daniel Aronchick, who at the time of its preparation was Marketing Manager at Thomas J. Lipton, Limited.

Exhibit 1
Past 12-month share of soap market (percent)

	Maritimes	Quebec	Ontario	Manitoba/ Saskatchewan	Alberta	British Columbia
Deodorant segment						
Zest	21.3%	14.2%	24.5%	31.2%	30.4%	25.5%
Dial	10.4	5.1	12.8	16.1	17.2	14.3
Lifebuoy	4.2	3.1	1.2	6.4	5.8	4.2
Protect	2.1	5.6	1.0	4.2	4.2	2.1
Beauty bar segment						
Camay	6.2	12.3	7.0	4.1	4.0	5.1
Lux	6.1	11.2	7.7	5.0	6.9	5.0
Dove	5.5	8.0	6.6	6.3	6.2	4.2
Lower-priced bars						
Ivory	11.2	6.5	12.4	5.3	5.2	9.0
Sunlight	6.1	3.2	8.2	4.2	4.1	8.0
All others (including stores' own brands)	26.9	30.8	18.6	17.2	16.0	22.6
Total soap market	100.0	100.0	100.0	100.0	100.0	100.0

Exhibit 2
Standard cases of three-ounce bars consumed per 1,000 people in 12 months

	Maritimes	Quebec	Ontario	Manitoba/ Saskatchewan	Alberta	British Columbia
Protect.............	4.1	10.9	1.9	8.1	4.1	6.2
Sales index	66	175	31	131	131	100

revealed that consumer top-of-mind awareness of the Protect brand differed greatly across Canada. This was true despite the even expenditure of advertising funds in past years. Also, trial of Protect was low in the Maritimes, Ontario, and B.C. (Exhibit 3).

The attitude portion of the research revealed that consumers who had heard of Protect were aware of its main attribute of deodorant protection via a high fragrance level. This was the main selling point in the copy strategy and it was well communicated through Protect's advertising. The other important finding was that consumers who had tried Protect were satisfied with the product. Some 72 percent of those trying Protect had repurchased the product at least twice.

One last pressing issue for Protect was the pending delisting of the brand by two key Ontario chains. These chains, which controlled about half the grocery volume in Ontario, were dissatisfied with the level at which Protect was moving off the shelves.

With this information before him, Mike now had to resolve the key aspect of the brand's marketing plan for the following year: how to allocate the advertising and sales promotion budget by region.

Protect's total advertising/sales promotion budget was 22 percent of sales. With forecasted sales of $3.2 million, this budget amounted to a $700M marketing expenditure. Traditionally such funds had been allocated in proportion to population (Exhibit 4).

Mike's inclination is to skew spending even more heavily into Ontario where the grocery chain delisting problem exists. In the previous year, 36 percent of Protect's budget was allocated to Ontario which ac-

counted for only 12 percent of Protect's sales. Mike wants to increase Ontario spending to 45 percent of the total budget by taking funds evenly from all other areas. Mike expects this will increase business in the key Ontario market which has over a third of Canada's population.

Mike then presented this plan to Gerry, his newly appointed group product manager. Gerry strongly disagreed. He had also been reviewing Protect's business and felt that advertising and rally promotion funds had historically been misallocated. It was his firm belief that, to use his words: "A brand should spend where its business is." Gerry believed that the first priority in allocating funds regionally was to support the areas of strength. He went on to suggest to Mike that there was more business to be had in the brand's strong areas, Quebec and the Prairies, than in chasing sales in Ontario. Therefore, Gerry suggested that spending for Protect in the coming year be proportional to the brand's sales by region rather than to regional population.

Mike felt this was wrong, particularly in light of the Ontario situation. He asked Gerry how the Ontario market should be handled. Gerry suggested the conservative way to build business in Ontario was to consider investing incremental marketing funds. However, before these incremental funds are invested, a test of this Ontario investment proposition should be conducted. Gerry recommended that in a small area or town in Ontario an investment-spending test market be conducted for 12 months to see if the incremental spending resulted in higher sales and profits—profits

Exhibit 3
Usage results (in percent)

	Maritimes	Quebec	Ontario	Manitoba/ Saskatchewan	Alberta	British Columbia
Respondents aware of Protect	20%	58%	28%	30%	32%	16%
Respondents ever trying Protect	3	18	2	8	6	4

Exhibit 4
Allocation of marketing budget, by population

	Maritimes	Quebec	Ontario	Manitoba/ Saskatchewan	Alberta	British Columbia	Canada
Percent of population	10%	27%	36%	8%	8%	11%	100%
Possible allocation of budget based on population	$70M	$190M	$253M	$55M	$55M	$77M	$700M
Percent of Protect business at present	7%	51%	12%	11%	11%	8%	100%

large enough to justify the higher spending. In other words, an investment payout would have to be assured before spending any extra money in Ontario.

Mike felt this approach would be a waste of time and unduly cautious, given the importance of the Ontario market.

Should Protect's advertising and promotional funds be allocated by region in proportion to past sales, by regional population, or in some other fashion?

NOTES

Chapter 1

1. Reavis Cox, *Distribution in a High-Level Economy* (Englewood Cliffs, N.J.: Prentice-Hall, 1965), p. 149; and Paul W. Stewart and J. Frederick Dewhurst, *Does Distribution Cost Too Much?* (New York: Twentieth Century Fund, 1963), pp. 117–18.

2. Malcolm P. McNair, "Marketing and the Social Challenge of Our Times," in *A New Measure of Responsibility for Marketing,* ed. Keith Cox and Ben M. Enis (Chicago: American Marketing Association, 1968.)

3. Peter F. Drucker, *Management: Tasks, Responsibilities, Practices* (New York: Harper & Row, 1973), pp. 64–65.

4. Paul A. Samuelson, *Economics: An Introductory Analysis,* 7th ed. (New York: McGraw-Hill, 1967), p. 5.

5. For more on this topic, see Reed Moyer, "Marketing in the Iron Curtain Countries," *Journal of Marketing,* October 1966, pp. 3–9; and G. Peter Lauter, "The Changing Role of Marketing in the Eastern European Socialist Economies," *Journal of Marketing,* October 1971, pp. 16–20.

6. See, for example, Milton Friedman, *Capitalism and Freedom* (Chicago: University of Chicago Press, 1962); and Murray L. Weidenbaum, *Business, Government, and the Public* (Englewood Cliffs, N.J.: Prentice-Hall, 1977).

7. Wroe Alderson, "Factors Governing the Development of Marketing Channels," in *Marketing Channels for Manufactured Products,* ed. Richard M. Clewett (Homewood, Ill.: Richard D. Irwin, 1954), p. 7.

8. Adapted from Wroe Alderson, "Factors Governing the Development of Marketing Channels."

9. Peter F. Drucker, "Marketing and Economic Development," *Journal of Marketing* (January 1958), p. 253. Reprinted from the *Journal of Marketing.*

10. Ragnar Nurkse, *Problems of Capital Formation in Underdeveloped Countries* (Oxford: Basil Blackwell, 1953), p. 4.

11. This discussion is based largely on William McInnes, "A Conceptual Approach to Marketing," in *Theory in Marketing,* second series, ed. Reavis Cox, Wroe Alderson, and Stanley J. Shapiro (Homewood, Ill.: Richard D. Irwin, 1964), pp. 51–67; see also J. F. Grashof and A. Kelman, *Introduction to Macro-Marketing* (Columbus, Ohio: Grid, 1973), pp. 69–78.

12. Adapted from McInnes, "A Conceptual Approach to Marketing," pp. 51–67.

13. This model was suggested by Professor A. A. Brogowicz of Western Michigan University.

14. *Forging America's Future: Strategies for National Growth and Development,* Report of the Advisory Committee on National Growth Policy Processes, reprinted in *Challenge,* January/February 1977.

Chapter 2

1. Robert J. Keith, "The Marketing Revolution," *Journal of Marketing,* January 1960, pp. 35–38.

2. Adapted from R. F. Vizza, T. E. Chambers, and E. J. Cook, *Adoption of the Marketing Concept—Fact or Fiction?* (New York: Sales Executive Club, 1967), pp. 13–15.

3. These charts are for a very large company which saw the need for many functional departments. Smaller companies would probably operate with many fewer managers. Nevertheless, a company which accepts the marketing concept would probably need to move many functions under the marketing manager in order to insure that proper integration of all of these functional activities actually did take place.

4. Edward S. McKay, "How to Plan and Set Up Your Marketing Program," *A Blueprint for an Effective Marketing Program, Marketing Series* No. 91 (New York: American Management Association, 1954), p. 15.

5. Philip Kotler, "Strategies for Introducing Marketing into Nonprofit Organizations," *Journal of Marketing,* vol. 43, January 1979, pp. 37–44; Karen F. A. Fox and Philip Kotler: "The Marketing of Social Causes: The First Ten Years," *Journal of Marketing,* Fall 1980, pp. 24–33; and Paul N. Bloom and William D. Novelli, "Problems and Challenges in Social Marketing," *Journal of Marketing,* Spring 1981, pp. 79–88.

6. Alfred P. Sloan, Jr., *My Years with General Motors* (New York: MacFadden Books, 1965), introduction, chaps. 4 and 9.

7. Daniel Yankelovich, "Psychological Market Segmentation," in *Some Bold New Theories of Advertising in Marketing,* ed. Jack Z. Sissors (Evanston, Ill.: Northwestern University, 1963), pp. 23–25.

8. "Falling Profit Prompts Timex to Shed Its Utilitarian Image," *The Wall Street Journal,* September 17, 1981, p. 27; "Japanese Heat on the Watch Industry," *Business Week,* May 5, 1980, pp. 92–106; "A Reclusive Tycoon Takes Over at Timex," *Business Week,* April 14, 1980, p. 32; "Texas Instruments Wrestles with the Consumer Market," *Fortune,* December 3, 1979, pp. 50–57; "The Great Digital Watch Shake-Out," *Business Week,* May 2, 1977, pp. 70–80; "The Digital Watch Becomes the World's Cheapest Timepiece," *The Wall Street Journal,* April 18, 1977, p. 11; "Gruen Industries Asks Chapter 11 Status," *The Wall Street Journal,* April 15, 1977, p. 9; "Why Gillette Stopped Its Digital Watches," *Business Week,* January 31, 1977, pp. 37–38; and "Digital Wristwatch Business Is Glowing, but Rivalry Winds Down Prices, Profits," *The Wall Street Journal,* August 24, 1976, p. 6.

Chapter 3

1. Gerald B. McCready, *Profile Canada: Social and Economic Projections* (Georgetown, Ont.: Irwin-Dorsey, Ltd., 1977), p. 58.

2. Adapted from M. Dale Beckman, "Canadian Life-Style: Values and Attributes of the Canadian Consumer," in *Problems in Canadian Marketing,* ed. Donald N. Thompson (Chicago: American Marketing Association, 1977), p. 44.

3. Peter M. Banting and Randolph E. Ross, "Canada: Obstacles and Opportunities," *Journal of the Academy of Marketing Science,* Winter 1975, pp. 11–13.

4. "Business out of Sync with Public, Pollster Says," *Advertising Age,* May 23, 1977, pp. 4 ff.

5. "Trudeau's New Rules for Foreign Investors," *Business Week,* August 24, 1974, pp. 58–59; *The Wall Street Journal,* May 1, 1972, p. 22; and "Ottawa Restricts U.S. Ads," *Business Week,* September 4, 1965, p. 36.

6. Murial Armstrong, *The Canadian Economy and Its Problems* (Scarborough, Ont.: Prentice-Hall of Canada, Ltd., 1970), pp. 148–49.

7. Donald N. Thompson, "Competition Policy and Marketing Regulation" in *Canadian Marketing: Problems and Prospects,* ed. Donald N. Thompson and David S. R. Leighton (Toronto: Wiley Publishers of Canada, Ltd., 1973), pp. 14–15.

8. Herb Gray, "Notes for Remarks to a York University Seminar on a Competition Policy," mimeographed (Toronto, January 25, 1974), pp. 5–7.

9. J. Allison Barnhill, "Marketing in the increasingly Controlled Economy of Canada," in *1976 Educators' Proceedings,* ed. K. L. Bernhardt (Chicago: American Marketing Association, 1976), pp. 456–60.

10. George C. Sawyer, "Social Issues and Social Change: Impact on Strategic Decisions," *MSU Business Topics,* Summer 1973, pp. 15–20.

11. "Oranges Start Coming Up Roses," *Business Week,* May 4, 1968, pp. 127–30; see also "Supermarket Sales of Orange Juice Died as Price Soars, with Further Rises Seen," *The Wall Street Journal,* February 13, 1981, p. 20.

12. *Business Week,* June 24, 1967, p. 85.

Chapter 4

1. Robert H. Hayes and William J. Abernathy, "Managing Our Way to Economic Decline," *Harvard Business Review,* July–August 1980, pp. 67–77, and Peter C. Riesz, "Revenge of the Marketing Concept," *Business Horizons,* June 1980, pp. 49–53.

2. "How Kodak Will Exploit Its New Instamatic," *Business Week,* March 18, 1972, pp. 46–48.

3. Igor Ansoff, *Corporate Strategy* (New York: McGraw-Hill, 1965).

4. Based on Charles H. Kline, "The Strategy of Product Policy," *Harvard Business Review,* July–August, 1955, pp. 91–100.

5. Charles H. Granger, "The Hierarchy of Objectives," *Harvard Business Review,* May–June 1964, p. 63.

6. Adapted from Peter F. Drucker, "Business Objectives and Survival Needs: Notes on a Discipline of Business Enterprise," *Journal of Business,* April 1958, pp. 181–90.

7. "A Turnaround 'Master' Takes on Kroehler," *Business Week,* June 16, 1980, pp. 86–89; "A Painful Attempt to Aid Ampex," *Business Week,* February 12, 1972, p. 17; "Ford Motor Company Adopts New Tactics to Boost Its 'Big Three' Standing," *The Wall Street Journal,* May 15, 1973, pp. 1 ff.; "RCA's New Vista: The Bottom Line," *Business Week,* July 4, 1977, pp. 38–44; "The Luster Dims at Westinghouse," *Business Week,* July 20, 1974, pp. 53–63; and "Market-Share-ROI Corporate Strategy Approach Can Be an 'Oversimplistic Share,'" *Marketing News,* December 15, 1978, pp. 1 ff.; "Owens-Illinois: Giving Market Share to Improve Profits," *Business Week,* May 11, 1981, p. 81–82; and "Profits Are What Count—At B. F. Goodrich Company," *Business Week,* January 26, 1981, p. 40.

8. Frank R. Bacon, Jr., and Thomas W. Butler, Jr., *Planned Innovation,* 2d ed., (Ann Arbor: Institute of Science and Technology, The University of Michigan, 1981).

9. M. G. Allen, "Strategic Problems Facing Today's Corporate Planner," a speech given to the Academy of Management, 36th annual meeting, Kansas City, Mo., 1976;

and "General Electric's 'Stoplight Strategy' for Planning," *Business Week,* April 28, 1974, p. 49. For other approches, see Frank R. Bacon, Jr., and T. W. Butler, Jr., *Planned Innovation,* 2d ed. (Ann Arbor: Institute of Science and Technology, The University of Michigan, 1981); and Y. Wind and H. J. Claycamp, "Planning Product Line Strategy: A Matrix Approach," *Journal of Marketing,* January 1976, pp. 2–9.

10. Ibid.

Chapter 5

1. *The Canadian Media Directors' Council Media Digest, 1981–82* (Published by Marketing).

2. Harper W. Boyd, Jr., Ralph Westfall, and Stanley F. Stasch, *Marketing Research: Texts and Cases,* 4th ed. (Homewood, Ill.: Richard D. Irwin, 1977).

3. J. G. Keane, "Some Observations on Marketing Research in Top Management Decision Making," *Journal of Marketing,* October 1969, pp. 10–15; B. A. Greenberg, Jac L. Goldstucker, and D. N. Bellenger, "What Techniques Are Used by Marketing Researchers in Business?" *Journal of Marketing,* April 1977, pp. 62–68; R. J. Small and L. J. Rosenberg, "The Marketing Researcher as a Decision Maker: Myth or Reality?" *Journal of Marketing,* January 1975, pp. 2–7; and Danny N. Bellenger, "The Marketing Manager's View of Marketing Research," *Business Horizons,* June 1979, pp. 59–65.

4. Arthur P. Felton, "Conditions of Marketing Leadership," *Harvard Business Review,* March–April 1956, pp. 117–27.

5. "Scouting the Trail for Marketers," *Business Week,* April 18, 1964, pp. 90–116.

6. Robert Hershey, "Commercial Intelligence on a Shoestring," *Harvard Business Review,* September–October, 1980, pp. 22–30; and Donald F. Mulvihill, "Marketing Research for the Small Company," *Journal of Marketing,* October 1951, pp. 179–82.

7. *The Role and Organization of Marketing Research,* Experiences in Marketing Management, No. 20 (New York: National Industrial Conference Board, 1969), 65 pp.

8. William A. Marsteller, "Can You Afford a Market Research Department?" *Industrial Marketing,* March 1951, pp. 36–37; see also "Top Executives Keep Tabs on the Consumer—or Contend They Do," *The Wall Street Journal,* July 1, 1976, pp. 1 ff.

9. For more discussion, see P. E. Green and D. S. Tull, *Research for Marketing Decisions,* 2d ed. (Englewood Cliffs, N.J.: Prentice-Hall, 1970), chap. 1.

10. Richard H. Brien and James E. Stafford, "Marketing Information Systems: A New Dimension for Marketing Research," *Journal of Marketing,* July 1968, p. 21; David B. Montgomery and Charles B. Weinberg, "Toward Strategic Intelligence Systems," *Journal of Marketing,* Fall 1979, pp. 41–52; and "Market Research by Scanner," *Business Week,* May 5, 1980, pp. 113–16.

Chapter 6

1. Statistics Canada, *Population and Dwelling Units Canada 1981, 1981 Interim Population and Dwellings; Canada and the Provinces,* January 7, 1982, *Population Projections for Canada and the Provinces, 1976–2001,* Cat. 91–520 (Ottawa: Minister of Industry, Trade and Commerce, February 1979).

2. For a very detailed study of Canada's future population, see Statistics Canada, *Population Projections for Canada and the Provinces, 1976–2001,* Cat. 91–520 (Ottawa: Minister of Industry, Trade and Commerce, February 1979).

3. Woods, Gordon & Co., *Tomorrow's Customers 1978,* April 1978, p. 4.

4. Based on an average of population projections from Statistics Canada, *Population Projections for Canada and the Provinces, 1976–2001,* Cat. 91–520, February, 1979.

5. Statistics Canada, *Household and Family Projections Canada, Provinces and Territories, 1926–2001,* Cat. 91–522 (Ottawa: Minister of Supply and Services Canada, December 1981).

6. Ibid.

7. Statistics Canada, *Vital Statistics: Volume 2, Marriages and Divorces, 1980,* Cat. 84–205 (Ottawa: Minister of Supply and Services Canada, March 1982).

8. Statistics Canada, *Perspectives III,* Cat. 11–511E (Ottawa: Minister of Supply and Services Canada, April 1980), p. 5.

9. Woods, Gordon & Co., *Tomorrow's Customers, 1978,* April 1978, p. 7.

10. Statistics Canada, The Conference Board of Canada, *Handbook of Canadian Consumer Markets, 1982,* 2d ed., p. 22.

11. Statistics Canada, *Dictionary of the 1971 Census Terms,* Cat. 12–540 (Ottawa: Information Canada, December 1972).

12. *New Population Census, 1981.*

13. P. M. Banting, *Canadian Marketing, A Case Approach* (Toronto: McGraw-Hill Ryerson Limited, 1977), p. 4.

14. "Canadians Top Movers: Study," *The Gazette,* October 12, 1976, p. 4.

15. Woods, Gordon & Co., *Tomorrow's Customers in Canada, 1982,* p. 13.

16. Statistics Canada, *Income Distributions by Size in Canada, Preliminary Estimates 1980,* Cat. 13–206 (Ottawa: Minister of Supply and Services Canada, September 1981).

17. Statistics Canada, *Income Distributions by Size in Canada, 1979,* Cat. 13–207 (Ottawa: Minister of Supply and Services Canada, May 1981).

18. Woods, Gordon & Co., *Tomorrow's Customers, 1981,* p. 14.

19. Statistics Canada, as found in *Handbook of Canadian Consumer Markets, 1982,* 2nd ed., p. 91.

20. Ibid., p. 100.

21. Statistics Canada, *Family Expenditure in Canada: Volume 3, All Canada—Urban and Rural, 1978,* Cat. 62–551 (Ottawa: Minister of Supply and Services Canada, January 1982).

22. "Young Market Becoming More Conventional," *Advertising Age,* May 16, 1977, p. 84; "On a Fast Track to the Good Life," *Fortune,* April 7, 1980, pp. 74–84; "Demography's Good News for the 80's," *Fortune,* November 5, 1979, pp. 92–106; and "The Upbeat Outlook for Family Incomes," *Fortune,* February 25, 1980, pp. 122–30.

23. Adapted from William D. Wells and George Gubar, "Life Cycle Concept in Marketing Research," *Journal of Marketing Research,* August 1968, p. 267.

24. "Motorcycles: The Dip Continues," *Business Week,* May 3, 1976, pp. 80–81.

25. "Why Gerber Makes an Inviting Target," *Business Week,* June 27, 1977, pp. 26–27.

26. P. M. Banting, *Canadian Marketing, A Case Approach.*

27. Statistics Canada, *Income Distributions by Size in Canada, 1979,* Cat. 13–207 (Ottawa: Minister of Supply and Services Canada, May 1981).

28. Woods, Gordon & Co., *Tomorrow's Customers, 1980,* April 1980, p. 5.

Chapter 7

1. K. H. Chung, *Motivational Theories and Practices* (Columbus, Ohio: Grid, 1977), pp. 40–43; and A. H. Maslow, *Motivation and Personality* (New York: Harper & Row, 1954).

2. Robert Ardrey, *African Genesis* (New York: Atheneum Publishers, 1961), chap. 4.

3. Donald G. Morrison, "Purchase Intentions and Purchase Behavior," *Journal of Marketing,* Spring 1979, pp. 65–74; Paul W. Miniard and Joel B. Cohen, "Isolating Attitudinal and Normative Influences in Behavioral Intentions Models," *Journal of Marketing Research,* February 1979, pp. 102–10; Russell I. Haley and Peter B. Case, "Testing Thirteen Attitude Scales for Agreement and Brand Discrimination," *Journal of Marketing,* Fall 1979, pp. 20–32; Paul R. Warshaw; "Predicting Purchase and Other Behaviors from General and Conceptually Specific Intentions," *Journal of Marketing Research,* February 1980, pp. 26–33; Paul R. Warshaw, "A New Model for Predicting Behavioral Intentions: An Alternative to Fishbein," *Journal of Marketing Research,* May 1980, pp. 153–72; Michael J. Ryan and E. H. Bonfield, "Fishbein's Intentions Model: A Test of External and Pragmatic Validity," *Journal of Marketing Research,* Spring 1980, pp. 82–95. This discussion is based on J. Pavasars and W. D. Wells, "Measures of Brand Attitudes Can Be Used to Predict Buying Behavior," *Marketing News,* April 11, 1975, p. 6; and F. E. Webster, Jr., *Social Aspects of Marketing* (Englewood Cliffs, N.J.: Prentice-Hall, 1974), pp. 44–46.

4. Joseph T. Plummer, "The Concept and Application of Life-Style Segmentation," *Journal of Marketing,* January 1974, pp. 33–37.

5. William D. Wells and Douglas J. Tigert, "Activities, Interests, and Opinions," in *Market Segmentation,* ed. James F. Engel et al. (New York: Holt, Rinehart & Winston, 1972), p. 258.

6. *Marketing News,* December 31, 1976, p. 8. See also Alvin C. Burns and Mary C. Harrison, "A Test of the Reliability of Psychographics," *Journal of Marketing Research,* February 1979, pp. 32–38; "Information on Values and Life-styles Needed to Identify Buying Patterns," *Marketing News,* October 5, 1979, pp. 1 ff.; "Life-Style Research Inappropriate for Some Categories of Products," *Marketing News,* June 17, 1977, p. 9; M. E. Goldberg, "Identifying Relevant Psychographic Segments: How Specifying Product Functions Can Help," *Consumer Research,* December 1976, pp. 163–69; and W. D. Wells, "Psychographics: A Critical Review," *Journal of Marketing Research,* May 1975, pp. 196–213.

7. W. H. Reynolds and James H. Meyers, "Marketing and the American Family," *Business Topics,* Spring 1966, pp. 58–59. See also G. M. Munsinger, J. E. Weber, and R. W. Hansen, "Joint Home Purchasing Decisions by Husbands and Wives," *Consumer Research,* March 1975, pp. 60–66; E. P. Cox III, "Family Purchase Decision Making and the Process of Adjustment," *Journal of Marketing Research,* May 1975, pp. 189–95; R. T. Green and I. C. M. Cunningham, "Feminine Role Perception and Family Purchasing Decisions," *Journal of Marketing Research,* August 1975, pp. 325–32; I. C. M. Cunningham and R. R. Green, "Purchasing Roles in the U.S. Family, 1955 & 1973," *Journal of Marketing,* October 1974, pp. 61–64; and Harry L. Davis, "Decision Making within the Household," *Journal of Consumer Research,* March 1976, pp. 241–60; Patrick E. Murphy and William A. Staples; "A Modernized Family Life Cycle," *Consumer Research,* June 1979, pp. 12–22; David J. Curry and Michael B. Menasco, "Some Effects of Differing Information Processing Strategies on Husband-Wife Joint Decisions," *Consumer Research,* September 1979, pp. 192–203; George J. Szybillo et al., "Family Member Influence in Household Decision Making," *Consumer Research,* December 1979, pp. 312–16; Harry L. Davis, "Decision Making within the Household," *Consumer Research,* March 1976, pp. 241–60; and Pierre Filiatrault, and J. R. Brent Ritchie, "Joint Purchasing Decisions: A Comparison of Influence Structure in Family and Couple Decision-Making Units," *Consumer Research,* September 1980, pp. 131–40.

8. Adapted from P. Martineau, *Motivation in Advertising* (New York: McGraw-Hill, 1957), p. 164. See also P. Martineau. "The Pattern of Social Classes," in *Marketing's Role in Scientific Management,* ed. R. L. Clewett (Chicago: American Marketing Association, 1957), pp. 246–47; James A. Carman, *The Application of Social Class in Market Segmentation* (Berkeley: Institute of Business and Economic Research, University of California, 1965); William H. Peters, "Relative Occupational Class Income: A Significant Variable in the Marketing of Automobiles," *Journal of Marketing,* April 1970, pp. 74–78; Arun K. Jain; "A Method for Investigating and Representing an Implicit Theory of Social Class," *Consumer Research,* June 1975, pp. 53–59; and Charles M. Schaninger, "Social Class versus Income Revisited: An Empirical Investigation," *Journal of Marketing Research,* May 1981, pp. 192–208.

9. For an especially useful collection of relatively recent articles on Canadian class structure see J. E. Curtis and W. G. Scott, *Social Stratification: Canada* (Scarborough, Ont.: Prentice-Hall of Canada, Ltd., 1973).

10. Martineau, "The Pattern of Social Classes," pp. 246–47.

11. Source: Adapted from work of Bureau of Applied Social Research, Columbia University, New York, N.Y. See also Donald W. Hendon, "A New and Empirical Look at the Influence of Reference Groups on Generic Product Category and Brand Choice: Evidence from Two Nations," in *Proceedings of the Academy of International Business: Asia-Pacific Dimensions of International Business* (Honolulu: College of Business Administration, University of Hawaii, December 18–20, 1979), pp. 752–61.

12. Carman, *The Application of Social Class in Market Segmentation,* pp. 21 and 61; and Elihu Katz and Paul E. Lazarsfeld, *Personal Influences* (Glencoe, Ill.: Free Press, 1955). See also John O. Summers, "The Identity of Women's Clothing Fashion Opinion Leaders," *Journal of Marketing Research,* May 1970, pp. 178–86; Charles W. King and John O. Summers, "Overlap of Opinion Leadership across Consumer Product Categories," *Journal of Marketing Research,* February 1970, pp. 43–50; and "Coke drinkers talk a lot," *The Wall Street Journal,* October 22, 1981, p. 25.

13. Walter A. Henry, "Cultural Values Do Correlate with Consumer Behavior," *Journal of Marketing Research,* May 1976, pp. 121–27.

14. Adapted from James H. Myers and William H. Reynolds, *Consumer Behavior and Marketing Management* (Boston: Houghton Mifflin, 1967), p. 49.

15. John A. Howard and Jagdish N. Sheth, *The Theory of Buyer Behavior* (New York: John Wiley & Sons, 1969), pp. 46–48. See also C. Whan Park, "Students and Housewives: Differences in Susceptibility to Reference Group Influence," *Consumer Research,* September 1977, pp. 102–10.

16. Adapted from E. M. Rogers, *The Diffusion of Innovations* (New York: Free Press, 1962); and E. M. Rogers with F. Schoemaker, *Communication of Innovation: A Cross-Cultural Approach* (New York: Free Press, 1968).

17. For further discussion on this topic, see James H. Myers and William H. Reynolds, *Consumer Behavior and Marketing Management* (Boston: Houghton Mifflin, 1967); and J. F. Engel, D. T. Kollat, and R. D. Blackwell, *Consumer Behavior* (New York: Holt Reinhart & Winston, 1968).

18. This section benefitted immeasurably from a careful review of an earlier draft by Prof. Robert Tamilia of the University of Quebec at Montreal. His contribution is reflected in many of the differences in both content and approach found in this edition as opposed to its predecessor.

19. P. C. Lefrancois and Gilles Chatel, "The French-Canadian Consumer: Fact and Fancy," in *New Ideas for Successful Marketing—Proceedings of the 1966 World Congress,* ed. J. S. Wright and J. L. Goldstucker (Chicago: American Marketing Association, 1966), p. 706.

20. The approach used in answering this question and the following one draws heavily upon Lefrancois and Chatel, but 1976 census figures have been utilized instead of the 1961 census data they employed.

21. Frederick Elkin, *Rebels and Colleagues: Advertising and Social Change in French Canada* (Montreal: McGill-Queen's Press, 1973), pp. 73.

22. The preceding are but a few of many drawn from numerous sources and cited by Bruce Mallen, "The Present State of Knowledge and Research in Marketing to the French-Canadian Market," in *Canadian Marketing: Problems and Prospects,* ed. Donald N. Thompson and David S. R. Leighton (Toronto: Wiley of Canada, Ltd., 1973), pp. 100–101.

23. Gerald B. McCready, *Canadian Marketing Trends* Georgetown, Ont.: Irwin-Dorsey, Ltd., 1972), pp. 64–65.

24. Jean M. Lefevre, "A Compilation of Empirical Studies of Family Roles in French-Canadian Families," (Mimeographed and undated).

25. Michael Patterson, "French Agencies have no Golden Touch—Just a Better feel for the Quebecois Taste," *Marketing,* October 27, 1975.

26. Robert D. Tamilia, "A Cross-Cultural Study of Source Effects in a Canadian Advertising Situation," in *Marketing 1978: New Trends in Canadian Marketing,* J. M. Boisvert and R. Savitt (Edmonton: Administrative Sciences Association of Canada, 1978), pp. 250–56.

27. Lefrancois and Chatel, "French-Canadian Consumer," pp. 710–15.

28. C. R. McGoldrick, "The French Canadian Consumer. The Past is Prologue," Speech before 4th Annual Conference, Association of Canadian Advertisers, in *Marketing: A Canadian Perspective,* ed. M. D. Beckman and R. H. Evans (Scarborough, Ont.: Prentice-Hall of Canada, Ltd., 1972), p. 92.

29. K. S. Palda, "A Comparison of Consumer Expenditures in Quebec and Ontario," *Canadian Journal of Economics and Political Science 33* (February 1967), p. 26. See also Dwight R. Thomas, "Culture and Consumption Behavior in English and French Canada," in *Marketing in the 1970s and Beyond,* ed. Bent Stidsen (Canadian Association of Administrative Sciences, Marketing Division, 1975), pp. 255–61.

30. Mallen, "The Present State of Knowledge and Research in Marketing to the French-Canadian Market," p. 105.

31. Cf. Yvan Allaire, "Le consommateur québécois: Methodologie ou Mythologie?" (Paper presented at the Montreal chapter of the American Marketing Association, March 1977).

32. D. J. Tigert, "Can A Separate Marketing Strategy for French Canada be Justified: Profiling English-French Markets through Life-Style Analysis," in Thompson and Leighton, eds., *Canadian Marketing,* p. 128.

33. Marion Plunkett, "The Differences between French- and English-Speaking Canadians" (Paper presented to the Academy of Marketing Science, Ohio, May 1977).

Chapter 8

1. The Vancouver User Service Office, Statistics Canada, May, 1982.

2. From an unpublished research paper by Shaheen Lalji, Simon Fraser University, 1982.

3. Patrick J. Robinson and Charles W. Faris, *Industrial Buying and Creative Marketing* (Boston: Allyn & Bacon, 1967), chap. 2. See also Frederick E. Webster, Jr., and Yoram Wind, "A General Model for Understanding Orga-

nizational Buying Behavior,'' *Journal of Marketing*, April 1972, pp. 12–19; Urban B. Ozanne and Gilbert A. Churchill, Jr., ''Five Dimensions of the Industrial Adoption Process,'' *Journal of Marketing Research*, August 1971, pp. 322–28; and Donald R. Lehmann and John O'Shaughnessy, ''Difference in Attribute Importance for Different Industrial Products,'' *Journal of Marketing*, April 1974, pp. 36–42; Lowell E. Crow, Richard W. Olshavsky, and John O. Summers, ''Industrial Buyers' Choice Strategies: A Protocol Analysis,'' *Journal of Marketing Research*, February 1980, pp. 34–44; and Robert E. Spekman and Louis W. Stern; ''Environmental Uncertainties and Buying Group Structure: An Empirical Investigation,'' *Journal of Marketing*, Spring 1979, pp. 54–64.

4. Patrick J. Robinson and Charles W. Faris, *Industrial Buying and Creative Marketing* (Boston: Allyn & Bacon, 1967), p. 33. Reprinted by permission of the publisher.

5. Donald F. Istvan, *Capital-Expenditure Decisions: How They Are Made in Large Corporations*, Indiana Business Report No. 33 (Bloomington: Indiana University, 1961), p. 97; and James D. Edwards, ''Investment Decision Making in a Competitive Society,'' *MSU Business Topics*, Autumn 1970, pp. 53–60.

6. For a detailed discussion of supermarket chain buying, see J. F. Grashof, ''Information Management for Supermarket Chain Product Mix Decisions,'' (Ph.D. thesis, Michigan State University, 1968). See also David B. Montgomery, ''New Product Distribution: An Analysis of Supermarket Buyer Decisions,'' *Journal of Marketing Research*, August 1975, pp. 255–64.

7. ''What's the Sales Potential of Those Products Taking Up Space on a Store's Valuable Shelves,'' *Systems Management*, January 1962, p. 35 ff.

8. ''Why Sears Stays the No. 1 Retailer,'' *Business Week*, January 20, 1968, pp. 65–73.

9. ''Monsanto Moves into Farmers' Back Yard,'' *Business Week*, February 6, 1965, pp. 60–62; see also ''Agricorporations Run into Growing Criticism as Their Role Expands,'' *The Wall Street Journal*, May 2, 1972, pp. 1 ff.; ''How the Family Farm Can Harvest Millions,'' *Business Week*, July 4, 1977, pp. 68–70; ''The Billion-Dollar Farm Coops Nobody Knows,'' *Business Week*, February 7, 1977, pp. 54–64; and ''It's up, down on the Farm,'' *Sales and Marketing Management*, April 6, 1981, pp. 31–38.

Chapter 9

1. Nelson N. Foote, ''Market Segmentation as a Competitive Strategy,'' in E. J. McCarthy et al., *Readings in Basic Marketing*, 3d ed. (Homewood, Ill.: Richard D. Irwin, 1981); and Alan J. Resnik; Peter B. B. Turney, and J. Barry Mason, ''Marketers Turn to 'Countersegmentation,''' *Harvard Business Review*, September–October 1979, pp. 100–106.

2. Abridged from E. J. McCarthy and Stanley J. Shapiro, *Basic Marketing*, 3d Canadian ed. (Homewood Ill.: Richard D. Irwin, 1983).

3. For a classic article on the subject, see Russell I. Haley, ''Benefit Segmentation: A Decision-Oriented Research Tool,'' *Journal of Marketing*, July 1968, pp. 30–35. See also Richard M. Johnson, ''Market Segmentation: A Strategic Management Tool,'' *Journal of Marketing Research*,

February 1971, pp. 13–18; James H. Myers, ''Benefit Structure Analysis: A New Tool for Product Planning,'' *Journal of Marketing*, October 1976, pp. 23–32; and Roger J. Calantone and Alan G. Sawyer, ''The Stability of Benefit Segments,'' *Journal of Marketing Research*, August 1978, pp. 395–404.

4. Adapted from *House and Home*, April 1965, pp. 94–99.

5. Frederick W. Winter, ''A Cost-Benefit Approach to Market Segmentation,'' *Journal of Marketing*, Fall 1979, pp. 103–11; Phillip E. Downs, ''Multidimensional Scaling versus the Hand-Drawn Technique,'' *Journal of Business Research*, December 1979, pp. 349–58; John R. Houser and Rank S. Koppelman, ''Alternative Perceptual Mapping Techniques: Relative Accuracy and Usefulness,'' *Journal of Marketing Research*, November 1979, pp. 495–506; Stephen John Arnold, ''A Test for Clusters,'' *Journal of Marketing Research*, November 1979, pp. 545–51; and Henry Assael, ''Segmenting Markets by Response Elasticity,'' *Journal of Advertising Research*, April 1976, pp. 27–35.

6. S. Arbeit and A. G. Sawyer, ''Benefit Segmentation in a Retail Banking Environment,'' presented at the American Marketing Association Fall Conference, Washington, D.C., August 1973.

7. ''Survey of Buying Power,'' *Sales & Marketing Management*, July 26, 1982, pp. D–9, D–10.

8. Checking the accuracy of forecasts is a difficult subject. See R. Ferber, W. J. Hawkes, Jr., and M. D. Plotkin, ''How Reliable Are National Retail Sales Estimates?'' *Journal of Marketing*, October 1976, pp. 13–22; D. J. Dalrymple, ''Sales Forecasting Methods and Accuracy,'' *Business Horizons*, December 1975, pp. 69–73; P. R. Wotruba and M. L. Thurlow, ''Sales Force Participation in Quota Setting and Sales Forecasting,'' *Journal of Marketing*, April 1976, pp. 11–16; R. Shoemaker and R. Staelin, ''The Effects of Sampling Variation on Sales Forecasts for New Consumer Products,'' *Journal of Marketing Research*, May 1976, pp. 138–43; R. Staelin and R. E. Turner, ''Error in Judgmental Sales Forecasts: Theory and Results,'' *Journal of Marketing Research*, February 1973, pp. 10–16; Reed Moyer, ''Forecasting Turning Points,'' *Business Horizons*, July–August 1981, pp. 57–61; and Gilbert Frisbie and Vincent A. Mabert, ''Crystal Ball vs. System—The Forecasting Dilemma,'' *Business Horizons*, September–October 1981, pp. 72–76.

Chapter 10

1. Stanley C. Hollander, ''Is There a Generic Demand for Services?'' *MSU Business Topics*, Spring 1979, pp. 41–46; John M. Rathmell, ''What Is Meant by Services?'' *Journal of Marketing*, October 1966, pp. 32–36; T. Levitt, ''The Industrialization of Service,'' *Harvard Business Review*, September–October 1976, pp. 63–74; R. W. Obenberger and S. W. Brown, ''A Marketing Alternative: Consumer Leasing and Renting,'' *Business Horizons*, October 1976, pp. 82–86; Richard B. Chase, ''Where Does the Customer Fit in a Service Operation?'' *Harvard Business Review*, November–December 1978, pp. 137–42; Dan R. E. Thomas, ''Strategy Is Different in Service Industries,'' *Harvard Business Review*, July–August 1978, pp. 158–65; Paul F. Anderson and William Lazer, ''Industrial

Lease Marketing," *Journal of Marketing*, January 1978, pp. 71–79; Robert E. Sabath, "How Much Service Do Customers Really Want?" *Business Horizons*, April 1978, pp. 26–32; "Sony's U.S. Operation Goes in for Repairs," *Business Week*, March 13, 1978, pp. 31–32; and Bernard Wysocki, Jr., "Branching Out: Major Retailers Offer Varied Services to Lure Customers, Lift Profits," *The Wall Street Journal*, June 12, 1978, pp. 1, 21.

2. Robert C. Blattberg, Peter Peacock, and S. K. Sen, "Purchasing Strategies across Product Categories," *Consumer Research*, December 1976, pp. 143–54; J. B. Mason and M. L. Mayer "Empirical Observations of Consumer Behavior as Related to Goods Classification and Retail Strategy," *Journal of Retailing*, Fall 1972, pp. 17–31; Arno K. Kleinenhagen, "Shopping, Specialty, or Convenience Goods?" *Journal of Retailing*, Winter 1966–67, pp. 32–39 ff.; Louis P. Bucklin, "Testing Propensities to Shop," *Journal of Marketing*, January 1966, pp. 22–27; William P. Dommermuth, "The Shopping Matrix and Marketing Strategy," *Journal of Marketing Research*, May 1965, pp. 128–32; Richard H. Holton, "The Distinction between Convenience Goods, Shopping Goods, and Specialty Goods," *Journal of Marketing*, July 1958, pp. 53–56; Perry Bliss, "Supply Considerations and Shopper Convenience," *Journal of Marketing*, July 1966, pp. 43–45; S. Kaish, "Cognitive Dissonance and the Classification of Consumer Goods," and W. P. Dommermuth and E. W. Cundiff, Shopping Goods, Shopping Centers, and Selling Strategies," *Journal of Marketing*, October 1967, pp. 28–36; Edward M. Tauber, "Why Do People Shop?" *Journal of Marketing*, October 1972, pp. 46–49; and Fred D. Reynolds and William R. Darden, "Intermarket Patronage: A Psychographic Study of Consumer Outshoppers," *Journal of Marketing*, October 1972, pp. 50–54.

3. M. Alexis, L. Simon, and K. Smith, "Some Determinants of Food Buying Behavior," in *Empirical Foundations of Marketing: Research Findings in the Behavioral and Applied Sciences*, ed. M. Alexis, R. Hancock, and R. J. Holloway (Skokie, Ill.: Rand McNally, 1969).

4. L. P. Feldman, "Prediction of the Spatial Pattern of Shopping Behavior," *Journal of Retailing*, Spring 1967, pp. 25–30 ff.

5. "If You Don't Give the Lady What She Wants, She'll Go Elsewhere," *Marketing News*, January 1, 1968, p. 11.

6. The number of people holding each view is indicated roughly by the size of the cluster. Suggested by Prof. Yusaku Furuhashi, University of Notre Dame.

7. "Switching the Charge on Batteries," *Business Week*, March 13, 1965, pp. 132–34.

8. J. E. Russo, "The Value of Unit Price Information," *Journal of Marketing Research*, May 1977, pp. 193–201; and K. B. Monroe and P. J. LaPlaca, "What Are the Benefits of Unit Pricing?" *Journal of Marketing*, July 1972, pp. 16–22.

9. Frank Presbrey, *The History and Development of Advertising* (New York: Doubleday, 1929).

10. *Business Week*, February 20, 1960, p. 71. See also Kent B. Monroe, "The Influence of Price Differences and Brand Familiarity on Brand Preferences," *Consumer Research*, June 1976, pp. 42–49.

11. The source of this discussion of Canadian trademark policy is B. E. Mallen, V. Kirpalani, and G. Lane, *Marketing in the Canadian Environment* (Toronto: Prentice-Hall of Canada, Ltd., 1973), p. 137.

12. "DuPont's Teflon Trademark Survives Attack," *Advertising Age*, July 14, 1975, p. 93; and George Miaoulis and Nancy D'Amato, "Consumer Confusion and Trademark Infringement," *Journal of Marketing*, April 1978, pp. 48–55; but see also "Miller Beer Wins Round over Use of Lite Name," *The Wall Street Journal*, October 10, 1980, p. 19.

13. "Generic Products Are Winning Noticeable Shares of Market from National Brands, Private Labels," *The Wall Street Journal*, August 10, 1979, p. 6; Betsy D. Gelb, " 'No-Name' Products: A Step Toward 'No-Name' Retailing," *Business Horizons*, June 1980, pp. 9–13; and a special report from A. C. Nielsen Company, *Generics in Supermarkets*, 1981.

14. *Marketing Communications*, August 1970, p. 13; "Is the Private Label Battle Heating up?" *Grey Matter*, vol. 44, no. 7 (July 1973); Zarrel V. Lambert; Paul L. Doering; Eric Goldstein; and William C. McCormick, "Predisposition toward Generic Drug Acceptance," *Consumer Research*, June 1980, pp. 14–23; "Private-Label Firms Aided by Inflation, Expected to Post Healthy Growth in 1980," *The Wall Street Journal*, March 31, 1980, p. 20; and "Generic Products in Supermarkets—Some New Perspectives," *The Nielsen Researcher*, no. 3 (1979), pp. 2–9.

15. E. Dichter, "Brand Loyalty and Motivation Research," *Food Business*, January—February 1956.

16. "Private Label Products Gain Increased Space on Many Retailers' Shelves," *The Wall Street Journal*, February 11, 1971, p. 1; "A&P's Own Brand of Consumerism," *Business Week*, April 11, 1970, p. 32; Victor J. Cook and T. F. Schutte, *Brand Policy Determination* (Boston: Allyn & Bacon, 1967); Arthur I. Cohen and Ana Loud Jones, "Brand Marketing in the New Retail Environment," *Harvard Business Review*, September–October 1978, pp. 141–48; "The Drugmaker's Rx for Living with Generics," *Business Week*, November 6, 1978, pp. 205–8; and "No-Name Goods Catching on with Grocers," *Detroit Free Press*, April 9, 1978, p. 16–D.

17. *Stage 1 Competition Policy*, Background Papers, Section 36(1)(c)—Misleading Warranties, Etc." (Ottawa: Consumer and Corporate Affairs), p. 42.

18. Arleen N. Hynd, Speech delivered to the Association of Canadian Advertisers, Toronto, October 8, 1975, p. 9.

Chapter 11

1. "Procter & Gamble's Profit Problem—Food," *Business Week*, January 26, 1981, pp. 52–60; "The Hot Frozen-Pizza Market Cools Down," *Business Week*, February 16, 1981, pp. 27–28; "For Volvo, a Shift away from Autos," *Business Week*, May 25, 1981, p. 75; "Levi Tries to Revive Sagging Jeans Business Amid Predictions of Denim Look's Demise," *The Wall Street Journal*, November 18, 1981, p. 25; "RCA to Cut Prices on Eight Color TVs in Promotion Effort," *The Wall Street Journal*, December 31, 1976, p. 16; "Decline in Color TV Sales Brings Worry that More Makers May Fall by Wayside," *The Wall Street Journal*, April 2, 1974, p. 36; "Sales of Major

Appliances, TV Sets Gain; But Profits Fail to Keep Up. Gap May Widen," *The Wall Street Journal,* August 21, 1972, p. 22; "What Do You Do When Snowmobiles Go on a Steep Slide?" *The Wall Street Journal,* March 8, 1978, pp. 1, 33; "Price of a Home Videotape Recorder Cut to $795 as U.S. Sales Efforts Accelerate," *The Wall Street Journal,* September 26, 1977, p. 8; "IBM Announces 2 New Processors for Big Systems," *The Wall Street Journal,* October 7, 1977, p. 4; "After Their Slow Year, Fast-Food Chains Use Ploys to Speed Up Sales," *The Wall Street Journal,* April 4, 1980, pp. 1 ff.; "Home Smoke Detectors Fall on Hard Times as Sales Apparently Peaked," *The Wall Street Journal,* April 3, 1980, p. 1; "As Once-Bright Market for CAT Scanners Dims, Smaller Makers of the X-ray Devices Fade Out," *The Wall Street Journal,* May 6, 1980, p. 40; and "Imports Fuzz the Future of Color TV Makers," *Business Week,* May 26, 1980, p. 51.

2. "The Short Happy Life," *Time,* March 29, 1963, p. 83.

3. Ibid.

4. "Xerox Unveils First of 'New Generation' of Copying Machines," *The Wall Street Journal,* May 20, 1970, p. 11.

5. "Getting Fat by Making Others Slim," *Business Week,* March 22, 1969, pp. 140–44.

6. "'Good Products Don't Die,' P&G Chairman Declares," *Advertising Age,* November 1, 1976, p. 8. See also "Detroit Brings Back the Fast, Flashy Auto to Aid Sluggish Sales," *The Wall Street Journal,* December 9, 1976, pp. 1 ff.

7. Adapted from Richard M. Johnson, "Market Segmentation: A Strategic Management Tool," *Journal of Marketing Research,* February 1971, p. 160.

8. Chester R. Wasson, "What is 'New' about New Products?" *Journal of Marketing,* July 1960, pp. 52–56; Patrick M. Dunne, "What Really Are New Products?" *Journal of Business,* December 1974, pp. 20–25; and S. H. Britt and V. M. Nelson, "The Marketing Importance of the 'Just Noticeable Difference,'" *Business Horizons,* August 1976, pp. 38–40.

9. *Business Week,* April 22, 1967, p. 120.

10. Adapted from Philip Kotler, "What Consumerism Means for Marketers," *Harvard Business Review,* May–June 1972, pp. 55–56.

11. "Inflation in Product Liability," *Business Week,* May 31, 1976, p. 60; Jane Mallor, "In Brief: Recent Products Liability Cases," *Business Horizons,* October 1979, pp. 47–49; and William L. Trombetta; "Products Liability: What New Court Ruling Means for Management," *Business Horizons,* August 1979, pp. 67–72.

12. See T. Levitt, "Innovative Imitation," *Harvard Business Review,* September–October 1966, pp. 63–70; and Roger A. Kerin, Michael G. Harvey, and James T. Rothe, "Cannibalism and New Product Development," *Business Horizons,* October 1978, pp. 25–31.

13. Adapted from Frank R. Bacon, Jr., and Thomas W. Butler, Jr., *Planned Innovation,* 2d ed. (Ann Arbor: Institute of Science and Technology, The University of Michigan, 1981; Edgar A. Pessemier, *Managing Innovation and New Product Development,* Marketing Science Institute

Report No. 75-122, December 1975: Phillip R. McDonald and Joseph O. Eastlack, Jr., "Top Management Involvement with New Products," *Business Horizons,* December 1971, pp. 23–31; William A. Bours III, "Imagination Wears Many Hats," *Journal of Marketing,* October 1966, pp. 59–61; John H. Murphy, "New Products Need Special Management," *Journal of Marketing,* October 1962, pp. 46–49; and E. J. McCarthy, "Organization for New-Product Development?" *Journal of Business of the University of Chicago,* April 1959, 128–32.

14. Benton & Bowles Research and *Printers' Ink,* April 13, 1962, pp. 22–23.

15. Paul Stillson and E. Leonard Arnof, "Product Search and Evaluation," *Journal of Marketing,* July 1957, p. 33. See also Frank R. Bacon, Jr., and T. W. Butler, Jr., *Planned Innovation* (Ann Arbor: Institute of Science and Technology, The University of Michigan, 1981); and Yoram Wind, John F. Grashof, and Joel D. Goldhar, "Market-Based Guidelines for Design of Industrial Products," *Journal of Marketing,* July 1978, pp. 27–37.

16. *Marketing News,* February 8, 1980; C. Merle Crawford, "Marketing Research and the New-Product Failure Rate," *Journal of Marketing,* April 1977, pp. 51–61.

17. Richard T. Hise and J. Patrick Kelly, "Product Management on Trial," *Journal of Marketing,* October 1978, pp. 28–33; Victor P. Buell, "The Changing Role of the Product Manager in Consumer Goods Companies," *Journal of Marketing,* July 1975, pp. 3–11.

18. Blair Little, "Characterizing the New Product for Better Evaluation and Planning," *Working Paper Series,* no. 21 (London, Canada: University of Western Ontario, July 1970); and Robert G. Cooper and Blair Little, "Reducing the Risk of Industrial New Product Development," *The Canadian Market,* Fall 1974, pp. 7–12.

19. Robert G. Cooper, "Why New Industrial Products Fail," *Industrial Marketing Management* 4 (1975), pp. 315–26.

20. Robert G. Cooper, *Winning the New Product Game* (Montreal: McGill Faculty of Management, 1976).

21. Roy Rothwell, "Factors for Success in Industrial Innovations," from *Project SAPPHO—A Comparative Study of Success and Failure in Industrial Innovation,* S.P.R.U., 1972; and Rothwell, Freeman, Horsley, Trevis, Robertson, and Townsend, "SAPPHO updated-project SAPPHO phase II," *Research Policy* 3(1974). pp. 258–91.

Chapter 12

1. Neil Suits, Suits News Company, Lansing, Michigan.

2. H. L. Purdy, *Transport Competition and Public Policy in Canada,* Section 7–3 (Vancouver: University of British Columbia Press, 1972), p. 59.

3. D. Philip Locklin, *Economics of Transportation,* 4th ed. (Homewood, Ill.: Richard D. Irwin, 1954), p. 35. © 1972 by Richard D. Irwin, Inc.

4. D. Philip Locklin, *Economics of Transportation,* 7th ed. (Homewood, Ill.: Richard D. Irwin, 1972), p. 57. © 1972 by Richard D. Irwin, Inc.

5. This discussion is based on the advantages and disadvantages discussed in *Vertical Integration in Marketing,* Bulletin 74, ed. Nugent Wedding (Urbana: Bureau of Eco-

nomic and Business Research, University of Illinois, 1952), pp. 11–12, 30.

6. Claude Raymond, "A Seminar with A. C. Nielsen," (Special presentation to Junior Advertising Sales Club of Montreal, April 18, 1978).

7. Tony Thompson, "Are the food chains really putting the big squeeze on their suppliers?" *Marketing*, July 3, 1978, p. 9.

8. Michael Levy and Dwight Grant, "Financial Terms of Sale and Control of Marketing Channel Conflict," *Journal of Marketing Research*, November 1980, pp. 524–30; F. Robert Dwyer, "Channel-Member Satisfaction: Laboratory Insights," *Journal of Retailing*, Summer 1980, pp. 45–65; Michael Etgar, "Selection of an Effective Channel Control Mix," *Journal of Marketing*, July 1978, pp. 53–58; Michael Etgar, "Intrachannel Conflict and Use of Power," *Journal of Marketing Research*, May 1978, pp. 273–74; and Robert F. Lusch, "Intrachannel Conflict and Use of Power: A Reply," *Journal of Marketing Research*, May 1978, pp. 275–76. For further discussion on channel control, see Robert F. Lusch, "Sources of Power: Their Impact on Intrachannel Conflict," *Journal of Marketing Research*, November 1976, pp. 382–90; William P. Dommermuth, "Profiting from Distribution Conflicts," *Business Horizons*, December 1976, pp. 4–13; Shelby D. Hunt and John R. Nevin, "Power in a Channel of Distribution: Sources and Consequences," *Journal of Marketing Research*, May 1974, pp. 186–93; Louis P. Bucklin, "A Theory of Channel Control," *Journal of Marketing*, January 1973, pp. 39–47; Ronald D. Michman and Stanley D. Sibley, *Marketing Channels and Strategies*, 2d ed. (Columbus, Ohio: Grid Publishing, 1980); and Joseph B. Mason, "Power and Channel Conflicts in Shopping Center Development," *Journal of Marketing*, April 1975, pp. 28–35.

9. D. J. Bowersox and E. J. McCarthy, "Strategic Development of Planned Vertical Marketing Systems," in *Vertical Marketing Systems* ed. Louis Bucklin (Glenview, Ill.: Scott, Foresman, 1970).

Chapter 13

1. Adapted from Louis Bucklin, "Retail Strategy and the Classification of Consumer Goods," *Journal of Marketing*, January 1963, pp. 50–55.

2. Statistics Canada, *Retail Trade March 1981*, Cat. 63-005 (Ottawa: Minister of Supply and Services Canada, June 1981).

3. Statistics Canada, *Department Stores in Canada, 1978*, Cat. 63-225 (Ottawa: Minister of Supply and Services Canada, June 1980).

4. Louis H. Grossman, "Merchandising Strategies of a Department Store Facing Change," *MSU Business Topics*, Winter 1970, pp. 31–42; "Suburban Malls Go Downtown," *Business Week*, November 10, 1973, pp. 90–94.

5. Statistics Canada, *Retail Chain and Department Stores, 1979*, Cat. 63-210 (Ottawa: Minister of Supply and Services Canada, December 1981).

6. Statistics Canada, *Direct Selling in Canada, 1980*, Cat. 63-218 (Ottawa: Minister of Supply and Services Canada, December 1981).

7. Statistics Canada, *Vending Machine Operators, 1980*, Cat. 63-213 (Ottawa: Minister of Supplies and Services Canada, February 1982).

8. Douglas J. Dalrymple, "Will Automatic Vending Topple Retail Precedence?" *Journal of Retailing*, Spring 1963, pp. 27–31.

9. A. C. Nielsen Company of Canada, taken from a Special Presentation to the Junior Advertising Sales Club of Montreal, April 18, 1978.

10. "Food Stores with Few Services Spring Up to Lure Increasingly Frugal Consumers," *The Wall Street Journal*, January 23, 1981, p. 36; Jonathan N. Goodrich and Jo Ann Hoffman, "Warehouse Retailing: The Trend of the Future?" *Business Horizons*, April 1979, pp. 45–50; and "K mart Corp. Gives Up on No-Frill Food Store," *The Wall Street Journal*, November 30, 1979, p. 35.

11. "Those 1,215 Ks Stand for Kresge, K mart, and the Key to Success," *The Wall Street Journal*, March 8, 1977, pp. 1 ff.; "Where K mart Goes Next Now that It's No. 2," *Business Week*, June 2, 1980, pp. 109–14.

12. Walter J. Salmon, Robert D. Buzzell, and Stanton G. Cort, "Today the Shopping Center, Tomorrow the Superstore," *Harvard Business Review*, January–February 1974, pp. 89–98; "Super-stores May Suit Customers to a T—a T-Shirt or a T-Bone," *The Wall Street Journal*, March 13, 1973, pp. 1 ff.; and *The Super-Store—Strategic Implications For the Seventies* (Cambridge, Mass.: The Marketing Science Institute, 1972).

13. Stanley C. Hollander, "Retailing: Cause or Effect?" in *Emerging Concepts in Marketing*, ed. William F. Decker (Chicago: American Marketing Association, December 1962), pp. 220–30.

14. Adapted from Bert C. McCammon, Jr., "The Future of Catalog Showrooms: Growth and Its Challenges to Management," Marketing Science Institute Working Paper (1973), p. 3.

15. For more discussion on segmenting of retail markets, see "Fast-Food Franchisers Invade the City," *Business Week*, April 22, 1974, pp. 92–93; "Korvettes Tries for a Little Chic," *Business Week*, May 12, 1973, pp. 124–26; Philip D. Cooper, "Will Success Produce Problems for the Convenience Store?" *MSU Business Topics*, Winter 1972, pp. 39–43; "Levitz: The Hot Name in 'Instant' Furniture," *Business Week*, December 4, 1971, pp. 90–93; David L. Appel, "Market Segmentation—A Response to Retail Innovation," *Journal of Marketing*, April 1970, pp. 64–67; Steven R. Flaster, "A Consumer Approach to the Specialty Store," *Journal of Retailing*, Spring 1969, pp. 21–31; A. Coskun Samli, "Segmentation and Carving a Niche in the Market Place," *Journal of Retailing*, Summer 1968, pp. 35–49; and Rom J. Markin and Calvin T. Duncan, "The Transformation of Retailing Institutions: Beyond the Wheel of Retailing and Life Cycle Theories," *Journal of Macromarketing*, Spring 1981, pp. 58–66.

16. The Vancouver User Service Office, Statistics Canada, May 1982.

17. Statistics Canada, *Retail Trade*, Cat. 63–005, March 1981.

18. E. H. Lewis and R. Hancock, *The Franchise System of Distribution* (Minneapolis: University of Minnesota Press,

1963). See also the special issue on franchising in *Journal of Retailing*, Winter 1968–69.

19. John A. Quelch and Hirotaka Takeuchi, "Nonstore Marketing: Fast Track or Slow?" *Harvard Business Review*, July–August 1981, pp. 75–84; and Larry J. Rosenberg and Elizabeth C. Herschman, "Retailing without Stores," *Harvard Business Review*, July–August 1980, pp. 103–12.

20. Bert Rosenbloom, "Strategic Planning and Retailing: Prospects and Problems," *Journal of Retailing*, Spring 1980, pp. 107–20; William R. Davidson and Alice L. Rodgers, "Changes and Challenges in Retailing," *Business Horizons*, January–February 1981, pp. 82–87; Alvin D. Star and Michael Z. Massel, "Survival Rates for Retailers," *Journal of Retailing*, Summer 1981, pp. 87–99; "Electronic Shopping Builds a Base," *Business Week*, October 26, 1981, pp. 125–30; "Discount Outlets Increasing in Malls, Irritating Many Full-Price Retailers," *The Wall Street Journal*, October 14, 1981, p. 27; "At Sears, 'Thumbs Up' to the Video Catalog," *Business Week*, May 11, 1981, pp. 33–34; Albert D. Bates, "The Troubled Future of Retailing" *Business Horizons*, August 1976, pp. 22–28; William R. Davidson, Albert D. Bates, and Stephen J. Bass, "Retail Life Cycle," *Harvard Business Review*, November–December 1976, pp. 89–96; "Investigating the Collapse of W. T. Grant," *Business Week*, July 19, 1976, pp. 60–62; "Shopping Center Boom Appears to Be Fading Due to Overbuilding," *The Wall Street Journal*, September 7, 1976, pp. 1 ff.; "Jewel Co. Discloses Operations Review in Search of a More Successful Strategy," *The Wall Street Journal*, March 23, 1977, p. 12; Ronald D. Michman, "Changing Patterns in Retailing," *Business Horizons*, October 1979, pp. 33–38; "The Discount Twist in Suburban Shopping Malls," *Business Week*, July 7, 1980, pp. 95–96; and "Sears Mulls Test of Catalog Sales via Warner Cable," *Advertising Age*, February 18, 1980, pp. 1 ff.

Chapter 14

1. Statistics Canada, *Merchandising Businesses Survey: Wholesale Merchants, 1975*, Cat. 63–601 (Ottawa: Information Canada, January 1978), p. 6.

2. Statistics Canada, The Vancouver User Service Office, May, 1982.

3. "Food Brokers: A Comprehensive Study of Their Growing Role in Marketing," *Grocery Manufacture*, December 1969. This and others available from the National Food Brokers Association, 1916 M Street, N.W., Washington, D.C. 20036.

4. S. G. Peitchinis, "The Role of the Wholesaler," *Business Quarterly*, Spring 1966. This article contains a full appraisal of the wholesaler's place in the distribution function.

5. Isiah A. Litvak and Peter M. Banting, "Manufacturers' Agent—Adaptation or Atrophy," *Industrial Canada*, January 1967, p. 25. This and five other articles by these authors appearing in *Industrial Canada* between October 1966 and March 1967 offer a good detailed view of wholesaling in Canada, its problems and prospects.

6. For more discussion, see F. E. Webster, Jr., "The Role of the Industrial Distributor in Marketing Strategy," *Journal of Marketing*, July 1976, pp. 10–16; and "Wetterau:

A Maverick Grocery Wholesaler," *Business Week*, February 14, 1977, pp. 121–22.

Chapter 15

1. Robert S. Mason, "What's a PR Director For, Anyway?" *Harvard Business Review*, September–October 1974, pp. 120–26; "Top Flacks Want Nobodies: Where the Power, Prestige and Big Bucks Are at More Firms," *The Wall Street Journal*, March 4, 1980, p. 1; and Raymond Simon, *Public Relations: Concepts and Practices*, 2d ed. (Columbus, Ohio: Grid Publishing, 1980).

2. Roger A. Strang, "Sales Promotion—Fast Growth, Faulty Management," *Harvard Business Review*, July–August 1976, pp. 115–24; "Now the Battling Airlines Try Mass Marketing," *Business Week*, April 18, 1980, p. 104; and Michel Chevalier, "Increase in Sales Due to In-Store Display," *Journal of Marketing Research*, November 1975, pp. 426–31.

3. Ibid., pp. 116–19.

4. For more discussion on sales promotion activities, see Alfred Gross, *Sales Promotion*, various editions (New York: Ronald Press); and Ovid Riso, *Sales Promotion Handbook*, 6th ed. (Chicago: Dartnell).

5. "More Firms Turn to Translation Experts to Avoid Costly Embarrassing Mistakes," *The Wall Street Journal*, January 13, 1977, p. 32.

6. M. S. Heidingsfield and A. B. Blankenship, *Marketing* (New York: Barnes & Noble, 1957), p. 149.

7. This curve is generally thought of as a normal curve. Here it is shown in its cumulative form.

8. For further discussion, see Gerald Zaltman, *Marketing: Contributions from the Behavioral Sciences*, (New York: Harcourt Brace & Jovanovich, 1965), pp. 45–56 and 23–37; Everett M. Rogers, *The Diffusion of Innovations* (New York: Free Press, 1962); Kenneth Uhl, Roman Andrus, and Lance Poulsen, "How Are Laggards Different? An Empirical Inquiry," *Journal of Marketing Research*, February 1970, pp. 51–54. See also C. W. King and J. O. Summers, "Overlap of Opinion Leadership across Consumer Product Categories," *Journal of Marketing Research*, February 1970, pp. 43–50; Joseph R. Mancuso, "Why Not Create Opinion Leaders for New Product Introductions?" *Journal of Marketing*, July 1969, pp. 20–25; Thomas S. Robertson, "The Process of Innovation and the Diffusion of Innovation," *Journal of Marketing*, January 1967, pp. 14–19; Robert A. Westbrook and Claes Fornel, "Patterns of Information Source Usage among Durable Goods Buyers," *Journal of Marketing Research*, August 1979, pp. 303–12; V. Mahajan and E. Muller, "Innovation Diffusion and New Products," *Journal of Marketing*, Fall 1979, pp. 55–68; L. E. Ostlund, "Perceived Innovation Attributes as Predictors of Innovativeness," *Consumer Research*, September 1974, pp. 23–29; Richard W. Olshavsky, "Time and the Rate of Adoption of Innovations," *Consumer Research*, March 1980, pp. 425–28; Thomas S. Robertson and Yoram Wind, "Organizational Psychographics and Innovativeness," *Consumer Research*, June 1980, pp. 24–31; and Peter C. Wilson and Edgar A. Pessemier, "Forecasting the Ultimate Acceptance of an Innovation: The Effects of Infor-

mation," *Journal of Consumer Research,* September 1981, pp. 162–71.

9. *Business Week,* January 26, 1981, p. 133; *Sales & Marketing Management,* February 21, 1977, p. 30; *Business Week,* November 19, 1979, p. 199; and *Sales & Marketing Management,* February 25, 1980.

10. *Business Week,* December 11, 1978, p. 145.

11. Edwin H. Lewis, "Sales Promotion Decisions," *Business News Notes* (Minneapolis: School of Business Administration, University of Minnesota, November 1954).

Chapter 16

1. Statistics Canada, *The Labour Force,* February 1982, Cat. 71–001 (Ottawa: Minister of Supply and Services Canada, March 1982).

2. Michael F. Lennon, "Don't Limit Customer's Horizon," *Printers' Ink,* June 30, 1961, p. 43.

3. "Making Sure the Goods Get on the Shelves," *Business Week,* July 22, 1972, pp. 46–47.

4. Adapted from Harold C. Cash and W. J. E. Crissy. "Ways of Looking at Selling," *Psychology of Selling,* 1957.

5. For further treatment, see W. J. Stanton and R. H. Buskirk, *Management of the Sales Force,* 4th ed. (Homewood, Ill.: Richard D. Irwin, 1973). See also A. F. Doody and W. G. Nickels, "Structuring Organizations for Strategic Selling," *MSU Business Topics,* Autumn 1972, pp. 27–34; Davis Fogg and Josef W. Rokus, "A Quantitative Method for Structuring a Profitable Sales Force," *Journal of Marketing,* July 1973, pp. 8–17; Leonard M. Lodish, " 'Vaguely Right' approach to Sales Force Allocations," *Harvard Business Review,* January–February 1974, pp. 119–24; Porter Henry, "Manage Your Sales Force as a System," *Harvard Business Review,* March–April 1975, pp. 85–94; Charles A. Beswick and David W. Cravens, "A Multistage Decision Model for Salesforce Management," *Journal of Marketing,* May 1977, pp. 135–44; Michael S. Herschel, "Effective Sales Territory Development," *Journal of Marketing,* April 1977, pp. 39–43; Stephen X. Doyle and Benson P. Shapiro, "What Counts Most in Motivating Your Sales Force," *Harvard Business Review,* May–June 1980, pp. 133–40; P. Ronald Stephenson, William L. Cron, and Gary L. Frazier, "Delegating Pricing Authority to the Sales Force: The Effects on Sales and Profit Performance," *Journal of Marketing,* Spring 1979, pp. 21–24; Kenneth Lawyer, *Training Salesmen to Serve Industrial Markets* (Washington, D.C.: Small Business Management Series No. 36, Small Business Administration, 1975); and Douglas J. Dalrymple, R. Ronald Stephenson, and William Cron, "Wage Levels and Sales Productivity," *Business Horizons,* December 1980, pp. 57–60.

Chapter 17

1. U.S. Data from *Advertising Age,* Canadian Data from MacLean Hunter Research Bureau.

2. Statistics Canada, *Advertising Expenditures in Canada, 1965,* Cat. 63–216, Table 19.

3. Statistics Canada as found in *A Report on Advertising Revenues in Canada,* November 1981, p. 11.

4. Elliot Research Corporation as reprinted in *Marketing Magazine,* April 19, 1982.

5. *Handbook of Canadian Consumer Markets, 1982,* 2d ed. (Ottawa: The Conference Board of Canada, February 1982) p. 220.

6. "A Pained Bayer Cries 'Foul,' " *Business Week,* July 25, 1977, p. 142.

7. "Product Pitches that Knock the Competition Creates New Troubles," *The Wall Street Journal,* April 16, 1976, pp. 1 ff.; "The FTC Broadens Its Attack on Ads," *Business Week,* June 20, 1977, pp. 27–28; William L. Wilkie and Paul W. Farris, "Comparison Advertising: Problems and Potential," *Journal of Marketing,* October 1975, pp. 7–15; V. K. Prasad, "Communications Effectiveness of Comparative Advertising: A Laboratory Analysis," *Journal of Marketing Research,* May 1976, pp. 128–37; Murphy A. Seawall and Michael H. Goldstein, "The Comparative Advertising Controversy: Consumer Perceptions of Catalog Showroom Reference Prices," *Journal of Marketing,* Summer 1979, pp. 85–92; Linda L. Golden, "Consumer Reactions to Explicit Brand Comparisons in Advertisements," *Journal of Marketing Research,* November 1979, pp. 517–32; Stephen Goodwin and Michael Etgar, "An Experimental Investigation of Comparative Advertising: Impact of Message Appeal, Information Load and Utility of Product Class," *Journal of Marketing Research,* May 1980, pp. 187–202; "Should an Ad Identify Brand X?" *Business Week,* September 24, 1979, pp. 156–61; George E. Belch, "An Examination of Comparative and Noncomparative Television Commercials," *Journal of Marketing Research,* August 1981, pp. 333–49; and "Comparative Ads: Battles That Wrote Dos and Don'ts," *Advertising Age,* September 29, 1980, pp. 59–64.

8. "Why Jockey Switched Its Ads from TV to Print," *Business Week,* July 26, 1976, pp. 140–42.

9. "Mailing-List Brokers Sell More than Names to Their Many Clients," *The Wall Street Journal,* February 19, 1974, pp. 1 ff.

10. *Bill C–227 Proposals for a New Competition Policy for Canada* (Ottawa: Department of Consumer and Corporate Affairs, November 1973), p. 5.

11. Denis Olorenshaw, "Misleading TV commercial led to legal precedent on liability of agency," *Marketing,* May 22, 1978, pp. 26, 29.

Chapter 18

1. W. Warren Haynes, *Pricing Decisions in Small Business* (Lexington: University of Kentucky Press, 1962); and Alan Reynolds, "A Kind Word for 'Cream Skimming,' " *Harvard Business Review,* November–December 1974, pp. 113–20.

2. For more discussion of the behavior of satisficers, see Herbert A. Simon, *Administrative Behavior,* 2d ed. (New York: Macmillan, 1961).

3. "Squeeze on Product Lines," *Business Week,* January 5, 1974, pp. 50 ff.; and "Pricing Strategy in an Inflation Economy," *Business Week,* April 6, 1974, pp. 43–49.

4. Joseph W. McGuire, John S. Y. Chiu, and Alvar O. Elving, "Executive Incomes, Sales and Profits," *American Economic Review,* September 1962, pp. 753–61; "For the Chief, Sales Sets the Pay," *Business Week,* September 30, 1967, p. 174; and Alfred Rappaport, "Executive Incentives versus Corporate Growth," *Harvard Business Review,* July–August 1978, pp. 81–88.

5. For an interesting discussion of the many variations from a one-price system in retailing, see Stanley C. Hollander, "The 'One-Price' System—Fact or Fiction?" *Journal of Retailing,* Fall 1955, pp. 127–44.

6. See, for example, "The Airline that Thrives on Discounting," *Business Week,* July 24, 1971, pp. 68–70. See also Zarrel V. Lambert, "Product Perception: An Important Variable in Pricing Strategy," *Journal of Marketing,* October 1970, pp. 68–76; "Price and Choice Behavior," *Journal of Marketing Research,* February 1972, pp. 35–40; and "United Takes on the Upstarts," *Business Week,* October 19, 1981, pp. 83–84.

7. For more discussion on price dealing, see Charles L. Hinkle, "The Strategy of Price Deals," *Harvard Business Review,* July–August 1965, pp. 75–85; B. C. Cotton and Emerson M. Babb, "Consumer Response to Promotional Deals," *Journal of Marketing,* July 1978, pp. 109–13; Robert Blattberg, Thomas Buesing, Peter Peacock, and Subrata Sen, "Identifying the Deal Prone Segment," *Journal of Marketing Research,* August 1978, pp. 369–77; Joe A. Dodson, Alice M. Tybout, and Brian Sternthal, "Impact of Deals and Deal Retraction on Brand Switching," *Journal of Marketing Research,* February 1978, pp. 72–81; and "Soda Makers' Rampant Discounts Have Some Worried over Effects," *The Wall Street Journal,* August 28, 1980, p. 17.

8. A. Haring and W. O. Yoder, eds., *Trading Stamps Practice and Pricing Policy,* Indiana Business Report no. 27, Bureau of Business Research (Bloomington: Indiana University, 1958), p. 301.

9. "Buyer's Choice: Stamps or Savings," *Business Week,* February 7, 1970, p. 106; "Sharp Drop in Gas-Station Business Brings Trading-Stamp Industry More Profit Woes," *The Wall Street Journal,* March 1, 1974, p. 26.

10. "Grocery Coupons Are Seen Threatened by Growth of Fraudulent Redemptions," *The Wall Street Journal,* April 12, 1976, p. 26.

11. For discussion concerning European countries, see *Market Power and the Law* (Washington, D.C.: Organization for Economic Cooperation and Development Publication Center, 1970), 206 pp.

12. For a complete summary of all court cases through late 1973 under the Combines Investigation Act, see Appendixes A and B of *Proposals for a New Competition Policy for Canada—First Stage Bill C–227* (Ottawa: Department of Consumer and Corporate Affairs, November 1973).

13. Bruce Mallen, "The Combines Investigation Act: Canada's Major Marketing Statute," in *Cases and Readings in Marketing,* ed. W. H. Kirpalani and R. H. Rotenberg (Toronto: Holt, Rinehart & Winston of Canada, Ltd., 1974), pp. 169–70. The same source was used in trying to assess the actual impact and the barriers to enforcement of other presently existing Combines Act Trade Practices provisions.

14. D. N. Thompson, "Competition Policy and Marketing Regulation," in *Canadian Marketing: Problems and Prospects,* D. N. Thompson and David S. R. Leighton (Toronto: Wiley Publishers of Canada Ltd., 1973), pp. 14–15; also D. N. Thompson, "Resale Price Maintenance and Refusal to Sell: Aspects of a Problem in Competition

of Policy," *University of Toronto Law Journal* 21, pp. 82–86.

Chapter 19

1. "Emergence of the Savvy Consumer Forces Some Painful Rethinking by Supermarkets," *The Wall Street Journal,* September 29, 1980, p. 25; and Super-Valu Study (New York: *Progressive Grocer,* 1957), pp. S-4–7.

2. John J. Wheatley, John S. Y. Chiu, and Arie H. Goldman, "Physical Quality, Price and Perceptions of Product Quality: Implications for Retailers," *Journal of Retailing,* September 1981, pp. 100–116; David R. Lambert, "Price as a Quality Cue in Industrial Buying," *Journal of the Academy of Marketing Science,* Summer 1981, pp. 227–38; "Research Suggests Consumers Will Increasingly Seek Quality," *The Wall Street Journal,* October 15, 1981, p. 25; John J. Wheatley and John S. Y. Chiu, "The Effects of Price, Store Image, and Product and Respondent Characteristics on Perceptions of Quality," *Journal of Marketing Research,* May 1977, pp. 181–86; Arthur G. Bedeian, "Consumer Perception of Price as an Indicator of Product Quality," *MSU Business Topics,* Summer 1971, pp. 59–65; David M. Gardner, "An Experimental Investigation of the Price/Quality Relationship," *Journal of Retailing,* Fall 1970, pp. 25–41; Kent B. Monroe, "Buyers' Subjective Perceptions of Price," *Journal of Marketing Research,* February 1973, pp. 70–80; and N. D. French, J. J. Williams, and W. A. Chance, "A Shopping Experiment on Price-Quality Relationships," *Journal of Retailing,* Fall 1972, pp. 3–16; Michael R. Hagerty, "Model Testing Techniques and Price-Quality Tradeoffs," *Consumer Research,* December 1978, pp. 194–205; Peter C. Riesz, "A Major Price-Perceived Quality Study Reexamined," *Journal of Marketing Research,* May 1980, pp. 259–62; and J. Douglas McConnell, "Comment on 'A Major Price-Perceived Quality Study Reexamined,'" *Journal of Marketing Research,* May 1980, pp. 263–64.

3. Dik W. Twedt, "Does the '9 Fixation in Retailing Really Promote Sales?" *Journal of Marketing,* October 1965, pp. 54–55; and H. J. Rudolph, "Pricing and Today's Market," *Printers' Ink,* May 29, 1954, pp. 22–24; "Strategic Mix of Odd, Even Prices Can Lead to Increased Retail Profits," *Marketing News,* March 7, 1980, p. 24.

4. E. R. Hawkins, "Price Policies and Theory," *Journal of Marketing,* January 1954, p. 236. See also B. P. Shapiro, "The Psychology of Pricing," *Harvard Business Review,* July–August 1968, pp. 14–25; C. Davis Fogg and Kent H. Kohnken, "Price-Cost Planning," *Journal of Marketing,* April 1978, pp. 97–106; and Benson P. Shapiro and Barbara B. Jackson, "Industrial Pricing to Meet Consumer Needs," *Harvard Business Review,* November–December 1978, pp. 119–27.

5. Stephen Paranka, "Competitive Bidding Strategy," *Business Horizons,* June 1971, pp. 39–43; Wayne J. Morse, "Probabilistic Bidding Models; A Synthesis," *Business Horizons,* April 1975, pp. 67–74; and Kenneth Simmonds and Stuart Slatter, "The Number of Estimators: A Critical Decision for Marketing under Competitive Bidding, *Journal of Marketing Research,* May 1978, pp. 203–13.

Chapter 20

1. Adapted from Statistics Canada, *Summary of External Trade, December 1981,* Cat. 65–001 (Ottawa: Minister of Supply and Services Canada).

2. The monthly reports and yearly summaries published by the External Trade Division of Statistics Canada provide detailed information on every product either exported from Canada or imported into the country from each of the nations with which Canada trades. See Statistics Canada Publications 65–001 through 65–007.

3. *Economic Review,* The Provincial Bank of Canada, Montreal, vol. 8, no. 2, March–April 1978, p. 3.

4. B. W. Wilkinson, "Canadian-United States Free Trade: The Issue for Canada" in *Cost and Management* 41 (November 1967) pp. 7–11. Reprinted in B. E. Mallen and E. A. Litvak, *Marketing Canada,* 2d ed. (Toronto: McGraw-Hill Book Co. of Canada, Ltd., 1968), pp. 328–35.

5. C. S. Mayer and J. E. Flynn, "Canadian Small Business Abroad: Opportunities, Aids and Experiences," *Business Quarterly* 38 (Winter 1973), pp. 33–47.

6. Rodman L. Drake and Lee M. Caudil, "Management of the Large Multinational—Trends and Future Challenges," *Business Horizons,* May–June 1981, pp. 83–91.

7. "How Coke Runs a Foreign Empire," *Business Week,* August 25, 1973, pp. 40–43; and "U.S. Companies Pro-Profit from Investments They Made Years Ago in Plants Overseas," *The Wall Street Journal,* March 11, 1981, p. 48.

8. "Multinational Companies," *Business Week,* April 20, 1963, pp. 62–86; "Multinational Firms Now Dominate Much of World's Production," *The Wall Street Journal,* April 18, 1973, pp. 1 ff.; "ITT Europe Rings up Profits; A Low Profile Keeps Troubles Minor," *The Wall Street Journal,* January 9, 1974, pp. 1 ff.; "Japanese Multinationals Covering the World with Investment," *Business Week,* June 16, 1980, pp. 92–99; David A. Heenan and Warren J. Keegan, "The Rise of Third World Multinationals," *Harvard Business Review,* January–February 1979, pp. 101–9; and Ulrich Wiechmann and Lewis G. Pringle, "Problems that Plague Multinational Marketers," *Harvard Business Review,* July–August 1979, pp. 118–24.

9. "Why So Many French Are Tackling the U.S.," *Business Week,* July 4, 1977, p. 30; and "An Appliance Maker Scouts for U.S. Sites," *Business Week,* May 30, 1977, pp. 38–39.

10. Franklin R. Root, "Public Policy Expectations of Multinational Managers," *MSU Business Topics,* Autumn 1973, pp. 5–12; "Domesticating the Multinationals," *Business Week,* May 26, 1973, p. 15; "Multinationals: The Public Gives Them Low Marks," *Business Week,* June 9, 1973, pp. 42–44; "The Unions Move against Multinationals," *Business Week,* July 24, 1971, pp. 48–52; John Kenneth Galbraith, "The Defense of the Multinational Company," *Harvard Business Review,* March–April 1978, pp. 83–93; Lawrence G. Franko, "Multinationals: The End of U.S. Dominance," *Harvard Business Review,* November–December 1978, pp. 93–101; and Frank Meissner, "Rise of the Third World 'Demands Marketing Be Stood on Its Head,'" *Marketing News,* October 6, 1978, pp. 1, 16.

11. "Big Business is beautiful, says the Royal Commission," *Financial Post* 300 (Summer 1978), p. 34.

12. Ibid.

13. H. H. Stikeman, Q. C., *Foreign Investment Review Act—Shape of Things to Come* (Toronto: Richard De Boo, Ltd., 1974), p. 15.

14. "McDonald's Brings Hamburger (with Beer) to Hamburg," *Advertising Age,* May 30, 1977, p. 61.

15. Adapted from Warren Keegan, "Multinational Product Planning: Strategic Alternatives," *Journal of Marketing,* January 1969, p. 59.

16. Warren J. Keegan, "A Conceptual Framework for Multinational Marketing, *Columbia Journal of World Business,* November 1972, pp. 67–78.

17. This discussion is based on William Copulsky, "Forecasting Sales in Underdeveloped Countries," *Journal of Marketing,* July 1959, pp. 36–37. Another set of stages is interesting although less marketing oriented; see W. W. Rostow, *The Stages of Economic Growth—A Non-Communist Manifesto* (New York: Cambridge University Press, 1960).

18. Ibid.

19. The *Statistical Abstract* and the U.S. Department of Commerce Bureau of International Commerce would be good places to start locating current data. In its publication *International Commerce,* the Department of Commerce issues a semiannual checklist of material it thinks will be helpful to business people interested in the world market. The *Statistical Year Book* of the Statistical Office of the United Nations is also a good source of basic data.

20. Drawn by J. F. McCarthy.

21. Adapted from Norton Ginsburg, *Atlas of Economic Development,* by permission of the University of Chicago Press. Copyright 1961 by the University of Chicago.

22. Donald G. Halper, "The Environment for Marketing in Peru," *Journal of Marketing,* July 1966, pp. 42–46.

23. (Lansing, Mich.) *State Journal,* February 10, 1970, p. D–7.

24. *Statistical Abstract of the U.S. 1979,* p. 885, and *Yearbook of National Accounts Statistics,* 1979, vol. 2 (New York: United Nations, 1980), pp. 3–9.

25. *Yearbook of National Accounts Statistics, 1979,* vol. 2 (New York: United Nations, 1980), pp. 3–9; and *Statistical Abstract of the U.S., 1979,* p. 895.

26. *The Wall Street Journal,* August 8, 1968, p. 1.

27. Norton Ginsburg, *Atlas of Economic Development* (Chicago: University of Chicago Press, 1961); and *Statistical Abstract of the U.S., 1979,* pp. 890–92.

28. Edward Marcus, "Selling the Tropical African Market," *Journal of Marketing,* July 1961, p. 30. See also Michael Colvin, Roger Heeler, and Jim Thorpe, "Developing International Advertising Strategy," *The Journal of Marketing,* Fall 1980, pp. 73–79.

29. Robert L. Brown, "The Common Market: What Its New Consumer Is Like," *Printers' Ink,* May 31, 1963, pp. 23–25.

Chapter 21

1. James U. McNeal, "Consumer Satisfaction: The Measure of Marketing Effectiveness," *MSU Business Topics,* Summer 1969, p. 33.

2. For an extensive discussion of the problems and mechanics of measuring the efficiency of marketing, see Stanley C. Hollander, "Measuring the Cost and Value of Marketing," *Business Topics,* Summer 1961, pp. 17–26; and Reavis Cox, *Distribution in a High-Level Economy* (Englewood Cliffs, N.J.: Prentice-Hall, 1965).

3. "New Harris Consumer Study Causes Few Shocks in Adland," *Advertising Age,* May 30, 1977, p. 2; and Hiram C. Barksdale and William D. Perreault, Jr., "Can Consumers Be Satisfied?" *MSU Business Topics,* Spring 1980, pp. 19–30.

4. B. Charles Ames, "Trappings vs. Substance in Industrial Marketing, *Harvard Business Review,* July–August 1970, pp. 93–102; and Merchant's Service, National Cash Register Co., *Establishing a Retail Store,* p. 3.

5. F. M. Nicosia, *Consumer Decision Processes* (Englewood Cliffs, N.J.: Prentice-Hall, 1966), p. 39.

6. E. H. Chamberlin, "Product Heterogeneity and Public Policy," *American Economic Review,* May 1950, p. 86.

7. Arnold J. Toynbee, *America and the World Revolution* (New York: Oxford University Press, 1966), pp. 144–45. See also John Kenneth Galbraith, *Economics and the Public Purpose* (Boston: Houghton Mifflin, 1973), pp. 144–45.

8. Russel J. Tomsen, "Take It Away," *Newsweek,* October 7, 1974, p. 21.

9. See Robert F. Hartley, *Marketing Mistakes* (Columbus, Ohio: Grid, 1976).

10. Jack L. Engledow, "Was Consumer Satisfaction a Pig in a Poke?" *MSU Business Topics,* April 1977, p. 92.

11. "Intellectuals Should Re-Examine the Marketplace; It Supports Them, Helps Keep Them Free, Prof. Stigler," *Advertising Age,* January 28, 1963. See also E. T. Grether, "Galbraith versus the Market: A Review Article," *Journal of Marketing,* January 1968, pp. 9–14; E. T. Grether, "Marketing and Public Policy: A Contemporary View, *Journal of Marketing,* July 1974, pp. 2–7; and James U. McNeal, "You Can Defend Advertising—But Not Every Advertisement," *Business Horizons,* September–October 1981, pp. 33–37.

12. Frederick Webster, *Social Aspects of Marketing* (Englewood Cliffs, N.J.: Prentice-Hall, 1974), p. 32.

13. See Richard P. Lundy, "How Many Service Stations Are 'Too Many'?" in *Theory in Marketing,* ed. Reavis Cox and Wroe Alderson (Homewood, Ill.: Richard D. Irwin, 1950), pp. 321–33.

14. Paul M. Mazur, "Does Distribution Cost Enough?" *Fortune,* November 1947.

15. John E. Smallwood, "The Product Life Cycle: A Key to Strategic Marketing Planning," *MSU Business Topics,* Winter 1973, pp. 29–35.

16. Irving Kristol, "The Corporation and the Dinosaur," *The Wall Street Journal,* February 14, 1974.

17. James T. Roth and Lissa Benson, "Intelligent Consumption: An Attractive Alternative to the Marketing Concept," *MSU Business Topics,* Winter 1974, pp. 30–34; and Robert E. Wilkes, "Fraudulent Behavior by Consumers," *Journal of Marketing,* October 1978, pp. 67–75; and "How Shoplifting Is Draining the Economy," *Business Week,* October 15, 1979, pp. 119–23.

18. "Dictating PRODUCT Safety," *Business Week,* May 18, 1974, pp. 56–62; Y. Hugh Furuhashi and E. Jerome McCarthy, *Social Issues of Marketing in the American Economy* (Columbus, Ohio: Grid, 1971); James Owens, "Business Ethics; Age-Old Ideal, Now Real," *Business Horizons,* February 1978, pp. 26–30; Steven F. Goodman, "Quality of Life: The Role of Business," *Business Horizons,* June 1978, pp. 36–37; William F. Dwyer, "Smoking: Free Choice," *Business Horizons,* June 1978, pp. 52–56; Stanley J. Shapiro, "Marketing in a Conserver Society," *Business Horizons,* April 1978, pp. 3–13; and Johan Arndt, "How Broad Should the Marketing Concept Be?" *Journal of Marketing,* January 1978, pp. 101–3.

PHOTO CREDITS

INDEX OF NAMES

INDEX OF SUBJECTS

This book has been set VideoComp CAP, in 10 and 9 point Spectra Light, leaded 2 points. Chapter numbers are 72 point Times Roman (regular), and chapter titles are 24 point Serif Gothic Bold. The size of the type page is 37 by 50 picas.